MtG

31

YEARS 2018-1988

NEET·AIPMT

CHAPTERWISE SOLUTIONS

CHEMISTRY

MtG Learning Media

MTG Learning Media (P) Ltd.

New Delhi | Gurgaon

Price : ₹ 300

Published by : **MTG Learning Media (P) Ltd., New Delhi**

Corporate Office : Plot 99, Sector 44 Institutional Area, Gurgaon, Haryana.
Phone : 0124 - 6601200. Web : mtg.in Email : info@mtg.in

Registered Office : 406, Taj Apt., Ring Road, Near Safdarjung Hospital, New Delhi-110029

Printed at Akash Press New Delhi 110020

Visit **www.mtg.in** for buying books online.

EVERY GENUINE COPY OF THE BOOK HAS A HOLOGRAM STICKER ON THE COVER

Move the book slightly to see the special features of the hologram

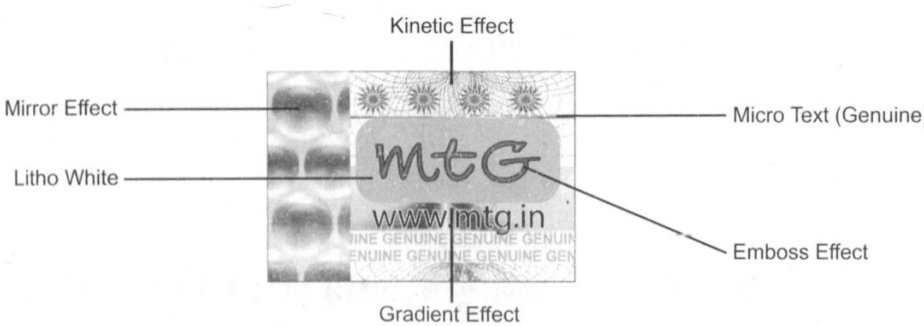

Contents

Syllabus*

UNIT I: SOME BASIC CONCEPTS OF CHEMISTRY

- General Introduction: Important and scope of chemistry.
- Laws of chemical combination, Dalton's atomic theory: concept of elements, atoms and molecules.
- Atomic and molecular masses; Mole concept and molar mass; percentage composition and empirical and molecular formula; chemical reactions, stoichiometry and calculations based on stoichiometry.

UNIT II: STRUCTURE OF ATOM

- Atomic number, isotopes and isobars. Concept of shells and subshells, dual nature of matter and light, de Broglie's relationship, Heisenberg uncertainty principle, concept of orbital, quantum numbers, shapes of *s*, *p* and *d* orbitals, rules for filling electrons in orbitals- Aufbau principle, Pauli exclusion principles and Hund's rule, electronic configuration of atoms, stability of half filled and completely filled orbitals.

UNIT III: CLASSIFICATION OF ELEMENTS AND PERIODICITY IN PROPERTIES

- Modern periodic law and long form of periodic table, periodic trends in properties of elements- atomic radii, ionic radii, ionization enthalpy, electron gain enthalpy, electronegativity, valence.

UNIT IV: CHEMICAL BONDING AND MOLECULAR STRUCTURE

- Valence electrons, ionic bond, covalent bond, bond parameters, Lewis structure, polar character of covalent bond, valence bond theory, resonance, geometry of molecules, VSEPR theory, concept of hybridization involving *s*, *p* and *d*-orbitals and shapes of some simple molecules, molecular orbital theory of homonuclear diatomic molecules (qualitative idea only). Hydrogen bond.

UNIT V: STATES OF MATTER: GASES AND LIQUIDS

- Three states of matter, intermolecular interactions, types of bonding, melting and boiling points, role of gas laws of elucidating the concept of the molecule, Boyle's law, Charles' law, Gay Lussac's law, Avogadro's law, ideal behaviour of gases, empirical derivation of gas equation. Avogadro number, ideal gas equation. Kinetic energy and molecular speeds (elementary idea), deviation from ideal behaviour, liquefaction of gases, critical temperature.
- Liquid State- Vapour pressure, viscosity and surface tension (qualitative idea only, no mathematical derivations).

**For details, refer to latest prospectus*

UNIT VI: THERMODYNAMICS

- First law of thermodynamics-internal energy and enthalpy, heat capacity and specific heat, measurement of ΔU and ΔH, Hess's law of constant heat summation, enthalpy of bond dissociation, combustion, formation, atomization, sublimation, phase transition, ionization, solution and dilution.
- Introduction of entropy as state function, Second law of thermodynamics, Gibbs energy change for spontaneous and non spontaneous process, criteria for equilibrium and spontaneity.
- Third law of thermodynamics- Brief introduction.

UNIT VII: EQUILIBRIUM

- Equilibrium in physical and chemical processes, dynamic nature of equilibrium, law of chemical equilibrium, equilibrium constant, factors affecting equilibrium- Le Chatelier's principle; ionic equilibrium- ionization of acids and bases, strong and weak electrolytes, degree of ionization, ionization of polybasic acids, acid strength, concept of pH., Hydrolysis of salts (elementary idea)., buffer solutions, Henderson equation, solubility product, common ion effect (with illustrative examples).

UNIT VIII: REDOX REACTIONS

- Concept of oxidation and reduction, redox reactions, oxidation number, balancing redox reactions in terms of loss and gain of electron and change in oxidation numbers.

UNIT IX: HYDROGEN

- Occurrence, isotopes, preparation, properties and uses of hydrogen; hydrides-ionic, covalent and interstitial; physical and chemical properties of water, heavy water; hydrogen peroxide-preparation, reactions, uses and structure.

UNIT X: *s*-BLOCK ELEMENTS (ALKALI AND ALKALINE EARTH METALS)

- Group 1 and group 2 elements:
- General introduction, electronic configuration, occurrence, anomalous properties of the first element of each group, diagonal relationship, trends in the variation of properties (such as ionization enthalpy, atomic and ionic radii), trends in chemical reactivity with oxygen, water, hydrogen and halogens; uses.
- Preparation and Properties of Some important Compounds: Sodium carbonate, sodium chloride, sodium hydroxide and sodium hydrogencarbonate, biological importance of sodium and potassium.
- Industrial use of lime and limestone, biological importance of Mg and Ca.

UNIT XI: SOME *p*-BLOCK ELEMENTS

- General Introduction to *p*-Block Elements.
- Group 13 elements: General introduction, electronic configuration, occurrence, variation of properties, oxidation states, trends in chemical reactivity, anomalous properties of first element of the group; Boron, some important compounds: borax, boric acids, boron hydrides. Aluminium: uses, reactions with acids and alkalies.
- General 14 elements: General introduction, electronic configuration, occurrence, variation of properties, oxidation states, trends in chemical reactivity, anomalous behaviour of first element. Carbon, allotropic forms, physical and chemical properties: uses of some important compounds: oxides.
- Important compounds of silicon and a few uses: silicon tetrachloride, silicones, silicates and zeolites, their uses.

UNIT XII: ORGANIC CHEMISTRY- SOME BASIC PRINCIPLES AND TECHNIQUES

- General introduction, methods of purification, qualitative and quantitative analysis, classification and IUPAC nomenclature of organic compounds.
- Electronic displacements in a covalent bond: inductive effect, electromeric effect, resonance and hyperconjugation.
- Homolytic and heterolytic fission of a covalent bond: free radicals, carbocations, carbanions; electrophiles and nucleophiles, types of organic reactions.

UNIT XIII: HYDROCARBONS

- Alkanes- Nomenclature, isomerism, conformations (ethane only), physical properties, chemical reactions including free radical mechanism of halogenation, combustion and pyrolysis.
- Alkenes-Nomenclature, structure of double bond (ethene), geometrical isomerism, physical properties, methods of preparation: chemical reactions: addition of hydrogen, halogen, water, hydrogen halides (Markovnikov's addition and peroxide effect), ozonolysis, oxidation, mechanism of electrophilic addition.
- Alkynes-Nomenclature, structure of triple bond (ethyne), physical properties, methods of preparation, chemical reactions: acidic character of alkynes, addition reaction of- hydrogen, halogens, hydrogen halides and water.
- Aromatic hydrocarbons- Introduction, IUPAC nomenclature; Benzene; resonance, aromaticity; chemical properties: mechanism of electrophilic substitution- Nitration, sulphonation, halogenation, Friedel Craft's alkylation and acylation; directive influence of functional group in mono-substituted benzene; carcinogenicity and toxicity.

UNIT XIV: ENVIRONMENTAL CHEMISTRY

- Environmental pollution: Air, water and soil pollution, chemical reactions in atmosphere, smogs, major atmospheric pollutants; acid rain, ozone and its reactions, effects of depletion of ozone layer, greenhouse effect and global warming-pollution due to industrial wastes; green chemistry as an alternative tool for reducing pollution, strategy for control of environmental pollution.

UNIT XV: SOLID STATE

- Classification of solids based on different binding forces; molecular, ionic, covalent and metallic solids, amorphous and crystalline solids (elementary idea), unit cell in two dimensional and three dimensional lattices, calculation of density of unit cell, packing in solids, packing efficiency, voids, number of atoms per unit cell in a cubic unit cell, point defects, electrical and magnetic properties, Band theory of metals, conductors, semiconductors and insulators.

UNIT XVI: SOLUTIONS

- Types of solutions, expression of concentration of solutions of solids in liquids, solubility of gases in liquids, solid solutions, colligative properties- relative lowering of vapour pressure, Raoult's law elevation of boiling point, depression of freezing point, osmotic pressure, determination of molecular masses using colligative properties, abnormal molecular mass, van't Hoff factor.

UNIT XVII: ELECTROCHEMISTRY

- Redox reactions, conductance in electrolytic solutions, specific and molar conductivity, variation of conductivity with concentration, Kohlrausch's Law, electrolysis and Laws of electrolysis (elementary idea), dry cell- electrolytic cells and Galvanic cells; lead accumulator, EMF of a cell, standard electrode potential, Relation between Gibbs energy change and EMF of a cell, fuel cells; corrosion.

UNIT XVIII: CHEMICAL KINETICS

- Rate of a reaction (average and instantaneous), factors affecting rates of reaction; concentration, temperature catalyst; order and molecularity of a reaction; rate law and specific rate constant, integrated rate equation and half life (only for zero and first order reactions); concept of collision theory (elementary idea, no mathematical treatment). Activation energy, Arrhenious equation.

UNIT XIX: SURFACE CHEMISTRY

- Adsorption-physisorption and chemisorption; factors affecting adsorption of gases on solids catalysis: homogeneous and heterogeneous, activity and selectivity: enzyme catalysis; colloidal state distinction between true solutions, colloids and suspensions; lyophillic, lyophobic, multimolecular an macromolecular colloids; properties of colloids; Tyndall effect, Brownian movement, electrophoresi coagulation; emulsions- types of emulsions.

UNIT XX: GENERAL PRINCIPLES AND PROCESSES OF ISOLATION OF ELEMENTS

- Principles and methods of extraction- concentration, oxidation, reduction, electrolytic method and refining; occurrence and principles of extraction of aluminium, copper, zinc and iron.

UNIT XXI: *p*- BLOCK ELEMENTS

- Group 15 elements: General introduction, electronic configuration, occurrence, oxidation states, trends in physical and chemical properties; preparation and properties of ammonia and nitric acid, oxides of nitrogen (structure only); Phosphorous- allotropic forms; compounds of phosphorous: preparation and properties of phosphine, halides (PCl_3, PCl_5) and oxoacids (elementary idea only).
- Group 16 elements: General introduction, electronic configuration, oxidation states, occurrence, trends in physical and chemical properties; dioxygen: preparation, properties and uses; classification of oxides; ozone. Sulphur – allotropic forms; compounds of sulphur: preparation, properties and uses of sulphur dioxide; sulphuric acid: industrial process of manufacture, properties and uses, oxoacids of sulphur (structures only).
- Group 17 elements: General introduction, electronic configuration, oxidation states, occurrence, trends in physical and chemical properties; compounds, of halogens: properties and uses of chlorine and hydrochloric acid, interhalogen compounds, oxoacids of halogens (structures only).
- Group 18 elements: General introduction, electronic configuration, occurrence, trends in physical and chemical properties, uses.

UNIT XXII: *d*- AND *f*- BLOCK ELEMENTS

- General introduction, electronic configuration, characteristics of transition metals, general trends in properties of the first row transition metals- metallic character, ionization enthalpy, oxidation states, ionic radii, colour, catalytic property, magnetic properties, interstitial compounds, alloy formation. Preparation and properties of $K_2Cr_2O_7$ and $KMnO_4$.
- Lanthanoids- electronic configuration, oxidation states, chemical reactivity, and lanthanoid contraction and its consequences.
- Actinoids: Electronic configuration, oxidation states and comparison with lanthanoids.

UNIT XXIII: COORDINATION COMPOUNDS

- Coordination compounds: Introduction, ligands, coordination number, colour, magnetic properties and shapes, IUPAC nomenclature of mononuclear coordination compounds, isomerism (structural and stereo) bonding, Werner's theory VBT,CFT; importance of coordination compounds (in qualitative analysis, biological systems).

UNIT XXIV: HALOALKANES AND HALOARENES

- Haloalkanes: Nomenclature, nature of C –*X* bond, physical and chemical properties, mechanism of substitution reactions, Optical rotation.
- Haloarenes: Nature of C-*X* bond, substitution reactions (directive influence of halogen for monosubstituted compounds only).
- Uses and environment effects of – dichloromethane, trichloromethane, tetrachloromethane, iodoform, freons, DDT.

UNIT XXV: ALCOHOLS, PHENOLS AND ETHERS

- Alcohols: Nomenclature, methods of preparation, physical and chemical properties (of primary alcohols only); identification of primary, secondary and tertiary alcohols; mechanism of dehydration, uses with special reference to methanol and ethanol.
- Phenols: Nomenclature, methods of preparation, physical and chemical properties, acidic nature of phenol, electrophilic substitution reactions, uses of phenols.
- Ethers: Nomenclature, methods of preparation, physical and chemical properties, uses.

UNIT XXVI: ALDEHYDES, KETONES AND CARBOXYLIC ACIDS

- Aldehydes and Ketones: Nomenclature, nature of carbonyl group, methods of preparation, physical and chemical properties; and mechanism of nucleophilic addition, reactivity of alpha hydrogen in aldehydes; uses.
- Carboxylic Acids: Nomenclature, acidic nature, methods of preparation, physical and chemical properties; uses.

UNIT XXVII: ORGANIC COMPOUNDS CONTAINING NITROGEN

- Amines: Nomenclature, classification, structure, methods of preparation, physical and chemical properties, uses, identification of primary, secondary and tertiary amines.
- Cyanides and Isocyanides- will be mentioned at relevant places.
- Diazonium salts: Preparation, chemical reactions and importance in synthetic organic chemistry.

UNIT XXVIII: BIOMOLECULES

- Carbohydrates- Classification (aldoses and ketoses), monosaccharide (glucose and fructose), *D, L*- configuration, oligosaccharides (sucrose, lactose, maltose), polysaccharides (starch, cellulose, glycogen): importance.
- Proteins- Elementary idea of – amino acids, peptide bond, polypeptides, proteins, primary structure, secondary structure, tertiary structure and quaternary structure (qualitative idea only), denaturation of proteins; enzymes.
- Hormones- Elementary idea (excluding structure).
- Vitamins- Classification and function.
- Nucleic Acids: DNA and RNA

UNIT XXIX: POLYMERS

- Classification- Natural and synthetic, methods of polymerization (addition and condensation), copolymerization. Some important polymers: natural and synthetic like polyesters, bakelite; rubber, Biodegradable and non-biodegradable polymers.

UNIT XXX: CHEMISTRY IN EVERYDAY LIFE

- Chemicals in medicines- analgesics, tranquilizers, antiseptics, disinfectants, antimicrobials, antifertility drugs, antibiotics, antacids, antihistamines.
- Chemicals in food- preservatives, artificial sweetening agents, elementary idea of antioxidants.
- Cleansing agents- soaps and detergents, cleansing action.

Chapter 1

Some Basic Concepts of Chemistry

1. A mixture of 2.3 g formic acid and 4.5 g oxalic acid is treated with conc. H_2SO_4. The evolved gaseous mixture is passed through KOH pellets. Weight (in g) of the remaining product at STP will be
(a) 1.4 (b) 3.0
(c) 2.8 (d) 4.4
(NEET 2018)

2. In which case is number of molecules of water maximum?
(a) 18 mL of water
(b) 0.18 g of water
(c) 0.00224 L of water vapours at 1 atm and 273 K
(d) 10^{-3} mol of water *(NEET 2018)*

3. Suppose the elements X and Y combine to form two compounds XY_2 and X_3Y_2. When 0.1 mole of XY_2 weighs 10 g and 0.05 mole of X_3Y_2 weighs 9 g, the atomic weights of X and Y are
(a) 40, 30 (b) 60, 40
(c) 20, 30 (d) 30, 20
(NEET-II 2016)

4. What is the mass of the precipitate formed when 50 mL of 16.9% solution of $AgNO_3$ is mixed with 50 mL of 5.8% NaCl solution? (Ag = 107.8, N = 14, O = 16, Na = 23, Cl = 35.5)
(a) 3.5 g (b) 7 g (c) 14 g (d) 28 g
(2015)

5. If Avogadro number N_A, is changed from 6.022×10^{23} mol^{-1} to 6.022×10^{20} mol^{-1}, this would change
(a) the mass of one mole of carbon
(b) the ratio of chemical species to each other in a balanced equation
(c) the ratio of elements to each other in a compound
(d) the definition of mass in units of grams.
(2015)

6. The number of water molecules is maximum in
(a) 1.8 gram of water
(b) 18 gram of water
(c) 18 moles of water
(d) 18 molecules of water. *(2015)*

7. A mixture of gases contains H_2 and O_2 gases in the ratio of 1 : 4 (w/w). What is the molar ratio of the two gases in the mixture?
(a) 16 : 1 (b) 2 : 1 (c) 1 : 4 (d) 4 : 1
(2015, Cancelled)

8. Equal masses of H_2, O_2 and methane have been taken in a container of volume V at temperature 27 °C in identical conditions. The ratio of the volumes of gases $H_2 : O_2$: methane would be
(a) 8 : 16 : 1 (b) 16 : 8 : 1
(c) 16 : 1 : 2 (d) 8 : 1 : 2 *(2014)*

9. When 22.4 litres of $H_{2(g)}$ is mixed with 11.2 litres of $Cl_{2(g)}$, each at S.T.P, the moles of $HCl_{(g)}$ formed is equal to
(a) 1 mol of $HCl_{(g)}$ (b) 2 mol of $HCl_{(g)}$
(c) 0.5 mol of $HCl_{(g)}$ (d) 1.5 mol of $HCl_{(g)}$.
(2014)

10. 1.0 g of magnesium is burnt with 0.56 g O_2 in a closed vessel. Which reactant is left in excess and how much? (At. wt. Mg = 24, O = 16)
(a) Mg, 0.16 g (b) O_2, 0.16 g
(c) Mg, 0.44 g (d) O_2, 0.28 g
(2014)

11. 6.02×10^{20} molecules of urea are present in 100 mL of its solution. The concentration of solution is
(a) 0.001 M (b) 0.1 M
(c) 0.02 M (d) 0.01 M
(NEET 2013)

12. In an experiment it showed that 10 mL of 0.05 M solution of chloride required 10 mL of 0.1 M solution of $AgNO_3$, which of the following

will be the formula of the chloride (X stands for the symbol of the element other than chlorine)
(a) X_2Cl_2 (b) XCl_2 (c) XCl_4 (d) X_2Cl
(Karnataka NEET 2013)

13. Which has the maximum number of molecules among the following?
(a) 44 g CO_2 (b) 48 g O_3
(c) 8 g H_2 (d) 64 g SO_2
(Mains 2011)

14. The number of atoms in 0.1 mol of a triatomic gas is ($N_A = 6.02 \times 10^{23}$ mol^{-1})
(a) 6.026×10^{22} (b) 1.806×10^{23}
(c) 3.600×10^{23} (d) 1.800×10^{22}
(2010)

15. 25.3 g of sodium carbonate, Na_2CO_3 is dissolved in enough water to make 250 mL of solution. If sodium carbonate dissociates completely, molar concentration of sodium ion, Na^+ and carbonate ions, CO_3^{2-} are respectively (Molar mass of Na_2CO_3 = 106 g mol^{-1})
(a) 0.955 M and 1.910 M
(b) 1.910 M and 0.955 M
(c) 1.90 M and 1.910 M
(d) 0.477 M and 0.477 M *(2010)*

16. 10 g of hydrogen and 64 g of oxygen were filled in a steel vessel and exploded. Amount of water produced in this reaction will be
(a) 3 mol (b) 4 mol
(c) 1 mol (d) 2 mol *(2009)*

17. What volume of oxygen gas (O_2) measured at 0°C and 1 atm, is needed to burn completely 1 L of propane gas (C_3H_8) measured under the same conditions?
(a) 5 L (b) 10 L (c) 7 L (d) 6 L
(2008)

18. How many moles of lead (II) chloride will be formed from a reaction between 6.5 g of PbO and 3.2 g HCl?
(a) 0.011 (b) 0.029 (c) 0.044 (d) 0.333
(2008)

19. An organic compound contains carbon, hydrogen and oxygen. Its elemental analysis gave C, 38.71% and H, 9.67%. The empirical formula of the compound would be
(a) CHO (b) CH_4O
(c) CH_3O (d) CH_2O *(2008)*

20. An element, X has the following isotopic composition:
^{200}X : 90% ^{199}X : 8.0% ^{202}X : 2.0%
The weighted average atomic mass of the naturally occurring element X is closest to
(a) 201 amu (b) 202 amu
(c) 199 amu (d) 200 amu *(2007)*

21. The maximum number of molecules is present in
(a) 15 L of H_2 gas at STP
(b) 5 L of N_2 gas at STP
(c) 0.5 g of H_2 gas
(d) 10 g of O_2 gas. *(2004)*

22. Which has maximum molecules?
(a) 7 g N_2 (b) 2 g H_2
(c) 16 g NO_2 (d) 16 g O_2 *(2002)*

23. Percentage of Se in peroxidase anhydrous enzyme is 0.5% by weight (at. wt. = 78.4) then minimum molecular weight of peroxidase anhydrous enzyme is
(a) 1.568×10^4 (b) 1.568×10^3
(c) 15.68 (d) 2.136×10^4
(2001)

24. Molarity of liquid HCl, if density of solution is 1.17 g/cc is
(a) 36.5 (b) 18.25
(c) 32.05 (d) 42.10 *(2001)*

25. Specific volume of cylindrical virus particle is 6.02×10^{-2} cc/g whose radius and length are 7 Å and 10 Å respectively. If $N_A = 6.02 \times 10^{23}$, find molecular weight of virus.
(a) 15.4 kg/mol (b) 1.54×10^4 kg/mol
(c) 3.08×10^4 kg/mol (d) 3.08×10^3 kg/mol
(2001)

26. In quantitative analysis of second group in laboratory, H_2S gas is passed in acidic medium for precipitation. When Cu^{2+} and Cd^{2+} react with KCN, then for product, true statement is
(a) $K_2[Cu(CN)_4]$ more soluble
(b) $K_2[Cd(CN)_4]$ less stable
(c) $K_3[Cu(CN)_2]$ less stable
(d) $K_2[Cd(CN)_3]$ more stable. *(2000)*

27. Volume of CO_2 obtained by the complete decomposition of 9.85 g of $BaCO_3$ is
(a) 2.24 L (b) 1.12 L
(c) 0.84 L (d) 0.56 L *(2000)*

28. Oxidation numbers of A, B, C are +2, +5 and –2 respectively. Possible formula of compound is
(a) $A_2(BC_2)_2$ (b) $A_3(BC_4)_2$
(c) $A_2(BC_3)_2$ (d) $A_3(B_2C)_2$ *(2000)*

29. The number of atoms in 4.25 g of NH_3 is approximately
(a) 4×10^{23} (b) 2×10^{23}
(c) 1×10^{23} (d) 6×10^{23} *(1999)*

30. Given the numbers: 161 cm, 0.161 cm, 0.0161 cm. The number of significant figures for the three numbers is
(a) 3, 3 and 4 respectively
(b) 3, 4 and 4 respectively
(c) 3, 4 and 5 respectively
(d) 3, 3 and 3 respectively. *(1998)*

31. Haemoglobin contains 0.334% of iron by weight. The molecular weight of haemoglobin is approximately 67200. The number of iron atoms (Atomic weight of Fe is 56) present in one molecule of haemoglobin is
(a) 4 (b) 6 (c) 3 (d) 2 *(1998)*

32. In the reaction,
$4NH_{3(g)} + 5O_{2(g)} \rightarrow 4NO_{(g)} + 6H_2O_{(l)}$
when 1 mole of ammonia and 1 mole of O_2 are made to react to completion :
(a) All the oxygen will be consumed.
(b) 1.0 mole of NO will be produced.
(c) 1.0 mole of H_2O is produced.
(d) All the ammonia will be consumed. *(1998)*

33. Among the following which one is not paramagnetic? [Atomic numbers; Be = 4, Ne = 10, As = 33, Cl = 17]
(a) Ne^{2+} (b) Be^+ (c) Cl^- (d) As^+ *(1998)*

34. 0.24 g of a volatile gas, upon vaporisation, gives 45 mL vapour at NTP. What will be the vapour density of the substance? (Density of H_2 = 0.089)
(a) 95.93 (b) 59.93 (c) 95.39 (d) 5.993 *(1996)*

35. The amount of zinc required to produce 224 mL of H_2 at STP on treatment with dilute H_2SO_4 will be
(a) 65 g (b) 0.065 g (c) 0.65 g (d) 6.5 g *(1996)*

36. The dimensions of pressure are the same as that of
(a) force per unit volume
(b) energy per unit volume
(c) force
(d) energy. *(1995)*

37. The number of moles of oxygen in one litre of air containing 21% oxygen by volume, under standard conditions, is
(a) 0.0093 mol (b) 2.10 mol
(c) 0.186 mol (d) 0.21 mol. *(1995)*

38. The total number of valence electrons in 4.2 g of N_3^- ion is (N_A is the Avogadro's number)
(a) 2.1 N_A (b) 4.2 N_A
(c) 1.6 N_A (d) 3.2 N_A *(1994)*

39. A 5 molar solution of H_2SO_4 is diluted from 1 litre to a volume of 10 litres, the normality of the solution will be
(a) 1 N (b) 0.1 N
(c) 5 N (d) 0.5 N *(1991)*

40. The number of gram molecules of oxygen in 6.02×10^{24} CO molecules is
(a) 10 g molecules (b) 5 g molecules
(c) 1 g molecules (d) 0.5 g molecules. *(1990)*

41. Boron has two stable isotopes, $^{10}B(19\%)$ and $^{11}B(81\%)$. Calculate average at. wt. of boron in the periodic table
(a) 10.8 (b) 10.2
(c) 11.2 (d) 10.0 *(1990)*

42. The molecular weight of O_2 and SO_2 are 32 and 64 respectively. At 15°C and 150 mmHg pressure, one litre of O_2 contains 'N' molecules. The number of molecules in two litres of SO_2 under the same conditions of temperature and pressure will be
(a) $N/2$ (b) N
(c) $2N$ (d) $4N$ *(1990)*

43. A metal oxide has the formula Z_2O_3. It can be reduced by hydrogen to give free metal and water. 0.1596 g of the metal oxide requires 6 mg of hydrogen for complete reduction. The atomic weight of the metal is
(a) 27.9 (b) 159.6
(c) 79.8 (d) 55.8 *(1989)*

44. Ratio of C_p and C_V of a gas 'X' is 1.4. The number of atoms of the gas 'X' present in 11.2 litres of it at NTP will be
(a) 6.02×10^{23} (b) 1.2×10^{23}
(c) 3.01×10^{23} (d) 2.01×10^{23}
(1989)

45. What is the weight of oxygen required for the complete combustion of 2.8 kg of ethylene?
(a) 2.8 kg (b) 6.4 kg (c) 9.6 kg (d) 96 kg
(1989)

46. The number of oxygen atoms in 4.4 g of CO_2 is
(a) 1.2×10^{23} (b) 6×10^{22}
(c) 6×10^{23} (d) 12×10^{23}
(1989)

47. At S.T.P. the density of CCl_4 vapour in g/L will be nearest to
(a) 6.87 (b) 3.42
(c) 10.26 (d) 4.57 *(1988)*

48. One litre hard water contains 12.00 mg Mg^{2+}. Milli-equivalents of washing soda required to remove its hardness is
(a) 1 (b) 12.16
(c) 1×10^{-3} (d) 12.16×10^{-3}
(1988)

49. 1 cc N_2O at NTP contains
(a) $\frac{1.8}{224} \times 10^{22}$ atoms
(b) $\frac{6.02}{22400} \times 10^{23}$ molecules
(c) $\frac{1.32}{224} \times 10^{23}$ electrons
(d) All the above. *(1988)*

Answer Key

1. (c)	**2.** (a)	**3.** (a)	**4.** (b)	**5.** (a)	**6.** (c)	**7.** (d)	**8.** (c)	**9.** (a)	**10.** (a)
11. (d)	**12.** (b)	**13.** (c)	**14.** (b)	**15.** (b)	**16.** (b)	**17.** (a)	**18.** (b)	**19.** (c)	**20.** (d)
21. (a)	**22.** (b)	**23.** (a)	**24.** (c)	**25.** (a)	**26.** (c)	**27.** (b)	**28.** (b)	**29.** (d)	**30.** (d)
31. (a)	**32.** (a)	**33.** (c)	**34.** (b)	**35.** (c)	**36.** (b)	**37.** (a)	**38.** (c)	**39.** (a)	**40.** (b)
41. (a)	**42.** (c)	**43.** (d)	**44.** (a)	**45.** (c)	**46.** (a)	**47.** (a)	**48.** (a)	**49.** (d)	

EXPLANATIONS

1. (c) : $HCOOH \xrightarrow[\text{conc. } H_2SO_4]{\text{Dehydrating agent}} CO + H_2O$

	$HCOOH$	CO	H_2O
n_i	$=\frac{2.3}{46}=\frac{1}{20}$	0	0
n_f	0	$\frac{1}{20}$	$\frac{1}{20}$

$H_2C_2O_4 \xrightarrow{\text{conc. } H_2SO_4} CO + CO_2 + H_2O$

	$H_2C_2O_4$	CO	CO_2	H_2O
n_i	$=\frac{4.5}{90}=\frac{1}{20}$	0	0	0
n_f	0	$\frac{1}{20}$	$\frac{1}{20}$	$\frac{1}{20}$

H_2O absorbed by H_2SO_4. Gaseous mixture (containing CO and CO_2) when passed through KOH pellets, CO_2 gets absorbed.

Moles of CO left (unabsorbed) $=\frac{1}{20}+\frac{1}{20}=\frac{1}{10}$

Mass of CO = moles × molar mass $=\frac{1}{10}\times 28 = 2.8$ g

2. (a) : (a) Mass of water $= V \times d = 18 \times 1 = 18$ g

Molecules of water = mole × $N_A = \frac{18}{18}N_A = N_A$

(b) Molecules of water = mole × $N_A = \frac{0.18}{18}N_A$
$= 10^{-2}\ N_A$

(c) Moles of water $=\frac{0.00224}{22.4}=10^{-4}$

Molecules of water = mole × $N_A = 10^{-4}\ N_A$

(d) Molecules of water = mole × $N_A = 10^{-3}\ N_A$

3. (a) : Let atomic weight of element X is x and that of element Y is y.

For XY_2, $n = \frac{w}{\text{Mol. wt.}}$

$0.1 = \frac{10}{x+2y} \Rightarrow x + 2y = \frac{10}{0.1} = 100$ ...(i)

For X_3Y_2, $n = \frac{w}{\text{Mol. wt.}}$

$0.05 = \frac{9}{3x+2y} \Rightarrow 3x + 2y = \frac{9}{0.05} = 180$ ...(ii)

On solving equations (i) and (ii), we get $y = 30$

$x + 2(30) = 100 \Rightarrow x = 100 - 60 = 40$

4. (b) : 16.9% solution of $AgNO_3$ means 16.9 g of $AgNO_3$ in 100 mL of solution.

16.9 g of $AgNO_3$ in 100 mL solution ≡ 8.45 g of $AgNO_3$ in 50 mL solution.

Similarly, 5.8% of NaCl in 100 mL solution
≡ 2.9 g of NaCl in 50 mL solution.

The reaction can be represented as :

	$AgNO_3$ +	NaCl	⟶ AgCl +	$NaNO_3$
Initial mole	8.45/170 = 0.049	2.9/58.5 = 0.049	0	0
Final moles	0	0	0.049	0.049

∴ Mass of AgCl precipitated = 0.049 × 143.3
= 7.02 ≈ 7 g

5. (a) : Mass of 1 mol (6.022×10^{23} atoms) of carbon = 12 g

If Avogadro number is changed to 6.022×10^{20} atoms then mass of 1 mol of carbon

$$=\frac{12\times 6.022\times 10^{20}}{6.022\times 10^{23}} = 12\times 10^{-3}\text{g}$$

6. (c) : 1.8 gram of water $=\frac{6.023\times 10^{23}}{18}\times 1.8$
$= 6.023 \times 10^{22}$ molecules

18 gram of water = 6.023×10^{23} molecules

18 moles of water = $18 \times 6.023 \times 10^{23}$ molecules

7. (d) : Number of moles of $H_2 = \frac{1}{2}$

Number of moles of $O_2 = \frac{4}{32}$

Hence, molar ratio $=\frac{1}{2}:\frac{4}{32} = 4:1$

8. (c) : According to Avogadro's hypothesis, ratio of the volumes of gases will be equal to the ratio of their no. of moles.

So, no. of moles $=\frac{\text{Mass}}{\text{Mol. mass}}$

$n_{H_2} = \frac{w}{2}$; $n_{O_2} = \frac{w}{32}$; $n_{CH_4} = \frac{w}{16}$

So, the ratio is $\frac{w}{2}:\frac{w}{32}:\frac{w}{16}$ or 16:1:2.

9. (a) : 1 mole ≡ 22.4 litres at S.T.P.

$n_{H_2} = \frac{22.4}{22.4} = 1$ mol ; $n_{Cl_2} = \frac{11.2}{22.4} = 0.5$ mol

Reaction is as,

	$H_{2(g)}$ +	$Cl_{2(g)}$ ⟶	$2HCl_{(g)}$
Initial	1 mol	0.5 mol	0
Final	(1 − 0.5) = 0.5 mol	(0.5 − 0.5) = 0 mol	2 × 0.5 = 1 mol

Here, Cl_2 is limiting reagent. So, 1 mole of $HCl_{(g)}$ is formed.

10. (a) : $n_{Mg} = \frac{1}{24} = 0.0416$ moles

$n_{O_2} = \frac{0.56}{32} = 0.0175$ moles

The balanced equation is

	Mg	+ $\frac{1}{2}O_2$	$\longrightarrow$ MgO
Initial	0.0416 moles	0.0175 moles	0
Final	(0.0416 – 2 × 0.0175) = 0.0066 moles (O_2 is limiting reagent.)	0	2 × 0.0175

∴ Mass of Mg left in excess = 0.0066 × 24 = 0.16 g

11. (d) : Moles of urea $= \frac{6.02\times10^{20}}{6.02\times10^{23}} = 0.001$

Concentration of solution $= \frac{0.001}{100} \times 1000 = 0.01$ M

12. (b) : Millimoles of solution of chloride = 0.05 × 10 = 0.5

Millimoles of $AgNO_3$ solution = 10 × 0.1 = 1

So, the millimoles of $AgNO_3$ are double than the chloride solution.

∴ $XCl_2 + 2AgNO_3 \rightarrow 2AgCl + X(NO_3)_2$

13. (c) : 8 g H_2 has 4 moles while the others has 1 mole each.

14. (b) : No. of atoms = N_A × No. of moles × 3 $= 6.023 \times 10^{23} \times 0.1 \times 3 = 1.806 \times 10^{23}$

15. (b) : Given that molar mass of Na_2CO_3 = 106 g

∴ Molarity of solution $= \frac{25.3\times1000}{106\times250}$

= 0.9547 M = 0.955 M

$Na_2CO_3 \rightarrow 2Na^+ + CO_3^{2-}$

$[Na^+] = 2[Na_2CO_3] = 2 \times 0.955 = 1.910$ M

$[CO_3^{2-}] = [Na_2CO_3] = 0.955$ M

16. (b) : $H_2 + 1/2O_2 \rightarrow H_2O$

2 g   16 g   18 g

1 mol   0.5   1 mol

10 g of H_2 = 5 mol and 64 g of O_2 = 2 mol

∴ In this reaction, oxygen is the limiting reagent so amount of H_2O produced depends on that of O_2.

Since 0.5 mol of O_2 gives 1 mol H_2O

∴ 2 mol of O_2 will give 4 mol H_2O

17. (a) : $C_3H_8 + 5O_2 \longrightarrow 3CO_2 + 4H_2O$ (balanced equation)

1 vol.   5 vol.   3 vol.   4 vol.

According to the above equation

1 vol. or 1 litre of propane requires to 5 vol. or 5 litre of O_2 to burn completely.

18. (b) : $PbO + 2HCl \rightarrow PbCl_2 + H_2O$

n mol $2n$ mol n mol

$\frac{6.5}{224}$ mol $\frac{3.2}{36.5}$ mol

0.029 mol   0.087 mol

Formation of moles of lead (II) chloride depends upon the no. of moles of PbO which acts as a limiting factor here. So, no. of moles of $PbCl_2$ formed will be equal to the no. of moles of PbO *i.e.* 0.029.

19. (c) :

Element	%	Atomic mass	mole ratio	simple ratio
C	38.71	12	$\frac{38.71}{12} = 3.22$	$\frac{3.22}{3.22} = 1$
H	9.67	1	$\frac{9.67}{1} = 9.67$	$\frac{9.67}{3.22} = 3$
O	51.62	16	$\frac{51.62}{16} = 3.22$	$\frac{3.22}{3.22} = 1$

Hence empirical formula of the compound would be CH_3O.

20. (d) : Average isotopic mass of X

$= \frac{200\times90+199\times8+202\times2}{90+8+2}$

$= \frac{18000+1592+404}{100} = 199.96$ a.m.u. ≈ 200 a.m.u.

21. (a) : At STP, 22.4 L $H_2 = 6.023 \times 10^{23}$ molecules

$15\text{ L } H_2 = \frac{6.023\times10^{23}\times15}{22.4} = 4.033\times10^{23}$

$5\text{ L } N_2 = \frac{6.023\times10^{23}\times5}{22.4} = 1.344\times10^{23}$

$2\text{ g } H_2 = 6.023 \times 10^{23}$

$0.5\text{ g } H_2 = \frac{6.023\times10^{23}\times0.5}{2} = 1.505\times10^{23}$

$32\text{ g } O_2 = 6.023 \times 10^{23}$

$10\text{ g of } O_2 = \frac{6.023\times10^{23}\times10}{32} = 1.882\times10^{23}$

22. (b) : 1 mole of any element contain 6.023×10^{23} number of molecules.

1 g mole of O_2 = 32 g O_2

⇒ 16 g of O_2 = 0.5 g mole O_2

1 g mole of N_2 = 28 g N_2

⇒ 7 g N_2 = 0.25 g mole N_2

1 g mole of H_2 = 2 g H_2

⇒ 2 g H_2 = 1.0 g mole H_2

1 g mole NO_2 = 14 + 16 × 2 = 46

⇒ 16 g of NO_2 = 0.35 mole NO_2

2 g H_2 (1 g mole H_2) contain maximum molecules.

23. (a) : In peroxidase anhydrous enzyme 0.5% Se is present means, 0.5 g Se is present in 100 g of enzyme. In a molecule of enzyme one Se atom must be present. Hence 78.4 g Se will be present in

$\frac{100}{0.5} \times 78.4 = 1.568 \times 10^4$

24. (c) : Density = 1.17 g/cc.

$\Rightarrow$ 1 cc. solution contains 1.17 g of HCl

$\therefore$ Molarity $= \frac{1.17 \times 1000}{36.5 \times 1} = 32.05$

25. (a) : Specific volume (vol. of 1 g) cylindrical virus particle $= 6.02 \times 10^{-2}$ cc/g

Radius of virus, $r = 7$ Å $= 7 \times 10^{-8}$ cm

Volume of virus $= \pi r^2 l$

$= \frac{22}{7} \times (7 \times 10^{-8})^2 \times 10 \times 10^{-8} = 154 \times 10^{-23}$ cc

wt. of one virus particle $= \frac{\text{Volume}}{\text{Specific volume}}$

$= \frac{154 \times 10^{-23}}{6.02 \times 10^{-2}}$ g

$\therefore$ Molecular wt. of virus = wt. of N_A particle

$= \frac{154 \times 10^{-23}}{6.02 \times 10^{-2}} \times 6.02 \times 10^{-23}$ g/mol.

= 15400 g/mol = 15.4 kg/mol

26. (c) : $K_3[Cu(CN)_2] = 3(+1) + x + 2(-1) = 0$

$\Rightarrow x = -1$

As the oxidation no. of 'Cu' is −1 (−ve), so this complex is unstable and is not formed.

27. (b) : $BaCO_3 \rightarrow BaO + CO_2$

197·34 g $\rightarrow$ 22·4 L at N.T.P.

$9{\cdot}85\text{ g} \rightarrow \frac{22{\cdot}4}{197{\cdot}34} \times 9{\cdot}85 = 1{\cdot}118$ L

$\Rightarrow$ 9·85 g $BaCO_3$ will produce 1.118 L CO_2 at N.T.P. on the complete decomposition.

28. (b) : In $A_3(BC_4)_2$, $(+2) \times 3 + 2[+5 + 4(-2)]$

$\Rightarrow +6 + 10 - 16 = 0$

Hence in the compound $A_3(BC_4)_2$, the oxidation no. of 'A', 'B' and 'C' are +2, +5 and −2 respectively.

29. (d) : No. of molecules in 4.25 g NH_3

$= \frac{4.25}{17} \times 6.023 \times 10^{23} = 2.5 \times 6.023 \times 10^{22}$

Number of atoms in 4.25 g NH_3

$= 4 \times 2.5 \times 6.023 \times 10^{22} = 6.023 \times 10^{23}$

30. (d) : Zeros placed left to the number are never significant, therefore the no. of significant figures for the numbers.

1 cm = 0.161 cm and 0.0161 cm are same, *i.e.* 3

31. (a) : Quantity of iron in one molecule

$= \frac{67200}{100} \times 0.334 = 224.45$ amu

No. of iron atoms in one molecule of haemoglobin

$= \frac{224.45}{56} = 4$

32. (a) : $4NH_{3(g)} + 5O_{2(g)} \rightarrow 4NO_{(g)} + 6H_2O_{(l)}$

4 mole + 5 mole $\rightarrow$ 4 mole + 6 mole

$\Rightarrow$ 1 mole of NH_3 requires $= \frac{5}{4} = 1.25$ mole of oxygen

while 1 mole of O_2 requires $= \frac{4}{5} = 0.8$ mole of NH_3.

As there is 1 mole of NH_3 and 1 mole of O_2, so all oxygen will be consumed.

33. (c) : $Ne^{2+}(8) \Rightarrow 1s^2 2s^2 2p_x^2 2p_y^1 2p_z^1$

$Be^+(3) \Rightarrow 1s^2 2s^1$

$Cl^-(18) \Rightarrow 1s^2 2s^2 2p^6 3s^2 3p^6$

$As^+(32) \Rightarrow 1s^2 2s^2 2p^6 3s^2 3p^6 4s^2 3d^{10} 4p_x^1 4p_y^1$

Cl^- is not paramagnetic, as it has no unpaired electron.

34. (b) : Weight of gas = 0.24 g, Volume of gas = 45 mL = 0.045 litre and density of H_2 = 0.089.

We know that weight of 45 mL of H_2 = Density × Volume $= 0.089 \times 0.045 = 4.005 \times 10^{-3}$ g

Therefore vapour density

$= \frac{\text{Weight of certain volume of substance}}{\text{Weight of same volume of hydrogen}}$

$= \frac{0.24}{4.005 \times 10^{-3}} = 59.93$

35. (c) : $\underset{(65\text{ g})}{Zn} + \underset{(22400\text{ mL})}{H_2SO_4} \rightarrow ZnSO_4 + H_2$

Since 65 g of zinc reacts to liberate 22400 mL of H_2 at STP, therefore amount of zinc needed to produce 224 mL of H_2 at STP

$= \frac{65}{22400} \times 224 = 0.65$ g

36. (b) : Pressure $= \frac{\text{Force}}{\text{Area}}$

Therefore dimensions of pressure $= \frac{MLT^{-2}}{L^2}$

$= ML^{-1}T^{-2}$

and dimensions of energy per unit volume

$= \frac{\text{Energy}}{\text{Volume}} = \frac{ML^2T^{-2}}{L^3} = ML^{-1}T^{-2}$

37. (a) : Volume of oxygen in one litre of air

$= \frac{21}{100} \times 1000 = 210$ mL

Therefore no. of mol $= \frac{210}{22400} = 0.0093$ mol

38. (c) : Each nitrogen atom has 5 valence electrons, therefore total number of electrons in N_3^- ion is 16. Since the molecular mass of N_3 is 42, therefore total number of electrons in 4.2 g of N_3^- ion

$$= \frac{4.2}{42} \times 16 \times N_A = 1.6\ N_A$$

39. (a) : 5 M H_2SO_4 = 10 N H_2SO_4

$N_1V_1 = N_2V_2 \Rightarrow 10 \times 1 = N_2 \times 10 \Rightarrow N_2 = 1$ N

40. (b) : Avogadro's No., $N_A = 6.02 \times 10^{23}$ molecules.

$\therefore 6.02 \times 10^{24}$ CO molecules = 10 moles CO

= 10 g atoms of O = 5 g molecules of O_2

41. (a) : Average atomic mass

$$= \frac{19 \times 10 + 81 \times 11}{100} = 10.81$$

42. (c) : If 1 L of one gas contains N molecules, 2 L of any gas under the same conditions will contain 2 N molecules.

43. (d) : $Z_2O_3 + 3H_2 \rightarrow 2Z + 3H_2O$

Valency of metal in Z_2O_3 = 3

0.1596 g of Z_2O_3 react with 6 mg of H_2.

[1 mg = 0.001 g = 10^{-3}g]

$$\therefore 1 \text{ g of } H_2 \text{ react with } = \frac{0.1596}{0.006} = 26.6 \text{ g of } Z_2O_3$$

$\therefore$ Eq. wt. of Z_2O_3 = 26.6

Now, Eq. wt. of Z + Eq. wt. of O = Eq. wt. of Z + 8 = 26.6

$\Rightarrow$ Eq. wt. of Z = 26.6 – 8 = 18.6

$\therefore$ At. wt. of Z = 18.6 × 3 = 55.8

$$\left[\because \text{Eq. wt.} = \frac{\text{Atomic wt.}}{\text{Valency of metal}}\right]$$

44. (a) : Here, C_p/C_V = 1.4, which shows that the gas is diatomic.

22.4 L at NTP = 6.02×10^{23} molecules

$\therefore$ 11.2 L at NTP = 3.01×10^{23} molecules

Since gas is diatomic.

$\therefore$ 11.2 L at NTP = 6.02×10^{23} atom

45. (c) : $C_2H_4 + 3O_2 \rightarrow 2CO_2 + 2H_2O$

28 g 96 g

$$2.8 \text{ kg } C_2H_4 = \frac{96 \text{ g}}{28 \text{ g}} \times 2.8 \text{ kg of } O_2$$

$$= \frac{96}{28} \times 2.8 \times 10^3 \text{ g} = 9.6 \times 10^3 \text{ g} = 9.6 \text{ kg of } O_2$$

46. (a) : 1 mol of CO_2 = 44 g of CO_2

$\therefore$ 4·4 g CO_2 = 0.1 mol CO_2 = 6×10^{22} molecules

[Since, 1 mole CO_2 = 6×10^{23} molecules]

= $2 \times 6 \times 10^{22}$ atoms of O = 1.2×10^{23} atoms of O

47. (a) : 1 mol CCl_4 vapour = 12 + 4 × 35.5

= 154 g = 22.4 L

$$\therefore \text{Density of } CCl_4 \text{ vapour } = \frac{154}{22.4} \text{ g L}^{-1}$$

= 6.875 g L^{-1}

48. (a) : $Mg^{2+} + Na_2CO_3 \rightarrow MgCO_3 + 2Na^+$

1g eq. 1g eq.

1g eq. of Mg^{2+} = 12g of Mg^{2+} = 12000 mg

Now, 1000 millieq. of Na_2CO_3 = 12000 mg of Mg^{2+}

$\therefore$ 1 millieq. of Na_2CO_3 = 12 mg of Mg^{2+}

49. (d) : As we know,

22400 cc of N_2O contain 6.02×10^{23} molecules

$$\therefore \quad 1 \text{ cc of } N_2O \text{ contain } \frac{6.02 \times 10^{23}}{22400} \text{ molecules}$$

Since in N_2O molecule there are 3 atoms

$$\therefore \quad 1 \text{ cc } N_2O = \frac{3 \times 6.02 \times 10^{23}}{22400} \text{ atoms}$$

$$= \frac{1.8 \times 10^{22}}{224} \text{ atoms}$$

No. of electrons in a molecule of N_2O = 7 + 7 + 8 = 2

$$\text{Hence, no. of electrons } = \frac{6.02 \times 10^{23}}{22400} \times 22 \text{ electron}$$

$$= \frac{1.32}{224} \times 10^{23} \text{ electrons}$$

Chapter 2
Structure of Atom

1. Which one is a wrong statement?
(a) Total orbital angular momentum of electron in s-orbital is equal to zero.
(b) An orbital is designated by three quantum numbers while an electron in an atom is designated by four quantum numbers.
(c) The electronic configuration of N atom is

$1s^2$	$2s^2$	$2p_x^1$	$2p_y^1$	$2p_z^1$
↑↓	↑↓	↑	↑	↓

(d) The value of m for d_{z^2} is zero.
(NEET 2018)

2. Which one is the wrong statement?
(a) The uncertainty principle is $\Delta E \times \Delta t \geq \dfrac{h}{4\pi}$
(b) Half filled and fully filled orbitals have greater stability due to greater exchange energy, greater symmetry and more balanced arrangement.
(c) The energy of $2s$-orbital is less than the energy of $2p$-orbital in case of hydrogen like atoms.
(d) de-Broglie's wavelength is given by $\lambda = \dfrac{h}{mv}$, where m = mass of the particle, v = group velocity of the particle.
(NEET 2017)

3. How many electrons can fit in the orbital for which $n = 3$ and $l = 1$?
(a) 2 (b) 6 (c) 10 (d) 14
(NEET-II 2016)

4. Which of the following pairs of d orbitals will have electron density along the axes?
(a) d_{z^2}, d_{xz} (b) d_{xz}, d_{yz}
(c) $d_{z^2}, d_{x^2-y^2}$ (d) $d_{xy}, d_{x^2-y^2}$
(NEET-II 2016)

5. Two electrons occupying the same orbital are distinguished by
(a) azimuthal quantum number
(b) spin quantum number
(c) principal quantum number
(d) magnetic quantum number.
(NEET-I 2016)

6. Which is the correct order of increasing energy of the listed orbitals in the atom of titanium? (At. no. $Z = 22$)
(a) $4s\ 3s\ 3p\ 3d$ (b) $3s\ 3p\ 3d\ 4s$
(c) $3s\ 3p\ 4s\ 3d$ (d) $3s\ 4s\ 3p\ 3d$
(2015)

7. The number of d-electrons in Fe^{2+} ($Z = 26$) is not equal to the number of electrons in which one of the following?
(a) d-electrons in Fe ($Z = 26$)
(b) p-electrons in Ne ($Z = 10$)
(c) s-electrons in Mg ($Z = 12$)
(d) p-electrons in Cl ($Z = 17$)
(2015, Cancelled)

8. The angular momentum of electron in 'd' orbital is equal to
(a) $2\sqrt{3}\hbar$ (b) $0\hbar$
(c) $\sqrt{6}\hbar$ (d) $\sqrt{2}\hbar$
(2015, Cancelled)

9. What is the maximum number of orbitals that can be identified with the following quantum numbers?
$n = 3, l = 1, m_l = 0$
(a) 1 (b) 2 (c) 3 (d) 4
(2014)

10. Calculate the energy in joule corresponding to light of wavelength 45 nm. (Planck's constant, $h = 6.63 \times 10^{-34}$ J s, speed of light, $c = 3 \times 10^8$ m s^{-1})
(a) 6.67×10^{15} (b) 6.67×10^{11}
(c) 4.42×10^{-15} (d) 4.42×10^{-18}
(2014)

11. Be^{2+} is isoelectronic with which of the following ions?
(a) H^+ (b) Li^+ (c) Na^+ (d) Mg^{2+}
(2014)

12. What is the maximum numbers of electrons that can be associated with the following set of quantum numbers?
$n = 3$, $l = 1$ and $m = -1$
(a) 4 (b) 2 (c) 10 (d) 6
(NEET 2013)

13. Based on equation $E = -2.178 \times 10^{-18}\ \text{J}\left(\frac{Z^2}{n^2}\right)$, certain conclusions are written. Which of them is not correct?
(a) Equation can be used to calculate the change in energy when the electron changes orbit.
(b) For $n = 1$, the electron has a more negative energy than it does for $n = 6$ which means that the electron is more loosely bound in the smallest allowed orbit.
(c) The negative sign in equation simply means that the energy of electron bound to the nucleus is lower than it would be if the electrons were at the infinite distance from the nucleus.
(d) Larger the value of n, the larger is the orbit radius. *(NEET 2013)*

14. The value of Planck's constant is 6.63×10^{-34} J s. The speed of light is 3×10^{17} nm s^{-1}. Which value is closest to the wavelength in nanometer of a quantum of light with frequency of 6×10^{15} s^{-1}?
(a) 50 (b) 75 (c) 10 (d) 25
(NEET 2013)

15. The outer electronic configuration of Gd (At. No. 64) is
(a) $4f^5\,5d^4\,6s^1$ (b) $4f^7\,5d^1\,6s^2$
(c) $4f^3\,5d^5\,6s^2$ (d) $4f^4\,5d^5\,6s^1$
(Karnataka NEET 2013)

16. According to law of photochemical equivalence the energy absorbed (in ergs/mole) is given as ($h = 6.62 \times 10^{-27}$ ergs, $c = 3 \times 10^{10}$ cm s^{-1}, $N_A = 6.02 \times 10^{-23}$ mol^{-1})
(a) $\frac{1.196\times10^{8}}{\lambda}$ (b) $\frac{2.859\times10^{5}}{\lambda}$
(c) $\frac{2.859\times10^{16}}{\lambda}$ (d) $\frac{1.196\times10^{16}}{\lambda}$
(Karnataka NEET 2013)

17. Maximum number of electrons in a subshell with $l = 3$ and $n = 4$ is
(a) 14 (b) 16 (c) 10 (d) 12
(2012)

18. The correct set of four quantum numbers for the valence electron of rubidium atom ($Z = 37$) is
(a) 5, 1, 1, +1/2 (b) 6, 0, 0, +1/2
(c) 5, 0, 0, +1/2 (d) 5, 1, 0, +1/2
(2012)

19. The orbital angular momentum of a p-electron is given as
(a) $\frac{h}{\sqrt{2}\pi}$ (b) $\sqrt{3}\frac{h}{2\pi}$ (c) $\sqrt{\frac{3}{2}}\frac{h}{\pi}$ (d) $\sqrt{6}\frac{h}{2\pi}$
(Mains 2012)

20. The total number of atomic orbitals in fourth energy level of an atom is
(a) 8 (b) 16 (c) 32 (d) 4
(2011)

21. The energies E_1 and E_2 of two radiations are 25 eV and 50 eV respectively. The relation between their wavelengths *i.e.*, λ_1 and λ_2 will be
(a) $\lambda_1 = \lambda_2$ (b) $\lambda_1 = 2\lambda_2$
(c) $\lambda_1 = 4\lambda_2$ (d) $\lambda_1 = \frac{1}{2}\lambda_2$ *(2011)*

22. If $n = 6$, the correct sequence for filling of electrons will be
(a) $ns \rightarrow (n-2)f \rightarrow (n-1)d \rightarrow np$
(b) $ns \rightarrow (n-1)d \rightarrow (n-2)f \rightarrow np$
(c) $ns \rightarrow (n-2)f \rightarrow np \rightarrow (n-1)d$
(d) $ns \rightarrow np \rightarrow (n-1)d \rightarrow (n-2)f$ *(2011)*

23. According to the Bohr theory, which of the following transitions in the hydrogen atom will give rise to the least energetic photon?
(a) $n = 6$ to $n = 1$ (b) $n = 5$ to $n = 4$
(c) $n = 6$ to $n = 5$ (d) $n = 5$ to $n = 3$
(Mains 2011)

24. A 0.66 kg ball is moving with a speed of 100 m/s. The associated wavelength will be ($h = 6.6 \times 10^{-34}$ J s)
(a) 6.6×10^{-32} m (b) 6.6×10^{-34} m
(c) 1.0×10^{-35} m (d) 1.0×10^{-32} m
(Mains 2010)

25. Maximum number of electrons in a subshell of an atom is determined by the following
(a) $2l + 1$ (b) $4l - 2$
(c) $2n^2$ (d) $4l + 2$ *(2009)*

26. Which of the following is not permissible arrangement of electrons in an atom?
(a) $n = 5, l = 3, m = 0, s = +1/2$
(b) $n = 3, l = 2, m = -3, s = -1/2$
(c) $n = 3, l = 2, m = -2, s = -1/2$
(d) $n = 4, l = 0, m = 0, s = -1/2$ *(2009)*

27. If uncertainty in position and momentum are equal, then uncertainty in velocity is
(a) $\frac{1}{m}\sqrt{\frac{h}{\pi}}$ (b) $\sqrt{\frac{h}{\pi}}$
(c) $\frac{1}{2m}\sqrt{\frac{h}{\pi}}$ (d) $\sqrt{\frac{h}{2\pi}}$ *(2008)*

28. The measurement of the electron position is associated with an uncertainty in momentum, which is equal to 1×10^{-18} g cm s^{-1}. The uncertainty in electron velocity is (mass of an electron is 9×10^{-28} g)
(a) 1×10^5 cm s^{-1} (b) 1×10^{11} cm s^{-1}
(c) 1×10^9 cm s^{-1} (d) 1×10^6 cm s^{-1}
(2008)

29. Consider the following sets of quantum numbers:

	n	l	m	s
(i)	3	0	0	+1/2
(ii)	2	2	1	+1/2
(iii)	4	3	−2	−1/2
(iv)	1	0	−1	−1/2
(v)	3	2	3	+1/2

Which of the following sets of quantum number is not possible?
(a) (i), (ii), (iii) and (iv)
(b) (ii), (iv) and (v)
(c) (i) and (iii)
(d) (ii), (iii) and (iv). *(2007)*

30. The orientation of an atomic orbital is governed by
(a) principal quantum number
(b) azimuthal quantum number
(c) spin quantum number
(d) magnetic quantum number. *(2006)*

31. Given : The mass of electron is 9.11×10^{-31} kg, Planck constant is 6.626×10^{-34} J s, the uncertainty involved in the measurement of velocity within a distance of 0.1 Å is
(a) 5.79×10^5 m s^{-1} (b) 5.79×10^6 m s^{-1}
(c) 5.79×10^7 m s^{-1} (d) 5.79×10^8 m s^{-1}
(2006)

32. The energy of second Bohr orbit of the hydrogen atom is −328 kJ mol^{-1}; hence the energy of fourth Bohr orbit would be
(a) − 41 kJ mol^{-1} (b) −82 kJ mol^{-1}
(c) −164 kJ mol^{-1} (d) −1312 kJ mol^{-1}
(2005)

33. The frequency of radiation emitted when the electron falls from $n = 4$ to $n = 1$ in a hydrogen atom will be (Given ionization energy of H = 2.18×10^{-18} J atom^{-1} and $h = 6.625 \times 10^{-34}$ J s)
(a) 1.54×10^{15} s^{-1} (b) 1.03×10^{15} s^{-1}
(c) 3.08×10^{15} s^{-1} (d) 2.00×10^{15} s^{-1}
(2004)

34. The value of Planck's constant is 6.63×10^{-34} J s. The velocity of light is 3.0×10^8 m s^{-1}. Which value is closest to the wavelength in nanometers of a quantum of light with frequency of 8×10^{15} s^{-1} ?
(a) 2×10^{-25} (b) 5×10^{-18}
(c) 4×10^1 (d) 3×10^7 *(2003)*

35. In hydrogen atom, energy of first excited state is −3.4 eV. Then find out *K.E.* of same orbit of hydrogen atom
(a) +3.4 eV (b) +6.8 eV
(c) −13.6 eV (d) +13.6 eV *(2002)*

36. Main axis of a diatomic molecule is z, molecular orbital p_x and p_y overlap to form which of the following orbitals.
(a) π molecular orbital
(b) σ molecular orbital
(c) δ molecular orbital
(d) No bond will form. *(2001)*

37. The following quantum numbers are possible for how many orbitals : $n = 3, l = 2, m = +2$?
(a) 1 (b) 2 (c) 3 (d) 4
(2001)

38. For given energy, $E = 3.03 \times 10^{-19}$ Joules corresponding wavelength is
($h = 6.626 \times 10^{-34}$ J sec, $c = 3 \times 10^8$ m/sec)

(a) 65.6 nm (b) 6.56 nm
(c) 3.4 nm (d) 656 nm *(2000)*

39. Isoelectronic species are
(a) CO, CN^-, NO^+, C_2^{2-}
(b) CO^-, CN, NO, C_2^-
(c) CO^+, CN^+, NO^-, C_2
(d) CO, CN, NO, C_2 *(2000)*

40. The uncertainty in momentum of an electron is 1×10^{-5} kg m/s. The uncertainty in its position will be ($h = 6.62 \times 10^{-34}$ kg m^2/s)
(a) 5.27×10^{-30} m (b) 1.05×10^{-26} m
(c) 1.05×10^{-28} m (d) 5.25×10^{-28} m *(1999)*

41. Who modified Bohr's theory by introducing elliptical orbits for electron path?
(a) Rutherford (b) Thomson
(c) Hund (d) Sommerfield *(1999)*

42. The de Broglie wavelength of a particle with mass 1 g and velocity 100 m/s is
(a) 6.63×10^{-35} m (b) 6.63×10^{-34} m
(c) 6.63×10^{-33} m (d) 6.65×10^{-35} m *(1999)*

43. The Bohr orbit radius for the hydrogen atom ($n = 1$) is approximately 0.530 Å. The radius for the first excited state ($n = 2$) orbit is (in Å)
(a) 4.77 (b) 1.06 (c) 0.13 (d) 2.12 *(1998)*

44. The position of both, an electron and a helium atom is known within 1.0 nm. Further the momentum of the electron is known within 5.0×10^{-26} kg m s^{-1}. The minimum uncertainty in the measurement of the momentum of the helium atom is
(a) 8.0×10^{-26} kg m s^{-1}
(b) 80 kg m s^{-1}
(c) 50 kg m s^{-1}
(d) 5.0×10^{-26} kg m s^{-1} *(1998)*

45. The ion that is isoelectronic with CO is
(a) CN^- (b) N_2^+ (c) O^{2-} (d) N_2^- *(1997)*

46. What will be the longest wavelength line in Balmer series of spectrum?
(a) 546 nm (b) 656 nm
(c) 566 nm (d) 556 nm *(1996)*

47. In a Bohr's model of an atom, when an electron jumps from $n = 1$ to $n = 3$, how much energy will be emitted or absorbed?
(a) 2.389×10^{-12} ergs
(b) 0.239×10^{-10} ergs
(c) 2.15×10^{-11} ergs
(d) 0.1936×10^{-10} ergs *(1996)*

48. Uncertainty in position of an electron (mass $= 9.1 \times 10^{-28}$ g) moving with a velocity of 3×10^4 cm/s accurate upto 0.001% will be (Use $h/(4\pi)$ in uncertainty expression where $h = 6.626 \times 10^{-27}$ erg second)
(a) 5.76 cm (b) 7.68 cm
(c) 1.93 cm (d) 3.84 cm *(1995)*

49. The radius of hydrogen atom in the ground state is 0.53 Å. The radius of Li^{2+} ion (atomic number = 3) in a similar state is
(a) 0.53 Å (b) 1.06 Å
(c) 0.17 Å (d) 0.265 Å *(1995)*

50. For which of the following sets of four quantum numbers, an electron will have the highest energy?

	n	l	m	s
(a)	3	2	1	+1/2
(b)	4	2	– 1	+1/2
(c)	4	1	0	–1/2
(d)	5	0	0	–1/2

(1994)

51. Which one of the following is not isoelectronic with O^{2-}?
(a) Tl^+ (b) Na^+ (c) N^{3-} (d) F^- *(1994)*

52. Electronic configuration of calcium atom can be written as
(a) [Ne] $4p^2$ (b) [Ar] $4s^2$
(c) [Ne] $4s^2$ (d) [Kr] $4p^2$ *(1992)*

53. The energy of an electron in the nth Bohr orbit of hydrogen atom is
(a) $\frac{13.6}{n^4}$ eV (b) $\frac{13.6}{n^3}$ eV
(c) $\frac{13.6}{n^2}$ eV (d) $\frac{13.6}{n}$ eV *(1992)*

54. In a given atom no two electrons can have the same values for all the four quantum numbers. This is called

(a) Hund's Rule
(b) Aufbau principle
(c) Uncertainty principle
(d) Pauli's Exclusion principle. *(1991)*

55. For azimuthal quantum number $l = 3$, the maximum number of electrons will be
(a) 2 (b) 6 (c) 0 (d) 14 *(1991)*

56. The order of filling of electrons in the orbitals of an atom will be
(a) $3d, 4s, 4p, 4d, 5s$
(b) $4s, 3d, 4p, 5s, 4d$
(c) $5s, 4p, 3d, 4d, 5s$
(d) $3d, 4p, 4s, 4d, 5s$ *(1991)*

57. The electronic configuration of Cu (atomic number 29) is
(a) $1s^2, 2s^22p^6, 3s^23p^6, 4s^23d^9$
(b) $1s^2, 2s^22p^6, 3s^23p^63d^{10}, 4s^1$
(c) $1s^2, 2s^22p^6, 3s^23p^6, 4s^24p^6, 5s^25p^1$
(d) $1s^2, 2s^22p^6, 3s^23p^6, 4s^24p^63d^3$ *(1991)*

58. The total number of electrons that can be accommodated in all the orbitals having principal quantum number 2 and azimuthal quantum number 1 are
(a) 2 (b) 4
(c) 6 (d) 8 *(1990)*

59. An ion has 18 electrons in the outermost shell, it is
(a) Cu^+ (b) Th^{4+}
(c) Cs^+ (d) K^+ *(1990)*

60. Which of the following statements do not form a part of Bohr's model of hydrogen atom?
(a) Energy of the electrons in the orbits are quantized.
(b) The electron in the orbit nearest the nucleus has the lowest energy.
(c) Electrons revolve in different orbits around the nucleus.
(d) The position and velocity of the electrons in the orbit cannot be determined simultaneously. *(1989)*

61. Number of unpaired electrons in N^{2+} is/are
(a) 2 (b) 0
(c) 1 (d) 3 *(1989)*

62. The maximum number of electrons in a subshell is given by the expression
(a) $4l - 2$ (b) $4l + 2$
(c) $2l + 2$ (d) $2n^2$ *(1989)*

63. The spectrum of He is expected to be similar to that
(a) H (b) Li^+
(c) Na (d) He^+ *(1988)*

64. The number of spherical nodes in $3p$ orbitals are/is
(a) one (b) three
(c) none (d) two *(1988)*

65. If r is the radius of the first orbit, the radius of nth orbit of H-atom is given by
(a) r_0n^2 (b) r_0n
(c) r_0/n (d) $r_0^2n^2$ *(1988)*

Answer Key

1. (c) **2.** (c) **3.** (a) **4.** (c) **5.** (b) **6.** (c) **7.** (d) **8.** (c) **9.** (a) **10.** (d)
11. (b) **12.** (b) **13.** (b) **14.** (a) **15.** (b) **16.** (a) **17.** (a) **18.** (c) **19.** (a) **20.** (b)
21. (b) **22.** (a) **23.** (c) **24.** (c) **25.** (d) **26.** (b) **27.** (c) **28.** (c) **29.** (b) **30.** (d)
31. (b) **32.** (b) **33.** (c) **34.** (c) **35.** (a) **36.** (a) **37.** (a) **38.** (d) **39.** (a) **40.** (a)
41. (d) **42.** (c) **43.** (d) **44.** (d) **45.** (a) **46.** (b) **47.** (d) **48.** (c) **49.** (c) **50.** (b)
51. (a) **52.** (b) **53.** (c) **54.** (d) **55.** (d) **56.** (b) **57.** (b) **58.** (c) **59.** (a) **60.** (d)
61. (c) **62.** (b) **63.** (b) **64.** (a) **65.** (a)

EXPLANATIONS

1. (c) : According to Hund's rule of maximum multiplicity, the correct configuration of 'N' is

$1s^2$	$2s^2$	$2p_x^1$	$2p_y^1$	$2p_z^1$
⇅	⇅	↑	↑	↑

2. (c) : In case of hydrogen like atoms, energy depends on the principal quantum number only. Hence, 2s-orbital will have energy equal to 2p-orbital.

3. (a) : For $n = 3$ and $l = 1$, the subshell is $3p$ and a particular $3p$ orbital can accommodate only 2 electrons.

4. (c) : $d_{x^2-y^2}$ and d_{z^2} orbitals have electron density along the axes while d_{xy}, d_{yz} and d_{xz} orbitals have electron density inbetween the axes.

5. (b) : For the two electrons occupying the same orbital values of n, l and m_l are same but m_s is different, *i.e.*, $+\frac{1}{2}$ and $-\frac{1}{2}$.

6. (c) : Ti(22) : $1s^2 2s^2 2p^6 3s^2 3p^6 4s^2 3d^2$

∴ Order of increasing energy is $3s$, $3p$, $4s$, $3d$

7. (d) : Number of d-electrons in $Fe^{2+} = 6$

Number of p-electrons in Cl = 11

8. (c) : Angular momentum $= \sqrt{l(l+1)}\,\hbar$

For d orbital, $l = 2$

Angular momentum $= \sqrt{2(2+1)}\,\hbar = \sqrt{6}\,\hbar$

9. (a) : Only one orbital, $3p_z$ has following set of quantum numbers, $n = 3$, $l = 1$ and $m_l = 0$.

10. (d) : $E = \frac{hc}{\lambda}$ [Given, $\lambda = 45$ nm $= 45 \times 10^{-9}$ m]

On putting the given values in the equation, we get

$$E = \frac{6.63\times10^{-34}\times3\times10^{8}}{45\times10^{-9}} = 4.42\times10^{-18}\text{ J}$$

11. (b):

Species	No. of electrons
Be^{2+}	2
H^+	0
Li^+	2
Na^+	10
Mg^{2+}	10

12. (b) : The orbital associated with $n = 3$, $l = 1$ is $3p$. One orbital (with $m = -1$) of $3p$-subshell can accomodate maximum 2 electrons.

13. (b) : The electron is more tightly bound in the smallest allowed orbit.

14. (a) : $c = \upsilon\lambda$

$$\lambda = \frac{c}{\upsilon} = \frac{3\times10^{17}}{6\times10^{15}} = 50\text{ nm}$$

15. (b) : The electronic configuration of Gd_{64} is $[Xe]4f^7 5d^1 6s^2$.

16. (a) : We know that, $E = \frac{hcN_A}{\lambda}$

$$= \frac{6.62\times10^{-27}\times3\times10^{10}\times6.02\times10^{23}}{\lambda}$$

$$= \frac{1.1955\times10^{8}}{\lambda} = \frac{1.196\times10^{8}}{\lambda}\text{ ergs mol}^{-1}$$

17. (a) : $l = 3$ and $n = 4$ represent $4f$. So, total number of electrons in a subshell $= 2(2l + 1) = 2(2 \times 3 + 1) = 14$ electrons. Hence f-subshell can contain maximum 14 electrons.

18. (c) : Rb(37) : $1s^2 2s^2 2p^6 3s^2 3p^6 4s^2 3d^{10} 4p^6 5s^1$

For $5s$, $n = 5$, $l = 0$, $m = 0$, $s = +1/2$ or $-1/2$

19. (a) : Orbital angular momentum

$$(m) = \sqrt{l(l+1)}\,\frac{h}{2\pi}$$

For p-electrons; $l = 1$

Thus, $m = \sqrt{1(1+1)}\,\frac{h}{2\pi} = \frac{\sqrt{2}\,h}{2\pi} = \frac{h}{\sqrt{2}\,\pi}$

20. (b) : Total number of atomic orbitals in any energy level is given by n^2.

21. (b) : $E_1 = \frac{hc}{\lambda_1}$ and $E_2 = \frac{hc}{\lambda_2}$;

$$\frac{E_1}{E_2} = \frac{hc}{\lambda_1}\times\frac{\lambda_2}{hc} = \frac{\lambda_2}{\lambda_1}$$

or $\frac{25}{50} = \frac{\lambda_2}{\lambda_1}$ or $\frac{1}{2} = \frac{\lambda_2}{\lambda_1} \Rightarrow \lambda_1 = 2\lambda_2$

22. (a)

23. (c) : We know that

$$\Delta E \propto \left[\frac{1}{n_1^2}-\frac{1}{n_2^2}\right],\text{ where } n_2 > n_1$$

∴ $n = 6$ to $n = 5$ will give least energetic photon.

24. (c) : According to de-Broglie equation, $\lambda = \frac{h}{mv}$

Given, $h = 6.6 \times 10^{-34}$ J s ; $m = 0.66$ kg ; $v = 100$ m s^{-1}

$$\therefore\ \lambda = \frac{6.6\times10^{-34}}{0.66\times100} = 1\times10^{-35}\text{ m}$$

25. (d) : For a given shell, l,

the number of subshells, $m_l = (2l + 1)$

Since each subshell can accommodate 2 electrons of opposite spin, so maximum number of electrons in a subshell $= 2(2l + 1) = 4l + 2$.

26. (b) : In an atom, for any value of n, the values of $l = 0$ to $(n - 1)$.
For a given value of l, the values of $m_l = -l$ to 0 to $+l$ and the value of $s = +1/2$ or $-1/2$.
In option (b), $l = 2$ and $m_l = -3$
This is not possible, as values of m_l which are possible for $l = 2$ are –2, –1, 0, +1 and +2 only.

27. (c) : From Heisenberg uncertainty principle

$$\Delta p \cdot \Delta x \geq \frac{h}{4\pi} \quad \text{or} \quad m\Delta v \times \Delta x \geq \frac{h}{4\pi}$$

$$\text{or} \quad (m\Delta v)^2 \geq \frac{h}{4\pi} \qquad (\because \Delta x = \Delta p)$$

$$\text{or} \quad \Delta v \geq \frac{1}{2m}\sqrt{\frac{h}{\pi}}$$

28. (c) : Uncertainty in momentum

$(m\Delta v) = 1 \times 10^{-18}$ g cm s^{-1}

Uncertainty in velocity,

$$(\Delta v) = \frac{1 \times 10^{-18}}{9 \times 10^{-28}} = 1.1 \times 10^9 \text{ cm s}^{-1}$$

29. (b) : (i) represents an electron in 3s orbital.
(ii) is not possible as value of l varies from 0, 1, ... $(n - 1)$.
(iii) represents an electron in 4f orbital.
(iv) is not possible as value of m varies from $-l$ ... $+l$.
(v) is not possible as value of m varies from $-l$ ... $+l$, it can never be greater than l.

30. (d) : Principal quantum number represents the name, size and energy of the shell to which the electron belongs. Azimuthal quantum number describes the spatial distribution of electron cloud and angular momentum. Magnetic quantum number describes the orientation or distribution of electron cloud. Spin quantum number represents the direction of electron spin around its own axis.

31. (b): $\Delta x \cdot m\Delta v = h/4\pi$

$$0.1 \times 10^{-10} \times 9.11 \times 10^{-31} \times \Delta v = \frac{6.626 \times 10^{-34}}{4 \times 3.143}$$

$$\Delta v = \frac{6.626 \times 10^{-34}}{0.1 \times 10^{-10} \times 9.11 \times 10^{-31} \times 4 \times 3.143}$$

$= 5.79 \times 10^6$ m s^{-1}

32. (b): $E_n = -K\left(\frac{Z}{n}\right)^2$

$Z = 1$ for hydrogen ; $n = 2$

$$E_2 = \frac{-K \times 1}{4} \Rightarrow E_2 = -328 \text{ kJ mol}^{-1} ; K = 4 \times 328$$

$$E_4 = \frac{-K \times 1}{16} \Rightarrow E_4 = -4 \times 328 \times \frac{1}{16} = -82 \text{ kJ mol}^{-1}$$

33. (c) : $E = h\upsilon$ or $\upsilon = E/h$

For H atom, $E = \dfrac{-21.76 \times 10^{-19}}{n^2}$ J atm^{-1}

$$\Delta E = -21.76 \times 10^{-19}\left(\frac{1}{4^2} - \frac{1}{1^2}\right) = 20.40 \times 10^{-19} \text{ J atm}^{-1}$$

$$\upsilon = \frac{20.40 \times 10^{-19}}{6.626 \times 10^{-34}} = 3.079 \times 10^{15} \text{ s}^{-1}$$

34. (c) : Applying $(\upsilon) = c/\lambda$,

$$\lambda = \frac{c}{\upsilon} = \frac{3 \times 10^8}{8 \times 10^{15}} = 37.5 \times 10^{-9} \text{ m} = 37.5 \text{ nm} \approx 4 \times 10^1 \text{ nm}$$

35. (a) : Kinetic energy $= \frac{1}{2}mv^2 = \left(\frac{\pi e^2}{nh}\right)^2 \times 2m$

$$\left[\because v = \frac{2\pi e^2}{nh}\right]$$

Total energy $E_n = -\dfrac{2\pi^2 me^4}{n^2h^2} = -\left(\dfrac{\pi e^2}{nh}\right)^2 \times 2m = -K.E.$

$\therefore$ Kinetic energy $= -E_n$

Energy of first excited state is –3.4 eV

$\therefore$ Kinetic energy of same orbit (n = 2) will be +3.4 eV.

36. (a) : For π overlap, the lobes of the atomic orbitals are perpendicular to the line joining the nuclei.

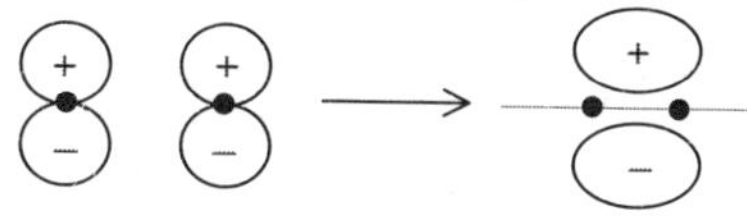

p_x p_y π-overlap

Hence, only sidewise overlapping takes place.

37. (a) : $n = 3, l = 2, m = +2$

It symbolises one of the five d-orbitals (3d).

$m =$	+2	+1	0	–1	–2

38. (d) : $E = \dfrac{hc}{\lambda} \Rightarrow \lambda = \dfrac{6 \cdot 6 \times 10^{-34} \times 3 \times 10^8}{3 \cdot 03 \times 10^{-19}}$

$= 656$ nm

39. (a) : Species having same no. of electrons are called isoelectronics.
The no. of electrons in $CO = CN^- = NO^+ = C_2^{2-} = 14$.
So these are isoelectronics.

40. (a) : $\Delta x \times \Delta p = \dfrac{h}{4\pi}$

(Heisenberg uncertainty principle)

$$\Rightarrow \Delta x = \frac{6.62 \times 10^{-34}}{4 \times 3.14 \times 10^{-5}} = 5.27 \times 10^{-30} \text{ m}$$

41. (d) : Sommerfield modified Bohr's theory considering that in addition to circular orbits electrons also move in elliptical orbits.

42. (c) : $\lambda = \frac{h}{mv} = \frac{6.63 \times 10^{-27}\ \text{erg sec}}{1\ \text{g} \times 10^4\ \text{cm/s}}$

$= 6.63 \times 10^{-31}$ cm $= 6.63 \times 10^{-33}$ m

43. (d) : For n^{th} orbit of 'H' atom, $r_n = n^2 \times r_1$

⇒ radius of 2nd Bohr's orbit.

$r_2 = 4 \times r_1 = 4 \times 0.530 = 2.120$ Å

44. (d) : According to uncertainty principle the product of uncertainty in position and uncertainty in momentum is constant for a particle.

i.e., $\Delta x \times \Delta p = \frac{h}{4\pi}$

As, Δx = 1.0 nm for both electron and helium atom, so Δp is also same for both the particles.

Thus uncertainty in momentum of the helium atom is also 5.0×10^{-26} kg m s^{-1}.

45. (a) : Since both CO and CN^- have 14 electrons, therefore these are isoelectronic (*i.e.* having same number of electrons).

46. (b) : The longest wavelength means the lowest energy. We know that relation for wavelength

$$\frac{1}{\lambda} = R_H\left(\frac{1}{n_1^2} - \frac{1}{n_2^2}\right)$$

here, $n_1 = 2$, $n_2 = 3$

R_H (Rydberg constant = 109677 cm^{-1}

$$\frac{1}{\lambda} = 109677\left(\frac{1}{(2)^2} - \frac{1}{(3)^2}\right) = 15233$$

or, $\lambda = \frac{1}{15233} = 6.56 \times 10^{-5}$ cm $= 6.56 \times 10^{-7}$ m $= 656$ nm

47. (d) : Energy of an atom when $n = 1$

$E_1 = -\frac{1312}{(1)^2} = -1312$ kJ mol^{-1}

Similarly energy when $n = 3$, $(E_3) = -\frac{1312}{(3)^2}$

$= -145.7$ kJ mol^{-1}

The energy absorbed when an electron jumps from $n = 1$ to $n = 3$

$E_3 - E_1 = -145.7 - (-1312) = 1166.3$ kJ mol^{-1}

$= \frac{1166.3}{6.023 \times 10^{23}} = 193.6 \times 10^{-23}$ kJ

$= 193.6 \times 10^{-20}$ J [1 Joule = 10^7 ergs]

⇒ 193.6×10^{-13} ergs $= 0.1936 \times 10^{-10}$ ergs

48. (c) : Mass of an electron $(m) = 9.1 \times 10^{-28}$ g

Velocity of electron $(v) = 3 \times 10^4$ cm/s

Accuracy = 0.001% = $\frac{0.001}{100}$ and Planck's constant $(h) = 6.626 \times 10^{-27}$ erg-second.

We know that actual velocity of the electron

$(\Delta v) = 3 \times 10^4 \times \frac{0.001}{100} = 0.3$ cm/s

Therefore, uncertainty in the position of the electron

$(\Delta x) = \frac{h}{4\pi m \Delta v} = \frac{6.626 \times 10^{-27}}{4\pi \times (9.1 \times 10^{-28}) \times 0.3} = 1.93$ cm

49. (c) : Due to ground state, state of hydrogen atom $(n) = 1$; Radius of hydrogen atom $(r) = 0.53$ Å

Atomic no. of Li $(Z) = 3$

Now, radius of Li^{2+} ion $= r \times \frac{n^2}{Z} = 0.53 \times \frac{(1)^2}{3} = 0.17$Å

50. (b) : Energy of electron depends on the value of $(n + l)$. The subshell are $3d$, $4d$, $4p$ and $5s$, $4d$ has highest energy.

51. (a) : The number of electrons in O^{2-}, N^{3-}, F^- and Na^+ is 10 each, but number of electrons in Tl^+ is 80.

52. (b) : Atomic No. of Ca = 20

∴ Electronic configuration of Ca = [Ar]$4s^2$

53. (c) : Energy of an electron in n^{th} Bohr orbit of hydrogen atom $= \frac{-13.6}{n^2}$ eV

54. (d) : This is a Pauli's Exclusion principle.

55. (d) : $l = 3$ means f-subshell

Maximum no. of electrons in f-subshell = 14

f-subshell = | ⇅ | ⇅ | ⇅ | ⇅ | ⇅ | ⇅ | ⇅ |

56. (b) : As per Aufbau Principle.

The principle states : In the ground state of the atoms, the orbitals are filled in order of thei increasing energies.

57. (b) : Electronic configuration of Cu

$= 1s^2 2s^2 2p^6 3s^2 3p^6 3d^{10} 4s^1$

58. (c) : $n = 2$, $l = 1$

It means $2p$-orbitals

Total no. of electrons that can be accomodated i $2p$ orbitals = 6

59. (a) : Electronic configuration of Cu^+ = [Ar]$3d$

60. (d) : It is uncertainty principle and not Bohr' postulate.

61. (c) : $N^{2+} = 1s^2 2s^2 2p_x^1$

∴ No. of unpaired electrons = 1

62. (b) : No. of orbitals in a subshell = $2l + 1$

⇒ No. of electrons = $2(2l + 1) = 4l + 2$

63. (b) : Both He and Li^+ contain 2 electrons each

64. (a) : No. of radial nodes in $3p$-orbital $= n - l -$

$= 3 - 1 - 1 =$

65. (a) : Radius of nth orbit of H-atom $= r_0 n^2$

where r_0 = radius of the first orbit

Chapter 3

Classification of Elements and Periodicity in Properties

1. Which of the following oxides is most acidic in nature?
(a) MgO (b) BeO
(c) BaO (d) CaO
(NEET 2018)

2. The correct order of atomic radii in group 13 elements is
(a) B < Al < In < Ga < Tl
(b) B < Al < Ga < In < Tl
(c) B < Ga < Al < Tl < In
(d) B < Ga < Al < In < Tl *(NEET 2018)*

3. The element Z = 114 has been discovered recently. It will belong to which of the following family/group and electronic configuration?
(a) Carbon family, [Rn] $5f^{14}\ 6d^{10}\ 7s^2\ 7p^2$
(b) Oxygen family, [Rn] $5f^{14}\ 6d^{10}\ 7s^2\ 7p^4$
(c) Nitrogen family, [Rn] $5f^{14}\ 6d^{10}\ 7s^2\ 7p^6$
(d) Halogen family, [Rn] $5f^{14}\ 6d^{10}\ 7s^2\ 7p^5$
(NEET 2017)

4. In which of the following options the order of arrangement does not agree with the variation of property indicated against it?
(a) I < Br < Cl < F (increasing electron gain enthalpy)
(b) Li < Na < K < Rb (increasing metallic radius)
(c) $Al^{3+} < Mg^{2+} < Na^+ < F^-$ (increasing ionic size)
(d) B < C < N < O (increasing first ionisation enthalpy) *(NEET-I 2016)*

5. The species Ar, K^+ and Ca^{2+} contain the same number of electrons. In which order do their radii increase?
(a) $Ca^{2+} < K^+ < Ar$ (b) $K^+ < Ar < Ca^{2+}$
(c) $Ar < K^+ < Ca^{2+}$ (d) $Ca^{2+} < Ar < K^+$
(2015, Cancelled)

6. Which of the following orders of ionic radii is correctly represented?
(a) $H^- > H^+ > H$ (b) $Na^+ > F^- > O^{2-}$
(c) $F^- > O^{2-} > Na^+$ (d) $Al^{3+} > Mg^{2+} > N^{3-}$
(2014)

7. Which one of the following arrangements represents the correct order of least negative to most negative electron gain enthalpy for C, Ca, Al, F and O?
(a) Al < Ca < O < C < F
(b) Al < O < C < Ca < F
(c) C < F < O < Al < Ca
(d) Ca < Al < C < O < F
(Karnataka NEET 2013)

8. Identify the wrong statement in the following.
(a) Amongst isoelectronic species, smaller the positive charge on the cation, smaller is the ionic radius.
(b) Amongst isoelectronic species, greater the negative charge on the anion, larger is the ionic radius.
(c) Atomic radius of the elements increases as one moves down the first group of the periodic table.
(d) Atomic radius of the elements decreases as one moves across from left to right in the 2nd period of the periodic table.
(2012)

9. What is the value of electron gain enthalpy of Na^+ if IE_1 of Na = 5.1 eV?
(a) –5.1 eV (b) –10.2 eV
(c) +2.55 eV (d) +10.2 eV
(Mains 2011)

10. The correct order of the decreasing ionic radii among the following isoelectronic species is
(a) $Ca^{2+} > K^+ > S^{2-} > Cl^-$
(b) $Cl^- > S^{2-} > Ca^{2+} > K^+$
(c) $S^{2-} > Cl^- > K^+ > Ca^{2+}$
(d) $K^+ > Ca^{2+} > Cl^- > S^{2-}$ *(2010)*

11. Which of the following represents the correct order of increasing electron gain enthalpy with negative sign for the elements O, S, F and Cl?
(a) Cl < F < O < S (b) O < S < F < Cl
(c) F < S < O < Cl (d) S < O < Cl < F
(2010)

12. Among the elements Ca, Mg, P and Cl, the order of increasing atomic radii is
(a) Mg < Ca < Cl < P (b) Cl < P < Mg < Ca
(c) P < Cl < Ca < Mg (d) Ca < Mg < P < Cl
(Mains 2010)

13. Among the following which one has the highest cation to anion size ratio?
(a) CsI (b) CsF (c) LiF (d) NaF
(Mains 2010)

14. Amongst the elements with following electronic configurations, which one of them may have the highest ionisation energy?
(a) Ne $[3s^2\,3p^2]$ (b) Ar $[3d^{10}\,4s^2\,4p^3]$
(c) Ne $[3s^2\,3p^1]$ (d) Ne $[3s^2\,3p^3]$
(2009)

15. Which one of the following arrangements does not give the correct picture of the trends indicated against it?
(a) $F_2 > Cl_2 > Br_2 > I_2$: Bond dissociation energy
(b) $F_2 > Cl_2 > Br_2 > I_2$: Electronegativity
(c) $F_2 > Cl_2 > Br_2 > I_2$: Oxidizing power
(d) $F_2 > Cl_2 > Br_2 > I_2$: Electron gain enthalpy
(2008)

16. Identify the correct order of the size of the following:
(a) $Ca^{2+} < K^+ < Ar < Cl^- < S^{2-}$
(b) $Ar < Ca^{2+} < K^+ < Cl^- < S^{2-}$
(c) $Ca^{2+} < Ar < K^+ < Cl^- < S^{2-}$
(d) $Ca^{2+} < K^+ < Ar < S^{2-} < Cl^-$ *(2007)*

17. With which of the following electronic configuration an atom has the lowest ionisation enthalpy?
(a) $1s^2\,2s^2\,2p^3$ (b) $1s^2\,2s^2\,2p^5\,3s^1$
(c) $1s^2\,2s^2\,2p^6$ (d) $1s^2\,2s^2\,2p^5$
(2007)

18. Which one of the following ionic species has the greatest proton affinity to form stable compound?
(a) NH_2^- (b) F^- (c) I^- (d) HS^-
(2007)

19. Which one of the following orders is not in accordance with the property stated against it?
(a) $F_2 > Cl_2 > Br_2 > I_2$: Bond dissociation energy
(b) $F_2 > Cl_2 > Br_2 > I_2$: Oxidising power
(c) $HI > HBr > HCl > HF$: Acidic property in water
(d) $F_2 > Cl_2 > Br_2 > I_2$: Electronegativity
(2006)

20. Which one of the following arrangements represents the correct order of electron gain enthalpy (with negative sign) of the given atomic species?
(a) S < O < Cl < F (b) Cl < F < S < O
(c) F < Cl < O < S (d) O < S < F < Cl
(2005)

21. Ionic radii are
(a) inversely proportional to effective nuclear charge
(b) inversely proportional to square of effective nuclear charge
(c) directly proportional to effective nuclear charge
(d) directly proportional to square of effective nuclear charge. *(2004)*

22. The ions O^{2-}, F^-, Na^+, Mg^{2+} and Al^{3+} are isoelectronic. Their ionic radii show
(a) a significant increase from O^{2-} to Al^{3+}
(b) a significant decrease from O^{2-} to Al^{3+}
(c) an increase from O^{2-} to F^- and then decrease from Na^+ to Al^{3+}
(d) a decrease from O^{2-} to F^- and then increase from Na^+ to Al^{3+}. *(2003)*

23. Which statement is wrong?
(a) Bond energy of $F_2 > Cl_2$
(b) Electronegativity of F > Cl
(c) F is more oxidising than Cl
(d) Electron affinity of Cl > F *(2000)*

24. Which of the following elements has the maximum electron affinity?
(a) I (b) Br (c) Cl (d) F
(1999)

25. The first ionization potentials (eV) of Be and B respectively are
(a) 8.29, 8.29 (b) 9.32, 9.32
(c) 8.29, 9.32 (d) 9.32, 8.29
(1998)

26. Which one of the following is correct order of the size of iodine species?
(a) $I^+ > I^- > I$ (b) $I^- > I > I^+$
(c) $I > I^- > I^+$ (d) $I > I^+ > I^-$
(1997)

27. Which of the following ion is the largest in size?
(a) K^+ (b) Ca^{2+} (c) Cl^- (d) S^{2-}
(1996)

28. Which of the following has the smallest size?
(a) Al^{3+} (b) F^- (c) Na^+ (d) Mg^{2+}
(1996)

29. The electronics configuration of an element is $1s^22s^22p^63s^23p^3$. What is the atomic number of the element, which is just below the above element in the periodic table?
(a) 33 (b) 34 (c) 36 (d) 49
(1995)

30. One would expect proton to have very large
(a) charge
(b) ionization potential
(c) hydration energy
(d) radius. *(1993)*

31. Na^+, Mg^{2+}, Al^{3+} and Si^{4+} are isoelectronic. the order of their ionic size is
(a) $Na^+ > Mg^{2+} < Al^{3+} < Si^{4+}$
(b) $Na^+ < Mg^{2+} > Al^{3+} > Si^{4+}$
(c) $Na^+ > Mg^{2+} > Al^{3+} > Si^{4+}$
(d) $Na^+ < Mg^{2+} > Al^{3+} < Si^{4+}$ *(1993)*

32. If the atomic number of an element is 33, it will be placed in the periodic table in the
(a) first group (b) third group
(c) fifth group (d) seventh group.
(1993)

33. In the periodic table from left to right in a period, the atomic volume
(a) decreases
(b) increases
(c) remains same
(d) first decrease then increases. *(1993)*

34. Which electronic configuration of an element has abnormally high difference between second and third ionization energy?
(a) $1s^2, 2s^2, 2p^6, 3s^1$
(b) $1s^2, 2s^2, 2p^6, 3s^13p^1$
(c) $1s^2, 2s^2, 2p^6, 3s^23p^2$
(d) $1s^2, 2s^2, 2p^6, 3s^2$ *(1993)*

35. One of the characteristic properties of non-metals is that they
(a) are reducing agents
(b) form basic oxides
(c) form cations by electron gain
(d) are electronegative. *(1993)*

36. Pauling's electronegativity values for elements are useful in predicting
(a) polarity of the molecules
(b) position in the E.M.F. series
(c) coordination numbers
(d) dipole moments. *(1989)*

37. The electronic configuration of four elements are given below. Which elements does not belong to the same family as others?
(a) $[Xe]4f^{14}5d^{10}1s^2$
(b) $[Kr]4d^{10}5s^2$
(c) $[Ne]3s^23p^5$
(d) $[Ar]3d^{10}4s^2$ *(1989)*

38. In the periodic table, with the increase in atomic number, the metallic character of an element
(a) decreases in a period and increases in a group
(b) increases in a period and decreases in a group
(c) increases both in a period and the group
(d) decreases in a period and the group.
(1989)

Answer Key

1. (b) **2.** (d) **3.** (a) **4.** (a, d) **5.** (a) **6.** (None) **7.** (d) **8.** (a)
9. (a) **10.** (c) **11.** (b) **12.** (b) **13.** (b) **14.** (d) **15.** (a, d) **16.** (a) **17.** (b) **18.** (a)
19. (a) **20.** (d) **21.** (a) **22.** (b) **23.** (a) **24.** (c) **25.** (d) **26.** (b) **27.** (d) **28.** (a)
29. (a) **30.** (c) **31.** (c) **32.** (c) **33.** (d) **34.** (d) **35.** (d) **36.** (a) **37.** (c) **38.** (a)

EXPLANATIONS

1. **(b)** : In metals, on moving down the group, metallic character increases, so basic nature increases hence most acidic will be BeO.

2. **(d)**

3. **(a)** : The electronic configuration of the element with $Z = 114$ (flerovium) is $[Rn]5f^{14}6d^{10}7s^2 7p^2$. Hence, it belongs to carbon family which has the same outer electronic configuration.

4. **(a, d)** : The correct order of increasing negative electron gain enthalpy is : I < Br < F < Cl and the correct order of increasing first ionisation enthalpy is B < C < O < N.

5. **(a)** : In case of isoelectronic species, radius decreases with increase in nuclear charge.

6. **(None)** : Cations lose electrons and are smaller in size than the parent atom, whereas anions add electrons and are larger in size than the parent atom. Hence, the order is $H^- > H > H^+$.
For isoelectronic species, the ionic radii decreases with increase in atomic number *i.e.* nuclear charge. Hence, the correct orders are
$O^{2-} > F^- > Na^+$ and $N^{3-} > Mg^{2+} > Al^{3+}$.

7. **(d)** : Electron gain enthalpy becomes less negative from top to bottom in a group while it becomes more negative from left to right within a period.

8. **(a)** : As positive charge on the cation increases, effective nuclear charge increases. Thus atomic size decreases.

9. **(a)** : $Na \rightarrow Na^+ + e^-$; $\Delta H = 5.1$ eV
$Na^+ + e^- \rightarrow Na$; $\Delta H = -5.1$ eV

10. **(c)** : $S^{2-} > Cl^- > K^+ > Ca^{2+}$
Among isoelectronic species, ionic radii increases with increase in negative charge. This happens because effective nuclear charge (Z_{eff}) decreases.
Similarly, ionic radii decreases with increase in positive charge as Z_{eff} increases.

11. **(b)** : Cl atom has the highest electron affinity in the periodic table. F being a member of group 17 has higher electron gain enthalpy than S which belongs to group 16. This in turn is higher than the electron affinity of O atom. Thus,
Cl > F > S > O
It is worth noting that the electron gain enthalpy of oxygen and fluorine, the members of the second period, have less negative values than the elements sulphur and chlorine of the third period.
This is due to small size of the atoms of oxygen and fluorine. As a result, there is a strong inter-electronic repulsion when extra electron is added to these atoms, *i.e.*, electron density is high and the addition of an extra electron is not easy.

12. **(b)** : The atomic radii decrease on moving from left to right in a period, thus order of sizes for Cl, P and Mg is Cl < P < Mg. Down the group size increases. Thus overall order is : Cl < P < Mg < Ca.

13. **(b)** : The cation to anion size ratio will be maximum when the cation is of largest size and the anion is of smallest size. Among the given species, Cs^+ has maximum size among given cations and F^- has smallest size among given anions, thus CsF has highest r_c/r_a ratio.

14. **(d)** : Among options (a), (c) and (d), option (d) has the highest ionisation energy because of extra stability associated with half-filled $3p$-orbital. In option (b), the presence of $3d^{10}$ electrons offers shielding effect, as a result the $4p^3$ electrons do not experience much nuclear charge and hence the electrons can be removed easily.

15. **(a,d)** : In case of diatomic molecules (X_2) of halogens the bond dissociation energy decreases in the order :
$Cl_2 > Br_2 > F_2 > I_2$
The oxidising power, electronegativity and reactivity decrease in the order :
$F_2 > Cl_2 > Br_2 > I_2$
Electron gain enthalpy of halogens follows the given order :
$Cl_2 > F_2 > Br_2 > I_2$
The low value of electron gain enthalpy (electron enthalpy) of fluorine is probably due to small size of fluorine atom.

16. **(a)** : Among isoelectronic ions, ionic radii of anions is more than that of cations. Further size of the anion increases with increase in negative charge and size of the cation decreases with increase in positive charge.

17. **(b)** : The larger the atomic size, smaller is the value of the ionisation enthalpy. Again higher the screening effect, lesser is the value of ionisation potential. Hence option (b) has lowest ionisation enthalpy.

18. **(a)** : In going from left to right across a period in the periodic table, the basicity (*i.e.* proton affinity) decreases as the electronegativity of the atom possessing the lone pair of electrons increases. Hence basicity of NH_2^- is higher than F^-. In moving down a group, as the atomic mass increases, basicity decreases. Hence F^- is more basic than I^- and HO^-

s more basic than HS^-. Hence among the given ionic pecies, NH_2^- has maximum proton affinity.

9. **(a) :** $X-X$ bond : F – F Cl – Cl Br – Br I – I

Bond dissociation energy (kcal/mol) :	38	57	45.5	35.6

The lower value of bond dissociation energy of fluorine is due to the high inter-electronic repulsion between non-bonding electrons in the $2p$-orbitals of fluorine. As a result F – F bond is weaker in comparison to Cl – Cl and Br – Br bonds.

0. **(d) :** The molar enthalpy change accompanying the addition of an electron to an atom (or ion) is known as electron gain enthalpy.

Generally it increases on moving from left to right in period and in a group it decreases as the size increases.

Exception: Because of the small size of F, electron-electron repulsion present in its relatively compact p-subshell, do not easily allow the addition of an extra electron. On the other hand, Cl because of its comparatively bigger size than F, allows the addition of an extra electron more easily.

$$\underset{-1.48}{O} < \underset{-2.0}{S} < \underset{-3.6}{F} < \underset{-3.8}{Cl}$$

1. **(a) :** Ionic radius in the nth orbit is given by

$$r_n = \frac{n^2 a_0}{Z^*} \quad \text{or,} \quad r_n \propto \frac{1}{Z^*}$$

where n is principal quantum number, a_0 the Bohr's radius of H-atom and Z^*, the effective nuclear charge.

2. **(b) :** Amongst isoelectronic ions, ionic radii of anions is more than that of cations. Further size of the anion increases with increase in –ve charge and size of cation decreases with increase in +ve charge. Hence, correct order is

$$O^{2-} > F^- > Na^+ > Mg^{2+} > Al^{3+}.$$

. **(a) :** Due to more repulsion in between non-bonding electron pair ($2p$) of two fluorines (due to small size of F-atom) in comparison to non-bonding electron pair ($3p$) in chlorine, the bond energy of F_2 less than Cl_2.

$BE\ (F_2) = 158{\cdot}5$ kJ/mole and

$BE\ (Cl_2) = 242{\cdot}6$ kJ/mole.

. **(c) :** Among the halogens the electron affinity value of 'F' should be maximum. But due to small size the 7-electrons in its valence shell are much more crowded, so that it feels difficulty in entry of new electrons. Thus, the E.A. value is slightly lower than chlorine and the order is

I < Br < F < Cl.

. **(d) :** $_4Be \rightarrow 1s^2\ 2s^2$, $_5B \rightarrow 1s^2\ 2s^2\ 2p^1$

Due to stable fully-filled 's'-orbital arrangement of electrons in 'Be' atom, more energy is required to remove an electron from the valence shell than 'B'atom. Therefore 'Be' has higher ionisaton potential than 'B',

26. **(b) :** Positive ion is always smaller and negative ion is always larger than the parent atom.

27. **(d) :** Since all of these ions contain 18 electrons each, so these are isoelectronic. For isoelectronic ions, smaller the positive nuclear charge, greater is the size of the ion.

28. **(a) :** These are isoelectronic ions (ions with same number of electrons) and for isoelectronic ions, greater the positive nuclear charge, greater is the force of attraction on the electrons by the nucleus and the smaller is the size of the ion. Thus, Al^{3+} has the smallest size.

29. **(a) :** Atomic no. of given element = 15, thus it belongs to 5th group.

Now, atomic no. of the element below the above element = 15 + 18 = 33

30. **(c) :** Proton (H^+) being very small in size would have very large hydration energy.

31. **(c) :** In isoelectronic ions, the size of the cation decreases as the magnitude of the positive charge increases.

32. **(c) :** Electronic configuration of an element is

$$1s^2 2s^2 2p^6 3s^2 3p^6 3d^{10} 4s^2 4p^3$$

Hence, it lies in fifth or 15th group.

33. **(d) :** Atomic volume is the volume occupied by one gram of an element. Within a period from left to right, atomic volume first decreases and then increases.

34. **(d) :** Abnormally high difference between 2nd and 3rd ionisation energy means that the element has two valence electrons, which is a case in configuration (d).

35. **(d)**

36. **(a) :** Pauling introduced the electronegativity concept. He introduced the idea that the ionic character of a bond varies with the difference in electronegativity. A large difference in electronegativity leads to a bond with high degree of polar character, *i.e.* the bond is predominantly ionic or vice versa.

37. **(c) :** Elements (a), (b) and (d) belong to the same group since each one of them has two electrons in valence shell. In contrast, element (c) has seven electrons in the valence shell, and hence it lies in other group.

38. **(a) :** Metallic character decreases in a period and increases in a group.

Chapter 4

Chemical Bonding and Molecular Structure

1. Consider the following species : CN^+, CN^-, NO and CN. Which one of these will have the highest bond order?
(a) NO (b) CN^-
(c) CN^+ (d) CN
(NEET 2018)

2. In the structure of ClF_3, the number of lone pairs of electrons on central atom 'Cl' is
(a) one (b) two
(c) four (d) three.
(NEET 2018)

3. Which of the following pairs of compounds is isoelectronic and isostructural?
(a) TeI_2, XeF_2 (b) IBr_2^-, XeF_2
(c) IF_3, XeF_2 (d) $BeCl_2$, XeF_2
(NEET 2017)

4. The species, having bond angles of 120° is
(a) ClF_3 (b) NCl_3
(c) BCl_3 (d) PH_3
(NEET 2017)

5. Which one of the following pairs of species have the same bond order?
(a) O_2, NO^+ (b) CN^-, CO
(c) N_2, O_2^- (d) CO, NO
(NEET 2017)

6. Which one of the following compounds shows the presence of intramolecular hydrogen bond?
(a) H_2O_2
(b) HCN
(c) Cellulose
(d) Concentrated acetic acid
(NEET-II 2016)

7. The hybridizations of atomic orbitals of nitrogen in NO_2^+, NO_3 and NH_4^+ respectively are
(a) sp, sp^3 and sp^2 (b) sp^2, sp^3 and sp
(c) sp, sp^2 and sp^3 (d) sp^2, sp and sp^3
(NEET-II 2016)

8. Which of the following pairs of ions i isoelectronic and isostructural?
(a) CO_3^{2-}, NO_3^- (b) ClO_3^-, CO_3^{2-}
(c) SO_3^{2-}, NO_3^- (d) ClO_3^-, SO_3^{2-}
(NEET-II 2016)

9. The correct geometry and hybridization fc XeF_4 are
(a) octahedral, sp^3d^2
(b) trigonal bipyramidal, sp^3d
(c) planar triangle, sp^3d^3
(d) square planar, sp^3d^2. *(NEET-II 2016)*

10. Among the following, which one is a wron statement?
(a) PH_5 and $BiCl_5$ do not exist.
(b) $p\pi$-$d\pi$ bonds are present in SO_2.
(c) SeF_4 and CH_4 have same shape.
(d) I_3^+ has bent geometry. *(NEET-II 201*

11. Consider the molecules CH_4, NH_3 and H_2 Which of the given statements is false?
(a) The H — O — H bond angle in H_2O smaller than the H — N — H bond ang in NH_3.
(b) The H — C — H bond angle in CH_4 is larg than the H — N — H bond angle in NH
(c) The H — C — H bond angle in CH_4, t H — N — H bond angle in NH_3, and t H — O — H bond angle in H_2O are greater than 90°.
(d) The H — O — H bond angle in H_2O is larg than the H — C — H bond angle in CH
(NEET-I 20

12. Predict the correct order among the followin
(a) bond pair - bond pair > lone pair - bond p > lone pair - lone p
(b) lone pair - bond pair > bond pair - bond p > lone pair - lone p
(c) lone pair - lone pair > lone pair - bond p > bond pair - bond p

(d) lone pair - lone pair > bond pair - bond pair > lone pair - bond pair *(NEET-I 2016)*

13. In which of the following pairs, both the species are not isostructural?
(a) Diamond, Silicon carbide
(b) NH_3, PH_3
(c) XeF_4, XeO_4
(d) $SiCl_4$, PCl_4^+ *(2015)*

14. Decreasing order of stability of O_2, O_2^-, O_2^+ and O_2^{2-} is
(a) $O_2^{2-} > O_2^- > O_2 > O_2^+$
(b) $O_2 > O_2^+ > O_2^{2-} > O_2^-$
(c) $O_2^- > O_2^{2-} > O_2^+ > O_2$
(d) $O_2^+ > O_2 > O_2^- > O_2^{2-}$ *(2015)*

15. Which of the following pairs of ions are isoelectronic and isostructural?
(a) SO_3^{2-}, NO_3^- (b) ClO_3^-, SO_3^{2-}
(c) CO_3^{2-}, SO_3^{2-} (d) ClO_3^-, CO_3^{2-}
(2015, Cancelled)

16. The correct bond order in the following species is
(a) $O_2^+ < O_2^- < O_2^{2+}$ (b) $O_2^- < O_2^+ < O_2^{2+}$
(c) $O_2^{2+} < O_2^+ < O_2^-$ (d) $O_2^{2+} < O_2^- < O_2^+$
(2015, Cancelled)

17. Which of the following options represents the correct bond order?
(a) $O_2^- > O_2 < O_2^+$ (b) $O_2^- < O_2 > O_2^+$
(c) $O_2^- > O_2 > O_2^+$ (d) $O_2^- < O_2 < O_2^+$
(2015, Cancelled)

18. Maximum bond angle at nitrogen is present in which of the following?
(a) NO_2^+ (b) NO_3^- (c) NO_2 (d) NO_2^-
(2015, Cancelled)

19. Which of the following molecules has the maximum dipole moment?
(a) CO_2 (b) CH_4 (c) NH_3 (d) NF_3
(2014)

20. Which one of the following species has plane triangular shape?
(a) N_3 (b) NO_3^- (c) NO_2^- (d) CO_2
(2014)

21. Which of the following is electron-deficient?
(a) $(BH_3)_2$ (b) PH_3
(c) $(CH_3)_2$ (d) $(SiH_3)_2$
(NEET 2013)

22. XeF_2 is isostructural with
(a) $SbCl_3$ (b) $BaCl_2$ (c) TeF_2 (d) ICl_2^-
(NEET 2013)

23. Which of the following is a polar molecule?
(a) SiF_4 (b) XeF_4 (c) BF_3 (d) SF_4
(NEET 2013)

24. Which of the following is paramagnetic?
(a) CN^- (b) NO^+ (c) CO (d) O_2^-
(NEET 2013)

25. Dipole-induced dipole interactions are present in which of the following pairs
(a) HCl and He atoms
(b) SiF_4 and He atoms
(c) H_2O and alcohol
(d) Cl_2 and CCl_4 *(NEET 2013)*

26. The pair of species that has the same bond order in the following is
(a) CO, NO^+ (b) NO^-, CN^-
(c) O_2, N_2 (d) O_2, B_2
(Karnataka NEET 2013)

27. The outer orbitals of C in ethene molecule can be considered to be hybridized to give three equivalent sp^2 orbitals. The total number of sigma (σ) and pi (π) bonds in ethene molecule is
(a) 3 sigma (σ) and 2 pi (π) bonds
(b) 4 sigma (σ) and 1 pi (π) bonds
(c) 5 sigma (σ) and 1 pi (π) bonds
(d) 1 sigma (σ) and 2 pi (π) bonds.
(Karnataka NEET 2013)

28. In which of the following pair both the species have sp^3 hybridization?
(a) SiF_4, BeH_2 (b) NF_3, H_2O
(c) NF_3, BF_3 (d) H_2S, BF_3
(Karnataka NEET 2013)

29. In which of the following ionization processes the bond energy increases and the magnetic behaviour changes from paramagnetic to diamagnetic.
(a) $O_2 \rightarrow O_2^+$ (b) $C_2 \rightarrow C_2^+$
(c) $NO \rightarrow NO^+$ (d) $N_2 \rightarrow N_2^+$
(Karnataka NEET 2013)

30. Which one of the following pairs is isostructural (*i.e.*, having the same shape and hybridization)?
(a) [BCl_3 and $BrCl_3$] (b) [NH_3 and NO_3^-]
(c) [NF_3 and BF_3] (d) [BF_4^- and NH_4^+]
(2012)

31. Bond order of 1.5 is shown by
(a) O_2^+ (b) O_2^- (c) O_2^{2-} (d) O_2
(2012)

32. Which of the following species contains three bond pairs and one lone pair around the central atom?
(a) H_2O (b) BF_3 (c) NH_2^- (d) PCl_3
(2012)

33. The pair of species with the same bond order is
(a) O_2^{2-}, B_2 (b) O_2^+, NO^+
(c) NO, CO (d) N_2, O_2
(2012)

34. During change of O_2 to O_2^- ion, the electron adds on which one of the following orbitals?
(a) π^* orbital (b) π orbital
(c) σ^* orbital (d) σ orbital
(Mains 2012)

35. Four diatomic species are listed below. Identify the correct order in which the bond order is increasing in them
(a) $NO < O_2^- < C_2^{2-} < He_2^+$
(b) $O_2^- < NO < C_2^{2-} < He_2^+$
(c) $C_2^{2-} < He_2^+ < O_2^- < NO$
(d) $He_2^+ < O_2^- < NO < C_2^{2-}$
(Mains 2012, 2008)

36. Which of the following has the minimum bond length?
(a) O_2^+ (b) O_2^- (c) O_2^{2-} (d) O_2
(2011)

37. Which of the two ions from the list given below that have the geometry that is explained by the same hybridization of orbitals, NO_2^-, NO_3^-, NH_2^-, NH_4^+, SCN^- ?
(a) NO_2^- and NO_3^- (b) NH_4^+ and NO_3^-
(c) SCN^- and NH_2^- (d) NO_2^- and NH_2^-
(2011)

38. The correct order of increasing bond length of C – H, C – O, C – C and C=C is
(a) C – H < C=C < C – O < C – C
(b) C – C < C=C < C – O < C – H
(c) C – O < C – H < C – C < C=C
(d) C – H < C – O < C – C < C=C *(2011)*

39. Which of the following structures is the most preferred and hence of lowest energy for SO_3?

(a) 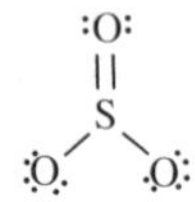

(b) 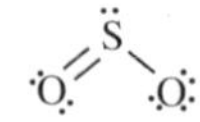

(c) 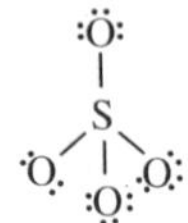

(d) 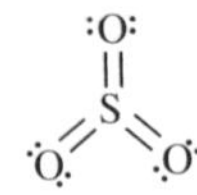

(Mains 2011)

40. The pairs of species of oxygen and their magnetic behaviour are noted below. Which of the following presents the correct description?
(a) O_2^-, O_2^{2-} - Both diamagnetic
(b) O^+, O_2^{2-} - Both paramagnetic
(c) O_2^+, O_2 - Both paramagnetic
(d) O, O_2^{2-} - Both paramagnetic *(2011)*

41. In which of the following pairs of molecules/ions, the central atoms have sp^2 hybridisation?
(a) NO_2^- and NH_3 (b) BF_3 and NO_2^-
(c) NH_2^- and H_2O (d) BF_3 and NH_2^-
(2010)

42. Which one of the following species does not exist under normal conditions?
(a) Be_2^+ (b) Be_2 (c) B_2 (d) Li_2
(2010)

43. In which one of the following species the central atom has the type of hybridization which is not the same as that present in the other three?
(a) SF_4 (b) I_3^-
(c) $SbCl_5^{2-}$ (d) PCl_5 *(2010)*

44. In which of the following molecules the central atom does not have sp^3 hybridization?
(a) CH_4 (b) SF_4 (c) BF_4^- (d) NH_4^+
(Mains 2010)

45. Some of the properties of the two species NO_3^- and H_3O^+ are described below. Which one of them is correct?
(a) Dissimilar in hybridization for the central atom with different structures.
(b) Isostructural with same hybridization for the central atom.
(c) Isostructural with different hybridization for the central atom.
(d) Similar in hybridization for the central atom with different structures. *(Mains 2010)*

46. What is the dominant intermolecular force or bond that must be overcome in converting liquid CH_3OH to a gas?
(a) Dipole-dipole interaction
(b) Covalent bonds
(c) London dispersion force
(d) Hydrogen bonding *(2009)*

47. According to MO theory which of the lists ranks the nitrogen species in terms of increasing bond order?
(a) $N_2^{2-} < N_2^- < N_2$ (b) $N_2 < N_2^{2-} < N_2^-$
(c) $N_2^- < N_2^{2-} < N_2$ (d) $N_2^- < N_2 < N_2^{2-}$ *(2009)*

48. In which of the following molecules/ions BF_3, NO_2^-, NH_2^- and H_2O, the central atom is sp^2 hybridised?
(a) NH_2^- and H_2O (b) NO_2^- and H_2O
(c) BF_3 and NO_2^- (d) NO_2^- and NH_2^- *(2009)*

49. The correct order of increasing bond angles in the following triatomic species is
(a) $NO_2^+ < NO_2 < NO_2^-$
(b) $NO_2^+ < NO_2^- < NO_2$
(c) $NO_2^- < NO_2^+ < NO_2$
(d) $NO_2^- < NO_2 < NO_2^+$ *(2008)*

50. In which of the following pairs, the two species are isostructural?
(a) SO_3^{2-} and NO_3^- (b) BF_3 and NF_3
(c) BrO_3^- and XeO_3 (d) SF_4 and XeF_4 *(2007)*

51. The correct order of C – O bond length among CO, CO_3^{2-}, CO_2 is
(a) $CO < CO_3^{2-} < CO_2$
(b) $CO_3^{2-} < CO_2 < CO$
(c) $CO < CO_2 < CO_3^{2-}$
(d) $CO_2 < CO_3^{2-} < CO$ *(2007)*

52. Which of the following is not a correct statement?
(a) Multiple bonds are always shorter than corresponding single bonds.
(b) The electron-deficient molecules can act as Lewis acids.
(c) The canonical structures have no real existence.
(d) Every AB_5 molecule does in fact have square pyramid structure. *(2006)*

53. Which of the following species has a linear shape?
(a) O_3 (b) NO_2^- (c) SO_2 (d) NO_2^+ *(2006)*

54. Which of the following is not isostructural with $SiCl_4$?
(a) NH_4^+ (b) SCl_4 (c) SO_4^{2-} (d) PO_4^{3-} *(2006)*

55. Which of the following molecules has trigonal planar geometry?
(a) BF_3 (b) NH_3 (c) PCl_3 (d) IF_3 *(2005)*

56. The correct order in which the O – O bond length increases in the following is
(a) $O_2 < H_2O_2 < O_3$ (b) $O_3 < H_2O_2 < O_2$
(c) $H_2O_2 < O_2 < O_3$ (d) $O_2 < O_3 < H_2O_2$ *(2005)*

57. The surface tension of which of the following liquid is maximum?
(a) C_2H_5OH (b) CH_3OH
(c) H_2O (d) C_6H_6 *(2005)*

58. Among the following, the pair in which the two species are not isostructural is
(a) SiF_4 and SF_4 (b) IO_3^- and XeO_3
(c) BH_4^- and NH_4^+ (d) PF_6^- and SF_6. *(2004)*

59. In a regular octahedral molecule, MX_6 the number of $X – M – X$ bonds at 180° is
(a) three (b) two (c) six (d) four. *(2004)*

60. H_2O is dipolar, whereas BeF_2 is not. It is because
(a) the electronegativity of F is greater than that of O
(b) H_2O involves hydrogen bonding whereas BeF_2 is a discrete molecule
(c) H_2O is linear and BeF_2 is angular
(d) H_2O is angular and BeF_2 is linear. *(2004)*

61. In BrF_3 molecule, the lone pairs occupy equatorial positions to minimize
(a) lone pair - bond pair repulsion only
(b) bond pair - bond pair repulsion only
(c) lone pair - lone pair repulsion and lone pair - bond pair repulsion
(d) lone pair - lone pair repulsion only. *(2004)*

62. Which one of the following statements is not correct for sigma- and pi- bonds formed between two carbon atoms?
(a) Sigma-bond is stronger than a pi-bond.
(b) Bond energies of sigma- and pi-bonds are of the order of 264 kJ/mol and 347 kJ/mol, respectively.
(c) Free rotation of atoms about a sigma-bond is allowed but not in case of a pi-bond.
(d) Sigma-bond determines the direction between carbon atoms but a pi-bond has no primary effect in this regard. *(2003)*

63. Which of the following has $p\pi - d\pi$ bonding?
(a) NO_3^- (b) SO_3^{2-} (c) BO_3^{3-} (d) CO_3^{2-}
(2002)

64. In NO_3^- ion number of bond pair and lone pair of electrons on nitrogen atom are
(a) 2, 2 (b) 3, 1 (c) 1, 3 (d) 4, 0.
(2002)

65. Which of the following is isoelectronic?
(a) CO_2, NO_2 (b) NO_2^-, CO_2
(c) CN^-, CO (d) SO_2, CO_2
(2002)

66. Which of the following two are isostructural?
(a) XeF_2, IF_2^- (b) NH_3, BF_3
(c) CO_3^{2-}, SO_3^{2-} (d) PCl_5, ICl_5
(2001)

67. In which of the following bond angle is maximum?
(a) NH_3 (b) NH_4^+ (c) PCl_3 (d) SCl_2
(2001)

68. Nitrogen forms N_2, but phosphorus does not form P_2, however, it converts P_4, reason is
(a) triple bond present between phosphorus atom
(b) $p\pi - p\pi$ bonding is weak
(c) $p\pi - p\pi$ bonding is strong
(d) multiple bonds form easily. *(2001)*

69. In $X - H - - - Y$, X and Y both are electronegative elements. Then
(a) electron density on X will increase and on H will decrease
(b) in both electron density will increase
(c) in both electron density will decrease
(d) on X electron density will decrease and on H increases. *(2001)*

70. $d\pi - p\pi$ bond present in
(a) CO_3^{2-} (b) PO_4^{3-} (c) NO_3^- (d) NO_2^-
(2000)

71. Right order of dissociation energy N_2 and N_2^+ is
(a) $N_2 > N_2^+$ (b) $N_2 = N_2^+$
(c) $N_2^+ > N_2$ (d) none. *(2000)*

72. Which species does not exhibit paramagnetism?
(a) N_2^+ (b) O_2^- (c) CO (d) NO
(2000)

73. The number of anti-bonding electron pairs in O_2^{2-} molecular ion on the basis of molecular orbital theory is (Atomic number of O is 8)
(a) 3 (b) 2 (c) 5 (d) 4
(1998)

74. In PO_4^{3-} ion, the formal charge on each oxygen atom and P—O bond order respectively are
(a) –0.75, 1.25 (b) –0.75, 1.0
(c) –0.75, 0.6 (d) –3, 1.25 *(1998)*

75. N_2 and O_2 are converted into monocations, N_2^+ and O_2^+ respectively. Which is wrong?
(a) In O_2 paramagnetism decreases.
(b) N_2^+ becomes diamagnetic.
(c) In N_2, the N–N bond weakens.
(d) In O_2, the O–O bond order increases.
(1997)

76. N_2 and O_2 are converted into monoanions N_2^- and O_2^- respectively, which of the following statements is wrong?
(a) In O_2, bond length increases.
(b) N_2^- becomes diamagnetic.
(c) In N_2, then N–N bond weakens.
(d) In O_2, the O–O bond order increases.
(1997)

77. The bond length between hybridised carbon atom and other carbon atom is minimum in
(a) propene (b) propyne
(c) propane (d) butane. *(1996)*

78. Which of the following has sp^2-hybridisation?
(a) $BeCl_2$ (b) C_2H_2 (c) C_2H_6 (d) C_2H_4
(1996)

79. Which of the following species is paramagnetic?
(a) CO (b) CN^- (c) O_2^{2-} (d) NO
(1995)

80. The correct order of the O–O bond length in O_2, H_2O_2 and O_3 is
(a) $O_2 > H_2O_2 > O_3$ (b) $H_2O_2 > O_3 > O_2$
(c) $O_2 > O_3 > H_2O_2$ (d) $O_3 > H_2O_2 > O_2$ *(1995)*

81. The ground state electronic configuration of valence shell electrons in nitrogen molecule (N_2) is written as $KK, \sigma 2s^2, \sigma^* 2s^2, \pi 2p_x^2 = \pi 2p_y^2 \sigma 2p_z^2$. Hence the bond order in nitrogen molecule is
(a) 2 (b) 3 (c) 0 (d) 1 *(1995)*

82. Which of the following molecules has the highest bond order?
(a) O_2^- (b) O_2 (c) O_2^+ (d) O_2^{2-} *(1994)*

83. Which of the following molecule does not possess a permanent dipole moment?
(a) CS_2 (b) SO_3 (c) H_2S (d) SO_2 *(1994)*

84. The table shown below gives the bond dissociation energies (E_{diss}) for single covalent bonds of carbon (C) atoms with element *A*, *B*, *C* and *D*. Which element has the smallest atoms?

Bond	E_{diss} (kJ mol^{-1})
C-*A*	240
C-*B*	328
C-*C*	276
C-*D*	485

(a) *C* (b) *D* (c) *A* (d) *B* *(1994)*

85. Among the following which compound will show the highest lattice energy?
(a) KF (b) NaF (c) CsF (d) RbF *(1993)*

86. Which one of the following is the correct order of interactions?
(a) Covalent < hydrogen bonding < van der Waals' < dipole-dipole
(b) van der Waals' < hydrogen bonding < dipole < covalent
(c) van der Waals' < dipole-dipole < hydrogen bonding < covalent
(d) Dipole-dipole < van der Waals' < hydrogen bonding < covalent. *(1993)*

87. Which one of the following has the shortest carbon carbon bond length?
(a) Benzene (b) Ethene
(c) Ethyne (d) Ethane *(1992)*

88. Which structure is linear?
(a) SO_2 (b) CO_2 (c) CO_3^{2-} (d) SO_4^{2-} *(1992)*

89. Strongest hydrogen bond is shown by
(a) water
(b) ammonia
(c) hydrogen fluoride
(d) hydrogen sulphide. *(1992)*

90. In compound *X*, all the bond angles are exactly 109°28′, *X* is
(a) chloromethane
(b) carbon tetrachloride
(c) iodoform
(d) chloroform. *(1991)*

91. Among LiCl, $BeCl_2$, BCl_3 and CCl_4, the covalent bond character follows the order
(a) $BeCl_2 > BCl_3 > CCl_4 < LiCl$
(b) $BeCl_2 < BCl_3 < CCl_4 < LiCl$
(c) $LiCl < BeCl_2 < BCl_3 < CCl_4$
(d) $LiCl > BeCl_2 > BCl_3 > CCl_4$ *(1990)*

92. The complex ion $[Co(NH_3)_6]^{3+}$ is formed by sp^3d^2 hybridisation. Hence the ion should possess
(a) octahedral geometry
(b) tetrahedral geometry
(c) square planar geometry
(d) tetragonal geometry. *(1990)*

93. Which statement is NOT correct?
(a) A sigma bond is weaker than a pi bond.
(b) A sigma bond is stronger than a pi bond.
(c) A double bond is stronger than a single bond.
(d) A double bond is shorter than a single bond. *(1990)*

94. Which one shows maximum hydrogen bonding?
(a) H_2O (b) H_2Se (c) H_2S (d) HF *(1990)*

95. Linear combination of two hybridized orbitals belonging to two atoms and each having one electron leads to the formation of

(a) sigma bond
(b) double bond
(c) co-ordinate covalent bond
(d) pi bond. *(1990)*

96. Which one of the following formulae does not correctly represent the bonding capacities of the two atoms involved?

(a) 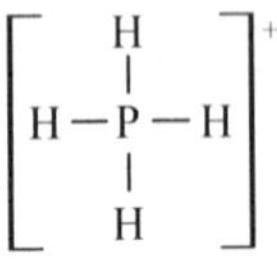

(b) 

(c) 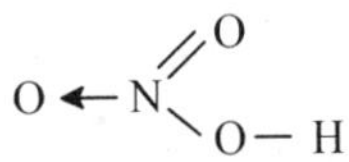

(d) 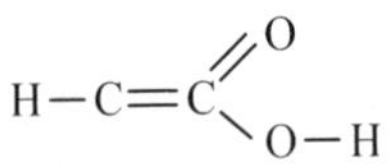 *(1990)*

97. Which of the following molecule does not have a linear arrangement of atoms?
(a) H_2S (b) C_2H_2 (c) Be_2 (d) CO_2 *(1989)*

98. Which of the following does not apply to metallic bond?
(a) Overlapping valence orbitals
(b) Mobile valence electrons
(c) Delocalized electrons
(d) Highly directed bonds *(1989)*

99. In which one of the following molecules the central atom can be said to adopt sp^2 hybridization?
(a) BeF_2 (b) BF_3 (c) C_2H_2 (d) NH_3 *(1989)*

100. H_2O has a net dipole moment while BeF_2 has zero dipole moment because
(a) H_2O molecule is linear while BeF_2 is bent
(b) BeF_2 molecule is linear while H_2O is bent
(c) fluorine has more electronegativity than oxygen
(d) beryllium has more electronegativity than oxygen. *(1989)*

101. The angle between the overlapping of one *s*-orbital and one *p*-orbital is
(a) 180° (b) 120°
(c) 109°28′ (d) 120°, 60° *(1988)*

102. Equilateral shape has
(a) *sp* hybridisation
(b) sp^2 hybridisation
(c) sp^3 hybridisation
(d) dsp^3 hybridisation. *(1988)*

Answer Key

1. (b)	**2.** (b)	**3.** (None)		**4.** (c)	**5.** (b)	**6.** (c)	**7.** (c)	**8.** (a,d)	**9.** (a)
10. (c)	**11.** (d)	**12.** (c)	**13.** (c)	**14.** (d)	**15.** (b)	**16.** (b)	**17.** (d)	**18.** (a)	**19.** (c)
20. (b)	**21.** (a)	**22.** (d)	**23.** (d)	**24.** (d)	**25.** (a)	**26.** (a)	**27.** (c)	**28.** (b)	**29.** (c)
30. (d)	**31.** (b)	**32.** (d)	**33.** (a)	**34.** (a)	**35.** (d)	**36.** (a)	**37.** (a)	**38.** (a)	**39.** (d)
40. (c)	**41.** (b)	**42.** (b)	**43.** (c)	**44.** (b)	**45.** (a)	**46.** (d)	**47.** (a)	**48.** (c)	**49.** (d)
50. (c)	**51.** (c)	**52.** (d)	**53.** (d)	**54.** (b)	**55.** (a)	**56.** (d)	**57.** (c)	**58.** (a)	**59.** (a)
60. (d)	**61.** (d)	**62.** (b)	**63.** (b)	**64.** (d)	**65.** (c)	**66.** (a)	**67.** (b)	**68.** (b)	**69.** (a)
70. (b)	**71.** (a)	**72.** (c)	**73.** (d)	**74.** (a)	**75.** (b)	**76.** (d)	**77.** (b)	**78.** (d)	**79.** (d)
80. (b)	**81.** (b)	**82.** (c)	**83.** (a)	**84.** (b)	**85.** (b)	**86.** (b)	**87.** (c)	**88.** (b)	**89.** (c)
90. (b)	**91.** (c)	**92.** (a)	**93.** (a)	**94.** (a)	**95.** (a)	**96.** (d)	**97.** (a)	**98.** (d)	**99.** (b)
100. (b)	**101.** (a)	**102.** (b)							

EXPLANATIONS

1. (b) : NO : $(\sigma 1s)^2, (\sigma^*1s)^2, (\sigma 2s)^2, (\sigma^*2s)^2, (\sigma 2p_z)^2, (\pi 2p_x)^2 = (\pi 2p_y)^2, (\pi^*2p_x)^1 = (\pi^*2p_y)^0$

$$B.O. = \frac{10-5}{2} = 2.5$$

CN^- : $(\sigma 1s)^2, (\sigma^*1s)^2, (\sigma 2s)^2, (\sigma^*2s)^2, (\pi 2p_x)^2 = (\pi 2p_y)^2, (\sigma 2p_z)^2$

$$B.O. = \frac{10-4}{2} = 3$$

CN : $(\sigma 1s)^2, (\sigma^*1s)^2, (\sigma 2s)^2, (\sigma^*2s)^2, (\pi 2p_x)^2 = (\pi 2p_y)^2, (\sigma 2p_z)^1$

$$B.O. = \frac{9-4}{2} = 2.5$$

CN^+ : $(\sigma 1s)^2, (\sigma^*1s)^2, (\sigma 2s)^2, (\sigma^*2s)^2, (\pi 2p_x)^2 = (\pi 2p_y)^2$

$$B.O. = \frac{8-4}{2} = 2$$

Hence, CN^- has highest bond order.

2. (b) : The structure of ClF_3 is

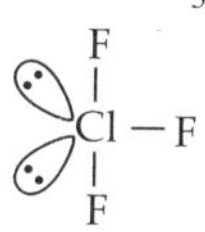

Hence, Cl has 2 lone pairs of electrons.

3. (None)

Species	No. of electrons	Structure
TeI_2	158	Bent
XeF_2	72	Linear
IBr_2^-	124	Linear
XeF_2	72	Linear
IF_3	80	T-shaped
XeF_2	72	Linear
$BeCl_2$	38	Linear
XeF_2	72	Linear

Note : In this question, in place of isoelectronic there should be same number of valence electrons.

4. (c) : BCl_3-Trigonal planar, sp^2-hybridised, 120° angle.

5. (b) : Molecular orbital electronic configurations and bond order values are :

$O_2 : \sigma 1s^2, \sigma^*1s^2, \sigma 2s^2, \sigma^*2s^2, \sigma 2p_z^2, \pi 2p_x^2 = \pi 2p_y^2, \pi^*2p_x^1 = \pi^*2p_y^1$

$$B.O. = \frac{1}{2}(N_b - N_a) = \frac{1}{2}(10-6) = 2$$

$NO^+ : \sigma 1s^2, \sigma^*1s^2, \sigma 2s^2, \sigma^*2s^2, \sigma 2p_z^2, \pi 2p_x^2 = \pi 2p_y^2$

$$B.O. = \frac{1}{2}(10-4) = 3$$

$CN^- : \sigma 1s^2, \sigma^*1s^2, \sigma 2s^2, \sigma^*2s^2, \pi 2p_x^2 = \pi 2p_y^2, \sigma 2p_z^2$

$$B.O. = \frac{1}{2}(10-4) = 3$$

$CO : \sigma 1s^2, \sigma^*1s^2, \sigma 2s^2, \sigma^*2s^2, \pi 2p_x^2 = \pi 2p_y^2, \sigma 2p_z^2$

$$B.O. = \frac{1}{2}(10-4) = 3$$

$N_2 : \sigma 1s^2, \sigma^*1s^2, \sigma 2s^2, \sigma^*2s^2, \pi 2p_x^2 = \pi 2p_y^2, \sigma 2p_z^2$

$$B.O. = \frac{1}{2}(10-4) = 3$$

$O_2^- = \sigma 1s^2, \sigma^*1s^2, \sigma 2s^2, \sigma^*2s^2, \sigma 2p_z^2, \pi 2p_x^2 = \pi 2p_y^2, \pi^*2p_x^2 = \pi^*2p_y^1$

$$B.O. = \frac{1}{2}(10-7) = 1.5$$

$NO : \sigma 1s^2, \sigma^*1s^2, \sigma 2s^2, \sigma^*2s^2, \sigma 2p_z^2, \pi 2p_x^2 = \pi 2p_y^2, \pi^*2p_x^1$

$$B.O. = \frac{1}{2}(10-5) = 2.5$$

6. (c) : H_2O_2, HCN and conc. CH_3COOH form intermolecular hydrogen bonding while cellulose has intramolecular hydrogen bonding.

7. (c) : $X = \frac{1}{2}(VE + MA - c + a)$

For NO_2^+, $X = \frac{1}{2}(5 + 0 - 1) = 2$ *i.e.*, *sp* hybridisation

For NO_3^-, $X = \frac{1}{2}(5 + 0 + 1) = 3$ *i.e.*, sp^2 hybridisation

For NH_4^+, $X = \frac{1}{2}(5 + 4 - 1) = 4$ *i.e.*, sp^3 hybridisation

8. (a, d) : (a) CO_3^{2-} : 6 + 24 + 2 = 32; sp^2; trigonal planar

NO_3^- : 7 + 24 + 1 = 32; sp^2; trigonal planar

Hence, these are isoelectronic as well as isostructural.

(b) ClO_3^- : 17 + 24 + 1 = 42; sp^3, trigonal pyramidal

CO_3^{2-} : 6 + 24 + 2 = 32; sp^2, trigonal planar

Hence, these are neither isoelectronic nor isostructural.

(c) SO_3^{2-} : 16 + 24 + 2 = 42; sp^3, trigonal pyramidal

NO_3^- : 7 + 24 + 1 = 32; sp^2, trigonal planar

These are neither isoelectronic nor isostructural

(d) ClO_3^- : $17 + 24 + 1 = 42$; sp^3, trigonal pyramidal

SO_3^{2-} : $16 + 24 + 2 = 42$; sp^3, trigonal pyramidal

9. (a) :

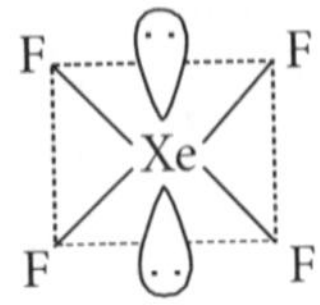

sp^3d^2 hybridisation (octahedral geometry, square planar shape)

10. (c) :

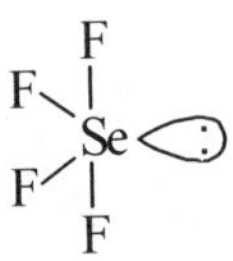

sp^3d hybridisation (see-saw shape)

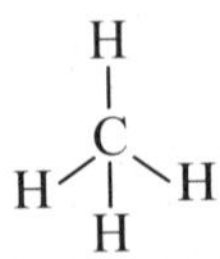

sp^3 hybridisation (tetrahedral)

11. (d) :

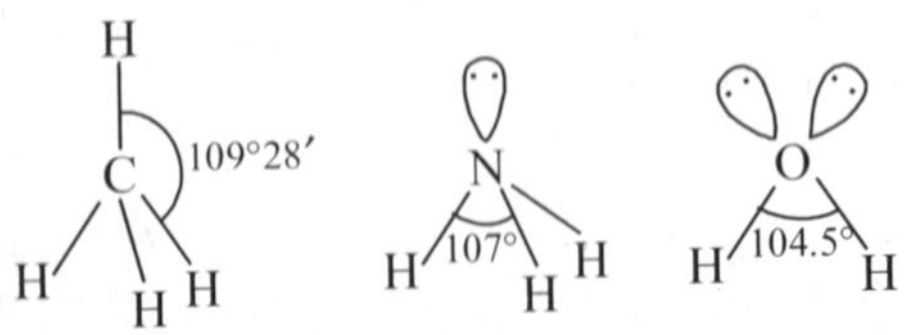

12. (c) : According to VSEPR theory, the repulsive forces between lone pair and lone pair are greater than between lone pair and bond pair which are further greater than bond pair and bond pair.

13. (c) : In diamond and silicon carbide, central atom is sp^3 hybridised and hence, both are isostructural.

NH_3 and PH_3, both are pyramidal and central atom in both cases is sp^3 hybridised.

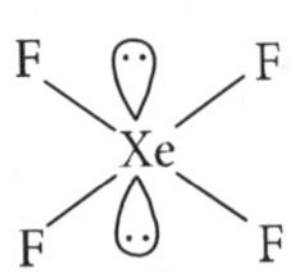

XeF_4

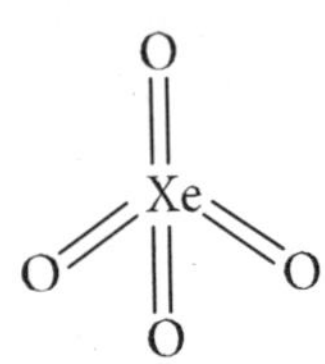

XeO_4

$SiCl_4$ and PCl_4^+, both are tetrahedral and central atom in both cases is sp^3 hybridised.

In XeF_4, Xe is sp^3d^2 hybridised and structure is square planar while in XeO_4, Xe is sp^3 hybridised and structure is tetrahedral.

14. (d) : $O_2(16) : KK\,\sigma 2s^2\,\sigma^*2s^2\,\sigma 2p_z^2\,\pi 2p_x^2 = \pi 2p_y^2$
$\pi^*2p_x^1 = \pi^*2p_y^1$

Bond order $= \frac{1}{2}(8-4) = 2$

$O_2^{2-}(18) : KK\,\sigma 2s^2\,\sigma^*2s^2\,\sigma 2p_z^2\,\pi 2p_x^2 = \pi 2p_y^2$
$\pi^*2p_x^2 = \pi^*2p_y^2$

Bond order $= \frac{1}{2}(8-6) = 1$

$O_2^-(17) : KK\,\sigma 2s^2\,\sigma^*2s^2\,\sigma 2p_z^2\,\pi 2p_x^2 = \pi 2p_y^2$
$\pi^*2p_x^2 = \pi^*2p_y^1$

Bond order $= \frac{1}{2}(8-5) = 1.5$

$O_2^+(15) : KK\,\sigma 2s^2\,\sigma^*2s^2\,\sigma 2p_z^2\,\pi 2p_x^2 = \pi 2p_y^2\,\pi^*2p_x^1$

Bond order $= \frac{1}{2}(8-3) = 2.5$

As, bond order $\propto$ stability

The decreasing order of stability is

$$O_2^+ > O_2 > O_2^- > O_2^{2-}$$

15. (b) :

Species	Hybridisation	Shape	No. of e^-s
SO_3^{2-}	sp^3	Pyramidal	42
ClO_3^-	sp^3	Pyramidal	42
CO_3^{2-}	sp^2	Triangular planar	32
NO_3^-	sp^2	Triangular planar	32

16. (b) :

	O_2^-	O_2	O_2^+	O_2^{2+}
B.O. :	1.5	2.0	2.5	3.0

17. (d) :

	O_2^-	<	O_2	<	O_2^+
B.O. :	1.5		2.0		2.5

18. (a) :

Species	NO_3^-	NO_2	NO_2^-	NO_2^+
Hybridisation	sp^2	sp^2	sp^2	sp(linear)
Bond angle	120°	134°	115°	180°

So, NO_2^+ has maximum bond angle.

19. (c) :

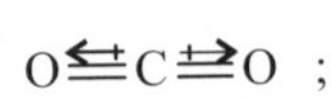

($\mu = 0$, symmetrical)

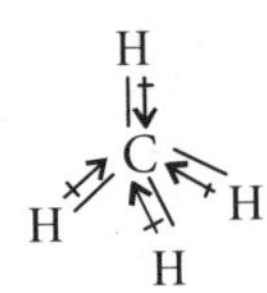

($\mu = 0$, symmetrical)

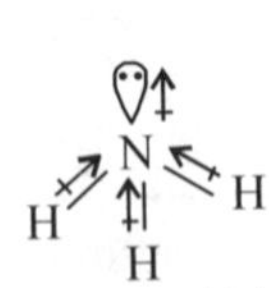

($\mu \neq 0$, pyramidal)

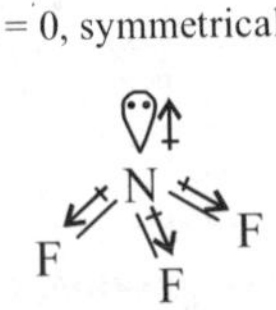

($\mu \neq 0$, pyramidal)

In NH_3, H is less electronegative than N and hence dipole moment of each N—H bond is towards N and create high net dipole moment whereas in NF_3, F is more electronegative than N, the dipole moment of each N—F bond is opposite to that of lone pair, hence reducing the net dipole moment.

20. (b): 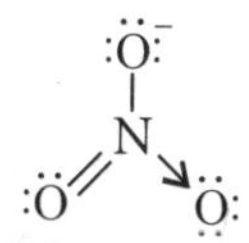

(sp^2-hybridised, trigonal planar)

21. (a): Boron hydrides are electron deficient compounds.

22. (d): F—Xe—F sp^3d, Linear

Cl—$\overset{\ominus}{\text{I}}$—Cl sp^3d, Linear

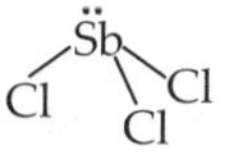 sp^3, Pyramidal

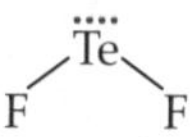 sp^3, V-shaped

23. (d): SF_4 has sp^3d-hybridisation and see-saw shape with (4 bp + 1lp)

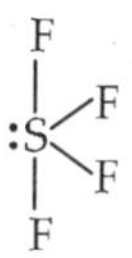 and resultant $\mu \neq 0$.

24. (d): $O_2^-(17)$ superoxide has one unpaired electron.

$\sigma 1s^2\ \sigma^*1s^2\ \sigma 2s^2\ \sigma^*2s^2\ \sigma 2p_z^{\ 2}\ \pi 2p_x^{\ 2} = \pi 2p_y^{\ 2}$
$\pi^*2p_x^{\ 2} = \pi^*2p_y^{\ 1}$

25. (a): HCl is polar ($\mu \neq 0$) and He is non-polar ($\mu = 0$) gives dipole-induced dipole interaction.

26. (a): CO = 6 + 8 = 14 electrons

$NO^+ = 7 + 8 - 1 = 14$ electrons

Both have electronic configuration :

$\sigma 1s^2\ \sigma^*1s^2\ \sigma 2s^2\ \sigma^*2s^2\ \sigma 2p_z^{\ 2}\ \pi 2p_x^{\ 2}\ \pi 2p_y^{\ 2}$

So, both have bond order = $\dfrac{10-4}{2} = 3$

27. (c): 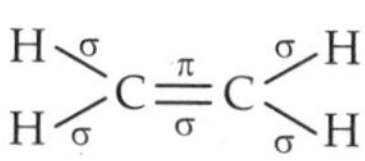

5 σ-bond and 1 π-bond

28. (b): NF_3 and H_2O are sp^3-hybridisation.

29. (c): Molecular orbital configuration of

$O_2 : \sigma 1s^2\ \sigma^*1s^2\ \sigma 2s^2\ \sigma^*2s^2\ \sigma 2p_z^{\ 2}\ \pi 2p_x^{\ 2}\ \pi 2p_y^{\ 2}\ \pi^*2p_x^1$
$\pi^*2p_y^1$

⇒ Paramagnetic

Bond order = $\dfrac{10-6}{2} = 2$

$O_2^+ : \sigma 1s^2\ \sigma^*1s^2\ \sigma 2s^2\ \sigma^*2s^2\ \sigma 2p_z^2\ \pi 2p_x^2\ \pi 2p_y^2\ \pi^*2p_x^1$

⇒ Paramagnetic

Bond order = $\dfrac{10-5}{2} = 2.5$

$C_2 : \sigma 1s^2\ \sigma^*1s^2\ \sigma 2s^2\ \sigma^*2s^2\ \pi 2p_x^{\ 2}\ \pi 2p_y^{\ 2}$

⇒ Diamagnetic

Bond order = $\dfrac{8-4}{2} = 2$

$C_2^+ : \sigma 1s^2\ \sigma^*1s^2\ \sigma 2s^2\ \sigma^*2s^2\ \pi 2p_x^{\ 2}\ \pi 2p_y^{\ 1}$

⇒ Paramagnetic

Bond order = $\dfrac{7-4}{2} = 1.5$

$NO : \sigma 1s^2\ \sigma^*1s^2\ \sigma 2s^2\ \sigma^*2s^2\ \sigma 2p_z^{\ 2}\ \pi 2p_x^{\ 2}\ \pi 2p_y^{\ 2}\ \pi^*2p_x^{\ 1}$

⇒ Paramagnetic

Bond order = $\dfrac{10-5}{2} = 2.5$

$NO^+ : \sigma 1s^2\ \sigma^*1s^2\ \sigma 2s^2\ \sigma^*2s^2\ \sigma 2p_z^{\ 2}\ \pi 2p_x^{\ 2}\ \pi 2p_y^{\ 2}$

⇒ Diamagnetic.

Bond order = $\dfrac{10-4}{2} = 3$

$N_2 : \sigma 1s^2\ \sigma^*1s^2\ \sigma 2s^2\ \sigma^*2s^2\ \pi 2p_x^{\ 2}\ \pi 2p_y^{\ 2}\ \sigma 2p_z^{\ 2}$

⇒ Paramagnetic

Bond order = $\dfrac{10-4}{2} = 3$

$N_2^+ : \sigma 1s^2\ \sigma^*1s^2\ \sigma 2s^2\ \sigma^*2s^2\ \pi 2p_x^{\ 2}\ \pi 2p_y^{\ 2}\ \sigma 2p_z^{\ 1}$

⇒ Paramagnetic

Bond order = $\dfrac{9-4}{2} = 2.5$

30. (d):

BCl_3 ⇒	sp^2,	trigonal planar
$BrCl_3$ ⇒	sp^3d,	T-shaped
NH_3 ⇒	sp^3,	pyramidal
NO_3^- ⇒	sp^2,	trigonal planar
NF_3 ⇒	sp^3,	pyramidal
BF_3 ⇒	sp^2,	trigonal planar
BF_4^- ⇒	sp^3,	tetrahedral
NH_4^+ ⇒	sp^3,	tetrahedral

31. (b): Configuration of O_2

$\sigma 1s^2\ \sigma^*1s^2\ \sigma 2s^2\ \sigma^*2s^2\ \sigma 2p_z^{\ 2}\ \pi 2p_x^{\ 2}\ \pi 2p_y^{\ 2}\ \pi^*2p_x^{\ 1}\ \pi^*2p_y^{\ 1}$

Bond order = $\dfrac{\text{No. of } e^- \text{ in bonding M.O.} - \text{No. of } e^- \text{ in antibonding M.O.}}{2}$

Bond order of $O_2^{\ +} = \dfrac{10-5}{2} = 2.5$

Bond order of $O_2^{\ -} = \dfrac{10-7}{2} = 1.5$

Bond order of $O_2^{\ 2-} = \dfrac{10-8}{2} = 1.0$

Bond order of $O_2 = \dfrac{10-6}{2} = 2$

32. (d): 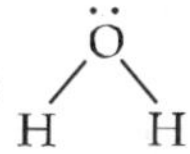 2 bond pairs, 1 lone pair

 3 bond pairs, 0 lone pair

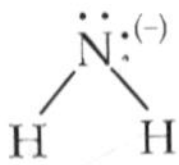 2 bond pairs, 2 lone pairs

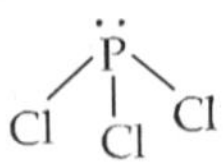 3 bond pairs, 1 lone pair

33. (a): $O_2^{2-} \rightarrow 1$ $\quad B_2 \rightarrow 1$
$O_2^{+} \rightarrow 2.5$ $\quad NO^{+} \rightarrow 3$
$NO \rightarrow 2.5$ $\quad CO \rightarrow 3$
$N_2 \rightarrow 3$ $\quad O_2 \rightarrow 2.0$

34. (a): Electronic configuration of O_2
$\sigma(1s)^2\, \sigma^*(1s)^2\, \sigma(2s)^2\, \sigma^*(2s)^2\, \sigma(2p_z)^2\, \pi(2p_x)^2 = \pi(2p_y)^2$
$\pi^*(2p_x)^1 = \pi^*(2p_y)^1$
Thus, the incoming electron will enter in π^*2p_x to form O_2^-.

35. (d):

Diatomic species	Bond order
NO	2.5
O_2^-	1.5
C_2^{2-}	3.0
He_2^+	0.5

Thus, increasing order : $He_2^+ < O_2^- < NO < C_2^{2-}$

36. (a) : Electronic configuration
$O_2 : KK(\sigma 2s)^2\, (\sigma^*2s)^2\, (\sigma 2p_x)^2\, (\pi 2p_y)^2\, (\pi 2p_z)^2\, (\pi^*2p_y)^1\, (\pi^*2p_z)^1$

Bond order $= \frac{1}{2}(8-4) = 2$

O_2^+ : Bond order $= \frac{1}{2}(8-3) = 2\frac{1}{2}$

O_2^- : Bond order $= \frac{1}{2}(8-5) = 1\frac{1}{2}$

O_2^{2-} : Bond order $= \frac{1}{2}(8-6) = 1$

As bond order increases, bond length decreases.

37. (a):

Ions	Hybridisation
NO_2^-	sp^2
NO_3^-	sp^2
NH_2^-	sp^3
NH_4^+	sp^3
SCN^-	sp

38. (a) : Increasing order of bond length is
C—H < C=C < C—O < C—C
107 pm 134 pm 141 pm 154 pm

39. (d) : 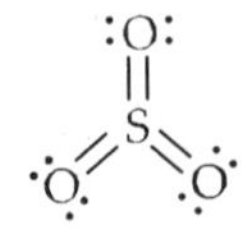 has maximum number of covalent bonds.

40. (c) : O_2^+ and O_2 are paramagnetic in nature as they contain one and two unpaired electrons respectively.

41. (b) : The hybridisation of the central atom can be calculated as

$$H = \frac{1}{2}\left[\begin{pmatrix}\text{No. of electrons}\\ \text{in valence shell}\\ \text{of atom}\end{pmatrix} + \begin{pmatrix}\text{No. of monovalent}\\ \text{atoms around}\\ \text{central atom}\end{pmatrix} - \begin{pmatrix}\text{Charge on}\\ \text{cation}\end{pmatrix} + \begin{pmatrix}\text{Charge on}\\ \text{anion}\end{pmatrix}\right]$$

$\therefore$ For BF_3, $H = \frac{1}{2}[(3)+(3)-(0)+(0)]$
$= 3 \Rightarrow sp^2$ hybridisation.

For NO_2^-, $H = \frac{1}{2}[(5)+(0)-(0)+(1)]$
$= 3 \Rightarrow sp^2$ hybridisation.

42. (b) : Be_2 does not exist.
Be_2 has an electronic configuration of :
$\sigma 1s^2\, \sigma^*1s^2\, \sigma 2s^2\, \sigma^*2s^2$

$\therefore$ Bond order $= \frac{4-4}{2} = 0$

Thus, Be_2 does not exist.

43. (c) : Hybridisation of the central atom can be calculated as:

$$H = \frac{1}{2}\left[\begin{pmatrix}\text{No. of valence}\\ \text{electrons in the}\\ \text{central atom}\end{pmatrix} + \begin{pmatrix}\text{No. of monovalent}\\ \text{atoms around}\\ \text{central atom}\end{pmatrix} - \begin{pmatrix}\text{Charge on}\\ \text{cation}\end{pmatrix} + \begin{pmatrix}\text{Charge on}\\ \text{anion}\end{pmatrix}\right]$$

Applying this formula we find that all the given species except $[SbCl_5]^{2-}$ have central atom with sp^3d (corresponding to H = 5) hybridization. In $[SbCl_5]^{2-}$, Sb is sp^3d^2 hybridized.

44. (b) : For neutral molecules,
No. of electron pairs = No. of atoms bonded to it + 1/2[Gp. no. of central atom – Valency of central atom]

$\therefore$ For CH_4, no. of e^- pairs $= 4 + \frac{1}{2}[4-4]$
$= 4$ (sp^3 hybridisation)

For SF_4, no. of e^- pairs $= 4 + \frac{1}{2}[6-4]$
$= 5$ (sp^3d hybridisation)

For ions,
No. of electron pairs = No. of atoms bonded to it + 1/2[Gp. no. of central atom – Valency of central atom ± No. of electrons]

$\therefore$ For BF_4^-, no. of e^- pairs $= 4 + \frac{1}{2}[3 - 4 + 1]$
$= 4$ (sp^3 hybridisation)

For NH_4^+, no. of e^- pairs $= 4 + \frac{1}{2}[5 - 4 - 1]$
$= 4$ (sp^3 hybridisation)

45. (a) : No. of electron pairs at the central atom = No. of atoms bonded to it + 1/2[Group number of central atom – Valency of the central atom ± no. of electrons]

No. of electron pairs at the central atom in NO_3^-
$= 3 + \frac{1}{2}[5 - 6 + 1] = 3$ (sp^2 hybridisation).

No. of electron pairs at the central atom in
$H_3O^+ = 3 + \frac{1}{2}[6 - 3 - 1] = 4$ (sp^3 hybridisation).

46. (d) : Methanol can undergo intermolecular association through H-bonding as the – OH group in alcohols is highly polarised.

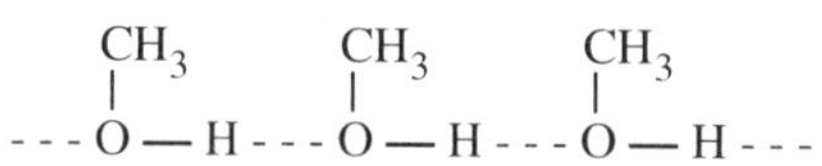

As a result, in order to convert liquid CH_3OH to gaseous state, the strong hydrogen bonds must be broken.

47. (a) : According to MOT, the molecular orbital electronic configuration of

$N_2 : (\sigma 1s)^2 (\sigma^* 1s)^2 (\sigma 2s)^2 (\sigma^* 2s)^2 (\pi 2p_x)^2 (\pi 2p_y)^2 (\sigma 2p_z)^2$

$\therefore$ $B.O = \frac{10-4}{2} = 3$

$N_2^- : (\sigma 1s)^2 (\sigma^* 1s)^2 (\sigma 2s)^2 (\sigma^* 2s)^2 (\pi 2p_x)^2 (\pi 2p_y)^2 (\sigma 2p_z)^2 (\pi^* 2p_x)^1$

$\therefore$ $B.O = \frac{10-5}{2} = 2.5$

$N_2^{2-} : (\sigma 1s)^2 (\sigma^* 1s)^2 (\sigma 2s)^2 (\sigma^* 2s)^2 (\pi 2p_x)^2 (\pi 2p_y)^2 (\sigma 2p_z)^2 (\pi^* 2p_x)^1 (\pi^* 2p_y)^1$

$\therefore$ $B.O. = \frac{10-6}{2} = 2$

Hence the order : $N_2^{2-} < N_2^- < N_2$

48. (c) : $BF_3 \rightarrow sp^2$, $NO_2^- \rightarrow sp^2$, $NH_2^- \rightarrow sp^3$, $H_2O \rightarrow sp^3$

49. (d) : Structures of NO_2^-, NO_2 and NO_2^+ is given as

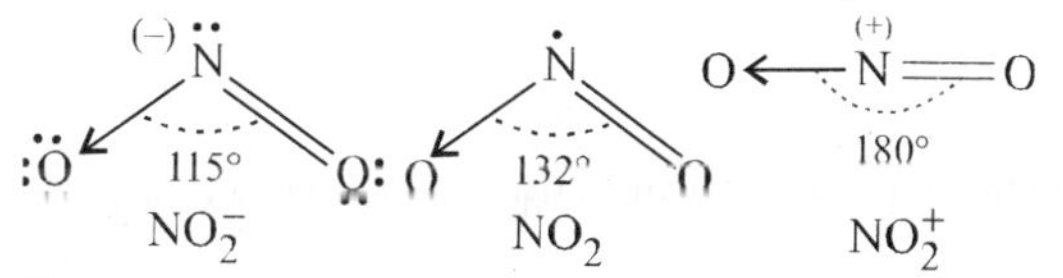

The correct order of increasing bond angles in the following triatomic species is
$NO_2^- < NO_2 < NO_2^+$

50. (c) : Hybridisation of Br in BrO_3^- :
$H = 1/2(7 + 0 - 0 + 1) = 4$ *i.e.* sp^3 hybridisation
Hybridisation of Xe in XeO_3 :
$H = \frac{1}{2}(8 + 0 - 0 + 0) = 4$ *i.e.* sp^3 hybridisation

In both BrO_3^- and XeO_3, the central atom is sp^3 hybridised and contains one lone pair of electrons, hence in both the cases, the structure is trigonal pyramidal.

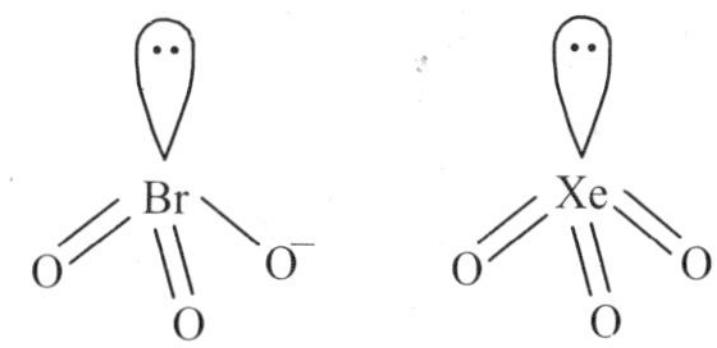

BrO_3^- XeO_3

51. (c) : $CO \Rightarrow :\overset{-}{C} \equiv \overset{+}{O}: \longleftrightarrow :C = \ddot{O}:$

$CO_3^{2-} \Rightarrow$

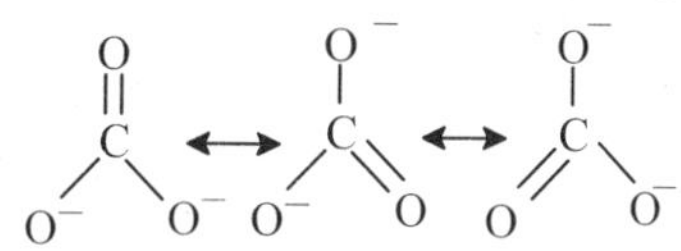

$CO_2 \Rightarrow :\ddot{O} = C = \ddot{O}: \longleftrightarrow :\overset{+}{O} \equiv C - \ddot{O}^-: \longleftrightarrow :\ddot{O}^- - C \equiv \overset{+}{O}:$

More single bond character in resonance hybrid, more is the bond length. Hence the increasing bond length is
$CO < CO_2 < CO_3^{2-}$

52. (d) : For AB_5 molecules, there are three possible geometries *i.e.* planar pentagonal, square pyramidal and trigonal bipyramidal.

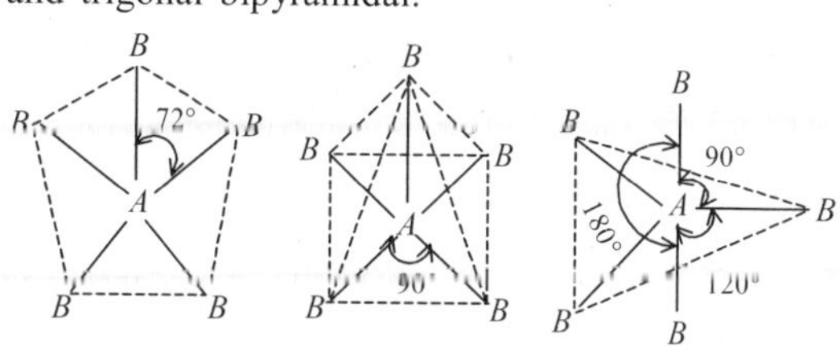

planar pentagonal square pyramidal trigonal bipyramidal

Out of these three geometries, it is only trigonal pyramidal shape in which bond pair-bond pair repulsions are minimum and hence this geometry is the most probable geometry of AB_5 molecule.

53. (d) : NO_2^- : Due to sp^2 hybridisation of N-atom and the presence of one lone pair on it, NO_2^- has angular shape.

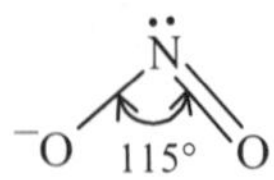

O_3 :  V-shaped

SO_2 : Due to the presence of one lone pair of electros in one of the three sp^2-hybrid orbitals and sp^2 hybridisation of S or S^+ atom, SO_2 molecule has angular (V-shaped) structure.

NO_2^+ : Due to sp hybridisation of N^+, NO_2^+ ion has linear shape.

$:\ddot{O}=\overset{+}{N}=\ddot{O}:$

54. (b) : $SiCl_4$, NH_4^+, SO_4^{2-} and PO_4^{3-} ions are the examples of molecules/ions which are of AB_4 type and have tetrahedral structure. SCl_4 is AB_4(lone pair) types species. Although the arrangement of five sp^3d hybrid orbitals in space is trigonal bipyramidal, due to the presence of one lone pair of electron in the basal hybrid orbital, the shape of AB_4 (lone pair) species gets distorted and becomes distorted tetrahedral or see-saw.

55. (a) :

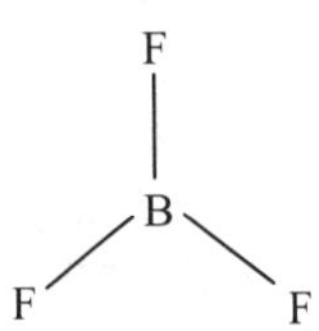

trigonal planar

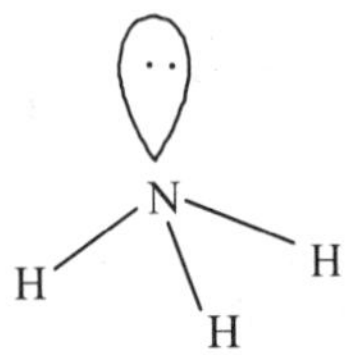

pyramidal

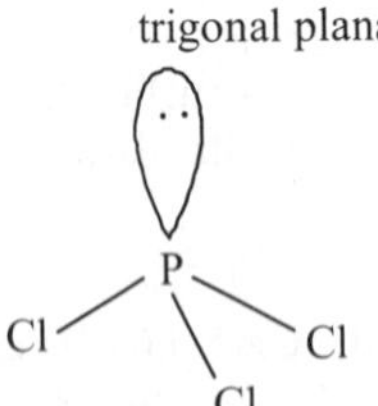

pyramidal

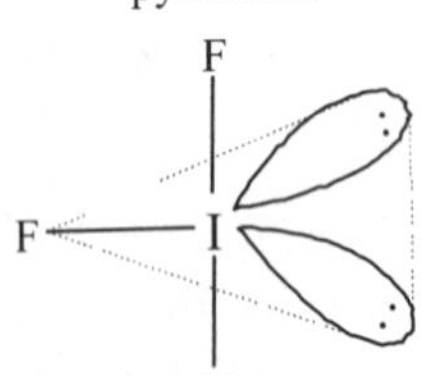

T-shape

56. (d) : Bond lengths of O – O in O_2 is 1.21Å, in H_2O_2 is 1.48Å and in O_3 is 1.28Å. Therefore, correct order of the O – O bond length is $H_2O_2 > O_3 > O_2$.

57. (c) : Hydrogen bonding in $H_2O > C_2H_5OH > CH_3OH$

Hence, H_2O has maximum surface tension.

58. (a) : SiF_4 has symmetrical tetrahedral shape which is due to sp^3 hybridisation of the central silicon atom in its excited state configuration.

SF_4 has distorted tetrahedral or sea-saw geometry which arises due to sp^3d hybridisation of central sulphur atom and due to the presence of one lone pair of electrons in one of the equatorial hybrid orbital.

59. (a) : In octahedral molecule six hybrid orbitals directed towards the corners of a regular octahedron with a bond angle of 90°.

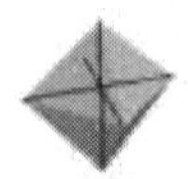 Octahedral 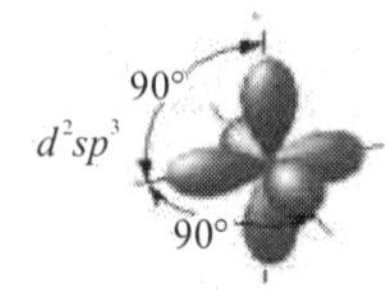

According to this geometry, the number of $X-M-X$ bonds at 180° must be three.

60. (d) : The overall value of the dipole moment of a polar molecule depends on its geometry and shape, *i.e.* vectorial addition of dipole moment of the constituent bonds. Water has angular structure with bond angle 105° as it has dipole moment. However BeF_2 is a linear molecule since dipole moment summation of all the bonds present in the molecule cancel each other.

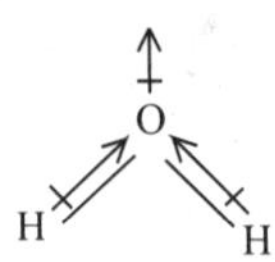

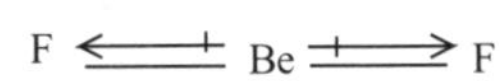

61. (d) :

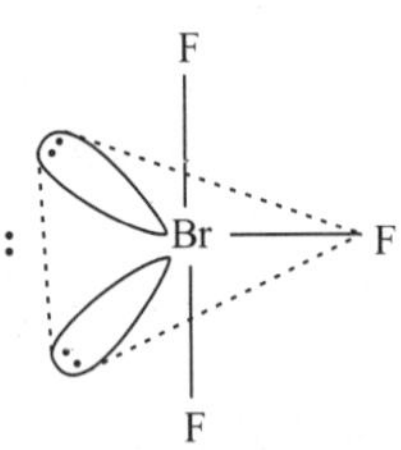

Bent T-shaped geometry in which both lone pairs occupy the equatorial positions of the trigonal bipyramid. Here (lp - lp) repulsion = 0, (lp - bp) repulsion = 4 and (bp - bp) repulsion = 2.

62. (b) : We know C – C = 347 kJ/mol

C = C = 619 kJ/mol

63. (b) : In sulphite ion the central atom sulphur is sp^3 hybridised.

Electronic structure of S atom in excited state

The three p electrons form σ bonds with three oxygen atoms - with one position (of the tetrahedron) being occupied by a lone pair. The d

electron (excluded from hybridisation) forms π bond with one oxygen atom. *i.e.* $p\pi$ - $d\pi$ bonding occurs.

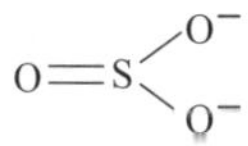

64. (d) : 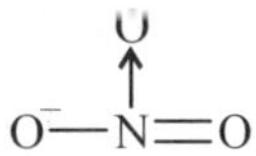

In NO_3^- ion, nitrogen has 4 bond pair of electrons and no lone pair of electrons.

65. (c) : In CO, the number of electrons
$= 6 + 8 = 14$ [Z of C = 6 and O = 8]

Electronic configuration of molecular orbital of CO :
$(\sigma 1s)^2(\sigma^*1s)^2(\sigma 2s)^2(\sigma^*2s)^2(\pi 2p_x)^2(\pi 2p_y)^2(\sigma 2p_z)^2$

CN^- have also get (6 + 7 + 1) 14 electrons and the configuration is similar to that of CO.

CN^- and CO are isoelectronic.

66. (a) : Compounds having same shape with same hybridisation are known as isostructural.
XeF_2, IF_2^- → both are sp^3d hybridised linear molecules.

67. (b) : Bond angle is maximum in NH_4^+ tetrahedral molecule with bond angle 109°.

68. (b) : For strong π-bonding, $p\pi$ - $p\pi$ bonding should be strong. In case of P, due to larger size as compared to N-atom, $p\pi$ - $p\pi$ bonding is not so strong.

69. (a)

70. (b) : In PO_4^{3-}, P atom has vacant *d*-orbitals, thus it can form $p\pi$-$d\pi$ bond. 'N' and 'C' have no vacant '*d*' orbital in their valence shell, so they cannot form such bond.

71. (a) : $N_2(14) \rightarrow (\sigma 1s)^2, (\sigma^*1s)^2, (\sigma 2s)^2, (\sigma^*2s)^2$
$(\sigma^*2s)^2, (\pi 2p_x)^2, (\pi 2p_y)^2, (\sigma 2p_z)^2$

In N_2, bond order $= \dfrac{N_b - N_a}{2} = \dfrac{10-4}{2} = 3$

In N_2^+, bond order $= \dfrac{9-4}{2} = 2\cdot 5$

As the bond order in N_2 is more than N_2^+ so the dissociation energy of N_2 is higher than N_2^+.

72. (c) : In 'CO' (14 electrons), there is no unpaired electron in its molecular orbital. Therefore, this does not exhibit paramagnetism.

73. (d) : $O_2^{2-}(18) \rightarrow (\sigma 1s)^2, (\sigma^*1s)^2(\sigma 2s)^2, (\sigma^*2s)^2$
$(\sigma 2p_x)^2, (\pi 2p_y)^2, (\pi 2p_z)^2, (\pi^*2p_y)^2, (\pi^*2p_z)^2$

Thus, the no. of antibonding electrons in O_2^{2-} ion is = 8(4 pairs)

74. (a) : The total charge = –3
So the average formal charge on each 'O' atom is
$-3/4 = -0.75$

Again total no. of electrons in the valence shell of PO_4^{3-} ion $= 5 + 8 = 13$

No. of electrons involved in bond formation in PO_4^{3-} ion $= 13 - 3 = 10$

No. of bonds in $PO_4^{3-} = \dfrac{10}{2} = 5$

$\Rightarrow$ Average P—O bond order $= \dfrac{5}{4} = 1.25$

75. (b) : Diamagnetism is caused due to the absence of unpaired electrons. But in N_2^+, there is unpaired electron. So, it is paramagnetic.

76. (d) : In O_2 bond, the order is 2 and in O_2^- bond, the order is 1.5.

77. (b) : The C–C bond length = 1.54 Å, C=C bond length = 1.34 Å and C≡C bond length = 1.20 Å. Since propyne has a triple bond, therefore it has minimum bond length.

78. (d) : $BeCl_2$ and C_2H_2 have *sp*-hybridisation and C_2H_6 has sp^3-hybridisation.

79. (d) : Paramagnetism is caused by the presence of atoms, ions or molecules with unpaired electrons, *i.e* $:\dot{N}=\ddot{O}:$

80. (b) : Bond length of O – O in O_2 is 1.21 Å (O = O); in H_2O_2 is 1.48 Å (HO – HO) and in O_3 is 1.28 Å 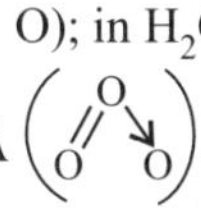.

81. (b) : Number of electrons in bonding orbitals N_b = 10 and number of electrons in antibonding orbitals N_a = 4.
Therefore bond order $= 1/2(N_b - N_a) = 1/2(10 - 4) = 3$

82. (c) : The bond order of $O_2^+ = 2.5$, $O_2^{2-} = 1$, $O_2^- = 1.5$ and that of $O_2 = 2$.

83. (a) : The structure of CS_2 is linear and therefore it does not have permanent dipole moment. It is represented as S—C—S.

84. (b) : Smaller the atom, stronger is the bond and greater the bond dissociation energy. Therefore the bond C-*D* has the greatest energy or smallest atoms.

85. (b) : For compounds containing ions of same charge, lattice energy increases as the size of ions decreases. Thus, NaF has highest lattice energy.

86. (b) : The strength of interaction follow the order van der Waals' < hydrogen-bond < dipole-dipole < covalent. It is so because bond length of H-bond is larger than that of a covalent bond.
And also covalent bond is strongest because, the greater the extent of overlapping, the stronger is the bond formed.

87. (c) : There is a triple bond in ethyne molecule $(H-C\equiv C-H)$ and due to this triple bond, carbon-carbon bond distance is shortest in ethyne.

88. (b) : CO_2 molecule is *sp*-hybridised and thus it is linear, while CO_3^{2-} is planar (sp^2 -hybridised), SO_2 is an angular molecule with sp^2 hybridisation
SO_4^{2-} is tetrahedral (sp^3-hybridised).

89. (c) : H – F shows strongest H-bonds because fluorine is most electronegative.

90. (b) : As all C – Cl bonds are directed towards the corner of a regular tetrahedron.

91. (c) : Along the period, electronegativity (*EN*) increases and hence as we move from Li → Be → B → C, the electronegativity increases and hence the *EN* difference between the element and Cl decreases and accordingly the covalent character increases.
Thus $LiCl < BeCl_2 < BCl_3 < CCl_4$ is correct.

92. (a) : According to VSEPR theory, a molecule with 6 bond pairs must be octahedral.

93. (a) : A σ-bond is stronger than a π-bond.

94. (a) : H_2O shows maximum H-bonding because each H_2O molecule is linked to four H_2O molecules through H-bonds.

95. (a)

96. (d) : $H-C=\overset{\overset{O}{||}}{C^*}-O-H$

The asterick (*) marked carbon has a valency of 5 and hence this formula is not correct because carbon has a maximum valency of 4.

97. (a) : For linear arrangement of atoms the hybridisation is *sp*. (bond angle = 180°).
Only H_2S has sp^3-hybridisation and hence it has angular shape while C_2H_2, BeH_2 and CO_2 all involve *sp*-hybridisation and hence has linear arrangement of atoms.

98. (d) : Metallic bonds have electrostatic attraction on all sides and hence do not have directional characteristics.

99. (b) : BF_3 involves sp^2-hybridisation

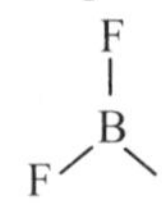

100. (b) : BeF_2 is linear and hence it has zero dipole moment.

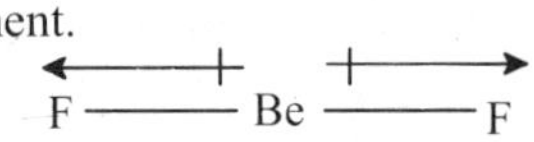

while H_2O is a bent molecule and hence it has a non-zero dipole moment

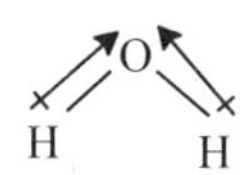

101. (a) : The type of overlap between *s*- and *p*-orbitals occurs along internuclear axis and hence the angle is 180°.

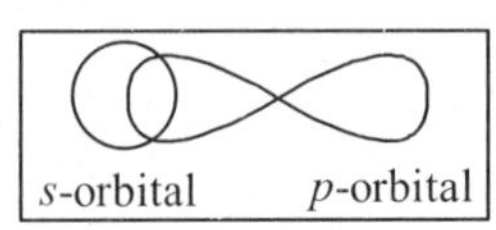

s-p overlapping

102. (b) : Equilateral or triangular planar shape involves sp^2 hybridisation. *e.g.* – BCl_3.

Chapter 5

States of Matter : Gases and Liquids

1. Given van der Waals' constant for NH_3, H_2, O_2 and CO_2 are respectively 4.17, 0.244, 1.36 and 3.59, which one of the following gases is most easily liquefied?
(a) NH_3 (b) H_2 (c) O_2 (d) CO_2
(NEET 2018)

2. The correction factor 'a' to the ideal gas equation corresponds to
(a) density of the gas molecules
(b) volume of the gas molecules
(c) electric field present between the gas molecules
(d) forces of attraction between the gas molecules. *(NEET 2018)*

3. Equal moles of hydrogen and oxygen gases are placed in a container with a pin-hole through which both can escape. What fraction of the oxygen escapes in the time required for one-half of the hydrogen to escape?
(a) 3/8 (b) 1/2 (c) 1/8 (d) 1/4
(NEET-I 2016)

4. A gas such as carbon monoxide would be most likely to obey the ideal gas law at
(a) low temperatures and high pressures
(b) high temperatures and high pressures
(c) low temperatures and low pressures
(d) high temperatures and low pressures.
(2015)

5. Maximum deviation from ideal gas is expected from
(a) $CH_{4(g)}$ (b) $NH_{3(g)}$ (c) $H_{2(g)}$ (d) $N_{2(g)}$
(NEET 2013)

6. What is the density of N_2 gas at 227°C and 5.00 atm. pressure? (R = 0.082 L atm $K^{-1}mol^{-1}$)
(a) 1.40 g/mL (b) 2.81 g/mL
(c) 3.41 g/mL (d) 0.29 g/mL
(Karnataka NEET 2013)

7. 50 mL of each gas A and of gas B takes 150 and 200 seconds respectively for effusing through a pin hole under the similar conditions. If molecular mass of gas B is 36, the molecular mass of gas A will be
(a) 96 (b) 128 (c) 32 (d) 64
(2012)

8. A certain gas takes three times as long to effuse out as helium. Its molecular mass will be
(a) 27 u (b) 36 u (c) 64 u (d) 9 u
(Mains 2012)

9. For real gases van der Waals equation is written as $\left(p+\frac{an^2}{V^2}\right)(V-nb)=nRT$
where a and b are van der Waals constants Two sets of gases are
(I) O_2, CO_2, H_2 and He
(II) CH_4, O_2 and H_2
The gases given in set-I in increasing order of b and gases given in set-II in decreasing order of a, are arranged below. Select the correct order from the following
(a) (I) $He < H_2 < CO_2 < O_2$ (II) $CH_4 > H_2 > O_2$
(b) (I) $O_2 < He < H_2 < CO_2$ (II) $H_2 > O_2 > CH_4$
(c) (I) $H_2 < He < O_2 < CO_2$ (II) $CH_4 > O_2 > H_2$
(d) (I) $H_2 < O_2 < He < CO_2$ (II) $O_2 > CH_4 > H_2$
(Mains 2012)

10. Equal volumes of two monatomic gases, A and B at same temperature and pressure are mixed. The ratio of specific heats (C_P/C_V) of the mixture will be
(a) 0.83 (b) 1.50 (c) 3.3 (d) 1.67
(2012)

11. By what factor does the average velocity of a gaseous molecule increase when the temperature (in Kelvin) is doubled?
(a) 2.0 (b) 2.8 (c) 4.0 (d) 1.4
(2011)

12. Two gases A and B having the same volume diffuse through a porous partition in 20 and 10 seconds respectively. The molecular mass of A is 49 u. Molecular mas of B will be
(a) 50.00 u (b) 12.25 u
(c) 6.50 u (d) 25.00 u *(2011)*

13. A gaseous mixture was prepared by taking equal mole of CO and N_2. If the total pressure of the mixture was found 1 atmosphere, the partial pressure of the nitrogen (N_2) in the mixture is
(a) 0.5 atm (b) 0.8 atm
(c) 0.9 atm (d) 1 atm *(2011)*

14. A bubble of air is underwater at temperature 15°C and the pressure 1.5 bar. If the bubble rises to the surface where the temperature is 25°C and the pressure is 1.0 bar, what will happen to the volume of the bubble?
(a) Volume will become greater by a factor of 1.6.
(b) Volume will become greater by a factor of 1.1.
(c) Volume will become smaller by a factor of 0.70.
(d) Volume will become greater by a factor of 2.5. *(Mains 2011)*

15. The pressure exerted by 6.0 g of methane gas in a 0.03 m^3 vessel at 129°C is (Atomic masses: C = 12.01, H = 1.01 and R = 8.314 J K^{-1} mol^{-1})
(a) 215216 Pa (b) 13409 Pa
(c) 41648 Pa (d) 31684 Pa
(Mains 2010)

16. The energy absorbed by each molecule (A_2) of a substance is 4.4×10^{-19} J and bond energy per molecule is 4.0×10^{-19} J. The kinetic energy of the molecule per atom will be
(a) 2.2×10^{-19} J (b) 2.0×10^{-19} J
(c) 4.0×10^{-20} J (d) 2.0×10^{-20} J
(2009)

17. If a gas expands at constant temperature, it indicates that
(a) kinetic energy of molecules remains the same
(b) number of the molecules of gas increases
(c) kinetic energy of molecules decreases
(d) pressure of the gas increases. *(2008)*

18. Volume occupied by one molecule of water (density = 1 g cm^{-3}) is
(a) 3.0×10^{-23} cm^3 (b) 5.5×10^{-23} cm^3
(c) 9.0×10^{-23} cm^3 (d) 6.023×10^{-23} cm
(2008

19. van der Waal's real gas, acts as an ideal gas at which conditions?
(a) High temperature, low pressure
(b) Low temperature, high pressure
(c) High temperature, high pressure
(d) Low temperature, low pressure *(2002*

20. Average molar kinetic energy of CO and N at same temperature is
(a) $KE_1 = KE_2$ (b) $KE_1 > KE_2$
(c) $KE_1 < KE_2$
(d) can't say any thing. Both volumes are n given. *(200*

21. At 25°C and 730 mm pressure, 380 mL of d oxygen was collected. If the temperature constant, what volume will the oxyge occupy at 760 mm pressure?
(a) 569 mL (b) 365 mL
(c) 265 mL (d) 621 mL
(199

22. Which of the following statements is wro for gases?
(a) Confined gas exerts uniform pressure the walls of its container in all directio
(b) Volume of the gas is equal to volume container confining the gas.
(c) Gases do not have a definite shape a volume.
(d) Mass of a gas cannot be determined weighing a container in which it enclosed. *(199*

23. The average kinetic energy of an ideal g per molecule in S.I. units, at 25°C will be
(a) 6.17×10^{-20} J (b) 7.16×10^{-20} J
(c) 61.7×10^{-21} J (d) 6.17×10^{-21} J
(199

24. At what temperature, the rate of effusion N_2 would be 1.625 times than the rate of S at 500°C?
(a) 373°C (b) 620°C
(c) 110°C (d) 173°C *(199*

25. Which of the following mixture of gases d not obey Dalton's Law of partial pressu
(a) Cl_2 and SO_2 (b) CO_2 and He
(c) O_2 and CO_2 (d) N_2 and O_2
(19

26. An ideal gas, obeying kinetic theory of gases can not be liquefied, because
(a) it solidifies before becoming a liquid
(b) forces acting between its molecules are negligible
(c) its critical temperature is above 0°C
(d) its molecules are relatively small in size. *(1995)*

27. 50 mL of hydrogen diffuses out through a small hole of a vessel, in 20 minutes. The time taken by 40 mL of oxygen to diffuse out is
(a) 32 minutes (b) 64 minutes
(c) 8 minutes (d) 12 minutes *(1994)*

28. The temperature of a gas is raised from 27°C to 927°C. The root mean square speed of the gas
(a) remains same
(b) gets $\sqrt{\frac{927}{27}}$ times
(c) gets halved
(d) gets doubled. *(1994)*

29. At STP, 0.50 mol H_2 gas and 1.0 mol He gas
(a) have equal average kinetic energies
(b) have equal molecular speeds
(c) occupy equal volumes
(d) have equal effusion rates. *(1993)*

30. Under what conditions will a pure sample of an ideal gas not only exhibit a pressure of 1 atm but also a concentration of 1 mole litre^{-1}? (R = 0.082 litre atm mol^{-1} deg^{-1})
(a) At STP
(b) When V = 22.4 litres
(c) When T = 12 K
(d) Impossible under any conditions. *(1993)*

31. Internal energy and pressure of a gas per unit volume are related as
(a) $P=\frac{2}{3}E$ (b) $P=\frac{3}{2}E$
(c) $P=\frac{1}{2}E$ (d) $P = 2E$ *(1993)*

32. The ratio among most probable velocity, mean velocity and root mean square velocity is given by
(a) 1 : 2 : 3 (b) $1:\sqrt{2}:\sqrt{3}$
(c) $\sqrt{2}:\sqrt{3}:\sqrt{8/\pi}$ (d) $\sqrt{2}:\sqrt{8/\pi}:\sqrt{3}$ *(1993)*

33. When is deviation more in the behaviour of a gas from the ideal gas equation $PV = nRT$?
(a) At high temperature and low pressure
(b) At low temperature and high pressure
(c) At high temperature and high pressure
(d) At low temperature and low pressure. *(1993)*

34. A closed flask contains water in all its three states solid, liquid and vapour at 0°C. In this situation, the average kinetic energy of water molecules will be
(a) the greatest in all the three states
(b) the greatest in vapour state
(c) the greatest in the liquid state
(d) the greatest in the solid state. *(1992)*

35. Which is not true in case of an ideal gas?
(a) It cannot be converted into a liquid.
(b) There is no interaction between the molecules.
(c) All molecules of the gas move with same speed.
(d) At a given temperature, PV is proportional to the amount of the gas. *(1992)*

36. The correct value of the gas constant 'R' is close to
(a) 0.082 litre-atmosphere K
(b) 0.082 litre-atmosphere K^{-1} mol^{-1}
(c) 0.082 litre-atmosphere^{-1} K mol^{-1}
(d) 0.082 litre^{-1} atmosphere^{-1} K mol. *(1992)*

37. An ideal gas can't be liquefied because
(a) its critical temperature is always above 0°C
(b) its molecules are relatively smaller in size
(c) it solidifies before becoming a liquid
(d) forces operative between its molecules are negligible. *(1992)*

38. Select one correct statement. In the gas equation, $PV = nRT$
(a) n is the number of molecules of a gas
(b) V denotes volume of one mole of the gas
(c) n moles of the gas have a volume V
(d) P is the pressure of the gas when only one mole of gas is present. *(1992)*

39. A gas is said to behave like an ideal gas when the relation PV/T = constant. When do you expect a real gas to behave like an ideal gas?
(a) When the temperature is low.
(b) When both the temperature and pressure are low.

(c) When both the temperature and pressure are high.
(d) When the temperature is high and pressure is low. *(1991)*

40. In a closed flask of 5 litres, 1.0 g of H_2 is heated from 300 to 600 K. Which statement is not correct?
(a) Pressure of the gas increases
(b) The rate of collision increases
(c) The number of moles of gas increases
(d) The energy of gaseous molecules increases *(1991)*

41. At constant temperature, in a given mass of an ideal gas
(a) the ratio of pressure and volume always remains constant
(b) volume always remains constant
(c) pressure always remains constant
(d) the product of pressure and volume always remains constant. *(1991)*

42. The root mean square velocity at STP for the gases H_2, N_2, and HBr are in the order
(a) $H_2 < N_2 < O_2 < HBr$
(b) $HBr < O_2 < N_2 < H_2$
(c) $H_2 < N_2 = O_2 < HBr$
(d) $HBr < O_2 < H_2 < N_2$ *(1991)*

43. Root mean square velocity of a gas molecule is proportional to
(a) $m^{1/2}$ (b) m^0 (c) $m^{-1/2}$ (d) m *(1990)*

44. Absolute zero is defined as the temperature
(a) at which all molecular motion ceases
(b) at which liquid helium boils
(c) at which ether boils
(d) all of the above. *(1990)*

45. In van der Waals equation of state for a non-ideal gas, the term that accounts for intermolecular forces is
(a) $(V - b)$ (b) $(RT)^{-1}$
(c) $\left(P + \frac{a}{V^2}\right)$ (d) RT *(1990)*

46. If P, V, M, T and R are pressure, volume, molar mass, temperature and gas constant respectively, then for an ideal gas, the density is given by
(a) $\frac{RT}{PM}$ (b) $\frac{P}{RT}$ (c) $\frac{M}{V}$ (d) $\frac{PM}{RT}$ *(1989)*

47. Pressure remaining the same, the volume of a given mass of an ideal gas increases for every degree centrigrade rise in temperature by definite fraction of its volume at
(a) 0°C
(b) its critical temperature
(c) absolute zero
(d) its Boyle temperature. *(1989)*

48. Correct gas equation is
(a) $\frac{V_1T_2}{P_1} = \frac{V_2T_1}{P_2}$ (b) $\frac{P_1V_1}{P_2V_2} = \frac{T_1}{T_2}$
(c) $\frac{P_1T_2}{V_1} = \frac{P_2V_2}{T_2}$ (d) $\frac{V_1V_2}{T_1T_2} = P_1P_2$ *(1989)*

Answer Key

1.	(a)	**2.**	(d)	**3.**	(c)	**4.**	(d)	**5.**	(b)	**6.**	(c)	**7.**	(None)	**8.**	(b)	**9.**	(c)
10.	(d)	**11.**	(d)	**12.**	(b)	**13.**	(a)	**14.**	(a)	**15.**	(c)	**16.**	(d)	**17.**	(a)	**18.**	(a)
19.	(a)																
20.	(a)	**21.**	(b)	**22.**	(d)	**23.**	(d)	**24.**	(b)	**25.**	(a)	**26.**	(b)	**27.**	(b)	**28.**	(d)
29.	(a)																
30.	(c)	**31.**	(a)	**32.**	(d)	**33.**	(b)	**34.**	(b)	**35.**	(c)	**36.**	(b)	**37.**	(d)	**38.**	(c)
39.	(d)																
40.	(c)	**41.**	(d)	**42.**	(b)	**43.**	(c)	**44.**	(a)	**45.**	(c)	**46.**	(d)	**47.**	(a)	**48.**	(b)

EXPLANATIONS

1. **(a) :** van der Waals' constant 'a' signifies the intermolecular forces of attraction between the particle of gas. So, higher the value of 'a', easier will be the liquefaction of gas.

2. **(d)**

3. **(c) :** Let the number of moles of each gas = x

Fraction of hydrogen escaped $= \frac{1}{2}x$

$$\frac{r_{O_2}}{r_{H_2}} = \sqrt{\frac{M_{H_2}}{M_{O_2}}} \Rightarrow \frac{n_{O_2}/t}{\frac{x}{2}/t} = \sqrt{\frac{2}{32}} = \sqrt{\frac{1}{16}} = \frac{1}{4}$$

$$\Rightarrow \frac{n_{O_2}/t}{\frac{x}{2}/t} = \frac{1}{4} \Rightarrow n_{O_2} = \frac{1}{8}x$$

Hence, fraction of oxygen escaped = $\frac{1}{8}$

4. **(d) :** Real gases show ideal gas behaviour at high temperatures and low pressures.

5. **(b) :** NH_3 is a polar molecule, thus more attractive forces between NH_3 molecule.

6. **(c) :** $PV = nRT$

$$PV = \frac{W}{M}RT \qquad \left[n = \frac{\text{Weight of the gas taken } (W)}{\text{Mol. mass of gas } (M)}\right]$$

$$P = \frac{W}{M} \times \frac{RT}{V}$$

$$P = \frac{dRT}{M} \qquad \left[\text{Density} = \frac{\text{Mass}}{\text{Volume}}\right]$$

$$d = \frac{PM}{RT} = \frac{5 \times 28}{0.0821 \times 500} = 3.41 \text{ g/mL}$$

7. **(None)**

According to Graham's law of diffusion,

$$\frac{r_1}{r_2} = \sqrt{\frac{d_2}{d_1}} = \sqrt{\frac{M_2}{M_1}}$$

$$r_A = \frac{V_A}{T_A}, \quad r_B = \frac{V_B}{T_B}$$

$$\frac{V_A/T_A}{V_B/T_B} = \sqrt{\frac{M_B}{M_A}}$$

$V_A = V_B$, $T_A = 150$ sec, $T_B = 200$ sec, $M_B = 36$, $M_A = ?$

$$\frac{T_B}{T_A} = \sqrt{\frac{M_B}{M_A}} \Rightarrow \frac{200}{150} = \sqrt{\frac{36}{M_A}}$$

$$\frac{4}{3} = \sqrt{\frac{36}{M_A}} \quad \text{or} \quad \frac{4 \times 4}{3 \times 3} = \frac{36}{M_A}$$

$$\text{or} \quad M_A = \frac{36}{4 \times 4} \times 3 \times 3 = 20.25$$

8. **(b):** According to Graham's law of diffusion

$$r \propto \frac{1}{\sqrt{d}} \propto \frac{1}{\sqrt{M}} \Rightarrow \frac{r_1}{r_2} = \sqrt{\frac{M_2}{M_1}}$$

$$\text{Rate of diffusion} = \frac{\text{Volume of gas diffused } (V)}{\text{Time taken } (t)}$$

$$\therefore \frac{V_1/t_1}{V_2/t_2} = \sqrt{\frac{M_2}{M_1}}$$

If same volume of two gases diffuse, then $V_1 = V_2$

$$\therefore \frac{t_2}{t_1} = \sqrt{\frac{M_2}{M_1}}$$

Here $t_2 = 3t_1$, $M_1 = 4$ u, $M_2 = ?$

$$\therefore \frac{3t_1}{t_1} = \sqrt{\frac{M_2}{4}} \Rightarrow 3 = \sqrt{\frac{M_2}{4}}$$

$$\Rightarrow 9 = \frac{M_2}{4} \Rightarrow M_2 = 36 \text{ u}$$

9. **(c) :** Van der Waal gas constant 'a' represent intermolecular force of attraction of gaseous molecules and Van der Waal gas constant 'b' represent effective size of molecules. Therefore order should be

(I) $H_2 < He < O_2 < CO_2$ (II) $CH_4 > O_2 > H_2$

10. **(d) :** C_P for monoatomic gas mixture of same volume $= \frac{5}{2}R$

$$C_V = \frac{3}{2}R$$

$$\therefore \frac{C_P}{C_V} = \frac{\frac{5}{2}R}{\frac{3}{2}R} = \frac{5}{3} = 1.67$$

11. **(d) :** Average velocity $= \sqrt{\frac{8RT}{\pi M}}$

12. **(b) :** We know that $\frac{r_A}{r_B} = \frac{v/t_A}{v/t_B} = \sqrt{\frac{M_B}{M_A}}$

$$\frac{t_B}{t_A} = \sqrt{\frac{M_B}{M_A}} \Rightarrow \frac{10}{20} = \sqrt{\frac{M_B}{49}}$$

$$\Rightarrow \left(\frac{10}{20}\right)^2 = \frac{M_B}{49} \Rightarrow \frac{100}{400} = \frac{M_B}{49}$$

$$\Rightarrow M_B = \frac{49 \times 100}{400} = 12.25 \text{ u}$$

13. (a) : $P_{CO} + P_{N_2} = 1$ atm

$2P_{N_2} = 1$ $\quad [\because n_{CO} = n_{N_2}]$

$P_{N_2} = \frac{1}{2} = 0.5$ atm

14. (a) : We know that from ideal equation,

$$V \propto \frac{T}{P}$$

Given $T_1 = 15 + 273 = 288$, $P_1 = 1.5$ bar

$T_2 = 25 + 273 = 298$, $P_2 = 1$ bar

$$V_1 \propto \frac{288}{1.5} \text{ i.e. } V_1 \propto 192 \text{ and } V_2 \propto \frac{298}{1}$$

$$\frac{V_2}{V_1} = \frac{298}{192} = 1.55 \approx 1.6$$

15. (c) : Given, mass of CH_4, $w = 6$ g

Volume of CH_4, $V = 0.03$ m^3

$T = 129°C = 129 + 273 = 402$ K

$R = 8.314$ J K^{-1} mol^{-1}

Molecular mass of CH_4, $M = 12.01 + 4 \times 1.01 = 16.05$

$$PV = nRT = \frac{w}{M}RT$$

$$\therefore \quad P = \frac{w}{M}\frac{RT}{V} = \frac{6}{16.05} \times \frac{8.314 \times 402}{0.03}$$

$$= 41647.7 \text{ Pa} \approx 41648 \text{ Pa}$$

16. (d) : Energy absorbed by each molecule $= 4.4 \times 10^{-19}$ J

Energy required to break the bond $= 4.0 \times 10^{-19}$ J

Remaining energy to get converted to kinetic energy

$= (4.4 \times 10^{-19} - 4.0 \times 10^{-19})$ J

$= 0.4 \times 10^{-19}$ J per molecule

$\therefore$ Kinetic energy per atom $= 0.2 \times 10^{-19}$ J or 2×10^{-20} J

17. (a) : The average translational *K.E.* of one molecule of an ideal gas will be given by

$$E_t = \frac{K.E.}{N_A} = \frac{3/2\,RT}{N_A} = \frac{3}{2}KT$$

When R/N_A = Boltzmann consant

i.e. $E_t \propto T$

So, at constant temperature *K.E.* of molecules remains same

18. (a) : Wt. of 6.023×10^{23} molecule of water = 18 g

$\therefore$ Volume occupied by 6.023×10^{23} molecule of water (density = 1g cm^{-3}) will be

$$= \frac{18 \text{ g}}{1 \text{ g cm}^{-3}} = 18 \text{ cm}^3 \text{ or mL}$$

$\therefore$ Volume occupied by one molecule of water

$$= \frac{18}{6.023 \times 10^{23}} = 2.988 \times 10^{-23} \approx 3.0 \times 10^{-23} \text{ cm}^3$$

19. (a) : At low pressure and high temperature van der Waals real gas acts as ideal gas and observed to obey $PV = nRT$ relation. At very low pressure when the gas-volume is quite large the space occupied by the molecules themselves becomes negligible comparatively and because the molecules are then far apart, the force of mutual attraction becomes too feeble, the real gas would satisfy the postulates of kinetic theory. As temperature is raised, the volume of the gas increases and we can consider $\left(P + \frac{n^2a}{V^2}\right)$ term as P and at low pressure $(V - nb)$ term as V.

$$\left(P + \frac{n^2a}{V^2}\right)(V - nb) = nRT$$

(van der Waals equation)

The gas equation becomes $PV = nRT$

This is ideal gas equation.

20. (a) : $KE = \frac{3}{2}RT$ (for one mole of a gas)

As temperatures are same and KE is independent of molecular mass, so $KE_1 = KE_2$.

21. (b) : $V_1 = 380$ mL, $P_1 = 730$ mm, $V_2 = ?$, $P_2 = 760$ mm.

From Boyle's law, $P_1V_1 = P_2V_2$

$$\Rightarrow V_2 = \frac{380 \times 730}{760} = 365 \text{ mL}$$

22. (d) : Mass of the gas = mass of the cylinder including gas – mass of empty cylinder.

So mass of a gas can be determined by weighing the container in which it is enclosed.

Thus, the statement (d) is wrong for gases.

23. (d) : Temperature $(T) = 25°C = 298$ K.

Therefore *K.E.* per molecule

$$= \frac{3RT}{2N_A} = \frac{3 \times 8.314 \times 298}{2 \times (6.02 \times 10^{23})} = 6.17 \times 10^{-21} \text{ J}$$

24. (b) : $R_1 = 1.625R_2$ and $T_2 = 500°C = 773$ K

We know that $\frac{R_1}{R_2} = \sqrt{\frac{M_1}{M_2} \times \frac{T_1}{T_2}}$

or $1.625 = \sqrt{\frac{64}{28} \times \frac{T_1}{773}}$

or $T_1 = \frac{(1.625)^2 \times 28 \times 773}{64} = 893 \text{ K} = 620°\text{C}$

25. (a) : $Cl_2 + SO_2 \xrightarrow{\text{Sunlight}} \underset{\text{(sulphuryl chloride)}}{SO_2Cl_2}$

Dalton's law of partial pressure is applicable only in those cases where gases are non-reacting. As Cl_2 and SO_2 reacts to form SO_2Cl_2 so this law is not obeyed in given case.

26. (b) : A gas can only be liquefied, if some forces of attraction are acting in its molecules. Since, an ideal gas is devoid of force of attraction in its molecules, therefore it can not be liquefied.

27. (b) : Volume of hydrogen = 50 mL; Time for diffusion (t) = 20 min and volume of oxygen = 40 mL.

Rate of diffusion of hydrogen $(r_1) = \frac{50}{20} = 2.5$ mL/min

Rate of diffusion of oxygen $(r_2) = \frac{40}{t}$ mL/min

Since the molecular mass of hydrogen (M_1) = 2 and that of oxygen (M_2) = 32, therefore

$\frac{r_1}{r_2} = \sqrt{\frac{M_2}{M_1}} \Rightarrow \frac{2.5}{40/t} = \sqrt{\frac{32}{2}}$

$\Rightarrow \frac{t}{16} = 4 \Rightarrow t = 64$ minutes

28. (d) : $T_1 = 27°\text{C} = 300$ K and
$T_2 = 927°\text{C} = 1200$ K

We know that root mean square speed $(v) \propto \sqrt{T}$. Therefore root mean square speed of the gas, when its temperature is raised $= \sqrt{\frac{T_2}{T_1}} = \sqrt{\frac{1200}{300}} = 2$

29. (a) : Because average kinetic energy depends only on temperature $KE = \frac{3}{2}nkT$

30. (c) : $PV = nRT$ or $P = \frac{n}{V}RT = CRT$

Hence, $1 = 1 \times 0.082 \times T$

is $T = \frac{1}{0.082} = 12$ K

31. (a) : $PV = \frac{1}{3}mnu^2 = \frac{1}{3}Mu^2$

$= \frac{2}{3} \cdot \frac{1}{2}Mu^2 = \frac{2}{3}E \qquad \left\{\because \frac{1}{2}Mu^2 = E\right\}$

or $P = \frac{2}{3}E$ per unit volume.

32. (d) : Most probable velocity, $(u_{mp}) = \sqrt{\frac{2RT}{M}}$

Mean velocity, $(\bar{v}) = \sqrt{\frac{8RT}{\pi M}}$

Root mean square velocity, $(u_{r.m.s}) = \sqrt{\frac{3RT}{M}}$

$\therefore \quad u_{mp} : \bar{v} : (u_{r.m.s}) = \sqrt{\frac{2RT}{M}} : \sqrt{\frac{8RT}{\pi M}} : \sqrt{\frac{3RT}{M}}$
$= \sqrt{2} : \sqrt{\frac{8}{\pi}} : \sqrt{3}$

33. (b) : At low temperature and high pressure, there is a deviation from the ideal behaviour in gases.

34. (b) : Velocity and hence average *K.E.* of water molecules is maximum in the gaseous state.

35. (c) : Molecules in an ideal gas move with different speeds. Due to collision between the particle their speed changes.

36. (b)

37. (d) : In an ideal gas, the intermolecular forces of attraction are negligible and hence it cannot be liquefied.

38. (c) : In the van der Waal's equation
$PV = nRT$
n moles of the gas have Volume V

39. (d) : At high temperature and low pressure the effect of a/V^2 and b is negligible.
As we know,
$PV = nRT$ (Ideal gas equation)

$PV = RT$ or $\frac{PV}{RT} = 1$

$\therefore \quad Z = 1$ [Z is compressibility factor]
Hence gas shows ideal behaviour.

40. (c) : Here volume is constant and mass of H_2 is fixed so the no. of moles of the gas do not change. As temperature increases the pressure also increases, therefore the rate of collision among the gas molecules and their energy also increases.

41. (d) : According to Boyle's law at constant temperature, $P \propto \frac{1}{V}$ or PV = constant

42. (b) : We know, $PV = \frac{1}{3}mnu^2 = \frac{1}{3}Mu^2$

or $u = \sqrt{3PV/M}$

At STP, $u \propto \sqrt{\frac{1}{M}}$

and molecular masses of H_2, N_2, O_2 and HBr are 2, 28, 32 and 81.

43. (c) : $PV = \frac{1}{3} mNu^2$,

here u = root mean square velocity.

Now $u^2 = \frac{3PV}{mN}$ or $u \propto \frac{1}{\sqrt{m}}$

44. (a) : Temperature at which all molecular motion ceases is called absolute zero.

45. (c) : van der Waal's equation for 1 mole is

$$\left(P + \frac{a}{V^2}\right)(V - b) = RT$$

Here, $\left(P + \frac{a}{V^2}\right)$ represents the intermolecular forces and $(V - b)$ is the corrected volume.

46. (d) : Ideal gas equation is

$$PV = nRT = \frac{m}{M} RT$$

or $PM = \frac{m}{V} RT = dRT$ [here d = density]

$$\Rightarrow d = \frac{PM}{RT}$$

47. (a) : According to Charles' law which states that The volume of the given mass of a gas increases or decreases by $\frac{1}{273}$ of its volume at 0°C for each degree rise or fall of temperature at constant pressure.

$$V_t = V_0\left(1 + \frac{t}{273}\right) \text{ at constant } P \text{ and } n$$

48. (b): $\frac{PV}{T}$ = constant or $\frac{P_1V_1}{T_1} = \frac{P_2V_2}{T_2} \Rightarrow \frac{P_1V_1}{P_2V_2} = \frac{T_1}{T_2}$

Chapter 6

Thermodynamics

1. The bond dissociation energies of X_2, Y_2 and XY are in the ratio of 1 : 0.5 : 1. ΔH for the formation of XY is –200 kJ mol^{-1}. The bond dissociation energy of X_2 will be
(a) 200 kJ mol^{-1} (b) 100 kJ mol^{-1}
(c) 800 kJ mol^{-1} (d) 400 kJ mol^{-1}
(NEET 2018)

2. For a given reaction, $\Delta H = 35.5$ kJ mol^{-1} and $\Delta S = 83.6$ J K^{-1} mol^{-1}. The reaction is spontaneous at (Assume that ΔH and ΔS do not vary with temperature.)
(a) $T > 425$ K (b) all temperatures
(c) $T > 298$ K (d) $T < 425$ K
(NEET 2017)

3. A gas is allowed to expand in a well insulated container against a constant external pressure of 2.5 atm from an initial volume of 2.50 L to a final volume of 4.50 L. The change in internal energy ΔU of the gas in joules will be
(a) –500 J (b) –505 J
(c) +505 J (d) 1136.25 J
(NEET 2017)

4. For a sample of perfect gas when its pressure is changed isothermally from p_i to p_f, the entropy change is given by
(a) $\Delta S = nR \ln\left(\frac{p_f}{p_i}\right)$ (b) $\Delta S = nR \ln\left(\frac{p_i}{p_f}\right)$
(c) $\Delta S = nRT \ln\left(\frac{p_f}{p_i}\right)$ (d) $\Delta S = RT \ln\left(\frac{p_i}{p_f}\right)$
(NEET-II 2016)

5. The correct thermodynamic conditions for the spontaneous reaction at all temperatures is
(a) $\Delta H < 0$ and $\Delta S > 0$
(b) $\Delta H < 0$ and $\Delta S < 0$
(c) $\Delta H < 0$ and $\Delta S = 0$
(d) $\Delta H > 0$ and $\Delta S < 0$ *(NEET-I 2016)*

6. Consider the following liquid-vapour equilibrium.
Liquid $\rightleftharpoons$ Vapour
Which of the following relations is correct?
(a) $\frac{d\ln P}{dT^2} = \frac{-\Delta H_v}{T^2}$ (b) $\frac{d\ln P}{dT} = \frac{\Delta H_v}{RT^2}$
(c) $\frac{d\ln G}{dT^2} = \frac{\Delta H_v}{RT^2}$ (d) $\frac{d\ln P}{dT} = \frac{-\Delta H_v}{RT}$
(NEET-I 2016)

7. The heat of combustion of carbon to CO_2 is –393.5 kJ/mol. The heat released upon formation of 35.2 g of CO_2 from carbon and oxygen gas is
(a) + 315 kJ (b) – 630 kJ
(c) – 3.15 kJ (d) – 315 kJ *(2015)*

8. Which of the following statements is correct for the spontaneous adsorption of a gas?
(a) ΔS is negative and, therefore ΔH should be highly positive.
(b) ΔS is negative and therefore, ΔH should be highly negative.
(c) ΔS is positive and therefore, ΔH should be negative.
(d) ΔS is positive and therefore, ΔH should also be highly positive. *(2014)*

9. For the reaction, $X_2O_{4(l)} \longrightarrow 2XO_{2(g)}$
$\Delta U = 2.1$ kcal, $\Delta S = 20$ cal K^{-1} at 300 K
Hence, ΔG is
(a) 2.7 kcal (b) – 2.7 kcal
(c) 9.3 kcal (d) – 9.3 kcal *(2014)*

10. A reaction having equal energies of activation for forward and reverse reactions has
(a) $\Delta H = 0$ (b) $\Delta H = \Delta G = \Delta S = 0$
(c) $\Delta S = 0$ (d) $\Delta G = 0$
(NEET 2013)

11. When 5 litres of a gas mixture of methane and propane is perfectly combusted at 0°C and 1 atmosphere, 16 litres of oxygen at the same temperature and pressure is consumed. The amount of heat released from this combustion in kJ ($\Delta H_{comb.}$ (CH_4) = 890 kJ mol^{-1}, $\Delta H_{comb.}$ (C_3H_8) = 2220 kJ mol^{-1}) is
(a) 38 (b) 317 (c) 477 (d) 32
(Karnataka NEET 2013)

12. Three thermochemical equations are given below
(i) $C_{(graphite)} + O_{2(g)} \rightarrow CO_{2(g)}$; $\Delta_r H^\circ = x$ kJ mol^{-1}
(ii) $C_{(graphite)} + \frac{1}{2}O_{2(g)} \rightarrow CO_{(g)}$; $\Delta_r H^\circ = y$ kJ mol^{-1}
(iii) $CO_{(g)} + \frac{1}{2}O_{2(g)} \rightarrow CO_{2(g)}$; $\Delta_r H^\circ = z$ kJ mol^{-1}
Based on the above equations, find out which of the relationship given below is correct.
(a) $z = x + y$ (b) $x = y + z$
(c) $y = 2z - x$ (d) $x = y - z$
(Karnataka NEET 2013)

13. In which of the following reactions, standard reaction entropy change (ΔS°) is positive and standard Gibbs energy change (ΔG°) decreases sharply with increasing temperature?
(a) $C_{(graphite)} + \frac{1}{2}O_{2(g)} \rightarrow CO_{(g)}$
(b) $CO_{(g)} + \frac{1}{2}O_{2(g)} \rightarrow CO_{2(g)}$
(c) $Mg_{(s)} + \frac{1}{2}O_{2(g)} \rightarrow MgO_{(s)}$
(d) $\frac{1}{2}C_{(graphite)} + \frac{1}{2}O_{2(g)} \rightarrow \frac{1}{2}CO_{2(g)}$
(2012)

14. The enthalpy of fusion of water is 1.435 kcal/mol. The molar entropy change for the melting of ice at 0°C is
(a) 10.52 cal/(mol K) (b) 21.04 cal/(mol K)
(c) 5.260 cal/(mol K) (d) 0.526 cal/(mol K)
(2012)

15. Standard enthalpy of vaporisation $\Delta_{vap}H^\circ$ for water at 100°C is 40.66 kJ mol^{-1}. The internal energy of vaporisation of water at 100°C (in kJ mol^{-1}) is
(a) +37.56 (b) −43.76
(c) +43.76 (d) +40.66
(Assume water vapour to behave like an ideal gas) *(2012)*

16. If the enthalpy change for the transition of liquid water to steam is 30 kJ mol^{-1} at 27°C, the entropy change for the process would be
(a) 10 J mol^{-1} K^{-1} (b) 1.0 J mol^{-1} K^{-1}
(c) 0.1 J mol^{-1} K^{-1} (d) 100 J mol^{-1} K^{-1}
(2011)

17. Enthalpy change for the reaction,
$4H_{(g)} \rightarrow 2H_{2(g)}$ is −869.6 kJ
The dissociation energy of H – H bond is
(a) − 434.8 kJ (b) − 869.6 kJ
(c) + 434.8 kJ (d) + 217.4 kJ *(2011)*

18. Which of the following is correct option for free expansion of an ideal gas under adiabatic condition?
(a) $q = 0, \Delta T \neq 0, w = 0$
(b) $q \neq 0, \Delta T = 0, w = 0$
(c) $q = 0, \Delta T = 0, w = 0$
(d) $q = 0, \Delta T < 0, w \neq 0$ *(2011)*

19. Consider the following processes:

	ΔH (kJ/mol)
$1/2A \rightarrow B$	+150
$3B \rightarrow 2C + D$	−125
$E + A \rightarrow 2D$	+350

For $B + D \rightarrow E + 2C$, ΔH will be
(a) 525 kJ/mol (b) −175 kJ/mol
(c) −325 kJ/mol (d) 325 kJ/mol
(Mains 2011)

20. For an endothermic reaction, energy of activation is E_a and enthalpy of reaction is ΔH (both of these in kJ/mol). Minimum value of E_a will be
(a) less than ΔH (b) equal to ΔH
(c) more than ΔH (d) equal to zero
(2010)

21. Standard entropies of X_2, Y_2 and XY_3 are 60, 40 and 50 J K^{-1} mol^{-1} respectively. For the reaction $1/2X_2 + 3/2Y_2 \rightleftharpoons XY_3$, $\Delta H = -30$ kJ to be at equilibrium, the temperature should be
(a) 750 K (b) 1000 K
(c) 1250 K (d) 500 K *(2010)*

22. Match List I (Equations) with List II (Type of processes) and select the correct option.

List I Equations	**List II Type of processes**
A. $K_p > Q$	(i) Non- spontaneous
B. $\Delta G^\circ < RT \ln Q$	(ii) Equilibrium
C. $K_p = Q$	(iii) Spontaneous and endothermic
D. $T > \frac{\Delta H}{\Delta S}$	(iv) Spontaneous

(a) A - (i), B - (ii), C - (iii), D - (iv)
(b) A - (iii), B - (iv), C - (ii), D - (i)
(c) A - (iv), B - (i), C - (ii), D - (iii)
(d) A - (ii), B - (i), C - (iv), D - (iii)
(Mains 2010)

23. Three moles of an ideal gas expanded spontaneously into vacuum. The work done will be
(a) infinite (b) 3 Joules
(c) 9 Joules (d) zero
(Mains 2010)

24. For vaporization of water at 1 atmospheric pressure, the values of ΔH and ΔS are 40.63 kJ mol^{-1} and 108.8 J K^{-1} mol^{-1}, respectively. The temperature when Gibb's energy change (ΔG) for this transformation will be zero, is
(a) 273.4 K (b) 393.4 K
(c) 373.4 K (d) 293.4 K
(Mains 2010)

25. The following two reactions are known
$Fe_2O_{3(s)} + 3CO_{(g)} \rightarrow 2Fe_{(s)} + 3CO_{2(g)}$; $\Delta H = -26.8$ kJ
$FeO_{(s)} + CO_{(g)} \rightarrow Fe_{(s)} + CO_{2(g)}$; $\Delta H = -16.5$ kJ
The value of ΔH for the following reaction
$Fe_2O_{3(s)} + CO_{(g)} \rightarrow 2FeO_{(s)} + CO_{2(g)}$ is
(a) + 10.3 kJ (b) – 43.3 kJ
(c) – 10.3 kJ (d) + 6.2 kJ
(Mains 2010)

26. The values of ΔH and ΔS for the reaction,
$C_{(graphite)} + CO_{2\,(g)} \rightarrow 2CO_{\,(g)}$
are 170 kJ and 170 J K^{-1}, respectively. This reaction will be spontaneous at
(a) 910 K (b) 1110 K
(c) 510 K (d) 710 K *(2009)*

27. From the following bond energies:
H — H bond energy : 431.37 kJ mol^{-1}
C = C bond energy : 606.10 kJ mol^{-1}
C — C bond energy : 336.49 kJ mol^{-1}
C — H bond energy : 410.50 kJ mol^{-1}
Enthalpy for the reaction,

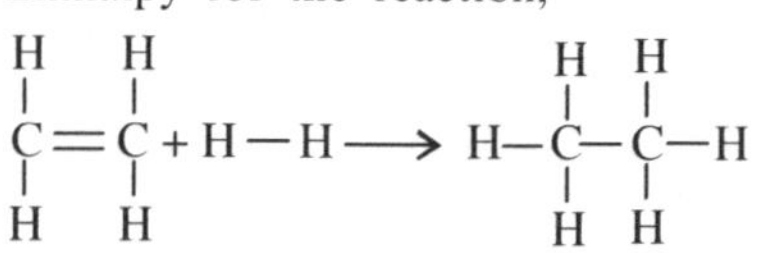

will be
(a) – 243.6 kJ mol^{-1} (b) – 120.0 kJ mol^{-1}
(c) 553.0 kJ mol^{-1} (d) 1523.6 kJ mol^{-1}
(2009)

28. Bond dissociation enthalpy of H_2, Cl_2 and HCl are 434, 242 and 431 kJ mol^{-1} respectively. Enthalpy of formation of HCl is
(a) –93 kJ mol^{-1} (b) 245 kJ mol^{-1}
(c) 93 kJ mol^{-1} (d) –245 kJ mol^{-1}
(2008)

29. For the gas phase reaction,
$PCl_{5\,(g)} \rightleftharpoons PCl_{3\,(g)} + Cl_{2\,(g)}$
which of the following conditions are correct?
(a) $\Delta H < 0$ and $\Delta S < 0$
(b) $\Delta H > 0$ and $\Delta S < 0$
(c) $\Delta H = 0$ and $\Delta S < 0$
(d) $\Delta H > 0$ and $\Delta S > 0$ *(2008)*

30. Which of the following are not state functions?
(I) $q + w$ (II) q
(III) w (IV) $H - TS$
(a) (I), (II) and (III) (b) (II) and (III)
(c) (I) and (IV) (d) (II), (III) and (IV)
(2008)

31. Consider the following reactions:
(i) $H^+_{(aq)} + OH^-_{(aq)} = H_2O_{(l)}$, $\Delta H = -X_1$ kJ mol^{-1}
(ii) $H_{2(g)} + 1/2O_{2(g)} = H_2O_{(l)}$, $\Delta H = -X_2$ kJ mol^{-1}
(iii) $CO_{2(g)} + H_{2(g)} = CO_{(g)} + H_2O_{(l)}$, $\Delta H = -X_3$ kJ mol^{-1}
(iv) $C_2H_{2(g)} + 5/2O_{2(g)} = 2CO_{2(g)} + H_2O_{(l)}$, $\Delta H = +X_4$ kJ mol^{-1}
Enthalpy of formation of $H_2O_{(l)}$ is
(a) $+X_3$ kJ mol^{-1} (b) $-X_4$ kJ mol^{-1}
(c) $+X_1$ kJ mol^{-1} (d) $-X_2$ kJ mol^{-1}.
(2007)

32. Given that bond energies of H – H and Cl – Cl are 430 kJ mol^{-1} and 240 kJ mol^{-1} respectively and ΔH_f for HCl is –90 kJ mol^{-1}, bond enthalpy of HCl is
(a) 380 kJ mol^{-1} (b) 425 kJ mol^{-1}
(c) 245 kJ mol^{-1} (d) 290 kJ mol^{-1}
(2007)

33. Identify the correct statement for change of Gibb's energy for a system (ΔG_{system}) at constant temperature and pressure.
(a) If $\Delta G_{system} < 0$, the process is not spontaneous.
(b) If $\Delta G_{system} > 0$, the process is spontaneous.
(c) If $\Delta G_{system} = 0$, the system has attained equilibrium.
(d) If $\Delta G_{system} = 0$, the system is still moving in a particular direction. *(2006)*

34. Assume each reaction is carried out in an open container. For which reaction will $\Delta H = \Delta E$?
(a) $2CO_{(g)} + O_{2(g)} \rightarrow 2CO_{2(g)}$
(b) $H_{2(g)} + Br_{2(g)} \rightarrow 2HBr_{(g)}$
(c) $C_{(s)} + 2H_2O_{(g)} \rightarrow 2H_{2(g)} + CO_{2(g)}$
(d) $PCl_{5(g)} \rightarrow PCl_{3(g)} + Cl_{2(g)}$ *(2006)*

35. The enthalpy and entropy change for the reaction: $Br_{2(l)} + Cl_{2(g)} \rightarrow 2BrCl_{(g)}$ are 30 kJ mol^{-1} and 105 J K^{-1} mol^{-1} respectively. The temperature at which the reaction will be in equilibrium is
(a) 300 K (b) 285.7 K
(c) 273 K (d) 450 K *(2006)*

36. The enthalpy of hydrogenation of cyclohexene is -119.5 kJ mol^{-1}. If resonance energy of benzene is -150.4 kJ mol^{-1}, its enthalpy of hydrogenation would be
(a) -358.5 kJ mol^{-1} (b) -508.9 kJ mol^{-1}
(c) -208.1 kJ mol^{-1} (d) -269.9 kJ mol^{-1} *(2006)*

37. Which of the following pairs of a chemical reaction is certain to result in a spontaneous reaction?
(a) Exothermic and increasing disorder
(b) Exothermic and decreasing disorder
(c) Endothermic and increasing disorder
(d) Endothermic and decreasing disorder *(2005)*

38. A reaction occurs spontaneously if
(a) $T\Delta S < \Delta H$ and both ΔH and ΔS are +ve
(b) $T\Delta S > \Delta H$ and ΔH is +ve and ΔS is –ve
(c) $T\Delta S > \Delta H$ and both ΔH and ΔS are +ve
(d) $T\Delta S = \Delta H$ and both ΔH and ΔS are +ve *(2005)*

39. The absolute enthalpy of neutralisation of the reaction:
$MgO_{(s)} + 2HCl_{(aq)} \rightarrow MgCl_{2(aq)} + H_2O_{(l)}$ will be
(a) -57.33 kJ mol^{-1}
(b) greater than -57.33 kJ mol^{-1}
(c) less than -57.33 kJ mol^{-1}
(d) 57.33 kJ mol^{-1} *(2005)*

40. If the bond energies of H–H, Br–Br, and H–Br are 433, 192 and 364 kJ mol^{-1} respectively, the $\Delta H°$ for the reaction $H_{2(g)} + Br_{2(g)} \rightarrow 2HBr_{(g)}$ is
(a) -261 kJ (b) $+103$ kJ
(c) $+261$ kJ (d) -103 kJ *(2004)*

41. Standard enthalpy and standard entropy changes for the oxidation of ammonia at 298 K are -382.64 kJ mol^{-1} and -145.6 kJ mol^{-1}, respectively. Standard Gibb's energy change for the same reaction at 298 K is
(a) -221.1 kJ mol^{-1} (b) -339.3 kJ mol^{-1}
(c) -439.3 kJ mol^{-1} (d) -523.2 kJ mol^{-1} *(2004)*

42. Considering entropy (S) as a thermodynamic parameter, the criterion for the spontaneity of any process is
(a) $\Delta S_{system} + \Delta S_{surroundings} > 0$
(b) $\Delta S_{system} - \Delta S_{surroundings} > 0$
(c) $\Delta S_{system} > 0$ only
(d) $\Delta S_{surroundings} > 0$ only. *(2004)*

43. The work done during the expansion of a gas from a volume of 4 dm^3 to 6 dm^3 against a constant external pressure of 3 atm is (1 L atm = 101.32 J)
(a) -6 J (b) -608 J
(c) $+304$ J (d) -304 J *(2004)*

44. For the reaction,
$C_3H_{8(g)} + 5O_{2(g)} \rightarrow 3CO_{2(g)} + 4H_2O_{(l)}$
at constant temperature, $\Delta H - \Delta E$ is
(a) $+RT$ (b) $-3RT$ (c) $+3RT$ (d) $-RT$ *(2003)*

45. The densities of graphite and diamond at 298 K are 2.25 and 3.31 g cm^{-3}, respectively. If the standard free energy difference ($\Delta G°$) is equal to 1895 J mol^{-1}, the pressure at which graphite will be transformed into diamond at 298 K is
(a) 9.92×10^8 Pa (b) 9.92×10^7 Pa
(c) 9.92×10^6 Pa (d) 9.92×10^5 Pa *(2003)*

46. What is the entropy change (in J K^{-1} mol^{-1}) when one mole of ice is converted into water at 0°C? (The enthalpy change for the conversion of ice to liquid water is 6.0 kJ mol^{-1} at 0°C.)
(a) 20.13 (b) 2.013 (c) 2.198 (d) 21.98 *(2003)*

47. Formation of a solution from two components can be considered as
(i) Pure solvent → separated solvent molecules, ΔH_1
(ii) Pure solute → separated solute molecules, ΔH_2
(iii) Separated solvent and solute molecules → solution, ΔH_3
Solution so formed will be ideal if
(a) $\Delta H_{soln} = \Delta H_1 + \Delta H_2 + \Delta H_3$
(b) $\Delta H_{soln} = \Delta H_1 + \Delta H_2 - \Delta H_3$
(c) $\Delta H_{soln} = \Delta H_1 - \Delta H_2 - \Delta H_3$
(d) $\Delta H_{soln} = \Delta H_3 - \Delta H_1 - \Delta H_2$ *(2003)*

48. For which one of the following equations is $\Delta H°_{react}$ equal to $\Delta H°_f$ for the product?
(a) $N_{2(g)} + O_{3(g)} \rightarrow N_2O_{3(g)}$
(b) $CH_{4(g)} + 2Cl_{2(g)} \rightarrow CH_2Cl_{2(l)} + 2HCl_{(g)}$
(c) $Xe_{(g)} + 2F_{2(g)} \rightarrow XeF_{4(g)}$
(d) $2CO_{(g)} + O_{2(g)} \rightarrow 2CO_{2(g)}$ *(2003)*

49. The molar heat capacity of water at constant pressure, C, is 75 J K^{-1} mol^{-1}. When 1.0 kJ of heat is supplied to 100 g of water which is

free to expand, the increase in temperature of water is
(a) 1.2 K (b) 2.4 K (c) 4.8 K (d) 6.6 K *(2003)*

50. Unit of entropy is
(a) $J\ K^{-1}\ mol^{-1}$ (b) $J\ mol^{-1}$
(c) $J^{-1}K^{-1}\ mol^{-1}$ (d) $J\ K\ mol^{-1}$ *(2002)*

51. In a closed insulated container a liquid is stirred with a paddle to increase the temperature which of the following is true?
(a) $\Delta E = W \neq 0, q = 0$ (b) $\Delta E = W = q \neq 0$
(c) $\Delta E = 0, W = q \neq 0$ (d) $W = 0, \Delta E = q \neq 0$. *(2002)*

52. Heat of combustion ΔH for $C_{(s)}$, $H_{2(g)}$ and $CH_{4(g)}$ are –94, –68 and –213 kcal/mol, then ΔH for $C_{(s)} + 2H_{2(g)} \rightarrow CH_{4(g)}$ is
(a) –17 kcal (b) –111 kcal
(c) –170 kcal (d) –85 kcal *(2002)*

53. Which reaction is not feasible?
(a) $2KI + Br_2 \rightarrow 2KBr + I_2$
(b) $2KBr + I_2 \rightarrow 2KI + Br_2$
(c) $2KBr + Cl_2 \rightarrow 2KCl + Br_2$
(d) $2H_2O + 2F_2 \rightarrow 4HF + O_2$ *(2002)*

54. 2 mole of ideal gas at 27°C temperature is expanded reversibly from 2 lit. to 20 lit. Find entropy change. (R = 2 cal/mol K)
(a) 92.1 (b) 0 (c) 4 (d) 9.2 *(2002)*

55. Change in enthalpy for reaction,
$2H_2O_{2(l)} \rightarrow 2H_2O_{(l)} + O_{2(g)}$
if heat of formation of $H_2O_{2(l)}$ and $H_2O_{(l)}$ are –188 and –286 kJ/mol respectively, is
(a) –196 kJ/mol (b) +196 kJ/mol
(c) +948 kJ/mol (d) –948 kJ/mole *(2001)*

56. When 1 mol of gas is heated at constant volume temperature is raised from 298 to 308 K. Heat supplied to the gas is 500 J. Then which statement is correct?
(a) $q = w = 500$ J, $\Delta E = 0$
(b) $q = \Delta E = 500$ J, $w = 0$
(c) $q = w = 500$ J, $\Delta E = 0$
(d) $\Delta E = 0, q = w = -500$ J *(2001)*

57. Enthalpy of $CH_4 + 1/2\ O_2 \rightarrow CH_3OH$ is negative. If enthalpy of combustion of CH_4 and CH_3OH are x and y respectively. Then which relation is correct?
(a) $x > y$ (b) $x < y$
(c) $x = y$ (d) $x\ ^3\ y$ *(2001)*

58. $PbO_2 \rightarrow PbO$; $\Delta G_{298} < 0$
$SnO_2 \rightarrow SnO$; $\Delta G_{298} > 0$
Most probable oxidation state of Pb and Sn will be
(a) Pb^{4+}, Sn^{4+} (b) Pb^{4+}, Sn^{2+}
(c) Pb^{2+}, Sn^{2+} (d) Pb^{2+}, Sn^{4+} *(2001)*

59. Cell reaction is spontaneous when
(a) $\Delta G°$ is negative (b) $\Delta G°$ is positive
(c) $\Delta E°_{red}$ is positive (d) $\Delta E°_{red}$ is negative. *(2000)*

60. $2Zn + O_2 \rightarrow 2ZnO$; $\Delta G° = -616$ J
$2Zn + S_2 \rightarrow 2ZnS$; $\Delta G° = -293$ J
$S_2 + 2O_2 \rightarrow 2SO_2$; $\Delta G° = -408$ J
$\Delta G°$ for the following reaction
$2ZnS + 3O_2 \rightarrow 2ZnO + 2SO_2$ is
(a) –731 J (b) –1317 J
(c) –501 J (d) +731 J *(2000)*

61. At 27°C latent heat of fusion of a compound is 2930 J/mol. Entropy change is
(a) 9.77 J/mol-K (b) 10.77 J/mol-K
(c) 9.07 J/mol-K (d) 0.977 J/mol-K *(2000)*

62. For the reaction,
$C_2H_5OH_{(l)} + 3O_{2(g)} \rightarrow 2CO_{2(g)} + 3H_2O_{(l)}$ which one is true
(a) $\Delta H = \Delta E - RT$ (b) $\Delta H = \Delta E + RT$
(c) $\Delta H = \Delta E + 2RT$ (d) $\Delta H = \Delta E - 2RT$ *(2000)*

63. In an endothermic reaction, the value of ΔH is
(a) negative (b) positive
(c) zero (d) constant. *(1999)*

64. In the reaction: $S + 3/2\ O_2 \rightarrow SO_3 + 2x$ kcal and $SO_2 + 1/2\ O_2 \rightarrow SO_3 + y$ kcal, the heat of formation of SO_2 is
(a) $(2x + y)$ (b) $(x - y)$
(c) $(x + y)$ (d) $(2x - y)$ *(1999)*

65. Identify the correct statement regarding entropy.
(a) At absolute zero of temperature, the entropy of all crystalline substances is taken to be zero.
(b) At absolute zero of temperature, the entropy of a perfectly crystalline substance is +ve.
(c) At absolute zero of temperature, entropy of a perfectly crystalline substance is taken to be zero.
(d) At 0°C, the entropy of a perfectly crystalline substance is taken to be zero. *(1998)*

66. One mole of an ideal gas at 300 K is expanded isothermally from an initial volume of 1 litre to 10 litres. The ΔE for this process is ($R = 2$ cal $mol^{-1}K^{-1}$)
(a) 1381.1 cal (b) zero
(c) 163.7 cal (d) 9 L atm *(1998)*

67. Given that $C + O_2 \rightarrow CO_2$, $\Delta H^o = -x$ kJ
$2CO + O_2 \rightarrow 2CO_2$, $\Delta H^o = -y$ kJ
The enthalpy of formation of carbon monoxide will be
(a) $\frac{y-2x}{2}$ (b) $2x - y$
(c) $y - 2x$ (d) $\frac{2x-y}{2}$ *(1997)*

68. Which of the following is the correct equation?
(a) $\Delta U = \Delta W + \Delta Q$ (b) $\Delta U = \Delta Q - W$
(c) $\Delta W = \Delta U + \Delta Q$ (d) None of these *(1996)*

69. If enthalpies of formation for $C_2H_{4(g)}$, $CO_{2(g)}$ and $H_2O_{(l)}$ at 25°C and 1 atm pressure are 52, – 394 and – 286 kJ/mol respectively, then enthalpy of combustion of $C_2H_{4(g)}$ will be
(a) + 141.2 kJ/mol (b) + 1412 kJ/mol
(c) – 141.2 kJ/mol (d) – 1412 kJ/mol *(1995)*

70. A chemical reaction is catalyzed by a catalyst *X*. Hence *X*
(a) reduces enthalpy of the reaction
(b) does not affect equilibrium constant of reaction
(c) decreases rate constant of the reaction
(d) increases activation energy of the reaction. *(1995)*

71. Standard state Gibbs free energy change for isomerization reaction *cis*-2-pentene $\rightleftharpoons$ *trans*-2-pentene is –3.67 kJ/mol at 400 K. If more *trans*-2-pentene is added to the reaction vessel, then
(a) equilibrium remains unaffected
(b) equilibrium is shifted in the forward direction
(c) more *cis*-2-pentene is formed
(d) additional *trans*-2-pentene is formed. *(1995)*

72. For a reaction to occur spontaneously
(a) ΔH must be negative
(b) ΔS must be negative
(c) $(\Delta H - T\Delta S)$ must be negative
(d) $(\Delta H + T\Delta S)$ must be negative. *(1995)*

73. During isothermal expansion of an ideal gas, its
(a) internal energy increases
(b) enthalpy decreases
(c) enthalpy remains unaffected
(d) enthalpy reduces to zero. *(1994, 91)*

74. Following reaction occurring in an automobile
$2C_8H_{18(g)} + 25O_{2(g)} \rightarrow 16CO_{2(g)} + 18H_2O_{(g)}$
The sign of ΔH, ΔS and ΔG would be
(a) –, +, + (b) +, +, –
(c) +, –, + (d) –, +, – *(1994)*

75. For the reaction $N_2 + 3H_2 \rightleftharpoons 2NH_3$, ΔH = ?
(a) $\Delta E + 2RT$ (b) $\Delta E - 2RT$
(c) $\Delta H = RT$ (d) $\Delta E - RT$ *(1991)*

76. If ΔH is the change in enthalpy and ΔE, the change in internal energy accompanying a gaseous reaction, then
(a) ΔH is always greater than ΔE
(b) $\Delta H < \Delta E$ only if the number of moles of the products is greater than the number of moles of the reactants
(c) ΔH is always less than ΔE
(d) $\Delta H < \Delta E$ only if the number of moles of products is less than the number of moles of the reactants. *(1990)*

Answer Key

1. (c) 2. (a) 3. (b) 4. (b) 5. (a, c) 6. (b) 7. (None) 8. (b) 9. (b)
10. (a) 11. (b) 12. (b) 13. (a) 14. (c) 15. (a) 16. (d) 17. (c) 18. (c) 19. (b)
20. (c) 21. (a) 22. (c) 23. (d) 24. (c) 25. (d) 26. (b) 27. (b) 28. (a) 29. (d)
30. (b) 31. (d) 32. (b) 33. (c) 34. (b) 35. (b) 36. (c) 37. (a) 38. (c) 39. (c)
40. (d) 41. (b) 42. (a) 43. (b) 44. (b) 45. (None) 46. (d) 47. (a) 48. (c)
49. (b) 50. (a) 51. (a) 52. (a) 53. (b) 54. (d) 55. (a) 56. (b) 57. (a) 58. (d)
59. (a) 60. (a) 61. (a) 62. (a) 63. (b) 64. (d) 65. (c) 66. (b) 67. (a) 68. (b)
69. (d) 70. (b) 71. (c) 72. (c) 73. (c) 74. (d) 75. (b) 76. (d)

EXPLANATIONS

1. **(c)** : Let B.E. of X_2, Y_2 and XY are x kJ mol^{-1}, $0.5x$ kJ mol^{-1} and x kJ mol^{-1} respectively.

$$\frac{1}{2}X_2+\frac{1}{2}Y_2 \rightarrow XY\ ;\ \Delta H=-200\ \text{kJ mol}^{-1}$$

$\Delta H = \Sigma(\text{B.E.})_{\text{Reactant}} - \Sigma(\text{B.E.})_{\text{Product}}$

$$\therefore\ -200=\left[\frac{1}{2}\times(x)+\frac{1}{2}\times(0.5x)\right]-[1\times(x)]$$

B.E. of $X_2 = x = 800$ kJ mol^{-1}

2. **(a)** : For a spontaneous reaction,
$\Delta G < 0$ *i.e.*, $\Delta H - T\Delta S < 0$

$$T>\frac{\Delta H}{\Delta S}$$

$$T>\left(\frac{35.5\times1000}{83.6}=424.6\approx425\text{ K}\right)$$

$\therefore\ T > 425$ K

3. **(b)** : $w = -P_{\text{ext}}\Delta V = -2.5(4.50 - 2.50)$
$= -5$ L atm $= -5 \times 101.325$ J $= -506.625$ J
$\Delta U = q + w$
As, the container is insulated, thus $q = 0$
Hence, $\Delta U = w = -506.625$ J

4. **(b)** : For an ideal gas undergoing reversible expansion, when temperature changes from T_i to T_f and pressure changes from p_i to p_f,

$$\Delta S=nC_p\ln\frac{T_f}{T_i}+nR\ln\frac{p_i}{p_f}$$

For an isothermal process, $T_i = T_f$ so, ln 1 = 0

$$\therefore\quad \Delta S=nR\ln\frac{p_i}{p_f}$$

5. **(a, c)** : $\Delta G = \Delta H - T\Delta S$
If $\Delta H < 0$ and $\Delta S > 0$
$\Delta G = (-\text{ve}) - T(+\text{ve})$
then at all temperatures, $\Delta G = -$ve, spontaneous reaction.
If $\Delta H < 0$ and $\Delta S = 0$
$\Delta G = (-\text{ve}) - T(0) = -$ve at all temperatures.

6. **(b)** : This is Clausius—Clapeyron equation.

7. **(None)** : Given :
$C_{(s)} + O_{2(g)} \longrightarrow CO_{2(g)}$, $\Delta H = -393.5$ kJ/mol
$\Rightarrow$ Amount of heat released on formation of 44 g CO_2 = 393.5 kJ
$\therefore$ Amount of heat released on formation of

$$35.2\text{ g }CO_2=\frac{393.5}{44}\times35.2=314.8\approx315\text{ kJ}$$

8. **(b)** : Using Gibb's-Helmholtz equation,
$\Delta G = \Delta H - T\Delta S$
During adsorption of a gas, entropy decreases *i.e.* $\Delta S < 0$
For spontaneous adsorption, ΔG should be negative, which is possible when ΔH is highly negative.

9. **(b)** : $\Delta H = \Delta U + \Delta n_g RT$
Given, $\Delta U = 2.1$ kcal, $\Delta n_g = 2$,
$R = 2 \times 10^{-3}$ kcal, $T = 300$ K
$\therefore\ \Delta H = 2.1 + 2 \times 2 \times 10^{-3} \times 300 = 3.3$ kcal
Again, $\Delta G = \Delta H - T\Delta S$
Given, $\Delta S = 20 \times 10^{-3}$ kcal K^{-1}
On putting the values of ΔH and ΔS in the equation, we get
$\Delta G = 3.3 - 300 \times 20 \times 10^{-3}$
$= 3.3 - 6 \times 10^3 \times 10^{-3} = -2.7$ kcal

10. **(a)** : $\Delta H = (E_a)_f - (E_a)_b = 0$

11. **(b)** : $CH_4 + 2O_2 \rightarrow CO_2 + 2H_2O$
$C_3H_8 + 5O_2 \rightarrow 3CO_2 + 4H_2O$

$$CH_4+C_3H_8=\frac{5}{22.4}=0.22\text{ moles}$$

$$O_2=\frac{16}{22.4}=0.71\text{ moles}$$

$2x + (0.22 - x)5 = 0.71$
$x = 0.13$
Heat liberated $= 0.13 \times 890 + 0.09 \times 2220 = 316$ kJ

12. **(b)** : According to Hess's law, equation (i) is equal to equations (ii) + (iii).

13. **(a)** : $C_{(\text{graphite})} + \frac{1}{2}O_{2(g)} \rightarrow CO_{(g)}$

$$\Delta n_g=1-\frac{1}{2}=\frac{1}{2}$$

As amount of gaseous substance is increasing in product, thus ΔS is positive for this reaction.
And we know that $\Delta G = \Delta H - T\Delta S$
As ΔS is positive, thus increase in temperature will make $T\Delta S$ more negative and ΔG will decrease.

14. **(c)** : $\Delta H_f = 1.435$ kcal/mol

$$\Delta S=\frac{\Delta H_f}{T_f}=\frac{1.435\times10^3}{273}=5.26\text{ cal/mol K}$$

15. **(a)** : $\Delta_{vap}H° = 40.66$ kJ mol^{-1}
$T = 100 + 273 = 373$ K, $\Delta E = ?$
$\Delta H = \Delta E + \Delta n_g RT \Rightarrow \Delta E = \Delta H - \Delta n_g RT$
Δn_g = number of gaseous moles of products − number of gaseous moles of reactants

$H_2O_{(l)} \rightleftharpoons H_2O_{(g)}$
$\Delta n_g = 1 - 0 = 1$
$\Delta E = \Delta H - RT$
$\Delta E = (40.66 \times 10^3) - (8.314 \times 373)$
$= 37559$ J/mol or 37.56 kJ/mol

16. (d) : We know that $\Delta G = \Delta H - T\Delta S$
$0 = \Delta H - T\Delta S \quad [\because \Delta G = 0]$
$$\Delta S = \frac{\Delta H}{T} = \frac{30 \times 10^3}{300} = 100 \text{ J mol}^{-1} \text{ K}^{-1}$$

17. (c) : The dissociation energy of H – H bond is
$$\frac{869.6}{2} = 434.8 \text{ kJ}$$

18. (c) : For free expansion of an ideal gas under adiabatic condition $q = 0$, $\Delta T = 0$, $w = 0$.

19. (b) : Adding all the equations

	ΔH
$A \rightarrow 2B$	300 kJ/mol
$3B \rightarrow 2C + D$	–125 kJ/mol
$2D \rightarrow A + E$	–350 kJ/mol

$B + D \rightarrow E + 2C$;
$\Delta H = (300 - 125 - 350) = -175$ kJ/mol

20. (c) : Refer to the figure.

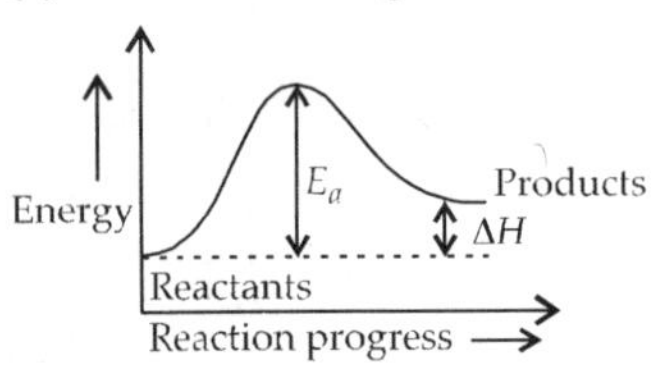

We find that the least E_a will be more than ΔH for an endothermic reaction since $E_{products} > E_{reactants}$.

21. (a) : Given reaction is :
$$\frac{1}{2}X_2 + \frac{3}{2}Y_2 \rightleftharpoons XY_3$$
We know, $\Delta S° = \Sigma S°_{\text{products}} - \Sigma S°_{\text{reactants}}$
$= 50 - (30 + 60) = -40 \text{ J K}^{-1} \text{ mol}^{-1}$
At equilibrium $\Delta G° = 0$
$\Delta H° = T\Delta S°$
$$\therefore \quad T = \frac{\Delta H°}{\Delta S°} = \frac{-30 \times 10^3 \text{ J mol}^{-1}}{-40 \text{ J K}^{-1} \text{ mol}^{-1}} = 750 \text{ K}$$

22. (c) : When $K_p > Q$, rate of forward reaction > rate of backward reaction.
$\therefore$ Reaction is spontaneous.
When $\Delta G° < RT \ln Q$, $\Delta G°$ is positive, reverse reaction is feasible, thus reaction is non spontaneous.
When $K_p = Q$, rate of forward reaction = rate of backward reaction.
$\therefore$ Reaction is in equilibrium.
When $T\Delta S > \Delta H$, ΔG will be negative only when ΔH = +ve.
$\therefore$ Reaction is spontaneous and endothermic.

23. (d) : Since the ideal gas expands spontaneously into vacuum, $P_{ext} = 0$, hence work done is also zero.

24. (c) : According to Gibbs equation,
$\Delta G = \Delta H - T\Delta S$
when $\Delta G = 0$, $\Delta H = T\Delta S$
Given, $\Delta H = 40.63 \text{ kJ mol}^{-1} = 40.63 \times 10^3 \text{ J mol}^{-1}$
$\Delta S = 108.8 \text{ J K}^{-1} \text{ mol}^{-1}$
$$\therefore \quad T = \frac{\Delta H}{\Delta S} = \frac{40.63 \times 10^3}{108.8} = 373.43 \text{ K}$$

25. (d) : $Fe_2O_{3(s)} + 3CO_{(g)} \rightarrow 2Fe_{(s)} + 3CO_{2(g)}$
$\Delta H = -26.8$ kJ ...(i)
$FeO_{(s)} + CO_{(g)} \rightarrow Fe_{(s)} + CO_{2(g)}$ $\Delta H = -16.5$ kJ ...(ii)
$Fe_2O_{3(s)} + CO_{(g)} \rightarrow 2FeO_{(s)} + CO_{2(g)}$ $\Delta H = ?$ ...(iii)
Eq. (iii) can be obtained as :
(i) – 2(ii)
$= -26.8 - 2(-16.5) = -26.8 + 33.0 = +6.2$ kJ

26. (b) : For the reaction to be spontaneous, ΔG = –ve.
Given, $\Delta H = 170 \text{ kJ} = 170 \times 10^3$ J
$\Delta S = 170 \text{ J K}^{-1} \text{ mol}^{-1}$
Applying, $\Delta G = \Delta H - T\Delta S$, the value of ΔG = –ve only when $T\Delta S > \Delta H$, which is possible only when $T = 1110$ K.
$\therefore \quad \Delta G = 170 \times 10^3 - (1110 \times 170) = -18700$ J
Thus, reaction is spontaneous at $T = 1110$ K

27. (b) : For the given reaction, enthalpy of reaction can be calculated as
= B.E.(reactant) – B.E.(product)
$= [\text{B.E.}_{(C=C)} + \text{B.E.}_{(H-H)} + 4 \times \text{B.E.}_{(C-H)}] - [\text{B.E.}_{(C-C)} + 6 \times \text{B.E.}_{(C-H)}]$
$= [606.10 + 431.37 + 4 \times 410.50] - [336.49 + 6 \times 410.50]$
$= 2679.47 - 2799.49 = -120.02 \text{ kJ mol}^{-1}$

28. (a) : $H_2 + Cl_2 \rightarrow 2HCl$
$\Delta H_{\text{reaction}} = \Sigma(\text{B.E})_{\text{reactant}} - \Sigma(\text{B.E})_{\text{product}}$
$= [(\text{B.E})_{H-H} + (\text{B.E})_{Cl-Cl}] - [2\text{B.E}_{(H-Cl)}]$
$= 434 + 242 - (431) \times 2$
$\Delta H_{\text{reaction}} = -186$ kJ
Heat of formation is the amount of heat absorbed or evolved when one mole of substance is directly obtained from its constituent element.

Hence, enthalpy of formation of HCl $= \frac{-186}{2}$ kJ
$= -93 \text{ kJ mol}^{-1}$

29. (d) : Gas phase reaction
$PCl_{5(g)} \rightleftharpoons PCl_{3(g)} + Cl_{2(g)}$
$\Delta H = \Delta E + \Delta n_g RT$

Δn_g = Change in number of moles of product and reactant species.
Since Δn_g = +ve, hence ΔH = +ve
also one mole of PCl_5 is dissociated into two moles of PCl_3 and Cl_2 in the same phase.
Therefore, $\Delta S = S_{product} - S_{reactant}$
ΔS = +ve.

30. (b) : State functions or state variables are those which depend only on the state of the system and not on how the state was reached.

$$\left.\begin{array}{l} q + w = \Delta E \text{ (internal energy)} \\ H - TS = G \text{ (free energy)} \end{array}\right\} \text{State functions}$$

Path function depends on the path followed during a process as well as the end states. Work and heat are the path functions.

31. (d) : The amount of heat absorbed or released when 1 mole of a substance is directly obtained from its constituent elements is called the heat of formation or enthalpy of formation.
Equation (i) represents neutralisation reaction, (iii) represents hydrogenation reaction and (iv) represents combustion reaction.

32. (b): $HCl \rightarrow \frac{1}{2}H_2 + \frac{1}{2}Cl_2$

$$\Delta H = \Sigma \text{ B.E.}_{(products)} - \Sigma \text{ B.E.}_{(reactants)}$$
$$= \frac{1}{2}[\text{B.E.}_{(H_2)} + \text{B.E.}_{(Cl_2)}] - \text{B.E.}_{(HCl)}$$
$$= \frac{1}{2}(430 + 240) - (-90) = \frac{1}{2} \times 670 + 90$$
$$= 335 + 90 = 425 \text{ kJ mol}^{-1}$$

33. (c) : The criteria for spontaneity of a process in terms of ΔG is as follows:
If ΔG is negative, the process is spontaneous.
If ΔG is positive, the process does not occur in the forward direction. It may occur in the backward direction.
If ΔG is zero, the system is in equilibrium.

34. (b) : $\Delta H = \Delta E + \Delta n_g RT$
or $H_{2(g)} + Br_{2(g)} \rightarrow 2HBr_{(g)}$
$\Delta n_g = 2 - (1 + 1) = 0.$ *i.e.* $\Delta H = \Delta E$

35. (b) : $Br_{2(l)} + Cl_{2(g)} \rightarrow 2BrCl_{(g)}$
$\Delta H = 30 \text{ kJ mol}^{-1}, \Delta S = 105 \text{ J K}^{-1} \text{ mol}^{-1}$

$$\Delta S = \frac{\Delta H}{T} \quad i.e. \quad 105 = \frac{30}{T} \times 1000$$
$$T = \frac{30 \times 1000}{105} = 285.7 \text{ K}$$

36. (c) : 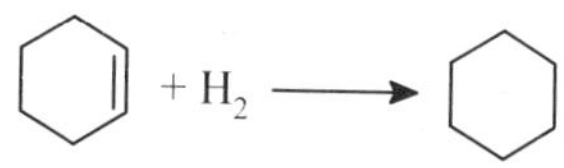

,
$\Delta H = -119.5 \text{ kJ mol}^{-1}$

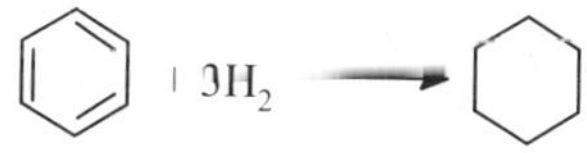

Enthalpy of hydrogenation of benzene
$= 3 \times \Delta H$ – resonance energy
$= 3 \times (-119.5) - (-150.4) = -358.5 + 150.4$
$= -208.1 \text{ kJ mol}^{-1}$

37. (a) : For spontaneous reaction ΔH = –ve, ΔS = +ve
Spontaneity depends upon both critical minimum energy and maximum randomness / disorder.

38. (c) : $\Delta G = \Delta H - T\Delta S$
ΔG = –ve for spontaneous reaction
When ΔS = +ve, ΔH = +ve
and $T\Delta S > \Delta H \Rightarrow \Delta G = -ve$

39. (c) : MgO is the oxide of weak base and we know that heat of neutralisation of 1 eq. of strong acid with strong base is –57.33 kJ/mol.
⇒ with weak base some heat is absorbed in dissociation of weak base.
⇒ Heat of neutralisation of weak base with strong acid will be less than –57.33 kJ/mol.

40. (d) : $H - H + Br - Br \rightarrow 2H - Br$

$H - H + Br - Br$	$2H - Br$
433 + 192	2 × 364
= 625	= 728
Energy absorbed	Energy released

Net energy released = 728 – 625 = 103 kJ
i.e. $\Delta H = -103$ kJ

41. (b) : $\Delta G = \Delta H - T\Delta S = -382.64 - 298\left(\frac{-145.6}{1000}\right)$
$= -382.64 + 43.38 = -339.3 \text{ kJ mol}^{-1}$

42. (a) : $\Delta S = R \ln \frac{V_2}{V_1}$
Here the volume of gas increases from V_1 to V_2 at constant temperature T.
Since $V_2 > V_1$, it is obvious that the spontaneous (irreversible) isothermal expansion of a gas is accompanied by an increase in the entropy of the system and its surroundings considered together.
$\Delta S_{sys} + \Delta S_{surr} > 0$

43. (b) : Work = $-P_{ext}$ × volume change
$= -3 \times 101.32 \times (6 - 4) = 6 \times 101.32$
$= -607.92 \text{ J} \approx -608 \text{ J}$

44. (b) : $C_3H_{8(g)} + 5O_{2(g)} \rightarrow 3CO_{2(g)} + 4H_2O_{(l)}$
$\Delta n_g = 3 - 6 = -3$
$\Delta H = \Delta E + P\Delta V$ or $\Delta H - \Delta E = P\Delta V$
$\Delta H - \Delta E = \Delta n_g RT = -3RT$

45. (None) $\Delta G = -P\Delta V$ = Work done

$$\Delta V = \left(\frac{12}{3.31} - \frac{12}{2.25}\right) \times 10^{-3} \text{ L} = -1.71 \times 10^{-3} \text{ L}$$

ΔG = Work done = $-(-1.71 \times 10^{-3}) \times P \times 101.3$ J

$$P = \frac{1895}{1.71 \times 10^{-3} \times 101.3} = 10.93 \times 10^3 \text{ atm}$$

$= 11.07 \times 10^8$ Pa

46. (d) : $S = \frac{q_{rev}}{T} = \frac{6000}{273} = 21.978 \text{ J K}^{-1} \text{ mol}^{-1}$

47. (a) : Heat of solution is defined as the amount of heat evolved or absorbed when one mole of the substance is dissolved in excess of the solvent. For hydrated salt and for salts which do not form hydrates, ΔH is positive and for anhydrous salts, it is negative.

48. (c) : For (c) $\Delta H^\circ_{\text{reaction}}$
$= \Delta H^\circ_f(\text{XeF}_4) - [\Delta H^\circ_f(\text{Xe}) + 2\Delta H^\circ_f(\text{F}_2)]$
Enthalpies of formation of elementary substances Xe and F_2 are taken as zero.
Thus, $\Delta H^\circ_{\text{reaction}} = \Delta H^\circ_f(\text{XeF}_4)$

49. (b) : Molar heat capacity = $75 \text{ J K}^{-1} \text{ mol}^{-1}$
18 g of water = 1 mole = $75 \text{ J K}^{-1} \text{ mol}^{-1}$

1 g of water = $\frac{75}{18} \text{ J K}^{-1}$

$Q = m \cdot C \cdot \Delta t$ or $1000 = 100 \times \frac{75}{18} \times \Delta t$

$\Rightarrow \Delta t = \frac{10 \times 18}{75} = 2.4$ K

50. (a) : Entropy change (dS) is given by $dS = \frac{q_{rev}}{T}$

$\therefore$ Unit of entropy = J/K mol (entropy per unit mole) $= \text{J K}^{-1}\text{mol}^{-1}$

51. (a) : The mathematical form of first law of thermodynamics : $q = \Delta E + W$
Since the system is closed and insulated, $q = 0$
Paddle work is done on system. $\therefore$ $W \neq 0$.
Temperature and hence internal energy of the system increases. $\therefore$ $\Delta E \neq 0$.

52. (a) : (i) $C_{(s)} + O_{2(g)} \rightarrow CO_{2(g)}$; $\Delta H_i = -94$ kcal/mole

(ii) $2H_{2(g)} + O_{2(g)} \rightarrow 2H_2O_{(l)}$; $\Delta H_{ii} = -68 \times 2$ kcal/mole

(iii) $CH_{4(g)} + 2O_{2(g)} \rightarrow CO_{2(g)} + 2H_2O_{(l)}$; $\Delta H_{iii} = -213$ kcal/mole

(iv) $C_{(s)} + 2H_{2(g)} \rightarrow CH_{4(g)}$; $\Delta H_{iv} = ?$

By applying Hess's law we can compute ΔH_{iv}.
$\therefore$ $\Delta H_{iv} = \Delta H_i + \Delta H_{ii} - \Delta H_{iii}$
$= (-94 - 68 \times 2 + 213)$ kcal $= -17$ kcal

53. (b) : The halogen are highly electronegative elements - their non-metallic character gradually decreases from fluorine to iodine. F > Cl > Br > I. Fluorine can displace chlorine, bromine and iodine. Chlorine can displace bromine and iodine and bromine can displace iodine from their salts. Iodine cannot displace flourine, chlorine and bromine. Hence reaction (b) is not feasible.

54. (d) : The change of entropy $dS = \frac{q_{rev}}{T}$

From the first law of thermodynamics,
$$dq = dU + PdV = C_V dT + PdV$$
$$\Rightarrow \frac{dq}{T} = C_V \frac{dT}{T} + \frac{P}{T} dV$$
$$\Rightarrow \frac{dq}{T} = C_V \frac{dT}{T} + \frac{RdV}{V} \quad \left[\frac{P}{T} = \frac{R}{V}\right]$$
$$\therefore \quad dS = C_V \frac{dT}{T} + R\frac{dV}{V}$$
$$\Rightarrow \quad \Delta S = C_V \ln\frac{T_2}{T_1} + R\ln\frac{V_2}{V_1}$$
[for one mole of ideal gas]

Here $T_2 = T_1 = 27°\text{C} = 300$ K. $\therefore$ $\ln\frac{T_2}{T_1} = 0$

$\therefore$ $\Delta S = R\ln\frac{V_2}{V_1} = 2\ln\frac{20}{2} = 2\ln 10 = 4.605$

$\therefore$ $\Delta S = 4.605$ cal/mol-K
Entropy change for 2 moles of gas
$= 2 \times 4.605$ cal/K = 9.2 cal/K

55. (a) : $\Delta H^\circ_f = \Sigma H^\circ_{f\text{ (product)}} - \Sigma H^\circ_{f\text{ (reactant)}}$
For the given reaction,
$$2H_2O_{2(l)} \rightarrow 2H_2O_{(l)} + O_{2(g)}$$
$\Delta H^\circ_f = 2 \times \Delta H^\circ_{f\,(H_2O)} - 2 \times \Sigma H^\circ_{f\,(H_2O_2)}$
$= 2 \times -286 \text{ kJ mol}^{-1} - 2 \times (-188) \text{ kJ mol}^{-1}$
$= -196 \text{ kJ mol}^{-1}$

56. (b) : $\Delta H = \Delta E + P\Delta V$
When $\Delta V = 0$; $w = 0$.
$\Delta H = \Delta E + 0$ or $\Delta H = \Delta E$
As $\Delta E = q + w$, $\Delta E = q$
In the present problem, $\Delta H = 500$ J,
$\Delta H = \Delta E = 500$ J, $q = 500$ J, $w = 0$

57. (a) : $CH_4 + 2O_2 \rightarrow CO_2 + 2H_2O$, $\Delta H_1 = -x$ kJ ...(i)

$CH_3OH + \frac{3}{2}O_2 \rightarrow CO_2 + 2H_2O$, $\Delta H_2 = -y$ kJ ...(ii)

Subtracting (ii) from (i), we get

$CH_4 + \frac{1}{2}O_2 \rightarrow CH_3OH$, $\Delta H_3 = -\text{ve}$

i.e., $-x - (-y) = -\text{ve}$
$y - x = -$ ve
Hence, $x > y$.

58. (d) : The sign and magnitude of Gibbs free energy is a criterion of spontaneity for a process. When $\Delta G > 0$ or +ve, it means $G_{product} > G_{reactant}$ as $\Delta G = G_{products} - G_{reactants}$
the reaction will not take place spontaneously, *i.e.* the reaction should be spontaneous in reverse direction.

$$\underset{+4}{SnO_2} \rightarrow \underset{+2}{SnO}\ ;\ \Delta G > 0$$
(more favourable)

$\Delta G < 0$ or –ve, the reaction or change occurs spontaneously.

$$\underset{+4}{PbO_2} \rightarrow \underset{+2}{PbO}\ ;\ \rightarrow \Delta G < 0$$
(more favourable)

59. (a) : For a cell reaction to be spontaneous $\Delta G°$ should be negative. As $\Delta G° = -nFE°_{cell}$, so the value will be –ve only when $E°_{cell}$ is +ve.

60. (a) : For the reactions,
$2ZnS \rightarrow 2Zn + S_2\ ;\ \Delta G° = +293$ J ...(1)
$2Zn + O_2 \rightarrow 2ZnO\ ;\ \Delta G° = -616$ J ...(2)
$S_2 + 2O_2 \rightarrow 2SO_2\ ;\ \Delta G° = -408$ J ...(3)
The $\Delta G°$ for the reaction,
$2ZnS + 3O_2 \rightarrow 2ZnO + 2SO_2$ can be obtained by adding eq. (1), (2) and (3).
So, $\Delta G° = 293 - 616 - 408 = -731$ J

61. (a) : $\Delta S = \frac{Q}{T} = \frac{2930}{300} = 9.77$ J/mol K

62. (a) : $\Delta H = \Delta E + P\Delta V$
Also $PV = nRT$ (ideal gas equation)
or $P\Delta V = \Delta n_g RT$
Δn_g = change in number of gaseous moles
$\therefore \Delta H = \Delta E + \Delta n_g RT \Rightarrow \Delta n_g = 2 - 3 = -1$
$\Rightarrow \Delta H = \Delta E - RT$

63. (b) : In endothermic reactions, energy of reactants is less than energy of products. Thus, $E_R < E_P$.
$\Delta H = E_P - E_R = +ve$

64. (d) : $S + \frac{3}{2}O_2 \rightarrow SO_3 + 2x$ kcal ...(i)

$SO_2 + \frac{1}{2}O_2 \rightarrow SO_3 + y$ kcal (ii)

By substracting equation (ii) from (i) we get,
$S + O_2 \rightarrow SO_2 + (2x - y)$ kcal
The heat of formation of SO_2 is $(2x - y)$ kcal/mole.

65. (c) : The entropy of a substance increases with increase in temperature. However at absolute zero the entropy of a perfectly crystalline substance is taken as zero, which is also called as third law of thermodynamics.

66. (b) : Change in internal energy depends upon temperature. At constant temperature, the internal energy of the gas remains constant, so $\Delta E = 0$

67. (a) : $C_{(s)} + O_{2(g)} \rightarrow CO_{2(g)}$; $\Delta H = -x$ kJ ...(i)

$CO_{(g)} + \frac{1}{2}O_{2(g)} \rightarrow CO_{2(g)}$; $\Delta H = -\frac{y}{2}$ kJ ...(ii)

By substracting equation (ii) from (i) we get,

$C_{(s)} + \frac{1}{2}O_{2(g)} \rightarrow CO_{(g)}$;

$$\Delta H = -x - \left(-\frac{y}{2}\right) = \frac{y - 2x}{2}\text{ kJ}$$

68. (b) : This is the mathematical relation of first law of thermodynamics. Here ΔU = change in internal energy; ΔQ = heat absorbed by the system and W = work done by the system.

69. (d) : $C_2H_4 + 3O_2 \rightarrow 2\,CO_2 + 2\,H_2O$
$\Delta H = \Delta H_{products} - \Delta H_{reactants}$
$= 2 \times (-394) + 2 \times (-286) - (52 + 0) = -1412$ kJ/mol

70. (b) : Since a catalyst affects equally both forward and backward reactions, therefore it does not affect equilibrium constant of reaction.

71. (c) : If more *trans*-2-pentene is added, then its concentration in right hand side will increase. But in order to maintain the constant K, concentration of *cis*-2-pentene will also increase. Therefore more *cis*-2-pentene will be formed.

72. (c) : For a reaction to be spontaneous, ΔG (Gibb's free energy change) must be negative.
$\Delta G = \Delta H - T\Delta S$
ΔH = change in enthalpy, ΔS = change in entropy.

73. (c) : During isothermal expansion of an ideal gas, $\Delta T = 0$.
Now we know $H = E + PV$
$\because \Delta H = \Delta E + \Delta(PV) = \Delta E + \Delta(nRT)$
$\therefore \Delta H = \Delta E + nR\Delta T = 0 + 0 = 0$

74. (d) : (i) The given reaction is a combustion reaction, therefore ΔH is less than 0. Hence, ΔH is negative.
(ii) Since there is increase in the number of moles, therefore ΔS is positive
(iii) Since reaction is spontaneous, therefore ΔG is negative.

75. (b) : $\Delta n_g = 2 - 4 = -2$, $\Delta H = \Delta E - 2RT$

76. (d) : If $n_p < n_r$; $\Delta n_g = n_p - n_r = -ve$.
Hence $\Delta H < \Delta E$.

Chapter 7

Equilibrium

1. Following solutions were prepared by mixing different volumes of NaOH and HCl of different concentrations :

A. $60\ \text{mL}\ \frac{M}{10}\ \text{HCl} + 40\ \text{mL}\ \frac{M}{10}\ \text{NaOH}$

B. $55\ \text{mL}\ \frac{M}{10}\ \text{HCl} + 45\ \text{mL}\ \frac{M}{10}\ \text{NaOH}$

C. $75\ \text{mL}\ \frac{M}{5}\ \text{HCl} + 25\ \text{mL}\ \frac{M}{5}\ \text{NaOH}$

D. $100\ \text{mL}\ \frac{M}{10}\ \text{HCl} + 100\ \text{mL}\ \frac{M}{10}\ \text{NaOH}$

pH of which one of them will be equal to 1?
(a) *B* (b) *A* (c) *D* (d) *C*
(NEET 2018)

2. The solubility of $BaSO_4$ in water is 2.42×10^{-3} g L^{-1} at 298 K. The value of its solubility product (K_{sp}) will be (Given molar mass of $BaSO_4$ = 233 g mol^{-1})
(a) 1.08×10^{-10} mol^2 L^{-2}
(b) 1.08×10^{-12} mol^2 L^{-2}
(c) 1.08×10^{-14} mol^2 L^{-2}
(d) 1.08×10^{-8} mol^2 L^{-2} *(NEET 2018)*

3. Which one of the following conditions will favour maximum formation of the product in the reaction
$A_{2(g)} + B_{2(g)} \rightleftharpoons X_{2(g)}$, $\Delta_r H = -X$ kJ ?
(a) Low temperature and high pressure
(b) Low temperature and low pressure
(c) High temperature and high pressure
(d) High temperature and low pressure
(NEET 2018)

4. The equilibrium constants of the following are
$N_2 + 3H_2 \rightleftharpoons 2NH_3$; K_1
$N_2 + O_2 \rightleftharpoons 2NO$; K_2
$H_2 + \frac{1}{2}O_2 \rightleftharpoons H_2O$; K_3

The equilibrium constant (K) of the reaction :
$2NH_3 + \frac{5}{2}O_2 \xrightleftharpoons{K} 2NO + 3H_2O$ will be
(a) $K_2K_3^3/K_1$ (b) K_2K_3/K_1
(c) $K_2^3K_3/K_1$ (d) $K_1K_3^3/K_2$
(NEET 2017, 2007, 2003)

5. Concentration of the Ag^+ ions in a saturated solution of $Ag_2C_2O_4$ is 2.2×10^{-4} mol L^{-1}. Solubility product of $Ag_2C_2O_4$ is
(a) 2.66×10^{-12} (b) 4.5×10^{-11}
(c) 5.3×10^{-12} (d) 2.42×10^{-8}
(NEET 2017)

6. A 20 litre container at 400 K contains $CO_{2(g)}$ at pressure 0.4 atm and an excess of SrO (neglect the volume of solid SrO). The volume of the container is now decreased by moving the movable piston fitted in the container. The maximum volume of the container, when pressure of CO_2 attains its maximum value will be
(Given that : $SrCO_{3(s)} \rightleftharpoons SrO_{(s)} + CO_{2(g)}$, K_p = 1.6 atm)
(a) 10 litre (b) 4 litre
(c) 2 litre (d) 5 litre
(NEET 2017)

7. The percentage of pyridine (C_5H_5N) that forms pyridinium ion ($C_5H_5\overset{+}{N}H$) in a 0.10 M aqueous pyridine solution (K_b for $C_5H_5N = 1.7 \times 10^{-}$[illegible]) is
(a) 0.0060% (b) 0.013%
(c) 0.77% (d) 1.6%
(NEET-II 2016)

8. The solubility of $AgCl_{(s)}$ with solubility product 1.6×10^{-10} in 0.1 M NaCl solution would be
(a) 1.26×10^{-5} M (b) 1.6×10^{-9} M
(c) 1.6×10^{-11} M (d) zero.
(NEET-II 201

9. Which of the following fluoro-compounds is most likely to behave as a Lewis base?
(a) BF_3 (b) PF_3 (c) CF_4 (d) SiF_4
(NEET-II 201

10. MY and NY_3, two nearly insoluble salts, have the same K_{sp} values of 6.2×10^{-13} at room temperature. Which statement would be true in regard to MY and NY_3?
(a) The salts MY and NY_3 are more soluble in 0.5 M KY than in pure water.
(b) The addition of the salt of KY to solution of MY and NY_3 will have no effect on their solubilities.
(c) The molar solubilities of MY and NY_3 in water are identical.
(d) The molar solubility of MY in water is less than that of NY_3. *(NEET-I 2016)*

11. If the equilibrium constant for

$N_{2(g)} + O_{2(g)} \rightleftharpoons 2NO_{(g)}$ is K, the equilibrium

constant for $\frac{1}{2}N_{2(g)} + \frac{1}{2}O_{2(g)} \rightleftharpoons NO_{(g)}$ will

be
(a) $\frac{1}{2}K$ (b) K
(c) K^2 (d) $K^{1/2}$ *(2015)*

12. What is the pH of the resulting solution when equal volumes of 0.1 M NaOH and 0.01 M HCl are mixed?
(a) 2.0 (b) 7.0
(c) 1.04 (d) 12.65 *(2015)*

13. Aqueous solution of which of the following compounds is the best conductor of electric current?
(a) Hydrochloric acid, HCl
(b) Ammonia, NH_3
(c) Fructose, $C_6H_{12}O_6$
(d) Acetic acid, $C_2H_4O_2$ *(2015)*

14. Which one of the following pairs of solution is not an acidic buffer?
(a) CH_3COOH and CH_3COONa
(b) H_2CO_3 and Na_2CO_3
(c) H_3PO_4 and Na_3PO_4
(d) $HClO_4$ and $NaClO_4$ *(2015)*

15. The K_{sp} of Ag_2CrO_4, AgCl, AgBr and AgI are respectively, 1.1×10^{-12}, 1.8×10^{-10}, 5.0×10^{-13}, 8.3×10^{-17}. Which one of the following salts will precipitate last if $AgNO_3$ solution is added to the solution containing equal moles of NaCl, NaBr, NaI and Na_2CrO_4?
(a) AgBr (b) Ag_2CrO_4
(c) AgI (d) AgCl
(2015, Cancelled)

16. Which of the following statements is correct for a reversible process in a state of equilibrium?
(a) $\Delta G° = -2.30\ RT \log K$
(b) $\Delta G° = 2.30\ RT \log K$
(c) $\Delta G = -2.30\ RT \log K$
(d) $\Delta G = 2.30\ RT \log K$ *(2015, Cancelled)*

17. If the value of equilibrium constant for a particular reaction is 1.6×10^{12}, then at equilibrium the system will contain
(a) mostly products
(b) similar amounts of reactants and products
(c) all reactants
(d) mostly reactants. *(2015, Cancelled)*

18. Which of the following salts will give highest pH in water?
(a) KCl (b) NaCl
(c) Na_2CO_3 (d) $CuSO_4$ *(2014)*

19. Using the Gibb's energy change, $\Delta G° = +63.3$ kJ, for the following reaction,

$$Ag_2CO_{3(s)} \rightleftharpoons 2Ag^+_{(aq)} + CO_3^{2-}{}_{(aq)}$$

the K_{sp} of $Ag_2CO_{3(s)}$ in water at 25 °C is ($R = 8.314$ J K^{-1} mol^{-1})
(a) 3.2×10^{-26} (b) 8.0×10^{-12}
(c) 2.9×10^{-3} (d) 7.9×10^{-2}
(2014)

20. For the reversible reaction,
$N_{2(g)} + 3H_{2(g)} \rightleftharpoons 2NH_{3(g)}$ + heat
The equilibrium shifts in forward direction
(a) by increasing the concentration of $NH_{3(g)}$
(b) by decreasing the pressure
(c) by decreasing the concentrations of $N_{2(g)}$ and $H_{2(g)}$
(d) by increasing pressure and decreasing temperature. *(2014)*

21. For a given exothermic reaction, K_p and K'_p are the equilibrium constants at temperatures T_1 and T_2, respectively. Assuming that heat of reaction is constant in temperature range between T_1 and T_2, it is readily observed that
(a) $K_p > K'_p$ (b) $K_p < K'_p$
(c) $K_p = K'_p$ (d) $K_p = \frac{1}{K'_p}$
(2014)

22. $KMnO_4$ can be prepared from K_2MnO_4 as per the reaction,

$$3MnO_4^{2-} + 2H_2O \rightleftharpoons 2MnO_4^- + MnO_2 + 4OH^-$$

The reaction can go to completion by removing OH^- ions by adding

(a) CO_2 (b) SO_2 (c) HCl (d) KOH *(NEET 2013)*

23. Which of these is least likely to act as a Lewis base?

(a) BF_3 (b) PF_3 (c) CO (d) F^- *(NEET 2013)*

24. Accumulation of lactic acid ($HC_3H_5O_3$), a monobasic acid in tissues leads to pain and a feeling of fatigue. In a 0.10 M aqueous solution, lactic acid is 3.7% dissociates. The value of dissociation constant, K_a, for this acid will be

(a) 1.4×10^{-5} (b) 1.4×10^{-4}
(c) 3.7×10^{-4} (d) 2.8×10^{-4} *(Karnataka NEET 2013)*

25. At 100°C the K_w of water is 55 times its value at 25°C. What will be the pH of neutral solution? (log 55 = 1.74)

(a) 7.00 (b) 7.87 (c) 5.13 (d) 6.13 *(Karnataka NEET 2013)*

26. The values of K_{sp} of $CaCO_3$ and CaC_2O_4 are 4.7×10^{-9} and 1.3×10^{-9} respectively at 25°C. If the mixture of these two is washed with water, what is the concentration of Ca^{2+} ions in water?

(a) 5.831×10^{-5} M (b) 6.856×10^{-5} M
(c) 3.606×10^{-5} M (d) 7.746×10^{-5} M *(Karnataka NEET 2013)*

27. The dissociation constant of a weak acid is 1×10^{-4}. In order to prepare a buffer solution with a pH = 5, the [Salt]/[Acid] ratio should be

(a) 4 : 5 (b) 10 : 1 (c) 5 : 4 (d) 1 : 10 *(Karnataka NEET 2013)*

28. pH of a saturated solution of $Ba(OH)_2$ is 12. The value of solubility product (K_{sp}) of $Ba(OH)_2$ is

(a) 3.3×10^{-7} (b) 5.0×10^{-7}
(c) 4.0×10^{-6} (d) 5.0×10^{-6} *(2012, 2010)*

29. Equimolar solutions of the following substances were prepared separately. Which one of these will record the highest pH value?

(a) $BaCl_2$ (b) $AlCl_3$ (c) LiCl (d) $BeCl_2$ *(2012)*

30. Buffer solutions have constant acidity and alkalinity because

(a) these give unionised acid or base on reaction with added acid or alkali
(b) acids and alkalies in these solutions are shielded from attack by other ions
(c) they have large excess of H^+ or OH^- ions
(d) they have fixed value of pH. *(2012)*

31. Given that the equilibrium constant for the reaction,

$$2SO_{2(g)} + O_{2(g)} \rightleftharpoons 2SO_{3(g)}$$

has a value of 278 at a particular temperature. What is the value of the equilibrium constant for the following reaction at the same temperature?

$$SO_{3(g)} \rightleftharpoons SO_{2(g)} + \frac{1}{2}O_{2(g)}$$

(a) 1.8×10^{-3} (b) 3.6×10^{-3}
(c) 6.0×10^{-2} (d) 1.3×10^{-5} *(Mains 2012)*

32. Given the reaction between 2 gases represented by A_2 and B_2 to give the compound $AB_{(g)}$.

$$A_{2(g)} + B_{2(g)} \rightleftharpoons 2AB_{(g)}$$

At equilibrium, the concentration of $A_2 = 3.0 \times 10^{-3}$ M, of $B_2 = 4.2 \times 10^{-3}$ M, of $AB = 2.8 \times 10^{-3}$ M

If the reaction takes place in a sealed vessel at 527°C, then the value of K_c will be

(a) 2.0 (b) 1.9 (c) 0.62 (d) 4.5 *(Mains 2012)*

33. The value of ΔH for the reaction $X_{2(g)} + 4Y_{2(g)} \rightleftharpoons 2XY_{4(g)}$ is less than zero. Formation of $XY_{4(g)}$ will be favoured at

(a) high temperature and high pressure
(b) low pressure and low temperature
(c) high temperature and low pressure
(d) high pressure and low temperature *(2011)*

34. A buffer solution is prepared in which the concentration of NH_3 is 0.30 M and the concentration of NH_4^+ is 0.20 M. If the equilibrium constant, K_b for NH_3 equals 1.8×10^{-5}, what is the pH of this solution? (log 2.7 = 0.43)

(a) 9.08 (b) 9.43 (c) 11.72 (d) 8.73 *(2011)*

35. Which of the following is least likely to behave as Lewis base?

(a) H_2O (b) NH_3 (c) BF_3 (d) OH^- *(2011)*

36. For the reaction, $N_{2(g)} + O_{2(g)} \rightleftharpoons 2NO_{(g)}$, the equilibrium constant is K_1. The equilibrium constant is K_2 for the reaction,
$2NO_{(g)} + O_{2(g)} \rightleftharpoons 2NO_{2(g)}$
What is K for the reaction,
$NO_{2(g)} \rightleftharpoons \frac{1}{2}N_{2(g)} + O_{2(g)}$?
(a) $\frac{1}{2K_1K_2}$ (b) $\frac{1}{4K_1K_2}$
(c) $\left[\frac{1}{K_1K_2}\right]^{1/2}$ (d) $\frac{1}{K_1K_2}$ *(2011)*

37. In qualitative analysis, the metals of group I can be separated from other ions by precipitating them as chloride salts. A solution initially contains Ag^+ and Pb^{2+} at a concentration of 0.10 M. Aqueous HCl is added to this solution until the Cl^- concentration is 0.10 M. What will the concentrations of Ag^+ and Pb^{2+} be at equilibrium?
(K_{sp} for AgCl = 1.8×10^{-10}, K_{sp} for $PbCl_2$ = 1.7×10^{-5})
(a) $[Ag^+] = 1.8 \times 10^{-7}$ M, $[Pb^{2+}] = 1.7 \times 10^{-6}$ M
(b) $[Ag^+] = 1.8 \times 10^{-11}$ M, $[Pb^{2+}] = 8.5 \times 10^{-5}$ M
(c) $[Ag^+] = 1.8 \times 10^{-9}$ M, $[Pb^{2+}] = 1.7 \times 10^{-3}$ M
(d) $[Ag^+] = 1.8 \times 10^{-11}$ M, $[Pb^{2+}] = 1.7 \times 10^{-4}$ M
(Mains 2011)

38. What is $[H^+]$ in mol/L of a solution that is 0.20 M in CH_3COONa and 0.10 M in CH_3COOH? (K_a for CH_3COOH = 1.8×10^{-5})
(a) 3.5×10^{-4} (b) 1.1×10^{-5}
(c) 1.8×10^{-5} (d) 9.0×10^{-6}
(2010)

39. In which of the following equilibrium K_c and K_p are not equal?
(a) $2NO_{(g)} \rightleftharpoons N_{2(g)} + O_{2(g)}$
(b) $SO_{2(g)} + NO_{2(g)} \rightleftharpoons SO_{3(g)} + NO_{(g)}$
(c) $H_{2(g)} + I_{2(g)} \rightleftharpoons 2HI_{(g)}$
(d) $2C_{(s)} + O_{2(g)} \rightleftharpoons 2CO_{2(g)}$ *(2010)*

40. In a buffer solution containing equal concentration of B^- and HB, the K_b for B^- is 10^{-10}. The pH of buffer solution is
(a) 10 (b) 7 (c) 6 (d) 4
(2010)

41. The reaction,
$2A_{(g)} + B_{(g)} \rightleftharpoons 3C_{(g)} + D_{(g)}$
is begun with the concentrations of A and B both at an initial value of 1.00 M. When equilibrium is reached, the concentration of D is measured and found to be 0.25 M. The value for the equilibrium constant for this reaction is given by the expression
(a) $[(0.75)^3(0.25)] \div [(1.00)^2(1.00)]$
(b) $[(0.75)^3(0.25)] \div [(0.50)^2(0.75)]$
(c) $[(0.75)^3(0.25)] \div [(0.50)^2(0.25)]$
(d) $[(0.75)^3(0.25)] \div [(0.75)^2(0.25)]$
(Mains 2010)

42. The dissociation constants for acetic acid and HCN at 25°C are 1.5×10^{-5} and 4.5×10^{-10} respectively. The equilibrium constant for the equilibrium,
$CN^- + CH_3COOH \rightleftharpoons HCN + CH_3COO^-$
would be
(a) 3.0×10^{-5} (b) 3.0×10^{-4}
(c) 3.0×10^{4} (d) 3.0×10^{5} *(2009)*

43. Which of the following molecules acts as a Lewis acid?
(a) $(CH_3)_2O$ (b) $(CH_3)_3P$
(c) $(CH_3)_3N$ (d) $(CH_3)_3B$ *(2009)*

44. The ionization constant of ammonium hydroxide is 1.77×10^{-5} at 298 K. Hydrolysis constant of ammonium chloride is
(a) 6.50×10^{-12} (b) 5.65×10^{-13}
(c) 5.65×10^{-12} (d) 5.65×10^{-10}
(2009)

45. What is the $[OH^-]$ in the final solution prepared by mixing 20.0 mL of 0.050 M HCl with 30.0 mL of 0.10 M $Ba(OH)_2$?
(a) 0.40 M (b) 0.0050 M
(c) 0.12 M (d) 0.10 M *(2009)*

46. The dissociation equilibrium of a gas AB_2 can be represented as :
$$2AB_{2(g)} \rightleftharpoons 2AB_{(g)} + B_{2(g)}$$
The degree of dissociation is x and is small compared to 1. The expression relating the degree of dissociation (x) with equilibrium constant K_P and total pressure P is
(a) $(2K_P/P)^{1/2}$ (b) (K_P/P)
(c) $(2K_P/P)$ (d) $(2K_P/P)^{1/3}$
(2008)

47. If the concentration of OH^- ions in the reaction $Fe(OH)_{3(s)} \rightleftharpoons Fe^{3+}_{(aq)} + 3OH^-_{(aq)}$
is decreased by 1/4 times, then equilibrium concentration of Fe^{3+} will increase by
(a) 64 times (b) 4 times
(c) 8 times (d) 16 times.
(2008)

48. Equal volumes of three acid solutions of pH 3, 4 and 5 are mixed in a vessel. What will be the H^+ ion concentration in the mixture?
(a) 3.7×10^{-3} M (b) 1.11×10^{-3} M
(c) 1.11×10^{-4} M (d) 3.7×10^{-4} M
(2008)

49. The value of equilibrium constant of the reaction,
$HI_{(g)} \rightleftharpoons \frac{1}{2}H_{2(g)} + \frac{1}{2}I_{2(g)}$
is 8.0. The equilibrium constant of the reaction
$H_{2(g)} + I_{2(g)} \rightleftharpoons 2HI_{(g)}$ will be
(a) 16 (b) 1/8 (c) 1/16 (d) 1/64
(2008)

50. The values of for the reactions,
$X \rightleftharpoons Y + Z$ ...(i)
$A \rightleftharpoons 2B$ ...(ii)
are in the ratio 9 : 1. If degree of dissociation of X and A be equal, then total pressure at equilibrium (i) and (ii) are in the ratio
(a) 36 : 1 (b) 1 : 1 (c) 3 : 1 (d) 1 : 9
(2008)

51. A weak acid, HA, has a K_a of 1.00×10^{-5}. If 0.100 mol of this acid is dissolved in one litre of water, the percentage of acid dissociated at equilibrium is closest to
(a) 1.00% (b) 99.9%
(c) 0.100% (d) 99.0% *(2007)*

52. Calculate the pOH of a solution at 25°C that contains 1×10^{-10} M of hydronium ions, *i.e.* H_3O^+.
(a) 4.000 (b) 9.000 (c) 1.000 (d) 7.000
(2007)

53. For the reaction:
$CH_{4(g)} + 2O_{2(g)} \rightleftharpoons CO_{2(g)} + 2H_2O_{(l)}$,
$\Delta H_r = -170.8$ kJ mol^{-1}. Which of the following statements is not true?
(a) The reaction is exothermic.
(b) At equilibrium, the concentrations of $CO_{2(g)}$ and $H_2O_{(l)}$ are not equal.
(c) The equilibrium constant for the reaction is given by $K_p = \frac{[CO_2]}{[CH_4][O_2]}$.
(d) Addition of $CH_{4(g)}$ or $O_{2(g)}$ at equilibrium will cause a shift to the right. *(2006)*

54. Which of the following pairs constitutes a buffer?
(a) HCl and KCl
(b) HNO_2 and $NaNO_2$
(c) NaOH and NaCl
(d) HNO_3 and NH_4NO_3 *(2006)*

55. The hydrogen ion concentration of a 10^{-8} M HCl aqueous solution at 298 K ($K_w = 10^{-14}$) is
(a) 1.0×10^{-8} M (b) 1.0×10^{-6} M
(c) 1.0525×10^{-7} M (d) 9.525×10^{-8} M
(2006)

56. At 25°C, the dissociation constant of a base, BOH, is 1.0×10^{-12}. The concentration of hydroxyl ions in 0.01 M aqueous solution of the base would be
(a) 1.0×10^{-5} mol L^{-1} (b) 1.0×10^{-6} mol L^{-1}
(c) 2.0×10^{-6} mol L^{-1} (d) 1.0×10^{-7} mol L^{-1}
(2005)

57. H_2S gas when passed through a solution of cations containing HCl precipitates the cations of second group of qualitative analysis but not those belonging to the fourth group. It is because
(a) presence of HCl decreases the sulphide ion concentration
(b) solubility product of group II sulphides is more than that of group IV sulphides
(c) presence of HCl increases the sulphide ion concentration
(d) sulphides of group IV cations are unstable in HCl. *(2005)*

58. Equilibrium constants K_1 and K_2 for the following equilibria:
$NO_{(g)} + \frac{1}{2}O_2 \xrightleftharpoons{K_1} NO_{2(g)}$ and
$2NO_{2(g)} \xrightleftharpoons{K_2} 2NO_{(g)} + O_{2(g)}$ are related as
(a) $K_2 = 1/K_1^2$ (b) $K_2 = K_1^2$
(c) $K_2 = 1/K_1$ (d) $K_2 = K_1/2$
(2005)

59. The solubility product of a sparingly soluble salt AX_2 is 3.2×10^{-11}. Its solubility (in moles/L) is
(a) 5.6×10^{-6} (b) 3.1×10^{-4}
(c) 2×10^{-4} (d) 4×10^{-4} *(2004)*

60. The rapid change of pH near the stoichiometric point of an acid-base titration is the basis of indicator detection. pH of the solution is related to ratio of the concentrations of the conjugate acid (HIn) and base (In^-) forms of the indicator by the expression
(a) $\log\frac{[In^-]}{[HIn]} = pK_{In} - pH$
(b) $\log\frac{[HIn]}{[In^-]} = pK_{In} - pH$

(c) $\log\frac{[\mathrm{HIn}]}{[\mathrm{In}^-]} = \mathrm{pH} - \mathrm{p}K_{\mathrm{In}}$

(d) $\log\frac{[\mathrm{In}^-]}{[\mathrm{HIn}]} - \mathrm{pH} - \mathrm{p}K_{\mathrm{In}}$ *(2004)*

61. In Haber process 30 litres of dihydrogen and 30 litres of dinitrogen were taken for reaction which yielded only 50 % of the expected product. What will be the composition of gaseous mixture under the aforesaid condition in the end?
(a) 20 litres ammonia, 20 litres nitrogen, 20 litres hydrogen
(b) 10 litres ammonia, 25 litres nitrogen, 15 litres hydrogen
(c) 20 litres ammonia, 10 litres nitrogen, 30 litres hydrogen
(d) 20 litres ammonia, 25 litres nitrogen, 15 litres hydrogen *(2003)*

62. The reaction quotient (Q) for the reaction $N_{2(g)} + 3H_{2(g)} \rightleftharpoons 2NH_{3(g)}$ is given by $Q = \frac{[NH_3]^2}{[N_2][H_2]^3}$. The reaction will proceed from right to left if
(a) $Q = K_c$ (b) $Q < K_c$
(c) $Q > K_c$ (d) $Q = 0$
where K_c is the equilibrium constant. *(2003)*

63. Which one of the following statements is not true?
(a) Among halide ions, iodide is the most powerful reducing agent.
(b) Fluorine is the only halogen that does not show a variable oxidation state.
(c) HOCl is a stronger acid than HOBr.
(d) HF is a stronger acid than HCl. *(2003)*

64. The solubility product of AgI at 25°C is 1.0×10^{-16} mol^2 L^{-2}. The solubility of AgI in 10^{-4} N solution of KI at 25°C is approximately (in mol L^{-1})
(a) 1.0×10^{-16} (b) 1.0×10^{-12}
(c) 1.0×10^{-10} (d) 1.0×10^{-8} *(2003)*

65. Reaction $BaO_{2(s)} \rightleftharpoons BaO_{(s)} + O_{2(g)}$; $\Delta H = +$ve. In equilibrium condition, pressure of O_2 depends on
(a) increase mass of BaO_2
(b) increase mass of BaO
(c) increase temperature on equilibrium
(d) increase mass of BaO_2 and BaO both. *(2002)*

66. Solubility of MX_2 type electrolytes is 0.5×10^{-4} mole/lit., then find out K_{sp} of electrolytes.
(a) 5×10^{-12} (b) 25×10^{-10}
(c) 1×10^{-13} (d) 5×10^{-13} *(2002)*

67. Which has highest pH?
(a) CH_3COOK (b) Na_2CO_3
(c) NH_4Cl (d) $NaNO_3$ *(2002)*

68. Solution of 0.1 N NH_4OH and 0.1 N NH_4Cl has pH 9.25. Then find out pK_b of NH_4OH.
(a) 9.25 (b) 4.75 (c) 3.75 (d) 8.25 *(2002)*

69. In HS^-, I^-, R–NH_2, NH_3 order of proton accepting tendency will be
(a) $I^- > NH_3 > R - NH_2 > HS^-$
(b) $NH_3 > R - NH_2 > HS^- > I^-$
(c) $R - NH_2 > NH_3 > HS^- > I^-$
(d) $HS^- > R - NH_2 > NH_3 > I^-$ *(2001)*

70. Ionisation constant of CH_3COOH is 1.7×10^{-5} and concentration of H^+ ions is 3.4×10^{-4}. Then find out initial concentration of CH_3COOH molecules.
(a) 3.4×10^{-4} (b) 3.4×10^{-3}
(c) 6.8×10^{-4} (d) 6.8×10^{-3} *(2001)*

71. Solubility of M_2S salt is 3.5×10^{-6} then find out solubility product.
(a) 1.7×10^{-6} (b) 1.7×10^{-16}
(c) 1.7×10^{-18} (d) 1.7×10^{-12} *(2001)*

72. Correct relation between dissociation constants of a dibasic acid is
(a) $K_{a_1} = K_{a_2}$ (b) $K_{a_1} > K_{a_2}$
(c) $K_{a_1} < K_{a_2}$ (d) $K_{a_1} = \frac{1}{K_{a_2}}$ *(2000)*

73. For any reversible reaction, if we increase concentration of the reactants, then effect on equilibrium constant
(a) depends on amount of concentration
(b) unchange
(c) decrease
(d) increase. *(2000)*

74. Conjugate acid of NH_2^- is
(a) NH_4OH (b) NH_4^+
(c) NH_2^- (d) NH_3 *(2000)*

75. Which statement is wrong about pH and H^+?
(a) pH of neutral water is not zero.
(b) Adding 1 N solution of CH_3COOH and 1 N solution of NaOH, pH will be seven.
(c) $[H^+]$ of dilute and hot H_2SO_4 is more than concentrated and cold H_2SO_4.
(d) Mixing solution of CH_3COOH and HCl, pH will be less than 7. *(2000)*

76. Equilibrium constant K_p for following reaction
$MgCO_{3(s)} \rightleftharpoons MgO_{(s)} + CO_{2(g)}$
(a) $K_p = P_{CO_2}$
(b) $K_p = P_{CO_2} \times \frac{P_{CO_2} \times P_{MgO}}{P_{MgCO_3}}$
(c) $K_p = \frac{P_{CO_2} + P_{MgO}}{P_{MgCO_3}}$
(d) $K_p = \frac{P_{MgCO_3}}{P_{CO_2} \times P_{MgO}}$ *(2000)*

77. The strongest conjugate base is
(a) SO_4^{2-} (b) Cl^-
(c) NO_3^- (d) CH_3COO^- *(1999)*

78. The concentration of $[H^+]$ and concentration of $[OH^-]$ of a 0.1 aqueous solution of 2% ionised weak acid is [ionic product of water $= 1 \times 10^{-14}$]
(a) 2×10^{-3} M and 5×10^{-12} M
(b) 1×10^{-3} M and 3×10^{-11} M
(c) 0.02×10^{-3} M and 5×10^{-11} M
(d) 3×10^{-2} M and 4×10^{-13} M *(1999)*

79. The solubility of a saturated solution of calcium fluoride is 2×10^{-4} moles per litre. Its solubility product is
(a) 22×10^{-11} (b) 14×10^{-4}
(c) 2×10^{-2} (d) 32×10^{-12} *(1999)*

80. If K_1 and K_2 are the respective equilibrium constants for the two reactions,
$XeF_{6(g)} + H_2O_{(g)} \rightarrow XeOF_{4(g)} + 2HF_{(g)}$
$XeO_{4(g)} + XeF_{6(g)} \rightarrow XeOF_{4(g)} + XeO_3F_{2(g)}$,
the equilibrium constant of the reaction,
$XeO_{4(g)} + 2HF_{(g)} \rightarrow XeO_3F_{2(g)} + H_2O_{(g)}$, will be
(a) K_1/K_2 (b) $K_1 \cdot K_2$
(c) $K_1/(K_2)^2$ (d) K_2/K_1 *(1998)*

81. A physician wishes to prepare a buffer solution at pH = 3.85 that efficiently resists changes in pH yet contains only small concentration of the buffering agents. Which of the following weak acids together with its sodium salt would be best to use?
(a) 2, 5-Dihydroxy benzoic acid ($pK_a = 2.97$)
(b) Acetoacetic acid ($pK_a = 3.58$)
(c) *m*-Chlorobenzoic acid ($pK_a = 3.98$)
(d) *p*-Chlorocinnamic acid ($pK_a = 4.41$) *(1997)*

82. The hydride ion H^- is stronger base than its hydroxide ion OH^-. Which of the following reaction will occur if sodium hydride (NaH) is dissolved in water?
(a) $H^- + H_2O \rightarrow$ no reaction
(b) $H^-_{(aq)} + H_2O \rightarrow H_2O$
(c) $H^-_{(aq)} + H_2O_{(l)} \rightarrow OH^- + H_2$
(d) None of these. *(1997)*

83. The solubility product of CuS, Ag_2S and HgS are 10^{-31}, 10^{-44} and 10^{-54} respectively. The solubilities of these sulphides are in the order
(a) HgS > Ag_2S > CuS
(b) CuS > Ag_2S > HgS
(c) Ag_2S > CuS > HgS
(d) AgS > HgS > CuS *(1997)*

84. The equilibrium constant for the reaction $N_2 + 3H_2 \rightleftharpoons 2NH_3$ is K, then the equilibrium constant for the equilibrium $2NH_3 \rightleftharpoons N_2 + 3H_2$ is
(a) $\sqrt{K}$ (b) $\sqrt{\frac{1}{K}}$ (c) $\frac{1}{K}$ (d) $\frac{1}{K^2}$ *(1996)*

85. The ionic product of water at 25°C is 10^{-14}. Its ionic product at 90°C will be,
(a) 1×10^{-14} (b) 1×10^{-16}
(c) 1×10^{-20} (d) 1×10^{-12} *(1996)*

86. If α is dissociation constant, then the total number of moles for the reaction,
$2HI \rightarrow H_2 + I_2$ will be
(a) 1 (b) 1 – α
(c) 2 (d) 2 – α *(1996)*

87. The pH value of *N*/10 NaOH solution is
(a) 12 (b) 13 (c) 10 (d) 11 *(1996)*

88. Which of the following is not a Lewis acid
(a) SiF_4 (b) C_2H_4 (c) BF_3 (d) $FeCl_3$ *(1996)*

89. The pH value of blood does not appreciably change by a small addition of an acid or base, because the blood
(a) can be easily coagulated
(b) contains iron as a part of the molecule
(c) is a body fluid
(d) contains serum protein which acts as buffer *(1995)*

90. The pH value of a 10 M solution of HCl is
(a) equal to 1 (b) equal to 2
(c) less than 0 (d) equal to 0
(1995)

91. The solubility of AgCl will be minimum in
(a) 0.01 M $CaCl_2$ (b) pure water
(c) 0.001 M $AgNO_3$ (d) 0.01 M NaCl
(1995)

92. In liquid-gas equilibrium, the pressure of vapours above the liquid is constant at
(a) constant temperature
(b) low temperature
(c) high temperature
(d) none of these. *(1995)*

93. Which one of the following is most soluble?
(a) Bi_2S_3 ($K_{sp} = 1 \times 10^{-70}$)
(b) Ag_2S ($K_{sp} = 6 \times 10^{-51}$)
(c) CuS ($K_{sp} = 8 \times 10^{-37}$)
(d) MnS ($K_{sp} = 7 \times 10^{-16}$) *(1994)*

94. At 80°C, distilled water has $[H_3O^+]$ concentration equal to 1×10^{-6} mole/litre. The value of K_w at this temperature will be
(a) 1×10^{-12} (b) 1×10^{-15}
(c) 1×10^{-6} (d) 1×10^{-9} *(1994)*

95. According to Le Chatelier's principle, adding heat to a solid and liquid in equilibrium will cause the
(a) temperature to increase
(b) temperature to decrease
(c) amount of liquid to decrease
(d) amount of solid to decrease. *(1993)*

96. 0.1 M solution of which one of these substances will act basic?
(a) Sodium borate
(b) Ammonium chloride
(c) Calcium nitrate
(d) Sodium sulphate *(1992)*

97. Which one of the following information can be obtained on the basis of Le Chatelier principle?
(a) Dissociation constant of a weak acid
(b) Entropy change in a reaction
(c) Equilibrium constant of a chemical reaction
(d) Shift in equilibrium position on changing value of a constraint *(1992)*

98. Aqueous solution of acetic acid contains
(a) CH_3COO^- and H^+
(b) CH_3COO^-, H_3O^+ and CH_3COOH
(c) CH_3COO^-, H_3O^+ and H^+
(d) CH_3COOH, CH_3COO^- and H^+ *(1991)*

99. K_1 and K_2 are equilibrium constant for reactions (i) and (ii)

$$N_{2(g)} + O_{2(g)} \rightleftharpoons 2NO_{(g)} \quad \text{....(i)}$$

$$NO_{(g)} \rightleftharpoons \frac{1}{2}N_{2(g)} + \frac{1}{2}O_{2(g)} \quad \text{...(ii)}$$

(a) $K_1 = \left(\frac{1}{K_2}\right)^2$ (b) $K_1 = K_2^2$

(c) $K_1 = \frac{1}{K_2}$ (d) $K_1 = (K_2)^0$

(1989)

100. The compound whose water solution has the highest pH is
(a) NaCl (b) $NaHCO_3$
(c) Na_2CO_3 (d) NH_4Cl *(1988)*

Answer Key

1. (d)	**2.** (a)	**3.** (a)	**4.** (a)	**5.** (c)	**6.** (d)	**7.** (b)	**8.** (b)	**9.** (b)	**10.** (d)
11. (d)	**12.** (d)	**13.** (a)	**14.** (d)	**15.** (b)	**16.** (a)	**17.** (a)	**18.** (c)	**19.** (b)	**20.** (d)
21. (a)	**22.** (a)	**23.** (a)	**24.** (b)	**25.** (d)	**26.** (d)	**27.** (b)	**28.** (b)	**29.** (a)	**30.** (a)
31. (c)	**32.** (c)	**33.** (d)	**34.** (b)	**35.** (c)	**36.** (c)	**37.** (c)	**38.** (d)	**39.** (d)	**40.** (d)
41. (b)	**42.** (c)	**43.** (d)	**44.** (d)	**45.** (d)	**46.** (d)	**47.** (a)	**48.** (d)	**49.** (d)	**50.** (a)
51. (a)	**52.** (a)	**53.** (c)	**54.** (b)	**55.** (c)	**56.** (d)	**57.** (a)	**58.** (a)	**59.** (c)	**60.** (d)
61. (b)	**62.** (c)	**63.** (d)	**64.** (b)	**65.** (c)	**66.** (d)	**67.** (b)	**68.** (b)	**69.** (c)	**70.** (d)
71. (b)	**72.** (b)	**73.** (b)	**74.** (d)	**75.** (b)	**76.** (a)	**77.** (d)	**78.** (a)	**79.** (d)	**80.** (d)
81. (b)	**82.** (d)	**83.** (b)	**84.** (c)	**85.** (d)	**86.** (c)	**87.** (b)	**88.** (b)	**89.** (d)	**90.** (c)
91. (a)	**92.** (a)	**93.** (d)	**94.** (a)	**95.** (d)	**96.** (a)	**97.** (d)	**98.** (b)	**99.** (a)	**100.** (c)

EXPLANATIONS

1. (d) : pH = 1, so $[H^+] = 10^{-1}$
For acid base mixture: $N_1V_1 - N_2V_2 = N_3V_3$
(For NaOH and HCl, Normality = Molarity)

$$A.\ M_1(H^+) = \frac{60\times\frac{1}{10} - 40\times\frac{1}{10}}{100} = 2\times10^{-3}\text{ M } i.e.\ \text{pH} = 2.7$$

$$B.\ M_2(H^+) = \frac{55\times\frac{1}{10} - 45\times\frac{1}{10}}{100} = \frac{1}{100} = 10^{-2}\text{ M } i.e.\ \text{pH} = 2$$

$$C.\ M_3(H^+) = \frac{75\times\frac{1}{5} - 25\times\frac{1}{5}}{100} = 10^{-1}\text{ M } i.e.\ \text{pH} = 1$$

$$D.\ M_4(H^+) = \frac{100\times\frac{1}{10} - 100\times\frac{1}{10}}{200} = 0\ i.e.\ \text{pH} = 7$$

2. (a) : Solubility of $BaSO_4$, $s = \frac{2.42\times10^{-3}}{233}$ mol L^{-1}
$= 1.04 \times 10^{-5}$ mol L^{-1}

$BaSO_4$ ionizes completely in the solution as :

$$BaSO_{4(s)} \rightleftharpoons \underset{s}{Ba^{2+}_{(aq)}} + \underset{s}{SO^{2-}_{4(aq)}}$$

$K_{sp} = [Ba^{2+}][SO_4^{2-}] = s^2$
$= (1.04 \times 10^{-5})^2 = 1.08 \times 10^{-10}$ mol^2 L^{-2}

3. (a) : On increasing the pressure and decreasing the temperature, equilibrium will shift in forward direction.

4. (a) : From the given equations,

$$2NH_3 \rightleftharpoons N_2 + 3H_2;\ \frac{1}{K_1} \quad ...(i)$$

$$N_2 + O_2 \rightleftharpoons 2NO;\ K_2 \quad ...(ii)$$

$$3H_2 + \frac{3}{2}O_2 \rightarrow 3H_2O;\ K_3^3 \quad ...(iii)$$

By adding equations (i), (ii) and (iii), we get

$$2NH_3 + \frac{5}{2}O_2 \overset{K}{\rightleftharpoons} 2NO + 3H_2O,\ K = \frac{K_2K_3^3}{K_1}$$

5. (c) : Let solubility of $Ag_2C_2O_4$ be s mol L^{-1}

$$\underset{s}{Ag_2C_2O_{4(s)}} \rightleftharpoons \underset{2s}{2Ag^+_{(aq)}} + \underset{s}{C_2O_4^{2-}{}_{(aq)}}$$

$K_{sp} = (2s)^2(s) = 4s^3$
$K_{sp} = 4 \times (1.1 \times 10^{-4})^3$ ($\because [Ag^+] = 2s = 2.2 \times 10^{-4}$)
$K_{sp} \approx 5.3 \times 10^{-12}$

6. (d) : $SrCO_{3(s)} \rightleftharpoons SrO_{(s)} + CO_{2(g)}$; $K_p = 1.6$ atm

$$K_p = \frac{p_{CO_2} \times p_{SrO}}{p_{SrCO_3}}$$

$\Rightarrow\ 1.6 = p_{CO_2}$ $\quad (\because p_{SrO} = p_{SrCO_3} = 1)$

$\therefore$ Maximum pressure of CO_2 = 1.6 atm

Let the maximum volume of the container when pressure of CO_2 is 1.6 atm be V L

During the process, PV = constant

$\therefore\ 0.4 \times 20 = 1.6 \times V$

$$\Rightarrow\ V = \frac{0.4\times20}{1.6} = 5\text{ L}$$

7. (b) : $\underset{0.10\text{ M}}{C_5H_5N} + H_2O \rightleftharpoons C_5H_5\overset{+}{N}H + OH^-$

$$\alpha = \sqrt{\frac{K_b}{C}} = \sqrt{\frac{1.7\times10^{-9}}{0.10}} = 1.30\times10^{-4}$$

$\therefore$ Percentage of pyridine that forms pyridinium ion $= 1.30 \times 10^{-4} \times 100 = 0.013\%$

8. (b) : Let s be the solubility of AgCl in moles per litre.

$$\underset{s}{AgCl_{(aq)}} \rightleftharpoons \underset{s}{Ag^+_{(aq)}} + \underset{(s+0.1)}{Cl^-_{(aq)}}$$

($\because$ 0.1 M NaCl solution also provides 0.1 M Cl^- ion)

$K_{sp} = [Ag^+][Cl^-]$; $1.6 \times 10^{-10} = s(s + 0.1)$
$1.6 \times 10^{-10} = s(0.1)$ $\quad (\because s <<<< 0.1)$

$$s = \frac{1.6\times10^{-10}}{0.1} = 1.6\times10^{-9}\text{ M}$$

9. (b) : $BF_3 \longrightarrow$ Lewis acid (incomplete octet)
$PF_3 \longrightarrow$ Lewis base (presence of lone pair on P atom)
$CF_4 \longrightarrow$ Complete octet
$SiF_4 \longrightarrow$ Lewis acid (empty d-orbital in Si-atom)

10. (d) : For MY : $K_{sp} = s_1^2$

$$\Rightarrow s_1 = \sqrt{K_{sp}} = \sqrt{6.2\times10^{-13}} = 7.87 \times 10^{-7}\text{ mol L}^{-1}$$

For NY_3 : $K_{sp} = 27s_2^4$

$$\Rightarrow\ s_2 = \sqrt[4]{\frac{6.2\times10^{-13}}{27}} = 3.89 \times 10^{-4}\text{ mol L}^{-1}$$

Hence, molar solubility of MY in water is less than that of NY_3.

11. (d) : If the reaction is multiplied by $\frac{1}{2}$, then new equilibrium constant, $K' = K^{1/2}$.

12. (d) : One mole of NaOH is completely neutralised by one mole of HCl
Hence, 0.01 mole of NaOH will be completely neutralised by 0.01 mole of HCl.

$\Rightarrow$ NaOH left unneutralised = 0.1 – 0.01 = 0.09 mol
As equal volumes of two solutions are mixed,

$$[OH]^- = \frac{0.09}{2} = 0.045 \text{ M}$$

$\Rightarrow$ pOH = –log(0.045) = 1.35

$\therefore$ pH = 14 – 1.35 = 12.65

13. (a) : HCl is a strong acid and dissociates completely into ions in aqueous solution.

14. (d) : Acidic buffer is a mixture of a weak acid and its salt with a strong base. $HClO_4$ is a strong acid.

15. (b) :

Salt	K_{sp}	**Solubility**
Ag_2CrO_4	$1.1 \times 10^{-12} = 4s^3$	$s = \sqrt[3]{\frac{K_{sp}}{4}} = 0.65 \times 10^{-4}$
AgCl	$1.8 \times 10^{-10} = s^2$	$s = \sqrt{K_{sp}} = 1.34 \times 10^{-5}$
AgBr	$5 \times 10^{-13} = s^2$	$s = \sqrt{K_{sp}} = 0.71 \times 10^{-6}$
AgI	$8.3 \times 10^{-17} = s^2$	$s = \sqrt{K_{sp}} = 0.9 \times 10^{-8}$

Solubility of Ag_2CrO_4 is highest thus, it will be precipitated at last.

16. (a)

17. (a) : The value of K is high which means reaction proceeds almost to completion *i.e.*, the system will contain mostly products.

18. (c) : Na_2CO_3 which is a salt of NaOH (strong base) and H_2CO_3 (weak acid) will produce a basic solution with pH greater than 7.

19. (b) : $\Delta G° = -2.303RT \log K_{sp}$

$63.3 \times 10^3 \text{ J} = -2.303 \times 8.314 \times 298 \log K_{sp}$

$63.3 \times 10^3 \text{ J} = -5705.84 \log K_{sp}$

$$\log K_{sp} = -\frac{63.3 \times 10^3}{5705.84} = -11.09$$

K_{sp} = antilog (–11.09) = 8.128×10^{-12}

20. (d) : As the forward reaction is exothermic and leads to lowering of pressure (produces lesser number of gaseous moles) hence, according to Le Chatelier's principle, at high pressure and low temperature, the given reversible reaction will shift in forward direction to form more product.

21. (a) : $\log \frac{K'_p}{K_p} = -\frac{\Delta H}{2.303R}\left[\frac{1}{T_2} - \frac{1}{T_1}\right]$

For exothermic reaction, ΔH = –ve *i.e.* heat is evolved. The temperature T_2 is higher than T_1.

Thus, $\left(\frac{1}{T_2} - \frac{1}{T_1}\right)$ is negative.

so, $\log K'_p - \log K_p$ = –ve or $\log K_p > \log K'_p$

or $K_p > K'_p$

22. (a) : HCl and SO_2 are reducing agents. So they can reduce MnO_4^-.
CO_2 is neither oxidising nor reducing agent, it will provide only acidic medium. It can shift the reaction in forward direction and the reaction can go to completion.

23. (a) : BF_3 is Lewis acid (e^- pair acceptor).

24. (b) : Degree of dissociation, $\alpha = \frac{3.7}{100} = 0.037$

According to Ostwald's formula,
$K_a = \alpha^2 C = (0.037)^2 \times 0.10 = 1.369 \times 10^{-4} \approx 1.4 \times 10^{-4}$

25. (d) : We know that, at 25°C, $K_w = 1 \times 10^{-14}$
At 100°C, $K_w = 55 \times 10^{-14}$

$H^+ = \sqrt{55 \times 10^{-14}}$

pH = – log [H^+]

$$pH = -\log\left[\sqrt{55 \times 10^{-14}}\right]$$

$$= \frac{1}{2}[-\log(55 \times 10^{-14})] = \frac{1}{2}[-\log 55 + 14 \log 10]$$

$$= \frac{1}{2}[-1.74 + 14] = \frac{1}{2}[12.26] = 6.13$$

26. (d) : $CaCO_3 \rightarrow Ca^{2+} + CO_3^{2-}$
$\qquad\qquad x \qquad x$

$CaC_2O_4 \rightarrow Ca^{2+} + C_2O_4^{2-}$
$\qquad\qquad y \qquad y$

Now, $[Ca^{2+}] = x + y$

and $x(x + y) = 4.7 \times 10^{-9}$ ...(i)

$y(x + y) = 1.3 \times 10^{-9}$ ...(ii)

Dividing equation (i) and (ii) we get

$$\frac{x}{y} = 3.6$$

$\therefore$ $x = 3.6y$

Putting this value in equation (ii), we get

$$y(3.6y + y) = 1.3 \times 10^{-9}$$

On solving, we get $y = 1.68 \times 10^{-5}$

and $x = 3.6 \times 1.68 \times 10^{-5} = 6.048 \times 10^{-5}$

$\therefore$ $[Ca^{2+}] = (x+y) = (1.68 \times 10^{-5}) + (6.048 \times 10^{-5})$

$\therefore$ $[Ca^{2+}] = 7.728 \times 10^{-5}$ M

27. (b) : $pH = pK_a + \log \frac{[Salt]}{[Acid]}$

$5 = -\log K_a + \log \frac{[Salt]}{[Acid]}$ $[\because pK_a = -\log K_a]$

$5 = -\log [1 \times 10^{-4}] + \log \frac{[Salt]}{[Acid]}$

$5 = 4 + \log \frac{[Salt]}{[Acid]}$

$5 - 4 = \log \frac{[Salt]}{[Acid]}$

$1 = \log \frac{[Salt]}{[Acid]}$

$\frac{[Salt]}{[Acid]} = 10$ *i.e.*, 10 : 1

28. (b) : pH of solution = 12

$[H^+] = 10^{-12}$

$[OH^-] = \frac{10^{-14}}{10^{-12}} = 10^{-2}$

$Ba(OH)_2 \rightleftharpoons \underset{s}{Ba^{2+}} + \underset{2s}{2OH^-}$

$2s = 10^{-2} \Rightarrow s = \frac{10^{-2}}{2}$

$K_{sp} = (s)(2s)^2 = 4s^3$

$= 4 \times \left(\frac{10^{-2}}{2}\right)^3 = \frac{4}{8} \times 10^{-6} = 5 \times 10^{-7}$

29. (a) : $BaCl_2$ is made up of $Ba(OH)_2$ and HCl.
$AlCl_3$ is made up of $Al(OH)_3$ and HCl.
LiCl is made up of LiOH and HCl.
$BeCl_2$ is made up of $Be(OH)_2$ and HCl.
$Ba(OH)_2$ is strongest base among the given options thus have maximum pH.

30. (a)

31. (c) : $2SO_{2(g)} + O_{2(g)} \rightleftharpoons 2SO_{3(g)}$, $K = 278$ ...(i)

By reversing the equation (i), we get

$2SO_{3(g)} \rightleftharpoons 2SO_{2(g)} + O_{2(g)}$ ...(ii)

Equilibrium constant for this reaction is

$K' = \frac{1}{K} = \frac{1}{278}$

By dividing the equation (ii) by 2, we get desired equation,

$SO_{3(g)} \rightleftharpoons SO_{2(g)} + \frac{1}{2}O_{2(g)}$ ...(iii)

Equilibrium constant for this reaction

$K'' = \sqrt{K'} = \sqrt{\frac{1}{K}} = \sqrt{\frac{1}{278}} = 0.0599 \approx 0.06$ or 6×10^{-2}

32. (c) : $A_{2(g)} + B_{2(g)} \rightleftharpoons 2AB_{(g)}$

$K_c = \frac{[AB]^2}{[A_2][B_2]}$

$= \frac{(2.8 \times 10^{-3})^2}{(3.0 \times 10^{-3})(4.2 \times 10^{-3})} = \frac{2.8 \times 2.8}{3.0 \times 4.2} = 0.62$

33. (d) : $X_{2(g)} + 4Y_{2(g)} \rightleftharpoons 2XY_{4(g)}$

$\Delta n_g = -ve$ and $\Delta H = -ve$

The reaction is favoured in forward direction at low temperature and high pressure.

34. (b) : $[NH_3] = 0.30$ M, $K_b = 1.8 \times 10^{-5}$

$[NH_4^+] = 0.20$ M

$pOH = pK_b + \log \frac{[salt]}{[base]} = 4.74 + \log \frac{0.2}{0.3} = 4.56$

$pH = (14 - 4.56) = 9.44$

35. (c) : BF_3 is an electron deficient species and acts as Lewis base.

36. (c) : $N_2 + O_2 \rightleftharpoons 2NO$; K_1

$2NO + O_2 \rightleftharpoons 2NO_2$; K_2

$NO_2 \rightleftharpoons \frac{1}{2}N_2 + O_2$; K

$K_1 = \frac{[NO]^2}{[N_2][O_2]}$; $K_2 = \frac{[NO_2]^2}{[NO]^2[O_2]}$

$K = \frac{[N_2]^{1/2}[O_2]}{[NO_2]} = \sqrt{\frac{[N_2][O_2] \times [NO]^2[O_2]}{[NO]^2 \times [NO_2]^2}}$

$K = \sqrt{\frac{1}{K_1 K_2}}$

37. (c) : $K_{sp}[AgCl] = [Ag^+][Cl^-]$

$[Ag^+] = \frac{1.8 \times 10^{-10}}{10^{-1}} = 1.8 \times 10^{-9}$ M

$K_{sp}[PbCl_2] = [Pb^{2+}][Cl^-]^2$

$[Pb^{2+}] = \frac{1.7 \times 10^{-5}}{10^{-1} \times 10^{-1}} = 1.7 \times 10^{-3}$ M

38. (d) : $\underset{C-x}{CH_3COOH} \rightleftharpoons \underset{x}{CH_3COO^-} + \underset{x}{H^+}$

$\underset{0.2\ M}{CH_3COONa} \rightarrow \underset{0.2\ M}{CH_3COO^-} + \underset{0.2\ M}{Na^+}$

$[CH_3COOH] = C - x \approx 0.1$ M
$[CH_3COO^-] = 0.2 + x \approx 0.2$ M
{acetic acid is a weak acid so, dissociation is minimum.

$\therefore \quad [H^+] = \dfrac{K_a[CH_3COOH]}{[CH_3COO^-]}$

$= \dfrac{1.8 \times 10^{-5} \times 10^{-1}}{2 \times 10^{-1}} = 9 \times 10^{-6}$ M

39. (d) : K_p and K_c are related by the equation,

$K_p = K_c(RT)^{\Delta n_g}$

where Δn_g = difference in the no. of moles of products and reactants in the gaseous state.

for $2C_{(s)} + O_{2(g)} \rightleftharpoons 2CO_{2(g)}$

$\Delta n_g = 2 - (1) = 1 \neq 0$

40. (d) : We know, $pOH = pK_b + \log\dfrac{[B^-]}{[HB]}$

Since, $[B^-] = [HB]$ (given)

$\therefore$ $pOH = pK_b \Rightarrow pOH = 10$

$\therefore$ $pH = 14 - 10 = 4$

41. (b): $2A_{(g)} + B_{(g)} \rightleftharpoons 3C_{(g)} + D_{(g)}$

	$2A_{(g)}$	$B_{(g)}$	$3C_{(g)}$	$D_{(g)}$
Initial moles :	1	1	0	0
Moles at eq. :	1 – (2×0.25) = 0.5	1 – 0.25 = 0.75	3×0.25 = 0.75	0.25 = 0.25

Equilibrium constant, $K = \dfrac{[C]^3[D]}{[A]^2[B]}$

$\therefore \quad K = \dfrac{(0.75)^3(0.25)}{(0.5)^2(0.75)}$

42. (c) : Given,

$CH_3COOH \rightleftharpoons CH_3COO^- + H^+$

$K_1 = \dfrac{[CH_3COO^-][H^+]}{[CH_3COOH]} = 1.5 \times 10^{-5}$

$HCN \rightleftharpoons H^+ + CN^-$

$K_2 = \dfrac{[CN^-][H^+]}{[HCN]} = 4.5 \times 10^{-10}$

$CN^- + CH_3COOH \rightleftharpoons HCN + CH_3COO^-$

$K = \dfrac{[HCN][CH_3COO^-]}{[CN^-][CH_3COOH]}$

$K = \dfrac{K_1}{K_2} = \dfrac{1.5 \times 10^{-5}}{4.5 \times 10^{-10}} \approx 0.3 \times 10^5$

or $K = 3 \times 10^4$

43. (d) : Lewis acids are electron deficient compounds, since $(CH_3)_3B$ is electron deficient (due to incomplete octect of B), it acts as a Lewis acid.

44. (d) : NH_4Cl is a salt of strong acid and weak base, so hydrolysis constant is

$K_h = \dfrac{K_w}{K_b}$

Given, $K_b(NH_4OH) = 1.77 \times 10^{-5}$

$K_w = 10^{-14}$

$\therefore \quad K_h = \dfrac{10^{-14}}{1.77 \times 10^{-5}} = 0.565 \times 10^{-9}$

or $K_h = 5.65 \times 10^{-10}$

45. (d) : Millimoles of H^+ produced = 20 × 0.05 = 1

Millimoles of OH^- produced = 30 × 0.1 × 2 = 6

($\because$ Each $Ba(OH)_2$ gives $2OH^-$.)

$\therefore$ Millimoles of OH^- remaining in solution = 6 – 1 = 5

Total volume of solution = 20 + 30 = 50 mL

$\therefore \quad [OH^-] = \dfrac{5}{50} = 0.1$ M

46. (d) : $2AB_{2(g)} \rightleftharpoons 2AB_{(g)} + B_{2(g)}$

$2AB_{2(g)}$	$2AB_{(g)}$	$B_{2(g)}$	
2	0	0	(initially)
2(1 – x)	2x	x	(at equilibrium)

Amount of moles at equilibrium = 2(1 – x) + 2x + x = 2 + x

$K_p = \dfrac{[p_{AB}]^2[p_{B_2}]}{[p_{AB_2}]^2}$

$K_p = \dfrac{\left(\dfrac{2x}{2+x} \times P\right)^2 \times \left(\dfrac{x}{2+x} \times P\right)}{\left(\dfrac{2(1-x)}{2+x} \times P\right)^2} = \dfrac{\dfrac{4x^3}{2+x} \times P}{4(1-x)^2}$

$K_p = \dfrac{4x^3 \times P}{2} \times \dfrac{1}{4} \qquad (\because \ 1 - x \approx 1 \ \& \ 2 + x \approx 2)$

$x = \left(\dfrac{8K_p}{4P}\right)^{1/3} \Rightarrow x = \left(\dfrac{2K_p}{P}\right)^{1/3}$

47. (a) : $Fe(OH)_{3(s)} \rightleftharpoons Fe^{3+}_{(aq)} + 3OH^-_{(aq)}$

$K = \dfrac{[Fe^{3+}][OH^-]^3}{[Fe(OH)_3]}$

$K = [Fe^{3+}][OH^-]^3$ (activity of solid is taken unity)

Concentration of OH^- ion in the reaction is decreased by 1/4 times then equilibrium concentration of Fe^{3+} will be increased by 64 times in order to keep the value of K constant.

48. (d) : $pH = -\log[H^+]$

or $[H^+] = 10^{-pH}$; $[H^+]$ of soln. 1 = 10^{-3}

$[H^+]$ of soln. 2 = 10^{-4}; $[H^+]$ of soln. 3 = 10^{-5}

Total concentration of $[H^+]$

$= 10^{-3}(1 + 1 \times 10^{-1} + 1 \times 10^{-2})$

$\Rightarrow \quad 10^{-3}\left(\dfrac{1}{1} + \dfrac{1}{10} + \dfrac{1}{100}\right) \Rightarrow 10^{-3}\left(\dfrac{100 + 10 + 1}{100}\right)$

$\Rightarrow\ 10^{-3}\left(\frac{111}{100}\right) = 1.11\times10^{-3}$

So, H^+ ion concentration in mixture of equal volume of these acid solution $= \frac{1.11\times10^{-3}}{3} = 3.7\times10^{-4}$ M

49. (d) : $HI_{(g)} \rightleftharpoons 1/2H_{2(g)} + 1/2I_{2(g)}$

i.e. $K = \frac{[H_2]^{1/2}[I_2]^{1/2}}{[HI]} = 8$

$H_{2(g)} + I_{2(g)} \rightleftharpoons 2HI_{(g)}$

$K' = \frac{[HI]^2}{[H_2][I_2]} = \left(\frac{1}{8}\right)^2 \Rightarrow K' = \frac{1}{64}$

50. (a) : $X \rightleftharpoons Y + Z$ ...(i)

$A \rightleftharpoons 2B$ ...(ii)

X	$\rightleftharpoons$ Y	+ Z	
1	0	0	Initially
$1-\alpha$	α	α	At equilibrium

Total no. of moles at equilibrium $= 1-\alpha+2\alpha = 1+\alpha$

Similarly,

A	$\rightleftharpoons 2B$	
1	0	Initially
$1-\alpha$	2α	At equilibrium

Total no. of moles at equilibrium $= 1-\alpha+2\alpha = 1+\alpha$

$$\therefore\ K_{p_1} = \frac{p_Y\times p_Z}{p_X} = \frac{\frac{\alpha}{1+\alpha}\times P_1\times\frac{\alpha}{1+\alpha}\times P_1}{\frac{1-\alpha}{1+\alpha}\times P_1}$$

$$K_{p_2} = \frac{(p_B)^2}{p_A} = \frac{\left(\frac{2\alpha}{1+\alpha}\times P_2\right)^2}{\frac{1-\alpha}{1+\alpha}\times P_2}$$

Now $\frac{K_{p_1}}{K_{p_2}} = \frac{P_1}{4P_2} \Rightarrow \frac{P_1}{P_2} = \frac{36}{1} = 36:1$

51. (a) : For a weak acid, degree of dissociation,

$$\alpha = \sqrt{\frac{K_a}{C}} = \sqrt{\frac{1\times10^{-5}}{0.1}} = 10^{-2}\quad i.e.\ 1.00\%$$

52. (a) : Given, $[H_3O^+] = 1\times10^{-10}$ or, pH = 10

Now at 25°C, pH + pOH = pK_w = 14

or, pOH = 14 – pH = 14 – 10 = 4

53. (c) : $CH_{4(g)} + 2O_{2(g)} \rightleftharpoons CO_{2(g)} + 2H_2O_{(l)}$

$$K_p = \frac{P_{CO_2}}{P_{CH_4}\cdot P_{O_2}^2}$$

54. (b) : HNO_2 and $NaNO_2$ are examples of acidic buffer.

55. (c) : 10^{-8} M HCl $= 10^{-8}$ M H^+

Also from water, $[H^+] = 10^{-7}$

Total $[H^+] = 10^{-7} + 0.10\times10^{-7} = 1.1\times10^{-7}$

56. (d) : $C = 0.01$ M

$K_b = 1\times10^{-12}$ at 25°C

	BOH	$\rightleftharpoons$ B^+	+ OH^-
	C	0	0
at eq.	$C - C\alpha$	$C\alpha$	$C\alpha$

$[OH^-] = C\alpha$

$[OH^-] = \sqrt{K_b C} = \sqrt{1\times10^{-12}\times10^{-2}}$

$[OH^-] = 10^{-7}$ mol L^{-1}

57. (a) : The cation of group II are precipitated as their sulphides.

Solubility product of sulphide of group II radicals are very low. Therefore, even with low conc. of S^{2-} ions, the ionic product exceeds the value of their solubility product and the radical of group II gets precipitated. The low conc. of S^{2-} ions is obtained by passing H_2S gas through the solution of the salt in the presence of dil. HCl which suppresses degree of ionisation of H_2S by common ion effect.

$$H_2S \rightleftharpoons \boxed{\begin{matrix}2H^+\\H^+\end{matrix}} \begin{matrix}+\ S^{2-}\\+\ Cl^-\end{matrix}$$

common ion

Note: Solubility product of group IV radicals are quite high.

It is necessary to suppress the conc. of S^{2-} ions, otherwise radical of group IV will also get precipitated along with group II radicals.

58. (a): $K_1 = \frac{p_{NO_2}}{p_{NO}\cdot(p_{O_2})^{1/2}}$ ...(1)

$K_2 = \frac{(p_{NO})^2\cdot p_{O_2}}{(p_{NO_2})^2}$ ...(2)

taking square root on both sides in eq. 2.

$\Rightarrow \sqrt{K_2} = \frac{p_{NO}\cdot(p_{O_2})^{1/2}}{p_{NO_2}}$

$\Rightarrow \sqrt{K_2} = \frac{1}{K_1}$; $\Rightarrow K_2 = \frac{1}{K_1^2}$

59. (c) : $K_{sp} = 3.2\times10^{-11}$

$AX_2 \rightleftharpoons A^{2+} + 2X^-$

$\qquad\qquad s \qquad 2s$

$K_{sp} = s\times(2s)^2 = 4s^3$; *i.e.*, $3.2\times10^{-11} = 4s^3$

or, $s^3 = 0.8 \times 10^{-11} = 8 \times 10^{-12}$

$\therefore \quad s = 2 \times 10^{-4}$

60. (d) : Let us consider the formation of a salt of a weak acid and a strong base.

$In^- + H_2O \rightleftharpoons HIn + OH^-$

$$K_h = \frac{[HIn][OH^-]}{[In^-]} \quad ...(i)$$

Other equations present in the solution are

$HIn \rightleftharpoons H^+ + In^-$

$H_2O \rightleftharpoons H^+ + OH^-$

$$K_{In} = \frac{[H^+][In^-]}{[HIn]} \quad ...(ii)$$

$$K_w = [H^+][OH^-] \quad ...(iii)$$

From (ii) and (iii),

$$\frac{K_w}{K_{In}} = \frac{[HIn][OH^-]}{[In^-]} = K_h \quad ...(iv)$$

$$[OH^-] = \frac{K_w}{K_{In}}\frac{[In^-]}{[HIn]}$$

$$\log [OH^-] = \log K_w - \log K_{In} + \log\frac{[In^-]}{[HIn]}$$

$$-pOH = -pK_w + pK_{In} + \log\frac{[In^-]}{[HIn]}$$

$$pK_w - pOH = pK_{In} + \log\frac{[In^-]}{[HIn]}$$

or, $pH = pK_{In} + \log\frac{[In^-]}{[HIn]}$

i.e. $\log\frac{[In^-]}{[HIn]} = pH - pK_{In}$

61. (b) : $3H_2 + N_2 \rightarrow 2NH_3$

$3H_2$	N_2	$2NH_3$
3	1	2
3/2	1/2	1
$10\times\frac{3}{2}$	$10\times\frac{1}{2}$	10×1
15	5	10

Composition of gaseous mixture under the aforesaid condition in the end

$H_2 = 30 - 15 = 15$ litres

$N_2 = 30 - 5 = 25$ litres

$NH_3 = 10$ litres

62. (c) : $N_{2(g)} + 3H_{2(g)} \rightleftharpoons 2NH_{3(g)}$

$$K_c = \frac{[NH_3]^2}{[N_2][H_2]^3} \; ; \quad \Delta n = 2 - 4 = -2$$

Thus, the reaction will shift in forward direction when $Q > K_c$.

63. (d) : Due to strong hydrogen-fluorine bond, proton is not given off easily and hence, HF is weakest acid.

64. (b) : $AgI \rightleftharpoons Ag^+ + I^-$

$1.0 \times 10^{-16} = s \times s$

Solubility of $Ag^+ = 1.0 \times 10^{-8}$ mol L^{-1}

Solubility of AgI in KI solution $= 1.0 \times 10^{-8} \times 10^{-4}$

$= 1.0 \times 10^{-12}$ mol L^{-1}

65. (c) : Pressure of O_2 does not depend on concentration terms of other reactants (because both are in solid state), since this is an endothermic reaction. If the temperature be raised dissociation of BaO_2 would occur, more O_2 is produced at equilibrium, pressure of O_2 increases.

66. (d) : If s is the solubility of the electrolyte MX_2

$C_{M^{2+}} = s, C_{X^-} = 2s$

Solubility product, $K_{sp} = s \times (2s)^2 = 4s^3$;

$s = 0.5 \times 10^{-4}$ mole/litre

$\therefore \quad K_{sp} = 4 \times (0.5 \times 10^{-4})^3$; $K_{sp} = 5 \times 10^{-13}$

67. (b) : NH_4OH is a weak base but HCl is a strong acid in solution, so pH of NH_4Cl solution is comparatively low.

$NaNO_3$ is a salt of strong base and strong acid, so pH of the solution will be 7.

Hydrolysis of potassium acetate (a salt of a weak acid and a strong alkali) gives a weakly alkaline solution, since the acetate ion acts as a weak base.

$$CH_3COOK + H_2O \rightarrow CH_3COOH + K^+ + OH^-$$

The pH of this solution ≈ 8.8.

Hydrolysis of sodium carbonate (a salt of strong alkali and a weak acid) gives an alkaline solution

$$Na_2CO_3 + 2H_2O \rightarrow 2(Na^+ + OH^-) + H_2CO_3$$

The pH of this solution is > 10.

68. (b) : Solution of 0.1 N NH_4OH and 0.1 N NH_4Cl is a buffer solution.

According to Henderson equation, the pH of a basic buffer,

$$pH = 14 - pK_b - \log\frac{C_{salt}}{C_{base}}$$

$$\Rightarrow pK_b = 14 - pH - \log\frac{C_{salt}}{C_{base}}$$

$$\Rightarrow pK_b = 14 - 9.25 - \log\frac{0.1}{0.1}$$

$\Rightarrow pK_b = 14 - 9.25 = 4.75$

$\therefore \quad pK_b$ of $NH_4OH = 4.75$

69. (c) : Proton accepting tendency is known as the strength of basicity.

In $R—\ddot{N}H_2$, N has lone pair of electron which intensify due to electron releasing R-group and increase the tendency to donate lone pair of electrons to H^+.

Secondly as the size of the ion increases there is less attraction for H^+ to form weaker bonds with H – atom and are less basic. The order of the given series: $RNH_2 > NH_3 > HS^- > I^-$.

70. (d) : $CH_3COOH \rightleftharpoons CH_3COO^- + H^+$

$$K_{ion} = \frac{[CH_3COO^-][H^+]}{[CH_3COOH]}$$

$$[CH_3COOH] = \frac{3.4\times10^{-4}\times3.4\times10^{-4}}{1.7\times10^{-5}} = 6.8\times10^{-3}$$

71. (b) : For reaction,

$$M_2S \rightleftharpoons 2M^+ + S^{2-}$$

Solubility = 3.5×10^{-6}

Solubility product, $K_{sp} = [M^+]^2\,[S^{2-}]$

$= (2s)^2\,s = 4s^3 = 4 \times (3.5 \times 10^{-6})^3 = 1.7 \times 10^{-16}$

72. (b) : (i) $H_2A \overset{K_{a_1}}{\rightleftharpoons} HA^- + H^+$

(ii) $HA^- \overset{K_{a_2}}{\rightleftharpoons} A^{2-} + H^+$

In the 1st step H^+ ion comes from neutral molecule, while in the 2nd step the H^+ ion comes from negatively charged ions. The presence of –ve charge makes the removal H^+ ion difficult. Thus, $K_{a_1} > K_{a_2}$.

73. (b) : For a reaction, $A + B \rightleftharpoons C + D$.

$$K_{eq} = \frac{[C]\,[D]}{[A]\,[B]}$$

Increase in conc. of reactants will proceed the equilibrium in the forward direction giving more products. So that the equilibrium constant value remains constant and independent of concentration.

74. (d) : $NH_2^- + H^+ \rightarrow NH_3$ (conjugate acid)

Substance + H^+ → conjugate acid

Substance – H^+ → conjugate base

75. (b) : After mixing 1 N solution of CH_3COOH (weak acid) and 1 N NaOH (strong base), the resulting solution will have free OH^- ions. Thus pH will be higher than 7.

76. (a) : $K_p = P_{CO_2}$

Solids do not exert pressure, so their partial pressure is taken as unity.

77. (d) : $CH_3COOH \rightleftharpoons CH_3COO^- + H^+$
Weak acid — Conjugate base

As CH_3COOH is the weakest acid, so its conjugate base (CH_3COO^-) is the strongest base. H_2SO_4, HCl, HNO_3 are strong acids, so their conjugate bases are weak.

78. (a) : $[H^+] = C\alpha = 0.1 \times 0.02 = 2 \times 10^{-3}$ M
(As degree of dissociation = 2% = 0.02)

Hence, $[OH^-] = \dfrac{10^{-14}}{2\times10^{-3}} = 5 \times 10^{-12}$ M

79. (d) : For CaF_2, decomposition is as follows:

$CaF_2 \rightarrow Ca^{2+} + 2F^-$
$\quad\quad\quad\;\; s \quad\quad 2s$

$\Rightarrow K_{sp} = [Ca^{2+}]\,[F^-]^2 = s \times (2s)^2$

or, $K_{sp} = 4s^3 \Rightarrow K_{sp} = 4s^3 = 4 \times (2 \times 10^{-4})^3$

$\Rightarrow K_{sp} = 32 \times 10^{-12}$

80. (d) : Given,

$XeF_6 + H_2O \rightleftharpoons XeOF_4 + 2HF, K_{eq} = K_1$

$XeOF_4 + 2HF \rightleftharpoons XeF_6 + H_2O, K_{eq} = 1/K_1$ ...(1)

and $XeO_4 + XeF_6 \rightleftharpoons XeOF_4 + XeO_3F_2, K_{eq} = K_2$ ...(2)

The reaction, $XeO_4 + 2HF \rightleftharpoons XeO_3F_2 + H_2O$, can be obtained by adding eq. (1) and eq.(2).

So, the equilibrium constant for the above reaction can be obtained by multiplying the equilibrium constants of eq. (1) and eq. (2).

Hence, the value is $= \dfrac{K_2}{K_1}$

81. (b) : $pH = pK_a + \log\dfrac{[Salt]}{[Acid]}$

For small concentration of buffering agent and fo[r] maximum buffer capacity [Salt]/[Acid] ≈ 1

i.e., pH = pK_a.

82. (d) : $NaH + H_2O \rightarrow NaOH + H_2$

or, $H^-_{(aq)} + H_2O_{(l)} \rightarrow OH^- + H_2\uparrow$

Hydride ions will abstract proton from NaOH an[d] hydrogen gas will evolve as a result of it.

83. (b) : The greater the solubility product, th[e] greater is the solubility.

84. (c) : The equilibrium constant for the revers[e] reaction will be $1/K$.

85. (d) : At high temperature, the value of ion product increases.

86. (c) : Total number of moles = $2(1 - \alpha) + 2\alpha$ =

87. (b) : Since NaOH is a strong base, therefore completely ionises. Thus, the hydroxyl io[n] concentration is equal to that of the base itself. W[e] know that concentration of OH^- in $N/10$ NaO[H] $= 0.1 = 10^{-}$

Therefore value of

$$\left[H_3O^+\right]=\frac{K_w}{\left[OH^-\right]}=\frac{1\times10^{-14}}{10^{-1}}=1\times10^{-13}$$

$$pH = -\log[H_3O^+] = -\log[1\times10^{-13}] = 13$$

88. (b) . In BF_3 and $FeCl_3$ molecules, the central atoms have incomplete octet and in SiF_4, the central atom has empty *d*-orbitals. Hence, according to Lewis concept, these are Lewis acids.

89. (d) : The pH value of the blood is maintained constant by buffer solution present in the blood itself. Buffer solutions resist the change in pH values.

90. (c) : Since HCl is a strong acid and it completely ionises, therefore H_3O^+ ions concentration is equal that of the acid itself *i.e.* $[H_3O^+] = [HCl] = 10$ M.

Therefore $pH = -\log[H_3O^+] = -\log[10] = -1$

91. (a) : There are greater number of particles (*i.e.* ions) compared to others. Hence, solubility will be minimum.

92. (a) : Vapour pressure is directly related to temperature. Greater is the temperature, greater will be the vapour pressure. So to keep it constant, temperature should be constant.

93. (d) : Higher the value of solubility product, greater is the solubility.

94. (a) : $[H_3O^+] = [OH^-] = 1\times10^{-6}$ mole/litre

$K_w = [H_3O^+][OH^-] = [1\times10^{-6}]\times[1\times10^{-6}] = 1\times10^{-12}$

95. (d) : When solid and liquid are in equilibrium, the increase in temperature results in increase in volume of liquid or decrease in the amount of solid.

$$\text{Solid} \rightleftharpoons \text{Liquid}$$

With increase in temperature equilibrium shifts in forward direction.

96. (a) : Sodium borate is a salt formed from strong base (NaOH) and weak acid (H_3BO_3). Hence, sodium borate will act basic.

97. (d) : According to Le Chatelier's principle, if an equilibrium is subjected to a change in concentration, pressure or temperature, etc. equilibrium shift in such a way so as to undo the effect of a change imposed.

98. (b) : $CH_3COOH + H_2O \rightleftharpoons CH_3COO^- + H_3O^+$

99. (a) : Reaction (ii) is the reversible reaction of (i) and is half of the reaction (i). Thus, rate constant can be given as:

$$K_2=\sqrt{\frac{1}{K_1}} \text{ or } K_1=\left[\frac{1}{K_2}\right]^2$$

100. (c) : NH_4Cl and $NaHCO_3$ are acidic in nature and NaCl is neutral. Only Na_2CO_3 is basic and thus have highest pH.

Chapter

8

Redox Reactions

1. Consider the change in oxidation state of bromine corresponding to different emf values as shown in the given diagram :

$$BrO_4^- \xrightarrow{1.82\ V} BrO_3^- \xrightarrow{1.5\ V} HBrO$$

$$Br^- \xleftarrow{1.0652\ V} Br_2 \xleftarrow{1.595\ V} HBrO$$

Then the species undergoing disproportionation is

(a) BrO_3^- (b) BrO_4^-

(c) Br_2 (d) HBrO

(NEET 2018)

2. The correct order of N-compounds in its decreasing order of oxidation states is

(a) HNO_3, NO, N_2, NH_4Cl

(b) HNO_3, NO, NH_4Cl, N_2

(c) HNO_3, NH_4Cl, NO, N_2

(d) NH_4Cl, N_2, NO, HNO_3 *(NEET 2018)*

3. For the redox reaction,

$MnO_4^- + C_2O_4^{2-} + H^+ \rightarrow Mn^{2+} + CO_2 + H_2O$

The correct coefficients of the reactants for the balanced equation are

	MnO_4^-	$C_2O_4^{2-}$	H^+
(a)	16	5	2
(b)	2	5	16
(c)	2	16	5
(d)	5	16	2

(NEET 2018)

4. Hot concentrated sulphuric acid is a moderately strong oxidizing agent. Which of the following reactions does not show oxidizing behaviour?

(a) $Cu + 2H_2SO_4 \rightarrow CuSO_4 + SO_2 + 2H_2O$

(b) $S + 2H_2SO_4 \rightarrow 3SO_2 + 2H_2O$

(c) $C + 2H_2SO_4 \rightarrow CO_2 + 2SO_2 + 2H_2O$

(d) $CaF_2 + H_2SO_4 \rightarrow CaSO_4 + 2HF$

(NEET-II 2016)

5. The pair of compounds that can exist together is

(a) $FeCl_3$, $SnCl_2$ (b) $HgCl_2$, $SnCl_2$

(c) $FeCl_2$, $SnCl_2$ (d) $FeCl_3$, KI *(2014)*

6. (I) $H_2O_2 + O_3 \longrightarrow H_2O + 2O_2$

(II) $H_2O_2 + Ag_2O \longrightarrow 2Ag + H_2O + O_2$

Role of hydrogen peroxide in the abov reactions is respectively

(a) oxidizing in (I) and reducing in (II)

(b) reducing in (I) and oxidizing in (II)

(c) reducing in (I) and (II)

(d) oxidizing in (I) and (II) *(2014*

7. In acidic medium, H_2O_2 changes $Cr_2O_7^{2-}$ t CrO_5 which has two (—O—O—) bonds Oxidation state of Cr in CrO_5 is

(a) +5 (b) +3 (c) +6 (d) –10

(2014

8. When Cl_2 gas reacts with hot and concentrate sodium hydroxide solution, the oxidatio number of chlorine changes from

(a) zero to +1 and zero to –5

(b) zero to –1 and zero to +5

(c) zero to –1 and zero to +3

(d) zero to +1 and zero to –3 *(2012*

9. A mixture of potassium chlorate, oxalic aci and sulphuric acid is heated. During th reaction which element undergoes maximu change in the oxidation number?

(a) S (b) H

(c) Cl (d) C *(2012*

10. Oxidation numbers of P in PO_4^{3-}, of S in SO and that of Cr in $Cr_2O_7^{2-}$ are respectively

(a) +3, +6 and +5 (b) +5, +3 and +6

(c) –3, +6 and +6 (d) +5, +6 and +6

(200

11. Number of moles of MnO_4^- required to oxidi one mole of ferrous oxalate completely in acid medium will be

(a) 7.5 moles (b) 0.2 moles

(c) 0.6 moles (d) 0.4 moles.

(200

12. Which is the best description of the behaviour of bromine in the reaction given below?
$H_2O + Br_2 \rightarrow HOBr + HBr$
(a) Proton acceptor only
(b) Both oxidised and reduced
(c) Oxidised only
(d) Reduced only *(2004)*

13. The oxidation states of sulphur in the anions SO_3^{2-}, $S_2O_4^{2-}$ and $S_2O_6^{2-}$ follow the order
(a) $S_2O_4^{2-} < SO_3^{2-} < S_2O_6^{2-}$
(b) $SO_3^{2-} < S_2O_4^{2-} < S_2O_6^{2-}$
(c) $S_2O_4^{2-} < S_2O_6^{2-} < SO_3^{2-}$
(d) $S_2O_6^{2-} < S_2O_4^{2-} < SO_3^{2-}$ *(2003)*

14. Oxidation state of Fe in Fe_3O_4 is
(a) $\frac{5}{4}$ (b) $\frac{4}{5}$
(c) $\frac{3}{2}$ (d) $\frac{8}{3}$ *(1999)*

15. Which of the following is redox reaction?
(a) Evaporation of H_2O
(b) Both oxidation and reduction
(c) H_2SO_4 with NaOH
(d) In atmosphere O_3 from O_2 by lighting. *(1997)*

16. The oxide, which cannot act as a reducing agent is
(a) CO_2 (b) ClO_2
(c) NO_2 (d) SO_2 *(1995)*

17. Which substance is serving as a reducing agent in the following reaction?
$14H^+ + Cr_2O_7^{2-} + 3Ni \rightarrow 7H_2O + 2Cr^{3+} + 3Ni^{2+}$
(a) H^+ (b) $Cr_2O_7^{2-}$
(c) H_2O (d) Ni *(1994)*

18. The oxidation state of I in $H_4IO_6^-$ is
(a) + 1 (b) – 1
(c) + 7 (d) + 5 *(1994)*

Answer Key

1.	(d)	**2.**	(a)	**3.**	(b)	**4.**	(d)	**5.**	(c)	**6.**	(c)	**7.**	(c)	**8.**	(b)	**9.**	(c)	**10.**	(d)
11.	(d)	**12.**	(b)	**13.**	(a)	**14.**	(d)	**15.**	(b)	**16.**	(a)	**17.**	(d)	**18.**	(c)				

EXPLANATIONS

1. (d) : For a reaction to be spontaneous, E°_{cell} should be positive.

$HBrO \longrightarrow Br_2 \quad E^\circ = 1.595\ V$, SRP (cathode)

$HBrO \longrightarrow BrO_3^- \quad E^\circ = -1.5\ V$, SOP (anode)

$2HBrO \longrightarrow Br_2 + BrO_3^-$

E°_{cell} = SRP (cathode) – SRP (anode)

$= 1.595 - 1.5 = 0.095\ V$

$E^\circ_{cell} > 0 \Rightarrow \Delta G^\circ < 0$ (spontaneous)

2. (a) : $\overset{+5}{HNO_3}, \overset{+2}{NO}, \overset{0}{N_2}, \overset{-3}{NH_4Cl}$

3. (b) : The correct balanced equation is

$2MnO_4^- + 5C_2O_4^{2-} + 16H^+ \longrightarrow 2Mn^{2+} + 10CO_2 + 8H_2O$

4. (d) : $CaF_2 + H_2SO_4 \rightarrow CaSO_4 + 2HF$

Here, the oxidation state of every atom remains the same so, it is not a redox reaction.

5. (c) : Both $FeCl_2$ and $SnCl_2$ are reducing agents with low oxidation numbers.

6. (c) :

Increase in oxidation state (reducing agent)

$\overset{-1}{H_2O_2} + O_3 \longrightarrow H_2O + 2\overset{0}{O_2}$

Increase in oxidation state (reducing agent)

$\overset{-1}{H_2O_2} + \overset{+1}{Ag_2O} \longrightarrow 2\overset{0}{Ag} + H_2O + \overset{0}{O_2}$

Decrease in oxidation state

H_2O_2 acts as reducing agent in all those reactions in which O_2 is evolved.

7. (c) : CrO_5 has butterfly structure having two peroxo bonds.

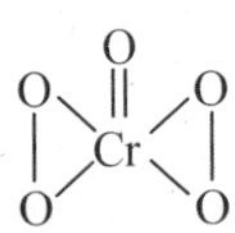

Peroxo oxygen has –1 oxidation state.

Let oxidation state of Cr be 'x'

$CrO_5 : x + 4(-1) + 1(-2) = 0 \Rightarrow x = +6$

8. (b) :

$3\overset{0}{Cl_2} + \underset{\text{(hot and conc.)}}{6NaOH} \longrightarrow 5Na\overset{-1}{Cl} + Na\overset{+5}{Cl}O_3 + 3H_2O$

This is an example of disproportionation reaction and oxidation state of chlorine changes from 0 to –1 and +5.

9. (c) : $K\overset{+1}{}\overset{+5}{Cl}\overset{-2}{O_3} + (COOH)_2 + H_2\overset{+6}{S}O_4 \longrightarrow K_2\overset{+6}{S}O_4 + K\overset{-1}{Cl} + CO_2 + H_2O$

Maximum change in oxidation number of chlorine, *i.e.*, from +5 to –1.

10. (d) : Let oxidation number of P in PO_4^{3-} be x.

$\therefore\ x + 4(-2) = -3 \Rightarrow x = +5$

Let oxidation number of S in SO_4^{2-} be y.

$\therefore\ y + 4(-2) = -2 \Rightarrow y = +6$

Let oxidation number of Cr in $Cr_2O_7^{2-}$ be z.

$\therefore\ 2z + 7(-2) = -2 \Rightarrow z = +6$

11. (d) : $[5e^- + MnO_4^- + 8H^+ \rightarrow Mn^{2+} + 4H_2O\ ..(i)] \times 2$

$[C_2O_4^{2-} \rightarrow 2e^- + 2CO_2\ ....(ii)] \times 5$

$2MnO_4^- + 16H^+ + 5C_2O_4^{2-} \rightarrow 2Mn^{2+} + 10CO_2$

2 moles of MnO_4^- required to oxidise 5 moles of oxalate.

$\therefore$ Number of moles of MnO_4^- required to oxidise 1 mole of oxalate = 2/5 = 0.4

12. (b) : $H_2O + \overset{0}{Br_2} \rightarrow HO\overset{+1}{Br} + H\overset{-1}{Br}$

In the above reaction the oxidation number of Br_2 increases from zero (in Br_2) to +1 (in HOBr) and decreases from zero (in Br_2) to –1 (in HBr). Thus Br_2 is oxidised as well as reduced and hence it is a redox reaction.

13. (a) : $SO_3^{2-} : x + (-2)3 = -2$

or $x - 6 = -2$ or $x = +4$

$S_2O_4^{2-} : 2x + (-2)4 = -2$

or $2x - 8 = -2$ or $2x = +6 \therefore x = +3$

$S_2O_6^{2-} : 2x + (-2)6 = -2$

or, $2x - 12 = -2$ or $2x = +10 \therefore x = +5$

Oxidation states follow the order:

$S_2O_4^{2-} < SO_3^{2-} < S_2O_6^{2-}$

14. (d) : $Fe_3O_4 \rightarrow 3x + 4(-2) = 0 \Rightarrow x = +\frac{8}{3}$

15. (b) : Redox reactions are those chemical reactions which involve transfer of electrons from one chemical species to another.

16. (a) : Since carbon is in maximum state of + 4, therefore carbon dioxide (CO_2) cannot act as a reducing agent.

17. (d) : Since the oxidation number of Ni increases from 0 to 2, therefore it acts as a reducing agent.

18. (c) : Let x = Oxidation state of I. Since oxidation state of H = + 1 and oxidation state of O = – 2, therefore for $H_4IO_6^-$, we get

$(4 \times 1) + x + (6 \times -2) = -1$

or $x = +7$

Chapter 9

Hydrogen

1. Which of the following statements about hydrogen is incorrect?
(a) Hydronium ion, H_3O^+ exists freely in solution.
(b) Dihydrogen does not act as a reducing agent.
(c) Hydrogen has three isotopes of which tritium is the most common.
(d) Hydrogen never acts as cation in ionic salts.
(NEET-I 2016)

2. Some statements about heavy water are given below:
(i) Heavy water is used as a moderator in nuclear reactors.
(ii) Heavy water is more associated than ordinary water.
(iii) Heavy water is more effective solvent than ordinary water.
Which of the above statements are correct?
(a) (i) and (ii) (b) (i), (ii) and (iii)
(c) (ii) and (iii) (d) (i) and (iii)
(Mains 2010)

3. The structure of H_2O_2 is
(a) spherical (b) non-planar
(c) planar (d) linear
(2003)

4. Which one of the following pairs of substances on reaction will not evolve H_2 gas?
(a) Copper and HCl (aqueous)
(b) Iron and steam
(c) Iron and H_2SO_4 (aqueous)
(d) Sodium and ethyl alcohol
(1998)

5. The volume strength of 1.5 N H_2O_2 solution is
(a) 8.8 (b) 8.4
(c) 4.8 (d) 5.2
(1997, 1996)

6. The O – O – H bond angle in H_2O_2 is
(a) 106° (b) 109°28′
(c) 120° (d) 97°
(1994)

7. Which of the following groups of ions makes the water hard?
(a) Sodium and bicarbonate
(b) Magnesium and chloride
(c) Potassium and sulphate
(d) Ammonium and chloride
(1994)

8. One would expect proton to have very large
(a) charge
(b) ionization potential
(c) hydration energy
(d) radius.
(1993)

9. At its melting point ice is lighter than water because
(a) H_2O molecules are more closely packed in solid state
(b) ice crystals have hollow hexagonal arrangement of H_2O molecules.
(c) on melting of ice the H_2O molecules shrinks in size
(d) ice forms mostly heavy water on first melting.
(1992)

10. Hydrogen peroxide molecules are
(a) monoatomic and form X_2^{2-} ions
(b) diatomic and form X^- ions
(c) diatomic and form X_2^- ions
(d) monoatomic and form X^- ions.
(1991)

11. The ionization of hydrogen atom would give rise to
(a) hydride ion (b) hydronium ion
(c) proton (d) hydroxyl ion.
(1990)

12. Which of the following metal evolves hydrogen on reacting with cold dilute HNO_3?
(a) Mg (b) Al (c) Fe (d) Cu
(1989)

13. Which of the following is the true structure of H_2O_2?

(a) H—O—O—H
(b) 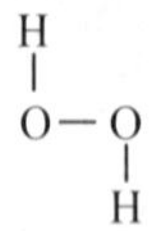
(c) 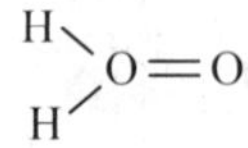
(d) 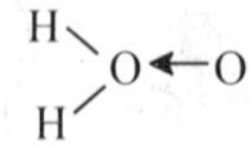
(1989)

14. The reaction of H_2O_2 with H_2S is an example of .... reaction.
(a) addition (b) oxidation
(c) reduction (d) acidic
(1988)

Answer Key

1. (b, c)	**2.** (a)	**3.** (b)	**4.** (a)	**5.** (b)	**6.** (d)	**7.** (b)	**8.** (c)	**9.** (b)	**10.** (b)
11. (c)	**12.** (a)	**13.** (b)	**14.** (b)						

EXPLANATIONS

1. **(b, c)** : Dihydrogen acts as a powerful reducing agent and reduces metal oxides such as CuO, ZnO, PbO and Fe_3O_4 to their respective metals.

$CuO + H_2 \rightarrow Cu + H_2O$

$ZnO + H_2 \rightarrow Zn + H_2O$

$Fe_3O_4 + 4H_2 \rightarrow 3Fe + 4H_2O$

Hydrogen has three isotopes of which protium is the most common and tritium is radioactive.

2. **(a)** : Heavy water is used for slowing down the speed of neutrons in nuclear reactors, hence used as moderator. Boiling point of heavy water is greater (374.42 K) than that of ordinary water (373 K), hence heavy water is more associated. Dielectric constant of ordinary water is greater than that of heavy water, hence ordinary water is a better solvent.

3. **(b)** : In H_2O_2, the O–H groups are not in the same plane. So it has non-planar structure. It has a half-opened book structure in which the two O–H groups lie on the two pages of the book. The angle between two pages of the book is 94° and H–O–O bond angle is 97°.

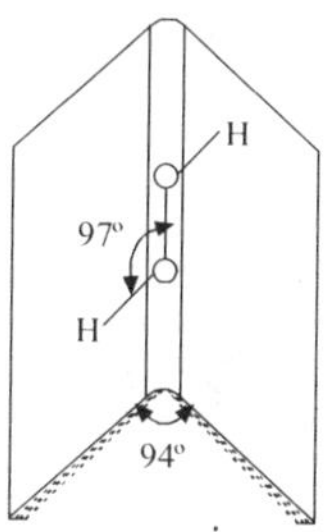

4. **(a)** : Copper is a noble metal, as it lies below hydrogen in the electrochemical series. Therefore it can't displace hydrogen from dilute HCl. While iron and sodium lie above hydrogen in the electrochemical series, so they can liberate H_2 either from steam or H_2SO_4 solution.

$C_2H_5-OH + Na \rightarrow C_2H_5-ONa + 1/2H_2$

$Fe + H_2SO_4 \rightarrow FeSO_4 + H_2$

$3Fe + 4H_2O \rightarrow Fe_3O_4 + 4H_2$

5. **(b)** : Normality $(N) = 1.5$

We know that equivalent weight of H_2O_2 is 17 and strength of H_2O_2 = Normality × Equivalent weight

$= 1.5 \times 17 = 25.5$

$2H_2O_2 \rightarrow 2H_2O + O_2$

$(2 \times 34 = 68\text{ g}) \quad (22.4\text{ L})$

Since 68 grams of H_2O_2 produces 22.4 litres oxygen at NTP, therefore 25.5 grams of H_2O_2 will produce

$= \frac{22.4}{68} \times 25.5 = 8.4$ litre of oxygen.

Thus, volume strength of given H_2O_2 solution is 8.4.

6. **(d)** : Bond angle of O – O – H in H_2O_2 is 97°.

7. **(b)** : Hardness of water, due to the presence of chlorides and sulphates of Ca and Mg is called permanent hardness. Hence, hard water will consist of Mg^{2+} and Cl^- ions.

8. **(c)** : Proton (H^+) ion being very small in size would have very large hydration energy.

9. **(b)** : When ice melts, its molecules move into the holes or open spaces and comes closer to each other than they were in solid state. Thus, ice has lower density than water and there is contraction in volume.

10. **(b)** : H_2O_2 is diatomic and forms $H^+ + HO_2^- (X^-)$ (hydroperoxide ion).

11. **(c)** : It gives rise to proton.

$H_{(g)} \rightarrow \underset{\text{Proton}}{H^+} + e^-$

12. **(a)** : Mg reacts with nitric acid to give $Mg(NO_3)_2$ and evolves H_2

$Mg + 2HNO_3 \rightarrow Mg(NO_3)_2 + H_2$

13. **(b)** : 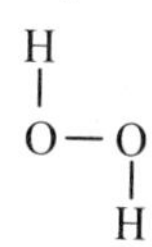 is the true structure.

14. **(b)** : It is an example of oxidation reaction.

$H_2S + H_2O_2 \rightarrow 2H_2O + S$

Chapter 10
s-Block Elements

1. Among CaH_2, BeH_2, BaH_2, the order of ionic character is
   (a) $BeH_2 < CaH_2 < BaH_2$
   (b) $CaH_2 < BeH_2 < BaH_2$
   (c) $BeH_2 < BaH_2 < CaH_2$
   (d) $BaH_2 < BeH_2 < CaH_2$ *(NEET 2018)*

2. Magnesium reacts with an element (X) to form an ionic compound. If the ground state electronic configuration of (X) is $1s^2\ 2s^2\ 2p^3$, the simplest formula for this compound is
   (a) Mg_2X_3 (b) MgX_2
   (c) Mg_2X (d) Mg_3X_2
   (NEET 2018)

3. Ionic mobility of which of the following alkali metal ions is lowest when aqueous solution of their salts are put under an electric field?
   (a) K (b) Rb
   (c) Li (d) Na
   (NEET 2017)

4. The suspension of slaked lime in water is known as
   (a) lime water (b) quick lime
   (c) milk of lime
   (d) aqueous solution of slaked lime.
   (NEET-II 2016)

5. In context with beryllium, which one of the following statements is incorrect?
   (a) It is rendered passive by nitric acid.
   (b) It forms Be_2C.
   (c) Its salts rarely hydrolyse.
   (d) Its hydride is electron-deficient and polymeric. *(NEET-II 2016)*

6. Which of the following statements is false?
   (a) Ca^{2+} ions are not important in maintaining the regular beating of the heart.
   (b) Mg^{2+} ions are important in the green parts of the plants.
   (c) Mg^{2+} ions form a complex with ATP.
   (d) Ca^{2+} ions are important in blood clotting.
   (NEET-I 2016)

7. The product obtained as a result of a reaction of nitrogen with CaC_2 is
   (a) $CaCN_3$ (b) Ca_2CN
   (c) $Ca(CN)_2$ (d) CaCN
   (NEET-I 2016)

8. On heating which of the following releases CO_2 most easily?
   (a) Na_2CO_3 (b) $MgCO_3$
   (c) $CaCO_3$ (d) K_2CO_3
   (2015)

9. 20.0 g of a magnesium carbonate sample decomposes on heating to give carbon dioxide and 8.0 g magnesium oxide. What will be the percentage purity of magnesium carbonate in the sample?
   (At. wt. of Mg = 24)
   (a) 96 (b) 60
   (c) 84 (d) 75 *(2015)*

10. The function of "Sodium pump" is a biological process operating in each and every cell of all animals. Which of the following biologically important ions is also a constituent of this pump?
    (a) K^+ (b) Fe^{2+}
    (c) Ca^{2+} (d) Mg^{2+}
    (2015, Cancelled)

11. Solubility of the alkaline earth metal sulphates in water decreases in the sequence
    (a) Sr > Ca > Mg > Ba
    (b) Ba > Mg > Sr > Ca
    (c) Mg > Ca > Sr > Ba
    (d) Ca > Sr > Ba > Mg *(2015, Cancelled)*

12. In Castner-Kellner cell for production of sodium hydroxide
    (a) brine is electrolyzed using graphite electrodes

(b) molten sodium chloride is electrolysed
(c) sodium amalgam is formed at mercury cathode
(d) brine is electrolyzed with Pt electrodes *(Karnataka NEET 2013)*

13. Which one of the alkali metals, forms only, the normal oxide, M_2O on heating in air?
(a) Rb (b) K
(c) Li (d) Na *(2012)*

14. The ease of adsorption of the hydrated alkali metal ions on an ion-exchange resins follows the order:
(a) $Li^+ < K^+ < Na^+ < Rb^+$
(b) $Rb^+ < K^+ < Na^+ < Li^+$
(c) $K^+ < Na^+ < Rb^+ < Li^+$
(d) $Na^+ < Li^+ < K^+ < Rb^+$ *(2012)*

15. Which of the following compounds has the lowest melting point?
(a) $CaCl_2$ (b) $CaBr_2$
(c) CaI_2 (d) CaF_2 *(2011)*

16. Which one of the following is present as an active ingredient in bleaching powder for bleaching action?
(a) $CaOCl_2$ (b) $Ca(OCl)_2$
(c) CaO_2Cl (d) $CaCl_2$ *(2011)*

17. Match List-I with List-II for the compositions of substances and select the correct answer using the code given:

List-I (Substances)	List-II (Composition)
(A) Plaster of Paris	(i) $CaSO_4 \cdot 2H_2O$
(B) Epsomite	(ii) $CaSO_4 \cdot 1/2\ H_2O$
(C) Kieserite	(iii) $MgSO_4 \cdot 7H_2O$
(D) Gypsum	(iv) $MgSO_4 \cdot H_2O$
	(v) $CaSO_4$

(a) (A)-(iii), (B)-(iv), (C)-(i), (D)-(ii)
(b) (A)-(ii), (B)-(iii), (C)-(iv), (D)-(i)
(c) (A)-(i), (B)-(ii), (C)-(iii), (D)-(v)
(d) (A)-(iv), (B)-(iii), (C)-(ii), (D)-(i) *(Mains 2011)*

18. Which of the following alkaline earth metal sulphates has hydration enthalpy higher than the lattice enthalpy?
(a) $CaSO_4$ (b) $BeSO_4$
(c) $BaSO_4$ (d) $SrSO_4$ *(2010)*

19. Property of the alkaline earth metals that increases with their atomic number
(a) solubility of their hydroxides in water
(b) solubility of their sulphates in water
(c) ionization energy
(d) electronegativity *(2010)*

20. Which one of the following compounds is a peroxide?
(a) KO_2 (b) BaO_2
(c) MnO_2 (d) NO_2 *(2010)*

21. The compound *A* on heating gives a colourless gas and a residue that is dissolved in water to obtain *B*. Excess of CO_2 is bubbled through aqueous solution of *B*, *C* is formed which is recovered in the solid form. Solid *C* on gentle heating gives back *A*. The compound is
(a) $CaCO_3$ (b) Na_2CO_3
(c) K_2CO_3 (d) $CaSO_4 \cdot 2H_2O$ *(Mains 2010)*

22. In the case of alkali metals, the covalent character decreases in the order
(a) $MF > MCl > MBr > MI$
(b) $MF > MCl > MI > MBr$
(c) $MI > MBr > MCl > MF$
(d) $MCl > MI > MBr > MF$ *(2009)*

23. Which of the following oxides is not expected to react with sodium hydroxide?
(a) CaO (b) SiO_2
(c) BeO (d) B_2O_3 *(2009)*

24. Equimolar solutions of the following were prepared in water separately. Which one of the solutions will record the highest pH?
(a) $MgCl_2$ (b) $CaCl_2$
(c) $SrCl_2$ (d) $BaCl_2$ *(2008)*

25. The sequence of ionic mobility in aqueous solution is
(a) $Rb^+ > K^+ > Cs^+ > Na^+$
(b) $Na^+ > K^+ > Rb^+ > Cs^+$
(c) $K^+ > Na^+ > Rb^+ > Cs^+$
(d) $Cs^+ > Rb^+ > K^+ > Na^+$ *(2008)*

26. The alkali metals form salt-like hydrides by the direct synthesis at elevated temperature. The thermal stability of these hydrides decreases in which of the following orders?
(a) NaH > LiH > KH > RbH > CsH
(b) LiH > NaH > KH > RbH > CsH
(c) CsH > RbH > KH > NaH > LiH
(d) KH > NaH > LiH > CsH > RbH *(2008)*

27. The correct order of increasing thermal stability of K_2CO_3, $MgCO_3$, $CaCO_3$ and $BeCO_3$ is
(a) $BeCO_3 < MgCO_3 < CaCO_3 < K_2CO_3$
(b) $MgCO_3 < BeCO_3 < CaCO_3 < K_2CO_3$
(c) $K_2CO_3 < MgCO_3 < CaCO_3 < BeCO_3$
(d) $BeCO_3 < MgCO_3 < K_2CO_3 < CaCO_3$
(2007)

28. In which of the following the hydration energy is higher than the lattice energy?
(a) $MgSO_4$ (b) $RaSO_4$
(c) $SrSO_4$ (d) $BaSO_4$ *(2007)*

29. The correct order of the mobility of the alkali metal ions in aqueous solution is
(a) $Rb^+ > K^+ > Na^+ > Li^+$
(b) $Li^+ > Na^+ > K^+ > Rb^+$
(c) $Na^+ > K^+ > Rb^+ > Li^+$
(d) $K^+ > Rb^+ > Na^+ > Li^+$ *(2006)*

30. The correct sequence of increasing covalent character is represented by
(a) $LiCl < NaCl < BeCl_2$
(b) $BeCl_2 < LiCl < NaCl$
(c) $NaCl < LiCl < BeCl_2$
(d) $BeCl_2 < NaCl < LiCl$ *(2005)*

31. A solid compound *X* on heating gives CO_2 gas and a residue. The residue mixed with water forms *Y*. On passing an excess of CO_2 through *Y* in water, a clear solution *Z* is obtained. On boiling *Z*, compound *X* is reformed. The compound *X* is
(a) $Ca(HCO_3)_2$ (b) $CaCO_3$
(c) Na_2CO_3 (d) K_2CO_3. *(2004)*

32. In which of the following processes, fused sodium hydroxide is electrolysed at a 330°C temperature for extraction of sodium?
(a) Castner's process (b) Down's process
(c) Cyanide process (d) Both (b) and (c).
(2000)

33. When a substance (*A*) reacts with water it produces a combustible gas (*B*) and a solution of substance (*C*) in water. When another substance (*D*) reacts with this solution of (*C*), it also produces the same gas (*B*) on warming but (*D*) can produce gas (*B*) on reaction with dilute sulphuric acid at room temperature. Substance (*A*) imparts a deep golden yellow colour to a smokeless flame of Bunsen burner. Then (*A*), (*B*), (*C*) and (*D*) respectively are
(a) Ca, H_2, $Ca(OH)_2$, Sn
(b) K, H_2, KOH, Al
(c) Na, H_2, NaOH, Zn
(d) CaC_2, C_2H_2, $Ca(OH)_2$, Fe *(1998)*

34. Calcium is obtained by the
(a) electrolysis of solution of calcium chloride in water
(b) electrolysis of molten anhydrous calcium chloride
(c) roasting of limestone
(d) reduction of calcium chloride with carbon.
(1997)

35. Sodium is made by the electrolysis of a molten mixture of about 40% NaCl and 60% $CaCl_2$ because
(a) Ca^{++} can reduce NaCl to Na
(b) Ca^{++} can displace Na from NaCl
(c) $CaCl_2$ helps in conduction of electricity
(d) this mixture has a lower melting point than NaCl. *(1995)*

36. The solubility in water of sulphate down the Be group is Be > Mg > Ca > Sr > Ba. This is due to
(a) decreasing lattice energy
(b) high heat of solvation for smaller ions like Be^{2+}
(c) increase in melting points
(d) increasing molecular weight. *(1995)*

37. Identify the correct statement.
(a) Plaster of Paris can be obtained by hydration of gypsum.
(b) Plaster of Paris is obtained by partial oxidation of gypsum.
(c) Gypsum contains a lower percentage of calcium than Plaster of Paris.
(d) Gypsum is obtained by heating Plaster of Paris. *(1995)*

38. Which of the following is known as fusion mixture?
(a) Mixture of $Na_2CO_3 + NaHCO_3$
(b) $Na_2CO_3.10H_2O$
(c) Mixture of $K_2CO_3 + Na_2CO_3$
(d) $NaHCO_3$ *(1994)*

39. All the following substances react with water. The pair that gives the same gaseous product is
(a) K and KO_2 (b) Na and Na_2O_2
(c) Ca and CaH_2 (d) Ba and BaO_2.
(1994)

40. Among the following oxides, the one which is most basic is

(a) ZnO (b) MgO
(c) Al_2O_3 (d) N_2O_5 *(1994)*

41. Which of the following metal ions play an important role in muscle contraction?

(a) K^+ (b) Na^+
(c) Mg^{2+} (d) Ca^{2+} *(1994)*

42. Which of the following statement is false?

(a) Strontium decomposes water readily than beryllium.
(b) Barium carbonate melts at a higher temperature than calcium carbonate.
(c) Barium hydroxide is more soluble in water than magnesium hydroxide.
(d) Beryllium hydroxide is more basic than barium hydroxide. *(1994)*

43. Which one of the following has minimum value of cation/anion ratio?

(a) NaCl (b) KCl
(c) $MgCl_2$ (d) CaF_2 *(1993)*

44. Which of the following has largest size?

(a) Na (b) Na^+
(c) Na^- (d) Can't be predicted. *(1993)*

45. Which compound will show the highest lattice energy?

(a) RbF (b) CsF
(c) NaF (d) KF *(1993)*

46. Strongest bond is in between

(a) CsF
(b) NaCl
(c) both (a) and (b)
(d) none of the above. *(1993)*

47. Electronic configuration of calcium atom may be written as

(a) [Ne] $4p^2$ (b) [Ar] $4s^2$
(c) [Ne] $4s^2$ (d) [Ar] $4p^2$ *(1992)*

48. Which one of the following substance is used in the laboratory for fast drying of neutral gases?

(a) Phosphorus pentoxide
(b) Active charcoal
(c) Anhydrous calcium chloride
(d) Na_3PO_4 *(1992)*

49. Compared with the alkaline earth metals, the alkali metals exhibit

(a) smaller ionic radii
(b) highest boiling points
(c) greater hardness
(d) lower ionization energies. *(1990)*

50. Washing soda has formula

(a) $Na_2CO_3.7H_2O$ (b) $Na_2CO_3.10H_2O$
(c) $Na_2CO_3.3H_2O$ (d) Na_2CO_3 *(1990)*

51. Which one of the following properties of alkali metals increases in magnitude as the atomic number rises?

(a) Ionic radius (b) Melting point
(c) Electronegativity
(d) First ionization energy *(1989)*

52. Which of the following atoms will have the smallest size?

(a) Mg (b) Na
(c) Be (d) Li *(1989)*

Answer Key

1.	(a)	**2.**	(d)	**3.**	(c)	**4.**	(c)	**5.**	(c)	**6.**	(a)	**7.**	(c)	**8.**	(b)	**9.**	(c)	**10.**	(a)
11.	(c)	**12.**	(c)	**13.**	(c)	**14.**	(b)	**15.**	(c)	**16.**	(b)	**17.**	(b)	**18.**	(b)	**19.**	(a)	**20.**	(b)
21.	(a)	**22.**	(c)	**23.**	(a)	**24.**	(d)	**25.**	(d)	**26.**	(b)	**27.**	(a)	**28.**	(a)	**29.**	(a)	**30.**	(c)
31.	(b)	**32.**	(a)	**33.**	(c)	**34.**	(b)	**35.**	(d)	**36.**	(b)	**37.**	(c)	**38.**	(c)	**39.**	(c)	**40.**	(b)
41.	(d)	**42.**	(d)	**43.**	(c)	**44.**	(c)	**45.**	(c)	**46.**	(a)	**47.**	(b)	**48.**	(a)	**49.**	(d)	**50.**	(b)
51.	(a)	**52.**	(c)																

EXPLANATIONS

1. **(a) :** $BeH_2 < CaH_2 < BaH_2$
On moving down the group, metallic character of metals increases. So, ionic character of metal hydrides increases. Hence, BeH_2 will be least ionic.

2. **(d) :** Electronic configuration of X is $1s^2, 2s^2, 2p^3$.
So, valency of X will be 3.
Magnesium ion = Mg^{2+}

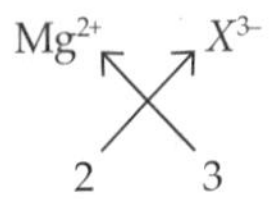

Formula : Mg_3X_2

3. **(c) :** The hydration enthalpy of alkali metal ions decreases with increase in ionic sizes *i.e.*,
$Li^+ > Na^+ > K^+ > Rb^+ > Cs^+$
Hence, lithium having maximum degree of hydration will be least mobile.
The order of ionic mobility is
$[Li_{(aq)}]^+ < [Na_{(aq)}]^+ < [K_{(aq)}]^+ < [Rb_{(aq)}]^+$

4. **(c) :** $\underset{\text{Quick lime}}{CaO} + H_2O \longrightarrow \underset{\text{Slaked lime}}{Ca(OH)_2} + \text{Heat}$
This process is known as slaking of lime.
The paste of lime in water (*i.e.*; suspension) is called milk of lime while the filtered and clear solution is known as lime water.

5. **(c) :** Beryllium salts are readily hydrolysed.

6. **(a) :** Ca^{2+} ions are required to trigger the contraction of muscles and to maintain the regular beating of the heart.

7. **(c) :** Read $Ca(CN)_2$ as $CaCN_2$.
$$CaC_2 + N_2 \longrightarrow \underset{\text{Nitrolim}}{CaCN_2} + C$$

8. **(b) :** Stability of carbonates increases down the group with increase in the size of metal ion. Also the alkali metal carbonates are more stable than alkaline earth metal carbonates.
Hence, $MgCO_3$ is least stable and it releases CO_2 most easily.
$$MgCO_3 \xrightarrow{\Delta} MgO + CO_2$$

9. **(c) :** $\underset{84\text{ g}}{MgCO_{3(s)}} \xrightarrow{\Delta} \underset{40\text{ g}}{MgO_{(s)}} + CO_{2(g)}$
84 g of $MgCO_3 \equiv 40$ g of MgO
$$\therefore \quad 20 \text{ g of } MgCO_3 \equiv \frac{40}{84} \times 20 = 9.52 \text{ g of MgO}$$
Actual yield = 8 g of MgO
$$\therefore \quad \% \text{ purity} = \frac{8}{9.52} \times 100 = 84\%$$

10. **(a)**

11. **(c) :** Solubility of alkaline earth metal sulphates decreases down the group because hydration energy decreases.

12. **(c) :** In Castner-Kellner cell, sodium amalgam is formed at mercury cathode.

13. **(c) :** When alkali metals heated in atmosphere of oxygen, the alkali metals ignite and form oxides. On combustion Li forms Li_2O; sodium gives the peroxide Na_2O_2 and potassium and rubidium give super oxide (MO_2).

14. **(b)**

15. **(c) :** As the covalent character in compound increases and ionic character decreases, melting point of the compound decreases. So, CaI_2 has the highest covalent character and lowest melting point.

16. **(b) :** Active ingredient in bleaching powder for bleaching action is $Ca(OCl)_2$.

17. **(b) :**

Plaster of Paris	- $CaSO_4 \cdot \frac{1}{2} H_2O$
Epsomite	- $MgSO_4 \cdot 7H_2O$
Kieserite	- $MgSO_4 \cdot H_2O$
Gypsum	- $CaSO_4 \cdot 2H_2O$

18. **(b) :** The hydration enthalpy of $BeSO_4$ is higher than its lattice energy. Within group 2, the hydration energy decreases down the group while lattice energy is almost the same.

19. **(a) :** The solubility of an ionic compound depends on two factors :
(a) lattice energy, and (b) hydration energy
In case of alkaline metal hydroxides, the lattice energy decreases as we move down the group. This decrease is more than the decrease in the hydration energy down the group.

20. **(b) :** BaO_2 has peroxide linkage.

21. **(a) :** The reactions can be summarised as follows:

$A \xrightarrow{\Delta}$ colourless gas + residue

Residue + $H_2O \rightarrow B \xrightarrow{\text{excess } CO_2} C \xrightarrow{\Delta} A$

This is possible only when A is $CaCO_3$. The reactions are as follows :

$$\underset{(A)}{CaCO_3} \xrightarrow{\Delta} \underset{\text{(colourless gas)}}{CO_2} + \underset{\text{(residue)}}{CaO}$$

$$CaO + H_2O \longrightarrow \underset{(B)}{Ca(OH)_2} \xrightarrow[\text{(excess)}]{CO_2} \underset{(C)}{Ca(HCO_3)_2} \xrightarrow{\Delta} \underset{(A)}{CaCO_3}$$

22. (c) : Alkali metals are highly electropositive and halogens are electronegative. Thus for the halides of a given alkali metal, the covalent character decreases with increase in electronegativity of halogens.

∴ Order of covalent character of halides is $MI > MBr > MCl > MF$.

23. (a) : CaO being a basic oxide does not react with NaOH, however SiO_2 (acidic oxide), BeO (amphoteric oxide) and B_2O_3 (acidic oxide) react with NaOH.

24. (d) : Equimolar solutions of the given chlorides when prepared in water forms their respective hydroxides.

$Be(OH)_2$ is amphoteric, but the hydroxides of other alkaline earth metals are basic. The basic strength increases down the group. Hence higher the basic character higher will be the pH.

25. (d) : Smaller the size of cation, higher will be the hydration and its effective size will increase and hence mobility in aqueous solution will decrease. Larger size ions have more ionic mobility due to less hydration. Thus the degree of hydration of M^+ ions decreases from Li^+ to Cs^+. Consequently the radii of the hydrated ion decreases from Li^+ to Cs^+. Hence the ionic conductance of these hydrated ions increases from Li^+ to Cs^+.

26. (b) : The ionic character of the bonds in hydrides increases from LiH to CsH so thermal stability of these hydrides decreases in the order of

LiH > NaH > KH > RbH > CsH

27. (a) : In all cases, for a particular set of *e.g.* Group 1 or Group 2 compounds, the thermal stability increases down the group as the ionic radius of the cation increases, and its polarising power decreases.

Group 1 compounds tend to be more thermally stable than group 2 compounds because the cation has a smaller charge and a larger ionic radius, and so a lower polarising power, particularly when adjacent metals on the same period are compared. Hence, the order of increasing thermal stability of K_2CO_3, $MgCO_3$, $CaCO_3$ and $BeCO_3$ is $BeCO_3 < MgCO_3 < CaCO_3 < K_2CO_3$.

28. (a) : When hydration energy exceeds lattice energy, the compound becomes soluble in water. The solubility of alkaline earth metal sulphates decreases in the order :

$$\underset{\text{very high}}{BeSO_4} > \underset{\text{high}}{MgSO_4} > \underset{\text{sparingly soluble}}{CaSO_4} > \underbrace{SrSO_4 > BaSO_4 > RaSO_4}_{\text{almost insoluble}}$$

The solubilities of $BeSO_4$ and $MgSO_4$ are due to high energy of solvation of smaller Be^{2+} and Mg^{2+} ions.

29. (a) : The alkali metal ions exist as hydrated ions $M^+(H_2O)_x$ in the aqueous solution. The degree of hydration, however, decreases with the ionic size as we move from Li^+ to Cs^+. In other words, Li^+ ion is most highly hydrated. *e.g.* $[Li(H_2O)_6]^+$. Since the mobility of ion is inversely proportional to the size of their hydrated ions, therefore, amongst the alkali metal ions, lithium has the lowest ionic mobility.

$Rb^+_{(aq)} > K^+_{(aq)} > Na^+_{(aq)} > Li^+_{(aq)}$

30. (c) : Covalent character in a compound is found by Fajan's Rule.

Fajan's Rule :

(i) Greater the size of the cation more will be the ionic character and

(ii) Greater the size of anion more will be its covalent character and charge on the cation is dominant over the size of the cation.

(iii) Greater the charge on the cation more will be its covalent character.

Hence, $BeCl_2 > LiCl > NaCl$ (In Covalent character).

31. (b) : The given compound X must be $CaCO_3$. It can be explained by following reactions:

$$CaCO_3 \xrightarrow{\Delta} CaO + CO_2\uparrow$$

$$CaO + H_2O \rightarrow \underset{(Y)}{Ca(OH)_2}$$

$$Ca(OH)_2 + 2CO_2 + H_2O \rightarrow \underset{(Z)}{Ca(HCO_3)_2}$$

$$Ca(HCO_3)_2 \xrightarrow{\Delta} \underset{(X)}{CaCO_3} + CO_2\uparrow + H_2O$$

32. (a) : In Castner's process, for production of sodium metal, sodium hydroxide (NaOH) is electrolysed at temperature 330°C.

33. (c) : Only 'Na' imparts golden colour to bunsen flame, therefore, A = Na, $B = H_2$, C = NaOH, D = Zn.

$2Na + 2H_2O \rightarrow 2NaOH + H_2$
(A) (C) (B)

$Zn + 2NaOH \rightarrow Na_2ZnO_2 + H_2$
(D) (C) (B)

$Zn + H_2SO_4 \rightarrow ZnSO_4 + H_2$
(D) (B)

34. (b) : Calcium is obtained by electrolysis of a fused mass consisting six parts calcium chloride and one part calcium fluoride at about 700°C.

$CaCl_2 \rightleftharpoons Ca^{2+} + 2Cl^-$

$2Cl^- \longrightarrow Cl_2 + 2e$

$Ca^{2+} + 2e \longrightarrow Ca$

35. (d) : Sodium is obtained by electrolytic reduction of its chloride. Melting point of chloride of sodium is high so in order to lower its melting point, calcium chloride is added to it.

36. (b) : As we move down the group from $BeSO_4$ to $BaSO_4$ the enthalpy of hydration of the positive ion becomes smaller due to increase in ionic size. Salts of heavier metal ions are less soluble than those of lighter ions.

37. (c) : Gypsum is $CaSO_4 \cdot 2H_2O$ and Plaster of Paris is $(CaSO_4)_2 \cdot H_2O$. Therefore gypsum contains a lower percentage of calcium than Plaster of Paris.

38. (c) : K_2CO_3 and Na_2CO_3 mixture is called as fusion mixture.

39. (c) : The pair which gives the same gaseous product is Ca and CaH_2.

$Ca + 2H_2O \rightarrow Ca(OH)_2 + H_2$

$CaH_2 + 2H_2O \rightarrow Ca(OH)_2 + 2H_2$

Whereas, K gives H_2 while KO_2 gives O_2 and H_2O_2.

$2K + 2H_2O \rightarrow 2KOH + H_2$

$2KO_2 + 2H_2O \rightarrow 2KOH + O_2 + H_2O_2$

Similarly, Na gives H_2, while Na_2O_2 gives H_2O_2.

$2Na + 2H_2O \rightarrow 2NaOH + H_2$

$Na_2O_2 + 2H_2O \rightarrow 2NaOH + H_2O_2$

Likewise Ba gives H_2 while BaO_2 gives H_2O_2.

$Ba + 2H_2O \rightarrow Ba(OH)_2 + H_2$

$BaO_2 + 2H_2O \rightarrow Ba(OH)_2 + H_2O_2$

40. (b) : Al_2O_3 and ZnO are amphoteric. N_2O_5 is strongly acidic.

41. (d) : Calcium is an essential element for the contraction of muscles. In the presence of calcium ions and energy from ATP, actin and myosin (contractile proteins) interact forming actomyosin which causes contraction of muscles.

42. (d) : Beryllium hydroxide although amphoteric, is however less basic than barium hydroxide.

43. (c) : The order of ionic size for given ions will be $K^+ > Ca^{2+} > Mg^{2+}$ and that of $Cl^- > F^-$. Therefore Mg^{2+}/Cl^- has minimum value of cation/anion ratio.

44. (c) : The cations are always smaller than the neutral atom and anions are always larger in size $Na^- > Na > Na^+$

45. (c) : With the same anion, smaller the size of the cation, higher is the lattice energy. Therefore, NaF will show the highest lattice energy among the given compounds.

46. (a) : According to Fajan rules, ionic character increases with increase in size of the cation (Cs > Rb > K > Na) and with decrease in size of the anion (F > Cl > Br > I). Thus, CsF has higher ionic character than NaCl and hence bond in CsF is stronger than in NaCl.

47. (b) : ${}_{20}Ca \longrightarrow 1s^2, 2s^22p^6, 3s^23p^6, 4s^2$

${}_{18}Ar \longrightarrow 1s^2, 2s^2\,2p^6, 3s^23p^6$

hence ${}_{20}Ca \longrightarrow [Ar]4s^2$

48. (a) : P_2O_5 absorbs moisture much readily than anhydrous $CaCl_2$.

49. (d) : The alkali metals are larger in size and have smaller nuclear charge thus they have lower ionization energy in comparison to alkaline earth metals.

50. (b) : $Na_2CO_3.10H_2O$ is washing soda.

51. (a) : In a group, ionic radius increases with increase in atomic number whereas the m.pt. decreases down in a group due to weakening of metallic bond. Similarly, electronegativity and the ionization energy also decreases down the group.

52. (c) : The atomic size decreases within a period from left to right, therefore Li > Be and Na > Mg. The size increases in a group from top to bottom. Hence, the size of Na is greater than Li. Overall order Na > Mg > Li > Be

Thus, Be has smallest size.

Chapter 11

p-Block Elements (Group 13 and 14)

1. Which one of the following elements is unable to form MF_6^{3-} ion?
(a) Ga (b) Al (c) B (d) In
(NEET 2018)

2. It is because of inability of ns^2 electrons of the valence shell to participate in bonding that
(a) Sn^{2+} is oxidising while Pb^{4+} is reducing
(b) Sn^{2+} and Pb^{2+} are both oxidising and reducing
(c) Sn^{4+} is reducing while Pb^{4+} is oxidising
(d) Sn^{2+} is reducing while Pb^{4+} is oxidising.
(NEET 2017)

3. Boric acid is an acid because its molecule
(a) contains replaceable H^+ ion
(b) gives up a proton
(c) accepts OH^- from water releasing proton
(d) combines with proton from water molecule.
(NEET-II 2016)

AlF_3 is soluble in HF only in presence of KF. It is due to the formation of
(a) $K_3[AlF_3H_3]$ (b) $K_3[AlF_6]$
(c) AlH_3 (d) $K[AlF_3H]$
(NEET-II 2016)

The stability of + 1 oxidation state among Al, Ga, In and Tl increases in the sequence
(a) Al < Ga < In < Tl (b) Tl < In < Ga < Al
(c) In < Tl < Ga < Al (d) Ga < In < Al < Tl
(2015, 2009)

Which of the following structure is similar to graphite?
(a) B_4C (b) B_2H_6
(c) BN (d) B *(NEET 2013)*

Which of these is not a monomer for a high molecular mass silicone polymer?
(a) Me_3SiCl (b) $PhSiCl_3$
(c) $MeSiCl_3$ (d) Me_2SiCl_2
(NEET 2013)

The basic structural unit of silicates is
(a) SiO_3^{2-} (b) SiO_4^{2-}
(c) SiO^- (d) SiO_4^{4-}
(NEET 2013)

9. Which statement is wrong?
(a) Beryl is an example of cyclic silicate.
(b) Mg_2SiO_4 is orthosilicate.
(c) Basic structural unit in silicates is the SiO_4 tetrahedron.
(d) Feldspars are not aluminosilicates.
(Karnataka NEET 2013)

10. Name the two type of the structure of silicate in which one oxygen atom of $[SiO_4]^{4-}$ is shared?
(a) Linear chain silicate (b) Sheet silicate
(c) Pyrosilicate (d) Three dimensional
(2011)

11. Which of the following statements is incorrect?
(a) Pure sodium metal dissolves in liquid ammonia to give blue solution.
(b) NaOH reacts with glass to give sodium silicate.
(c) Aluminium reacts with excess NaOH to give $Al(OH)_3$.
(d) $NaHCO_3$ on heating gives Na_2CO_3.
(Mains 2011)

12. Which of the following oxide is amphoteric?
(a) SnO_2 (b) CaO
(c) SiO_2 (d) CO_2
(Mains 2011)

13. Which one of the following molecular hydrides acts as a Lewis acid?
(a) NH_3 (b) H_2O
(c) B_2H_6 (d) CH_4 *(2010)*

14. The tendency of BF_3, BCl_3 and BBr_3 to behave as Lewis acid decreases in the sequence
(a) $BCl_3 > BF_3 > BBr_3$ (b) $BBr_3 > BCl_3 > BF_3$
(c) $BBr_3 > BF_3 > BCl_3$ (d) $BF_3 > BCl_3 > BBr_3$
(2010)

15. The straight chain polymer is formed by
(a) hydrolysis of CH_3SiCl_3 followed by condensation polymerisation
(b) hydrolysis of $(CH_3)_4Si$ by addition polymerisation

(c) hydrolysis of $(CH_3)_2SiCl_2$ followed by condensation polymerisation
(d) hydrolysis of $(CH_3)_3SiCl$ followed by condensation polymerisation. *(2009)*

16. Which of the following oxidation states are the most characteristic for lead and tin respectively?
(a) +2, +4 (b) +4, +4
(c) +2, +2 (d) +4, +2. *(2007)*

17. Which of the following anions is present in the chain structure of silicates?
(a) $(Si_2O_5^{2-})_n$ (b) $(SiO_3^{2-})_n$
(c) SiO_4^{4-} (d) $Si_2O_7^{6-}$ *(2007)*

18. Which of the following is the most basic oxide?
(a) SeO_2 (b) Al_2O_3
(c) Sb_2O_3 (d) Bi_2O_3 *(2006)*

19. The correct order regarding the electronegativity of hybrid orbitals of carbon is
(a) $sp < sp^2 < sp^3$ (b) $sp > sp^2 < sp^3$
(c) $sp > sp^2 > sp^3$ (d) $sp < sp^2 > sp^3$
(2006)

20. Which one of the following statements about the zeolite is false?
(a) They are used as cation exchangers.
(b) They have open structure which enables them to take up small molecules.
(c) Zeolites are aluminosilicates having three dimensional network.
(d) Some of the SiO_4^{4-} units are replaced by AlO_4^{5-} and AlO_6^{9-} ions in zeolites. *(2004)*

21. Which one of the following compounds is not a protonic acid?
(a) $B(OH)_3$ (b) $PO(OH)_3$
(c) $SO(OH)_2$ (d) $SO_2(OH)_2$ *(2003)*

22. Which compound is electron deficient?
(a) $BeCl_2$ (b) BCl_3
(c) CCl_4 (d) PCl_5 *(2000)*

23. Which of the following does not show electrical conduction?
(a) Diamond (b) Graphite
(c) Potassium (d) Sodium *(1999)*

24. The type of hybridisation of boron in diborane is
(a) sp^3-hybridisation (b) sp^2-hybridisation
(c) sp-hybridisation (d) sp^3d^2-hybridisation
(1999)

25. Percentage of lead in lead pencil is
(a) 80 (b) 20
(c) zero (d) 70 *(1999)*

26. In graphite, electrons are
(a) localised on each C-atom
(b) localised on every third C-atom
(c) spread out between the structure
(d) present in antibonding orbital.
(1997, 1993)

27. Boron compounds behave as Lewis acids, because of their
(a) ionisation property
(b) electron deficient nature
(c) acidic nature
(d) covalent nature. *(1996)*

28. Aluminium (III) chloride forms a dimer becaus[e] aluminium
(a) belongs to 3rd group
(b) can have higher coordination number
(c) cannot form a trimer
(d) has high ionization energy. *(1995*

29. The BCl_3 is a planar molecule whereas NCl_3 i[s] pyramidal because
(a) nitrogen atom is smaller than boron ator[m]
(b) BCl_3 has no lone pair but NCl_3 has a lon[e] pair of electrons
(c) B—Cl bond is more polar than N—Cl bon[d]
(d) N—Cl bond is more covalent than B—C[l] bond. *(1995*

30. Method used for obtaining highly pure silico[n] used as a semiconductor material, is
(a) crystallization (b) zone refining
(c) oxidation (d) electrochemical
(199

31. Carbon and silicon belong to (IV) group. Th[e] maximum coordination number of carbon [in] commonly occurring compounds is 4, where[as] that of silicon is 6. This is due to
(a) availability of low lying d-orbitals in silic[on]
(b) large size of silicon
(c) more electropositive nature of silicon
(d) both (b) and (c). *(199*

32. Which of the following statements abo[ut] H_3BO_3 is not correct?
(a) It has a layer structure in which planar B[O_3] units are joined by hydrogen bonds.
(b) It does not act as proton donor but ac[ts] as a Lewis acid by accepting hydroxyl io[n]
(c) It is a strong tribasic acid.
(d) It is prepared by acidifying an aqueo[us] solution of borax. *(199*

33. Na^+, Mg^{2+}, Al^{3+} and Si^{4+} are isoelectronic, their ionic size will follow the order
(a) $Na^+ > Mg^{2+} < Al^{3+} < Si^{4+}$
(b) $Na^+ < Mg^{2+} < Al^{3+} < Si^{4+}$
(c) $Na^+ > Mg^{2+} > Al^{3+} > Si^{4+}$
(d) $Na^+ < Mg^{2+} > Al^{3+} < Si^{4+}$ *(1993)*

34. Which of the following types of forces bind together the carbon atoms in diamond?
(a) Ionic (b) Covalent
(c) Dipolar (d) van der Waals *(1992)*

35. Water gas is produced by
(a) passing steam through a red hot coke
(b) saturating hydrogen with moisture
(c) mixing oxygen and hydrogen in the ratio of 1 : 2
(d) heating a mixture of CO_2 and CH_4 in petroleum refineries. *(1992)*

36. Which of the following is an insulator?
(a) Graphite (b) Aluminum
(c) Diamond (d) Silicon *(1992)*

37. Glass is a
(a) liquid
(b) solid
(c) supercooled liquid
(d) transparent organic polymer. *(1991)*

38. The ability of a substance to assume two or more crystalline structures is called
(a) isomerism (b) polymorphism
(c) isomorphism (d) amorphism. *(1990)*

39. The substance used as a smoke screen in warfare is
(a) $SiCl_4$ (b) PH_3
(c) PCl_5 (d) acetylene. *(1989)*

Answer Key

.	(c)	**2.**	(d)	**3.**	(c)	**4.**	(b)	**5.**	(a)	**6.**	(c)	**7.**	(a)	**8.**	(d)	**9.**	(d)	**10.**	(c)
1.	(c)	**12.**	(a)	**13.**	(c)	**14.**	(b)	**15.**	(c)	**16.**	(a)	**17.**	(b)	**18.**	(d)	**19.**	(c)	**20.**	(d)
1.	(a)	**22.**	(b)	**23.**	(a)	**24.**	(a)	**25.**	(c)	**26.**	(b)	**27.**	(b)	**28.**	(b)	**29.**	(b)	**30.**	(b)
1.	(a)	**32.**	(c)	**33.**	(c)	**34.**	(b)	**35.**	(a)	**36.**	(c)	**37.**	(c)	**38.**	(b)	**39.**	(a)		

EXPLANATIONS

1. (c) : Boron does not have vacant *d*-orbitals in its valence shell, so it cannot extend its covalency beyond 4. *i.e.*, 'B' cannot form the ions like MF_6^{3-}.

2. (d) : The inertness of *s*-subshell electrons towards bond formation is known as inert pair effect. This effect increases down the group thus, for Sn, +4 oxidation state is more stable, whereas, for Pb, +2 oxidation state is more stable, *i.e.*, Sn^{2+} is reducing while Pb^{4+} is oxidising.

3. (c) : Boric acid behaves as a Lewis acid, by accepting a pair of electrons from OH^- ion of water thereby releasing a proton.

$$H{-}OH + B(OH)_3 \longrightarrow [B(OH)_4]^- + H^+$$

4. (b) : AlF_3 is insoluble in anhydrous HF because the F^- ions are not available in hydrogen bonded HF but, it becomes soluble in presence of little amount of KF due to formation of complex, $K_3[AlF_6]$. $AlF_3 + 3KF \rightarrow K_3[AlF_6]$

5. (a) : In group 13 elements, stability of +3 oxidation state decreases down the group while that of +1 oxidation state increases due to inert pair effect. Hence, stability of +1 oxidation state increases in the sequence : Al < Ga < In < Tl.

6. (c) : BN is known as inorganic graphite and has structure similar to graphite.

7. (a) : It can form only dimer.

8. (d) : SiO_4^{4-} orthosilicate is basic unit of silicates.

9. (d): Feldspars are three dimensional aluminosilicates.

10. (c) : Pyrosilicate contains two units of SiO_4^{4-} joined along a corner containing oxygen atom.

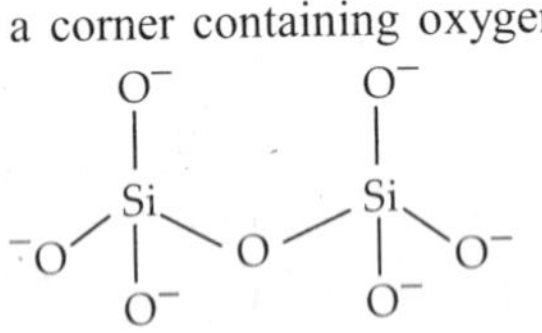

11. (c) : Al reacts with NaOH to give sodium metaaluminate.

12. (a) : SnO_2 reacts with acid as well as base. So SnO_2 is an amphoteric.

$SnO_2 + 4HCl \rightarrow SnCl_2 + 2H_2O$

$SnO_2 + 2NaOH \rightarrow Na_2SnO_3 + H_2O$

CaO is basic in nature while SiO_2 and CO_2 are acidic in nature.

13. (c) : Compounds that are electron deficient act as Lewis acids. Out of the given hydrides B_2H_6 satisfies this condition and is therefore a Lewis acid.

14. (b) : The relative Lewis acid character of boron trihalides is found to follow the following order,

$BBr_3 > BCl_3 > BF_3$

but the expected order on the basis of electronegativity of the halogens (electronegativity of halogens decreases from F to I) should be,

$BF_3 > BCl_3 > BBr_3$

This anomaly is explained on the basis of the relative tendency of the halogen atom to back donate its unutilised electrons to vacant *p*-orbital of boron atom. In BF_3, boron has a vacant 2*p*-orbital and each flourine has fully filled unutilised 2*p*-orbitals. Fluorine transfers two electrons to vacant 2*p*-orbital of boron, thus forming $p\pi$-$p\pi$ bond

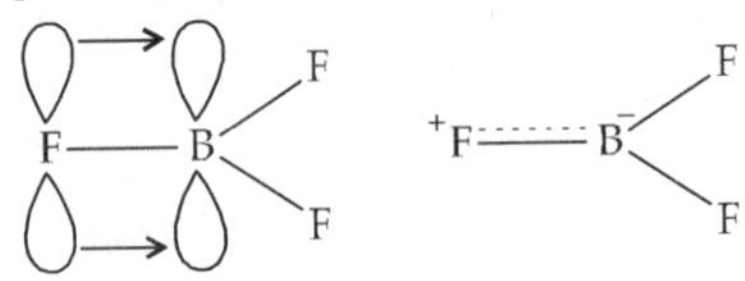

This type of bond has some double bond character and is known as dative or back bonding. All the three bond lengths are same. It is possible when double bond is delocalized. The delocalization may be represented as :

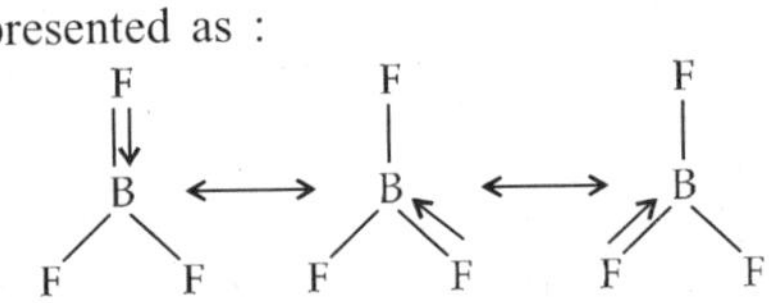

The tendency to back donate decreases from F to I as energy level difference between B and halogen atom increases from F to I. So, the order is $BF_3 < BCl_3 < BBr_3$.

15. (c) : Hydrolysis of substituted chlorosilanes yields corresponding silanols which undergo polymerisation. Out of the given chlorosilanes, only $(CH_3)_2SiCl_2$ will give linear polymer on hydrolysis followed by polymerisation.

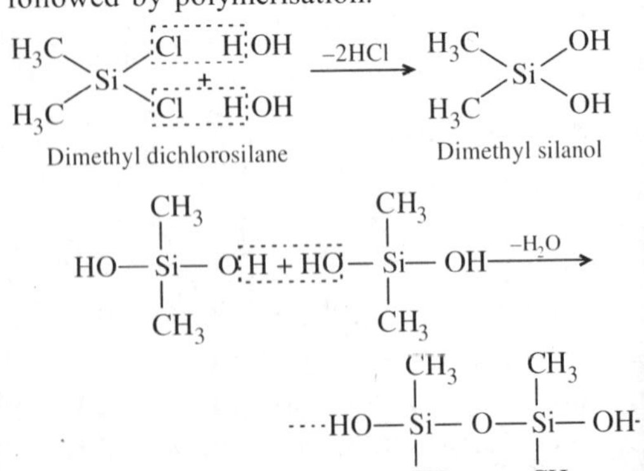

16. (a) : When ns^2 electrons of outermost shell do not participate in bonding then these ns^2 electrons are called inert pair and the effect is called inert pair effect. Due to this inert pair effect Ge, Sn and Pb of group IV have a tendency to form both +4 and +2 ions. Now the inert pair effect increases down the group, hence the stability of M^{2+} ions increases and M^{4+} ions decreases down the group. For this reason, Pb^{2+} is more stable than Pb^{4+} and Sn^{4+} is more stable than Sn^{2+}.

17. (b) : Chain silicates are formed by sharing two oxygen atoms by each tetrahedra. Anions of chain silicate have two general formula :

(i) $(SiO_3)_n^{2n-}$ (ii) $(Si_4O_{11})_n^{6n-}$

18. (d) : $SeO_2 \rightarrow$ acidic oxide

$Al_2O_3 \rightarrow$ amphoteric, $Sb_2O_3 \rightarrow$ amphoteric

$Bi_2O_3 \rightarrow$ basic oxide.

19. (c) : Electronegativity of carbon atom is not fixed. It varies with the state of hybridisation. Electronegativity of carbon increases as the *s*-character of the hybrid orbital increases.

$C\ (sp) > C\ (sp^2) > C\ (sp^3)$

20. (d) : Zeolites have SiO_4 and AlO_4 tetrahedrons, linked together in a three dimensional open structure in which four or six membered rings predominate. Due to open chain structure, they have cavities and can take up water and other small molecules.

21. (a) : $B(OH)_3$ in aqueous medium coordinates a molecule of water to form the hydrated species $H_2O \rightarrow B(OH)_3$. In this species, B^{3+} ion, because of its small size, exercises a high polarizing power thereby pulling the sigma electron charge of the coordinated O atom towards itself. The coordinated oxygen, in turn, pulls the sigma electron charge of the OH bond of the attached water molecule towards itself. This facilitates the removal of H^+ ion from the O – H bond.

$$H_2O \rightarrow B(OH)_3 \rightleftharpoons [B(OH)_4]^- + H^+$$

Thus, the solution of $B(OH)_3$ in water acts as a weak acid, and it is not a protonic acid.

22. (b) : In BCl_3 the central atom 'B' is sp^2 hybridised and contains only 'six' electrons in its valence shell. Therefore it is electron deficient.

23. (a) : Except diamond other three conduct electricity. Potassium and sodium are metallic conductors, while graphite is a non-metallic conductor.

24. (a) : Each 'B' atom in diborane (B_2H_6) is sp^3-hybridised. Of the 4-hybrid orbitals, three have one electron each, while the 4th is empty. Two orbitals of each form σ bonds with two 'H'-atoms, while one of the remaining hybrid orbital (either filled or empty), 1*s* orbital of 'H' atom and one of the hybrid orbitals of other 'B' atom overlap to form three centered two electron bond. So there exists two such type of three centered bonds.

25. (c) : Lead pencil contains graphite and clay. It does not contain lead.

26. (b) : In graphite each carbon atom undergoes sp^2-hybridisation and is covalently bonded to three other carbon atoms by single bonds. The fourth electron forms π bond. A graphite consists of two layers which are separated by a distance of 340 pm.

27. (b) : Lewis acids are those substances which can accept a pair of electrons and boron compounds usually are deficient in electrons.

28. (b) : $AlCl_3$ forms a dimer as there is unsaturation in coordination. Also it enables Al atoms to complete their octets.

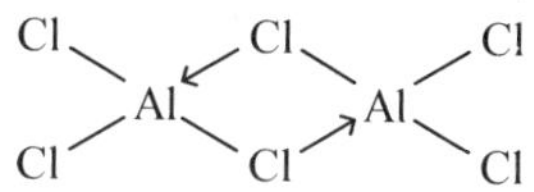

29. (b) : There is no lone pair on boron in BCl_3 hence no repulsion takes place. There is a lone pair on nitrogen in NCl_3 hence repulsion takes place. Therefore BCl_3 is planar molecule but NCl_3 is pyramidal molecule.

30. (b) : Pure silicon is made by the reduction of highly purified silicon tetrachloride ($SiCl_4$) with dihydrogen.

$SiCl_4 + 2H_2 \rightarrow Si + 4HCl$

The silicon obtained is purified further by the zone refining process. A method of refining metals some inorganic and organic compounds depending on the difference in solubility of impurities in the liquid and solid states is called zone refining process.

31. (a) : Carbon has no *d*-orbitals, while silicon contains *d*-orbitals in its valence shell which can be used for bonding purposes.

32. (c) : H_3BO_3 is a weak monobasic acid. We know that $B(OH)_3 + H_2O \rightarrow [B(OH)_4]^- + H^+$. Therefore it is a weak monobasic acid.

33. (c) : In isoelectronic species as the charge on cations increases, their sizes decrease in that order. Thus the ionic sizes of the given cation (isoelectronic) decrease in the order:

$Na^+ > Mg^{2+} > Al^{3+} > Si^{4+}$

34. (b) : In diamond each carbon atom is sp^3 hybridized and thus forms covalent bonds with four other carbon atoms lying at the corners of a regular tetrahedron.

35. (a) : $\underset{\text{Steam}}{H_2O} + \underset{\text{Red hot}}{C} \rightarrow \underbrace{H_2 + CO}_{\text{Water gas}}$

36. (c) : All the above are conductors except diamond. Hence diamond is an insulator.

37. (c) : Glass is a supercooled liquid which forms a non-crystalline solid without a regular lattice.

38. (b) : The phenomenon of existence of a substance in two or more crystalline structures is called polymorphism. Polymorphism of elements is known as allotropy.

39. (a) : $SiCl_4$ gets hydrolysed in moist air and gives white fumes which are used as a smoke screen in warfare.

Chapter 12
Organic Chemistry – Some Basic Principles and Techniques

1. Which of the following is correct with respect to $-I$ effect of the substituents? (R = alkyl)
   (a) $-NH_2 < -OR < -F$
   (b) $-NR_2 < -OR < -F$
   (c) $-NH_2 > -OR > -F$
   (d) $-NR_2 > -OR > -F$ *(NEET 2018)*

2. Which of the following carbocations is expected to be most stable?

   (a) 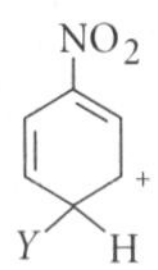
   (b) 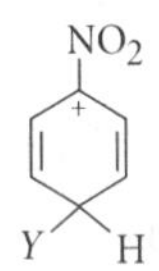
   (c) 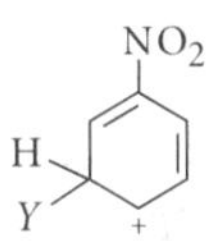
   (d) 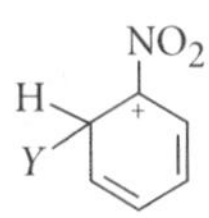

   (NEET 2018)

3. Which of the following molecules represents the order of hybridisation sp^2, sp^2, sp, sp from left to right atoms?
   (a) $HC \equiv C - C \equiv CH$
   (b) $CH_2 = CH - C \equiv CH$
   (c) $CH_2 = CH - CH = CH_2$
   (d) $CH_3 - CH = CH - CH_3$ *(NEET 2018)*

4. The most suitable method of separation of 1 : 1 mixture of *ortho* and *para*-nitrophenols is
   (a) chromatography (b) crystallisation
   (c) steam distillation (d) sublimation.
   (NEET 2017, 1999, 1993)

5. The IUPAC name of the compound

   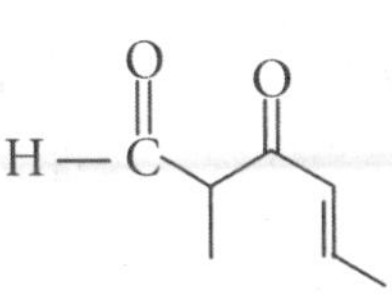

   is ________.

   (a) 5-formylhex-2-en-3-one
   (b) 5-methyl-4-oxohex-2-en-5-al
   (c) 3-keto-2-methylhex-5-enal
   (d) 3-keto-2-methylhex-4-enal *(NEET 2017)*

6. The correct statement regarding electrophile is
   (a) electrophile is a negatively charged species and can form a bond by accepting a pair of electrons from another electrophile
   (b) electrophiles are generally neutral species and can form a bond by accepting a pair of electrons from a nucleophile
   (c) electrophile can be either neutral or positively charged species and can form a bond by accepting a pair of electrons from a nucleophile
   (d) electrophile is a negatively charged species and can form a bond by accepting a pair of electrons from a nucleophile.
   (NEET 2017)

7. Which among the given molecules can exhibit tautomerism?

    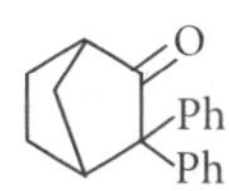 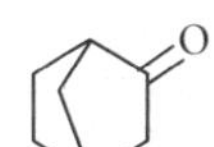

   I II III

   (a) III only (b) Both I and III
   (c) Both I and II (d) Both II and III
   (NEET-II 2016)

8. Which of the following statements is not correct for a nucleophile?
   (a) Ammonia is a nucleophile.
   (b) Nucleophiles attack low e^- density sites.
   (c) Nucleophiles are not electron seeking.
   (d) Nucleophile is a Lewis acid. *(2015)*

9. Which of the following is not the product of dehydration of 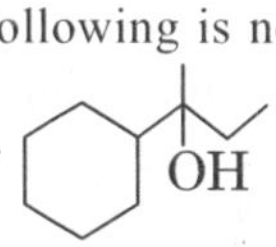 ?

   (a) 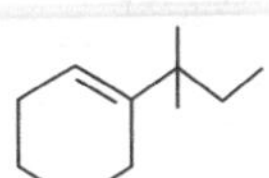
   (b) 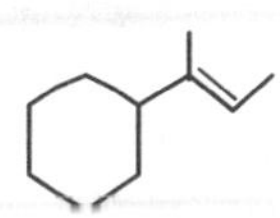
   (c) 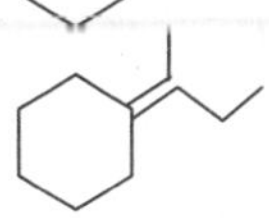
   (d) 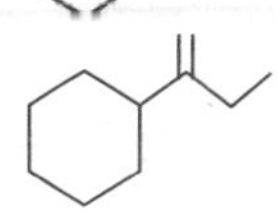

   (2015)

10. Treatment of cyclopentanone 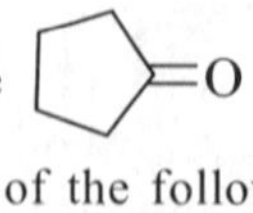 with methyl lithium gives which of the following species?

(a) Cyclopentanonyl radical
(b) Cyclopentanonyl biradical
(c) Cyclopentanonyl anion
(d) Cyclopentanonyl cation

(2015, Cancelled)

11. The total number of π-bond electrons in the following structure is

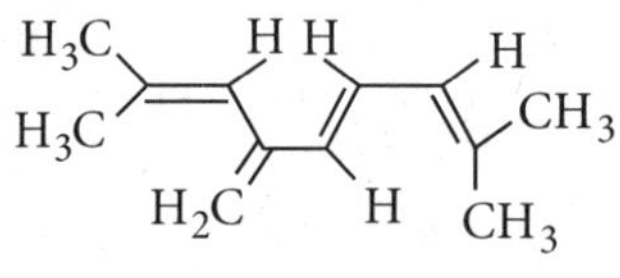

(a) 12 (b) 16
(c) 4 (d) 8

(2015, Cancelled)

12. Which of the following species contains equal number of σ- and π-bonds?

(a) $(CN)_2$ (b) $CH_2(CN)_2$
(c) HCO_3^- (d) XeO_4

(2015, Cancelled)

13. Given :

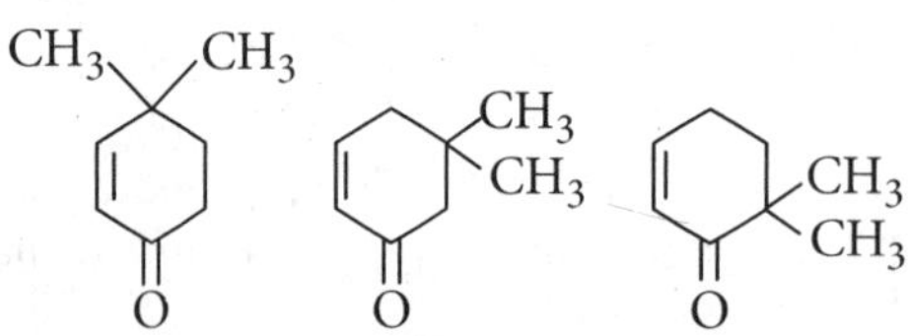

(I) (II) (III)

Which of the given compounds can exhibit tautomerism?

(a) II and III (b) I, II and III
(c) I and II (d) I and III

(2015, Cancelled)

14. Which of the following is the most correct electron displacement for a nucleophilic reaction to take place?

(a) 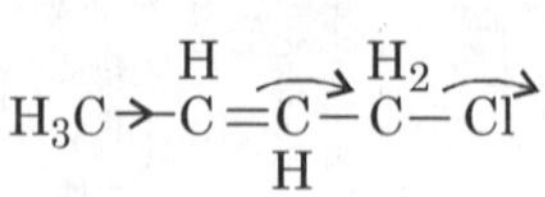

(b) 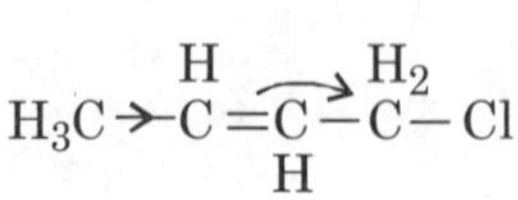

(c) 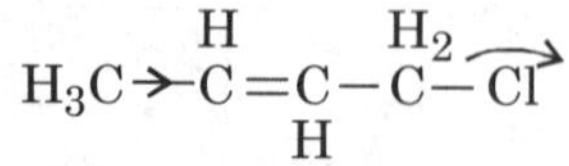

(d) 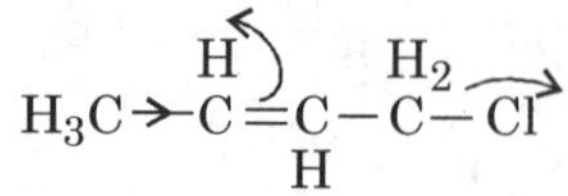

(2015, Cancelled)

15. In Duma's method for estimation of nitrogen, 0.25 g of an organic compound gave 40 mL of nitrogen collected at 300 K temperature and 725 mm pressure. If the aqueous tension at 300 K is 25 mm, the percentage of nitrogen in the compound is

(a) 16.76 (b) 15.76
(c) 17.36 (d) 18.20

(2015, Cancelled)

16. Consider the following compounds :

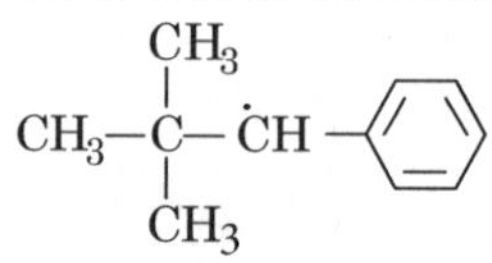 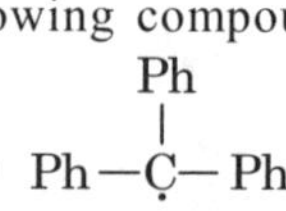 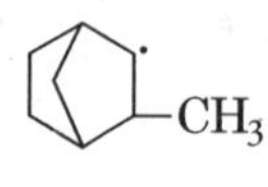

(I) (II) (III)

Hyperconjugation occurs in

(a) III only (b) I and III
(c) I only (d) II only.

(2015, Cancelled)

17. The enolic form of ethyl acetoacetate as shown below has

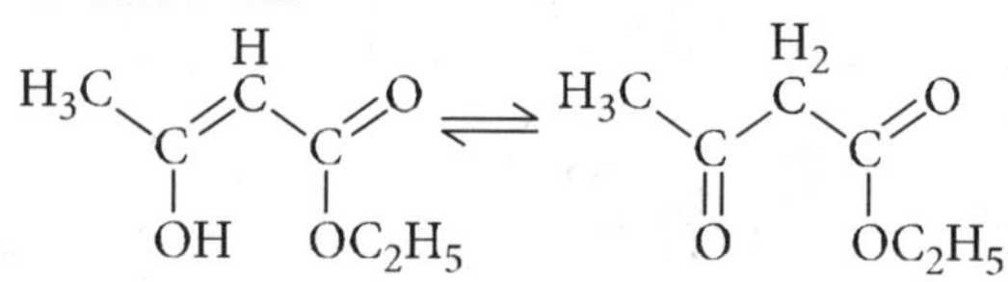

(a) 9 sigma bonds and 2 pi-bonds
(b) 9 sigma bonds and 1 pi-bond
(c) 18 sigma bonds and 2 pi-bonds
(d) 16 sigma bonds and 1 pi-bond.

(2015, Cancelled)

18. In which of the following compounds, the C—Cl bond ionisation shall give most stable carbonium ion?

(a) 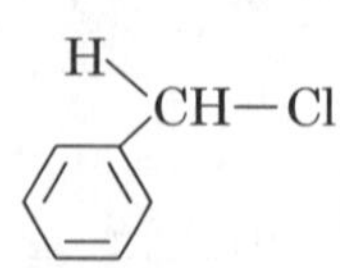 (b) 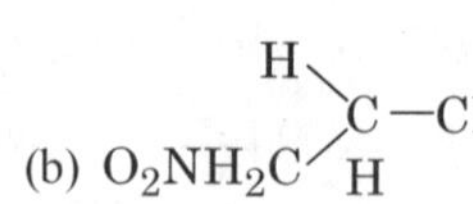

(c) 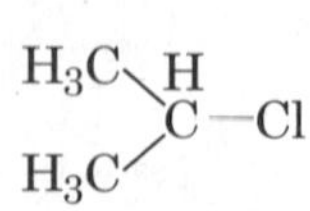 (d) 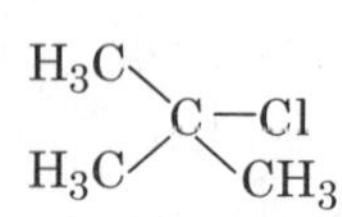

(2015, Cancelled)

19. In the Kjeldahl's method for estimation of nitrogen present in a soil sample, ammonia evolved from 0.75 g of sample neutralized 10 mL of 1 M H_2SO_4. The percentage of nitrogen in the soil is

(a) 37.33 (b) 45.33
(c) 35.33 (d) 43.33 *(2014)*

20. The radical, 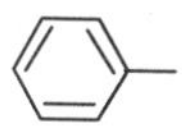 $\dot{C}H_2$ is aromatic because it has

(a) 7 *p*-orbitals and 7 unpaired electrons
(b) 6 *p*-orbitals and 7 unpaired electrons
(c) 6 *p*-orbitals and 6 unpaired electrons
(d) 7 *p*-orbitals and 6 unpaired electrons.

(NEET 2013)

21. The structure of isobutyl group in an organic compound is

(a) $CH_3—CH_2—CH_2—CH_2—$

(b) $CH_3—\overset{CH_3}{\underset{CH_3}{C}}—$ (c) $(CH_3)_2>CH—CH_2—$

(d) $CH_3—\underset{|}{C}H—CH_2—CH_3$ *(NEET 2013)*

22. Structure of the compound whose IUPAC name is 3-Ethyl-2-hydroxy-4-methylhex-3-en-5-ynoic acid is

(a) 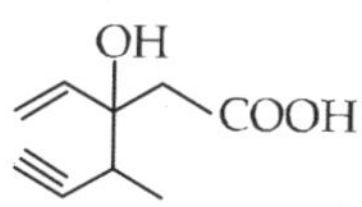 (b) 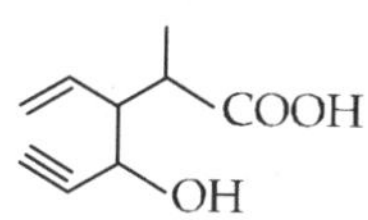

(c) 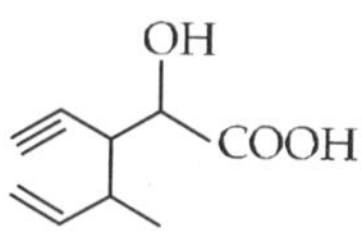 (d) 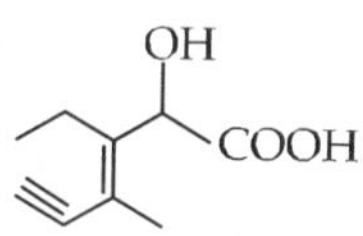

(NEET 2013)

23. Some *meta*-directing substituents in aromatic substitution are given. Which one is most deactivating?

(a) —COOH (b) $—NO_2$
(c) $—C\equiv N$ (d) $—SO_3H$

(NEET 2013)

24. Arrange the following in increasing order of stability

1. $(CH_3)_2—\overset{+}{C}—CH_2—CH_3$
2. $(CH_3)_3—\overset{+}{C}$ 3. $(CH_3)_2\ \overset{+}{C}H$
4. $CH_3—\overset{+}{C}H_2$ 5. $\overset{+}{C}H_3$

(a) 5 < 4 < 3 < 1 < 2 (b) 4 < 5 < 3 < 1 < 2
(c) 1 < 5 < 4 < 3 < 2 (d) 5 < 4 < 3 < 2 < 1

(Karnataka NEET 2013)

25. What is the hybridisation state of benzyl carbonium ion 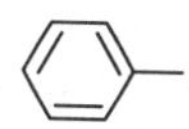 $\overset{+}{C}H_2$?

(a) sp^2 (b) spd^2
(c) sp^2d (d) sp^3

(Karnataka NEET 2013)

26. Nitrogen detection in an organic compound is carried out by Lassaigne's test. The blue colour formed corresponds to which of the following formulae?

(a) $Fe_3[Fe(CN)_6]_2$ (b) $Fe_4[Fe(CN)_6]_3$
(c) $Fe_4[Fe(CN)_6]_2$ (d) $Fe_3[Fe(CN)_6]_3$

(Karnataka NEET 2013)

27. Homolytic fission of the following alkanes forms free radicals $CH_3—CH_3$, $CH_3—CH_2—CH_3$, $(CH_3)_2CH—CH_3$, $CH_3—CH_2—CH(CH_3)_2$. Increasing order of stability of the radicals is

(a) $(CH_3)_2\dot{C}—CH_2CH_3 < CH_3—\dot{C}H—CH_3 < CH_3—\dot{C}H_2 < (CH_3)_3C^{\bullet}$
(b) $CH_3—\dot{C}H_2 < CH_3—\dot{C}H—CH_3 < (CH_3)_2\dot{C}—CH_2—CH_3 < (CH_3)_3\dot{C}$
(c) $CH_3—\dot{C}H_2 < CH_3—\dot{C}H—CH_3 < (CH_3)_3\dot{C} < (CH_3)_2\dot{C}—CH_2CH_3$
(d) $(CH_3)_3\dot{C} < (CH_3)_2\dot{C}—CH_2CH_3 < CH_3—\dot{C}H—CH_3 < CH_3—\dot{C}H_2$

(Karnataka NEET 2013)

28. Among the following compounds the one that is most reactive towards electrophilic nitration is

(a) benzoic acid (b) nitrobenzene
(c) toluene (d) benzene

(2012, 1992)

29. Which nomenclature is not according to IUPAC system?

(a) $Br-CH_2-CH=CH_2$
1-Bromoprop-2-ene

(b) $CH_3-CH_2-\overset{CH_3}{\underset{Br}{C}}-CH_2-\underset{CH_3}{CHCH_3}$
4-Bromo-2,4-dimethylhexane

(c) 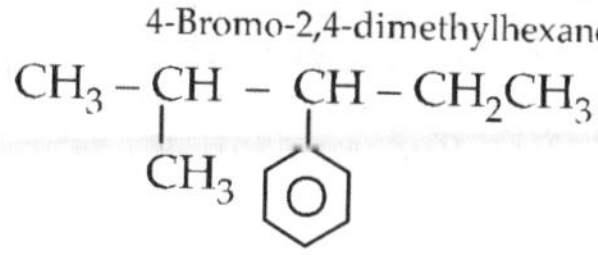
2-Methyl-3-phenylpentane

(d) $CH_3-\underset{O}{\underset{||}{C}}-CH_2-CH_2-CH_2COOH$
5-oxohexanoic acid

(2012)

30. Considering the state of hybridization of carbon atoms, find out the molecule among the following which is linear?
(a) $CH_3 - CH{=}CH - CH_3$
(b) $CH_3 - C{\equiv}C - CH_3$
(c) $CH_2{=}CH - CH_2 - C{\equiv}CH$
(d) $CH_3 - CH_2 - CH_2 - CH_3$ *(2011)*

31. Which one of the following is most reactive towards electrophilic reagent?

(a) 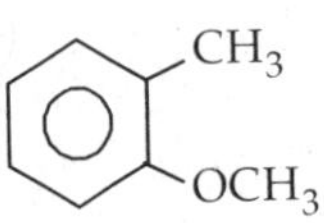
(b) 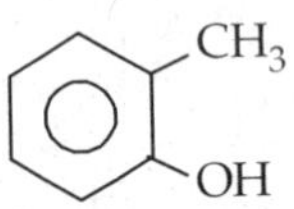
(c) 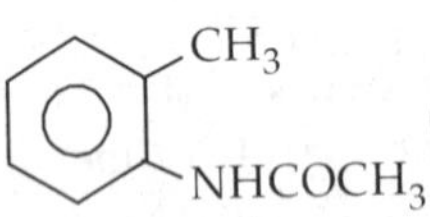
(d) 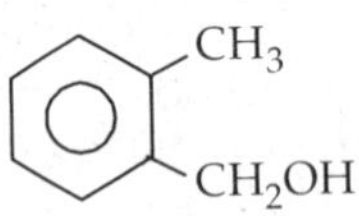

(2011, 2010)

32. The correct IUPAC name for the compound

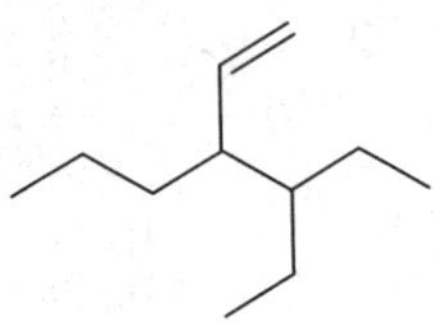

is

(a) 4-ethyl-3-propylhex-1-ene
(b) 3-ethyl-4-ethenylheptane
(c) 3-ethyl-4-propylhex-5-ene
(d) 3-(1-ethylpropyl)hex-1-ene. *(2011)*

33. In Dumas' method of estimation of nitrogen 0.35 g of an organic compound gave 55 mL of nitrogen collected at 300 K temperature and 715 mm pressure. The percentage composition of nitrogen in the compound would be (aqueous tension at 300 K = 15 mm).
(a) 15.45 (b) 16.45
(c) 17.45 (d) 14.45 *(2011)*

34. Which one is a nucleophilic substitution reaction among the following?

(a) $CH_3 - CH{=}CH_2 + H_2O \xrightarrow{H^+} CH_3 - \underset{\substack{|\\ OH}}{CH} - CH_3$

(b) $RCHO + R'MgX \longrightarrow R - \underset{\substack{|\\ OH}}{CH} - R'$

(c) $CH_3 - CH_2 - \overset{\substack{CH_3\\ |}}{CH} - CH_2Br + NH_3 \longrightarrow CH_3 - CH_2 - \overset{\substack{CH_3\\ |}}{CH} - CH_2NH_2$

(d) $CH_3CHO + HCN \longrightarrow CH_3CH(OH)CN$ *(2011)*

35. The Lassaigne's extract is boiled with conc. HNO_3 while testing for halogens. By doing so it
(a) decomposes Na_2S and NaCN, formed
(b) helps in the precipitation of AgCl
(c) increases the solubility product of AgCl
(d) increases the concentration of NO_3^- ions *(2011)*

36. Which of the following compounds undergoes nucleophilic substitution reaction most easily?

(a) 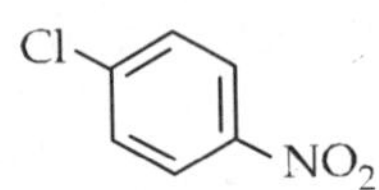
(b) 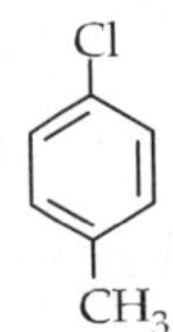
(c) 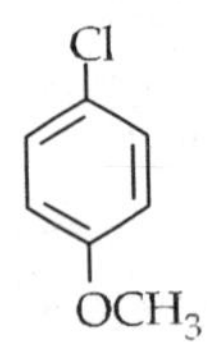
(d) 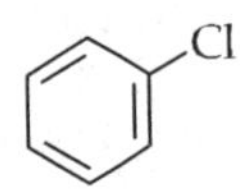

(Mains 2011)

37. The IUPAC name of the following compound is

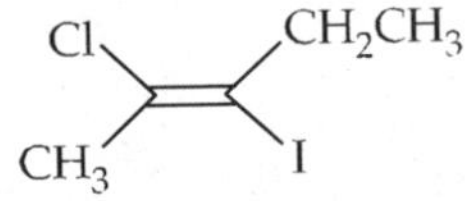

(a) *trans*-2-chloro-3-iodo-2-pentene
(b) *cis*-3-iodo-4-chloro-3-pentane
(c) *trans*-3-iodo-4-chloro-3-pentene
(d) *cis*-2-chloro-3-iodo-2-pentene. *(Mains 2011, 1998)*

38. Which of the following species is not electrophilic in nature?
(a) $\overset{\oplus}{Cl}$ (b) BH_3
(c) $H_3\overset{\oplus}{O}$ (d) $\overset{\oplus}{NO_2}$ *(Mains 2010)*

39. The IUPAC name of the compound $CH_3CH{=}CHC{\equiv}CH$ is
(a) pent-4-yn-2-ene (b) pent-3-en-1-yne
(c) pent-2-en-4-yne (d) pent-1-yn-3-ene *(Mains 2010)*

40. The IUPAC name of the compound having the formula $CH{\equiv}C{-}CH{=}CH_2$ is
(a) 1-butyne-3-ene (b) but-1-yne-3-ene
(c) 1-butene-3-yne (d) 3-butene-1-yne.
(2009)

41. Base strength of

$$H_3C\overset{\ominus}{C}H_2,\ H_2C{=}\overset{\ominus}{C}H \text{ and } H-C{\equiv}\overset{\ominus}{C}$$
(i) (ii) (iii)

is in the order of
(a) (i) > (iii) > (ii) (b) (i) > (ii) > (iii)
(c) (ii) > (i) > (iii) (d) (iii) > (ii) > (i)
(2008)

42. Which one of the following is most reactive towards electrophilic attack?

(a) 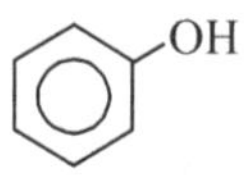 (b) 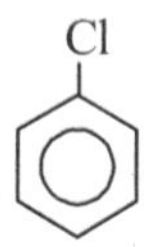

(c) 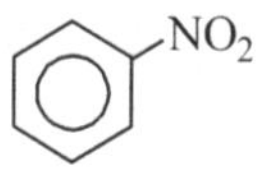 (d) 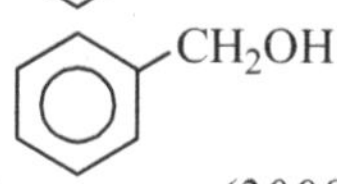
(2008)

43. The stability of carbanions in the following.

(i) $RC{\equiv}\overset{\ominus}{C}$ (ii) 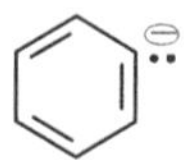

(iii) $R_2C{=}\overset{\ominus}{C}H$ (iv) $R_3C{-}\overset{\ominus}{C}H_2$

is in the order of
(a) (iv) > (ii) > (iii) > (i)
(b) (i) > (iii) > (ii) > (iv)
(c) (i) > (ii) > (iii) > (iv)
(d) (ii) > (iii) > (iv) > (i) *(2008)*

44. For (i) I^-, (ii) Cl^-, (iii) Br^-, the increasing order of nucleophilicity would be
(a) $Cl^- < Br^- < I^-$ (b) $I^- < Cl^- < Br^-$
(c) $Br^- < Cl^- < I^-$ (d) $I^- < Br^- < Cl^-$
(2007)

45. The order of decreasing reactivity towards an electrophilic reagent, for the following would be
(i) benzene (ii) toluene
(iii) chlorobenzene (iv) phenol
(a) (ii) > (iv) > (i) > (iii) (b) (iv) > (iii) > (ii) > (i)
(c) (iv) > (ii) > (i) > (iii) (d) (i) > (ii) > (iii) > (iv)
(2007)

46. The general molecular formula, which represents the homologous series of alkanols is
(a) $C_nH_{2n}O$ (b) $C_nH_{2n}O_2$
(c) $C_nH_{2n+2}O$ (d) $C_nH_{2n+1}O$
(2006)

47. The IUPAC name of 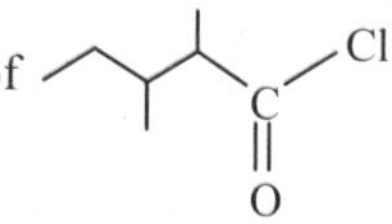 is
(a) 1-chloro-1-oxo-2,3-dimethylpentane
(b) 2-ethyl-3-methylbutanoyl chloride
(c) 2,3-dimethylpentanoyl chloride
(d) 3,4-dimethylpentanoyl chloride. *(2006)*

48. Names of some compounds are given. Which one is not in IUPAC system?

(a) $CH_3-CH_2-CH_2-\underset{\displaystyle CH_2CH_3}{\underset{|}{C}H}-\overset{\displaystyle CH_3}{\overset{|}{C}H}-CH_2CH_3$
3-Methyl-4-ethylheptane

(b) $CH_3-\underset{\displaystyle OH}{\underset{|}{C}H}-\underset{\displaystyle CH_3}{\underset{|}{C}H}-CH_3$
3-Methyl-2-butanol

(c) $CH_3-CH_2-\underset{\displaystyle CH_2}{\underset{||}{C}}-\underset{\displaystyle CH_3}{\underset{|}{C}H}-CH_3$
2-Ethyl-3-methylbut-1-ene

(d) $CH_3-C{\equiv}C-CH(CH_3)_2$
4-Methyl-2-pentyne *(2005)*

49. Which amongst the following is the most stable carbocation?

(a) $\overset{+}{C}H_3$ (b) $CH_3\overset{+}{C}H_2$

(c) $CH_3-\underset{\displaystyle CH_3}{\underset{|}{\overset{+}{C}H}}$ (d) $CH_3\underset{\displaystyle CH_3}{\underset{|}{\overset{\displaystyle CH_3}{\overset{|}{C^+}}}}$ *(2005)*

50. Which one of the following pairs represents stereoisomerism?
(a) Structural isomerism and geometrical isomerism
(b) Optical isomerism and geometrical isomerism
(c) Chain isomerism and rotational isomerism
(d) Linkage isomerism and geometrical isomerism. *(2005)*

51. The best method for the separation of naphthalene and benzoic acid from their mixture is
(a) distillation (b) sublimation
(c) chromatography (d) crystallisation.
(2005)

52. The – OH group of an alcohol or the – COOH group of a carboxylic acid can be replaced by – Cl using
(a) phosphorus pentachloride
(b) hypochlorous acid
(c) chlorine
(d) hydrochloric acid. *(2004)*

53. The molecular formula of diphenyl methane,

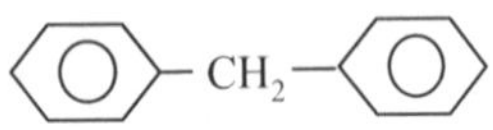

is $C_{13}H_{12}$.

How many structural isomers are possible when one of the hydrogen is replaced by a chlorine atom?
(a) 6 (b) 4
(c) 8 (d) 7 *(2004)*

54. Name of the compound given below is

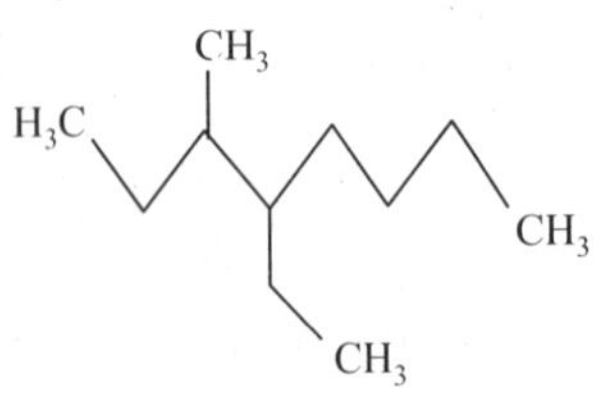

(a) 4-ethyl-3-methyloctane
(b) 3-methyl-4-ethyloctane
(c) 2,3-diethylheptane
(d) 5-ethyl-6-methyloctane *(2003)*

55. Which one of the following orders of acid strength is correct?
(a) $RCOOH > ROH > HOH > HC\equiv CH$
(b) $RCOOH > HOH > ROH > HC\equiv CH$
(c) $RCOOH > HOH > HC\equiv CH > ROH$
(d) $RCOOH > HC\equiv CH > HOH > ROH$ *(2003)*

56. IUPAC name of the following is
$CH_2 = CH - CH_2 - CH_2 - C \equiv CH$
(a) 1,5-hexenyne (b) 1-hexene-5-yne
(c) 1-hexyne-5-ene (d) 1,5-hexynene. *(2002)*

57. Geometrical isomers differ in
(a) position of functional group
(b) position of atoms
(c) spatial arrangement of atoms
(d) length of carbon chain. *(2002)*

58. The incorrect IUPAC name is
(a) $CH_3-C(=O)-CH(CH_3)-CH_3$ -2-methyl-3-butanone
(b) $CH_3-CH(CH_3)-CH(CH_2CH_3)-CH_3$ -2,3-dimethylpentane
(c) $CH_3-C\equiv CCH(CH_3)_2$-4-methyl-2-pentyne
(d) $CH_3CH(Cl)CH(Br)CH_3$-3-bromo-2-chlorobutane. *(2001)*

59. In steam distillation of toluene, the pressure of toluene in vapour is
(a) equal to pressure of barometer
(b) less than pressure of barometer
(c) equal to vapour pressure of toluene in simple distillation
(d) more than vapour pressure of toluene in simple distillation. *(2001)*

60. Which one of the following orders is correct regarding the – I effect of the substituents?
(a) $-NR_2 < -OR < -F$ (b) $-NR_2 > -OR > -F$
(c) $-NR_2 < -OR > -F$ (d) $-NR_2 > -OR < -F$ *(1998)*

61. The following reaction is described as

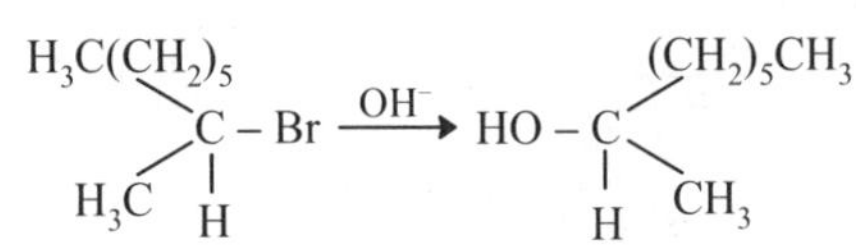

(a) S_N2 (b) S_N0
(c) S_E2 (d) S_N1 *(1997)*

62. Tautomerism is exhibited by
(a) R_3CNO_2 (b) RCH_2NO_2
(c) $(CH_3)_3CNO$ (d) $(CH_3)_2NH$ *(1997)*

63. Which of the following technique is most suitable for purification of cyclohexanone from a mixture containing benzoic acid, isoamyl alcohol, cyclohexane and cyclohexanone?
(a) Sublimation (b) Evaporation
(c) Crystallisation (d) IR spectroscopy *(1997)*

64. The number of isomers in $C_4H_{10}O$ will be
(a) 7 (b) 8
(c) 5 (d) 6 *(1996)*

65. The IUPAC name of $(CH_3)_2CH - CH_2 - CH_2Br$ is
(a) 1-bromo 3-methylbutane
(b) 2-methyl-3-bromopropane
(c) 1-bromopentane
(d) 2-methyl-4-bromobutane. *(1996)*

66. Which of the following is used as an antiknocking material?
(a) Glyoxal (b) Freon
(c) T.E.L. (d) Ethyl alcohol
(1996)

67. In which of the following compounds there is more than one kind of hybridization (sp, sp^2, sp^3) for carbon?
(a) $CH_2=CH-CH=CH_2$
(b) $H-C\equiv C-H$
(c) $CH_3CH_2CH_2CH_3$
(d) $CH_3-CH = CH-CH_3$ *(1995)*

68. The IUPAC name for
$CH_3CH=CHCH_2\underset{\underset{NH_2}{|}}{CH}CH_2COOH$ is
(a) 3-amino-5-heptenoic acid
(b) β-amino-δ-heptenoic acid
(c) 5-amino-2-heptenoic acid
(d) 5-amino-hex-2-enecarboxylic acid. *(1995)*

69. Which of the following statements is not correct?
(a) Double bond is shorter than a single bond.
(b) Sigma bond is weaker than a π (pi) bond.
(c) Double bond is stronger than a single bond.
(d) Covalent bond is stronger than hydrogen bond. *(1993)*

70. When the hybridization state of carbon atom changes from sp^3 to sp^2 and finally to sp, the angle between the hybridized orbitals
(a) decreases gradually
(b) decreases considerably
(c) is not affected
(d) increases progressively. *(1993)*

71. Which of the following fertilizers has the highest nitrogen percentage?
(a) Ammonium sulphate
(b) Calcium cyanamide
(c) Urea
(d) Ammonium nitrate *(1993)*

72. 2-Methyl-2-butene will be represented as
(a) $CH_3-\overset{\overset{CH_3}{|}}{CH}-CH_2CH_3$
(b) $CH_3-\underset{\underset{CH_3}{|}}{C}=CH-CH_3$
(c) $CH_3-CH_2-\underset{\underset{CH_3}{|}}{C}=CH_2$
(d) $CH_3-\underset{\underset{CH_3}{|}}{CH}-CH=CH_2$ *(1992)*

73. The IUPAC name of
$CH_3-\underset{\underset{OH}{|}}{CH}-CH=\underset{\underset{CH_3}{|}}{C}-CHO$
(a) 4-hydroxy-1-methylpentanal
(b) 4-hydroxy-2-methylpent-2-en-1al
(c) 2-hydroxy-4-methylpent-3-en-5-al
(d) 2-hydroxy-3-methylpent-2-en-5-al *(1992)*

74. Isomers of a substance must have the same
(a) structural formula
(b) physical properties
(c) chemical properties
(d) molecular formula. *(1991)*

75. Which of the following is the most stable carbocation (carbonium ion)?
(a) $CH_3\overset{+}{C}H_2$ (b) $(CH_3)_2\overset{+}{C}H$
(c) $(CH_3)_3\overset{+}{C}$ (d) $C_6H_5\overset{+}{C}H_2$
(1991)

76. In sodium fusion test of organic compounds, the nitrogen of the organic compound is converted into
(a) sodamide (b) sodium cyanide
(c) sodium nitrite (d) sodium nitrate.
(1991)

77. The shortest C–C bond distance is found in
(a) diamond (b) ethane
(c) benzene (d) acetylene.
(1991)

78. A sp^3 hybrid orbital contains
(a) 1/4 s-character (b) 1/2 s-character
(c) 1/3 s-character (d) 2/3 s-character.
(1991)

79. A straight chain hydrocarbon has the molecular formula C_8H_{10}. The hybridization of the carbon atoms from one end of the chain to the other are respectively sp^3, sp^2, sp^2, sp^3, sp^2, sp^2, sp and sp. The structural formula of the hydrocarbon would be
(a) $CH_3C\equiv CCH_2-CH=CHCH=CH_2$
(b) $CH_3CH_2-CH=CHCH=CHC\equiv CH$
(c) $CH_3CH=CHCH_2-C\equiv CCH=CH_2$
(d) $CH_3CH=CHCH_2-CH=CHC\equiv CH$
(1991)

80. Kjeldahl's method is used in the estimation of
(a) nitrogen (b) halogens
(c) sulphur (d) oxygen. *(1990)*

81. An organic compound X(molecular formula $C_6H_7O_2N$) has six carbon atoms in a ring system, two double bonds and a nitro group as substituent, X is
(a) homocyclic but not aromatic
(b) aromatic but not homocyclic
(c) homocyclic and aromatic
(d) heterocyclic and aromatic. *(1990)*

82. Which one of the following can exhibit *cis-trans* isomerism?
(a) $CH_3-CHCl-COOH$
(b) $H-C\equiv C-Cl$
(c) $ClCH=CHCl$
(d) $ClCH_2-CH_2Cl$ *(1989)*

83. Which of the following possesses a *sp*-carbon in its structure?
(a) $CH_2=CCl-CH=CH_2$
(b) $CCl_2=CCl_2$
(c) $CH_2=C=CH_2$
(d) $CH_2=CH-CH=CH_2$ *(1989)*

84. Cyclic hydrocarbon 'A' has all the carbon and hydrogen atoms in a single plane. All the carbon -carbon bonds have the same length, less than 1.54 Å, but more than 1.34 Å. The bond angle will be
(a) 109°28′ (b) 100°
(c) 180° (d) 120° *(1989)*

85. Lassaigne's test is used in qualitative analysis to detect
(a) nitrogen (b) sulphur
(c) chlorine (d) all of these. *(1989)*

86. How many chain isomers could be obtained from the alkane C_6H_{14}?
(a) Four (b) Five
(c) Six (d) Seven *(1988)*

87. The Cl–C–Cl angle in 1, 1, 2, 2-tetrachloroethene and tetrachloromethane respectively will be about
(a) 120° and 109.5° (b) 90° and 109.5°
(c) 109.5°and 90° (d) 109.5° and 120°. *(1988)*

Answer Key

1.	(a,b)	**2.**	(c)	**3.**	(b)	**4.**	(c)	**5.**	(d)	**6.**	(c)	**7.**	(a)	**8.**	(d)	**9.**	(a)	**10.**	(c)
11.	(d)	**12.**	(d)	**13.**	(b)	**14.**	(a)	**15.**	(a)	**16.**	(a)	**17.**	(c)	**18.**	(d)	**19.**	(a)	**20.**	(c)
21.	(c)	**22.**	(d)	**23.**	(b)	**24.**	(a)	**25.**	(a)	**26.**	(b)	**27.**	(b)	**28.**	(c)	**29.**	(a)	**30.**	(b)
31.	(b)	**32.**	(a)	**33.**	(b)	**34.**	(c)	**35.**	(a)	**36.**	(a)	**37.**	(a)	**38.**	(c)	**39.**	(b)	**40.**	(c)
41.	(b)	**42.**	(a)	**43.**	(c)	**44.**	(a)	**45.**	(c)	**46.**	(c)	**47.**	(c)	**48.**	(a)	**49.**	(d)	**50.**	(b)
51.	(b)	**52.**	(a)	**53.**	(b)	**54.**	(a)	**55.**	(b)	**56.**	(b)	**57.**	(c)	**58.**	(a)	**59.**	(b)	**60.**	(a)
61.	(a)	**62.**	(b)	**63.**	(d)	**64.**	(a)	**65.**	(a)	**66.**	(c)	**67.**	(d)	**68.**	(a)	**69.**	(b)	**70.**	(d)
71.	(c)	**72.**	(b)	**73.**	(b)	**74.**	(d)	**75.**	(c)	**76.**	(b)	**77.**	(d)	**78.**	(a)	**79.**	(d)	**80.**	(a)
81.	(a)	**82.**	(c)	**83.**	(c)	**84.**	(d)	**85.**	(d)	**86.**	(b)	**87.**	(a)						

EXPLANATIONS

1. (a, b) : $-I$ effect increases on increasing the electronegativity of atom.

$\therefore \; -NH_2 < -OR < -F \quad -I$ effect

Also, $-NR_2 < -OR < -F \quad -I$ effect

2. (c) : $-NO_2$ group is *meta*-directing, thus will stabilize a electrophile at *m*-position.

3. (b) : $\overset{sp^2}{CH_2}=\overset{sp^2}{CH}-\overset{sp}{C}\equiv\overset{sp}{CH}$

4. (c) : The *o*- and *p*-nitrophenols are separated by steam distillation since *o*-isomer is steam volatile due to intramolecular H-bonding while *p*-isomer is not steam volatile due to association of molecules by intermolecular H-bonding.

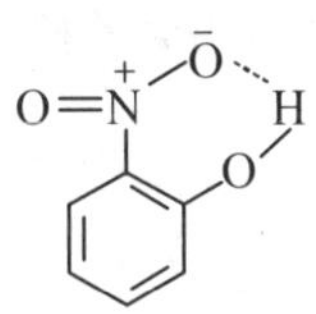

(*o*-Nitrophenol)

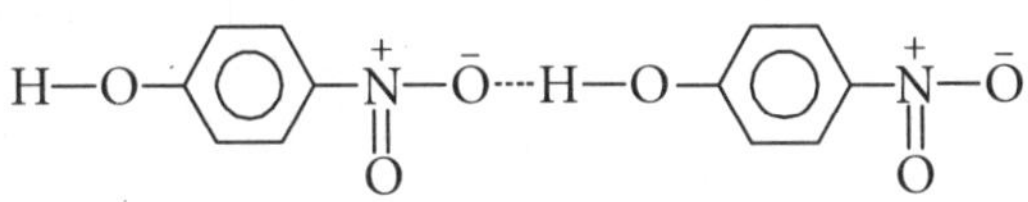

Intermolecular H-bonding (*p*-Nitrophenol)

5. (d) :

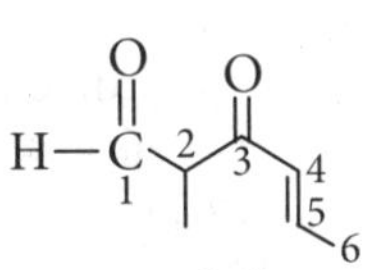

3-Keto-2-methylhex-4-enal

6. (c)

7. (a) : α-Hydrogen at bridge carbon never participate in tautomerism. Thus, only (III) exhibits tautomerism.

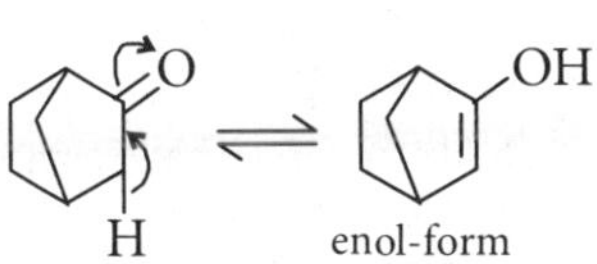

keto-form (III) enol-form

8. (d) : Nucleophiles are electron rich species hence, they are Lewis bases.

9. (a) :

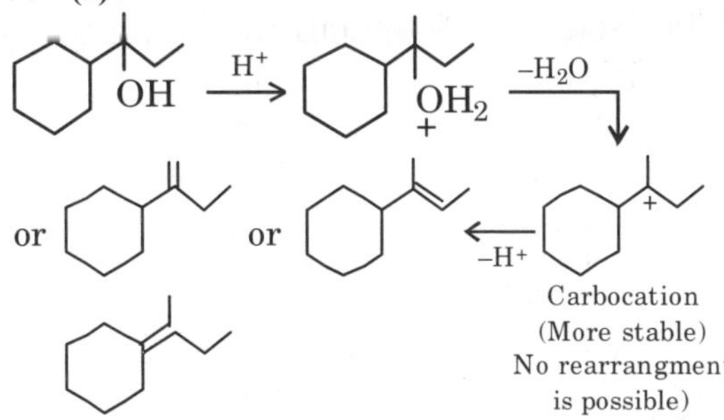

10. (c) :

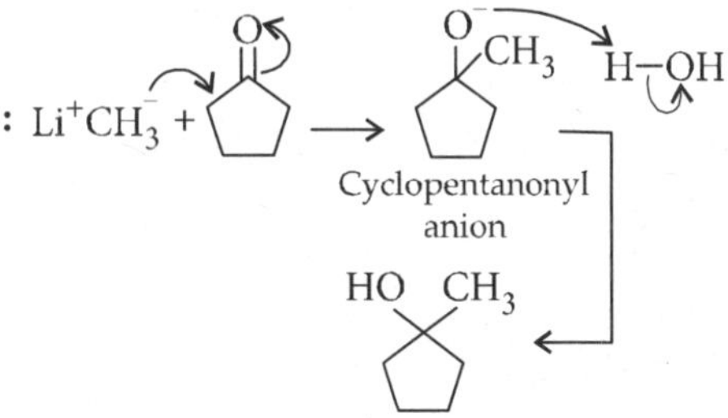

11. (d) : There are four double bonds. Hence, no. of π-electrons = 2 × 4 = 8

12. (d) : $CH_2(CN)_2$, $N\equiv C-CH_2-C\equiv N$ $(6\,\sigma + 4\,\pi)$

HCO_3^-,

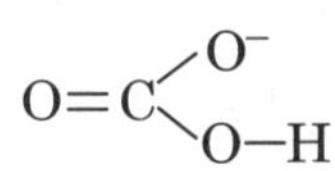

$(4\,\sigma + 1\,\pi)$

XeO_4,

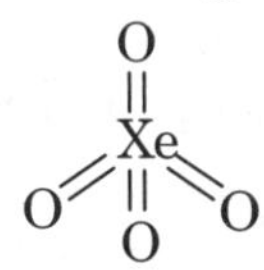

$(4\,\sigma + 4\,\pi)$

$(CN)_2$, $N\equiv C-C\equiv N$ $(3\,\sigma + 4\,\pi)$

13. (b) : In keto-enol tautomerism,

(I)

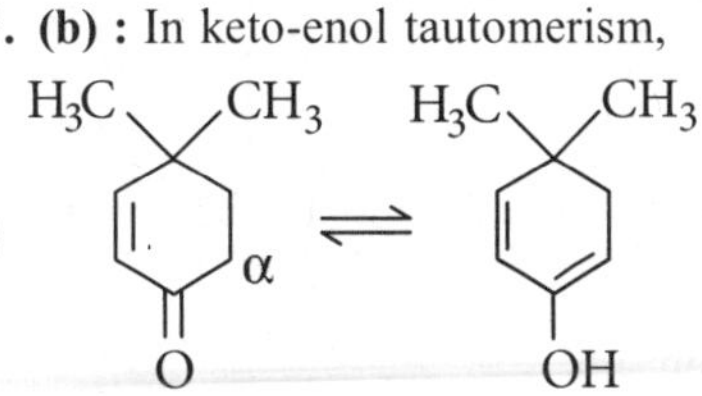

here, α-H participates.

(II)

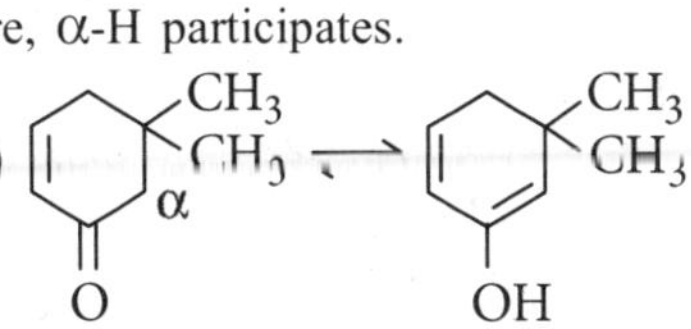

here, α-H participates.

(III) 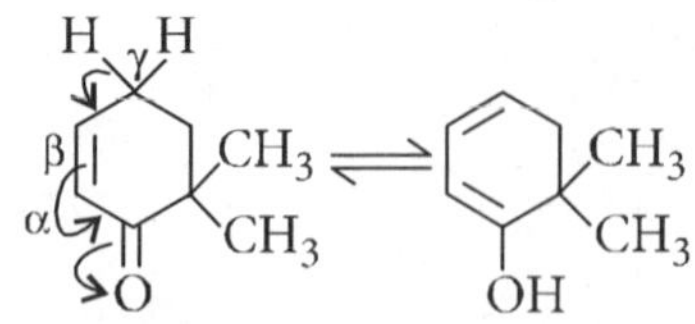

here, γ-H participates (*p*-tautomerism).

14. (a) : Nucleophile will attack a stable carbocation (S_N1 reaction).

$H_3C \rightarrow CH{=}CH{-}CH_2{-}Cl \longrightarrow H_3C \rightarrow \overset{+}{C}H{-}CH{=}CH_2$

(Stable due to $+I$ effect of $-CH_3$ group)

15. (a) : Mass of organic compound = 0.25 g

Experimental values, At STP,

$V_1 = 40$ mL

$V_2 = ?$

$T_1 = 300$ K

$T_2 = 273$ K

$P_1 = 725 - 25 = 700$ mm

$P_2 = 760$ mm

$$\frac{P_1V_1}{T_1} = \frac{P_2V_2}{T_2}$$

$$V_2 = \frac{P_1V_1T_2}{T_1P_2} = \frac{700 \times 40 \times 273}{300 \times 760} = 33.52 \text{ mL}$$

22400 mL of N_2 at STP weighs = 28 g

$$\therefore \; 33.52 \text{ mL of } N_2 \text{ at STP weighs} = \frac{28 \times 33.52}{22400} = 0.0419 \text{ g}$$

$$\% \text{ of N} = \frac{\text{Mass of nitrogen at STP}}{\text{Mass of organic compound taken}} \times 100$$

$$= \frac{0.0419}{0.25} \times 100 = 16.76\%$$

16. (a) : Hyperconjugation can occur only in compound III as it has α-hydrogen atoms.

17. (c)

18. (d) : $H_3C{-}\overset{CH_3}{\underset{CH_3}{C^+}}$ is most stable due to hyperconjugation.

19. (a) : $H_2SO_4 + 2NH_3 \rightarrow (NH_4)_2SO_4$

10 mL of 1 M H_2SO_4 = 10 mmol

$[\because M \times V_{(mL)} = \text{mmol}]$

NH_3 consumed = 20 mmol

Acid used for the absorption of ammonia

= 20 – 10 mmol

= 10 mL of 2 N (or 1 M) H_2SO_4

$$\% \text{ of N} = \frac{1.4 \times N \times V}{W} = \frac{1.4 \times 2 \times 10}{0.75} = 37.33\%$$

20. (c) **21. (c)**

22. (d): 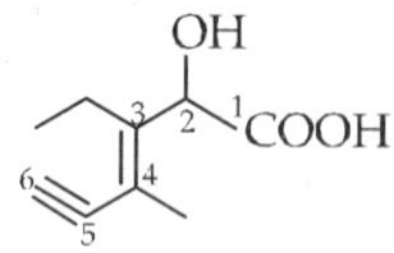

IUPAC name of the structure is 3-Ethyl-2-hydroxy-4-methylhex-3-en-5-ynoic acid.

23. (b) : $-NO_2$ is most deactivating due to $-I$ and $-M$ effect.

24. (a) : Greater the number of electron donating alkyl groups ($+I$ effect), greater is the stability of carbocations.

$+I$ effect is in the order :

$$CH_3{-}\underset{CH_3}{\overset{CH_3}{C}}{-} > CH_3{-}\overset{CH_3}{CH}{-} > CH_3{-}CH_2{-} > CH_3{-}$$

Hence the order of stability of carbocations is $5 < 4 < 3 < 1 < 2$

25. (a)

26. (b) : $\underset{\text{Sodium ferrocyanide}}{3Na_4[Fe(CN)_6]} + 2Fe_2(SO_4)_3 \rightarrow \underset{\text{Ferric ferrocyanide (Prussian blue)}}{Fe_4[Fe(CN)_6]_3} + 6Na_2SO_4$

27. (b) : More the number of hyperconjugative structures, the greater is the stability.

28. (c) : As the $+I$ effect increases reactivity towards electrophilic reactions increases and as $-I$ or $-M$ effect increases reactivity towards electrophilic reactions decreases. Thus, the order is

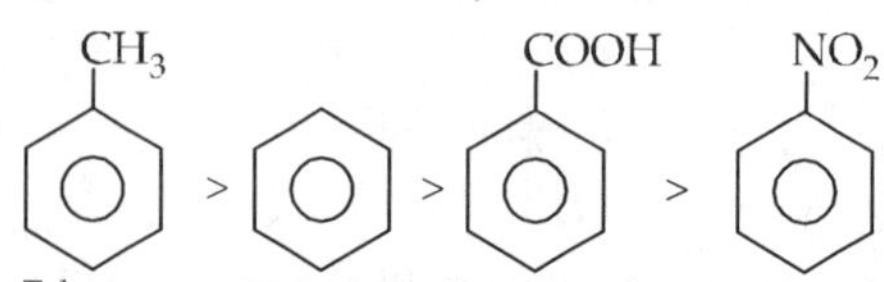

Toluene > Benzene > Benzoic acid > Nitrobenzene

29. (a) : $Br - \overset{3}{C}H_2 - \overset{2}{C}H = \overset{1}{C}H_2$

3-Bromopropene

30. (b) : $CH_3 - C \equiv C - CH_3$

In case of sp^3 hybridised carbon, bond angle is 109° 28′; sp^2 hybridised carbon, bond angle is 120° and sp hybridised carbon, bond angle is 180°.

So, only $CH_3 - \underset{sp}{C} \equiv \underset{sp}{C} - CH_3$ is linear.

31. (b) : $+R$ effect of $-$OH group is greater than that of $-OCH_3$ group.

32. (a): 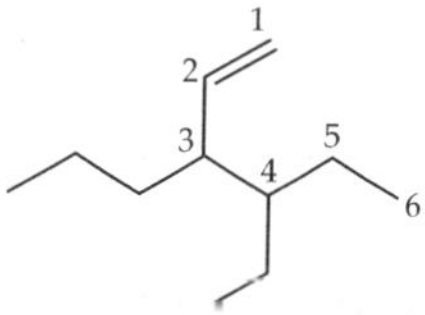

33. (b): Given $V_1 = 55$ mL, $V_2 = ?$
$P_1 = 715 - 15 = 700$ mm, $P_2 = 760$ mm
$T_1 = 300$ K, $T_2 = 273$ K

General gas equation, $\frac{P_1V_1}{T_1} = \frac{P_2V_2}{T_2}$

Volume of nitrogen at STP,

$$V_2 = \frac{P_1V_1T_2}{P_2T_1} = \frac{700 \times 55 \times 273}{760 \times 300} = 46.099 \text{ mL}$$

% of nitrogen = $\frac{V_2}{8W}$, were W = the mass of organic compound.

$$\% \text{ of N} = \frac{46.099}{8 \times 0.35} = 16.46$$

34. (c): Nucleophilic substitution reaction involves he displacement of a nucleophile by another.

35. (a): In case of Lassaigne's test of halogens, it s necessary to remove sodium cyanide and sodium ulphide from the sodium extract if nitrogen and ulphur are present. This is done by boiling the odium extract with conc. HNO_3.
$NaCN + HNO_3 \rightarrow NaNO_3 + HCN\uparrow$
$Na_2S + 2HNO_3 \rightarrow 2NaNO_3 + H_2S\uparrow$

6. (a): Electron withdrawing groups like $-NO_2$ acilitates nucleophilic substitution reaction in hlorobenzene.

7. (a): 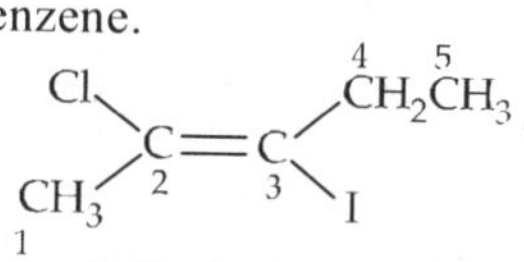

trans-2-chloro-3-iodo-2-pentene

8. (c)

9. (b): $\overset{5}{C}H_3\overset{4}{C}H=\overset{3}{C}H\overset{2}{C}\equiv\overset{1}{C}H$

Pent-3-en-1-yne

act : If a molecule contains both carbon-carbon ouble or triple bonds, the two are treated as per in eking the lowest number combination. However, the sum of numbers turns out to be the same arting from either of the carbon chain, then lowest umber is given to the C=C double bond.

. (c): $\overset{4}{C}H\equiv\overset{3}{C}-\overset{2}{C}H=\overset{1}{C}H_2$

1-Butene-3-yne

nce the sum of numbers starting from either side the carbon chain turns out to be the same, so west number is given to the C=C end.

41. (b): $\underset{sp}{H-C}\equiv\underset{sp}{C}-H > \underset{sp^2}{CH_2}=\underset{sp^2}{CH_2} > \underset{sp^3}{CH_3CH_3}$
(Acidic character)

Conjugate base of the given acid :

$\overset{\ominus}{C}\equiv C-H < \overset{\ominus}{C}H=CH_2 < \overset{\ominus}{C}H_2CH_3$
(Basic character)

Conjugate base of stronger acid is weaker and vice-versa.

42. (a): Groups like, –Cl and $-NO_2$ shows $-I$ effect. $-I$ groups attached to the benzene ring decrease the electron density and hence less prone to electrophilic attack. –OH not only shows $-I$ effect but also $+M$ effect which predominates the $-I$ character and electron density is increased in the benzene ring which facilitates electrophilic attack.

43. (c): Higher the no. of electron releasing group lower will be stability of carbanion, and vice-versa. So the order of stability of carbanions is

$RC\equiv C^{\ominus}$ > 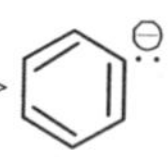 > $R_2C=\bar{C}H > R_3C-\bar{C}H_2$

44. (a): In case of different nucleophiles, but present in the same group in the periodic table, then larger is the atomic mass, higher is the nucleophilicity. Hence the decreasing order of nucleophilicity of the halide ions is
$I^- > Br^- > Cl^- > F^-$.

45. (c): Electrophiles are electron loving chemical species. They attack at the highest electron density site of the substrate. Electron donating substances ($+I$ effect) increases the electron density of the molecule. $+I$ effect decreases in the order:
$-OH > -CH_3 > -H > -Cl$.
Hence order of decreasing reactivity towards electrophile is
$C_6H_5OH > C_6H_5CH_3 > C_6H_6 > C_6H_5Cl$.

46. (c): General molecular formula for alkanols is $C_nH_{2n+2}O$ or $[C_nH_{2n+1}OH]$.

47. (c): 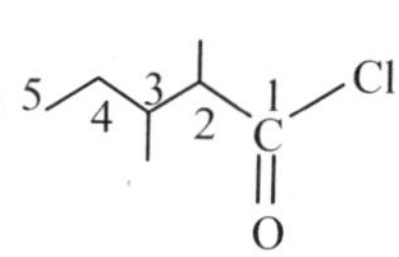

It is 2,3-dimethylpentanoyl chloride.

48. (a): $\overset{7}{C}H_3-\overset{6}{C}H_2\overset{5}{C}H_2\overset{4}{C}H(CH_2CH_3)-\overset{3}{C}H(CH_3)-\overset{2}{C}H_2\overset{1}{C}H_3$

4-Ethyl-3-methylheptane

49. (d) : $H_3C \rightarrow \overset{\overset{CH_3}{\downarrow}}{\underset{\underset{CH_3}{\uparrow}}{C^+}}$

3°C is more stable due to the stabilization of the charge by three methyl groups (or inductive effect). It can also be explained on the basis of hyperconjugation.

50. (b):

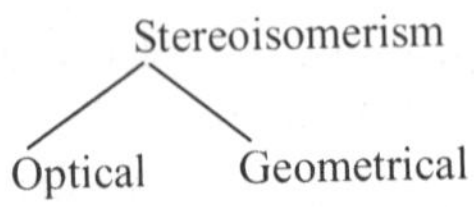

51. (b): Sublimation method is used for those organic substances which pass directly from solid to vapour state on heating and vice-versa on cooling. *e.g.* benzoic acid, naphthalene, camphor, anthracene, etc. Naphthalene is volatile and benzoic acid is non-volatile due to the formation of the dimer.

52. (a) : $ROH + PCl_5 \rightarrow RCl + POCl_3 + HCl$
$RCOOH + PCl_5 \rightarrow RCOCl + POCl_3 + HCl$

53. (b) : Only four structural isomers are possible for diphenyl methane.

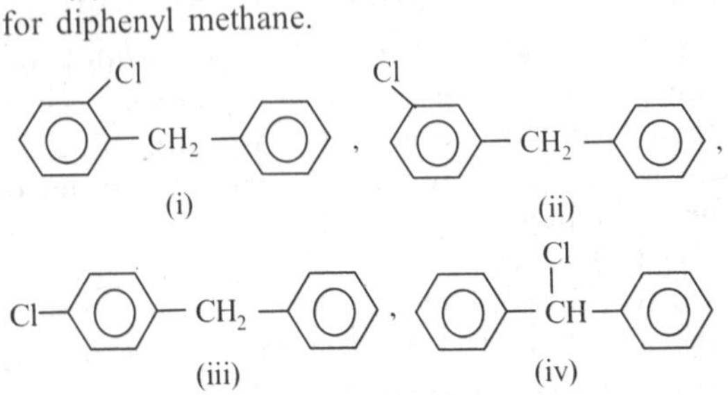

54. (a) :

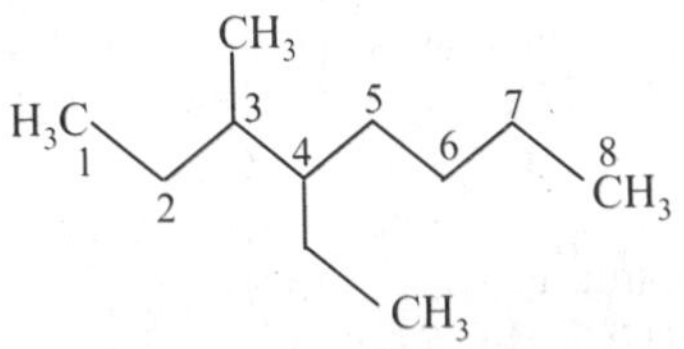

4-ethyl-3-methyloctane

55. (b) : Carboxylic acid is much stronger than water and alcohol. Since the carboxylate ion after the removal of proton is stabilised by resonating structures. The – OH in alcohols is almost neutral. Acetylene is also weakest acid.

56. (b) : $\overset{1}{C}H_2 = \overset{2}{C}H - \overset{3}{C}H_2 - \overset{4}{C}H_2 - \overset{5}{C} \equiv \overset{6}{C}H$

The double bond gets priority over triple bond. Therefore correct IUPAC name is 1-hexene-5-yne.

57. (c) : Geometrical isomers are those isomers which possess the same molecular and structural formula but differ in the arrangement of atoms or groups in space due to hindered rotation around the double bonded atoms.

58. (a) : $\overset{4}{C}H_3 - \underset{\underset{O}{\|}}{\overset{3}{C}} - \underset{\underset{CH_3}{|}}{\overset{2}{C}H} - \overset{1}{C}H_3$ (wrong numbering)

The $-\overset{\overset{O}{\|}}{C}-$ group should get priority over methy group.

$\therefore$ Correct IUPAC name is

$\overset{1}{C}H_3 - \underset{\underset{O}{\|}}{\overset{2}{C}} - \underset{\underset{CH_3}{|}}{\overset{3}{C}H} - \overset{4}{C}H_3$ 3-Methyl-2-butanone

59. (b) : Steam distillation is essentially Co distillation with water and is carried out when a soli or liquid is insoluble in water and is volatile wit steam but the impurities are non-volatile.

60. (a) : The electronegativity of F, O, and N follow the order: N < O < F

Therefore the negative inductive effect of – NR_2 –*OR* and –F follows the order:

$-NR_2 < -OR < -F$

61. (a) : S_N2 reaction are bimolecular reaction where rate of reaction depends on the concentratio of both substrate and nucleophile. When OH attacks the substrate from the opposite side of th leaving group *i.e.*, Br^- a transition state results, i which both OH and Br are partially bonded t carbon atom.

62. (b) : It is a special type of functional isomerisr in which both the isomers are represented by or and the same substance and are always present equilibrium. It is exhibited by nitroalka (RCH_2NO_2) and isonitroalkane.

63. (d) : In the IR spectroscopy, each function group appears at a certain peak (in cm^{-1}). S cyclohexanone can be identified by carbonyl pea

64. (a) : There are 7 isomers in $C_4H_{10}O$. Out these, 4 are alcohols and 3 are ethers.

$CH_3CH_2 - O - CH_2CH_3$, $CH_3OCH_2CH_2CH$

$CH_3OCH\begin{matrix} CH_3 \\ CH_3 \end{matrix}$

$CH_3CH_2CH_2CH_2OH$, $CH_3CH_2\underset{\underset{OH}{|}}{C}H - CH_3$

$\begin{matrix} CH_3 \\ CH_3 \end{matrix} CH - CH_2OH$, $CH_3 - \underset{\underset{OH}{|}}{\overset{\overset{CH_3}{|}}{C}} - CH_3$

65. (a) : $H_3C - \underset{\underset{CH_3}{|}}{\overset{\overset{H}{|}}{C}} - \underset{\underset{H}{|}}{\overset{\overset{H}{|}}{C}} - \underset{\underset{H}{|}}{\overset{\overset{H}{|}}{C}} - Br$

1-Bromo-3-methylbutane

66. (c) : Tetraethyl lead $(C_2H_5)_4Pb$, is used as an antiknocking agent in gasoline used for running automobiles.

67. (d) : $\underset{sp^3}{CH_3} - \underset{sp^2}{CH} = \underset{sp^2}{CH} - \underset{sp^3}{CH_3}$

68. (a) :

$$\overset{7}{CH_3} - \overset{6}{CH} = \overset{5}{CH} - \overset{4}{CH_2} - \underset{NH_2}{\overset{3}{CH}} - \overset{2}{CH_2} - \overset{1}{COOH}$$

As – COOH group is highest priority group, it is numbered one. So, the IUPAC name is 3-amino-5-heptenoic acid.

69. (b) : Sigma bond is stronger than π-bond because of better overlap. All single bonds are σ bonds and all multiple bonds contain one σ and other π bonds.

70. (d) : Angle increases progressively
$sp^3(109°28')$, $sp^2(120°)$, $sp(180°)$

71. (c) : Urea (46.6% N). % of N in other compounds are : $(NH_4)_2SO_4$ = 21.2%; $CaCN_2$ = 35.0% and NH_4NO_3 = 35.0%

72. (b) : $^{1}CH_3 - {}^{2}\overset{CH_3}{C} = {}^{3}CH - {}^{4}CH_3$

2-Methyl-2-butene

73. (b) : $^{5}CH_3 - {}^{4}\underset{OH}{CH} - {}^{3}CH = {}^{2}\underset{CH_3}{C} - {}^{1}CHO$

4-Hydroxy-2-methylpent-2-en-1-al

74. (d) : Isomers must have same molecular formula but different structural formula.

75. (c) : 3° > 2° > 1° more the delocalisation of positive charge, more is its stability.

76. (b) : Sodium cyanide (Na + C + N → NaCN).

77. (d) : Shortest C–C distance (1.20 Å) is in acetylene.

78. (a) : sp^3 orbital has 1/4 (25%) *s*-character.

79. (d) : $\overset{sp^3}{CH_3}\overset{sp^2}{CH} = \overset{sp^2}{C}H\overset{sp^3}{CH_2} - \overset{sp^2}{CH} = \overset{sp^2}{C}H\overset{sp}{C} \equiv \overset{sp}{CH}$

80. (a)

81. (a) : 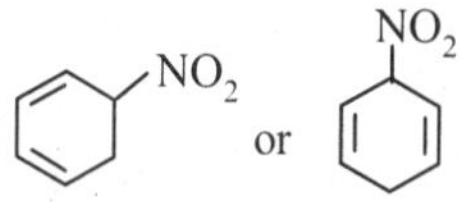

Hence it is homocyclic (as the ring system is made of one type of atoms, *i.e.*, carbon) but not aromatic.

82. (c) :

Cl – C – H ‖ Cl – C – H	Cl – C – H ‖ H – C – Cl
(*cis*)	(*trans*)

1, 2-dichloroethene exhibits *cis-trans* (geometrical) isomerism.

83. (c) : $\overset{sp^2}{CH_2} = \overset{sp}{C} = \overset{sp^2}{CH_2}$

84. (d) : All the properties mentioned in the question suggest that it is a benzene molecule. Since in benzene all carbons are sp^2-hybridized, therefore, C – C – C angle is 120°.

85. (d) : All the three (N, S, halogens).

86. (b) : 5-chain isomers are obtained from alkane C_6H_{14}.

(i) $CH_3CH_2CH_2CH_2CH_2CH_3$

(ii) $CH_3 - \underset{CH_3}{CH} - CH_2 - CH_2 - CH_3$

(iii) $CH_3 - \underset{CH_3}{\overset{CH_3}{C}} - CH_2CH_3$

(iv) $CH_3 - \underset{CH_3}{CH} - \underset{CH_3}{CH} - CH_3$

(v) $CH_3CH_2\underset{CH_3}{CH} - CH_2CH_3$

87. (a) : Tetrachloroethene being an alkene has sp^2-hybridized C-atoms and hence the angle Cl – C – Cl is 120° while in tetrachloromethane, carbon is sp^3 hybridized, therefore the angle Cl – C – Cl is 109°28′.

Chapter 13

Hydrocarbons

1. Hydrocarbon (A) reacts with bromine by substitution to form an alkyl bromide which by Wurtz reaction is converted to gaseous hydrocarbon containing less than four carbon atoms. (A) is

(a) $CH\equiv CH$ (b) $CH_2=CH_2$
(c) CH_3-CH_3 (d) CH_4

(NEET 2018)

2. Which one is the correct order of acidity?

(a) $CH\equiv CH > CH_3-C\equiv CH > CH_2=CH_2 > CH_3-CH_3$
(b) $CH\equiv CH > CH_2=CH_2 > CH_3-C\equiv CH > CH_3-CH_3$
(c) $CH_3-CH_3 > CH_2=CH_2 > CH_3-C\equiv CH > CH\equiv CH$
(d) $CH_2=CH_2 > CH_3-CH=CH_2 > CH_3-C\equiv CH > CH\equiv CH$

(NEET 2017)

3. Predict the correct intermediate and product in the following reaction :

$$H_3C-C\equiv CH \xrightarrow[HgSO_4]{H_2O,\ H_2SO_4} \underset{(A)}{\text{Intermediate}} \rightarrow \underset{(B)}{\text{Product}}$$

(a) $A: H_3C-\underset{OH}{\underset{|}{C}}=CH_2$ $B: H_3C-\underset{SO_4}{\underset{|}{C}}=CH_2$

(b) $A: H_3C-\underset{O}{\underset{\|}{C}}-CH_3$ $B: H_3C-C\equiv CH$

(c) $A: H_3C-\underset{OH}{\underset{|}{C}}=CH_2$ $B: H_3C-\underset{O}{\underset{\|}{C}}-CH_3$

(d) $A: H_3C-\underset{SO_4}{\underset{|}{C}}=CH_2$ $B: H_3C-\underset{O}{\underset{\|}{C}}-CH_3$

(NEET 2017)

4. With respect to the conformers of ethane, which of the following statements is true?

(a) Bond angle changes but bond length remains same.
(b) Both bond angle and bond length change
(c) Both bond angle and bond length remain same.
(d) Bond angle remains same but bond length changes.

(NEET 2017)

5. Which of the following can be used as the halide component for Friedel–Crafts reaction?

(a) Chlorobenzene
(b) Bromobenzene
(c) Chloroethene
(d) Isopropyl chloride

(NEET-II 2016)

6. In which of the following molecules, all atom are coplanar?

(a) 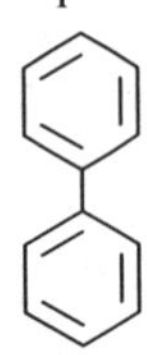

(b) 

(c) 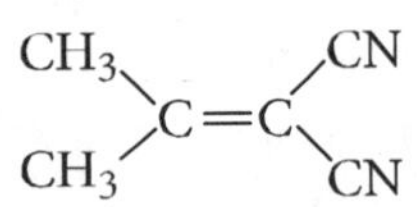

(d) 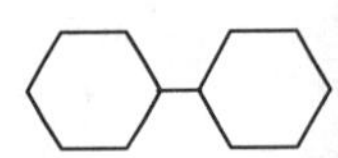

(NEET-II 2016)

7. In pyrrole the electron density is maximum o

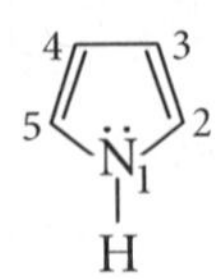

(a) 2 and 3 (b) 3 and 4
(c) 2 and 4 (d) 2 and 5

(NEET-II 201

8. Which of the following compounds shall n produce propene by reaction with HBr followe by elimination or direct only eliminatio reaction?

(a) 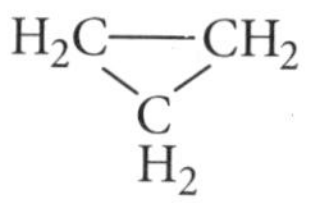

(b) $H_3C-\overset{H_2}{C}-CH_2OH$

(c) $H_2C=C=O$

(d) $H_3C-\overset{H_2}{C}-CH_2Br$ *(NEET-II 2016)*

9. In the given reaction,

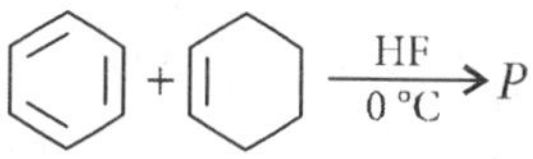

the product P is

(a) 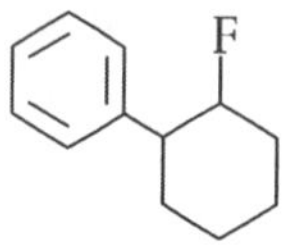

(b) 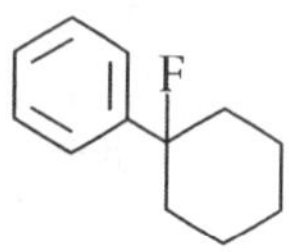

(c) 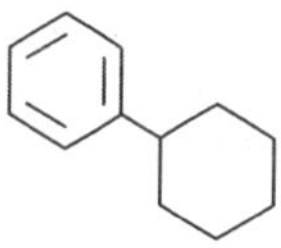

(d) 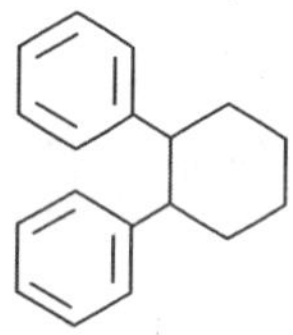

(NEET-II 2016)

10. The compound that will react most readily with gaseous bromine has the formula

(a) C_3H_6 (b) C_2H_2

(c) C_4H_{10} (d) C_2H_4

(NEET-II 2016)

11. The correct statement regarding the comparison of staggered and eclipsed conformations of ethane, is

(a) the eclipsed conformation of ethane is more stable than staggered conformation even though the eclipsed conformation has torsional strain

(b) the staggered conformation of ethane is more stable than eclipsed conformation, because staggered conformation has no torsional strain

(c) the staggered conformation of ethane is less stable than eclipsed conformation, because staggered conformation has torsional strain

(d) the eclipsed conformation of ethane is more stable than staggered conformation, because eclipsed conformation has no torsional strain. *(NEET-I 2016)*

12. Consider the nitration of benzene using mixed conc. H_2SO_4 and HNO_3. If a large amount of $KHSO_4$ is added to the mixture, the rate of nitration will be

(a) unchanged (b) doubled

(c) faster (d) slower.

(NEET-I 2016)

13. The pair of electrons in the given carbanion, $CH_3C\equiv C^-$, is present in which of the following orbitals?

(a) sp^2 (b) sp

(c) $2p$ (d) sp^3

(NEET-I 2016)

14. In the reaction

$$H-C\equiv CH \xrightarrow[\text{(ii) } CH_3CH_2Br]{\text{(i) } NaNH_2/\text{liq. } NH_3} X \xrightarrow[\text{(ii) } CH_3CH_2Br]{\text{(i) } NaNH_2/\text{liq. } NH_3} Y,$$

X and Y are

(a) X = 2-Butyne, Y = 2-Hexyne

(b) X = 1-Butyne, Y = 2-Hexyne

(c) X = 1-Butyne, Y = 3-Hexyne

(d) X = 2-Butyne, Y = 3-Hexyne. *(NEET-I 2016)*

15. In the reaction with HCl, an alkene reacts in accordance with the Markovnikov's rule to give a product 1-chloro-1-methylcyclohexane. The possible alkene is

(a) 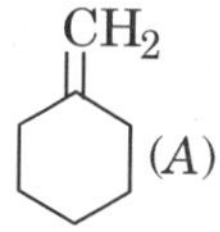 (A)

(b) 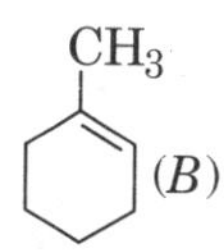 (B)

(c) (A) and (B)

(d) 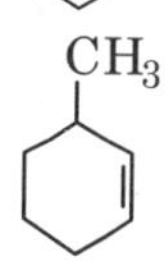 *(2015)*

16. 2,3-Dimethyl-2-butene can be prepared by heating which of the following compounds with a strong acid?

(a) $(CH_3)_3CCH=CH_2$

(b) $(CH_3)_2C=CHCH_2CH_3$

(c) $(CH_3)_2CHCH_2CH=CH_2$

(d) $(CH_3)_2CH-\underset{\underset{CH_3}{|}}{CH}-CH=CH_2$ *(2015)*

17. A single compound of the structure,

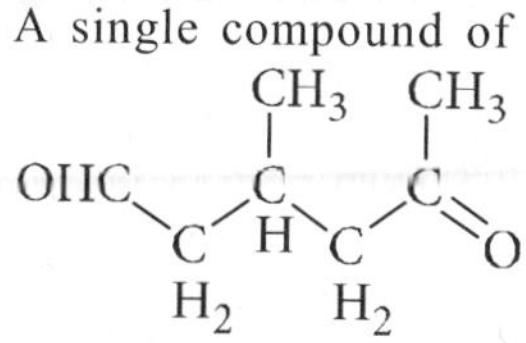

is obtainable from ozonolysis of which of the following cyclic compounds?

(a) 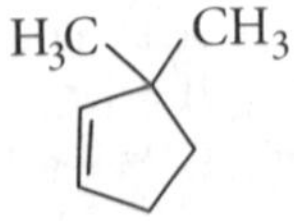 (b) 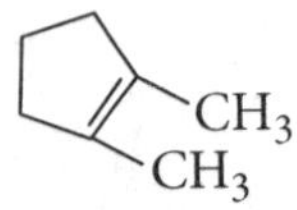

(c) 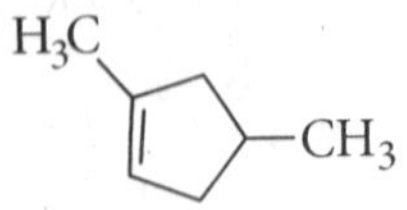 (d) 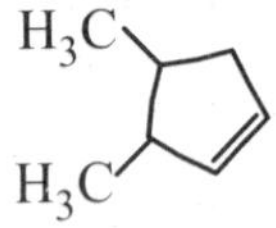

(2015, Cancelled)

18. Given :

I. 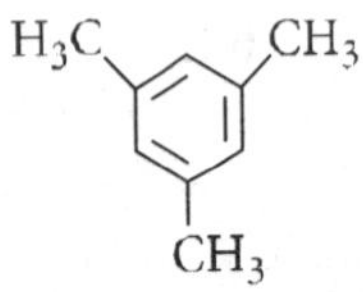 II. 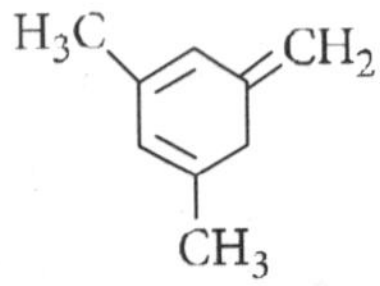

III. 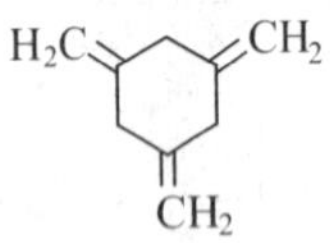

The enthalpy of hydrogenation of these compounds will be in the order as

(a) II > III > I (b) II > I > III
(c) I > II > III (d) III > II > I *(2015, Cancelled)*

19. What products are formed when the following compound is treated with Br_2 in the presence of $FeBr_3$?

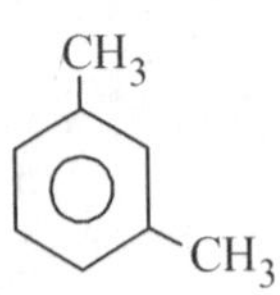

(a) 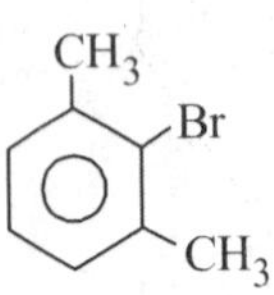 and 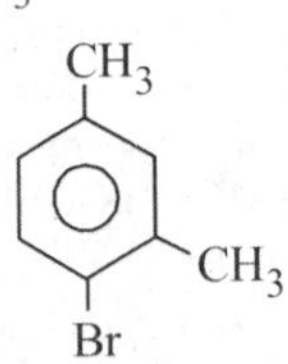

(b) 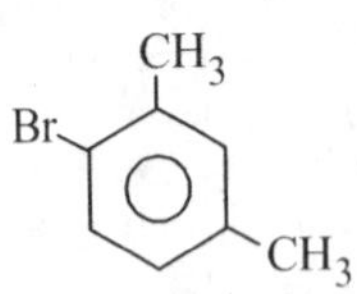 and 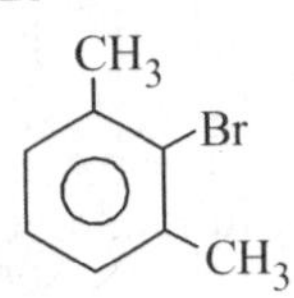

(c) 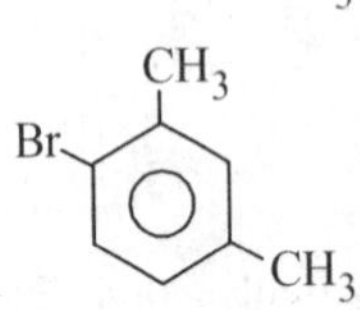 and 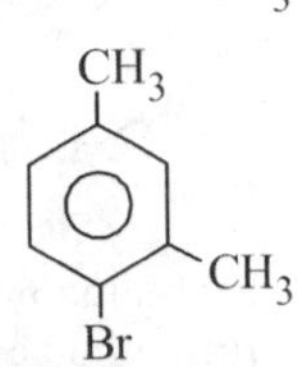

(d) 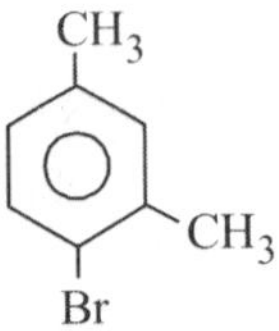 and 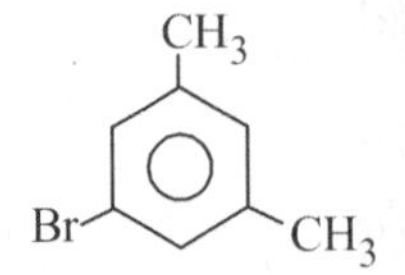

(2014)

20. Identify Z in the sequence of reactions :

$$CH_3CH_2CH=CH_2 \xrightarrow{HBr/H_2O_2} Y \xrightarrow{C_2H_5ONa} Z$$

(a) $CH_3-(CH_2)_3-O-CH_2CH_3$
(b) $(CH_3)_2CH-O-CH_2CH_3$
(c) $CH_3(CH_2)_4-O-CH_3$
(d) $CH_3CH_2-CH(CH_3)-O-CH_2CH_3$ *(2014)*

21. Which of the following organic compounds has same hybridization as its combustion product (CO_2)?

(a) Ethane (b) Ethyne
(c) Ethene (d) Ethanol *(2014)*

22. Which of the following compounds will not undergo Friedel-Crafts reaction easily?

(a) Nitrobenzene (b) Toluene
(c) Cumene (d) Xylene *(NEET 2013)*

23. Which of the following chemical system is non aromatic?

(a)  (b) 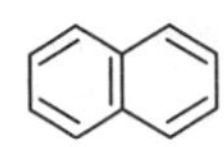

(c)  (d) 

(Karnataka NEET 2013)

24. In the following reaction:

$$HC\equiv CH \xrightarrow[Hg^{2+}]{H_2SO_4} 'P'$$

Product 'P' will not give

(a) Tollens' reagent test
(b) Brady's reagent test
(c) Victor Meyer test
(d) Iodoform test *(Karnataka NEET 2013)*

25. In the following reaction

$$H_3C-\overset{CH_3}{\underset{CH_3}{C}}-CH=CH_2 \xrightarrow{H_2O/H^{\oplus}} \underset{\text{Major product}}{A} + \underset{\text{Minor product}}{B}$$

The major product is

(a) $H_3C-\underset{OH}{\overset{CH_3}{C}}-\underset{CH_3}{CH}-CH_3$

(b) 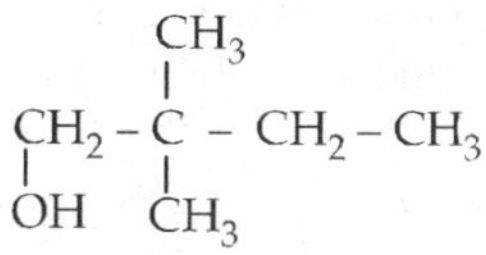

(c) 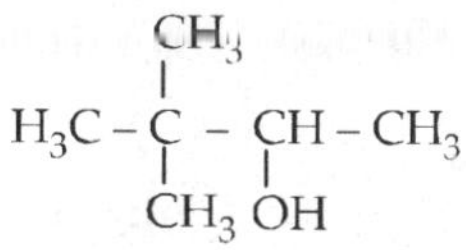

(d) 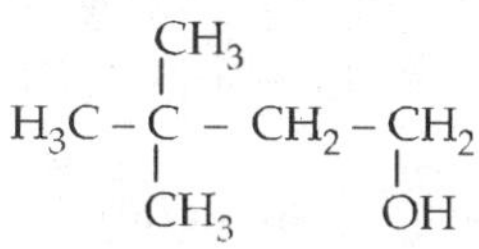 *(2012)*

26. Which of the following reagents will be able to distinguish between 1-butyne and 2-butyne?
(a) $NaNH_2$ (b) HCl
(c) O_2 (d) Br_2 *(Mains 2012)*

27. In the following the most stable conformation of *n*-butane is

(a) 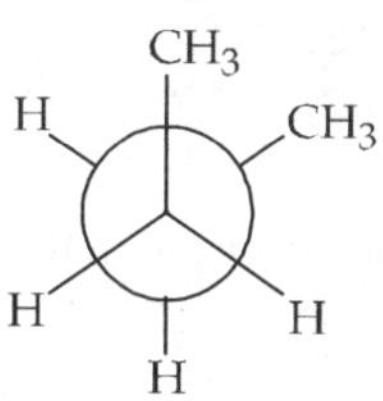

(b) 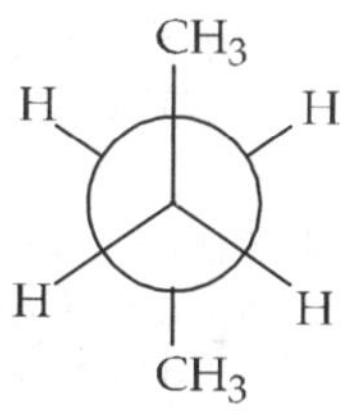

(c) 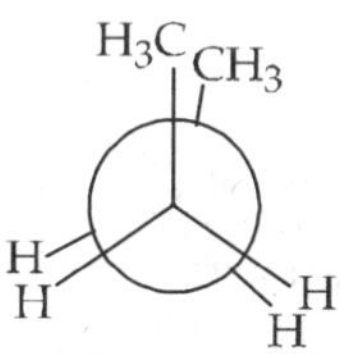

(d) 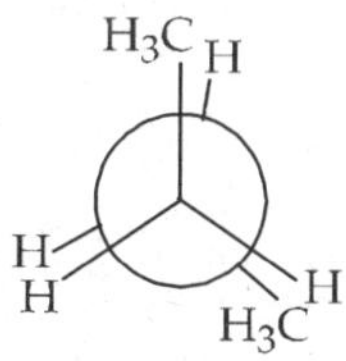

(2010)

28. Liquid hydrocarbons can be converted to a mixture of gaseous hydrocarbons by
(a) oxidation
(b) cracking
(c) distillation under reduced pressure
(d) hydrolysis. *(2010)*

29. The reaction of toluene with Cl_2 in presence of $FeCl_3$ gives *X* and reaction in presence of light gives *Y*. Thus, *X* and *Y* are
(a) *X* = Benzal chloride, *Y* = *o*-chlorotoluene
(b) *X* = *m*-chlorotoluene, *Y* = *p*-chlorotoluene
(c) *X* = *o* and *p* chlorotoluene,
Y = Trichloromethyl benzene
(d) *X* = Benzyl chloride, *Y* = *m*-chlorotoluene *(2010)*

30. In a set of reactions, ethylbenzene yielded a product *D*.

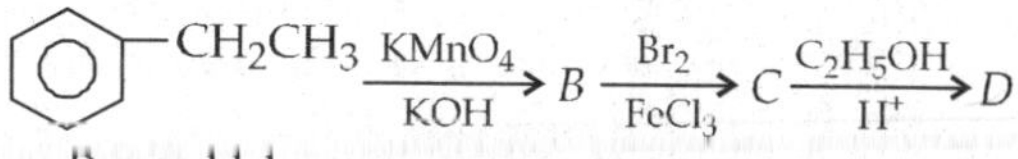

D would be

(a) 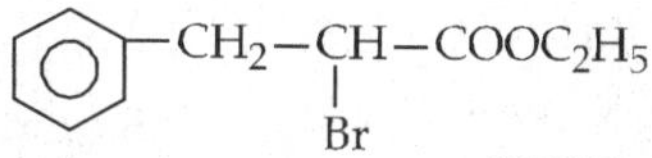

(b) 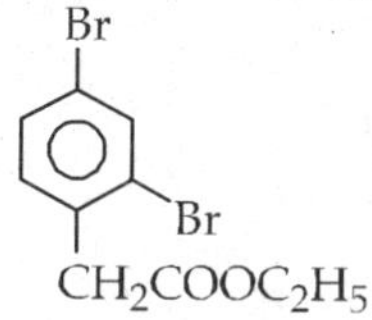

(c) 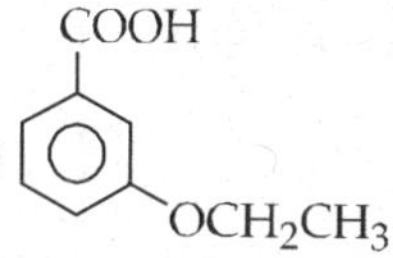

(d) 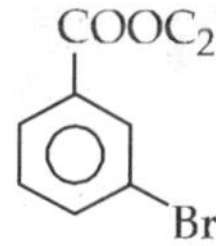 *(2010)*

31. Which of the following conformers for ethylene glycol is most stable?

(a) 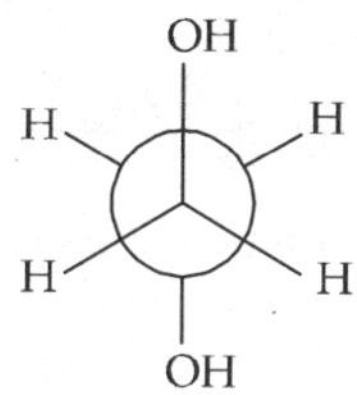

(b) 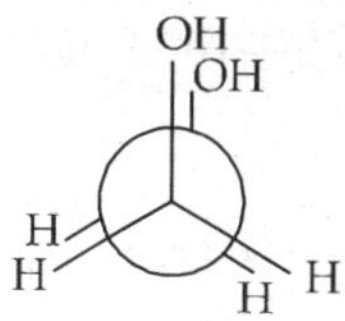

(c) 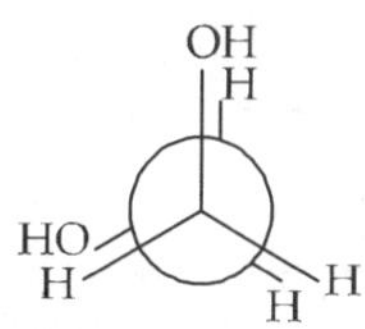

(d) 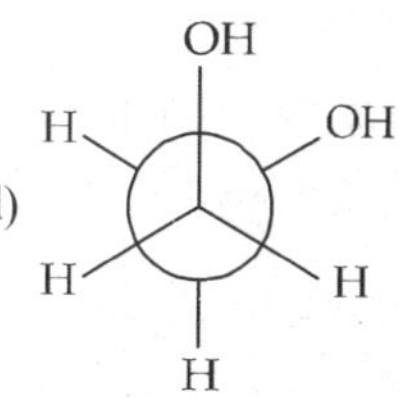

(Mains 2010)

32. The state of hybridisation of C_2, C_3, C_5 and C_6 of the hydrocarbon,

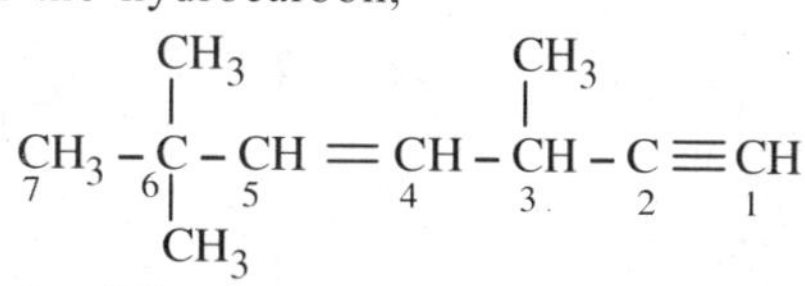

is in the following sequence
(a) sp^3, sp^2, sp^2 and sp
(b) sp, sp^2, sp^2 and sp^3
(c) sp, sp^2, sp^3 and sp^2
(d) sp, sp^3, sp^2 and sp^3 *(2009)*

33. Which of the following compounds will exhibit *cis-trans* (geometrical) isomerism?
(a) Butanol (b) 2-Butyne
(c) 2-Butenol (d) 2-Butene *(2009)*

34. Benzene reacts with CH_3Cl in the presence of anhydrous $AlCl_3$ to form
(a) chlorobenzene (b) benzyl chloride
(c) xylene (d) toluene. *(2009)*

35. $H_3C-\underset{\displaystyle CH_3}{\underset{|}{CH}}-CH=CH_2+HBr \longrightarrow A$

A (predominantly) is
(a) $CH_3-\underset{Br}{\underset{|}{CH}}-\underset{CH_3}{\underset{|}{CH}}-CH_3$
(b) $CH_3-\underset{CH_3}{\underset{|}{CH}}-\underset{Br}{\underset{|}{CH}}-CH_3$
(c) $CH_3-\underset{CH_3}{\underset{|}{CH}}-CH_2-CH_2Br$
(d) $CH_3-\overset{Br}{\overset{|}{\underset{CH_3}{\underset{|}{C}}}}-CH_2CH_3$ *(2008)*

36. In the hydrocarbon,
$\underset{6}{CH_3}-\underset{5}{CH}=\underset{4}{CH}-\underset{3}{CH_2}-\underset{2}{C}\equiv\underset{1}{CH}$
The state of hybridization of carbons 1, 3 and 5 are in the following sequence
(a) sp, sp^2, sp^3 (b) sp^3, sp^2, sp
(c) sp^2, sp, sp^3 (d) sp, sp^3, sp^2
(2008)

37. Predict the product *C* obtained in the following reaction of 1-butyne.
$CH_3CH_2-C\equiv CH + HCl \longrightarrow B \xrightarrow{HI} C$
(a) $CH_3-CH_2-CH_2-\overset{I}{\overset{|}{\underset{Cl}{\underset{|}{C}}}}-H$
(b) $CH_3-CH_2-\overset{I}{\overset{|}{CH}}-CH_2Cl$
(c) $CH_3CH_2-\overset{I}{\overset{|}{\underset{Cl}{\underset{|}{C}}}}-CH_3$
(d) $CH_3-\underset{Cl}{\underset{|}{CH}}-CH_2CH_2I$ *(2007)*

38. Which of the compound with molecular formula C_5H_{10} yields acetone on ozonolysis?
(a) 3-Methyl-1-butene (b) Cyclopentane
(c) 2-Methyl-1-butene (d) 2-Methyl-2-butene
(2007)

39. Which one of the following alkenes will react faster with H_2 under catalytic hydrogenation conditions?
(a) 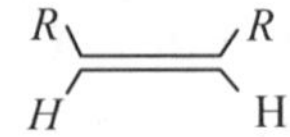 (b) 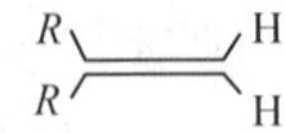
(c) 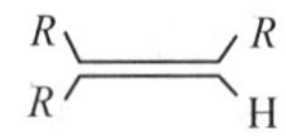 (d) 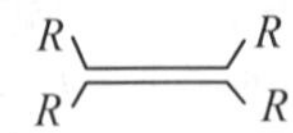
(*R* = alkyl substituent)
(2005)

40. Products of the following reaction :
$CH_3C\equiv CCH_2CH_3 \xrightarrow[\text{(ii) hydrolysis}]{\text{(i) } O_3}$ are
(a) $CH_3COOH + CO_2$
(b) $CH_3COOH + HOOCCH_2CH_3$
(c) $CH_3CHO + CH_3CH_2CHO$
(d) $CH_3COOH + CH_3COCH_3$ *(2005)*

41. Using anhydrous $AlCl_3$ as catalyst, which one of the following reactions produces ethylbenzene (PhEt)?
(a) $H_3C-CH_2OH + C_6H_6$
(b) $CH_3-CH=CH_2 + C_6H_6$
(c) $H_2C=CH_2 + C_6H_6$
(d) $H_3C-CH_3 + C_6H_6$ *(2004)*

42. Reaction of HBr with propene in the presence of peroxide gives
(a) isopropyl bromide
(b) 3-bromopropane
(c) allyl bromide
(d) *n*-propyl bromide. *(2004)*

43. The compound $CH_3-\overset{CH_3}{\overset{|}{C}}=CH-CH_3$ on reaction with $NaIO_4$ in the presence of $KMnO_4$ gives
(a) CH_3COCH_3
(b) $CH_3COCH_3+CH_3COOH$
(c) $CH_3COCH_3+CH_3CHO$
(d) $CH_3CHO+CO_2$ *(2003)*

44. Which one of the following is a free-radical substitution reaction?
(a) 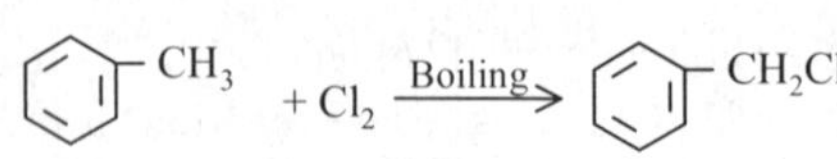
(b) 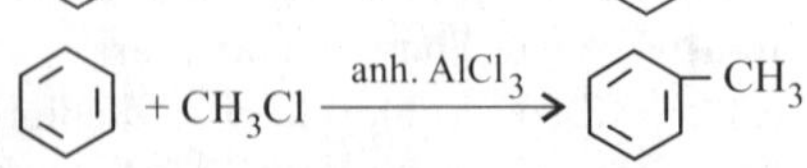
(c) 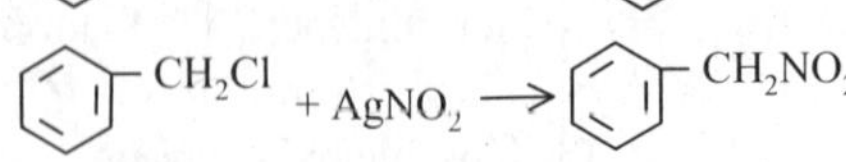
(d) $CH_3CHO + HCN \rightarrow CH_3CH(OH)CN$
(2003)

45. The correct order of reactivity towards the electrophilic substitution of the compounds aniline (I), benzene (II) and nitrobenzene (III) is
(a) III > II > I (b) II > III > I
(c) I < II > III (d) I > II > III
(2003)

46. When $CH_3CH_2CHCl_2$ is treated with $NaNH_2$, the product formed is
(a) $CH_3-CH=CH_2$ (b) $CH_3-C\equiv CH$
(c) 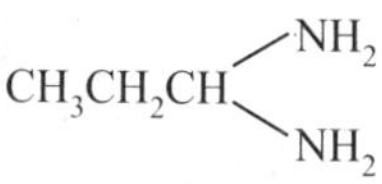 (d) 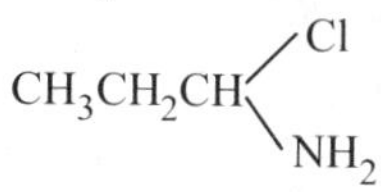
(2002)

47. In preparation of alkene from alcohol using Al_2O_3 which is the effective factor?
(a) Porosity of Al_2O_3
(b) Temperature
(c) Concentration
(d) Surface area of Al_2O_3. *(2001)*

48. The correct acidic order of the following is
I. 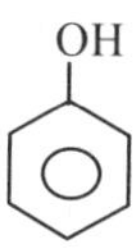 II.  III. 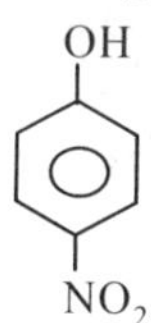
(a) I > II > III (b) III > I > II
(c) II > III > I (d) I > III > II
(2001)

49. Increasing order of electrophilic substitution for following compounds
(I)  (II) 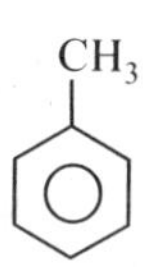
(III)  (IV) 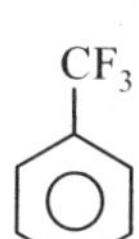
(a) IV < I < II < III (b) III < II < I < IV
(c) I < IV < III < II (d) II < III < I < IV
(2000)

50. In Friedel-Crafts reaction, toluene can be prepared by
(a) $C_6H_6 + CH_3Cl$ (b) $C_6H_5Cl + CH_4$
(c) $C_6H_6 + CH_2Cl_2$ (d) $C_6H_6 + CH_3COCl$
(2000)

51. Which reagent converts propene to 1-propanol?
(a) H_2O, H_2SO_4
(b) B_2H_6, H_2O_2, OH^-
(c) $Hg(OAc)_2$, $NaBH_4/H_2O$
(d) Aq. KOH *(2000)*

52. Which is maximum stable?
(a) 1-Butene (b) *cis*-2-Butene
(c) *trans*-2-Butene
(d) All have same stability. *(2000)*

53. 2-Butene shows geometrical isomerism due to
(a) restricted rotation about double bond
(b) free rotation about double bond
(c) free rotation about single bond
(d) chiral carbon. *(2000)*

54. Dihedral angle in staggered form of ethane is
(a) 0° (b) 120°
(c) 60° (d) 180° *(2000)*

55. When acetylene is passed through dil. H_2SO_4 in the presence of $HgSO_4$, the compound formed is
(a) acetic acid (b) ketone
(c) ether (d) acetaldehyde
(1999)

56. In Friedel-Crafts alkylation, besides $AlCl_3$ the other reactants are
(a) $C_6H_6 + CH_3Cl$ (b) $C_6H_6 + CH_4$
(c) $C_6H_6 + NH_3$ (d) $C_6H_6 + CH_3COCl$
(1999)

57. Which of the following compounds will be most easily attacked by an electrophile?
(a) 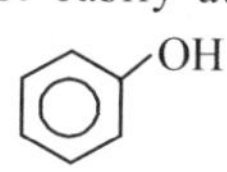 (b) 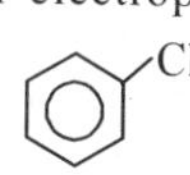
(c)  (d) 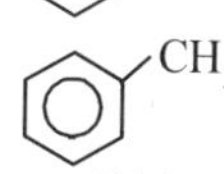
(1999, 1998)

58. Which one of these is not compatible with arenes?
(a) Electrophilic additions
(b) Delocalisation of π-electrons
(c) Greater stability
(d) Resonance *(1998)*

59. 2-Bromopentane is heated with potassium ethoxide in ethanol. The major product obtained is
(a) *trans*-2-pentene (b) 1-pentene
(c) 2-ethoxy pentane (d) 2-*cis*-pentene
(1998)

60. Which of the following reaction is expected to readily give a hydrocarbon product in good yields?

(a) $CH_3CH_3 \xrightarrow[h\nu]{Cl_2}$

(b) $(CH_3)_2CHCl \xrightarrow{C_2H_5OH}$

(c) $RCOOK \xrightarrow[\text{Oxidation}]{\text{Electrolysis}}$

(d) $RCOOAg \xrightarrow{I_2}$ *(1997)*

61. In a reaction, $CH_2{=}CH_2 \xrightarrow[\text{acid}]{\text{Hypochlorous}} M \xrightarrow{R} \begin{matrix} CH_2OH \\ | \\ CH_2OH \end{matrix}$

where M = Molecule and R = Reagent. M and R are

(a) CH_3CH_2OH and HCl

(b) $CH_2{=}CH_2$ and heat

(c) CH_3CH_2Cl and NaOH

(d) $CH_2Cl - CH_2OH$ and aq. $NaHCO_3$. *(1997)*

62. The cylindrical shape of an alkyne is due to

(a) two sigma C – C and one π C – C bonds

(b) one sigma C – C and two π C – C bonds

(c) three sigma C – C bonds

(d) three π C – C bonds. *(1997)*

63. In the commercial gasolines, the type of hydrocarbons which are more desirable is

(a) linear unsaturated hydrocarbon

(b) toluene

(c) branched hydrocarbon

(d) straight-chain hydrocarbon. *(1997)*

64. Among the following compounds (I-III) the correct reaction with electrophile is

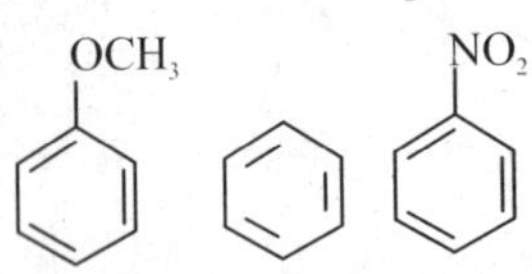

I II III

(a) I > II > III (b) I = II > III

(c) II > III > I (d) III < I < II *(1997)*

65. The most stable conformation of n-butane is

(a) gauche (b) staggered

(c) skew boat (d) eclipsed. *(1997)*

66. Electrophile in the case of chlorination of benzene in the presence of $FeCl_3$ is

(a) Cl (b) $FeCl_3$

(c) Cl^+ (d) Cl^- *(1996)*

67. The reaction,

$CH_2 = CH - CH_3 + HBr \rightarrow CH_3CHBr - CH_3$ is

(a) electrophilic substitution

(b) free radical addition

(c) nucleophilic addition

(d) electrophilic addition. *(1996)*

68. Which of the following has zero dipole moment?

(a) 1-Butene (b) 2-Methyl-1-propene

(c) *cis*-2-Butene (d) *trans*-2-Butene *(1996)*

69. The alkene $R - CH = CH_2$ reacts readily with B_2H_6 and the product on oxidation with alkaline hydrogen peroxides produces

(a) $R{-}C({=}O){-}CH_3$ (b) $R{-}CH(OH){-}CH_2(OH)$

(c) $R - CH_2 - CHO$

(d) $R - CH_2 - CH_2{-}OH$ *(1995)*

70. One of the following which does not observe the anti-Markownikoff's addition of HBr, is

(a) pent-2-ene (b) propene

(c) but-2-ene (d) but-1-ene *(1994)*

71. The reactive species in the nitration of benzene is

(a) NO_3 (b) HNO_3

(c) NO_2^+ (d) NO_2^- *(1994)*

72. $R - CH_2 - CCl_2 - R \xrightarrow{\text{Reagent}} R - C \equiv C - R$

The reagent is

(a) Na (b) HCl in H_2O

(c) KOH in C_2H_5OH (d) Zn in alcohol. *(1993)*

73. Reduction of 2-butyne with sodium in liquid ammonia gives predominantly

(a) *cis*-2-butene (b) no reaction

(c) *trans*-2-butene (d) n-butane. *(1993)*

74. A compound is treated with $NaNH_2$ to give sodium salt. Identify the compound.

(a) C_2H_2 (b) C_6H_6

(c) C_2H_6 (d) C_2H_4 *(1993)*

75. Reactivity of hydrogen atoms attached to different carbon atoms in alkanes has the order

(a) tertiary > primary > secondary
(b) primary > secondary > tertiary
(c) both (a) and (b)
(d) tertiary > secondary > primary. *(1993)*

76. Which is the correct symbol relating the two Kekule structures of benzene?
(a) $\rightleftharpoons$ (b) $\longrightarrow$
(c) $\equiv$ (d) $\longleftrightarrow$
(1993)

77. The restricted rotation about carbon carbon double bond in 2-butene is due to
(a) overlap of one s and sp^2-hybridized orbitals
(b) overlap of two sp^2-hybridized orbitals
(c) overlap of one p and one sp^2-hybridized orbitals
(d) sideways overlap of two p-orbitals. *(1993)*

78. Select the true statement about benzene amongst the following
(a) because of unsaturation benzene easily undergoes addition
(b) there are two types of C – C bonds in benzene molecule
(c) there is cyclic delocalisation of π-electrons in benzene
(d) monosubstitution of benzene gives three isomeric products. *(1992)*

79. Acetylenic hydrogens are acidic because
(a) sigma electron density of C – H bond in acetylene is nearer to carbon, which has 50% s-character
(b) acetylene has only open hydrogen in each carbon
(c) acetylene contains least number of hydrogens among the possible hydrocarbons having two carbons
(d) Acetylene belongs to the class of alkynes with molecular formula, C_nH_{2n-2}. *(1989)*

80. Which is the most suitable reagent among the following to distinguish compound (3) from rest of the compounds?
(1) $CH_3-C\equiv C-CH_3$
(2) $CH_3-CH_2-CH_2-CH_3$
(3) $CH_3-CH_2C\equiv CH$
(4) $CH_3-CH=CH_2$
(a) Bromine in carbon tetrachloride
(b) Bromine in acetic acid
(c) Alk. $KMnO_4$
(d) Ammoniacal silver nitrate. *(1989)*

Answer Key

1.	(d)	**2.**	(a)	**3.**	(c)	**4.**	(c)	**5.**	(d)	**6.**	(a)	**7.**	(d)	**8.**	(c)	**9.**	(c)	**10.**	(a)
11.	(b)	**12.**	(d)	**13.**	(b)	**14.**	(c)	**15.**	(c)	**16.**	(a)	**17.**	(c)	**18.**	(d)	**19.**	(c)	**20.**	(a)
21.	(b)	**22.**	(a)	**23.**	(d)	**24.**	(c)	**25.**	(a)	**26.**	(a)	**27.**	(b)	**28.**	(b)	**29.**	(c)	**30.**	(d)
31.	(d)	**32.**	(d)	**33.**	(d)	**34.**	(d)	**35.**	(d)	**36.**	(d)	**37.**	(c)	**38.**	(d)	**39.**	(a)	**40.**	(b)
41.	(c)	**42.**	(d)	**43.**	(b)	**44.**	(a)	**45.**	(d)	**46.**	(b)	**47.**	(b)	**48.**	(b)	**49.**	(a)	**50.**	(a)
51.	(b)	**52.**	(c)	**53.**	(a)	**54.**	(c)	**55.**	(d)	**56.**	(a)	**57.**	(a)	**58.**	(a)	**59.**	(a)	**60.**	(c)
61.	(d)	**62.**	(b)	**63.**	(c)	**64.**	(a)	**65.**	(b)	**66.**	(c)	**67.**	(d)	**68.**	(d)	**79.**	(d)	**70.**	(c)
71.	(c)	**72.**	(c)	**73.**	(c)	**74.**	(a)	**75.**	(d)	**76.**	(d)	**77.**	(d)	**78.**	(c)	**79.**	(a)	**80.**	(d)

EXPLANATIONS

1. (d) : $\underset{(A)}{CH_4} \xrightarrow{Br_2/h\nu} CH_3Br \xrightarrow[\text{Wurtz reaction}]{\text{Na/dry ether}} CH_3-CH_3$

(Less than 4 carbon atoms)

2. (a) : Alkanes, alkenes and alkynes follow the following trend in their acidic behaviour :

$\overset{sp}{H}C\equiv\overset{sp}{C}H > H_2\overset{sp^2}{C}=\overset{sp^2}{C}H_2 > \overset{sp^3}{C}H_3-\overset{sp^3}{C}H_3$

This is because *sp*-hybridised carbon is more electronegative than sp^2-hybridised carbon which is further more electronegative than sp^3-hybridised carbon. Hence, in ethyne proton can be released more easily than ethene and ethane.

Among alkynes the order of acidity is :

$HC\equiv CH > CH_3-C\equiv CH >> CH_3-C\equiv C-CH_3$

This is due to $+I$ effect of $-CH_3$ group.

3. (c) : In case of unsymmetrical alkynes addition of H_2O occurs in accordance with Markownikoff's rule.

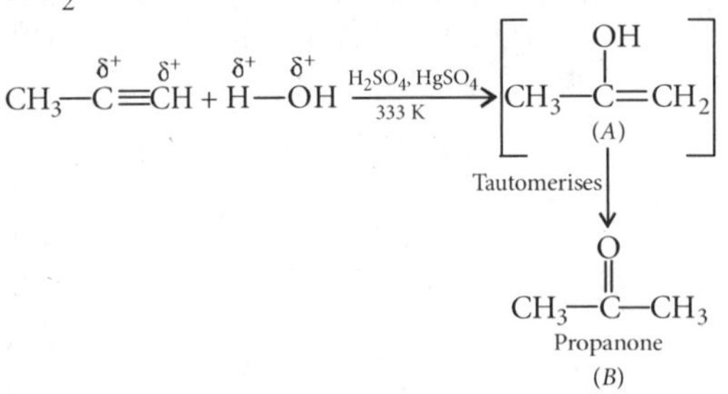

4. (c) : Conformers of ethane have different dihedral angles.

5. (d) : Friedel–Crafts reaction :

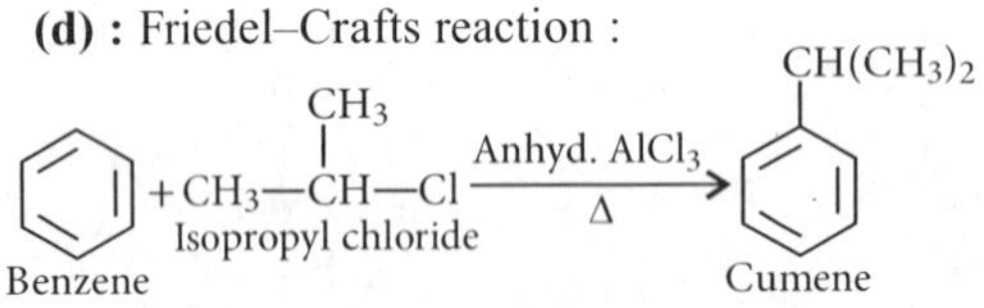

Chlorobenzene, bromobenzene and chloroethene are not suitable halide components as C–*X* bond acquires some double bond character due to resonance of lone pair of electrons with π bond.

6. (a) : Biphenyl is coplanar as all C-atoms are sp^2 hybridised.

7. (d) : Pyrrole has maximum electron density on 2 and 5. It generally reacts with electrophiles at the C-2 or C-5 due to the highest degree of stability of the protonated intermediate.

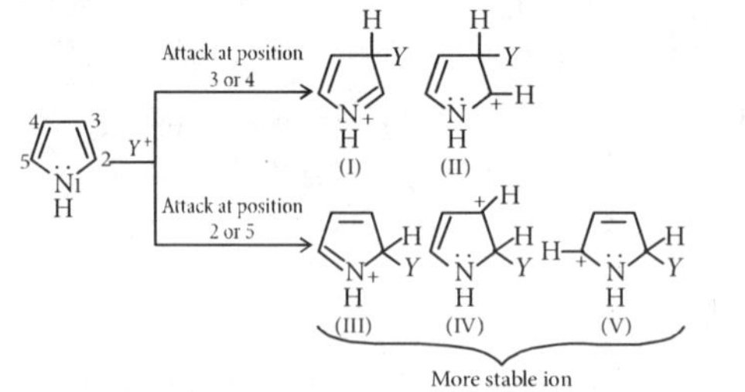

Attack at position 3 or 4 yields a carbocation that is a hybrid of structures (I) and (II). Attack at position 2 or 5 yields a carbocation that is a hybrid not only of structures (III) and (IV) (analogous to I and II) but also of structure (V). The extra stabilization conferred by (V) makes this ion the more stable one.

Also, attack at position 2 or 5 is faster because the developing positive charge is accommodated by three atoms of the ring instead of by only two.

8. (c) :

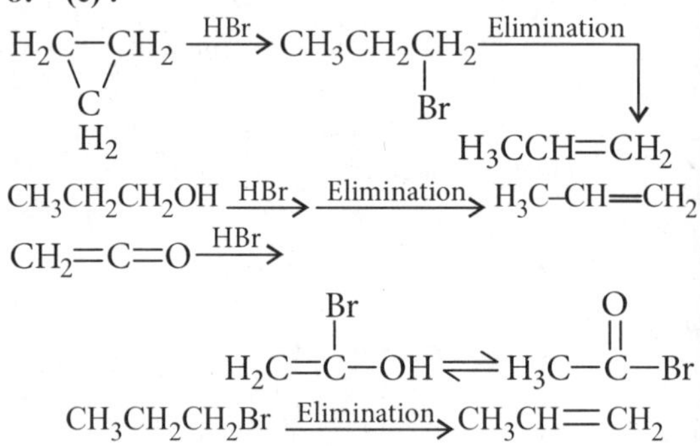

9. (c) :

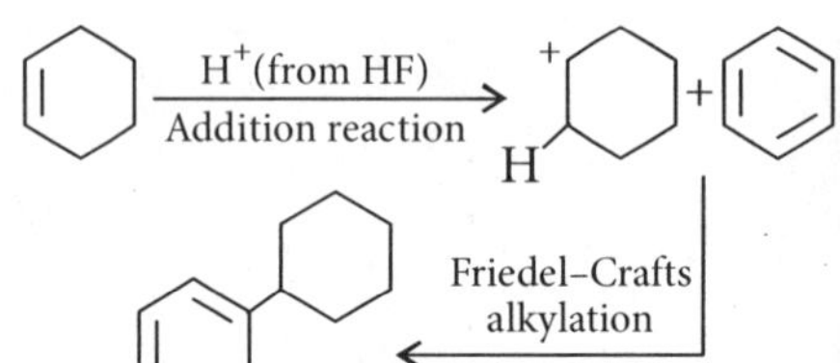

10. (a)

11. (b) :

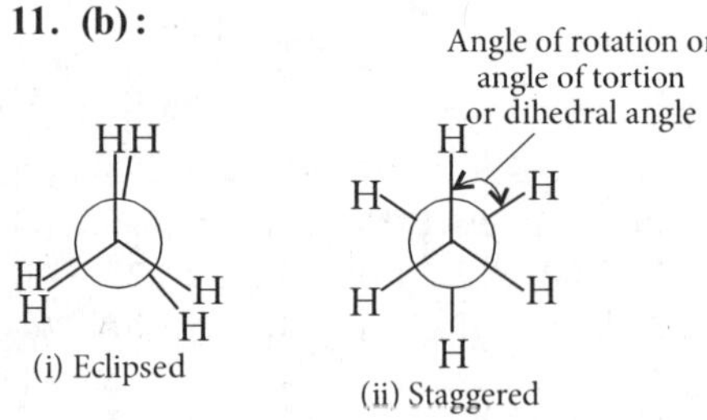

Newman's projections of ethane

Magnitude of torsional strain depends upon the angle of rotation about C—C bond. Staggered form has the least torsional strain and the eclipsed form has the maximum torsional strain. So, the staggered conformation of ethane is more stable than the eclipsed conformation.

12. (d) : Mechanism of nitration is :

$$HNO_3 + 2H_2SO_4 \longrightarrow NO_2^+ + 2HSO_4^- + H_3O^+$$

If a large amount of $KHSO_4$ is added then conc. of HSO_4^- ions increases and the reaction will be shifted in backward direction hence, the rate of nitration will be slower.

13. (b) : $CH_3-\overset{sp}{C}\equiv\overset{sp}{C}^-$

Thus, pair of electrons is present in *sp*-hybridised orbital.

14. (c) :

$$HC\equiv CH \xrightarrow{NaNH_2/liq.NH_3} HC\equiv CNa \xrightarrow{CH_3CH_2Br} \underset{\text{1-Butyne }(X)}{CH_3CH_2C\equiv CH}$$

$$CH_3CH_2C\equiv CH \xrightarrow{NaNH_2/liq.\ NH_3} CH_3CH_2C\equiv CNa \xrightarrow{CH_3CH_2Br} \underset{\text{3-Hexyne }(Y)}{CH_3CH_2C\equiv CCH_2CH_3}$$

15. (c) :

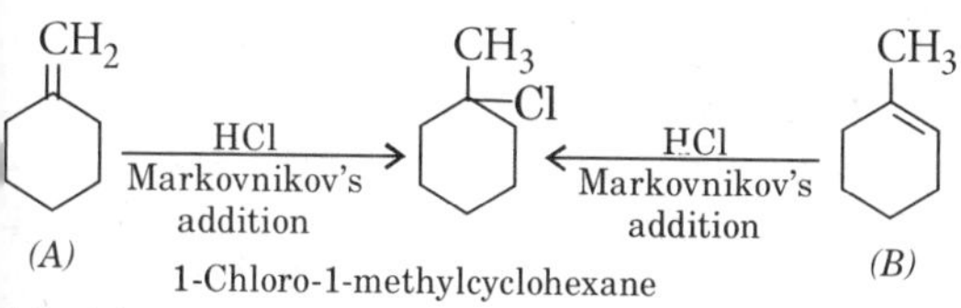

16. (a) :

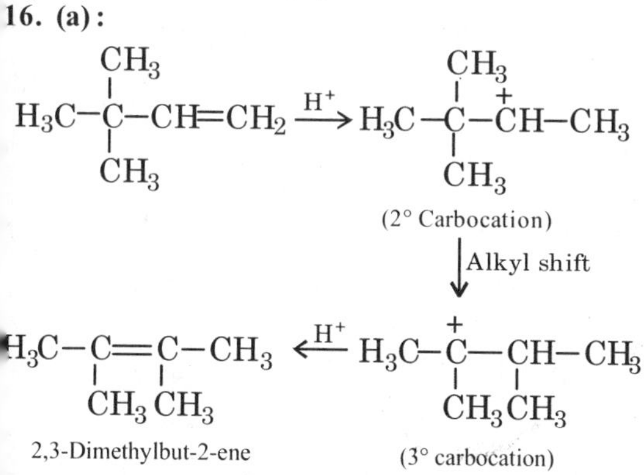

17. (c) :

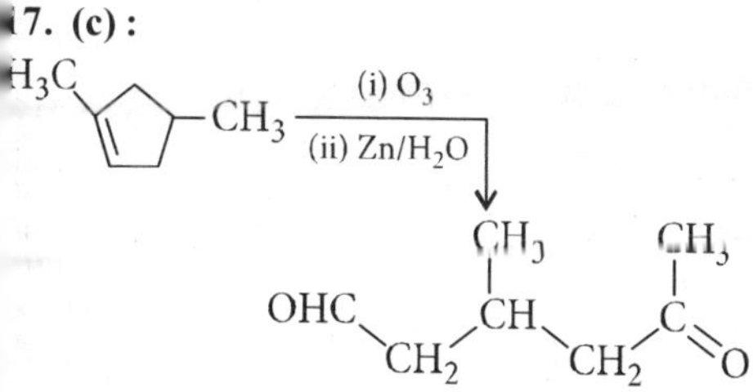

18. (d) : Enthalpy of hydrogenation is inversely proportional to the stability of alkenes.
Stability of alkenes : I > II > III
Enthalpy of hydrogenation : I < II < III

19. (c) : $-CH_3$ group is *o,p*-directing. Because of crowding, no substitution occurs at the carbon atom between the two $-CH_3$ groups in *m*-Xylene, even though two $-CH_3$ groups activate that position.

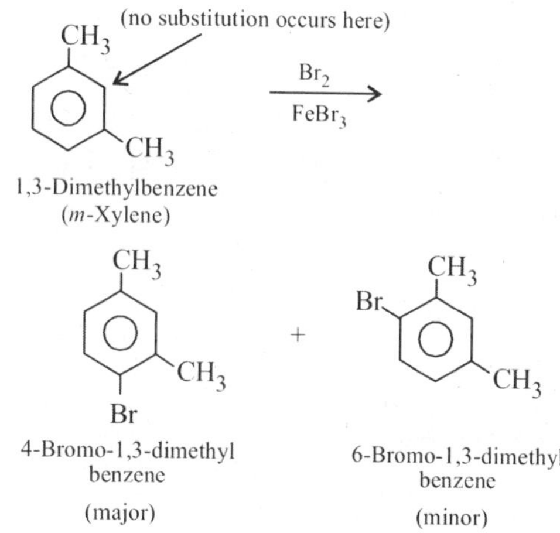

20. (a) :

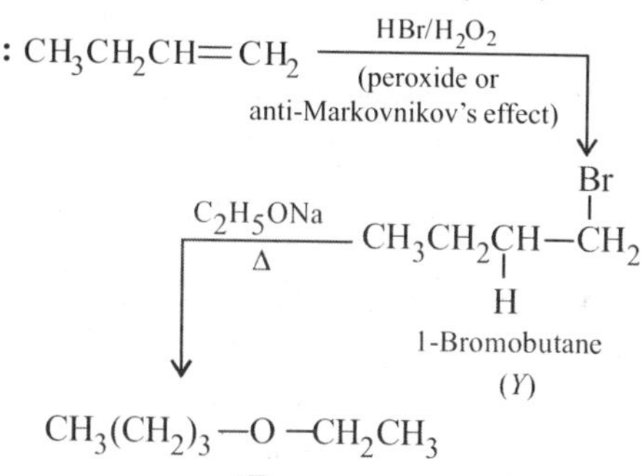

21. (b) : $C_2H_2 + \frac{5}{2}O_2 \longrightarrow 2CO_2 + H_2O$

Both ethyne and CO_2 have *sp*-hybridisation.

$$O=\overset{sp}{C}=O \qquad H\overset{sp}{C}\equiv\overset{sp}{C}H$$

22. (a) : Nitrobenzene is strongly deactivated, hence will not undergo Friedel-Crafts reaction.

23. (d) : The molecules which do not satisfy Huckel rule or $(4n + 2)\pi$-electron rule are said to be non-aromatic. The compound (d) has total $4\pi e^-$. It does not follow $(4n + 2)$ rule. So it is non-aromatic compound. All other compounds (a, b, c) are planar and have $6\pi e^-$, so they are aromatic.

24. (c) : 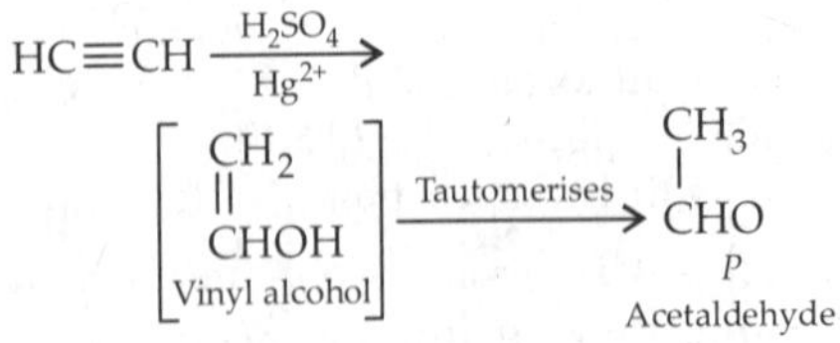

Acetaldehyde does not give Victor Meyer test.

25. (a) : 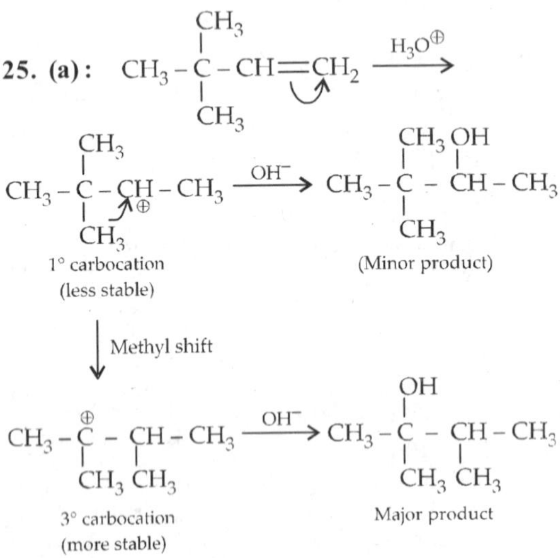

26. (a) : Terminal alkynes (1-butyne) react with $NaNH_2$ to form sodium acetylide and evolve hydrogen but 2-butyne do not.

27. (b) : The anti-conformation is the most stable conformation of *n*-butane. In this, the bulky methyl groups are as far apart as possible thereby keeping steric repulsion at a minimum.

28. (b) : Cracking : The process of cracking converts higher alkanes into smaller alkanes and alkenes. This process can be used for production of natural gas.

29. (c) : The reaction of Cl_2, in presence of $FeCl_3$, with benzene yields a ring substitution product.

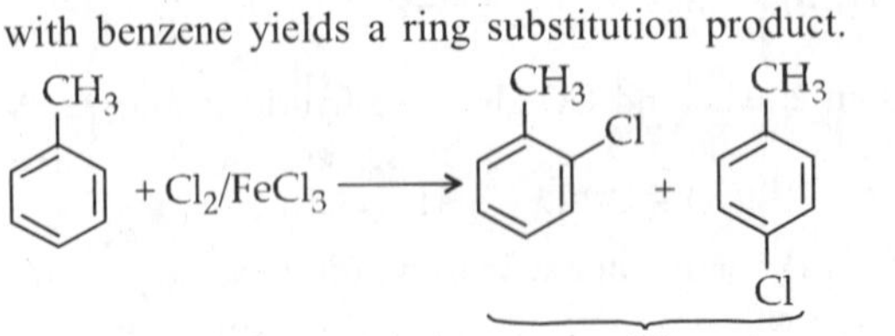

(X)

In presence of sunlight, free radical reaction takes place.

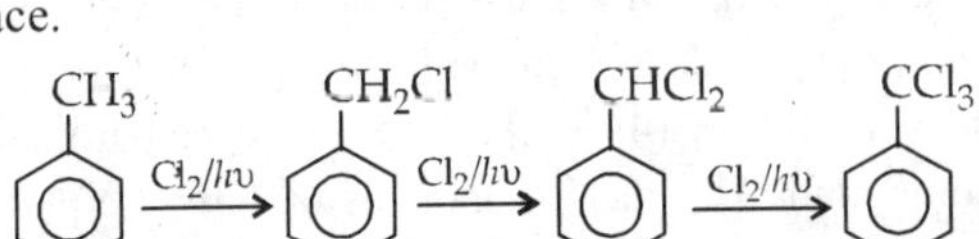

(Y)

30. (d) :

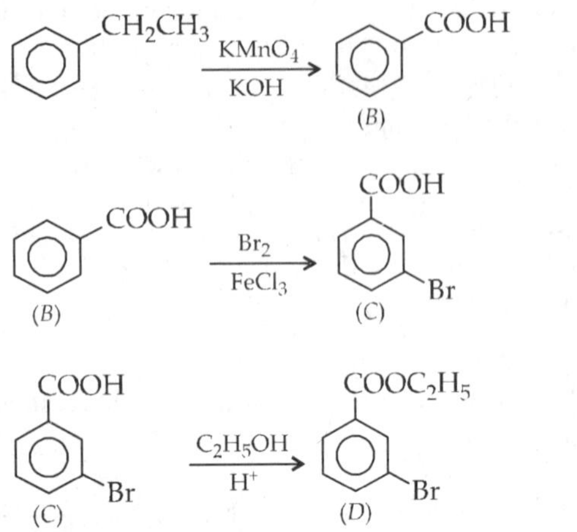

31. (d) : The conformation (d) is most stable because of intermolecular H-bonding.

32. (d) : 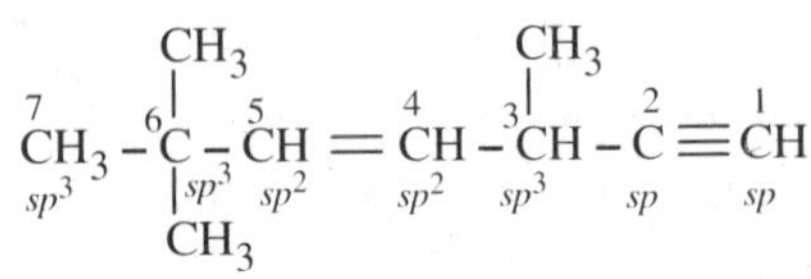

$\therefore$ C_2 - *sp*, C_3 - sp^3, C_5 - sp^2 and C_6 - sp^3

33. (d) : *Cis-trans* isomerism is exhibited by compounds having C=C, C=N and N=N groups, due to restricted rotation around the double bond. Among the given options only 2-butene qualifies to exhibit geometrical isomerism.

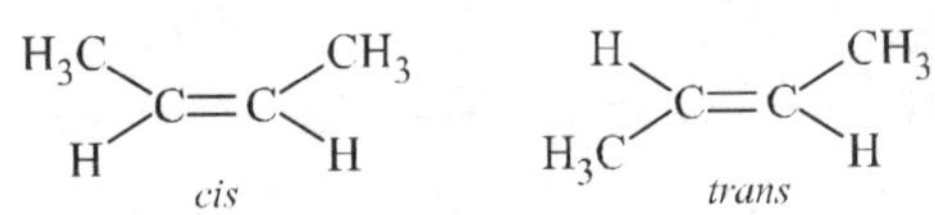

34. (d) : This is Friedel-Crafts alkylation.

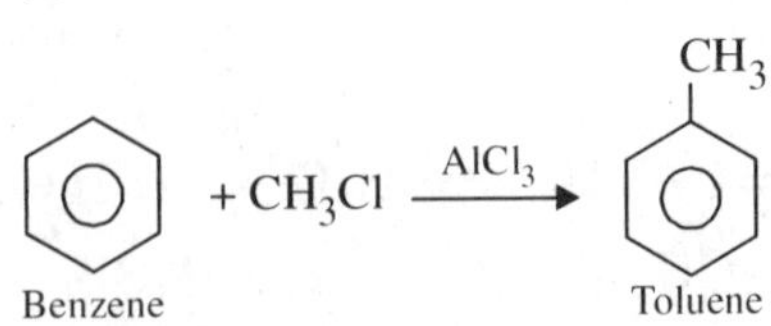

Mechanism: $CH_3Cl + AlCl_3 \rightarrow AlCl_4^- + CH_3^+$

Lewis acid Electrophile

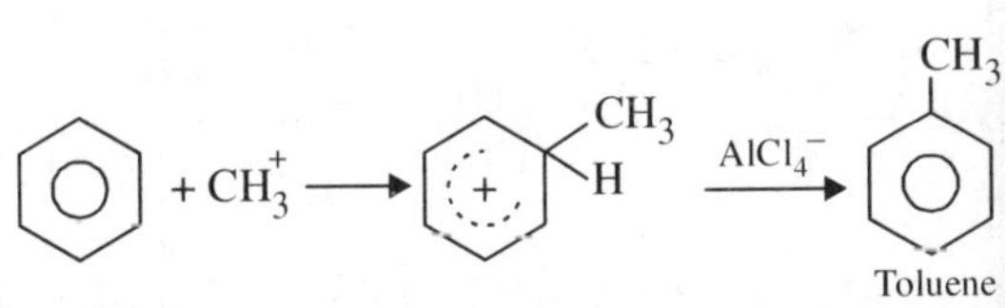

$+ AlCl_3 + HCl$

35. (d) : $CH_3-\underset{\substack{|\\ CH_3}}{CH}-CH=CH_2 \xrightarrow{\overset{\delta+\ \ \delta-}{H-Br}} A$

3-Methylbut-1-ene

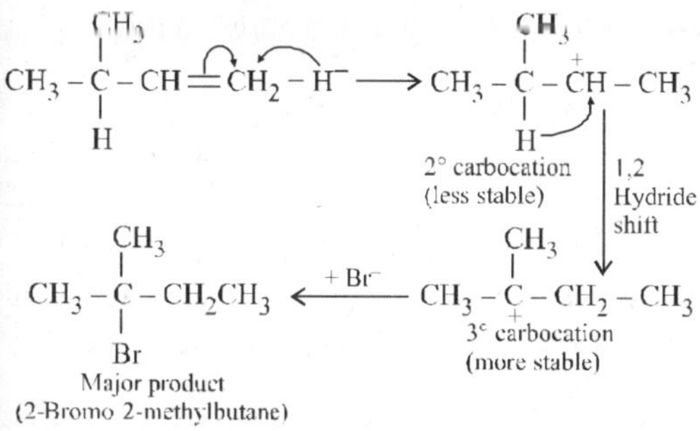

36. (d) : $\underset{6}{\overset{sp^3}{CH_3}}-\underset{5}{\overset{sp^2}{CH}}=\underset{4}{\overset{sp^2}{CH}}-\underset{3}{\overset{sp^3}{CH_2}}-\underset{2}{\overset{sp}{C}}\equiv\underset{1}{\overset{sp}{CH}}$

The state of hybridisation of carbon in 1, 3 and 5 position are sp, sp^3 sp^2.

37. (c) : $CH_3-CH_2-C\equiv CH + HCl \longrightarrow$

$$\underset{(B)}{CH_3-CH_2-\underset{\substack{|\\ Cl}}{C}=CH_2} \xrightarrow{HI} \underset{(C)}{CH_3-CH_2-\overset{\substack{I\\ |}}{\underset{\substack{|\\ Cl}}{C}}-CH_3}$$

According to Markownikoff's rule, during hydrohalogenation to unsymmetrical alkene, the negative part of the addendum adds to less hydrogenated (*i.e.* more substituted) carbon atom.

38. (d) : (a) $H_3C-\underset{\substack{|\\ CH_3}}{CH}-CH=CH_2 \xrightarrow[\text{(ii) Zn/H}_2\text{O}_2]{\text{(i) O}_3}$

3-Methyl-1-butene

$H_3C-\underset{\substack{|\\ CH_3}}{CH}-CH=O$ (2-Methylpropanal) $+$ CH_2O (Formaldehyde)

(b) 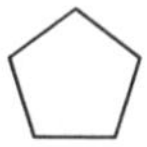 $\xrightarrow[\text{(ii) Zn/H}_2\text{O}_2]{\text{(i) O}_3}$ no reaction

(c) $H_3C-CH_2-\underset{\substack{|\\ CH_3}}{C}=CH_2 \xrightarrow[\text{(ii) Zn/H}_2\text{O}_2]{\text{(i) O}_3}$

2-Methyl-1-butene

$H_3C-CH_2-\underset{\substack{|\\ CH_3}}{C}=O$ (Ethylmethylketone) $+$ CH_2O (Formaldehyde)

(d) $H_3C-\underset{\substack{|\\ CH_3}}{C}=CH-CH_3 \xrightarrow[\text{(ii) Zn/H}_2\text{O}_2]{\text{(i) O}_3}$

2-Methyl-2-butene

$H_3C-\underset{\substack{|\\ CH_3}}{\overset{\substack{O\\ \|}}{C}}$ (Acetone) $+$ CH_3CHO (Acetaldehyde)

39. (a) : The relative rates of hydrogenation decrease with the increase of steric hindrance. In order of stability of alkene, most stable the alkene slowly it gives the product.

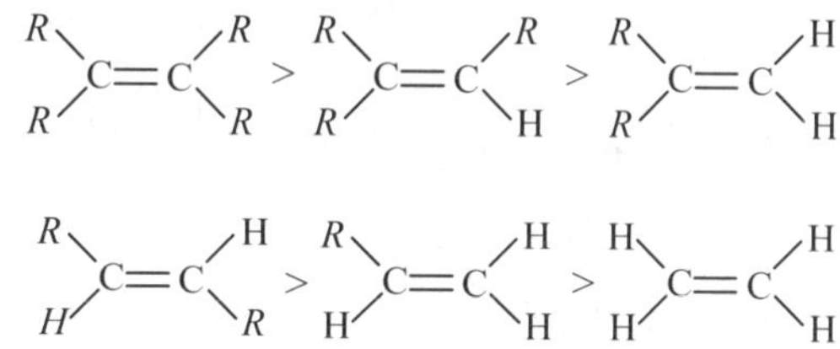

Hence alkene which will react faster with H_2 is that which is most unstable.

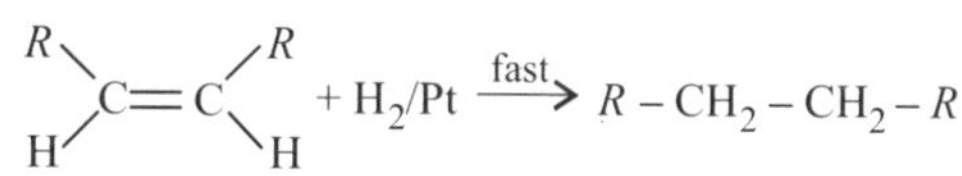

40. (b) : On ozonolysis, higher alkynes form diketones which are further oxidised to dicarboxylic acid.

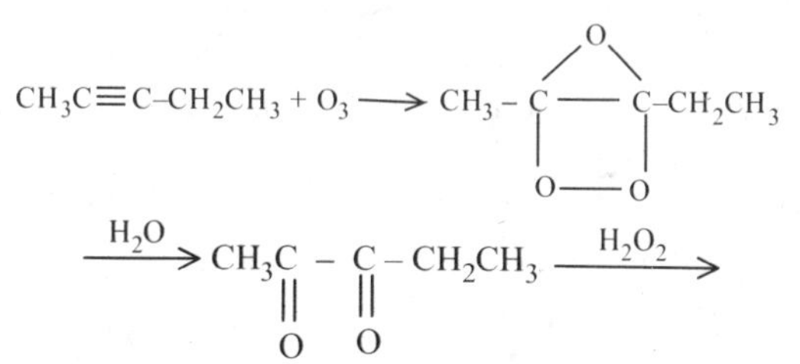

$CH_3COOH + CH_3CH_2COOH$

41. (c) : $C_6H_5H + H_2C=CH_2 \xrightarrow[95°,\ \text{pressure}]{AlCl_3,\ HCl} C_6H_5CH_2CH_3$

42. (d) : The formation of *n*-propyl bromide in presence of peroxide can be explained as follows:

Step 1 : Peroxide undergoes fission to give free radicals.

$$R-O-O-R \longrightarrow 2R-\dot{O}$$

Step 2 : HBr combines with free radical to form bromine free radical.

$$R-\dot{O} + HBr \longrightarrow R-OH + \dot{Br}$$

Step 3 : $\dot{Br}$ attacks the double bond of the alkene to form a more stable free radical.

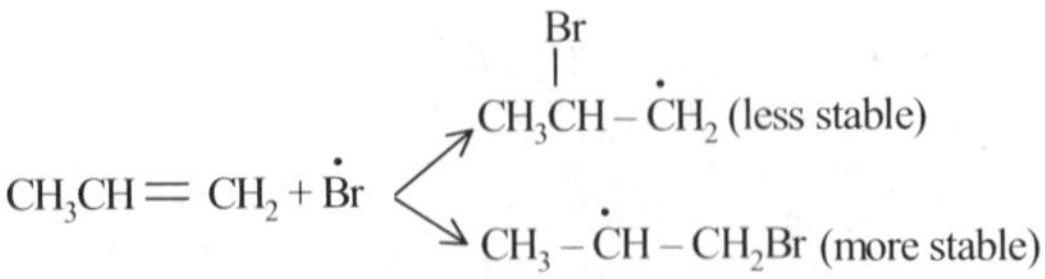

Step 4 : More stable free radical attacks on HBr.

$$CH_3\dot{C}HCH_2Br + HBr \longrightarrow \underset{n\text{-propyl bromide}}{CH_3CH_2CH_2Br} + \dot{B}r$$

Step 5 : $\dot{B}r + \dot{B}r \longrightarrow Br_2$

43. (b) :

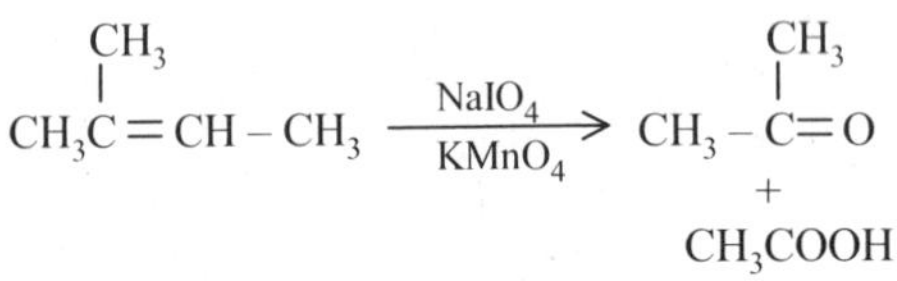

44. (a) :

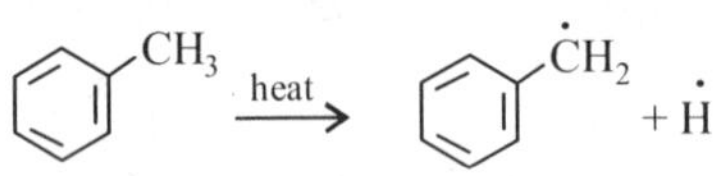

Benzyl free radical

$$Cl_2 \xrightarrow[\text{sunlight}]{\text{Energy}} 2\dot{C}l$$

45. (d) :

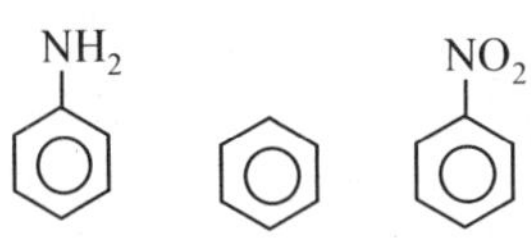

I II III

$-NH_2$ group is electron donating hence increases electron density on ring. Benzene is also electron rich due to delocalisation of electrons. $-NO_2$ group is electron withdrawing hence, decreases electron density on ring. Thus, correct order for electrophilic substitution is I > II > III.

46. (b) : $CH_3CH_2CHCl_2 \xrightarrow{NaNH_2} CH_3C\equiv CH$

47. (b) : Alcohols may be dehydrated to the corresponding olefins. The order of ease of dehydration is

3° alcohol > 2° alcohol > 1° alcohol.

$$CH_3CH_2OH \xrightarrow[-H_2O]{Al_2O_3,\ 620\text{ K}} CH_2{=}CH_2$$

48. (b) : Phenol exists as a resonance hybrid of the following structures.

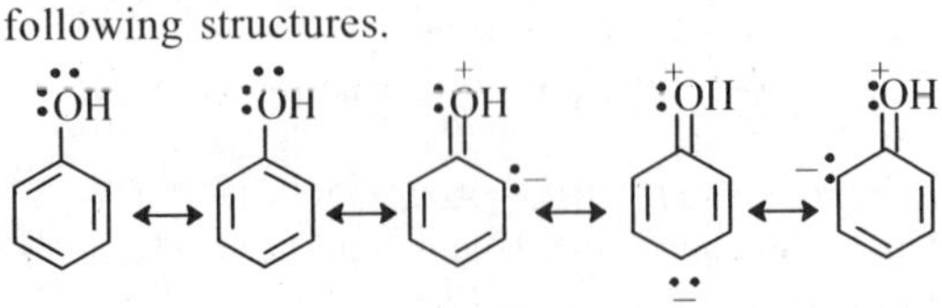

Thus, due to resonance the oxygen atom of the – OH group acquires a positive charge and hence attracts electron pair of the O – H bond leading to the release of hydrogen atom as proton.

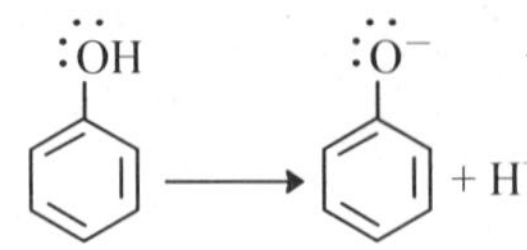

Phenoxide ion

Once the phenoxide ion is formed it stabilises itself by resonance which is more stable than the parent phenol as there is no charge separation.

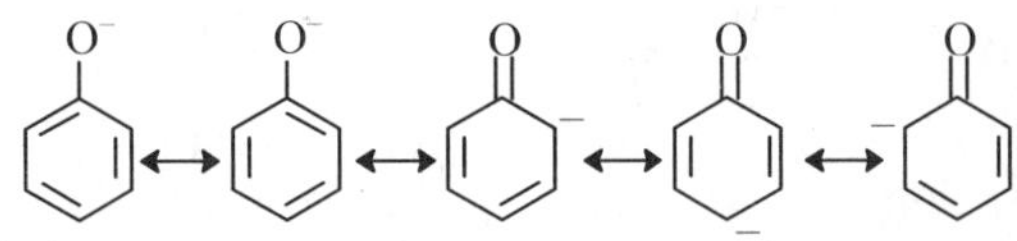

Effect of substituent → Presence of electron withdrawing groups ($-NO_2$, $-X$, $-CN$) increase the acidity of phenols while the presence of electron releasing groups ($-NH_2$, $-CH_3$) decrease the acidity of phenols. This explains the following order of acidity.

p-nitrophenol > phenol > *p*-cresol.

49. (a) : Due to $-I$ effect of F atom, CF_3 in benzene ring deactivates the ring and does not favour electrophilic substitution. While $-CH_3$ and $-OCH_3$ are '$+I$ group' which favours electrophilic substitution in the benzene ring at '*ortho*' and '*para*' positions. The $+I$ effect of $-OCH_3$ is more than $-CH_3$, therefore the correct order for electrophilic substitution is

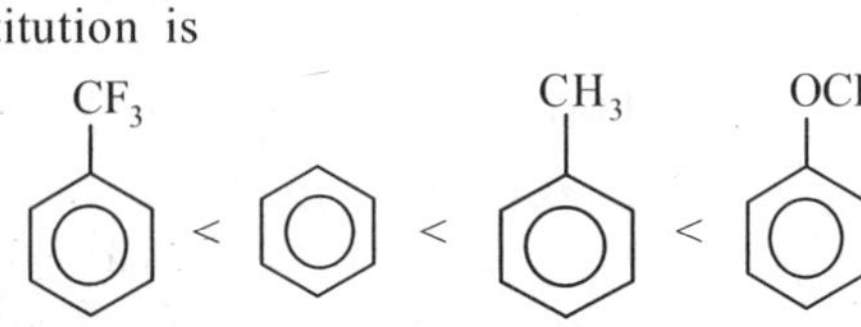

50. (a) : In Friedel-Crafts reaction toluene is obtained by the action of CH_3Cl on benzene in presence of $AlCl_3$.

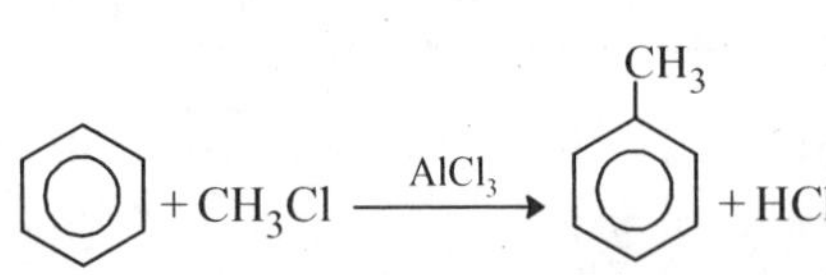

Toluene

51. (b) : Propene adds to diborane (B_2H_6) giving an addition product. The addition compound on oxidation gives 1-propanol. Here addition of water takes place according to anti-Markownikoff's rule.

52. (c) : 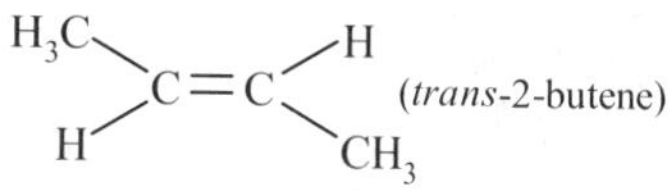

This is most stable as the repulsion between two methyl groups is least.

53. (a) : Due to restricted rotation about double bond, 2-butene shows geometrical isomerism.

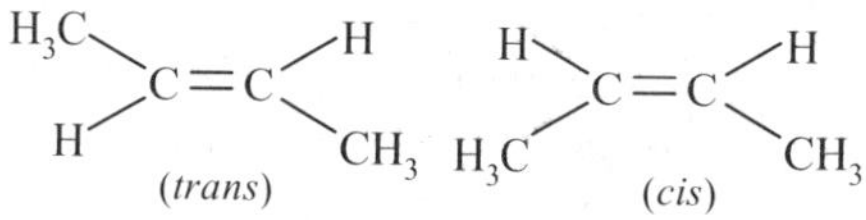

54. (c) : The staggered form of ethane has the following structure and the dihedral angle is 60°, which means 'H' atoms are at an angle of 60° to each other.

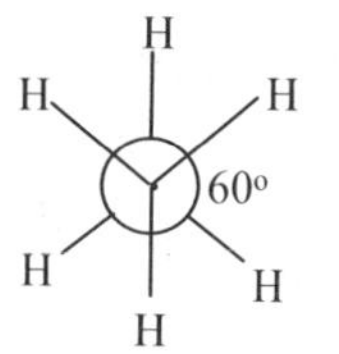

55. (d):

$$\underset{\text{Acetylene (unstable)}}{CH{\equiv}CH + H_2O} \xrightarrow[HgSO_4]{\text{dil. } H_2SO_4} CH_2{=}CH{-}OH \longrightarrow \underset{\text{Acetaldehyde}}{CH_3{-}\overset{\displaystyle O}{\overset{\|}{C}}{-}H}$$

56. (a) : In Friedel-Crafts reaction, an alkyl group is introduced into the benzene ring in presence of a Lewis acid ($AlCl_3$) catalyst. The reaction is

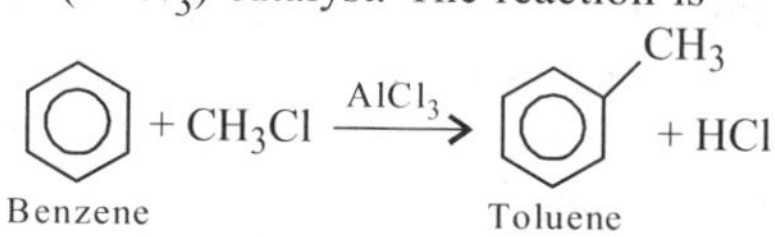

57. (a) : – OH, – Cl and – CH_3 groups in benzene are *ortho-para* directing groups and activate the ring towards electrophilic substitution reaction. But among these –OH group is strongly activating while –CH_3 is weakly activating and –Cl is deactivating. Thus, phenol will be most easily attacked by an electrophile.

58. (a) : Arenes undergo nucleophilic substitution reaction and are resistant to addition reactions, due to delocalisation of π-electrons. These are also stabilized by resonance.

59. (a) : $\underset{\text{2-Bromopentane}}{CH_3-\underset{|}{\overset{}{C}}H(Br)-CH_2-CH_2-CH_3} + C_2H_5-{}^{-}OK^{+}$

$$\rightarrow \underset{trans\text{-2-Pentene}}{CH_3-CH{=}CH-CH_2-CH_3} + KBr + C_2H_5-OH$$

60. (c) : When an aqueous solution of sodium or potassium salt of carboxylic acid is electrolysed, hydrocarbon is evolved at anode.

$$2RCOOK \xrightarrow[\text{Oxidation}]{\text{Electrolysis}} \underset{\text{Anode}}{2RCOO^-} + \underset{\text{Cathode}}{2K^+}$$

At anode: $2RCOO^- - 2e^- \rightarrow \underset{\text{Alkne}}{R-R} + 2CO_2$

61. (d) :

$$CH_2{=}CH_2 + HOCl \longrightarrow \begin{matrix} CH_2OH \\ | \\ CH_2Cl \end{matrix} \xrightarrow{\text{aq. } NaHCO_3} \begin{matrix} CH_2OH \\ | \\ CH_2OH \end{matrix}$$

Therefore, $M = CH_2Cl{-}CH_2OH$ and R = aq.$NaHCO_3$

62. (b) : In alkyne, two carbon atoms constituting the triple bond are *sp*-hybridised. Carbon undergoes *sp*-hybridisation to form two *sp*-hybrid orbitals. The two 2*p*-orbitals remain unhybridised. Hybrid orbitals form one sigma bond while two π-bonds are formed by unhybridised orbitals.

63. (c) : The branching of chain increases the octane number of a fuel. High octane number means better fuel.

64. (a) : In structure III, withdrawal of electrons by – NO_2 causes decrease in reaction rate while in structure I, there is electron releasing effect by – OCH_3 group which accelerates the reaction.

65. (b) : $CH_3CH_2CH_2CH_3$ - *n*-butane

Newman projection for *n*-butane is

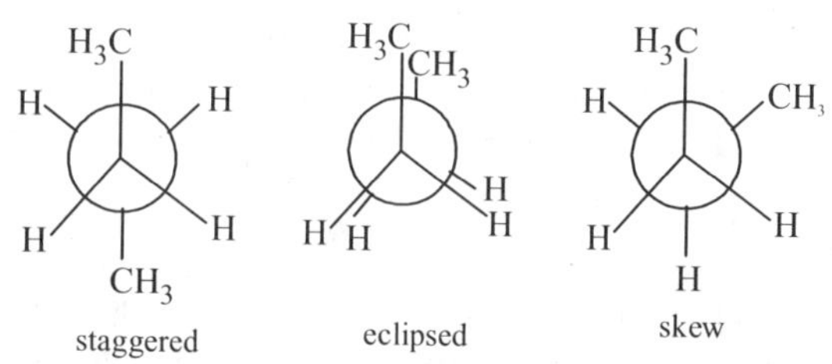

The staggered conformation has minimum repulsion between the hydrogen atoms attached tetrahedrally to the two carbon atoms. Thus, it is the most stable conformation.

66. (c) : $Cl_2 + FeCl_3 \rightarrow FeCl_4^- + Cl^+$

67. (d) : In this reaction, HBr undergoes heterolytic fission as $HBr \rightarrow H^+ + Br^-$

$$CH_2 = CH - CH_3 + HBr \longrightarrow CH_3 - \overset{\oplus}{C}H - CH_3$$

$$\xrightarrow{Br^-} CH_3 - CHBr - CH_3$$

68. (d) : 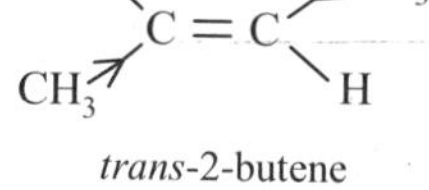

trans-2-butene

Both methyl group cancel each other. So net zero dipole moment exists.

69. (d) : $6(\underset{\text{Alkene}}{R-CH=CH_2}) \xrightarrow[\text{Ether, 0°C}]{B_2H_6} 2R(CH_2CH_2)_3B$

$\xrightarrow[\text{NaOH}]{H_2O_2} RCH_2CH_2OH + 2H_3BO_3$

70. (c) : In the case of but-2-ene ($CH_3-CH=CH-CH_3$) both double bonded carbons are identical. Therefore, it does not observe the anti-Markownikoff's addition of HBr.

71. (c) : Nitronium ion (NO_2^+) is an electrophile that actually attacks the benzene ring.

72. (c) : KOH in C_2H_5OH, when reacts with 1,1-dihaloalkanes form alkynes.

73. (c) : Reduction of non-terminal alkynes with Na in liq. NH_3 at 195 - 200 K gives *trans*-2-butene.

$$CH_3-C\equiv C-CH_3 \xrightarrow[195-200\text{ K}]{\text{Na in liq. }NH_3} \underset{\textit{trans}\text{-But-2-ene}}{(CH_3)(H)C=C(H)(CH_3)}$$

(Birch reduction)

74. (a) : Alkynes react with strong bases like $NaNH_2$ to form sodium acetylide derivative known as acetylides.

$$H-C\equiv C-H + NaNH_2 \longrightarrow H-C\equiv \bar{C}-\overset{+}{Na} + 1/2H_2$$

75. (d) : The reactivity of H-atom depends upon the stability of free radicals, therefore reactivity of H-atom follows the order:

$$3° > 2° > 1°$$

76. (d) : Benzene shows Kekule structures which are resonating structures and these structures are separated by a double headed arrow (↔).

77. (d) : $>C=C<$,

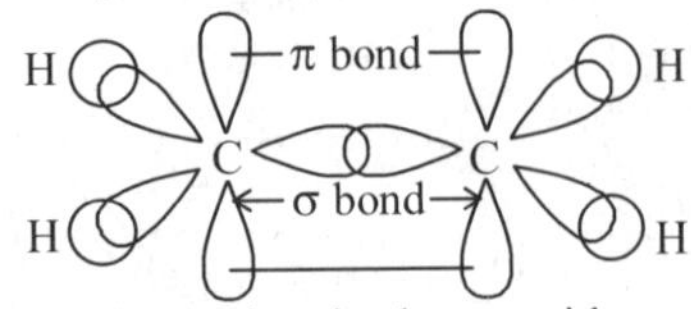

Restricted rotation is due to sideways overlap of two *p*-orbitals.

78. (c) : Due to resonance all the C – C bonds in the benzene possess same nature and the resonating structures are obtained because of the delocalisation of π-electrons.

79. (a) :

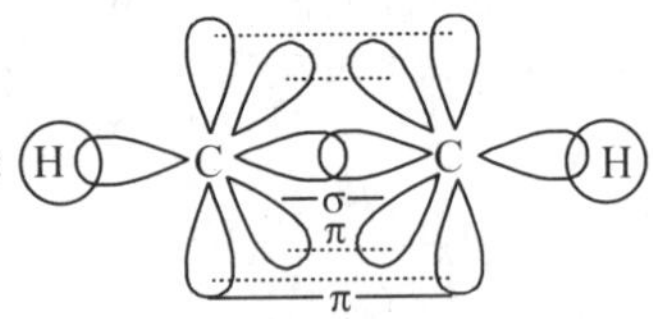

The formation of C – H bond in acetylene involves *sp*-hybridised carbon atom. Since *s*-electrons are closer to the nucleus than *p* electrons, the electrons present in a bond having more *s*-character will be more closer to the nucleus. In alkynes *s* character is 50%, the electrons constituting this bond are more strongly bonded by the carbon nucleus. Thus, acetylenic C-atom becomes more electronegative in comparison to sp^2, sp^3 and hence the hydrogen atom present on carbon atom ($\equiv C-H$) can be easily removed.

80. (d) : All the three reagents except ammoniacal $AgNO_3$ reacts with 1, 2 and 4 compounds. The compound 3 possessing the terminal alkyne only reacts with ammoniacal $AgNO_3$ and thus can be distinguished from 1, 2 and 4 compounds.

Chapter 14

Environmental Chemistry

1. Which oxide of nitrogen is not a common pollutant introduced into the atmosphere both due to natural and human activity?
(a) N_2O_5 (b) NO_2
(c) N_2O (d) NO
(NEET 2018)

2. Which of the following is a sink for CO?
(a) Microorganisms present in the soil
(b) Oceans
(c) Plants
(d) Haemoglobin *(NEET 2017)*

3. Which one of the following is not a common component of Photochemical smog?
(a) Ozone
(b) Acrolein
(c) Peroxyacetyl nitrate
(d) Chlorofluorocarbons *(2014)*

4. Which one of the following statements is not true?
(a) Clean water would have a BOD value of 5 ppm.
(b) Fluoride deficiency in drinking water is harmful. Soluble fluoride is often used to bring its concentration upto 1 ppm.
(c) When the pH of rain water is higher than 6.5, it is called acid rain.
(d) Dissolved Oxygen (DO) in cold water can reach a concentration upto 10 ppm.
(Karnataka NEET 2013)

5. Which one of the following statements regarding photochemical smog is not correct?
(a) Carbon monoxide does not play any role in photochemical smog formation.
(b) Photochemical smog is an oxidising agent in character.
(c) Photochemical smog is formed through photochemical reaction involving solar energy.
(d) Photochemical smog does not cause irritation in eyes and throat. *(2012)*

6. Which one of the following statement is not true?
(a) pH of drinking water should be between 5.5 – 9.5
(b) Concentration of DO below 6 ppm is good for the growth of fish.
(c) Clean water would have a BOD value of less than 5 ppm.
(d) Oxides of sulphur, nitrogen and carbon, are the most widespread air pollutant.
(2011)

7. Green chemistry means such reactions which
(a) are related to the depletion of ozone layer
(b) study the reactions in plants
(c) produce colour during reactions
(d) reduce the use and production of hazardous chemicals *(2008)*

8. Which one of the following is responsible for depletion of the ozone layer in the upper strata of the atmosphere?
(a) Polyhalogens (b) Ferrocene
(c) Fullerenes (d) Freons *(2004)*

Answer Key

1. (a) **2.** (a, d) **3.** (d) **4.** (c) **5.** (d) **6.** (b) **7.** (d) **8.** (d)

EXPLANATIONS

1. (a)

2. (a, d) : Microorganisms present in the soil consume atmospheric CO. Haemoglobin has higher affinity for CO and it combines with CO to form carboxyhaemoglobin.

3. (d)

4. (c) : When pH of rain water drops below 5.6 it is called acid rain.

5. (d)

6. (b): Fish dies in water bodies polluted by sewage due to decrease in dissolved oxygen (D.O).

7. (d) : Green chemistry is the design, development, and implementation of chemical products and processes to reduce or eliminate the use and generation of substances hazardous to human health and the environment. Green chemistry also refers to the redesign of chemical products and processes with the goal of reducing or eliminating any negative environmental or health effects.

8. (d) : Fluorocarbons such as freon-1 ($CFCl_3$) and freon-12 (CF_2Cl_2) emitted as propellants in aerosol spray cans, refrigerators, fire fighting reagents etc. are stable compoundsand chemically inert. They do not react with any substance with which they come in contact and thus float through the atmosphere unchanged and eventually enter the stratosphere. There they absorb UV radiations and break down liberating free atomic chlorine which causes decomposition of ozone. This results in the depletion of the ozone layer.

$$\dot{Cl} + O_3 \rightarrow Cl\dot{O} + O_2$$

$$Cl\dot{O} + O_3 \rightarrow \dot{Cl} + 2O_2$$

Chapter 15

Solid State

Iron exhibits *bcc* structure at room temperature. Above 900°C, it transforms to *fcc* structure. The ratio of density of iron at room temperature to that at 900°C (assuming molar mass and atomic radii of iron remains constant with temperature) is

(a) $\frac{\sqrt{3}}{\sqrt{2}}$ (b) $\frac{4\sqrt{3}}{3\sqrt{2}}$

(c) $\frac{3\sqrt{3}}{4\sqrt{2}}$ (d) $\frac{1}{2}$ *(NEET 2018)*

Which is the incorrect statement?

(a) Density decreases in case of crystals with Schottky defect.

(b) $NaCl_{(s)}$ is insulator, silicon is semiconductor, silver is conductor, quartz is piezoelectric crystal.

(c) Frenkel defect is favoured in those ionic compounds in which sizes of cation and anions are almost equal.

(d) $FeO_{0.98}$ has non-stoichiometric metal deficiency defect. *(NEET 2017)*

In calcium fluoride, having the fluorite structure, the coordination numbers for calcium ion (Ca^{2+}) and fluoride ion (F^-) are

(a) 4 and 2 (b) 6 and 6

(c) 8 and 4 (d) 4 and 8 *(NEET-II 2016)*

Lithium has a *bcc* structure. Its density is 530 kg m^{-3} and its atomic mass is 6.94 g mol^{-1}. Calculate the edge length of a unit cell of lithium metal. ($N_A = 6.02 \times 10^{23}$ mol^{-1})

(a) 527 pm (b) 264 pm

(c) 154 pm (d) 352 pm *(NEET-I 2016)*

The ionic radii of A^+ and B^- ions are 0.98×10^{-10} m and 1.81×10^{-10} m. The coordination number of each ion in *AB* is

(a) 8 (b) 2

(c) 6 (d) 4 *(NEET-I 2016)*

The vacant space in *bcc* lattice unit cell is

(a) 48% (b) 23%

(c) 32% (d) 26% *(2015)*

7. The correct statement regarding defects in crystalline solids is

(a) Frenkel defects decrease the density of crystalline solids

(b) Frenkel defect is a dislocation defect

(c) Frenkel defect is found in halides of alkaline metals

(d) Schottky defects have no effect on the density of crystalline solids. *(2015)*

8. A given metal crystallises out with a cubic structure having edge length of 361 pm. If there are four metal atoms in one unit cell, what is the radius of one atom?

(a) 80 pm (b) 108 pm

(c) 40 pm (d) 127 pm *(2015, Cancelled)*

9. If a is the length of the side of a cube, the distance between the body centered atom and one corner atom in the cube will be

(a) $\frac{2}{\sqrt{3}}a$ (b) $\frac{4}{\sqrt{3}}a$

(c) $\frac{\sqrt{3}}{4}a$ (d) $\frac{\sqrt{3}}{2}a$ *(2014)*

10. A metal has a *fcc* lattice. The edge length of the unit cell is 404 pm. The density of the metal is 2.72 g cm^{-3}. The molar mass of the metal is

(N_A Avogadro's constant = 6.02×10^{23} mol^{-1})

(a) 27 g mol^{-1} (b) 20 g mol^{-1}

(c) 40 g mol^{-1} (d) 30 g mol^{-1} *(NEET 2013)*

11. The number of carbon atoms per unit cell of diamond unit cell is

(a) 6 (b) 1

(c) 4 (d) 8 *(NEET 2013)*

12. A metal crystallises with a face-centred cubic lattice. The edge of the unit cell is 408 pm. The diameter of the metal atom is

(a) 288 pm (b) 408 pm

(c) 144 pm (d) 204 pm *(2012)*

13. The number of octahedral void(s) per atom present in a cubic close-packed structure is

(a) 1 (b) 3
(c) 2 (d) 4 (2012)

14. Structure of a mixed oxide is cubic close packed (*ccp*). The cubic unit cell of mixed oxide is composed of oxide ions. One fourth of the tetrahedral voids are occupied by divalent metal *A* and the octahedral voids are occupied by a monovalent metal *B*. The formula of the oxide is
(a) ABO_2 (b) A_2BO_2
(c) $A_2B_3O_4$ (d) AB_2O_2 (Mains 2012)

15. A solid compound *XY* has NaCl structure. If the radius of the cation is 100 pm, the radius of the anion (Y^-) will be
(a) 275.1 pm (b) 322.5 pm
(c) 241.5 pm (d) 165.7 pm (Mains 2011)

16. *AB* crystallizes in a body centred cubic lattice with edge length '*a*' equal to 387 pm. The distance between two oppositely charged ions in the lattice is
(a) 335 pm (b) 250 pm
(c) 200 pm (d) 300 pm (2010)

17. Lithium metal crystallises in a body-centred cubic crystal. If the length of the side of the unit cell of lithium is 351 pm, the atomic radius of lithium will be
(a) 151.8 pm (b) 75.5 pm
(c) 300.5 pm (d) 240.8 pm (2009)

18. Copper crystallises in a face-centred cubic lattice with a unit cell length of 361 pm. What is the radius of copper atom in pm?
(a) 157 (b) 181
(c) 108 (d) 128 (2009)

19. Percentage of free space in a body centred cubic unit cell is
(a) 34% (b) 28%
(c) 30% (d) 32% (2008)

20. Which of the following statements is not correct?
(a) The number of carbon atoms in a unit cell of diamond is 4.
(b) The number of Bravais lattices in which a crystal can be categorized is 14.
(c) The fraction of the total volume occupied by the atoms in a primitive cell is 0.48.
(d) Molecular solids are generally volatile. (2008)

21. With which one of the following elements silicon should be doped so as to give *p*-type of semiconductor?
(a) Selenium (b) Boron
(c) Germanium (d) Arsenic (2008)

22. If *a* stands for the edge length of the cubi systems: simple cubic, body centred cubi and face centred cubic, then the ratio of rad of the spheres in these systems will b respectively
(a) $\frac{1}{2}a : \frac{\sqrt{3}}{2}a : \frac{\sqrt{2}}{2}a$
(b) $1a : \sqrt{3}a : \sqrt{2}a$
(c) $\frac{1}{2}a : \frac{\sqrt{3}}{4}a : \frac{1}{2\sqrt{2}}a$
(d) $\frac{1}{2}a : \sqrt{3}a : \frac{1}{\sqrt{2}}a$ (2008

23. The fraction of total volume occupied by th atoms present in a simple cube is
(a) $\frac{\pi}{3\sqrt{2}}$ (b) $\frac{\pi}{4\sqrt{2}}$
(c) $\frac{\pi}{4}$ (d) $\frac{\pi}{6}$ (200

24. If NaCl is doped with 10^{-4} mol % of $SrCl_2$, th concentration of cation vacancies will b ($N_A = 6.02 \times 10^{23}$ mol^{-1})
(a) 6.02×10^{16} mol^{-1} (b) 6.02×10^{17} mol
(c) 6.02×10^{14} mol^{-1} (d) 6.02×10^{15} mol (200

25. The appearance of colour in solid alkali met halides is generally due to
(a) interstitial positions
(b) *F*-centres
(c) Schottky defect
(d) Frenkel defect. (200

26. CsBr crystallises in a body centred cubic lattic The unit cell length is 436.6 pm. Given th the atomic mass of Cs = 133 and that Br = 80 amu and Avogadro number bei 6.02×10^{23} mol^{-1}, the density of CsBr is
(a) 4.25 g/cm^3 (b) 42.5 g/cm^3
(c) 0.425 g/cm^3 (d) 8.25 g/cm^3 (200

27. In a face-centered cubic lattice, a unit cell shared equally by how many unit cells?
(a) 2 (b) 4
(c) 6 (d) 8 (200

28. A compound formed by elements *X* and crystallises in a cubic structure in which th *X* atoms are at the corners of a cube and th *Y* atoms are at the face-centres. The formu of the compound is
(a) XY_3 (b) X_3Y
(c) XY (d) XY_2 (200

29. The pyknometric density of sodium chloride crystal is 2.165×10^3 kg m^{-3} while its X-ray density is 2.178×10^3 kg m^{-3}. The fraction of unoccupied sites in sodium chloride crystal is
(a) 5.96 (b) 5.96×10^{-2}
(c) 5.96×10^{-1} (d) 5.96×10^{-3}
(2003)

30. When Zn converts from melted state to its solid state, it has *hcp* structure, then find the number of nearest atoms.
(a) 6 (b) 8
(c) 12 (d) 4 *(2001)*

31. Cation and anion combines in a crystal to form following type of compound
(a) ionic (b) metallic
(c) covalent (d) dipole-dipole.
(2000)

32. In cube of any crystal *A*-atom placed at every corners and *B*-atom placed at every centre of face. The formula of compound is
(a) AB (b) AB_3
(c) A_2B_2 (d) A_2B_3 *(2000)*

33. In crystals of which one of the following ionic compounds would you expect maximum distance between centres of cations and anions?
(a) CsI (b) CsF
(c) LiF (d) LiI *(1998)*

34. The second order Bragg diffraction of X-rays with $\lambda = 1.00$ Å from a set of parallel planes in a metal occurs at an angle 60°. The distance between the scattering planes in the crystal is
(a) 2.00 Å (b) 1.00 Å
(c) 0.575 Å (d) 1.15 Å *(1998)*

35. The edge length of face centred unit cubic cells is 508 pm. If the radius of the cation is 110 pm, the radius of the anion is
(a) 144 pm (b) 398 pm
(c) 288 pm (d) 618 pm *(1998)*

36. Schottky defect in crystals is observed when
(a) density of the crystal is increased
(b) unequal number of cations and anions are missing from the lattice
(c) an ion leaves its normal site and occupies an interstitial site
(d) equal number of cations and anions are missing from the lattice. *(1998)*

37. The high density of water compared to ice is due to
(a) dipole-induced dipole interactions
(b) induced dipole induced dipole interactions
(c) hydrogen bonding interactions
(d) dipole-dipole interactions. *(1997)*

38. For two ionic solids CaO and KI, identify the wrong statement among the following
(a) CaO has high melting point
(b) Lattice energy of CaO is much larger than that of KI
(c) KI has high melting point
(d) KI is soluble in benzene. *(1997)*

39. The intermetallic compound LiAg crystallizes in cubic lattice in which both lithium and silver have coordination number of eight. The crystal class is
(a) face-centred cube (b) simple cube
(c) body-centred cube (d) none of these.
(1997)

40. The *fcc* crystal contains how many atoms in each unit cell?
(a) 6 (b) 8
(c) 4 (d) 5 *(1996)*

41. If we mix a pentavalent impurity in a crystal lattice of germanium, what type of semiconductor formation will occur?
(a) *n*-type semiconductor
(b) *p*-type semiconductor
(c) both (a) and (b)
(d) None of these. *(1996)*

42. An element (atomic mass = 100 g/mol) having *bcc* structure has unit cell edge 400 pm. The density of element is
(a) 7.289 g/cm^3 (b) 2.144 g/cm^3
(c) 10.376 g/cm^3 (d) 5.188 g/cm^3
(1996)

43. The number of atoms in 100 g of a *fcc* crystal with density $d = 10$ g/cm^3 and cell edge equal to 100 pm, is equal to
(a) 2×10^{25} (b) 1×10^{25}
(c) 4×10^{25} (d) 3×10^{25} *(1994)*

44. Ionic solids, with Schottky defects, contain in their structure
(a) cation vacancies only
(b) cation vacancies and interstitial cations
(c) equal number of cation and anion vacancies
(d) anion vacancies and interstitial anions.
(1994)

45. The pure crystalline substance on being heated gradually first forms a turbid liquid at constant temperature and still at higher temperature turbidity completely disappears. The behaviour is a characteristic of substance forming

(a) allotropic crystals
(b) liquid crystals
(c) isomeric crystals
(d) isomorphous crystals. *(1993)*

46. On doping Ge metal with a little of In or Ga, one gets
(a) *p*-type semiconductor
(b) *n*-type semiconductor
(c) insulator
(d) rectifier. *(1993)*

47. In the fluorite structure, the coordination number of Ca^{2+} ion is
(a) 4 (b) 6
(c) 8 (d) 3 *(1993)*

48. The number of atoms contained in a *fcc* unit cell of a monoatomic substance is
(a) 1 (b) 2
(c) 4 (d) 6 *(1993)*

49. For orthorhombic system axial ratios are $a \neq b \neq c$ and the axial angles are
(a) $\alpha = \beta = \gamma \neq 90°$
(b) $\alpha = \beta = \gamma = 90°$
(c) $\alpha = \gamma = 90°, \beta \neq 90°$
(d) $\alpha \neq \beta \neq \gamma \neq 90°$ *(1991)*

50. Most crystals show good cleavage because their atoms, ions or molecules are
(a) weakly bonded together
(b) strongly bonded together
(c) spherically symmetrical
(d) arranged in planes. *(1991)*

Answer Key

1.	(c)	**2.**	(c, d)	**3.**	(c)	**4.**	(d)	**5.**	(c)	**6.**	(c)	**7.**	(b)	**8.**	(d)	**9.**	(d)	**10.**	(a)
11.	(d)	**12.**	(a)	**13.**	(a)	**14.**	(d)	**15.**	(c)	**16.**	(a)	**17.**	(a)	**18.**	(d)	**19.**	(d)	**20.**	(c)
21.	(b)	**22.**	(c)	**23.**	(d)	**24.**	(b)	**25.**	(b)	**26.**	(a)	**27.**	(c)	**28.**	(a)	**29.**	(d)	**30.**	(c)
31.	(a)	**32.**	(b)	**33.**	(a)	**34.**	(d)	**35.**	(a)	**36.**	(d)	**37.**	(c)	**38.**	(d)	**39.**	(c)	**40.**	(c)
41.	(a)	**42.**	(d)	**43.**	(c)	**44.**	(c)	**45.**	(b)	**46.**	(a)	**47.**	(c)	**48.**	(c)	**49.**	(b)	**50.**	(d)

EXPLANATIONS

1. (c) : For *bcc* lattice : $Z = 2,\ a = \frac{4r}{\sqrt{3}}$

For *fcc* lattice : $Z = 4,\ a = 2\sqrt{2}\,r$

$$\therefore\ \frac{d_{\text{R.T.}}}{d_{900°\text{C}}} = \frac{\left(\frac{ZM}{N_A a^3}\right)_{bcc}}{\left(\frac{ZM}{N_A a^3}\right)_{fcc}}$$

Given, molar mass and atom radii are constant.

$$= \frac{2}{4}\left(\frac{2\sqrt{2}r}{\frac{4r}{\sqrt{3}}}\right)^3 = \frac{3\sqrt{3}}{4\sqrt{2}}$$

2. (c, d) : Frenkel defect is favoured in those ionic compounds in which there is large difference in the size of cations and anions.

Non-stoichiometric defects due to metal deficiency is shown by Fe_xO where $x = 0.93$ to 0.96.

3. (c) : In fluorite structure, Ca^{2+} ions are in the face centred cubic arrangement. Each Ca^{2+} is connected to 4 F^- ions below it and to another set of 4 F^- ions above it *i.e.* Ca^{2+} has a coordination number of 8 and each F^- ion has a coordination number 4.

4. (d) : For *bcc*, $Z = 2$, $\rho = 530\ \text{kg m}^{-3}$, at. mass of Li $= 6.94\ \text{g mol}^{-1}$, $N_A = 6.02 \times 10^{23}\ \text{mol}^{-1}$

$$\rho = 530\ \text{kg m}^{-3} = \frac{530 \times 1000\ \text{g}}{1 \times (100)^3\ \text{cm}^3} = 0.53\ \text{g cm}^{-3}$$

$$\rho = \frac{Z \times \text{At. mass}}{N_A \times a^3}$$

$$a^3 = \frac{Z \times \text{At. mass}}{N_A \times \rho} = \frac{2 \times 6.94}{6.02 \times 10^{23} \times 0.53}$$

$$= 43.5 \times 10^{-24}\ \text{cm}^3$$

$$\Rightarrow\ a = 352 \times 10^{-10}\ \text{cm} = 352\ \text{pm}$$

5. (c) : Radius ratio, $\frac{r^+}{r^-} = \frac{0.98 \times 10^{-10}}{1.81 \times 10^{-10}} = 0.541$

It lies in the range of 0.414 to 0.732 hence, coordination number of each ion will be 6 as the compound will have NaCl type structure *i.e.*, octahedral arrangement.

6. (c) : Packing efficiency of *bcc* lattice = 68%

Hence, empty space = 32%.

7. (b) : Frenkel defect is a dislocation defect as smaller ions (usually cations) are dislocated from normal sites to interstitial sites. Frenkel defect is shown by compounds having large difference in the size of cations and anions hence, alkali metal halides do not show Frenkel defect. Also, Schottky defect decreases the density of crystal while Frenkel defect has no effect on the density of crystal.

8. (d) : $Z = 4$, *i.e.*, structure is *fcc*.

Hence, $r = \frac{a}{2\sqrt{2}} = \frac{361}{2\sqrt{2}} = 127.65\ \text{pm} \approx 127\ \text{pm}$

9. (d) : The distance between the body centered atom and one corner atom is $\frac{\sqrt{3}a}{2}$ *i.e.* half of the body diagonal.

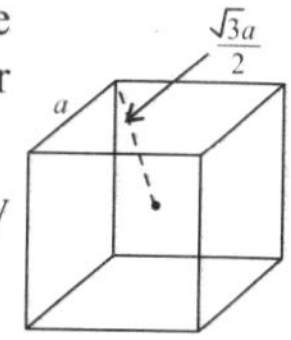

10. (a) : $d = \frac{ZM}{N_A a^3}$ ($Z = 4$ for *fcc*)

$$M = \frac{d \times N_A \times a^3}{Z} = \frac{2.72 \times 6.023 \times 10^{23} \times (404 \times 10^{-10})^3}{4}$$

$M = 26.99 \approx 27\ \text{g mol}^{-1}$

11. (d) : Diamond is like ZnS (Zinc blende). Carbon forming *ccp* (*fcc*) and also occupying half of tetrahedral voids.

Total no. of carbon atoms per unit cell

$$= \underset{\text{(Corners)}}{8 \times \frac{1}{8}} + \underset{\text{(Face centrered)}}{6 \times \frac{1}{2}} + \underset{\text{(Tetrahedral void)}}{4} = 8$$

12. (a) : For a face centred cubic (*fcc*) structure,

$r = \frac{a}{2\sqrt{2}}$, $a = 408$ pm, $r = \frac{408}{2\sqrt{2}} = 144$ pm

Diameter $= 2r = 2 \times 144 = 288$ pm

13. (a) : Number of octahedral voids is same as number of atoms.

14. (d) : Number of atoms in *ccp* $= 4 = O^{2-}$

Number of tetrahedral voids $= 2 \times N = 2 \times 4$

Number of A^{2+} ions $= 8 \times \frac{1}{4} = 2$

Number of octahedral voids

= Number of B^+ ions $= N = 4$

Ratio, $O^{2-} : A^{2+} : B^+ = 4 : 2 : 4 = 2 : 1 : 2$

Formula of oxide $= AB_2O_2$

15. (c) : For NaCl, $\frac{r^+}{r^-} = 0.414$

Given radius of cation = 100 pm

$$\frac{100}{r^-} = 0.414 \Rightarrow \frac{100}{0.414} = r^- \Rightarrow r^- = 241.5 \text{ pm}$$

16. (a) : For a *bcc* lattice, $2(r^+ + r^-) = \sqrt{3}a$

where r^+ = radius of cation, r^- = radius of anion

a = edge length

$$\therefore (r^+ + r^-) = \frac{\sqrt{3} \times 387}{2} = 335.142 \text{ pm} \approx 335 \text{ pm}$$

17. (a) : Since Li crystallises in body-centred cubic crystal, atomic radius, $r = \frac{\sqrt{3}a}{4}$ (a = edge length)

$$\therefore r = \frac{\sqrt{3}}{4} \times 351 = 151.8 \text{ pm (given } a = 351 \text{ pm)}$$

18. (d) : Since Cu crystallises in a face-centred cubic lattice,

Atomic radius, $r = \frac{a}{2\sqrt{2}}$ (a = edge length = 361 pm)

$$\therefore r = \frac{361}{2\sqrt{2}} = 127.6 \approx 128 \text{ pm}$$

19. (d) : The ratio of volumes occupied by atoms in unit cell to the total volume of the unit cell is called as packing fraction or density of packing. For body centred cubic structure, packing fraction = 0.68 *i.e.*, 68% of the unit cell is occupied by atoms and 32% is empty.

20. (c) : Packing fraction for a cubic unit cell is

given by $f = \frac{z \times \frac{4}{3}\pi r^3}{a^3}$

where a = edge length, r = radius of cation and anion. Efficiency of packing in simple cubic or primitive cell = $\pi/6$ = 0.52 *i.e.* 52% of unit cell is occupied by atoms and 48% is empty.

21. (b) : If silicon is doped with any of the element of group III (B, Al, Ga, In, Th) of the periodic table, *p*-type of semiconductor will be obtained.

22. (c) : For Simple cubic : $r^+ + r^- = a/2$

For Body centred : $r^+ + r^- = a\sqrt{3}/4$

where a = edge length, $r^+ + r^-$ = interatomic distance.

For Face centered: $r^+ + r^- = \frac{a}{2\sqrt{2}}$

$\therefore$ Ratio of radii of the three will be $\frac{a}{2} : \frac{a\sqrt{3}}{4} : \frac{a}{2\sqrt{2}}$

23. (d) : The maximum properties of the available volume which may be filled by hard sphere in simple cubic arrangement is $\pi/6$ or 0.52.

24. (b) : As each Sr^{2+} ion introduces one cation vacancy, therefore, concentration of cation vacancies = mole % of $SrCl_2$ added.

$\therefore$ Concentration of cation vacancies

$$= 10^{-4} \text{ mole\%} = \frac{10^{-4}}{100} \times 6.023 \times 10^{23} = 6.023 \times 10^{17}$$

25. (b) : *F*-centres are the sites where anions are missing and instead electrons are present. They are responsible for colours.

26. (a) : Density of CsBr = $\frac{Z \times M}{V \times N_A}$

$$= \frac{1 \times 213}{(436.6 \times 10^{-10})^3 \times 6.023 \times 10^{23}} = 4.25 \text{ g/cm}^3$$

27. (c) : Here given unit cell is shared equally by six faces in the *fcc* which is shared equally by six different unit cells.

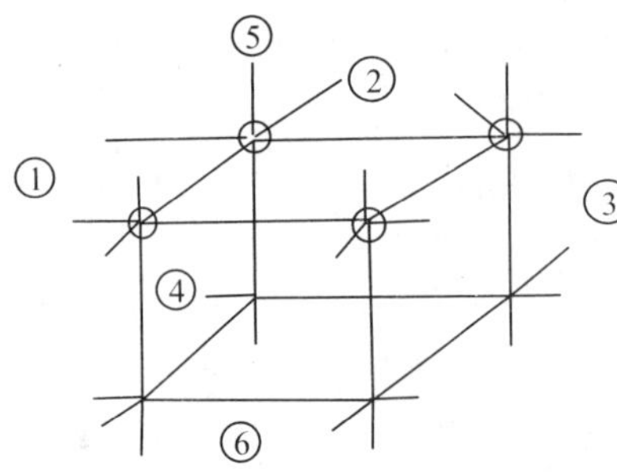

28. (a) : In a unit cell, X atoms at the corners

$$= \frac{1}{8} \times 8 = 1$$

Y atoms at the face centres = $\frac{1}{2} \times 6 = 3$

Ratio of X and Y = 1 : 3. Hence formula is XY_3.

29. (d) : Molar volume from pyknometric density

$$= \frac{M}{2.165 \times 10^3} \text{ m}^3$$

Molar volume from X-ray density

$$= \frac{M}{2.178 \times 10^3} \text{ m}^3$$

$$\text{Volume unoccupied} = \frac{M}{10^3}\left(\frac{1}{2.165} - \frac{1}{2.178}\right) \text{m}^3$$

raction unoccupied

$$= \left(\frac{0.013\,M \times 10^{-3}}{2.165 \times 2.178}\right) \Big/ \left(\frac{M \times 10^{-3}}{2.165}\right) = 5.96 \times 10^{-3}$$

0. (c) : *hcp* is a closed packed arrangement in hich the unit cell is hexagonal and coordination umber is 12.

1. (a) : The electrostatic force of attraction which xists between oppositely charged ions is called as nic bond.

2. (b) : 'A' atoms are at '8' corners of the cube. Thus,

). of 'A' atoms per unit cell $= 8 \times \frac{1}{8} = 1$

' atoms are at the face centre of six faces. Thus, no.

 'B' atoms per unit cell $= 6 \times \frac{1}{2} = 3$

he formula is AB_3.

3. (a) : As Cs^+ ion has larger size than Li^+ and has larger size than F^-, so maximum distance tween centres of cations and anions is in CsI.

4. (d) : According to Bragg's equation.
$n\lambda = 2d \sin\theta$
s, $n = 2$, $\lambda = 1.00$Å, $\theta = 60°$, $d = ?$

$d = \frac{1}{\sin 60°} = \frac{2}{\sqrt{3}} = 1.15$Å

5. (a) : In the face centred cubic lattice, the edge ngth of the unit cell, $a = r + 2R + r$
here r = Radius of cation
R = Radius of anion
$508 = 2 \times 110 + 2R \Rightarrow R = 144$ pm

6. (d) : In Schottky defect equal no. of cations d anions are missing from the lattice. So the ystal remains neutral. Such defect is more common highly ionic compounds of similar cationic and ionic size, *i.e.* NaCl.

7. (c) : Due to polar nature, water molecules are ld together by intermolecular hydrogen bonds. e structure of ice is open with large number of cant spaces. Thus the density of ice is less.

8. (d) : KI is an ionic compound while benzene is not.

9. (c) : A body centred cubic unit cell consists of atoms at the corners and one atom at the centre.

0. (c) : The contribution of eight atoms of face ntred cubic unit cell $= 8 \times \frac{1}{8} = 1$ atom. There is one atom at each of six faces, which is shared by 2 unit cells each. The contribution of 6 face centred atoms $= 6 \times \frac{1}{2} = 3$. Therefore $n = 1 + 3 = 4$

41. (a) : When an impurity atom with 5 valence electrons (as arsenic) is introduced in a germanium crystal, it replaces one of the germanium atoms. Four of the five valence electrons of the impurity atom form covalent bonds with each valence electron of four germanium atoms and fifth valence electron becomes free to move in the crystal structure. This free electron acts as a charge carrier. Such as an impure germanium crystal is called n-type semiconductor because in it charge carriers are negative (free electrons).

42. (d) : Cell edge = 400 pm; Number of atoms in *bcc* (Z) = 2 and atomic mass = 100 g/mol.

Since atomic mass is 100 g/mol, therefore mass of each atom $(m) = \frac{100}{6.023 \times 10^{23}} = 16.6 \times 10^{-23}$ g

We know that volume of unit cell $= (400 \text{ pm})^3$
$= (64 \times 10^6)\text{pm}^3 = 64 \times 10^{-24}$ cm^3 and
mass of unit cell $= Z \times m = 2 \times (16.6 \times 10^{-23})$
$= 33.2 \times 10^{-23}$ g

Therefore density $= \frac{\text{Mass of unit cell}}{\text{Volume of unit cell}}$

$= \frac{33.2 \times 10^{-23}}{64 \times 10^{-24}} = 5.188 \text{ g/cm}^3$

43. (c) : Mass (m) = 100 g; Density (d) = 10 g/cm^3 and length (l) = 100 pm = 100×10^{-12} m
$= 100 \times 10^{-10}$ cm

We know that volume of the unit cell
$= (l)^3 = (100 \times 10^{-10} \text{ cm})^3 = 10^{-24}\text{cm}^3$

and volume of 100 g of element $= \frac{\text{Mass}}{\text{Density}} = \frac{100}{10} = 10 \text{ cm}^3$

Therefore number of unit cells $= \frac{10}{10^{-24}} = 1 \times 10^{25}$

Since each *fcc* cube contains 4 atoms, therefore total number of atoms in 100 g
$= 4 \times (1 \times 10^{25}) = 4 \times 10^{25}$

44. (c) : When an atom is missing from its normal lattice site, a lattice vacancy is created. Such a defect, which involves equal number of cation and anion vacancies in the crystal lattice is called a Schottky defect.

45. (b) : Liquid crystals on heating first become turbid and then on further heating turbidity completely disappears.

46. (a) : *p*-type of semiconductors are produced (a) due to metal deficiency defects (b) by adding impurity containing less electrons (*i.e.* atoms of group 13). Ge belongs to Group 14 and In to Group 13. Hence on doping *p*-type semiconductor is obtained.

This doping of Ge with In increase the electrical conductivity of the Ge crystal.

47. (c) : In fluorite (CaF_2) structure, C.N. of $Ca^{2+} = 8$, C.N. of $F^- = 4$.

48. (c) : *fcc* crystal contains

$$= 8 \times \frac{1}{8} + 6 \times \frac{1}{2} = 4 \text{ atoms in a unit cell}$$

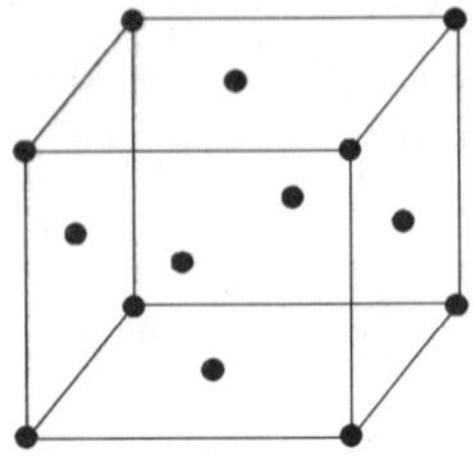

49. (b) : For orthorhombic system $\alpha = \beta = \gamma = 90^{\circ}$

50. (d) : Crystals show good cleavage because their constituent particles are arranged in planes.

Chapter 16

Solutions

1. If molality of the dilute solution is doubled, the value of molal depression constant (K_f) will be
(a) halved (b) tripled
(c) unchanged (d) doubled.
(NEET 2017)

2. Which of the following is dependent on temperature?
(a) Molarity (b) Mole fraction
(c) Weight percentage (d) Molality
(NEET 2017)

3. The van't Hoff factor (i) for a dilute aqueous solution of the strong electrolyte barium hydroxide is
(a) 0 (b) 1
(c) 2 (d) 3
(NEET-II 2016)

4. Which one of the following is incorrect for ideal solution?
(a) $\Delta H_{mix} = 0$ (b) $\Delta U_{mix} = 0$
(c) $\Delta P = P_{obs} - P_{\text{calculated by Raoult's law}} = 0$
(d) $\Delta G_{mix} = 0$ *(NEET-II 2016)*

5. Which of the following statements about the composition of the vapour over an ideal 1 : 1 molar mixture of benzene and toluene is correct? Assume that the temperature is constant at 25°C. (Given, vapour pressure data at 25°C, benzene = 12.8 kPa, toluene = 3.85 kPa)
(a) The vapour will contain equal amounts of benzene and toluene.
(b) Not enough information is given to make a prediction.
(c) The vapour will contain a higher percentage of benzene.
(d) The vapour will contain a higher percentage of toluene. *(NEET-I 2016)*

6. At 100°C the vapour pressure of a solution of 6.5 g of a solute in 100 g water is 732 mm. If $K_b = 0.52$, the boiling point of this solution will be
(a) 102°C (b) 103°C
(c) 101°C (d) 100°C
(NEET-I 2016)

7. What is the mole fraction of the solute in a 1.00 m aqueous solution?
(a) 1.770 (b) 0.0354
(c) 0.0177 (d) 0.177
(2015, 2011)

8. The boiling point of 0.2 mol kg^{-1} solution of X in water is greater than equimolal solution of Y in water. Which one of the following statements is true in this case?
(a) Molecular mass of X is less than the molecular mass of Y.
(b) Y is undergoing dissociation in water while X undergoes no change.
(c) X is undergoing dissociation in water.
(d) Molecular mass of X is greater than the molecular mass of Y. *(2015, Cancelled)*

9. Which one of the following electrolytes has the same value of van't Hoff factor (i) as that of $Al_2(SO_4)_3$ (if all are 100% ionised)?
(a) $Al(NO_3)_3$ (b) $K_4[Fe(CN)_6]$
(c) K_2SO_4 (d) $K_3[Fe(CN)_6]$
(2015, Cancelled)

10. Which of them is not equal to zero for an ideal solution?
(a) ΔV_{mix}
(b) $\Delta P = P_{observed} - P_{Raoult}$
(c) ΔH_{mix} (d) ΔS_{mix}
(2015, Cancelled)

11. Of the following 0.10 m aqueous solutions, which one will exhibit the largest freezing point depression?
(a) KCl (b) $C_6H_{12}O_6$
(c) $Al_2(SO_4)_3$ (d) K_2SO_4
(2014)

12. How many grams of concentrated nitric acid solution should be used to prepare 250 mL of 2.0 M HNO_3? The concentrated acid is 70% HNO_3.
(a) 70.0 g conc. HNO_3
(b) 54.0 g conc. HNO_3
(c) 45.0 g conc. HNO_3
(d) 90.0 g conc. HNO_3 *(NEET 2013)*

13. Which condition is not satisfied by an ideal solution?
(a) $\Delta_{mix} V = 0$ (b) $\Delta_{mix} S = 0$
(c) Obeyance to Raoult's Law
(d) $\Delta_{mix} H = 0$ *(Karnataka NEET 2013)*

14. p_A and p_B are the vapour pressure of pure liquid components, A and B, respectively of an ideal binary solution. If x_A represents the mole fraction of component A, the total pressure of the solution will be
(a) $p_A + x_A(p_B - p_A)$ (b) $p_A + x_A(p_A - p_B)$
(c) $p_B + x_A(p_B - p_A)$ (d) $p_B + x_A(p_A - p_B)$
(2012)

15. Vapour pressure of chloroform ($CHCl_3$) and dichloromethane (CH_2Cl_2) at 25°C are 200 mm Hg and 41.5 mm Hg respectively. Vapour pressure of the solution obtained by mixing 25.5 g of $CHCl_3$ and 40 g of CH_2Cl_2 at the same temperature will be
(Molecular mass of $CHCl_3$ = 119.5 u and molecular mass of CH_2Cl_2 = 85 u)
(a) 173.9 mm Hg (b) 615.0 mm Hg
(c) 347.9 mm Hg (d) 285.5 mm Hg
(Mains 2012)

16. The freezing point depression constant for water is $-1.86°$ C m^{-1}. If 5.00 g Na_2SO_4 is dissolved in 45.0 g H_2O, the freezing point is changed by -3.82°C. Calculate the van't Hoff factor for Na_2SO_4.
(a) 2.05 (b) 2.63
(c) 3.11 (d) 0.381 *(2011)*

17. The van't Hoff factor i for a compound which undergoes dissociation in one solvent and association in other solvent is respectively
(a) less than one and greater than one
(b) less than one and less than one
(c) greater than one and less than one
(d) greater than one and greater than one.
(2011)

18. A 0.1 molal aqueous solution of a weak acid is 30% ionized. If K_f for water is 1.86°C/m, the freezing point of the solution will be
(a) -0.18°C (b) -0.54°C
(c) -0.36°C (d) -0.24°C
(Mains 2011)

19. 200 mL of an aqueous solution of a protein contains its 1.26 g. The osmotic pressure of this solution at 300 K is found to be 2.57×10^{-3} bar. The molar mass of protein will be
(R = 0.083 L bar mol^{-1} K^{-1})
(a) 51022 g mol^{-1} (b) 122044 g mol^{-1}
(c) 31011 g mol^{-1} (d) 61038 g mol^{-1}
(Mains 2011)

20. An aqueous solution is 1.00 molal in KI. Which change will cause the vapour pressure of the solution to increase?
(a) Addition of NaCl
(b) Addition of Na_2SO_4
(c) Addition of 1.00 molal KI
(d) Addition of water *(2010)*

21. A solution of sucrose (molar mass = 342 g mol^{-1}) has been prepared by dissolving 68.5 g of sucrose in 1000 g of water. The freezing point of the solution obtained will be (K_f for water = 1.86 K kg mol^{-1})
(a) -0.372°C (b) -0.520°C
(c) $+0.372$°C (d) -0.570°C
(2010)

22. A 0.0020 m aqueous solution of an ionic compound $[Co(NH_3)_5(NO_2)]Cl$ freezes at -0.00732°C. Number of moles of ions which 1 mol of ionic compound produces on being dissolved in water will be
($K_f = -1.86$°C/m)
(a) 3 (b) 4
(c) 1 (d) 2 *(2009)*

23. 0.5 molal aqueous solution of a weak acid (HX) is 20% ionised. If K_f for water is 1.86 K kg mol^{-1}, the lowering in freezing point of the solution is
(a) 0.56 K (b) 1.12 K
(c) -0.56 K (d) -1.12 K
(2007)

24. Concentrated aqueous sulphuric acid is 98% H_2SO_4 by mass and has a density of 1.80 g mL^{-1}. Volume of acid required to make one litre of 0.1 M H_2SO_4 solution is
(a) 16.65 mL (b) 22.20 mL
(c) 5.55 mL (d) 11.10 mL
(2007)

5. During osmosis, flow of water through a semipermeable membrane is
   (a) from solution having lower concentration only
   (b) from solution having higher concentration only
   (c) from both sides of semipermeable membrane with equal flow rates
   (d) from both sides of semipermeable membrane with unequal flow rates. *(2006)*

6. A solution of acetone in ethanol
   (a) obeys Raoult's law
   (b) shows a negative deviation from Raoult's law
   (c) shows a positive deviation from Raoult's law
   (d) behaves like a near ideal solution. *(2006)*

7. 1.00 g of a non-electrolyte solute (molar mass 250 g mol^{-1}) was dissolved in 51.2 g of benzene. If the freezing point depression constant, K_f of benzene is 5.12 K kg mol^{-1}, the freezing point of benzene will be lowered by
   (a) 0.2 K (b) 0.4 K
   (c) 0.3 K (d) 0.5 K *(2006)*

8. A solution containing 10 g per dm^3 of urea (molecular mass = 60 g mol^{-1}) is isotonic with a 5% solution of a nonvolatile solute is
   (a) 200 g mol^{-1} (b) 250 g mol^{-1}
   (c) 300 g mol^{-1} (d) 350 g mol^{-1} *(2006)*

9. The mole fraction of the solute in one molal aqueous solution is
   (a) 0.009 (b) 0.018
   (c) 0.027 (d) 0.036 *(2005)*

0. The vapour pressure of two liquids P and Q are 80 and 60 torr, respectively. The total vapour pressure of solution obtained by mixing 3 mole of P and 2 mol of Q would be
   (a) 72 torr (b) 140 torr
   (c) 68 torr (d) 20 torr *(2005)*

1. A solution has a 1 : 4 mole ratio of pentane to hexane. The vapour pressures of the pure hydrocarbons at 20°C are 440 mm Hg for pentane and 120 mm Hg for hexane. The mole fraction of pentane in the vapour phase would be
   (a) 0.200 (b) 0.549
   (c) 0.786 (d) 0.478 *(2005)*

32. A solution of urea (mol. mass 56 g mol^{-1}) boils at 100.18°C at the atmospheric pressure. If K_f and K_b for water are 1.86 and 0.512 K kg mol^{-1} respectively, the above solution will freeze at
   (a) 0.654°C (b) – 0.654°C
   (c) 6.54°C (d) – 6.54°C *(2005)*

33. A solution containing components A and B follows Raoult's law
   (a) A - B attraction force is greater than A - A and B - B
   (b) A - B attraction force is less than A - A and B - B
   (c) A - B attraction force remains same as A - A and B - B
   (d) volume of solution is different from sum of volume of solute and solvent. *(2002)*

34. A solution contains non volatile solute of molecular mass M_2. Which of the following can be used to calculate the molecular mass of solute in terms of osmotic pressure?
   (a) $M_2 = \left(\frac{m_2}{\pi}\right)VRT$
   (b) $M_2 = \left(\frac{m_2}{V}\right)\frac{RT}{\pi}$
   (c) $M_2 = \left(\frac{m_2}{V}\right)\pi RT$
   (d) $M_2 = \left(\frac{m_2}{V}\right)\frac{\pi}{RT}$
   (m_2 = mass of solute, V = volume of solution, π = osmotic pressure) *(2002)*

35. 2.5 litre of 1 M NaOH solution is mixed with another 3 litre of 0.5 M NaOH solution. Then find out molarity of resultant solution.
   (a) 0.80 M (b) 1.0 M
   (c) 0.73 M (d) 0.50 M *(2002)*

36. The beans are cooked earlier in pressure cooker because
   (a) boiling point increases with increasing pressure
   (b) boiling point decreases with increasing pressure
   (c) extra pressure of pressure cooker softens the beans
   (d) internal energy is not lost while cooking in pressure cooker. *(2001)*

37. Pure water can be obtained from sea water by
   (a) centrifugation (b) plasmolysis
   (c) reverse osmosis (d) sedimentation. *(2001)*

38. From the colligative properties of solution, which one is the best method for the determination of molecular weight of proteins and polymers?
(a) Osmotic pressure
(b) Lowering in vapour pressure
(c) Lowering in freezing point
(d) Elevation in boiling point *(2000)*

39. The vapour pressure of benzene at a certain temperature is 640 mm of Hg. A non-volatile and non-electrolyte solid, weighing 2.175 g is added to 39.08 of benzene. The vapour pressure of the solution is 600 mm of Hg. What is the molecular weight of solid substance?
(a) 69.5 (b) 59.6
(c) 49.50 (d) 79.8 *(1999)*

40. How many g of dibasic acid (mol. weight 200) should be present in 100 mL of the aqueous solution to give strength of 0.1 N?
(a) 10 g (b) 2 g
(c) 1 g (d) 20 g *(1999)*

41. If 0.15 g of a solute, dissolved in 15 g of solvent, is boiled at a temperature higher by 0.216°C, than that of the pure solvent. The molecular weight of the substance (Molal elevation constant for the solvent is 2.16°C) is
(a) 10.1 (b) 100
(c) 1.01 (d) 1000 *(1999)*

42. The vapour pressure of a solvent decreased by 10 mm of mercury when a non-volatile solute was added to the solvent. The mole fraction of the solute in the solution is 0.2. What should be the mole fraction of the solvent if the decrease in the vapour pressure is to be 20 mm of mercury?
(a) 0.4 (b) 0.6
(c) 0.8 (d) 0.2 *(1998)*

43. A 5% solution of cane sugar (mol. wt. = 342) is isotonic with 1% solution of a substance *X*. The molecular weight of *X* is
(a) 68.4 (b) 171.2
(c) 34.2 (d) 136.8 *(1998)*

44. Which of the following 0.10 m aqueous solution will have the lowest freezing point?
(a) KI (b) $C_{12}H_{22}O_{11}$
(c) $Al_2(SO_4)_3$ (d) $C_5H_{10}O_5$
(1997)

45. What is the molarity of H_2SO_4 solution, tha has a density 1.84 g/cc at 35°C and contain 98% by weight?
(a) 18.4 M (b) 18 M
(c) 4.18 M (d) 8.14 M *(1996*

46. The vapour pressure of CCl_4 at 25°C is 143 mm Hg If 0.5 g of a non-volatile solute (mol weight = 65) is dissolved in 100 mL CCl_4, th vapour pressure of the solution will be
(a) 199.34 mm Hg (b) 143.99 mm H
(c) 141.43 mm Hg (d) 94.39 mm Hg
(1996

47. The relationship between osmotic pressur at 273 K when 10 g glucose (p_1), 10 g ure (p_2), and 10 g sucrose (p_3) are dissolved i 250 mL of water is
(a) $p_2 > p_1 > p_3$
(b) $p_2 > p_3 > p_1$
(c) $p_1 > p_2 > p_3$
(d) $p_3 > p_1 > p_2$ *(1996*

48. The concentration unit, independent o temperature, would be
(a) normality
(b) weight volume percent
(c) molality
(d) molarity. *(1995, 1992*

49. According to Raoult's law, the relative lowerin of vapour pressure for a solution is equal t
(a) mole fraction of solute
(b) mole fraction of solvent
(c) moles of solute
(d) moles of solvent. *(1995*

50. How many grams of CH_3OH should be adde to water to prepare 150 mL solution of 2 M CH_3OH?
(a) 9.6×10^3 (b) 2.4×10^3
(c) 9.6 (d) 2.4 *(1994*

51. At 25°C, the highest osmotic pressure i exhibited by 0.1 M solution of
(a) glucose (b) urea
(c) $CaCl_2$ (d) KCl. *(1994*

52. Which of the following salt has the same valu of vant's Hoff factor (i) as that of $K_3[Fe(CN)_6]$
(a) Na_2SO_4 (b) $Al(NO_3)_3$
(c) $Al_2(SO_4)_3$ (d) NaCl *(1994*

3. If 0.1 M solution of glucose and 0.1 M solution of urea are placed on two sides of the semipermeable membrane to equal heights, then it will be correct to say that
   (a) there will be no net movement across the membrane
   (b) glucose will flow towards glucose solution
   (c) urea will flow towards glucose solution
   (d) water will flow from urea solution to glucose. *(1992)*

4. Which one is a colligative property?
   (a) Boiling point (b) Vapour pressure
   (c) Osmotic pressure (d) Freezing point *(1992)*

5. Blood cells retain their normal shape in solution which are
   (a) hypotonic to blood
   (b) isotonic to blood
   (c) hypertonic to blood
   (d) equinormal to blood. *(1991)*

6. Which of the following aqueous solution has minimum freezing point?
   (a) 0.01 m NaCl
   (b) 0.005 m C_2H_5OH
   (c) 0.005 m MgI_2
   (d) 0.005 m $MgSO_4$ *(1991)*

57. The relative lowering of the vapour pressure is equal to the ratio between the number of
   (a) solute molecules to the solvent molecules
   (b) solute molecules to the total molecules in the solution
   (c) solvent molecules to the total molecules in the solution
   (d) solvent molecules to the total number of ions of the solute. *(1991)*

58. All form ideal solution except
   (a) C_6H_6 and $C_6H_5CH_3$
   (b) C_2H_6 and C_2H_5I
   (c) C_6H_5Cl and C_6H_5Br
   (d) C_2H_5I and C_2H_5OH *(1988)*

59. An ideal solution is formed when its components
   (a) have no volume change on mixing
   (b) have no enthalpy change on mixing
   (c) have both the above characteristics
   (d) have high solubility. *(1988)*

Answer Key

. (c) **2.** (a) **3.** (d) **4.** (d) **5.** (c) **6.** (c) **7.** (c) **8.** (c) **9.** (b) **10.** (d)
1. (c) **12.** (c) **13.** (b) **14.** (d) **15.** (None) **16.** (b) **17.** (c) **18.** (d) **19.** (d)
0. (d) **21.** (a) **22.** (d) **23.** (b) **24.** (c) **25.** (d) **26.** (c) **27.** (b) **28.** (c) **29.** (b)
0. (a) **31.** (d) **32.** (b) **33.** (c) **34.** (b) **35.** (c) **36.** (a) **37.** (c) **38.** (a) **39.** (a)
0. (c) **41.** (b) **42.** (b) **43.** (a) **44.** (c) **45.** (a) **46.** (c) **47.** (a) **48.** (c) **49.** (a)
0. (c) **51.** (c) **52.** (b) **53.** (a) **54.** (c) **55.** (b) **56.** (a) **57.** (a) **58.** (d) **59.** (c)

EXPLANATIONS

1. **(c)** : The value of molal depression constant, K_f is constant for a particular solvent, thus, it will be unchanged when molality of the dilute solution is doubled.

2. **(a)**

3. **(d)** : Being a strong electrolyte, $Ba(OH)_2$ undergoes 100% dissociation in a dilute aqueous solution,

$Ba(OH)_{2(aq)} \longrightarrow Ba^{2+}_{(aq)} + 2OH^-_{(aq)}$

Thus, van't Hoff factor $i = 3$.

4. **(d)** : For an ideal solution, $\Delta H_{mix} = 0, \Delta V_{mix} = 0,$

Now, $\Delta U_{mix} = \Delta H_{mix} - P\Delta V_{mix}$

$\therefore \quad \Delta U_{mix} = 0$

Also, for an ideal solution,

$p_A = x_A p_A^\circ, p_B = x_B p_B^\circ$

$\therefore \quad \Delta P = P_{obs} - P_{\text{calculated by Raoult's law}} = 0$

$\Delta G_{mix} = \Delta H_{mix} - T\Delta S_{mix}$

For an ideal solution, $\Delta S_{mix} \neq 0$

$\therefore \quad \Delta G_{mix} \neq 0$

5. **(c)** : $p_{Benzene} = x_{Benzene} p^\circ_{Benzene}$

$p_{Toluene} = x_{Toluene} p^\circ_{Toluene}$

For an ideal 1 : 1 molar mixture of benzene and toluene, $x_{Benzene} = \frac{1}{2}$ and $x_{Toluene} = \frac{1}{2}$

$p_{Benzene} = \frac{1}{2} p^\circ_{Benzene} = \frac{1}{2} \times 12.8 \text{ kPa} = 6.4 \text{ kPa}$

$p_{Toluene} = \frac{1}{2} p^\circ_{Toluene} = \frac{1}{2} \times 3.85 \text{ kPa} = 1.925 \text{ kPa}$

Thus, the vapour will contain a high percentage of benzene as the partial vapour pressure of benzene is higher as compared to that of toluene.

6. **(c)** : Given : $W_B = 6.5$ g, $W_A = 100$ g, $p_s = 732$ mm, $K_b = 0.52$, $T_b^\circ = 100°C$, $p^\circ = 760$ mm

$\frac{p^\circ - p_s}{p^\circ} = \frac{n_2}{n_1} \Rightarrow \frac{760 - 732}{760} = \frac{n_2}{100/18}$

$\Rightarrow n_2 = \frac{28 \times 100}{760 \times 18} = 0.2046 \text{ mol}$

$\Delta T_b = K_b \times m$

$T_b - T_b^\circ = K_b \times \frac{n_2 \times 1000}{W_A(g)}$

$T_b - 100°C = \frac{0.52 \times 0.2046 \times 1000}{100} = 1.06$

$T_b = 100 + 1.06 = 101.06°C$

7. **(c)** : 1 molal aqueous solution means 1 mole of solute is present in 1000 g of water.

$\therefore \quad x_{solute} = \frac{1}{1 + \frac{1000}{18}} = \frac{1}{56.5} = 0.0177$

8. **(c)** : $\Delta T_b = iK_b m$

For equimolal solutions, elevation in boiling poi will be higher if solution undergoes dissociati *i.e.*, $i > 1$.

9. **(b)** : $Al_2(SO_4)_3 \longrightarrow 2Al^{3+} + 3SO_4^{2-}, i = 5$

$Al(NO_3)_3 \longrightarrow Al^{3+} + 3NO_3^-, i = 4$

$K_4[Fe(CN)_6] \longrightarrow 4K^+ + [Fe(CN)_6]^{4-}, i = 5$

$K_2SO_4 \longrightarrow 2K^+ + SO_4^{2-}, i = 3$

$K_3[Fe(CN)_6] \longrightarrow 3K^+ + [Fe(CN)_6]^{3-}, i = 4$

10. **(d)** : For an ideal solution, $\Delta S_{mix} > 0$ while ΔH ΔV_{mix} and $\Delta P = 0$.

11. **(c)** : $\Delta T_f = i \times K_f \times m$

So, $\Delta T_f \propto i$ (van't Hoff factor)

Salt	i
KCl	2
$C_6H_{12}O_6$	1
$Al_2(SO_4)_3$	5
K_2SO_4	3

Hence, i is maximum *i.e.*, 5 for $Al_2(SO_4)_3$.

12. **(c)** : Molarity $= \frac{W \times 1000}{M_w \times V_{sol(mL)}} \Rightarrow 2 = \frac{W}{63} \times \frac{100}{25}$

$W = \frac{63}{2}$ g; Mass of acid $\times \frac{70}{100} = \frac{63}{2}$

Mass of acid = 45 g

13. **(b)** : An ideal solution is follow:

- Volume change (ΔV) of mixing should be ze
- Heat change (ΔH) on mixing should be ze
- Obey Raoult's law at every range of concentrati

14. **(d)** : According to Raoult's law,

$P = x_A p_A + x_B p_B$ ...

For binary solutions,

$x_A + x_B = 1, \quad x_B = 1 - x_A$ ...

Putting value of x_B from eqn. (ii) to eqn. (i)

$P = x_A p_A + (1 - x_A)p_B = x_A p_A + p_B - x_A p_B$

$P = p_B + x_A(p_A - p_B)$

15. **(None)** :

$P^\circ_{CHCl_3} = 200$ mm Hg, $P^\circ_{CH_2Cl_2} = 41.5$ mm Hg

Moles of $CHCl_3$

$= \frac{\text{Weight}}{\text{Molecular weight}} = \frac{25.5}{119.5} = 0.213$

Moles of $CH_2Cl_2 = \frac{40}{85} = 0.470$

$X_{CHCl_3} = \frac{0.213}{0.213+0.470} = 0.31$

$X_{CH_2Cl_2} = \frac{0.470}{0.213+0.470} = 0.69$

$P_T = P°_{CHCl_3} X_{CHCl_3} + P°_{CH_2Cl_2} X_{CH_2Cl_2}$

$= 200 \times 0.31 + 41.5 \times 0.69 = 62 + 28.63 = 90.63$

16. (b) : We know that $\Delta T_f = i \times K_f \times \frac{w_B \times 1000}{m_B \times w_A}$

Given : $\Delta T_f = 3.82$, $K_f = 1.86$,

$w_B = 5$, $m_B = 142$, $w_A = 45$

$$i = \frac{\Delta T \times m_B \times w_A}{K_f \times w_B \times 1000} = \frac{3.82 \times 142 \times 45}{1.86 \times 5 \times 1000} = 2.63$$

17. (c) : From the value of van't Hoff factor i it is possible to determine the degree of dissociation or association. In case of dissociation, i is greater than 1 and in case of association i is less than 1.

18. (d) : We know that $\Delta T_f = i \times K_f \times m$

Here i is van't Hoff's factor.

i for weak acid is $1 + \alpha$.

Here α is degree of dissociation *i.e.*, $30/100 = 0.3$

$\therefore \quad i = 1 + \alpha = 1 + 0.3 = 1.3$

$\Delta T_f = i \times K_f \times m = 1.3 \times 1.86 \times 0.1 = 0.24$

$\therefore$ Freezing point $= -0.24$

19. (d) : We know that $\pi V = nRT$, where $n = \frac{w}{M}$

$$\pi V = \frac{w}{M} RT$$

$$M = \frac{wRT}{\pi V} = \frac{1.26 \times 0.083 \times 300}{2.57 \times 10^{-3} \times \frac{200}{1000}} = \frac{1.26 \times 0.083 \times 300}{2.57 \times 10^{-3} \times 0.2}$$

$= 61038$ g mol^{-1}

20. (d) : Addition of water to an aqueous solution of KI causes the concentration of the solution to decrease thereby increasing the vapour pressure. In the other three options the electrolytes undergo ionization, which leads to lowering of vapour pressure.

21. (a) : We know, $\Delta T_f = K_f m$

$$m = \frac{w_B}{M_B} \times \frac{1000}{W_A} = \frac{68.5 \times 1000}{342 \times 1000} = \frac{68.5}{342}$$

$$\Delta T_f = 1.86 \times \frac{68.5}{342} = 0.372°C$$

$\therefore \quad T_f = 0 - 0.372°C = -0.372°C$

22. (d) : The number of moles of ions produced by 1 mol of ionic compound $= i$

Applying, $\Delta T_f = i \times K_f \times m$

$0.00732 = i \times 1.86 \times 0.002$

$$\Rightarrow \quad i = \frac{0.00732}{1.86 \times 0.002} = 1.96 \approx 2$$

23. (b) : $HX \rightleftharpoons H^+ + X^-$

$1 - \alpha \qquad \alpha \qquad \alpha$

Total $= 1 + \alpha$

$\therefore \quad i = 1 + \alpha = 1 + 0.2 = 1.2$

$\Delta T_f = i \times K_f \times m = 1.2 \times 1.86 \times 0.5$

$= 1.116 \text{ K} \approx 1.12 \text{ K}$

24. (c) : H_2SO_4 is 98% by weight.

Weight of H_2SO_4 = 98 g

Weight of solution = 100 g

$\therefore$ Volume of solution $= \frac{\text{mass}}{\text{density}} = \frac{100}{1.80}$ mL

$= 55.55 \text{ mL} = 0.0555 \text{ L}$

Molarity of solution $= \frac{98}{98 \times 0.0555}$ M $= 18.02$ M

Let V mL of this H_2SO_4 are used to prepare 1 litre of 0.1 M H_2SO_4.

$\therefore$ mM of concentrated H_2SO_4 = mM of dilute H_2SO_4

or, $V \times 18.02 = 1000 \times 0.1 \Rightarrow V = \frac{1000 \times 0.1}{18.02} = 5.55$ mL

25. (d) : Osmosis is the phenomenon of flow of pure solvent from the solvent to the solution or from a less concentrated solution to a more concentrated solution through a semipermeable membrane. Common semipermeable membranes are permeable to certain solute particles also. Infact, there is no perfect semipermeable membrane. Therefore we can say that flow of water through a semipermeable membrane takes place both sides with unequal rates.

26. (c) : Both the components escape easily showing higher vapour pressure than the expected value.

27. (b): $m = \frac{1000 \times K_f \times w}{W \times \Delta T}$ or, $250 = \frac{1000 \times 5.12 \times 1}{51.2 \times \Delta T}$

$$\therefore \quad \Delta T = \frac{1000 \times 5.12 \times 1}{51.2 \times 250} = 0.4 \text{ K}$$

28. (c) : For isotonic solution,

osmotic pressure of urea = osmotic pressure of non-volatile solute

$$\frac{10}{60 \times 1000} = \frac{5}{m \times 100} \Rightarrow m = 300 \text{ g mol}^{-1}$$

29. (b) : 1 mole of solute present in 1 kg of H_2O

1 mole of solute present in $\frac{1000}{18}$ g mole of H_2O

$$X_{solute} = \frac{1}{\frac{1000}{18} + 1} = \frac{18}{1018} = 0.01768 \sim 0.018$$

30. (a) : By Raoult's Law

$P_T = P_P^{\circ} X_P^{\circ} + P_Q^{\circ} X_Q$

where $P_P^\circ = 80$ torr, $P_Q^\circ = 60$ torr, $X_P = \frac{3}{5}, X_Q = \frac{2}{5}$

$$P_T = 80 \times \frac{3}{5} + 60 \times \frac{2}{5} = 48 + 24 = 72 \text{ torr}$$

31. (d) : $\frac{n_{C_5H_{12}}}{n_{C_6H_{14}}} = \frac{1}{4}$

$\Rightarrow X_{C_5H_{12}} = \frac{1}{5}$ and $X_{C_6H_{14}} = \frac{4}{5}$

$$P^\circ_{C_5H_{12}} = 440 \text{ mm Hg}; \quad P^\circ_{C_6H_{14}} = 120 \text{ mm Hg}$$

$$P_T = P^\circ_{C_5H_{12}} X_{C_5H_{12}} + P^\circ_{C_6H_{14}} X_{C_6H_{14}}$$

$$= 440 \times \frac{1}{5} + 120 \times \frac{4}{5} = 88 + 96 = 184 \text{ mm of Hg}$$

By Raoult's Law, $P_{C_5H_{12}} = P^\circ_{C_5H_{12}} X_{C_5H_{12}}$ ...(1)

$X_{C_5H_{12}} \rightarrow$ mole fraction of pentane in solution

By Dalton's Law, $P_{C_5H_{12}} = X'_{C_5H_{12}} P$ ...(2)

$X'_{C_5H_{12}} \rightarrow$ mole fraction of pentane above the solution.

From (1) and (2),

$$P_{C_5H_{12}} = 440 \times \frac{1}{5} = 88 \text{ mm of Hg} \Rightarrow 88 = X'_{C_5H_{12}} \times 184$$

$$X' = \frac{88}{184};\ X' = 0.478$$

32. (b): $\Delta T_f = K_f m$ ...(1) ; $\Delta T_b = K_b m$ ...(2) $\Rightarrow \frac{\Delta T_f}{\Delta T_b} = \frac{K_f}{K_b}$ ...(3)

$\Delta T_f \rightarrow$ depression in freezing point

$\Delta T_b \rightarrow$ elevation in b.p.

b.p. of water = 100°C; K_f = 1.86 K kg mol^{-1}

b.p. of urea in water = 100.18°C

K_b = 0.512 K kg mol^{-1} $\Rightarrow \Delta T_b = 0.18$

f.p. of water = 0°C

f.p. of urea in water = $-T$°C

$\Rightarrow \Delta T_f = T$

$\Rightarrow$ from eq. (3), $\frac{T}{0.18} = \frac{1.86}{0.512} \Rightarrow T = 0.6539$

$\Rightarrow$ f.p. of urea in water = – 0.654°C

33. (c) : Raoult's law is valid for ideal solution only. The element of non-ideality enters into the picture when the molecules of the solute and solvent affect each others intermolecular forces. A solution containing components of A and B behaves as ideal solution when $A - B$ attraction force remains same as $A - A$ and $B - B$.

34. (b) : For dilute solution, the van't Hoff equation is $\pi = \frac{n}{V} RT$

$$\Rightarrow \pi V = \frac{m_2}{M} RT \Rightarrow M = \frac{m_2 RT}{\pi V}$$

35. (c) : Molecular weight of NaOH = 40

2.5 litre of 1 M NaOH solution contain 40 × 2.5 g of NaOH

3 litre of 0.5 M NaOH solution contain 40 × 0.5 × 3 g of NaOH

If these two solutions are mixed, the volume of the resultant solution = (2.5 + 3) = 5.5 litre.

5.5 litre of the resultant solution contain 40(2.5 + 1.5) g of NaOH

1 litre of the resultant solution contain

$\frac{40 \times 4}{5.5}$ g of NaOH = $\frac{40 \times 4}{5.5 \times 40}$ mole of NaOH

The molarity of the resultant solution = 0.727 ≈ 0.73 M

36. (a) : More is the pressure, greater will be the boiling point.

37. (c)

38. (a) : Polymers and proteins are covalent compounds, therefore by measuring osmotic pressure of their solution, the molecular weight can be determined.

$PV = nRT$ or, $\pi V = \frac{W}{M} RT$

$$\Rightarrow M = \frac{WRT}{\pi V} = \frac{CRT}{\pi}$$

39. (a) : P° = 640 mm, P_s = 600 mm, w = 2.175 g. W = 39.08 g

From Raoult's law

$$\frac{P^\circ - P_s}{P^\circ} = \frac{w \times M}{W \times m} \Rightarrow \frac{640 - 600}{640} = \frac{2.175 \times 78}{39.08 \times m}$$

$\Rightarrow m = 69.5$

40. (c) : The strength of the solution is 0.1 N

$\frac{w}{E} = \frac{V \times N}{1000}$ (Equivalent weight = $\frac{200}{2}$ = 100)

$$\Rightarrow w = \frac{100 \times 0.1 \times 100}{1000} = 1 \text{ g}$$

41. (b) : w = 0.15 g, W = 15 g, ΔT_b = 0.216°C

K_b = 2.16, m = ?

As $\Delta T_b = \frac{1000 \times K_b \times w}{m \times W}$

$$\Rightarrow m = \frac{1000 \times 2.16 \times 0.15}{0.216 \times 15} = 100$$

42. (b) : x_1 (mole fraction of solute) = 0.2

From Raoult's law,

$$\frac{P^\circ - P_s}{P^\circ} = x_1 \Rightarrow \frac{10}{P^\circ} = 0.2 \Rightarrow P^\circ = 50 \text{ mm}$$

Again, when $P^\circ - P_s$ = 20 mm, then

$$\frac{P^\circ - P_s}{P^\circ} = \text{mole fraction of solute} = \frac{20}{50} = 0.4$$

$\Rightarrow$ mole fraction of solvent = 1 – 0.4 = 0.6

43. (a) :

'*Cane Sugar*'	'*X*'
W_1 = 5 g	W_2 = 1 g
V_1 = 100 mL = 0.1 L	V_2 = 100 mL = 0.1 L
M_1 = 342	M_2 = ?

For isotonic solutions, $C_1 = C_2$

$$\frac{W_1}{M_1 V_1} = \frac{W_2}{M_2 V_2} \Rightarrow \frac{5}{342 \times 0.1} = \frac{1}{M_2 \times 0.1}$$

$$\Rightarrow M_2 = \frac{342}{5} = 68.4$$

44. (c) : Since $Al_2(SO_4)_3$ gives maximum number of ions on dissociation, therefore it will have the lowest freezing point.

45. (a) : We know that 98% H_2SO_4 by weight means 98 g of H_2SO_4 is present in 100 g of solution in water.

Therefore, its weight is 98 and moles of H_2SO_4

$$= \frac{\text{Weight of } H_2SO_4}{\text{Molecular Weight}} = \frac{98}{98} = 1$$

and volume of solution = $\frac{\text{Mass}}{\text{Density}}$

$$= \frac{100}{1.84} = 54.35 \text{ mL} = \frac{54.35}{1000} \text{ L}$$

Therefore, molarity of H_2SO_4

$$= \frac{\text{Moles of } H_2SO_4}{\text{Volume (in litres)}} = \frac{1 \times 1000}{54.35} = 18.4 \text{ M}$$

46. (c) : Vapour pressure of pure solvent (P_A°) = 143 mm Hg, weight of solute (w) = 0.5 gram, weight of solvent (W) = 100 grams, molecular weight of solute (m) = 65 and molecular weight of solvent (M) = 154.

$$\frac{P_A^\circ - P}{P_A^\circ} = \frac{wM}{mW} \text{ or } \frac{143 - P}{143} = \frac{0.5 \times 154}{65 \times 100} = 0.01$$

or $P = 141.31$ mm Hg

47. (a) : Weight of glucose = 10 g,
Weight of urea = 10 g and weight of sucrose = 10 g.
We know that the number of moles of glucose

$$(n_1) = \frac{\text{Weight}}{\text{Molecular weight}} = \frac{10}{180} = 0.05$$

Similarly number of moles of urea $(n_2) = \frac{10}{60} = 0.16$

and the number of moles of sucrose

$$(n_3) = \frac{10}{342} = 0.03$$

The osmotic pressure is a colligative property and it depends upon the number of moles of a solute. Since $n_2 > n_1 > n_3$, therefore $p_2 > p_1 > p_3$.

48. (c) : The molality involves weights of the solute and the solvent. Since the weight does not change with the temperatures, therefore molality does not depend upon the temperature.

49. (a) : Since relative lowering of vapour pressure is a colligative property, therefore it depends upon the number of solute particles or mole fraction of solute.

50. (c) : Since the molecular mass of CH_3OH is 32, therefore quantity of CH_3OH to prepare 150 mL solution of 2 M $CH_3OH = \left(\frac{2}{1000}\right) \times 150 \times 32 = 9.6$ g

51. (c) : In solution, $CaCl_2$ gives three ions, KCl gives two ions while glucose and urea are covalent molecules so they do not undergo ionisation. Since osmotic pressure is a colligative property and it depends upon the number of solute particles (ions), therefore, 0.1 M solution of $CaCl_2$ exhibits the highest osmotic pressure.

52. (b) : $K_3[Fe(CN)_6] \rightleftharpoons 3K^+ + [Fe(CN)_6]^{3-}$ and
$Al(NO_3)_3 \rightleftharpoons Al^{3+} + 3NO_3^-$

Since both $Al(NO_3)_3$ and $K_3[Fe(CN)_6]$ give the same number of ions, therefore they have the same van't Hoff factor.

53. (a) : There is no net movement of the solvent through the semipermeable membrane between two solutions of equal concentration.

54. (c) : The properties which depend only upon the number of solute particles present in the solution irrespective of their nature are called as colligative properties. Lowering in vapour pressure, elevation in boiling point, depression in freezing point and osmotic pressure are colligative properties.

55. (b) : Blood cells neither swell nor shrink in isotonic solution.
The solutions having same osmotic pressure are called isotonic sdutions.

56. (a) : Here, $\Delta T_f = i \times K_f \times m$
van't Hoff factor, i = 2 for NaCl, so conc. = 0.02, which is maximum in the present case.
Hence, ΔT_f is maximum or freezing point is minimum in 0.01 m NaCl.

57. (a) : $\frac{P^\circ_{\text{solvent}} - P_{\text{solution}}}{P^\circ_{\text{solvent}}} = x_{\text{solute}}$

Here, $P_A^\circ - P_A$ (difference in vapour pressure of pure solvent and solution) = lowering in vapour pressure ...(i)

Now, P_A° = vapour pressure of pure solvent ...(ii)

by dividing (i) and (ii), we get $\frac{P_A^\circ - P_A}{P_A^\circ}$

which is relative lowering in vapour pressure

58. (d) : Because C_2H_5I and C_2H_5OH are dissimilar liquids.

59. (c) : For ideal solution,
$\Delta V_{\text{mixing}} = 0$ and $\Delta H_{\text{mixing}} = 0$

Chapter 17

Electrochemistry

1. In the electrochemical cell : $Zn|ZnSO_4(0.01\ M)||CuSO_4(1.0\ M)|Cu$, the emf of this Daniell cell is E_1. When the concentration of $ZnSO_4$ is changed to 1.0 M and that of $CuSO_4$ changed to 0.01 M, the emf changes to E_2. From the followings, which one is the relationship between E_1 and E_2? (Given, $RT/F = 0.059$)
(a) $E_1 < E_2$ (b) $E_1 > E_2$
(c) $E_2 = 0 \neq E_1$ (d) $E_1 = E_2$
(NEET 2017)

2. The molar conductivity of a 0.5 mol/dm^3 solution of $AgNO_3$ with electrolytic conductivity of $5.76 \times 10^{-3}\ S\ cm^{-1}$ at 298 K is
(a) 2.88 $S\ cm^2/mol$ (b) 11.52 $S\ cm^2/mol$
(c) 0.086 $S\ cm^2/mol$ (d) 28.8 $S\ cm^2/mol$
(NEET-II 2016)

3. During the electrolysis of molten sodium chloride, the time required to produce 0.10 mol of chlorine gas using a current of 3 amperes is
(a) 55 minutes (b) 110 minutes
(c) 220 minutes (d) 330 minutes.
(NEET-II 2016)

4. If the E°_{cell} for a given reaction has a negative value, which of the following gives the correct relationships for the values of ΔG° and K_{eq} ?
(a) $\Delta G^\circ > 0; K_{eq} < 1$ (b) $\Delta G^\circ > 0; K_{eq} > 1$
(c) $\Delta G^\circ < 0; K_{eq} > 1$ (d) $\Delta G^\circ < 0; K_{eq} < 1$
(NEET-II 2016, 2011)

5. The number of electrons delivered at the cathode during electrolysis by a current of 1 ampere in 60 seconds is (charge on electron $= 1.60 \times 10^{-19}$ C)
(a) 6×10^{23} (b) 6×10^{20}
(c) 3.75×10^{20} (d) 7.48×10^{23}
(NEET-II 2016)

6. Zinc can be coated on iron to produce galvanized iron but the reverse is not possible. It is because
(a) zinc is lighter than iron
(b) zinc has lower melting point than iron
(c) zinc has lower negative electrode potential than iron
(d) zinc has higher negative electrode potential than iron. *(NEET-II 2016)*

7. The pressure of H_2 required to make the potential of H_2 electrode zero in pure water at 298 K is
(a) 10^{-10} atm (b) 10^{-4} atm
(c) 10^{-14} atm (d) 10^{-12} atm
(NEET-I 2016)

8. A device that converts energy of combustion of fuels like hydrogen and methane, directly into electrical energy is known as
(a) dynamo (b) Ni-Cd cell
(c) fuel cell (d) electrolytic cell.
(2015, Cancelled)

9. When 0.1 mol MnO_4^{2-} is oxidised the quantity of electricity required to completely oxidise MnO_4^{2-} to MnO_4^- is
(a) 96500 C (b) 2×96500 C
(c) 9650 C (d) 96.50 C *(2014)*

10. The weight of silver (at. wt. = 108) displaced by a quantity of electricity which displaces 5600 mL of O_2 at STP will be
(a) 5.4 g (b) 10.8 g
(c) 54.0 g (d) 108.0 g *(2014)*

11. At 25°C molar conductance of 0.1 molar aqueous solution of ammonium hydroxide is 9.54 $ohm^{-1}\ cm^2\ mol^{-1}$ and at infinite dilution its molar conductance is 238 $ohm^{-1}\ cm^2\ mol^{-1}$. The degree of ionisation of ammonium hydroxide at the same concentration and temperature is
(a) 4.008% (b) 40.800%
(c) 2.080% (d) 20.800%
(NEET 2013)

12. A button cell used in watches function as following:
$$Zn_{(s)} + Ag_2O_{(s)} + H_2O_{(l)} \rightleftharpoons 2Ag_{(s)} + Zn^{2+}_{(aq)} + 2OH^-_{(aq)}$$
If half cell potentials are
$Zn^{2+}_{(aq)} + 2e^- \rightarrow Zn_{(s)};\ E^\circ = -0.76$ V
$Ag_2O_{(s)} + H_2O_{(l)} + 2e^- \rightarrow 2Ag_{(s)} + 2OH^-_{(aq)}$, $E^\circ - 0.34$ V
The cell potential will be
(a) 0.84 V (b) 1.34 V
(c) 1.10 V (d) 0.42 V
(NEET 2013)

13. A hydrogen gas electrode is made by dipping platinum wire in a solution of HCl of pH = 10 and by passing hydrogen gas around the platinum wire at one atm pressure. The oxidation potential of electrode would be
(a) 0.118 V (b) 1.18 V
(c) 0.059 V (d) 0.59 V
(NEET 2013)

14. Consider the half-cell reduction reaction
$Mn^{2+} + 2e^- \rightarrow Mn$, $E° = -1.18$ V
$Mn^{2+} \rightarrow Mn^{3+} + e^-$, $E° = -1.51$ V
The $E°$ for the reaction $3Mn^{2+} \rightarrow Mn^0 + 2Mn^{3+}$, and possibility of the forward reaction are respectively
(a) – 4.18 V and yes (b) + 0.33 V and yes
(c) + 2.69 V and no (d) – 2.69 V and no
(Karnataka NEET 2013)

15. How many gram of cobalt metal will be deposited when a solution of cobalt(II) chloride is electrolyzed with a current of 10 amperes for 109 minutes (1 Faraday = 96,500 C; Atomic mass of Co = 59 u)
(a) 4.0 (b) 20.0
(c) 40.0 (d) 0.66
(Karnataka NEET 2013)

16. Limiting molar conductivity of NH_4OH [*i.e.* $\Lambda^\circ_{m(NH_4OH)}$] is equal to
(a) $\Lambda^\circ_{m(NH_4Cl)} + \Lambda^\circ_{m(NaCl)} - \Lambda^\circ_{m(NaOH)}$
(b) $\Lambda^\circ_{m(NaOH)} + \Lambda^\circ_{m(NaCl)} - \Lambda^\circ_{m(NH_4Cl)}$
(c) $\Lambda^\circ_{m(NH_4OH)} + \Lambda^\circ_{m(NH_4Cl)} - \Lambda^\circ_{m(HCl)}$
(d) $\Lambda^\circ_{m(NH_4Cl)} + \Lambda^\circ_{m(NaOH)} - \Lambda^\circ_{m(NaCl)}$ *(2012)*

17. Standard reduction potentials of the half reactions are given below :
$F_{2(g)} + 2e^- \rightarrow 2F^-_{(aq)}$; $E° = +2.85$ V
$Cl_{2(g)} + 2e^- \rightarrow 2Cl^-_{(aq)}$; $E° = +1.36$ V
$Br_{2(l)} + 2e^- \rightarrow 2Br^-_{(aq)}$; $E° = +1.06$ V
$I_{2(s)} + 2e^- \rightarrow 2I^-_{(aq)}$; $E° = +0.53$ V
The strongest oxidising and reducing agents respectively are
(a) F_2 and I^- (b) Br_2 and Cl^-
(c) Cl_2 and Br^- (d) Cl_2 and I_2
(Mains 2012)

18. Molar conductivities (Λ°_m) at infinite dilution of NaCl, HCl and CH_3COONa are 126.4, 425.9 and 91.0 S cm^2 mol^{-1} respectively. (Λ°_m) for CH_3COOH will be
(a) 425.5 S cm^2 mol^{-1} (b) 180.5 S cm^2 mol^{-1}
(c) 290.8 S cm^2 mol^{-1} (d) 390.5 S cm^2 mol^{-1}
(Mains 2012)

19. The Gibb's energy for the decomposition of Al_2O_3 at 500°C is as follows

$$\frac{2}{3}Al_2O_3 \rightarrow \frac{4}{3}Al + O_2,\ \Delta_rG = +960 \text{ kJ mol}^{-1}$$

The potential difference needed for the electrolytic reduction of aluminium oxide (Al_2O_3) at 500 °C is at least
(a) 4.5 V (b) 3.0 V
(c) 2.5 V (d) 5.0 V
(Mains 2012)

20. Standard electrode potentials of three metals *X*, *Y* and *Z* are –1.2 V, + 0.5 V and – 3.0 V respectively. The reducing power of these metals will be
(a) $Y > Z > X$ (b) $Y > X > Z$
(c) $Z > X > Y$ (d) $X > Y > Z$
(2011)

21. The electrode potentials for
$Cu^{2+}_{(aq)} + e^- \rightarrow Cu^+_{(aq)}$ and $Cu^+_{(aq)} + e^- \rightarrow Cu_{(s)}$ are + 0.15 V and + 0.50 V respectively. The value of $E°_{Cu^{2+}/Cu}$ will be
(a) 0.500 V (b) 0.325 V
(c) 0.650 V (d) 0.150 V *(2011)*

22. Standard electrode potential for Sn^{4+}/Sn^{2+} couple is + 0.15 V and that for the Cr^{3+}/Cr couple is – 0.74 V. These two couples in their standard state are connected to make a cell. The cell potential will be
(a) + 1.19 V (b) + 0.89 V
(c) + 0.18 V (d) + 1.83 V *(2011)*

23. A solution contains Fe^{2+}, Fe^{3+} and I^- ions. This solution was treated with iodine at 35 °C. $E°$ for Fe^{3+}/Fe^{2+} is + 0.77 V and $E°$ for $I_2/2I^- = 0.536$ V. The favourable redox reaction is
(a) I_2 will be reduced to I^-
(b) there will be no redox reaction
(c) I^- will be oxidised to I_2
(d) Fe^{2+} will be oxidised to Fe^{3+}
(Mains 2011)

24. For the reduction of silver ions with copper metal, the standard cell potential was found to be + 0.46 V at 25°C. The value of standard Gibbs energy, $\Delta G°$ will be
(F = 96500 C mol^{-1})
(a) – 89.0 kJ (b) – 89.0 J
(c) – 44.5 kJ (d) – 98.0 kJ *(2010)*

25. An increase in equivalent conductance of a strong electrolyte with dilution is mainly due to
(a) increase in ionic mobility of ions
(b) 100% ionisation of electrolyte at normal dilution
(c) increase in both *i.e.*, number of ions and ionic mobility of ions
(d) increase in number of ions. *(2010)*

26. Which of the following expressions correctly represents the equivalent conductance at infinite dilution of $Al_2(SO_4)_3$. Given that $\overset{\circ}{\Lambda}_{Al^{3+}}$ and $\overset{\circ}{\Lambda}_{SO_4^{2-}}$ are the equivalent conductances at infinite dilution of the respective ions?
(a) $2\overset{\circ}{\Lambda}_{Al^{3+}} + 3\overset{\circ}{\Lambda}_{SO_4^{2-}}$
(b) $\overset{\circ}{\Lambda}_{Al^{3+}} + \overset{\circ}{\Lambda}_{SO_4^{2-}}$
(c) $(\overset{\circ}{\Lambda}_{Al^{3+}} + \overset{\circ}{\Lambda}_{SO_4^{2-}}) \times 6$
(d) $\frac{1}{3}\overset{\circ}{\Lambda}_{Al^{3+}} + \frac{1}{2}\overset{\circ}{\Lambda}_{SO_4^{2-}}$ *(Mains 2010)*

27. Consider the following relations for emf of an electrochemical cell
(i) EMF of cell = (Oxidation potential of anode) – (Reduction potential of cathode)
(ii) EMF of cell = (Oxidation potential of anode) + (Reduction potential of cathode)
(iii) EMF of cell = (Reductional potential of anode) + (Reduction potential of cathode)
(iv) EMF of cell = (Oxidation potential of anode) – (Oxidation potential of cathode)
Which of the above relations are correct?
(a) (iii) and (i) (b) (i) and (ii)
(c) (iii) and (iv) (d) (ii) and (iv)
(Mains 2010)

28. Given :
(i) $Cu^{2+} + 2e^- \rightarrow Cu$, $E^\circ = 0.337$ V
(ii) $Cu^{2+} + e^- \rightarrow Cu^+$, $E^\circ = 0.153$ V
Electrode potential, E° for the reaction,
$Cu^+ + e^- \rightarrow Cu$, will be
(a) 0.90 V (b) 0.30 V
(c) 0.38 V (d) 0.52 V *(2009)*

29. Al_2O_3 is reduced by electrolysis at low potentials and high currents. If 4.0×10^4 amperes of current is passed through molten Al_2O_3 for 6 hours, what mass of aluminium is produced? (Assume 100% current efficiency, at. mass of Al = 27 g mol^{-1}).
(a) 8.1×10^4 g (b) 2.4×10^5 g
(c) 1.3×10^4 g (d) 9.0×10^3 g
(2009)

30. The equivalent conductance of $M/32$ solution of a weak monobasic acid is 8.0 mho cm^2 and at infinite dilution is 400 mho cm^2. The dissociation constant of this acid is
(a) 1.25×10^{-6} (b) 6.25×10^{-4}
(c) 1.25×10^{-4} (d) 1.25×10^{-5}
(2009)

31. On the basis of the following E° values, the strongest oxidizing agent is
$[Fe(CN)_6]^{4-} \rightarrow [Fe(CN)_6]^{3-} + e^-$; $E^\circ = -0.35$ V
$Fe^{2+} \rightarrow Fe^{3+} + e^-$; $E^\circ = -0.77$ V
(a) Fe^{3+} (b) $[Fe(CN)_6]^{3-}$
(c) $[Fe(CN)_6]^{4-}$ (d) Fe^{2+} *(2008)*

32. Kohlrausch's law states that at
(a) Infinite dilution, each ion makes definite contribution to conductance of an electrolyte whatever be the nature of the other ion of the electrolyte
(b) Infinite dilution, each ion makes definite contribution to equivalent conductance of an electrolyte, whatever be the nature of the other ion of the electrolyte
(c) Finite dilution, each ion makes definite contribution to equivalent conductance of an electrolyte, whatever be the nature of the other ion of the electrolyte
(d) Infinite dilution each ion makes definite contribution to equivalent conductance of an electrolyte depending on the nature of the other ion of the electrolyte.
(2008)

33. Standard free energies of formation (in kJ/mol) at 298 K are –237.2, –394.4 and –8.2 for $H_2O_{(l)}$, $CO_{2(g)}$ and pentane $_{(g)}$ respectively. The value of E°_{cell} for the pentane-oxygen fuel cell is
(a) 1.0968 V (b) 0.0968 V
(c) 1.968 V (d) 2.0968 V *(2008)*

34. The equilibrium constant of the reaction: $Cu_{(s)} + 2Ag^+_{(aq)} \rightarrow Cu^{2+}_{(aq)} + 2Ag_{(s)}$; $E^\circ = 0.46$ V at 298 K is
(a) 2.0×10^{10} (b) 4.0×10^{10}
(c) 4.0×10^{15} (d) 2.4×10^{10}
(2007)

35. The efficiency of a fuel cell is given by
(a) $\Delta G/\Delta S$ (b) $\Delta G/\Delta H$
(c) $\Delta S/\Delta G$ (d) $\Delta H/\Delta G$ *(2007)*

36. A hypothetical electrochemical cell is shown below.

$A \mid A^+ (xM) \parallel B^+ (yM) \mid B$

The emf measured is + 0.20 V. The cell reaction is

(a) $A + B^+ \rightarrow A^+ + B$
(b) $A^+ + B \rightarrow A + B^+$
(c) $A^+ + e^- \rightarrow A$; $B^+ + e^- \rightarrow B$
(d) the cell reaction cannot be predicted. *(2006)*

37. $E^\circ_{Fe^{2+}/Fe} = -0.441$ V and $E^\circ_{Fe^{3+}/Fe^{2+}} = 0.771$ V, the standard EMF of the reaction $Fe + 2Fe^{3+} \rightarrow 3Fe^{2+}$ will be

(a) 0.111 V (b) 0.330 V
(c) 1.653 V (d) 1.212 V *(2006)*

38. 4.5 g of aluminium (at. mass 27 amu) is deposited at cathode from Al^{3+} solution by a certain quantity of electric charge. The volume of hydrogen produced at STP from H^+ ions in solution by the same quantity of electric charge will be

(a) 44.8 L (b) 22.4 L
(c) 11.2 L (d) 5.6 L *(2005)*

39. The mass of carbon anode consumed (giving only carbon dioxide) in the production of 270 kg of aluminium metal from bauxite by the Hall process is

(a) 270 kg (b) 540 kg
(c) 90 kg (d) 180 kg
(Atomic mass : Al = 27) *(2005)*

40. The standard e.m.f. of a galvanic cell involving cell reaction with $n = 2$ is found to be 0.295 V at 25°C. The equilibrium constant of the reaction would be

(a) 2.0×10^{11} (b) 4.0×10^{12}
(c) 1.0×10^{2} (d) 1.0×10^{10}
(Given $F = 96500$ C mol^{-1}, $R = 8.314$ J K^{-1} mol^{-1}) *(2004)*

41. The e.m.f. of a Daniell cell at 298 K is E_1.

$$Zn \left| \begin{matrix} ZnSO_4 \\ (0.01\ M) \end{matrix} \right\| \begin{matrix} CuSO_4 \\ (1.0\ M) \end{matrix} \bigg| Cu$$

When the concentration of $ZnSO_4$ is 1.0 M and that of $CuSO_4$ is 0.01 M, the e.m.f. changed to E_2. What is the relationship between E_1 and E_2?

(a) $E_1 > E_2$ (b) $E_1 < E_2$
(c) $E_1 = E_2$ (d) $E_2 = 0 \neq E_1$ *(2003)*

42. On the basis of the information available from the reaction,
$4/3Al + O_2 \rightarrow 2/3Al_2O_3, \Delta G = -827$ kJ mol^{-1} of O_2, the minimum e.m.f. required to carry out an electrolysis of Al_2O_3 is ($F = 96500$ C mol^{-1})

(a) 2.14 V (b) 4.28 V
(c) 6.42 V (d) 8.56 V *(2003)*

43. In electrolysis of NaCl when Pt electrode is taken then H_2 is liberated at cathode while with Hg cathode it forms sodium amalgam

(a) Hg is more inert than Pt
(b) More voltage is required to reduce H^+ at Hg than at Pt
(c) Na is dissolved in Hg while it does not dissolve in Pt
(d) Conc. of H^+ ions is larger when Pt electrode is taken. *(2002)*

44. Standard electrode potentials are Fe^{2+}/Fe; $E^\circ = -0.44$ and Fe^{3+}/Fe^{2+}; $E^\circ = 0.77$ Fe^{2+}, Fe^{3+} and Fe blocks are kept together, then

(a) Fe^{3+} increases
(b) Fe^{3+} decreases
(c) Fe^{2+}/Fe^{3+} remains unchanged
(d) Fe^{2+} decreases. *(2001)*

45. Equivalent conductances of Ba^{2+} and Cl^- ions are 127 and 76 ohm^{-1} cm^{-1} eq^{-1} respectively. Equivalent conductance of $BaCl_2$ at infinite dilution is

(a) 139.5 (b) 101.5
(c) 203 (d) 279 *(2000)*

46. For the disproportionation of copper
$2Cu^+ \rightarrow Cu^{2+} + Cu$, E° is (Given: E° for Cu^{2+}/Cu is 0.34 V and E° for Cu^{2+}/Cu^+ is 0.15 V.)

(a) 0.49 V (b) –0.19 V
(c) 0.38 V (d) –0.38 V *(2000)*

47. The specific conductance of a 0.1 N KCl solution at 23°C is 0.012 ohm^{-1} cm^{-1}. The resistance of cell containing the solution at the same temperature was found to be 55 ohm. The cell constant will be

(a) 0.918 cm^{-1} (b) 0.66 cm^{-1}
(c) 1.142 cm^{-1} (d) 1.12 cm^{-1} *(1999)*

48. For the cell reaction,
$Cu^{2+} (C_1.aq) + Zn_{(s)} \rightleftharpoons Zn^{2+}(C_2.aq) + Cu_{(s)}$
of an electrochemical cell, the change in free energy ΔG at a given temperature is a function of

(a) $\ln (C_2)$ (b) $\ln (C_2/C_1)$
(c) $\ln (C_1)$ (d) $\ln (C_1 + C_2)$ *(1998)*

49. E° for the cell, $Zn \mid Zn^{2+}_{(aq)} \parallel Cu^{2+}_{(aq)} \mid Cu$ is 1.10V at 25°C, the equilibrium constant for the reaction $Zn + Cu^{2+}_{(aq)} \rightleftharpoons Cu + Zn^{2+}_{(aq)}$ is the order of

(a) 10^{+18} (b) 10^{+17}
(c) 10^{-28} (d) 10^{-37} *(1997)*

50. The molar conductances of NaCl, HCl and CH_3COONa at infinite dilution are 126.45, 426.16 and 91 ohm^{-1} cm^2 mol^{-1} respectively. The molar conductance of CH_3COOH at infinite dilution (Λ_m^∞) is
(a) 698.28 ohm^{-1} cm^2 mol^{-1}
(b) 540.48 ohm^{-1} cm^2 mol^{-1}
(c) 201.28 ohm^{-1} cm^2 mol^{-1}
(d) 390.71 ohm^{-1} cm^2 mol^{-1} *(1997)*

51. A 5 ampere current is passed through a solution of zinc sulphate for 40 minutes. The amount of zinc deposited at the cathode is
(a) 0.4065 g (b) 65.04 g
(c) 40.65 g (d) 4.065 g *(1996)*

52. Reduction potential for the following half-cell reactions are
$Zn = Zn^{2+} + 2e^-$; $E^\circ = +0.76$ V;
$Fe = Fe^{2+} + 2e^-$; $E^\circ = +0.44$ V.
The EMF for the cell reaction
$Fe^{2+} + Zn \rightarrow Zn^{2+} + Fe$ will be
(a) – 0.32 V (b) + 1.20 V
(c) – 1.20 V (d) + 0.32 V *(1996)*

53. An electrochemical cell is set up as : Pt; H_2 (1 atm)|HCl(0.1 M) || CH_3COOH (0.1 M) |H_2 (1 atm); Pt. The e.m.f. of this cell will not be zero, because
(a) acids used in two compartments are different
(b) e.m.f. depends on molarities of acids used
(c) the temperature is constant
(d) pH of 0.1 M HCl and 0.1 M CH_3COOH is not same. *(1995)*

54. On heating one end of a piece of a metal, the other end becomes hot because of
(a) energised electrons moving to the other end
(b) minor perturbation in the energy of atoms
(c) resistance of the metal
(d) mobility of atoms in the metal. *(1995)*

55. Standard reduction potentials at 25°C of Li^+|Li, Ba^{2+}|Ba, Na^+|Na and Mg^{2+}|Mg are – 3.05, – 2.90, – 2.71 and – 2.37 volt respectively. Which one of the following is the strongest oxidising agent?
(a) Ba^{2+} (b) Mg^{2+}
(c) Na^+ (d) Li^+ *(1994)*

56. On electrolysis of dilute sulphuric acid using platinum electrodes, the product obtained at the anode will be
(a) hydrogen (b) oxygen
(c) hydrogen sulphide (d) sulphur dioxide. *(1992)*

Answer Key

1. (b)	**2.** (b)	**3.** (b)	**4.** (a)	**5.** (c)	**6.** (d)	**7.** (c)	**8.** (c)	**9.** (c)	**10.** (d)
11. (a)	**12.** (c)	**13.** (d)	**14.** (d)	**15.** (b)	**16.** (d)	**17.** (a)	**18.** (d)	**19.** (c)	**20.** (c)
21. (b)	**22.** (b)	**23.** (c)	**24.** (a)	**25.** (a)	**26.** (b)	**27.** (d)	**28.** (d)	**29.** (a)	**30.** (d)
31. (a)	**32.** (a)	**33.** (a)	**34.** (c)	**35.** (b)	**36.** (a)	**37.** (d)	**38.** (d)	**39.** (c)	**40.** (d)
41. (a)	**42.** (a)	**43.** (b)	**44.** (b)	**45.** (a)	**46.** (c)	**47.** (b)	**48.** (b)	**49.** (d)	**50.** (d)
51. (d)	**52.** (d)	**53.** (d)	**54.** (a)	**55.** (b)	**56.** (b)				

EXPLANATIONS

1. **(b)** : $E_{cell} = E^\circ_{cell} - \frac{0.059}{n}\log\frac{[Zn^{2+}]}{[Cu^{2+}]}$

$E_1 = E^\circ - \frac{0.059}{2}\log\frac{0.01}{1}$

$E_1 = E^\circ - \frac{0.059}{2}(-2) = E^\circ + 0.059$

$E_2 = E^\circ - \frac{0.059}{2}\log\frac{1}{0.01} = E^\circ - 0.059$

Hence, $E_1 > E_2$

2. **(b)** : $\Lambda_m = \frac{\kappa \times 1000}{\text{Molarity}(M)}$

$= \frac{5.76\times10^{-3}\,\text{S cm}^{-1}\times1000}{0.5\ \text{mol cm}^{-3}} = 11.52\ \text{S cm}^2\ \text{mol}^{-1}$

3. **(b)** : During the electrolysis of molten sodium chloride,

At cathode : $2Na^+ + 2e^- \longrightarrow 2Na$

At anode : $2Cl^- \longrightarrow Cl_2 + 2e^-$

Net reaction: $2Na^+ + 2Cl^- \longrightarrow 2Na + Cl_2$

According to Faraday's first law of electrolysis,

$w = Z \times I \times t$

$w = \frac{E}{96500} \times I \times t$

No. of moles of Cl_2 gas × Mol. wt. of Cl_2 gas

$= \frac{\text{Eq. wt. of } Cl_2 \text{ gas} \times I \times t}{96500}$

$0.10 \times 71 = \frac{35.5\times3\times t}{96500}$

$t = \frac{0.10\times71\times96500}{35.5\times3} = 6433.33\ \text{sec}$

$t = \frac{6433.33}{60}\ \text{min} = 107.22\ \text{min} \approx 110\ \text{min}$

4. **(a)** : $\Delta G^\circ = -nFE^\circ_{cell}$

If E°_{cell} – ve then ΔG° = +ve *i.e.*; $\Delta G^\circ > 0$.

$\Delta G^\circ = -nRT\log K_{eq}$

For ΔG° = +ve, K_{eq} = –ve *i.e.*, $K_{eq} < 1$.

5. **(c)** : $Q = I \times t$

$Q = 1 \times 60 = 60$ C

Now, 1.60×10^{-19} C ≡ 1 electron

$\therefore 60\ \text{C} \equiv \frac{60}{1.6\times10^{-19}} = 37.5\times10^{19}$

$= 3.75\times10^{20}$ electrons

6. **(d)** : Reduction potential values of $E^\circ_{Zn^{2+}/Zn} = -0.76$ V and $E^\circ_{Fe^{2+}/Fe} = -0.44$ V

Thus, due to higher negative electrode potential value of zinc than iron, iron cannot be coated on zinc.

7. **(c)** : pH = 7 for water.

$-\log[H^+] = 7 \Rightarrow [H^+] = 10^{-7}$

$2H^+_{(aq)} + 2e^- \longrightarrow H_{2(g)}$

$E_{cell} = E^\circ_{cell} - \frac{0.0591}{2}\log\frac{p_{H_2}}{[H^+]^2}$

$0 = 0 - \frac{0.0591}{2}\log\frac{p_{H_2}}{(10^{-7})^2}$

$\log\frac{p_{H_2}}{(10^{-7})^2} = 0 \Rightarrow \frac{p_{H_2}}{(10^{-7})^2} = 1$ [∵ log 1 = 0]

$p_{H_2} = 10^{-14}$ atm

8. **(c)**

9. **(c)** : The oxidation reaction is

$\overset{+6}{MnO_4^{2-}} \longrightarrow \overset{+7}{MnO_4^-} + e^-$

0.1 mol 0.1 mol

$Q = 0.1 \times F = 0.1 \times 96500\ \text{C} = 9650$ C

10. **(d)** : According to Faraday's second law,

$\frac{W_{Ag}}{E_{Ag}} = \frac{W_{O_2}}{E_{O_2}}$ or $\frac{W_{Ag}}{108} = \frac{\frac{5600}{22400}\times32}{8}$

or $\frac{W_{Ag}}{108} = \frac{8}{8} \Rightarrow W_{Ag} = 108$ g

11. **(a)** : Degree of dissociation

$(\alpha) = \frac{\text{Molar conductivity at conc. } C(\Lambda_m^c)}{\text{Molar conductivity at infinite dilution } (\Lambda_m^\infty)}$

$\alpha = \frac{9.54\ \Omega^{-1}\text{cm}^2\ \text{mol}^{-1}}{238\ \Omega^{-1}\text{cm}^2\ \text{mol}^{-1}} = 0.04008 = 4.008\%$

12. **(c)** : $E^\circ_{cell} = E^\circ_{O.P.} + E^\circ_{R.P.}$

$= 0.76 + 0.34 = 1.10$ V

13. **(d)** : $\underset{1\text{ atm}}{H_2} \longrightarrow \underset{10^{-10}}{2H^+} + 2e^-$

$$E_{H_2/H^+} = 0 - \frac{0.059}{2}\log\frac{(10^{-10})^2}{1}$$

$$E_{H_2/H^+} = +0.59 \text{ V}$$

14. (d) : $Mn^{2+} + 2e^- \rightarrow Mn;\ E^\circ = -1.18$ V

$2Mn^{2+} \rightarrow 2Mn^{3+} + 2e^-;\quad E^\circ = -1.51$ V

For the cell,

$3Mn^{2+} \rightarrow Mn + 2Mn^{3+};\quad E^\circ = -2.69$ V

Since the E° value is negative, so the process is non-spontaneous.

15. (b) : $W = \frac{ItE}{96500}$

$$= \frac{10 \times 109 \times 60 \times 59}{96500 \times 2} = 19.99 \approx 20$$

16. (d)

17. (a) : More negative the value of reduction potential, stronger will be the reducing agent thus I^- is strongest reducing agent. More positive value of reduction potential shows good oxidising properties thus strongest oxidising agent is F_2.

18. (d) : $\Lambda^\circ_{NaCl} = 126.4$ S cm^2 mol^{-1}

$\Lambda^\circ_{HCl} = 425.9$ S cm^2 mol^{-1}

$\Lambda^\circ_{CH_3COONa} = 91.0$ S cm^2 mol^{-1}

$\Lambda^\circ_{CH_3COOH} = \Lambda^\circ_{CH_3COONa} + \Lambda^\circ_{HCl} - \Lambda^\circ_{NaCl}$

$= 91.0 + 425.9 - 126.4 = 390.5$ S cm^2 mol^{-1}

19. (c) : $\Delta G^\circ = -nFE^\circ$

$F = 96500,\ \Delta G^\circ = +960 \times 10^3$ J/mol

$$\frac{2}{3}Al_2O_3 \rightarrow \frac{4}{3}Al + O_2$$

Total number of Al atoms in $Al_2O_3 = \frac{2}{3} \times 2 = \frac{4}{3}$

$Al^{3+} + 3e^- \rightarrow Al$

As $3e^-$ change occur for each Al atom

$\therefore$ Total $n = \frac{4}{3} \times 3 = 4$

$$E^\circ = -\frac{\Delta G^\circ}{nF} = -\frac{960 \times 1000}{4 \times 96500} \Rightarrow E^\circ = -2.48 \approx -2.5 \text{ V}$$

20. (c) : As the electrode potential drops, reducing power increases.

So, $Z\ (-3.0 \text{ V}) > X\ (-1.2 \text{ V}) > Y\ (+0.5 \text{ V})$

21. (b) : $Cu^{2+}_{(aq)} + e^- \rightarrow Cu^+_{(aq)};\quad E_1^\circ = 0.15$ V

$Cu^+_{(aq)} + e^- \rightarrow Cu_{(s)};\ E_2^\circ = 0.50$ V

$Cu^{2+} + 2e^- \rightarrow Cu$

Now, $\Delta G^\circ = \Delta G_1^\circ + \Delta G_2^\circ$

or, $-nFE^\circ = -n_1FE_1^\circ - n_2FE_2^\circ$

or, $E^\circ = \frac{n_1E_1^\circ + n_2E_2^\circ}{n} = \frac{1 \times 0.15 + 1 \times 0.50}{2} = 0.325$ V

22. (b) : $E^\circ_{cell} = E^\circ_{cathode} - E^\circ_{anode}$

$= 0.15 - (-0.74) = 0.15 + 0.74 = 0.89$ V

23. (c) : Since the reduction potential of Fe^{3+}/Fe^{2+} is greater than that of I_2/I^-, Fe^{3+} will be reduced and I^- will be oxidised.

$2Fe^{3+} + 2I^- \rightarrow 2Fe^{2+} + I_2$

24. (a) : The cell reaction can be written as

$Cu + 2Ag^+ \rightarrow Cu^{2+} + 2Ag$

We know, $\Delta G^\circ = -nFE^\circ_{cell}$

$= -2 \times 96500 \times 0.46 = -88780$ J

$= -88.780$ kJ ≈ -89 kJ

25. (a) : Strong electrolytes are completely ionised at all concentrations. On increasing dilution the no. of ions remains the same but the ionic mobility increases and the equivalent conduction increases.

26. (b) : At infinite dilution, when dissociation is complete, each ion makes a definite contribution towards molar conductance of the electrolyte irrespective of the nature of the other ion with which it is associated.

Hence, $\overset{\circ}{\Lambda}_{Al_2(SO_4)_3} = \overset{\circ}{\Lambda}_{Al^{3+}} + \overset{\circ}{\Lambda}_{SO_4^{2-}}$

27. (d) : EMF of a cell = Reduction potential of cathode − Reduction potential of anode

= Reduction potential of cathode + Oxidation potential of anode

= Oxidation potential of anode − Oxidation potential of cathode.

28. (d) : Given,

$Cu^{2+} + 2e^- \rightarrow Cu;\quad E_1^\circ = 0.337$ V

$Cu^{2+} + e^- \rightarrow Cu^+;\quad E_2^\circ = 0.153$ V

The required reaction is

$Cu^+ + e^- \rightarrow Cu;\quad E_3^\circ = ?$

Applying, $\Delta G^\circ = -nFE^\circ$,

$$\Delta G_3^\circ = \Delta G_1^\circ - \Delta G_2^\circ$$

$$-(n_3FE_3^\circ) = -(n_1FE_1^\circ) - (-n_2FE_2^\circ)$$

or $E_3^\circ = 2 \times E_1^\circ - E_2^\circ$

or $E_3^\circ = (2 \times 0.337) - 0.153 = 0.52$ V

29. (a) : Applying $E = Z \times 96500$

$$\frac{27}{3} = Z \times 96500 \Rightarrow Z = \frac{9}{96500}$$

Now applying the formula, $W = Z \times I \times t$

$$W = \frac{9}{96500} \times 4 \times 10^4 \times 6 \times 60 \times 60 = 8.1 \times 10^4 \text{ g}$$

30. (d) : Given, $\Lambda = 8$ mho cm^2

$\Lambda_\infty = 400$ mho cm^2

Degree of dissociation, $\alpha = \frac{\Lambda}{\Lambda_\infty}$

$\Rightarrow \alpha = \frac{8}{400} = 2 \times 10^{-2}$

Dissociation constant, $K = C\alpha^2$

Given, $C = M/32$

$\therefore K = \frac{1}{32} \times 2 \times 10^{-2} \times 2 \times 10^{-2}$

$K = 1.25 \times 10^{-5}$

31. (a) : $[Fe(CN)_6]^{3-} \rightarrow [Fe(CN)_6]^{4-}$, $E° = +0.35V$
$Fe^{3+} \rightarrow Fe^{2+}$; $E° = +0.77V$

Higher the +ve reduction potential, stronger will be the oxidising agent. Oxidising agent oxidises other compounds and gets itself reduced easily.

32. (a) : At infinite dilution, when dissociation is complete each ion makes a definite contribution towards molar conductance of the electrolyte irrespective of the nature of the other ion with which it is associated and that the molar conductance of any electrolyte at infinite dilution is given by the sum of the contributions of two ions. This is called Kohlrausch's law.

$\Lambda_m^\infty = \Lambda_+^\infty + \Lambda_-^\infty$, Λ_+^∞ and Λ_-^∞ are molar ionic conductance at infinite dilution for cations and anions, respectively.

33. (a) : $C_5H_{12(g)} + 8O_{2(g)} \rightarrow 5CO_{2(g)} + 6H_2O_{(l)}$

$\Delta G° = [(-394.4 \times 5) + (-237.2 \times 6)] - [(-8.2) + (8 \times 0)]$

$= -3387.5$ kJ

Note that the standard free energy change of elementary substances is taken as zero.

For the fuel cell, the complete cell reaction is :

$C_5H_{12(g)} + 8O_{2(g)} \rightarrow 5CO_{2(g)} + 6H_2O_{(l)}$

Which is the combination of the following two half reactions :

$C_5H_{12(g)} + 10H_2O_{(l)} \rightarrow 5CO_{2(g)} + 32H^+ + 32e^-$

and $8O_{2(g)} + 32H^+ + 32e^- \rightarrow 16H_2O_{(l)}$

Therefore, the number of electrons exchanged is 32 here, means $n = 32$. This is the trickiest part of the problem.

$\Delta G° = -nFE° = -3387.5 \times 10^3$ J

$= -32 \times 96500$ J/Volt $\times E°$

Thus $E° = 1.09698$ V

34. (c) : For a cell reaction in equilibrium at 298 K,

$$E°_{cell} = \frac{0.0591}{n}\log K_C$$

where K_C = equilibrium constant, n = number of electrons involved in the electrochemical cell reaction.

Given, $E°_{cell} = 0.46$ V, $n = 2$

$\therefore 0.46 = \frac{0.0591}{2} \times \log K_C$

or, $\log K_C = \frac{2 \times 0.46}{0.0591} = 15.57$

or, $K_C = 3.7 \times 10^{15} \approx 4 \times 10^{15}$

35. (b) : The thermal efficiency, η of a fuel conversion device is the amount of useful energy produced relative to the change in enthalpy, ΔH between the product and feed streams.

$$\eta = \frac{\text{useful energy}}{\Delta H}$$

In an ideal case of an electrochemical convertor, such as a fuel cell, the change in Gibb's free energy, ΔG of the reaction is available as useful electric energy at that temperature of the conversion.

Hence $\eta_{ideal} = \frac{\Delta G}{\Delta H}$

36. (a) : From the given expression:

At anode : $A \rightarrow A^+ + e^-$

At cathode : $B^+ + e^- \rightarrow B$

Overall reaction is : $A + B^+ \rightarrow A^+ + B$

37. (d) : $Fe^{2+} + 2e^- \rightarrow Fe$; $E° = -0.441$ V ... (i)

$Fe^{3+} + e^- \rightarrow Fe^{2+}$; $E° = 0.771$ V ... (ii)

$Fe + 2Fe^{3+} \rightarrow 3Fe^{2+}$; $E° = ?$

To get the above equation, (ii) × 2 – (i)

$2Fe^{3+} + 2e^- \rightarrow 2Fe^{2+}$; $E° = 0.771$ V

$-Fe^{2+} - 2e^- \rightarrow -Fe$; $E° = -0.441$ V

$2Fe^{3+} + Fe \rightarrow 2Fe^{2+}$; $E° = 1.212$ V

38. (d) : We know that,

1 Faraday charge liberates 1 eq. of substance. This is the Faraday Law.

eq. wt. of Al = $\frac{27}{3} = 9$

no. of eq. of Al = $\frac{\text{wt. of Al}}{\text{eq. wt.}} = \frac{4.5}{9} = 0.5$

no. of Faraday required = 0.5

$\Rightarrow$ no. of eq. of H_2 produced = 0.5 eq.

Volume occupied by 1 eq. of $H_2 = \frac{22.4}{2} = 11.2$ L

$\Rightarrow$ Volume occupied by 0.5 = 11.2 × 0.5

= 5.6 L at STP

39. (c) : $3C + 2Al_2O_3 \longrightarrow 4Al + 3CO_2$
(from bauxite)

4 moles of Al is produced by 3 moles of C

1 mole of Al is produced by $\frac{3}{4}$ mole of C

10^4 moles of Al is produced by $\frac{3}{4} \times 10^4$ moles of C

Amount of carbon used = $\frac{3}{4} \times 10^4 \times 12$ g

$= \frac{3}{4} \times 10 \times 12$ kg = 90 kg

40. (d) : $E = E^\circ - \frac{0.0591}{n}\log_{10} Q$ at 25°C

At equilibrium, $E = 0$, $Q = K$

$$0 = E^\circ - \frac{0.0591}{n}\log_{10} K$$

or, $K = \text{antilog}\left[\frac{nE^\circ}{0.0591}\right]$

or, $K = \text{antilog}\left[\frac{2\times 0.295}{0.0591}\right] = \text{antilog}\left[\frac{0.590}{0.0591}\right]$

$= \text{antilog } 10 = 1 \times 10^{10}$

41. (a)

42. (a) : For O_2, $\Delta G = -nFE^\circ$

$$E^\circ = \frac{\Delta G}{-nF} = \frac{-827000}{-2\times 96500} = 4.28$$

Minimum EMF required to carry out electrolysis of Al_2O_3 = $\frac{4.28}{2} = 2.14$ V

43. (b) : When sodium chloride is dissolved in water, it ionises as $NaCl \rightleftharpoons Na^+ + Cl^-$. Water also dissociates as : $H_2O \rightleftharpoons H^+ + OH^-$.
During passing of electric current through this solution using platinum electrode, Na^+ and H^+ ions move towards cathode. However, only H^+ ions are discharged more readily than Na^+ ion because of their low discharge potential (In the electromotive series hydrogen is lower than sodium). These H^+ ions gain electrons and change into neutral atoms.

At cathode $H^+ + e \rightarrow H$, $H + H \rightarrow H_2$

Cl^- and OH^- ions move towards anode. Cl^- ions lose electrons and change into neutral atom. At anode, $Cl^- - e \rightarrow Cl$, $Cl + Cl \rightarrow Cl_2$

If mercury is used as cathode H^+ ions are not discharged at mercury cathode because mercury has a high hydrogen overvoltage. Na^+ ions are discharged at the cathode in perference to H^+ ions, yielding sodium, which dissolves in mercury to form sodium amalgam. At cathode : $Na^+ + e = Na$

44. (b) : The metals having higher negative values of their electrode potential can displace metals having lower values from their salt solutions.

45. (a) : $\lambda_\infty = \frac{1}{n^+}\lambda_+^\infty + \frac{1}{n^-}\lambda_-^\infty$

So, $\lambda_\infty(BaCl_2) = \frac{1}{2}\times\lambda^\infty_{Ba^{2+}} + \frac{1}{1}\times\lambda^\infty_{Cl^-}$

$= \frac{1}{2}\times 127 + 76 = 63\cdot5 + 76 = 139\cdot5$

46. (c) : For the reaction $2Cu^+ \rightarrow Cu^{2+} + Cu$ the cathode is Cu^+/Cu and anode is Cu^+/Cu^{2+}.

Given, $Cu^{2+} + 2e^- \rightarrow Cu$; $E_1^\circ = 0.34$ V ...(1)

$Cu^{2+} + e^- \rightarrow Cu^+$; $E_2^\circ = 0\cdot15$ V ...(2)

$Cu^+ + e^- \rightarrow Cu$; $E_3^\circ = ?$ ...(3)

Now $\Delta G^\circ_1 - nFE^\circ_1 = -2\times 0\cdot34\times F$

$\Delta G^\circ_2 = -1\times 0\cdot15\times F$, $\Delta G_3^\circ = -1\times E_3^\circ \times F$

Again $\Delta G_1^\circ = \Delta G_2^\circ + \Delta G_3^\circ \Rightarrow -0\cdot68 F$

$= -0.15 F - E_3^\circ \times F$

$\Rightarrow E_3^\circ = 0\cdot68 - 0\cdot15 = 0\cdot53$ V

As, $E^\circ_{cell} = E^\circ_{cathode}(Cu^+/Cu) - E^\circ_{anode}(Cu^{2+}/Cu^+)$

$= 0\cdot53 - 0\cdot15 = 0\cdot38$ V

47. (b) : $\kappa = 0.012\ ohm^{-1}cm^{-1}$

$R = 55$ ohm $\Rightarrow C = \frac{1}{R} = \frac{1}{55} = ohm^{-1}$

Cell Constant $\left(\frac{l}{a}\right) = \frac{\text{Specific Conductance}}{\text{Conductance}}$

$= \frac{0.012}{1/55} = 55 \times 0.012 = 0.66\ cm^{-1}$

48. (b) : We know $\Delta G = nFE$

Again according to Nernst equation,

$$E = \frac{0.059}{n}\log\frac{[Zn^{2+}]}{[Cu^{2+}]},\text{ at 25°C}$$

So ΔG (free energy change) in an electrochemical cell at a given temperature is a function of

$$\ln\frac{[Zn^{2+}]}{[Cu^{2+}]} = \ln\left(\frac{C_2}{C_1}\right)$$

49. (d) : Nernst equation is $E = E^\circ - \frac{0.059}{2}\log K$

$\Rightarrow E^\circ = \frac{0.059}{2}\log K$ ($E = 0$ at equilibrium condition)

$\Rightarrow 1.1 = \frac{0.059}{2}\log K \Rightarrow K = 10^{37}$

50. (d) : Molar conductance (Λ_m^∞) NaCl

$= 126.45\ ohm^{-1}cm^2mol^{-1}$;

HCl $= 426.16\ ohm^{-1}cm^2mol^{-1}$ and

$CH_3COONa = 91\ ohm^{-1}cm^2mol^{-1}$.

We know that molar conductance of CH_3COOH

$$= \Lambda_m^\infty (CH_3COONa) + \Lambda_m^\infty (HCl) - \Lambda_m^\infty (NaCl)$$

$$= 91 + 426.16 - 126.45 = 390.71 \text{ ohm}^{-1}\text{cm}^2\text{mol}^{-1}$$

51. (d) : Current (I) = 5 ampere and time (t) = 40 minutes = 2400 seconds.

Amount of electricity passed

$$(Q) = I \times t = 5 \times 2400 = 12000 \text{ C}$$

Now $Zn^{2+} + 2e^- \rightarrow Zn$ (1 mole = 65.39)

Since two charges (*i.e.* 2 × 96500 C) deposits 65.39 gm of zinc, therefore 12000 C will deposit

$$= \frac{65.39 \times 12000}{2 \times 96500} = 4.065 \text{ g of zinc}$$

52. (d) : $E^\circ_{Zn/Zn^{2+}} = +0.76$ V

$$E^\circ_{Fe/Fe^{2+}} = 0.44 \text{ V} \rightarrow E^\circ_{Fe^{2+}/Fe} = -0.44 \text{ V}$$

E.M.F. = + 0.76 – 0.44 = + 0.32 V

53. (d) : Since it is a concentration cell and the concentration of ions in two electrolyte solutions (HCl and CH_3COOH) are different, therefore e.m.f. of this cell will not be zero.

54. (a) : Conductivity of heat in metals is due to the presence of free electrons, which move due to increase in temperature.

55. (b) : A cation with maximum value of standard reduction potential, has the strongest oxidising power.

56. (b) : Product obtained at anode will be oxygen.

At anode : $2OH^- \rightleftharpoons H_2O + 1/2O_2$

Chapter 18

Chemical Kinetics

1. The correct difference between first and second order reactions is that
   (a) the rate of a first-order reaction does not depend on reactant concentrations; the rate of a second-order reaction does depend on reactant concentrations
   (b) the half-life of a first-order reaction does not depend on $[A]_0$; the half-life of a second-order reaction does depend on $[A]_0$
   (c) a first-order reaction can be catalysed; a second-order reaction cannot be catalysed
   (d) the rate of a first-order reaction does depend on reactant concentrations; the rate of a second-order reaction does not depend on reactant concentrations. *(NEET 2018)*

2. When initial concentration of the reactant is doubled, the half-life period of a zero order reaction
   (a) is halved (b) is doubled
   (c) is tripled
   (d) remains unchanged. *(NEET 2018)*

3. Mechanism of a hypothetical reaction $X_2 + Y_2 \rightarrow 2XY$, is given below :
   (i) $X_2 \rightarrow X + X$ (fast)
   (ii) $X + Y_2 \rightleftarrows XY + Y$ (slow)
   (iii) $X + Y \rightarrow XY$ (fast)
   The overall order of the reaction will be
   (a) 2 (b) 0
   (c) 1.5 (d) 1 *(NEET 2017)*

4. A first order reaction has a specific reaction rate of 10^{-2} sec^{-1}. How much time will it take for 20 g of the reactant to reduce to 5 g?
   (a) 138.6 sec (b) 346.5 sec
   (c) 693.0 sec (d) 238.6 sec *(NEET 2017)*

5. The decomposition of phosphine (PH_3) on tungsten at low pressure is a first-order reaction. It is because the
   (a) rate is proportional to the surface coverage
   (b) rate is inversely proportional to the surface coverage
   (c) rate is independent of the surface coverage
   (d) rate of decomposition is very slow. *(NEET-II 2016)*

6. The rate of first-order reaction is 0.04 mol L^{-1} s^{-1} at 10 seconds and 0.03 mol L^{-1} s^{-1} at 20 seconds after initiation of the reaction. The half-life period of the reaction is
   (a) 44.1 s (b) 54.1 s
   (c) 24.1 s (d) 34.1 s *(NEET-I 2016)*

7. The addition of a catalyst during a chemical reaction alters which of the following quantities?
   (a) Enthalpy (b) Activation energy
   (c) Entropy (d) Internal energy *(NEET-I 2016)*

8. The rate constant of the reaction $A \longrightarrow B$ is 0.6×10^{-3} mol L^{-1} s^{-1}. If the concentration of A is 5 M, then concentration of B after 20 minutes is
   (a) 3.60 M (b) 0.36 M
   (c) 0.72 M (d) 1.08 M *(2015)*

9. The activation energy of a reaction can be determined from the slope of which of the following graphs?
   (a) $\ln k$ vs $\frac{1}{T}$ (b) $\frac{T}{\ln k}$ vs $\frac{1}{T}$
   (c) $\ln k$ vs T (d) $\frac{\ln k}{T}$ vs T *(2015, Cancelled)*

10. When initial concentration of a reactant is doubled in a reaction, its half-life period is not affected. The order of the reaction is
    (a) second
    (b) more than zero but less than first
    (c) zero
    (d) first. *(2015, Cancelled)*

11. What is the activation energy for a reaction if its rate doubles when the temperature is raised from 20°C to 35°C?
    (R = 8.314 J mol^{-1} K^{-1})

(a) 34.7 kJ mol^{-1} (b) 15.1 kJ mol^{-1}
(c) 342 kJ mol^{-1} (d) 269 kJ mol^{-1}

(NEET 2013)

12. For a reaction between A and B the order with respect to A is 2 and the other with respect to B is 3. The concentrations of both A and B are doubled, the rate will increase by a factor of
(a) 12 (b) 16
(c) 32 (d) 10

(Karnataka NEET 2013)

13. A reaction is 50% complete in 2 hours and 75% complete in 4 hours. The order of reaction is
(a) 1 (b) 2
(c) 3 (d) 0

(Karnataka NEET 2013)

14. In a reaction, $A + B \rightarrow$ product, rate is doubled when the concentration of B is doubled, and rate increases by a factor of 8 when the concentration of both the reactants (A and B) are doubled, rate law for the reaction can be written as
(a) rate = $k[A][B]^2$ (b) rate = $k[A]^2[B]^2$
(c) rate = $k[A][B]$ (d) rate = $k[A]^2[B]$

(2012)

15. In a zero-order reaction, for every 10°C rise of temperature, the rate is doubled. If the temperature is increased from 10°C to 100°C, the rate of the reaction will become
(a) 256 times (b) 512 times
(c) 64 times (d) 128 times *(2012)*

16. Activation energy (E_a) and rate constants (k_1 and k_2) of a chemical reaction at two different temperatures (T_1 and T_2) are related by

(a) $\ln\frac{k_2}{k_1} = -\frac{E_a}{R}\left(\frac{1}{T_1}-\frac{1}{T_2}\right)$

(b) $\ln\frac{k_2}{k_1} = -\frac{E_a}{R}\left(\frac{1}{T_2}-\frac{1}{T_1}\right)$

(c) $\ln\frac{k_2}{k_1} = -\frac{E_a}{R}\left(\frac{1}{T_2}+\frac{1}{T_1}\right)$

(d) $\ln\frac{k_2}{k_1} = \frac{E_a}{R}\left(\frac{1}{T_1}-\frac{1}{T_2}\right)$ *(Mains 2012)*

17. Which one of the following statements for the order of a reaction is incorrect?
(a) Order can be determined only experimentally.
(b) Order is not influenced by stoichiometric coefficient of the reactants.
(c) Order of a reaction is sum of power to the concentration terms of reactants to express the rate of reaction.
(d) Order of reaction is always whole number.

(2011)

18. The rate of the reaction : $2N_2O_5 \rightarrow 4NO_2 + O_2$ can be written in three ways.

$$\frac{-d[N_2O_5]}{dt} = k[N_2O_5]$$

$$\frac{d[NO_2]}{dt} = k'[N_2O_5]; \quad \frac{d[O_2]}{dt} = k''[N_2O_5]$$

The relationship between k and k' and between k and k'' are
(a) $k' = 2k$; $k'' = k$ (b) $k' = 2k$; $k'' = k/2$
(c) $k' = 2k$; $k'' = 2k$ (d) $k' = k$; $k'' = k$

(Mains 2011)

19. The unit of rate constant for a zero order reaction is
(a) mol L^{-1} s^{-1} (b) L mol^{-1} s^{-1}
(c) L^2 mol^{-2} s^{-1} (d) s^{-1}

(Mains 2011)

20. The half-life of a substance in a certain enzyme-catalysed reaction is 138 s. The time required for the concentration of the substance to fall from 1.28 mg L^{-1} to 0.04 mg L^{-1} is
(a) 414 s (b) 552 s (c) 690 s (d) 276 s

(Mains 2011)

21. For the reaction $N_2O_{5(g)} \rightarrow 2NO_{2(g)} + 1/2O_{2(g)}$ the value of rate of disappearance of N_2O_5 is given as 6.25×10^{-3} mol $L^{-1}s^{-1}$. The rate of formation of NO_2 and O_2 is given respectively as
(a) 6.25×10^{-3} mol $L^{-1}s^{-1}$ and 6.25×10^{-3} mol $L^{-1}s^{-1}$
(b) 1.25×10^{-2} mol $L^{-1}s^{-1}$ and 3.125×10^{-3} mol $L^{-1}s^{-1}$
(c) 6.25×10^{-3} mol $L^{-1}s^{-1}$ and 3.125×10^{-3} mol $L^{-1}s^{-1}$
(d) 1.25×10^{-2} mol $L^{-1}s^{-1}$ and 6.25×10^{-3} mol $L^{-1}s^{-1}$

(2010)

22. During the kinetic study of the reaction, $2A + B \rightarrow C + D$, following results were obtained

Run	$[A]$/mol L^{-1}	$[B]$/mol L^{-1}	Initial rate of formation of D/mol L^{-1} min^{-1}
I.	0.1	0.1	6.0×10^{-3}
II.	0.3	0.2	7.2×10^{-2}
III.	0.3	0.4	2.88×10^{-1}
IV.	0.4	0.1	2.40×10^{-2}

Based on the above data which one of the following is correct?

(a) Rate = $k[A]^2[B]$ (b) Rate = $k[A][B]$
(c) Rate = $k[A]^2[B]^2$ (d) Rate = $k[A][B]^2$
(2010)

23. The rate of the reaction, $2NO + Cl_2 \rightarrow 2NOCl$ is given by the rate equation rate = $k[NO]^2[Cl_2]$. The value of the rate constant can be increased by
(a) increasing the temperature
(b) increasing the concentration of NO
(c) increasing the concentration of the Cl_2
(d) doing all of these. *(Mains 2010)*

24. For the reaction, $N_2 + 3H_2 \rightarrow 2NH_3$, if $\frac{d[NH_3]}{dt} = 2\times10^{-4}$ mol L^{-1}s^{-1}, the value of $\frac{-d[H_2]}{dt}$ would be
(a) 4×10^{-4} mol L^{-1} s^{-1}
(b) 6×10^{-4} mol L^{-1} s^{-1}
(c) 1×10^{-4} mol L^{-1} s^{-1}
(d) 3×10^{-4} mol L^{-1} s^{-1} *(2009)*

25. In the reaction,
$BrO^-_{3(aq)} + 5Br^-_{(aq)} + 6H^+ \rightarrow 3Br_{2(l)} + 3H_2O_{(l)}$.
The rate of appearance of bromine (Br_2) is related to rate of disappearance of bromide ions as
(a) $\frac{d[Br_2]}{dt} = -\frac{5}{3}\frac{d[Br^-]}{dt}$
(b) $\frac{d[Br_2]}{dt} = \frac{5}{3}\frac{d[Br^-]}{dt}$
(c) $\frac{d[Br_2]}{dt} = \frac{3}{5}\frac{d[Br^-]}{dt}$
(d) $\frac{d[Br_2]}{dt} = -\frac{3}{5}\frac{d[Br^-]}{dt}$ *(2009)*

26. Half-life period of a first order reaction is 1386 seconds. The specific rate constant of the reaction is
(a) 0.5×10^{-2} s^{-1} (b) 0.5×10^{-3} s^{-1}
(c) 5.0×10^{-2} s^{-1} (d) 5.0×10^{-3} s^{-1}.
(2009)

27. For the reaction $A + B \rightarrow$ products, it is observed that
(i) on doubling the initial concentration of A only, the rate of reaction is also doubled and
(ii) on doubling the initial concentration of both A and B, there is a change by a factor of 8 in the rate of the reaction.
The rate of this reaction is given by
(a) rate = $k[A][B]^2$ (b) rate = $k[A]^2[B]^2$
(c) rate = $k[A][B]$ (d) rate = $k[A]^2[B]$
(2009)

28. The bromination of acetone that occurs in acid solution is represented by this equation.
$CH_3COCH_{3(aq)} + Br_{2(aq)} \rightarrow CH_3COCH_2Br_{(aq)} + H^+_{(aq)} + Br^-_{(aq)}$
These kinetic data were obtained for given reaction concentrations.

Initial concentrations, M			Initial rate, disappearance of Br_2, Ms^{-1}
$[CH_3COCH_3]$	$[Br_2]$	$[H^+]$	
0.30	0.05	0.05	5.7×10^{-5}
0.30	0.10	0.05	5.7×10^{-5}
0.30	0.10	0.10	1.2×10^{-4}
0.40	0.05	0.20	3.1×10^{-4}

Based on these data, the rate equation is
(a) Rate = $k[CH_3COCH_3][Br_2][H^+]^2$
(b) Rate = $k[CH_3COCH_3][Br_2][H^+]$
(c) Rate = $k[CH_3COCH_3][H^+]$
(d) Rate = $k[CH_3COCH_3][Br_2]$ *(2008)*

29. The rate constants k_1 and k_2 for two different reactions are $10^{16} \cdot e^{-2000/T}$ and $10^{15} \cdot e^{-1000/T}$ respectively. The temperature at which $k_1 = k_2$ is
(a) 2000 K (b) $\frac{1000}{2.303}$ K
(c) 1000 K (d) $\frac{2000}{2.303}$ K *(2008)*

30. If 60% of a first order reaction was completed in 60 minutes, 50% of the same reaction would be completed in approximately
(log 4 = 0.60, log 5 = 0.69)
(a) 45 minutes (b) 60 minutes
(c) 40 minutes (d) 50 minutes.
(2007)

31. In a first-order reaction $A \rightarrow B$, if k is rate constant and initial concentration of the reactant A is 0.5 M, then the half-life is
(a) $\frac{\log 2}{k}$ (b) $\frac{\log 2}{k\sqrt{0.5}}$
(c) $\frac{\ln 2}{k}$ (d) $\frac{0.693}{0.5k}$ *(2007)*

32. The reaction of hydrogen and iodine monochloride is given as:
$$H_{2(g)} + 2ICl_{(g)} \rightarrow 2HCl_{(g)} + I_{2(g)}$$
This reaction is of first order with respect to $H_{2(g)}$ and $ICl_{(g)}$, following mechanisms were proposed.
Mechanism A :
$$H_{2(g)} + 2ICl_{(g)} \rightarrow 2HCl_{(g)} + I_{2(g)}$$

Mechanism B :

$H_{2(g)} + ICl_{(g)} \rightarrow HCl_{(g)} + HI_{(g)}$; slow

$HI_{(g)} + ICl_{(g)} \rightarrow HCl_{(g)} + I_{2(g)}$; fast

Which of the above mechanism(s) can be consistent with the given information about the reaction?

(a) *A* and *B* both (b) Neither *A* nor *B*
(c) *A* only (d) *B* only. *(2007)*

33. Consider the reaction: $N_{2(g)} + 3H_{2(g)} \rightarrow 2NH_{3(g)}$

The equality relationship between $\frac{d[NH_3]}{dt}$ and $-\frac{d[H_2]}{dt}$ is

(a) $\frac{d[NH_3]}{dt} = -\frac{d[H_2]}{dt}$

(b) $\frac{d[NH_3]}{dt} = -\frac{1}{3}\frac{d[H_2]}{dt}$

(c) $+\frac{d[NH_3]}{dt} = -\frac{2}{3}\frac{d[H_2]}{dt}$

(d) $+\frac{d[NH_3]}{dt} = -\frac{3}{2}\frac{d[H_2]}{dt}$ *(2006)*

34. For the reaction, $2A + B \rightarrow 3C + D$, which of the following does not express the reaction rate?

(a) $-\frac{d[A]}{2dt}$ (b) $-\frac{d[C]}{3dt}$
(c) $-\frac{d[B]}{dt}$ (d) $\frac{d[D]}{dt}$ *(2006)*

35. The rate of reaction between two reactants *A* and *B* decreases by a factor of 4 if the concentration of reactant *B* is doubled. The order of this reaction with respect to reactant *B* is

(a) 2 (b) –2
(c) 1 (d) –1 *(2005)*

36. For a first order reaction $A \rightarrow B$ the reaction rate at reactant concentration of 0.01 M is found to be 2.0×10^{-5} mol L^{-1} s^{-1}. The half-life period of the reaction is

(a) 30 s (b) 220 s
(c) 300 s (d) 347 s *(2005)*

37. The rate of a first order reaction is 1.5×10^{-2} mol L^{-1} min^{-1} at 0.5 M concentration of the reactant. The half-life of the reaction is

(a) 0.383 min (b) 23.1 min
(c) 8.73 min (d) 7.53 min *(2004)*

38. The temperature dependence of rate constant (*k*) of a chemical reaction is written in terms of Arrhenius equation, $k = A \cdot e^{-E^*/RT}$. Activation energy (E^*) of the reaction can be calculated by plotting

(a) k *vs* T (b) k *vs* $\frac{1}{\log T}$

(c) $\log k$ *vs* $\frac{1}{T}$ (d) $\log k$ *vs* $\frac{1}{\log T}$ *(2003)*

39. If the rate of the reaction is equal to the rate constant, the order of the reaction is

(a) 0 (b) 1
(c) 2 (d) 3 *(2003)*

40. The reaction $A \rightarrow B$ follows first order kinetics. The time taken for 0.8 mole of *A* to produce 0.6 mole of *B* is 1 hour. What is the time taken for conversion of 0.9 mole of *A* to produce 0.675 mole of *B* ?

(a) 1 hour (b) 0.5 hour
(c) 0.25 hour (d) 2 hours *(2003)*

41. The activation energy for a simple chemical reaction $A \rightleftharpoons B$ is E_a in forward direction. The activation energy for reverse reaction

(a) is negative of E_a
(b) is always less than E_a
(c) can be less than or more than E_a
(d) is always double of E_a. *(2003)*

42. $2A \rightarrow B + C$ It would be a zero order reaction when

(a) the rate of reaction is proportional to square of concentration of *A*
(b) the rate of reaction remains same at any concentration of *A*
(c) the rate remains unchanged at any concentration of *B* and *C*
(d) the rate of reaction doubles if concentration of *B* is increased to double. *(2002)*

43. $3A \rightarrow 2B$, rate of reaction $\frac{+d[B]}{dt}$ is equal to

(a) $-\frac{3}{2}\frac{d[A]}{dt}$ (b) $-\frac{2}{3}\frac{d[A]}{dt}$

(c) $-\frac{1}{3}\frac{d[A]}{dt}$ (d) $+2\frac{d[A]}{dt}$ *(2002)*

44. When a biochemical reaction is carried out in laboratory, outside the human body in absence of enzyme, then rate of reaction obtained is 10^{-6} times, the activation energy of reaction in the presence of enzyme is

(a) $6/RT$ (b) *P* is required
(c) different from E_a obtained in laboratory
(d) can't say anything. *(2001)*

45. For the reaction; $2N_2O_5 \rightarrow 4NO_2 + O_2$ rate and rate constant are 1.02×10^{-4} and 3.4×10^{-5} sec^{-1} respectively, then concentration of N_2O_5 at that time will be

(a) 1.732 (b) 3
(c) 1.02×10^{-4} (d) 3.4×10^{5}

(2001)

46. How enzymes increases the rate of reactions
(a) by lowering activation energy
(b) by increasing activation energy
(c) by changing equilibrium constant
(d) by forming enzyme substrate complex.

(2000)

47. For the reaction $H^+ + BrO_3^- + 3Br^- \rightarrow 5Br_2 + H_2O$ which of the following relation correctly represents the consumption and formation of products.

(a) $\frac{d[Br^-]}{dt} = -\frac{3}{5}\frac{d[Br_2]}{dt}$

(b) $\frac{d[Br^-]}{dt} = \frac{3}{5}\frac{d[Br_2]}{dt}$

(c) $\frac{d[Br^-]}{dt} = -\frac{5}{3}\frac{d[Br_2]}{dt}$

(d) $\frac{d[Br^-]}{dt} = \frac{5}{3}\frac{d[Br_2]}{dt}$ *(2000)*

48. For a first-order reaction, the half-life period is independent of
(a) first power of final concentration
(b) cube root of initial concentration
(c) initial concentration
(d) square root of final concentration

(1999)

49. Activation energy of a chemical reaction can be determined by
(a) evaluating rate constants at two different temperatures
(b) evaluating velocities of reaction at two different temperatures
(c) evaluating rate constant at standard temperature
(d) changing concentration of reactants.

(1998)

50. The experimental data for the reaction,
$2A + B_2 \rightarrow 2AB$ is

Experiment	$[A]$	$[B_2]$	Rate (mole s^{-1})
1	0.50	0.50	1.6×10^{-4}
2	0.50	1.00	3.2×10^{-4}
3	1.00	1.00	3.2×10^{-4}

The rate equation for the above data is
(a) Rate = $k[A]^2[B]^2$ (b) Rate = $k[A]^2[B]$
(c) Rate = $k[B_2]$ (d) Rate = $k[B_2]^2$

(1997)

51. For the reaction $H_{2(g)} + I_{2(g)} \rightleftharpoons 2HI_{(g)}$, the rate of reaction is expressed as

(a) $\frac{\Delta[H_2]}{\Delta t} = \frac{1}{2}\frac{\Delta[I_2]}{\Delta t} = -\frac{\Delta[HI]}{\Delta t}$

(b) $-\frac{\Delta[I_2]}{\Delta t} = -\frac{\Delta[H_2]}{\Delta t} = \frac{1}{2}\frac{\Delta[HI]}{\Delta t}$

(c) $\frac{\Delta[I_2]}{\Delta t} = \frac{\Delta[H_2]}{\Delta t} = \frac{\Delta[HI]}{2\Delta t}$

(d) none of these. *(1997)*

52. The given reaction,
$2FeCl_3 + SnCl_2 \rightarrow 2FeCl_2 + SnCl_4$
is an example of
(a) third order reaction
(b) first order reaction
(c) second order reaction
(d) none of these. *(1996)*

53. The data for the reaction $A + B \rightarrow C$, is

Exp.	$[A]_0$	$[B]_0$	Initial rate
1	0.012	0.035	0.10
2	0.024	0.070	0.80
3	0.024	0.035	0.10
4	0.012	0.070	0.80

The rate law corresponds to the above data is
(a) Rate = $k[A][B]^3$ (b) Rate = $k[A]^2[B]^2$
(c) Rate = $k[B]^3$ (d) Rate = $k[B]^4$.

(1994)

54. By the action of enzymes, the rate of biochemical reaction
(a) does not change
(b) increases
(c) decreases
(d) either (a) or (c). *(1994)*

Answer Key

1.	(b)	**2.**	(b)	**3.**	(c)	**4.**	(a)	**5.**	(a)	**6.**	(c)	**7.**	(b)	**8.**	(c)	**9.**	(a)	**10.**	(d)
11.	(a)	**12.**	(c)	**13.**	(a)	**14.**	(d)	**15.**	(b)	**16.**	(b, d)	**17.**	(d)	**18.**	(b)	**19.**	(a)	**20.**	(c)
21.	(b)	**22.**	(d)	**23.**	(a)	**24.**	(d)	**25.**	(d)	**26.**	(b)	**27.**	(a)	**28.**	(c)	**29.**	(b)	**30.**	(a)
31.	(c)	**32.**	(d)	**33.**	(c)	**34.**	(b)	**35.**	(b)	**36.**	(d)	**37.**	(b)	**38.**	(c)	**39.**	(a)	**40.**	(a)
41.	(c)	**42.**	(b)	**43.**	(b)	**44.**	(c)	**45.**	(b)	**46.**	(a)	**47.**	(a)	**48.**	(c)	**49.**	(a)	**50.**	(c)
51.	(b)	**52.**	(a)	**53.**	(c)	**54.**	(b)												

EXPLANATIONS

1. (b) : For the first order reaction, $t_{1/2} = \dfrac{0.693}{k}$ which is independent of initial concentration $[A]_0$.

For second order reaction, $t_{1/2} = \dfrac{1}{k[A]_0}$

Half-life depends on initial concentration of reactant.

2. (b) : $(t_{1/2})_{zero} = \dfrac{[A]_0}{2k}$

As the half-life of a zero order reaction is directly proportional to initial concentration.

$\therefore$ If $[A_0]$ = doubled then, $t_{1/2}$ = doubled.

3. (c) : Note : Correct the reactions given in question as

$X_2 \rightleftharpoons X + X$ (fast)

$X + Y_2 \rightarrow XY + Y$ (slow)

Slow step is the rate determining step.

$$\text{Rate} = k[X][Y_2] \quad ...(i)$$

Equilibrium constant for fast step, $K = \dfrac{[X]^2}{[X_2]}$

$[X] = \sqrt{K[X_2]}$

By substituting $[X]$ in equation (i), we get

$\text{Rate} = k\sqrt{K[X_2]}\,[Y_2] = k'[X_2]^{1/2}[Y_2]$

$\therefore$ Order of reaction $= \dfrac{1}{2} + 1 = \dfrac{3}{2} = 1.5$

4. (a) : For a first order reaction,

$$k = \frac{2.303}{t}\log\frac{[A]_0}{[A]_t}$$

$$10^{-2} = \frac{2.303}{t}\log\frac{20}{5}$$

$$10^{-2} = \frac{2.303 \times 0.6020}{t}$$

$t = 138.6$ sec

5. (a) : At low pressure, rate is proportional to the surface coverage and is of first order while at high pressure, it follows zero order kinetics due to complete coverage of surface area.

6. (c) : For a first order reaction, $A \rightarrow$ Products and for concentration of the reactant at two different times,

$$k = \frac{2.303}{t_2 - t_1}\log\frac{[A]_1}{[A]_2}$$

$$\therefore \quad k = \frac{2.303}{t_2 - t_1}\log\frac{(\text{rate})_1}{(\text{rate})_2} \quad (\because \text{rate} \propto [A])$$

$$k = \frac{2.303}{(20-10)}\log\left(\frac{0.04}{0.03}\right) = 0.0287\ \text{sec}^{-1}$$

$$t_{1/2} = \frac{0.693}{k} = \frac{0.693}{0.0287\ \text{sec}^{-1}} = 24.14\ \text{sec}$$

7. (b) : A catalyst provides an alternate path to the reaction which has lower activation energy.

8. (c) : Reaction is of zero order as the unit of rate constant is mol L^{-1} s^{-1}.

$\therefore$ Concentration of $B = k \times t$

$= 0.6 \times 10^{-3} \times 20 \times 60 = 0.72$ M

9. (a) : According to Arrhenius equation,

$k = Ae^{-E_a/RT}$

$\ln k = \ln A - \dfrac{E_a}{RT}$

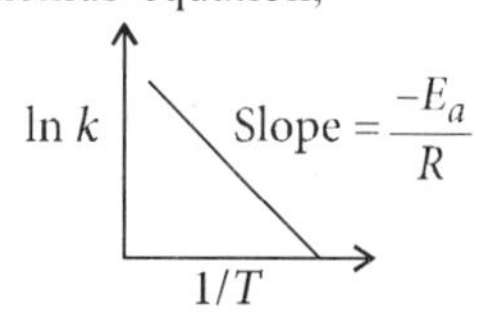

Hence, if ln k is plotted against $1/T$, slope of the line will be $-\dfrac{E_a}{R}$.

10. (d) : Half-life period of a first order reaction is independent of initial concentration,

$t_{1/2} = \dfrac{0.693}{k}$.

11. (a) : $\log\dfrac{k_2}{k_1} = \dfrac{E_a}{2.303R}\left(\dfrac{1}{T_1} - \dfrac{1}{T_2}\right)$

$k_2 = 2k_1$, $T_1 = 20 + 273 = 293$ K

or $T_2 = 35 + 273 = 308$ K

$R = 8.314$ J mol^{-1} K^{-1}

$$\log 2 = \frac{E_a}{2.303 \times 8.314}\left(\frac{1}{293} - \frac{1}{308}\right)$$

$$0.3010 = \frac{E_a}{19.147} \times \frac{15}{293 \times 308}$$

$E_a = 34673$ J mol^{-1} = 34.7 kJ mol^{-1}

12. (c) : $\text{Rate}_1 = k[A]^2[B]^3$

$\text{Rate}_2 = k[2A]^2[2B]^3$

$\text{Rate}_2 = 32k[A]^2[B]^3$

$\therefore$ $\text{Rate}_2 = 32(\text{Rate}_1)$

13. (a) : As $t_{75\%} = 2 \times t_{50\%}$, the order of the reaction is one, A is a first order reaction.

14. (d) :

$[A]$	$[B]$	Rate	
x	y	R	... (i)
x	$2y$	$2R$	... (ii)
$2x$	$2y$	$8R$	... (iii)

Let the rate law ; rate = $k[A]^a[B]^b$

From data given, $(x)^a(y)^b = R$ ... (iv)

$(x)^a(2y)^b = 2R$ ... (v)

Dividing eqn. (v) by (iv),

$$\frac{(2y)^b}{(y)^b} = \frac{2R}{R} \Rightarrow (2)^b = 2$$

Thus, $b = 1$

From data of (iii) experiment,

$(2x)^a(2y)^b = 8R$ ... (vi)

From eqn. (v) and (vi),

$$\frac{(2x)^a}{(x)^a} = \frac{8R}{2R} \Rightarrow (2)^a = 4$$

Thus, $a = 2$. By replacing the values of a and b in rate law; rate = $k[A]^2[B]$

15. (b) : At 10°C rise, rate increases by 2.

$$\frac{r_{100°C}}{r_{10°C}} = 2^{\left(\frac{100-10}{10}\right)} = 2^9 = 512 \text{ times}$$

16. (b, d) : $k_1 = Ae^{-E_a/RT_1}$, $k_2 = Ae^{-E_a/RT_2}$

$\ln k_1 = \ln A - E_a/RT_1$ ...(i)

$\ln k_2 = \ln A - E_a/RT_2$ ...(ii)

From eq.(i) and (ii), we have

$$\ln k_2 - \ln k_1 = \ln A - \frac{E_a}{RT_2} - \ln A + \frac{E_a}{RT_1}$$

$$\Rightarrow \ln\frac{k_2}{k_1} = \frac{E_a}{R}\left(\frac{1}{T_1} - \frac{1}{T_2}\right)$$

$$\Rightarrow \ln\frac{k_2}{k_1} = -\frac{E_a}{R}\left(\frac{1}{T_2} - \frac{1}{T_1}\right)$$

17. (d) : Order of a reaction is not always whole number. It can be zero, or fractional also.

18. (b) : $2N_2O_5 \rightarrow 4NO_2 + O_2$

$$-\frac{1}{2}\frac{d[N_2O_5]}{dt} = +\frac{1}{4}\frac{d[NO_2]}{dt} = +\frac{d[O_2]}{dt}$$
$$\quad k \qquad\qquad k' \qquad\qquad k''$$

$$\frac{1}{2}k = \frac{1}{4}k' = k'', \; k' = 2k; \; k'' = \frac{1}{2}k$$

19. (a) : The units are mol L^{-1} s^{-1}.

20. (c) : Fall of concentration from 1.28 mg L^{-1} to 0.04 mg L^{-1} requires 5 half-lives.

$\therefore$ Time required = $5 \times t_{1/2} = 5 \times 138 = 690$ s

21. (b) : $N_2O_{5(g)} \rightarrow 2NO_{2(g)} + 1/2O_{2(g)}$

For the given reaction the rate law may be written as :

$$\frac{-d[N_2O_5]}{dt} = \frac{1}{2}\frac{d[NO_2]}{dt} = \frac{2d[O_2]}{dt}$$

given that $\frac{-d[N_2O_5]}{dt} = 6.25 \times 10^{-3}$ mol L^{-1} s^{-1}

$$\therefore \frac{d[NO_2]}{dt} = 2 \times 6.25 \times 10^{-3} = 1.25 \times 10^{-2} \text{ mol L}^{-1}\text{s}^{-1}$$

$$\text{and } \frac{d[O_2]}{dt} = \frac{6.25 \times 10^{-3}}{2} = 3.125 \times 10^{-3} \text{ mol L}^{-1}\text{s}^{-1}$$

22. (d) : Let the rate of reaction be given by : rate = $k[A]^a[B]^b$.

Now consider II and III where $[A]$ is constant.

$$\frac{7.2 \times 10^{-2}}{2.88 \times 10^{-1}} = \frac{[0.3]^a[0.2]^b}{[0.3]^a[0.4]^b}$$

$$\frac{1}{4} = \left(\frac{1}{2}\right)^b \Rightarrow b = 2$$

Now consider I and IV

$$\frac{6.0 \times 10^{-3}}{2.4 \times 10^{-2}} = \frac{[0.1]^a[0.1]^b}{[0.4]^a[0.1]^b}$$

$$\frac{1}{4} = \left(\frac{1}{4}\right)^a \Rightarrow a = 1$$

$\therefore$ Rate = $k[A][B]^2$

23. (a) : Rate constant is independent of the initial concentration of the reactants. It has a constant value at fixed temperature. Hence the value of rate constant can be increased by increasing the temperature.

24. (d) : For reaction, $N_2 + 3H_2 \rightarrow 2NH_3$

$$\text{Rate} = \frac{1}{2}\frac{d[NH_3]}{dt} = -\frac{1}{3}\frac{d[H_2]}{dt} = -\frac{d[N_2]}{dt}$$

Given, $\frac{d[NH_3]}{dt} = 2 \times 10^{-4}$ mol L^{-1} s^{-1}

$$\therefore -\frac{d[H_2]}{dt} = \frac{3}{2}\frac{d[NH_3]}{dt} = \frac{3}{2} \times 2 \times 10^{-4}$$

$$\Rightarrow -\frac{d[H_2]}{dt} = 3 \times 10^{-4} \text{ mol L}^{-1}\text{ s}^{-1}$$

25. (d) : For the given reaction,

$BrO_{3(aq)}^- + 5Br^-_{(aq)} + 6H^+ \rightarrow 3Br_{2(l)} + 3H_2O_{(l)}$

Rate of reaction in terms of Br_2 and Br^- is,

$$\text{Rate} = \frac{1}{3}\frac{d[Br_2]}{dt} = -\frac{1}{5}\frac{d[Br^-]}{dt}$$

$$\therefore \frac{d[Br_2]}{dt} = -\frac{3}{5}\frac{d[Br^-]}{dt}$$

26. (b) : Given, $t_{1/2} = 1386$ s

For a first order reaction,

$$t_{1/2} = \frac{0.693}{k} \quad (k = \text{rate constant})$$

$\Rightarrow \quad 1386 = \dfrac{0.693}{k}$

$\Rightarrow \quad k = 5 \times 10^{-4}\ s^{-1} = 0.5 \times 10^{-3}\ s^{-1}$

27. (a) : $R = k[A]^m[B]^n$ ... (i)
$2R = k[2A]^m[B]^n$ ... (ii)
$8R = k[2A]^m[2B]^n$ ... (iii)
from (i), (ii) and (iii), $m = 1,\ n = 2$
So, rate $= k[A][B]^2$

28. (c) : From the first two experiments, it is clear that when concentration of Br_2 is doubled, the initial rate of disappearance of Br_2 remains unaltered. So, order of reaction with respect to Br_2 is zero. The probable rate law for the reaction will be : $k[CH_3COCH_3][H^+]$

29. (b) : $k_1 = 10^{16}e^{-2000/T},\ k_2 = 10^{15}e^{-1000/T}$
The temperature at which $k_1 = k_2$ will be

$$10^{16}e^{-2000/T} = 10^{15}e^{-1000/T}$$

$$\Rightarrow \frac{e^{-2000/T}}{e^{-1000/T}} = \frac{10^{15}}{10^{16}}$$

$$\Rightarrow e^{\frac{-1000}{T}} = 10^{-1} \Rightarrow \log_e e^{\frac{-1000}{T}} = \log_e 10^{-1}$$

$$\Rightarrow 2.303\log_{10} e^{\frac{-1000}{T}} = 2.303 \times \log_{10} 10^{-1}$$

$$\Rightarrow \frac{-1000}{T} \times \log_{10} e = -1 \Rightarrow T = \frac{1000}{2.303}\text{ K}$$

30. (a) : For a first order reaction,

$$k = \frac{2.303}{t}\log\frac{a}{a-x}$$

$$k = \frac{2.303}{60}\log\frac{100}{40} = \frac{2.303}{60} \times \log 2.5 = 0.0153$$

$$\text{Again, } t_{1/2} = \frac{2.303}{k}\log\frac{100}{50} = \frac{2.303}{0.0153} \times \log 2$$

$= 45.31$ min.

31. (c) : For a 1st order kinetics,

$$k = \frac{2.303}{t}\log_{10}\frac{a}{a-x}$$

$$\text{At } t_{1/2},\ k = \frac{2.303}{t_{1/2}}\log_{10}\frac{a}{a-\frac{a}{2}}$$

$$\text{or, } t_{1/2} = \frac{2.303}{k}\log_{10} 2 = \frac{\ln 2}{k}$$

32. (d) : The slow step is the rate determining step and it involves 1 molecule of $H_{2(g)}$ and 1 molecule of $ICl_{(g)}$. Hence the rate will be,

$r = k[H_{2(g)}]\,[ICl_{(g)}]$

i.e. the reaction is 1st order with respect to $H_{2(g)}$ and $ICl_{(g)}$.

33. (c) : $N_{2(g)} + 3H_{2(g)} \rightarrow 2NH_{3(g)}$

$$\text{Rate} = \frac{-d[N_2]}{dt} = -\frac{d[H_2]}{3dt} = +\frac{d[NH_3]}{2dt}$$

$$\text{Hence, } +\frac{d[NH_3]}{dt} = -\frac{2}{3}\frac{d[H_2]}{dt}$$

34. (b) : $2A + B \rightarrow 3C + D$

$$\text{rate} = \frac{-d[A]}{2dt} = -\frac{d[B]}{dt} = \frac{d[C]}{3dt} = \frac{d[D]}{dt}$$

Negative sign shows the decrease in concentration.

35. (b) : Rate of reaction $= k\,[A_0]^\alpha\,[B_0]^\beta$
$\alpha \rightarrow$ order of reaction w.r.t. A
$\beta \rightarrow$ order of reaction w.r.t. B
$[B] = [2B_0]$

$$\frac{r_1}{r_2} = \frac{k\,[A_0]^\alpha[B_0]^\beta}{[A_0]^\alpha[2B_0]^\beta} \Rightarrow 4 = \left(\frac{1}{2}\right)^\beta = \beta = -2$$

36. (d) : $A \longrightarrow B$
rate of reaction $= 2 \times 10^{-5}$ mol L^{-1} s^{-1}
$\Rightarrow$ order of reaction is $n = 1$, rate $= k\,[A]^n$
$k \rightarrow$ rate or velocity constant
$[A] = 0.01$ M

$$\Rightarrow k = \frac{2\times10^{-5}}{0.01} = 2 \times 10^{-3},\ k = \frac{0.693}{t_{1/2}}$$

$$t_{1/2} = \frac{0.693}{2\times10^{-3}} = 346.5\text{ s} \approx 347\text{ s}$$

37. (b) : Rate $\left(\dfrac{dx}{dt}\right) = kC$

i.e., $1.5 \times 10^{-2} = k \times 0.5$ or, $k = \dfrac{1.5\times10^{-2}}{0.5}$

For first order reaction,

$$t_{1/2} = \frac{0.693}{k} = \frac{0.693\times0.5}{1.5\times10^{-2}} = 23.1\text{ min}$$

38. (c) : On plotting log k *vs* $1/T$, we get a straight line, the slope indicates the value of activation energy.

39. (a) : $A \rightarrow$ products

If $-\dfrac{dx}{dt} = k$, it means $-\dfrac{dx}{dt} = k\,[A]^0 = k$

Hence order of reaction must be zero.

40. (a) :

In case I		**In case II**	
A	$\rightarrow B$	A	$\rightarrow B$
0.8	0	0.9	0
0.2	0.6	0.225	0.675
1	3	1	3

The time taken for the completion of same fraction of change is independent of initial concentration.

41. (c) : Activation energy is the minimum amount of energy required to convert reactant into product. It is affected by the presence of catalyst.

42. (b) : $2A \rightarrow B + C$
The rate equation of this equation may be expressed as $r = k\,[A]^0$. [Order = 0]. $r = k$.
$\therefore$ The rate is independent of concentration.

43. (b) : $3A \rightarrow 2B$

Rate of the reaction $= \frac{1}{2}\frac{d[B]}{dt} = -\frac{1}{3}\frac{d[A]}{dt}$

$\Rightarrow \frac{d[B]}{dt} = -\frac{2}{3}\frac{d[A]}{dt}$

44. (c) : For a given chemical reaction,
$k = Ae^{-E_a/RT}$ (Arrhenius equation)

45. (b) : $2N_2O_5 \rightarrow 4NO_2 + O_2$
This is a first order reaction.
$\therefore$ rate $= k\,[N_2O_5]$;

$[N_2O_5] = \text{rate}/k = \frac{1.02\times10^{-4}}{3.4\times10^{-5}} = 3$

46. (a) : Enzymes act like catalyst in biochemical reactions. Presence of an enzyme increases the rate of reaction by lowering the activation energy of the reactant.

47. (a) : $-\frac{1}{3}\frac{d[Br^-]}{dt} = +\frac{1}{5}\frac{d[Br_2]}{dt}$ = rate of reaction

$\Rightarrow \frac{d[Br^-]}{dt} = -\frac{3}{5}\frac{d[Br_2]}{dt}$

48. (c) : For the first order reaction, rate constant is given by, $k_1 = \frac{1}{t}\ln\frac{a}{a-x}$
a = initial concentration, $(a-x)$ = concentration at t time
At $t = t_{1/2}$, $x = a/2$

$\Rightarrow k_1 = \frac{1}{t_{1/2}}\ln\frac{a}{a-a/2} \Rightarrow k_1 = \frac{1}{t_{1/2}}\ln 2$

$\Rightarrow k_1 = \frac{0.693}{t_{1/2}}$

49. (a) : According to Arrhenius equation:

$\log\frac{k_2}{k_1} = \frac{E_a}{2.303R}\left[\frac{T_2-T_1}{T_2T_1}\right]$

where E_a = activation energy
R = gas constant = 8.314 J K^{-1} mol^{-1}
k_1 and k_2 are rate constants of the reaction at two different temperatures T_1 and T_2 respectively.
Therefore, $t_{1/2}$ is independent of initial concentration.

50. (c) : For the reaction $2A + B_2 \rightleftharpoons 2AB$,
Rate $\propto [A]^x[B_2]^y$. On substituting the given data, we get

From experiment 1, $1.6\times10^{-4} \propto [0.50]^x\,[0.50]^y$ ...(i)
From experiment 2, $3.2\times10^{-4} \propto [0.50]^x\,[1.00]^y$ ...(ii)
From experiment 3, $3.2\times10^{-4} \propto [1.00]^x\,[1.00]^y$ ..(iii)
On dividing equation (iii) by (ii), we get ,

$1 = \left[\frac{1.00}{0.50}\right]^x \Rightarrow 1 = 2^x \Rightarrow 2^0 = 2^x \Rightarrow x = 0$

Now, divide equation (ii) by equation (i) we get,

$2 = \left[\frac{1.00}{0.50}\right]^y \Rightarrow 2 = 2^y \Rightarrow y = 1$

Thus rate equation is : Rate $= k[A]^0\,[B_2]^1 = k[B_2]$.

51. (b) : For $H_{2(g)} + I_{2(g)} \rightleftharpoons 2HI_{(g)}$, the rate of reaction is

$$-\frac{\Delta[H_2]}{\Delta t} = -\frac{\Delta[I_2]}{\Delta t} = \frac{1}{2}\frac{\Delta[HI]}{\Delta t}$$

Negative sign shows disappearance of reactant and positive sign shows the appearance of product.

52. (a) : For a general reaction
$xA + yB + zC \rightarrow$ product, the order of reaction is $x + y + z$. Since three molecules undergo change in concentration, therefore it is a third order reaction.

53. (c) : $A + B \rightarrow C$
Let rate $= k(A)^x\,(B)^y$
where order of reaction is $(x + y)$.
Putting the values of exp. 1, 2, and 3, we get following equations.
$0.10 = k\,[0.012]^x\,[0.035]^y$ ...(i)
$0.80 = k\,[0.024]^x\,[0.070]^y$ ...(ii)
$0.10 = k\,[0.024]^x\,[0.035]^y$ ...(iii)
Dividing (ii) by (i), we get

$\frac{0.80}{0.10} = \left(\frac{0.070}{0.035}\right)^y \Rightarrow 2^y = 8 \Rightarrow y = 3$

Keeping $[A]$ constant, $[B]$ is doubled, rate becomes 8 times.
Dividing eq. (iii) by eq. (i), we get

$\frac{0.10}{0.10} = \left(\frac{0.024}{0.012}\right)^x \Rightarrow 2^x = 1 \Rightarrow x = 0.$

Keeping $[B]$ constant, $[A]$ is doubled, rate remains unaffected. Hence rate is independent of $[A]$.
rate $\propto [B]^3$.

54. (b) : Since the enzymes are regarded as biological catalysts, therefore their action increases the rate of biological reaction.

Chapter 19

Surface Chemistry

1. On which of the following properties does the coagulating power of an ion depend?
   (a) The magnitude of the charge on the ion alone
   (b) Size of the ion alone
   (c) Both magnitude and sign of the charge on the ion
   (d) The sign of charge on the ion alone
   (NEET 2018)

2. Which one of the following statements is not correct?
   (a) The value of equilibrium constant is changed in the presence of a catalyst in the reaction at equilibrium.
   (b) Enzymes catalyse mainly biochemical reactions.
   (c) Coenzymes increase the catalytic activity of enzyme.
   (d) Catalyst does not initiate any reaction.
   (NEET 2017)

3. The coagulation values in millimoles per litre of the electrolytes used for the coagulation of As_2S_3 are given below :
   I. $(NaCl) = 52$, II. $(BaCl_2) = 0.69$,
   III. $(MgSO_4) = 0.22$
   The correct order of their coagulating power is
   (a) I > II > III (b) II > I > III
   (c) III > II > I (d) III > I > II
   (NEET-II 2016)

4. Fog is a colloidal solution of
   (a) solid in gas (b) gas in gas
   (c) liquid in gas (d) gas in liquid.
   (NEET-I 2016)

5. Which one of the following characteristics is associated with adsorption?
   (a) ΔG and ΔH are negative but ΔS is positive.
   (b) ΔG and ΔS are negative but ΔH is positive.
   (c) ΔG is negative but ΔH and ΔS are positive.
   (d) ΔG, ΔH and ΔS all are negative.
   (NEET-I 2016)

6. Which property of colloidal solution is independent of charge on the colloidal particles?
   (a) Electroosmosis (b) Tyndall effect
   (c) Coagulation (d) Electrophoresis
   (2015, Cancelled)

7. Which property of colloids is not dependent on the charge on colloidal particles?
   (a) Coagulation (b) Electrophoresis
   (c) Electro-osmosis (d) Tyndall effect
   (2014)

8. In Freundlich adsorption isotherm, the value of $1/n$ is
   (a) between 0 and 1 in all cases
   (b) between 2 and 4 in all cases
   (c) 1 in case of physical absorption
   (d) 1 in case of chemisorption. *(2012)*

9. Which one of the following statements is incorrect about enzyme catalysis?
   (a) Enzymes are mostly proteinous in nature.
   (b) Enzyme action is specific.
   (c) Enzymes are denatured by ultraviolet rays and at high temperature.
   (d) Enzymes are least reactive at optimum temperature. *(2012)*

10. The protecting power of lyophilic colloidal sol is expressed in terms of
    (a) coagulation value
    (b) gold number
    (c) critical micelle concentration
    (d) oxidation number. *(2012)*

11. If x is amount of adsorbate and m is amount of adsorbent, which of the following relations is not related to adsorption process?
    (a) $x/m = f(p)$ at constant T
    (b) $x/m = f(T)$ at constant p
    (c) $p = f(T)$ at constant (x/m)
    (d) $\frac{x}{m} = p \times T$ *(2011)*

12. The Langmuir adsorption isotherm is deduced using the assumption
   (a) the adsorption sites are equivalent in their ability to adsorb the particles
   (b) the heat of adsorption varies with coverage
   (c) the adsorbed molecules interact with each other
   (d) the adsorption takes place in multilayers. *(2007)*

13. A plot of $\log(x/m)$ versus $\log p$ for the adsorption of a gas on a solid gives a straight line with slope equal to
   (a) $\log K$ (b) $-\log K$
   (c) n (d) $1/n$ *(2006)*

14. Which one of the following forms micelles in aqueous solution above certain concentration?
   (a) Dodecyl trimethyl ammonium chloride
   (b) Glucose (c) Urea
   (d) Pyridinium chloride *(2005)*

15. The enzyme which hydrolyses triglycerides to fatty acids and glycerol is called
   (a) maltase (b) lipase
   (c) zymase (d) pepsin. *(2004)*

16. According to the adsorption theory of catalysis, the speed of the reaction increases because
   (a) the concentration of reactant molecules at the active centres of the catalyst becomes high due to adsorption
   (b) in the process of adsorption, the activation energy of the molecules becomes large
   (c) adsorption produces heat which increases the speed of the reaction
   (d) adsorption lowers the activation energy of the reaction. *(2003)*

17. Position of non polar and polar part in micelle
   (a) polar at outer surface but non polar at inner surface
   (b) polar at inner surface non polar at outer surface
   (c) distributed over all the surface
   (d) are present in the surface only. *(2002)*

18. Which is not correct regarding the adsorption of a gas on surface of a solid?
   (a) On increasing temperature adsorption increases continuously.
   (b) Enthalpy and entropy change is negative.
   (c) Adsorption is more for some specific substance.
   (d) It is a reversible reaction. *(2001)*

19. Which one of the following method is commonly used method for destruction of colloid?
   (a) Dialysis
   (b) Condensation
   (c) Filteration by animal membrane
   (d) By adding electrolyte *(2000)*

20. At the critical micelle concentration (CMC) the surfactant molecules
   (a) associate
   (b) dissociate
   (c) decompose
   (d) become completely soluble *(1998)*

21. The ability of anion, to bring about coagulation of a given colloid, depends upon
   (a) magnitude of the charge
   (b) both magnitude and charge
   (c) its charge only
   (d) sign of the charge alone. *(1997)*

22. A colloidal system has particles of which o the following size?
   (a) 10^{-9} m to 10^{-12} m (b) 10^{-6} m to 10^{-9} m
   (c) 10^{-4} m to 10^{-10} m (d) 10^{-5} m to 10^{-7} m *(1996)*

23. When a few typical solutes are separated by a particular selective membrane such as protein particles, blood corpuscles, this process is called
   (a) transpiration (b) endosmosis
   (c) dialysis (d) diffusion. *(1996)*

24. For the adsorption of a gas on a solid, the plot of log (x/m) versus log P is linear with slope equal to
   (a) n (b) $1/n$
   (c) k (d) $\log k$. *(1994)*

Answer Key

1.	(c)	2.	(a)	3.	(c)	4.	(c)	5.	(d)	6.	(b)	7.	(d)	8.	(a)	9.	(d)	10.	(b)
11.	(d)	12.	(a)	13.	(d)	14.	(a)	15.	(b)	16.	(d)	17.	(a)	18.	(a)	19.	(d)	20.	(a)
21.	(b)	22.	(b)	23.	(c)	24.	(b)												

EXPLANATIONS

1. **(c) :** According to Hardy-Schulze rule, the coagulating power of an electrolyte depends on both magnitude and sign of the charge of the effective ion or electrolyte.

2. **(a) :** Calatyst does not change the value of equilibrium constant as they affect forward as well as backward reactions equally.

3. **(c) :** Coagulating power $\propto \dfrac{1}{\text{Coagulation value}}$

Lower the coagulation value, higher is the coagulating power so, the correct order is :

$MgSO_4 > BaCl_2 > NaCl$
(III) (II) (I)

4. **(c) :** Fog is an example of aerosol in which dispersed phase is liquid and dispersion medium is gas.

5. **(d) :** As the molecules of the adsorbate are held on the surface of the solid adsorbent, entropy decreases *i.e.*, $\Delta S = -\text{ve}$. As $\Delta G = \Delta H - T\Delta S$

For the adsorption to occur, $\Delta G = -\text{ve}$ and it is possible only if $\Delta H = -\text{ve}$.

6. **(b) :** Tyndall effect is scattering of light by colloidal particles which is independent of charge on them.

7. **(d) :** Tyndall effect is due to the scattering of light by colloidal particles and not due to the charge.

8. **(a) :** Freundlich adsorption isotherm:

$$\frac{x}{m} = k \cdot P^{1/n} \;; \qquad 0 \le \frac{1}{n} \le 1$$

9. **(d) :** The enzyme activity rises rapidly with temperature and becomes maximum at definite temperature, called optimum temperature.

10. **(b)**

11. **(d) :** $\dfrac{x}{m} = p \times T$

12. **(a) :** Langmuir adsorption isotherm is based on the assumption that every adsorption site is equivalent and that the ability of a particle to bind there is independent of whether nearby sites are occupied or not occupied.

13. **(d) :**

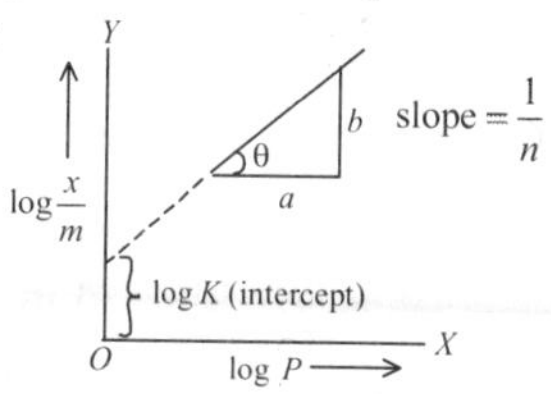

This is according to Freundlich adsorption isotherm.

14. **(a) :**

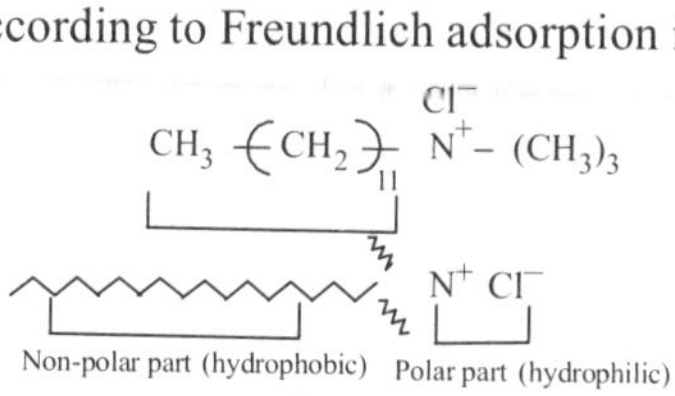

15. **(b) :**

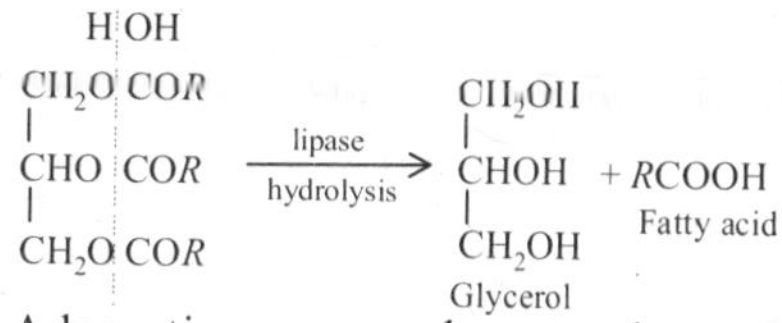

16. **(d) :** Adsorption causes decrease in surface energy which appears as heat. Thus adsorption is an exothermic process and hence lowers the activation energy of the reaction.

17. **(a) :** Micelles are the clusters or aggregates formed in solution by association of colloids. Usually such molecules have a lyophobic group and a lyophilic group. The long hydrocarbon is the lyophobic portion which tries to recede away from the solvent water and the ionisable lyophilic group which tends to go into water resulting into ions. As the concentration is increased the lyophobic parts receding away from the solvent approach each other and form a cluster, the lyophobic ends are in the interior lyophilic groups projecting outward in contact with the solvent.

18. **(a) :** Adsorption is the ability of a substance to concentrate or hold gases, liquids or dissolved substances upon its surface. Solids adsorb greater amounts of substances at lower temperature. In general, adsorption decreases with increase in temperature.

19. **(d) :** By adding electrolytes the colloidal particles are precipitated. The electrolytes neutralise the charge of colloids leading to their coagulation and thus destroy the colloid.

20. **(a) :** The soap conc. at which micelles (spherical colloid molecules) first appear is called as critical micellar concentration (CMC). At this condition the surfactant molecules associate with each other.

21. **(b) :** Both magnitude of charge and nature of charge effect coagulation of a given colloid. Greater the magnitude of the charge, quicker will be the coagulation.

22. **(b) :** Particle size lies in the range of 10^{-6} m to 10^{-9} m. Particles themselves are invisible even under the most powerful microscope.

23. **(c) :** Dialysis is the process of separating the particles of colloids from the particles of crystalloids by means of diffusion through a selective membrane placed in water.

24. **(b) :** According to Freundlich adsorption isotherm,

$$\log\left(\frac{x}{m}\right) = \log k + \left(\frac{1}{n}\right) \log P$$

Chapter 20 General Principles and Processes of Isolation of Elements

1. Considering Ellingham diagram, which of the following metals can be used to reduce alumina?
(a) Fe (b) Zn
(c) Mg (d) Cu
(NEET 2018)

2. Extraction of gold and silver involves leaching with CN^- ion. Silver is later recovered by
(a) distillation (b) zone refining
(c) displacement with Zn (d) liquation
(NEET 2017)

3. Match items of Column I with the items of Column II and assign the correct code :

Column I	Column II
(A) Cyanide process	(i) Ultrapure Ge
(B) Froth floatation process	(ii) Dressing of ZnS
(C) Electrolytic reduction	(iii) Extraction of Al
(D) Zone refining	(iv) Extraction of Au
	(v) Purification of Ni

Code :

	A	B	C	D
(a)	(i)	(ii)	(iii)	(iv)
(b)	(iii)	(iv)	(v)	(i)
(c)	(iv)	(ii)	(iii)	(i)
(d)	(ii)	(iii)	(i)	(v)

(NEET-I 2016)

4. In the extraction of copper from its sulphide ore, the metal is finally obtained by the reduction of cuprous oxide with
(a) carbon monoxide
(b) copper (I) sulphide
(c) sulphur dioxide
(d) iron (II) sulphide. *(2015, 2012)*

5. "Metals are usually not found as nitrates in their ores." Out of the following two (I and II) reasons which is/are true for the above observation?
I. Metal nitrates are highly unstable.
II. Metal nitrates are highly soluble in water.
(a) I is false but II is true.
(b) I is true but II is false.
(c) I and II are true.
(d) I and II are false *(2015, Cancelled)*

6. Roasting of sulphides gives the gas *X* as a byproduct. This is a colourless gas with choking smell of burnt sulphur and causes great damage to respiratory organs as a result of acid rain. Its aqueous solution is acidic, acts as a reducing agent and its acid has never been isolated.
The gas *X* is
(a) CO_2 (b) SO_3
(c) H_2S (d) SO_2
(NEET 2013)

7. The metal oxide which cannot be reduced to metal by carbon is
(a) Al_2O_3 (b) PbO
(c) ZnO (d) Fe_2O_3
(Karnataka NEET 2013)

8. Aluminium is extracted from alumina (Al_2O_3) by electrolysis of a molten mixture of
(a) $Al_2O_3 + HF + NaAlF_4$
(b) $Al_2O_3 + CaF_2 + NaAlF_4$
(c) $Al_2O_3 + Na_3AlF_6 + CaF_2$
(d) $Al_2O_3 + KF + Na_3AlF_6$ *(2012)*

9. Which one of the following is a mineral of iron?
(a) Malachite (b) Cassiterite
(c) Pyrolusite (d) Magnetite
(2012)

10. Which of the following elements is present as the impurity to the maximum extent in the pig iron?
(a) Manganese (b) Carbon
(c) Silicon (d) Phosphorus
(2011)

1. Which of the following pairs of metals is purified by van Arkel method?
(a) Ga and In (b) Zr and Ti
(c) Ag and Au (d) Ni and Fe
(2011)

2. The following reactions take place in the blast furnace in the preparation of impure iron. Identify the reaction pertaining to the formation of the slag.
(a) $Fe_2O_{3(s)} + 3CO_{(g)} \rightarrow 2Fe_{(l)} + 3CO_{2(g)}$
(b) $CaCO_{3(s)} \rightarrow CaO_{(s)} + CO_{2(g)}$
(c) $CaO_{(s)} + SiO_{2(s)} \rightarrow CaSiO_{3(s)}$
(d) $2C_{(s)} + O_{2(g)} \rightarrow 2CO_{(g)}$ *(Mains 2011)*

3. Sulphide ores of metals are usually concentrated by froth floatation process. Which one of the following sulphide ores offer an exception and is concentrated by chemical leaching?
(a) Galena (b) Copper pyrite
(c) Sphalerite (d) Argentite
(2007)

4. Which of the following statements, about the advantage of roasting of sulphide ore before reduction is not true?
(a) The ΔG_f° of the sulphide is greater than those for CS_2 and H_2S.
(b) The ΔG_f° is negative for roasting of sulphide ore to oxide.
(c) Roasting of the sulphide to the oxide is thermodynamically feasible.
(d) Carbon and hydrogen are suitable reducing agents for metal sulphides.
(2007)

15. The method of zone refining of metals is based on the principle of
(a) greater mobility of the pure metal than that of the impurity
(b) higher melting point of the impurity than that of the pure metal
(c) greater noble character of the solid metal than that of the impurity
(d) greater solubility of the impurity in the molten state than in the solid *(2003)*

16. Cassiterite is an ore of
(a) Sb (b) Ni
(c) Mn (d) Sn *(1999)*

17. Purification of aluminium, by electrolytic refining, is known as
(a) Hoope's process
(b) Bayer's process
(c) Hall's process
(d) Serpeck's process *(1999)*

18. Calcium is obtained by
(a) reduction of calcium chloride with carbon
(b) electrolysis of molten anhydrous calcium chloride
(c) roasting of limestone
(d) electrolysis of solution of calcium chloride in H_2O. *(1997)*

Answer Key

1.	(c)	**2.**	(c)	**3.**	(c)	**4.**	(b)	**5.**	(a)	**6.**	(d)	**7.**	(a)	**8.**	(c)	**9.**	(d)	**10.**	(b)
11.	(b)	**12.**	(c)	**13.**	(d)	**14.**	(d)	**15.**	(d)	**16.**	(d)	**17.**	(a)	**18.**	(b)				

EXPLANATIONS

1. **(c) :** Any metal oxide with lower value of $\Delta G°$ is more stable than a metal oxide with higher $\Delta G°$. This implies that the metal oxide placed higher in the diagram can be reduced by the metal involved in the formation of the oxide placed lower in the diagram.
The relative tendency of the various metals to act as reducing agents is : Ca > Mg > Al > Cr > Zn > Fe > Cu. Thus, Mg being more reducing in nature, can reduce aluminium oxide (alumina).

2. **(c) :** Extraction of gold and silver involves leaching the metal with CN^- and the metals silver and gold are later recovered by displacement method.

$$4M_{(s)} + 8CN^-_{(aq)} + 2H_2O_{(aq)} + O_{2(g)} \rightarrow 4[M(CN)_2]^-_{(aq)} + 4OH^-_{(aq)}$$

$$2[M(CN)_2]^-_{(aq)} + Zn_{(s)} \rightarrow 2M_{(s)} + [Zn(CN)_4]^{2-}_{(aq)}$$

3. **(c)**

4. **(b) :** It is an example of auto reduction.
$2Cu_2O + Cu_2S \rightarrow 6Cu + SO_2$

5. **(a) :** All nitrates are soluble in water and are quite stable as they do not decompose easily on heating.

6. **(d)**

7. **(a) :** Oxides of less reactive metals (like PbO, ZnO, Fe_2O_3) can be reduced by carbon. While oxides of very reactive metals (like Al_2O_3) can be reduced only by the electrolytic method.

8. **(c) :** Electrolytic mixture contains alumina (Al_2O_3), cryolite (Na_3AlF_6) and fluorspar (CaF_2) in the ratio of 20 : 40 : 20. Due to presence of these conductivity of alumina increases and fusion temperature decreases from 2000°C to 900°C.

9. **(d) :** Magnetite is Fe_3O_4 and contains upto 70% of the metal.

10. **(b) :** Pig iron contains about 4% carbon and many impurities such as Mn, P, Si, etc. in minor amount.

11. **(b) :** Van Arkel method is used for purification of Zr and Ti.

12. **(c) :** Slag is formed by the reaction
$CaO + SiO_2 \rightarrow CaSiO_3$

13. **(d) :** Leaching process involves the treatmen of the ore with a suitable reagent as to make i soluble while impurities remain insoluble. The or is recovered from the solution by suitable chemica method. Argentite or silver glance, Ag_2S is an or of silver. Silver is extracted from argentite by th Mac-Arthur and Forest cyanide process (leachin process).

$$Ag_2S + 4NaCN \rightarrow 2NaAg(CN)_2 + Na_2S$$
$$2NaAg(CN)_2 + Zn \rightarrow Na_2Zn(CN)_4 + 2Ag$$

14. **(d) :** The standard free energies of formatio ($\Delta G_f°$) of most of the sulphides are greater tha those of CS_2 and H_2S. Hence, neither carbon no hydrogen can reduce metal sulphides to metal. Th standard free energies of formation of oxides ar much lower than those of SO_2. Therefore, oxidatio of metal sulphides to metal oxides i thermodynamically favourable. Hence sulphide or is roasted to the oxide before reduction.

15. **(d) :** Elements which are used as semiconductor such as Si, Ge, Ga, etc. are refined by this method which is based on the difference in solubility o impurities in molten and solid state of the metal

16. **(d) :** Cassiterite is also called as Tin stone (SnO_2) an ore of tin (Sn).

17. **(a) :** Aluminium metal obtained from Hoope' electrolytic refining process is about 99.9% pure The cell used for this process consists of thre layers. The upper layer is pure 'Al', acts as cathode the middle layer is mixture of fluorides of Al an Ba, which acts as electrolyte. The lowest layer i impure 'Al', which acts as anode. On electrolysi Pure 'Al' is transferred from the bottom to the to layer, through the middle layer.

18. **(b) :** Calcium is obtained by the electrolysis o a fused mixture of anhydrous $CaCl_2$ and CaF_2 in graphite linked tank which serves as anode. Th cathode is a hollow movable iron rod which is kep cool. During electrolysis, calcium is deposited a cathode while Cl_2 is liberated at anode.

Chapter 21

p-Block Elements (Group 15 to 18)

1. Which of the following statements is not true for halogens?
   (a) All form monobasic oxyacids.
   (b) All are oxidizing agents.
   (c) All but fluorine show positive oxidation states.
   (d) Chlorine has the highest electron-gain enthalpy. *(NEET 2018)*

2. Match the interhalogen compounds of column-I with the geometry in column-II and assign the correct code.

Column I	Column II
(A) XX'	(i) T-shape
(B) XX'_3	(ii) Pentagonal bipyramidal
(C) XX'_5	(iii) Linear
(D) XX'_7	(iv) Square pyramidal
	(v) Tetrahedral

Code :

	A	B	C	D
(a)	(iii)	(i)	(iv)	(ii)
(b)	(v)	(iv)	(iii)	(ii)
(c)	(iv)	(iii)	(ii)	(i)
(d)	(iii)	(iv)	(i)	(ii)

(NEET 2017)

3. In which pair of ions both the species contain S — S bond?
   (a) $S_4O_6^{2-}, S_2O_3^{2-}$
   (b) $S_2O_7^{2-}, S_2O_8^{2-}$
   (c) $S_4O_6^{2-}, S_2O_7^{2-}$
   (d) $S_2O_7^{2-}, S_2O_3^{2-}$ *(NEET 2017)*

4. Match the compounds given in column I with the hybridisation and shape given in column II and mark the correct option.

Column I	Column II
(A) XeF_6	(i) distorted octahedral
(B) XeO_3	(ii) square planar
(C) $XeOF_4$	(iii) pyramidal
(D) XeF_4	(iv) square pyramidal

Code :

	A	B	C	D
(a)	(iv)	(iii)	(i)	(ii)
(b)	(iv)	(i)	(ii)	(iii)
(c)	(i)	(iii)	(iv)	(ii)
(d)	(i)	(ii)	(iv)	(iii)

(NEET-I 2016)

5. Which is the correct statement for the given acids?
   (a) Phosphinic acid is a monoprotic acid while phosphonic acid is a diprotic acid.
   (b) Phosphinic acid is a diprotic acid while phosphonic acid is a monoprotic acid.
   (c) Both are diprotic acids.
   (d) Both are triprotic acids. *(NEET-I 2016)*

6. Which one of the following orders is correct for the bond dissociation enthalpy of halogen molecules?
   (a) $Br_2 > I_2 > F_2 > Cl_2$
   (b) $F_2 > Cl_2 > Br_2 > I_2$
   (c) $I_2 > Br_2 > Cl_2 > F_2$
   (d) $Cl_2 > Br_2 > F_2 > I_2$ *(NEET-I 2016)*

7. When copper is heated with conc. HNO_3 it produces
   (a) $Cu(NO_3)_2$, NO and NO_2
   (b) $Cu(NO_3)_2$ and N_2O
   (c) $Cu(NO_3)_2$ and NO_2
   (d) $Cu(NO_3)_2$ and NO *(NEET-I 2016)*

8. Among the following, the correct order of acidity is
   (a) $HClO_2 < HClO < HClO_3 < HClO_4$
   (b) $HClO_4 < HClO_2 < HClO < HClO_3$
   (c) $HClO_3 < HClO_4 < HClO_2 < HClO$
   (d) $HClO < HClO_2 < HClO_3 < HClO_4$ *(NEET-I 2016)*

9. Strong reducing behaviour of H_3PO_2 is due to
   (a) high electron gain enthalpy of phosphorus
   (b) high oxidation state of phosphorus
   (c) presence of two –OH groups and one P—H bond
   (d) presence of one –OH group and two P—H bonds. *(2015)*

10. The variation of the boiling points of the hydrogen halides is in the order HF > HI > HBr > HCl.
What explains the higher boiling point of hydrogen fluoride?
(a) There is strong hydrogen bonding between HF molecules.
(b) The bond energy of HF molecules is greater than in other hydrogen halides.
(c) The effect of nuclear shielding is much reduced in fluorine which polarises the HF molecule.
(d) The electronegativity of fluorine is much higher than for other elements in the group.
(2015)

11. Which of the statements given below is incorrect?
(a) O_3 molecule is bent.
(b) ONF is isoelectronic with O_2N^-.
(c) OF_2 is an oxide of fluorine.
(d) Cl_2O_7 is an anhydride of perchloric acid.
(2015)

12. The formation of the oxide ion, $O^{2-}_{(g)}$ from oxygen atom requires first an exothermic and then an endothermic step as shown below :
$O_{(g)} + e^- \rightarrow O^-_{(g)}$; $\Delta_f H^\circ = -141$ kJ mol^{-1}
$O^-_{(g)} + e^- \rightarrow O^{2-}_{(g)}$; $\Delta_f H^\circ = +780$ kJ mol^{-1}
Thus, process of formation of O^{2-} in gas phase is unfavourable even though O^{2-} is isoelectronic with neon. It is due to the fact that,
(a) O^- ion has comparatively smaller size than oxygen atom
(b) oxygen is more electronegative
(c) addition of electron in oxygen results in larger size of the ion
(d) electron repulsion outweighs the stability gained by achieving noble gas configuration.
(2015)

13. Nitrogen dioxide and sulphur dioxide have some properties in common. Which property is shown by one of these compounds, but not by the other?
(a) Is soluble in water.
(b) Is used as a food preservative.
(c) Forms 'acid-rain'.
(d) Is a reducing agent. *(2015, Cancelled)*

14. Acidity of diprotic acids in aqueous solutions increases in the order
(a) $H_2S < H_2Se < H_2Te$
(b) $H_2Se < H_2S < H_2Te$
(c) $H_2Te < H_2S < H_2Se$
(d) $H_2Se < H_2Te < H_2S$ *(2014)*

15. Which is the strongest acid in the following?
(a) $HClO_4$ (b) H_2SO_3
(c) H_2SO_4 (d) $HClO_3$
(NEET 2013)

16. Which one of the following molecules contains no π bond?
(a) SO_2 (b) NO_2
(c) CO_2 (d) H_2O
(NEET 2013)

17. Which of the following does not give oxygen on heating?
(a) $K_2Cr_2O_7$ (b) $(NH_4)_2Cr_2O_7$
(c) $KClO_3$ (d) $Zn(ClO_3)_2$
(NEET 2013)

18. Identify the incorrect statement, regarding the molecule XeO_4 :
(a) XeO_4 molecule is square planar.
(b) There are four $p\pi$ - $d\pi$ bonds.
(c) There are four sp^3 - p, σ bonds.
(d) XeO_4 molecule is tetrahedral.
(Karnataka NEET 2013)

19. In which of the following compounds, nitrogen exhibits highest oxidation state?
(a) N_2H_4 (b) NH_3
(c) N_3H (d) NH_2OH
(2012)

20. Which of the following statements is not valid for oxoacids of phosphorus?
(a) Orthophosphoric acid is used in the manufacture of triple superphosphate.
(b) Hypophosphorous acid is a diprotic acid.
(c) All oxoacids contain tetrahedral four coordinated phosphorus.
(d) All oxoacids contain atleast one P═O unit and one P—OH group. *(2012)*

21. Sulphur trioxide can be obtained by which of the following reaction?
(a) $CaSO_4 + C \xrightarrow{\Delta}$
(b) $Fe_2(SO_4)_3 \xrightarrow{\Delta}$
(c) $S + H_2SO_4 \xrightarrow{\Delta}$
(d) $H_2SO_4 + PCl_5 \xrightarrow{\Delta}$ *(2012)*

22. In which of the following arrangements the given sequence is not strictly according to the property indicated against it?

(a) $HF < HCl < HBr < HI$: increasing acidic strength
(b) $H_2O < H_2S < H_2Se < H_2Te$: increasing pK_a values
(c) $NH_3 < PH_3 < AsH_3 < SbH_3$: increasing acidic character
(d) $CO_2 < SiO_2 < SnO_2 < PbO_2$: increasing oxidising power *(Mains 2012)*

23. Oxidation states of P in $H_4P_2O_5$, $H_4P_2O_6$, $H_4P_2O_7$ are respectively
(a) +3, +5, +4
(b) +5, +3, +4
(c) +5, +4, +3
(d) +3, +4, +5 *(2010)*

24. The correct order of increasing bond angles in the following species is
(a) $Cl_2O < ClO_2 < ClO_2^-$
(b) $ClO_2 < Cl_2O < ClO_2^-$
(c) $Cl_2O < ClO_2^- < ClO_2$
(d) $ClO_2^- < Cl_2O < ClO_2$ *(2010)*

25. How many bridging oxygen atoms are present in P_4O_{10}?
(a) 6
(b) 4
(c) 2
(d) 5 *(Mains 2010)*

26. Among the following which is the strongest oxidising agent?
(a) Br_2
(b) I_2
(c) Cl_2
(d) F_2 *(2009)*

27. The angular shape of ozone molecule (O_3) consists of
(a) 1σ and 1π bond
(b) 2σ and 1π bond
(c) 1σ and 2π bonds
(d) 2σ and 2π bonds *(2008)*

28. Which one of the following orders correctly represents the increasing acid strengths of the given acids?
(a) $HOClO < HOCl < HOClO_3 < HOClO_2$
(b) $HOClO_2 < HOClO_3 < HOClO < HOCl$
(c) $HOClO_3 < HOClO_2 < HOClO < HOCl$
(d) $HOCl < HOClO < HOClO_2 < HOClO_3$ *(2007, 2005)*

29. The electronegativity difference between N and F is greater than that between N and H yet the dipole moment of NH_3 (1.5 D) is larger than that of NF_3 (0.2 D). This is because
(a) in NH_3 the atomic dipole and bond dipole are in the opposite directions whereas in NF_3 these are in the same direction
(b) in NH_3 as well as in NF_3 the atomic dipole and bond dipole are in the same direction
(c) in NH_3 the atomic dipole and bond dipole are in the same direction whereas in NF_3 these are in opposite directions
(d) in NH_3 as well as in NF_3 the atomic dipole and bond dipole are in opposite directions. *(2006)*

30. Which one of the following orders is not in accordance with the property stated against it?
(a) $F_2 > Cl_2 > Br_2 > I_2$: Bond dissociation energy
(b) $F_2 > Cl_2 > Br_2 > I_2$: Oxidising power
(c) $HI > HBr > HCl > HF$: Acidic property in water
(d) $F_2 > Cl_2 > Br_2 > I_2$: Electronegativity. *(2006)*

31. In which of the following molecules are all the bonds are not equal?
(a) NF_3
(b) ClF_3
(c) BF_3
(d) AlF_3 *(2006)*

32. What is the correct relationship between the pH of isomolar solutions of sodium oxide, Na_2O (pH_1), sodium sulphide, Na_2S (pH_2), sodium selenide, Na_2Se (pH_3) and sodium telluride Na_2Te (pH_4)?
(a) $pH_1 > pH_2 > pH_3 > pH_4$
(b) $pH_1 > pH_2 \approx pH_3 > pH_4$
(c) $pH_1 < pH_2 < pH_3 < pH_4$
(d) $pH_1 < pH_2 < pH_3 \approx pH_4$ *(2005)*

33. Which one of the following oxides is expected to exhibit paramagnetic behaviour?
(a) CO_2
(b) SiO_2
(c) SO_2
(d) ClO_2 *(2005)*

34. Which of the following would have a permanent dipole moment?
(a) SiF_4
(b) SF_4
(c) XeF_4
(d) BF_3 *(2005)*

35. Among K, Ca, Fe and Zn, the element which can form more than one binary compound with chlorine is
(a) Fe
(b) Zn
(c) K
(d) Ca *(2004)*

36. Which of the following statement is true?
(a) Silicon exhibits 4 coordination number in its compound.
(b) Bond energy of F_2 is less than Cl_2.
(c) Mn(III) oxidation state is more stable than Mn(II) in aqueous state.
(d) Elements of 15th gp shows only + 3 and +5 oxidation states. *(2002)*

37. Which of the following order is wrong?
(a) $NH_3 < PH_3 < AsH_3$ – acidic
(b) $Li < Be < B < C$ – 1st IP
(c) $Al_2O_3 < MgO < Na_2O < K_2O$ – basic
(d) $Li^+ < Na^+ < K^+ < Cs^+$ – ionic radius. *(2002)*

38. Correct order of 1st ionisation potential among following elements Be, B, C, N, O is
(a) $B < Be < C < O < N$
(b) $B < Be < C < N < O$
(c) $Be < B < C < N < O$
(d) $Be < B < C < O < N$ *(2001)*

39. Which compound has planar structure?
(a) XeF_4 (b) $XeOF_2$
(c) XeO_2F_2 (d) XeO_4 *(2000)*

40. Which of the following oxides is most acidic?
(a) As_2O_5 (b) P_2O_5
(c) N_2O_5 (d) Sb_2O_5 *(1999)*

41. Which of the following phosphorus is the most reactive?
(a) Scarlet phosphorus
(b) White phosphorus
(c) Red phosphorus
(d) Violet phosphorus *(1999)*

42. Which of the following is used in the preparation of chlorine?
(a) Both MnO_2 and $KMnO_4$
(b) Only $KMnO_4$ (c) Only MnO_2
(d) Either MnO_2 or $KMnO_4$ *(1999)*

43. Repeated use of which one of the following fertilizers would increase the acidity of the soil?
(a) Ammonium sulphate
(b) Superphosphate of lime
(c) Urea
(d) Potassium nitrate *(1998)*

44. Which of the following has the highest dipole moment?
(a) SbH_3 (b) AsH_3
(c) NH_3 (d) PH_3 *(1997)*

45. The structural formula of hypophosphorous acid is

(a) 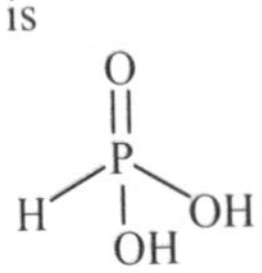

(b) 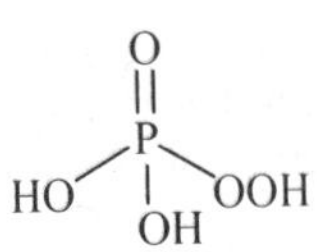

(c) 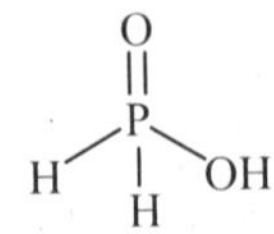

(d) None of these *(1997)*

46. Which of the following bonds has the highest energy?
(a) S–S (b) O–O
(c) Se–Se (d) Te–Te *(1996)*

47. The basic character of hydrides of the V group elements decreases in the order
(a) $NH_3 > PH_3 > AsH_3 > SbH_3$
(b) $SbH_3 > AsH_3 > PH_3 > NH_3$
(c) $SbH_3 > PH_3 > AsH_3 > NH_3$
(d) $NH_3 > SbH_3 > PH_3 > AsH_3$ *(1996)*

48. Among the following oxides, the lowest acidic is
(a) As_4O_6 (b) As_4O_{10}
(c) P_4O_6 (d) P_4O_{10} *(1996)*

49. Which of the following has the greatest electron affinity?
(a) I (b) Br
(c) F (d) Cl *(1996)*

50. Which of the following represents calcium chlorite?
(a) $Ca(ClO_3)_2$ (b) $Ca(ClO_2)_2$
(c) $CaClO_2$ (d) $Ca(ClO_4)_2$ *(1996)*

51. Reaction of sodium thiosulphate with iodine gives
(a) tetrathionate ion (b) sulphide ion
(c) sulphate ion (d) sulphite ion. *(1996)*

52. About 20 km above the earth, there is an ozone layer. Which one of the following statement about ozone and ozone layer is true?
(a) It is beneficial to us as it stops U.V. radiation
(b) Conversion of O_3 to O_2 is an endothermic reaction.
(c) Ozone has a triatomic linear molecule.
(d) It is harmful as it stops useful radiation *(199*

53. The electronic configuration of an element $1s^2\ 2s^2\ 2p^6\ 3s^2\ 3p^3$. What is the atomic number of the element, which is just below the above element in the periodic table?
(a) 36 (b) 49
(c) 33 (d) 34 *(199*

54. Which of the following oxides of nitrogen paramagnetic?

(a) NO_2 (b) N_2O_3
(c) N_2O (d) N_2O_5 *(1994)*

5. Which of the following displaces Br_2 from an aqueous solution containing bromide ions?
(a) I_2 (b) I_3^-
(c) Cl_2 (d) Cl^- *(1994)*

6. Which of the following fluorides does not exist?
(a) NF_5 (b) PF_5
(c) AsF_5 (d) SbF_5 *(1993)*

7. Which of the following species has four lone pairs of electrons?
(a) I (b) O
(c) Cl^- (d) He *(1993)*

8. Which of the following sets has strongest tendency to form anions?
(a) Ga, Ni, Tl (b) Na, Mg, Al
(c) N, O, F (d) V, Cr, Mn. *(1993)*

. A solution of potassium bromide is treated with each of the following. Which one would liberate bromine?
(a) Hydrogen iodide
(b) Sulphur dioxide
(c) Chlorine (d) Iodine *(1993)*

. Which of the following elements is extracted commercially by the electrolysis of an aqueous solution of its compound?
(a) Cl (b) Br
(c) Al (d) Na *(1993)*

. Number of electrons shared in the formation of nitrogen molecule is
(a) 6 (b) 10
(c) 2 (d) 8 *(1992)*

. Sugarcane on reaction with nitric acid gives
(a) CO_2 and SO_2
(b) $(COOH)_2$
(c) 2HCOOH(two moles)
(d) no reaction. *(1992)*

Nitrogen is relatively inactive element because
(a) its atom has a stable electronic configuration
(b) it has low atomic radius
(c) its electronegativity is fairly high
(d) dissociation energy of its molecule is fairly high. *(1992)*

H_3PO_2 is the molecular formula of an acid of phosphorus. Its name and basicity respectively are
(a) phosphorous acid and two
(b) hypophosphorous acid and two
(c) hypophosphorous acid and one
(d) hypophosphoric acid and two. *(1992)*

65. Which of the following bonds will be most polar?
(a) N – Cl (b) O – F
(c) N – F (d) N – N *(1992)*

66. Elements of which of the following groups will form anions most readily?
(a) Oxygen family (b) Nitrogen family
(c) Halogens (d) Alkali metals *(1992)*

67. Strongest hydrogen bonding is shown by
(a) water (b) ammonia
(c) hydrogen fluoride
(d) hydrogen sulphide. *(1992)*

68. When chlorine is passed over dry slaked lime at room temperature, the main reaction product is
(a) $Ca(ClO_2)_2$ (b) $CaCl_2$
(c) $CaOCl_2$ (d) $Ca(OCl)_2$ *(1992)*

69. In the manufacture of bromine from sea water, the mother liquor containing bromides is treated with
(a) carbon dioxide (b) chlorine
(c) iodine
(d) sulphur dioxide. *(1992)*

70. Which would quickly absorb oxygen?
(a) Alkaline solution of pyrogallol
(b) Conc. H_2SO_4
(c) Lime water
(d) Alkaline solution of $CuSO_4$. *(1991)*

71. Oleum is
(a) castor oil (b) oil of vitriol
(c) fuming H_2SO_4 (d) none of these. *(1991)*

72. Aqueous solution of ammonia consists of
(a) H^+ (b) OH^-
(c) NH_4^+ (d) NH_4^+ and OH^-. *(1991)*

73. P_2O_5 is heated with water to give
(a) hypophosphorous acid
(b) phosphorous acid
(c) hypophosphoric acid
(d) orthophosphoric acid. *(1991)*

74. Basicity of orthophosphoric acid is
(a) 2 (b) 3
(c) 4 (d) 5 *(1991)*

75. PCl_3 reacts with water to form
(a) PH_3 (b) H_3PO_3, HCl
(c) $POCl_3$ (d) H_3PO_4 *(1991)*

76. PH_4I + NaOH forms
(a) PH_3 (b) NH_3
(c) P_4O_6 (d) P_4O_{10} *(1991)*

77. Pure nitrogen is prepared in the laboratory by heating a mixture of
(a) NH_4OH + NaCl (b) NH_4NO_3 + NaCl
(c) NH_4Cl + NaOH (d) NH_4Cl + $NaNO_2$. *(1991)*

78. The bleaching action of chlorine is due to
(a) reduction (b) hydrogenation
(c) chlorination (d) oxidation. *(1991)*

79. Which of the following statement is not correct for nitrogen?
(a) Its electronegativity is very high.
(b) *d*-orbitals are available for bonding.
(c) It is a typical non-metal.
(d) Its molecular size is small. *(1990)*

80. Which of the following compound does not exist?
(a) NCl_5 (b) AsF_5
(c) $SbCl_5$ (d) PF_5 *(1989)*

81. Each of the following is true for white and red phosphorus except that they
(a) are both soluble in CS_2
(b) can be oxidised by heating in air
(c) consist of the same kind of atoms
(d) can be converted into one another. *(1989)*

82. When orthophosphoric acid is heated to 600°C, the product formed is
(a) PH_3 (b) P_2O_5
(c) H_3PO_3 (d) HPO_3 *(1989)*

83. Which one has the lowest boiling point?
(a) NH_3 (b) PH_3
(c) AsH_3 (d) SbH_3 *(1989*

84. Oxygen will directly react with each of th following elements except
(a) P (b) Cl
(c) Na (d) S *(1989*

85. The gases respectively absorbed by alkalin pyrogallol and oil of cinnamon are
(a) O_3, CH_4 (b) O_2, O_3
(c) SO_2, CH_4 (d) N_2O, O_3. *(198*

86. It is possible to obtain oxygen from air b fractional distillation because
(a) oxygen is in a different group of th periodic table from nitrogen
(b) oxygen is more reactive than nitrogen
(c) oxygen has higher b.p. than nitrogen
(d) oxygen has a lower density than nitroge *(198*

87. Bleaching powder reacts with a few drops conc. HCl to give
(a) chlorine
(b) hypochlorous acid
(c) calcium oxide
(d) oxygen. *(198*

88. Which of the following is a nitric acid anhydric
(a) NO (b) NO_2
(c) N_2O_5 (d) N_2O_3 *(198*

89. Bleaching powder is obtained by the action chlorine gas and
(a) dilute solution of $Ca(OH)_2$
(b) concentrated solution of $Ca(OH)_2$
(c) dry CaO
(d) dry slaked lime. *(198*

Answer Key

1. (c) **2.** (a) **3.** (a) **4.** (c) **5.** (a) **6.** (d) **7.** (c) **8.** (d) **9.** (d) **10.** (
11. (c) **12.** (d) **13.** (b) **14.** (a) **15.** (a) **16.** (d) **17.** (b) **18.** (a) **19.** (c) **20.** (
21. (b) **22.** (b) **23.** (d) **24.** (d) **25.** (a) **26.** (d) **27.** (b) **28.** (d) **29.** (c) **30.** (
31. (b) **32.** (a) **33.** (d) **34.** (b) **35.** (a) **36.** (b) **37.** (b) **38.** (a) **39.** (a) **40.** (
41. (b) **42.** (a) **43.** (a) **44.** (c) **45.** (c) **46.** (a) **47.** (a) **48.** (a) **49.** (d) **50.** (
51. (a) **52.** (a) **53.** (c) **54.** (a) **55.** (c) **56.** (a) **57.** (b) **58.** (c) **59.** (c) **60.** (
61. (a) **62.** (b) **63.** (d) **64.** (c) **65.** (c) **66.** (c) **67.** (c) **68.** (c) **69.** (b) **70.** (
71. (c) **72.** (d) **73.** (d) **74.** (b) **75.** (b) **76.** (a) **77.** (d) **78.** (d) **79.** (b) **80.** (
81. (a) **82.** (d) **83.** (b) **84.** (b) **85.** (b) **86.** (c) **87.** (a) **88.** (c) **89.** (d)

EXPLANATIONS

1. (c): All halogens show both positive and negative oxidation states while fluorine shows only negative oxidation state except +1 in HOF.

2. (a)

3. (a):

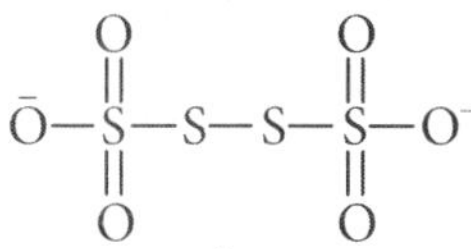

$(S_4O_6^{2-})$

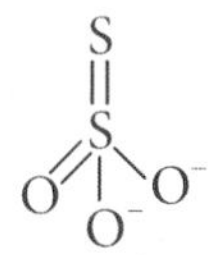

$(S_2O_3^{2-})$

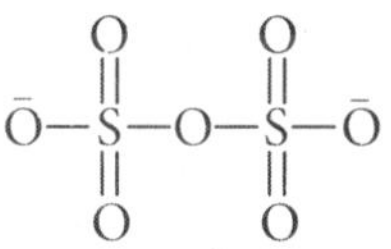

$(S_2O_7^{2-})$

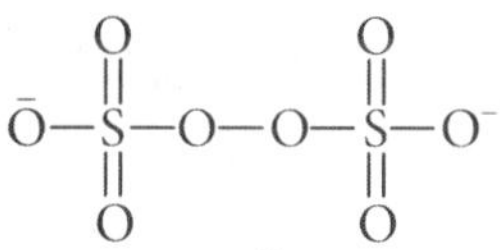

$(S_2O_8^{2-})$

4. (c) :

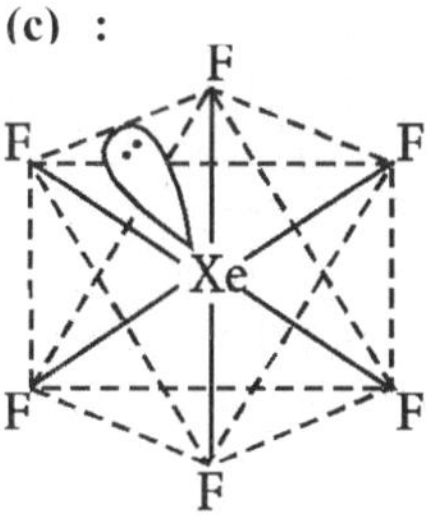

XeF_6
Distorted octahedral
sp^3d^3

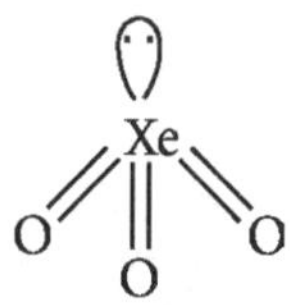

XeO_3
Pyramidal
sp^3

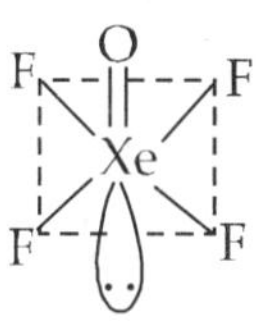

$XeOF_4$
Square pyramidal
sp^3d^2

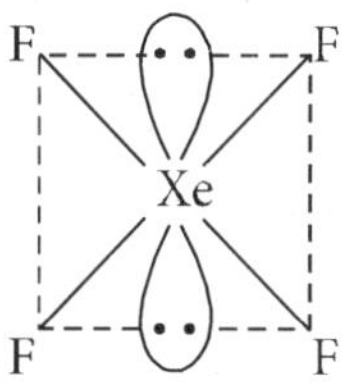

XeF_4
Square planar
sp^3d^2

5. (a) :

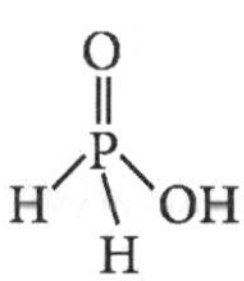

H_3PO_2
Hypophosphorous acid or Phosphinic acid (Monobasic)

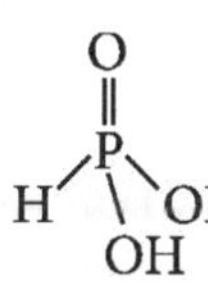

H_3PO_3
Orthophosphorous acid or Phosphonic acid (Dibasic)

6. (d): The order of bond dissociation enthalpy is :
$Cl_2 > Br_2 > F_2 > I_2$

7. (c): $Cu + 4HNO_3(conc.) \longrightarrow Cu(NO_3)_2 + 2NO_2 + 2H_2O$

8. (d): The acidic character of the oxoacids increases with increase in oxidation number of the halogen atom *i.e.*, $HClO < HClO_2 < HClO_3 < HClO_4$. This can be explained on the basis of relative stability of the anions left after removal of a proton. Since the stability of the anion decreases in the order : $ClO_4^- > ClO_3^- > ClO_2^- > ClO^-$, acid strength also decreases in the same order.

9. (d) : All oxyacids of phosphorus which have P—H bonds act as strong reducing agents. H_3PO_2 has two P—H bonds hence, it acts as a strong reducing agent.

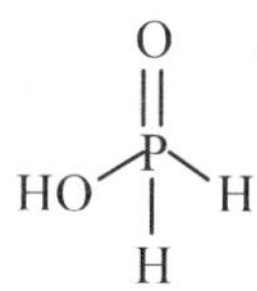

10. (a) : HF forms strong intermolecular H-bonding due to high electronegativity of F. Hence, the boiling point of HF is abnormally high. Boiling points of other hydrogen halides gradually increase from HCl to HI due to increase in size of halogen atoms from Cl to I which further increase the magnitude of van der Waals forces.

11. (c) : OF_2 (oxygen difluoride) is a fluoride of oxygen because fluorine is more electronegative than oxygen.

12. (d)

13. (b) : NO_2 is not used as a food preservative.

14. (a) : As the atomic size increases down the group, the bond length increases and the bond strength decreases and the cleavage of *E*–H bond becomes easier thus, more will be the acidity. Thus, the correct order is : $H_2S < H_2Se < H_2Te$.

15. (a): $H\overset{7}{\underline{Cl}}O_4$ with highest oxidation number and its conjugate base is resonance stabilised, hence it is most acidic. Cl is more electronegative than S.

16. (d): 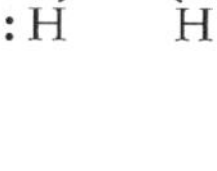

17. (b): $(NH_4)_2Cr_2O_7 \xrightarrow{\Delta} N_2 + Cr_2O_3 + 4H_2O$

$Zn(ClO_3)_2 \xrightarrow{\Delta} ZnCl_2 + 3O_2$

$KClO_3 \xrightarrow{\Delta} KCl + 3/2O_2$

$2K_2Cr_2O_7 \xrightarrow{\Delta} 2K_2CrO_4 + Cr_2O_3 + 3/2O_2$

18. (a): 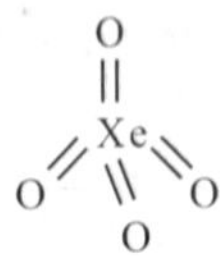

Tetrahedral (sp^3)

19. (c): $N_2H_4 \Rightarrow 2x + 4(+1) = 0 \Rightarrow 2x + 4 = 0$
$\Rightarrow x = -2$
$NH_3 \Rightarrow x + 3(+1) = 0 \Rightarrow x = -3$
$N_3H \Rightarrow 3x + 1(+1) = 0 \Rightarrow 3x + 1 = 0 \Rightarrow x = -1/3$
$NH_2OH \Rightarrow x + 2 + 1(-2) + 1 = 0 \Rightarrow x + 1 = 0$
$\Rightarrow x = -1$
Thus, highest oxidation state is –1/3.

20. (b): Hypophosphorous acid is a monoprotic acid.

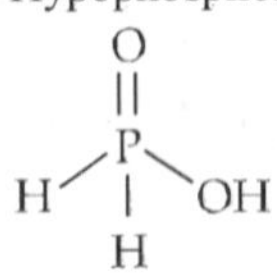

21. (b): $Fe_2(SO_4)_3 \xrightarrow{\Delta} Fe_2O_3 + 3SO_3$

22. (b): Acidic strength of hydrides increase with increase in molecular mass.
Thus order of acidic strength is

$HF < HCl < HBr < HI$
$H_2O < H_2S < H_2Se < H_2Te$
$NH_3 < PH_3 < AsH_3 < SbH_3$

And as acidic strength increases, pK_a decreases.
Thus order of pK_a

$H_2O > H_2S > H_2Se > H_2Te$

23. (d): The oxidation state can be calculated as :
$H_4P_2O_5: +4 + 2x + 5(-2) = 0 \Rightarrow 2x - 6 = 0 \Rightarrow x = +3$
$H_4P_2O_6: +4 + 2x + 6(-2) = 0 \Rightarrow 2x - 8 = 0 \Rightarrow x = +4$
$H_4P_2O_7: +4 + 2x + 7(-2) = 0 \Rightarrow 2x - 10 = 0 \Rightarrow 2x = 10$
$\Rightarrow x = +5$

24. (d)

25. (a): 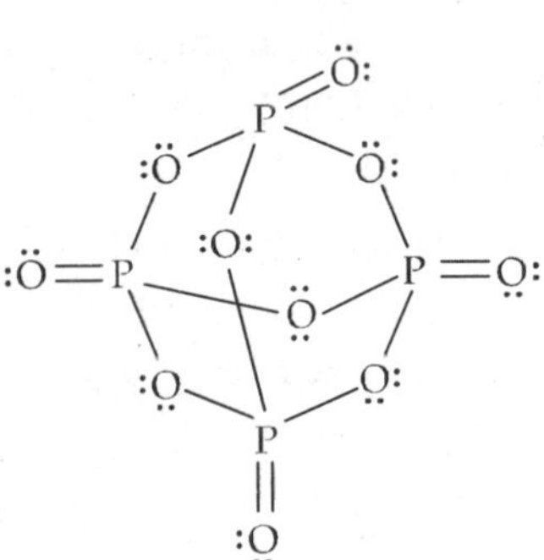

26. (d): Standard reduction potentials of halogens are positive and decrease from fluorine to iodine. So, F_2 is the strongest oxidising agent.

27. (b) : The angular shape of ozone molecule (O_3)

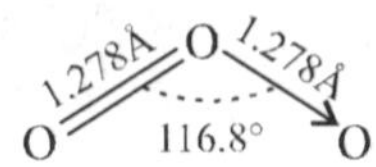

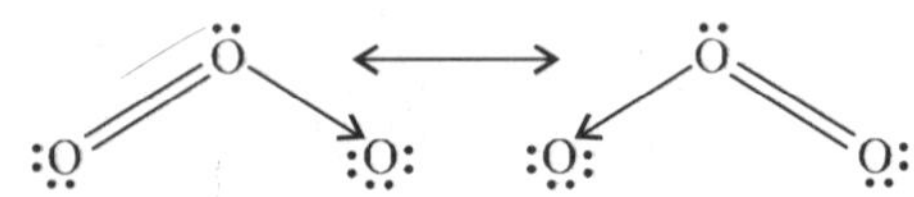

O_3 molecules can be represented by the following two lewis structures.

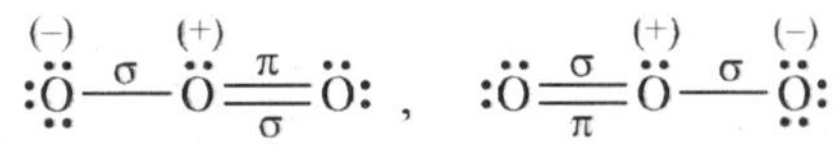

Structure I Structure II

28. (d): $\overset{+1}{HOCl} < \overset{+3}{HClO_2} < \overset{+5}{HClO_3} < \overset{+7}{HClO_4}$

As the number of oxygen atom increases, an increasing amount of electron density shifts from Cl atom to more electronegative O atom. Hence as the oxidation number of Cl atom increases, the amount of actual positive charge on Cl atom increases which in turn attracts the electron density from O – H bond, hence the O – H bond is weakened and proton is easily released and acidity increases.

29. (c) : The dipole moment of NF_3 is 0.24 D and of NH_3 is 1.48 D. The difference is due to fact that while the dipole moment due to N – F bonds in NF_3 are in opposite direction to the direction of the dipole moment of the lone pair on N atom which partly cancel out, the dipole moment of N – H bonds in NH_3 are in the same direction of the dipole moment of the lone pair on N atom which adds up as shown:

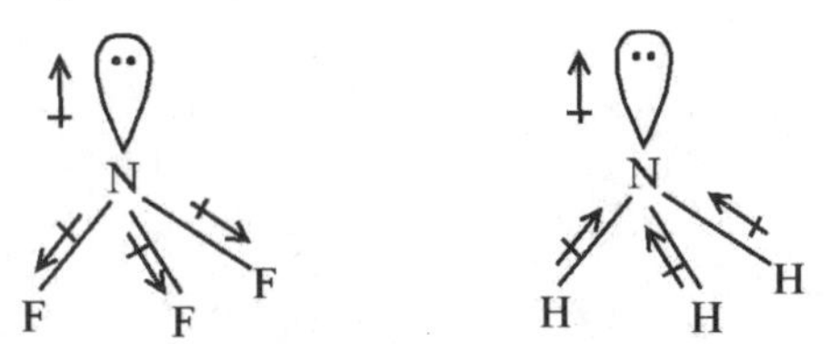

NF_3 (moments subtract) NH_3 (moments add)

30. (a) :

$X-X$ bond	F – F	Cl – Cl	Br – Br	I – I
Bond dissociation energy (kcal/mol)	38	57	45.5	35.6

The lower value of bond dissociation energy of fluorine is due to the high inter-electronic repulsions between non-bonding electrons in the 2*p*-orbitals of fluorine. As a result F – F bond is weaker in comparison to Cl – Cl and Br – Br bonds.

31. (b) : The Cl – F (Cl – F_{eq}) bond length is equal to 1.60 Å while each of the two axial Cl – F (Cl – F_a) bond length is equal to 1.70 Å.

32. (a) : Na_2O, Na_2S, Na_2Se, Na_2Te — basic character decreases down the group. Means Na_2O is most basic.

We know that more the basic compound more is the pH [pH ∝ basic character]

Hence $pH_1 > pH_2 > pH_3 > pH_4$

33. (d) : O=C=O diamagnetic O=Si=O diamagnetic

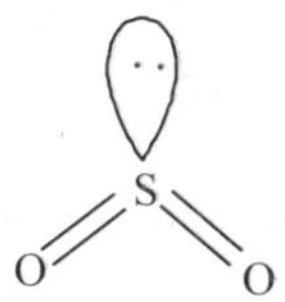

diamagnetic

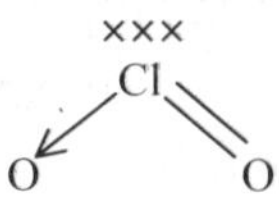

paramagnetic

34. (b) : For dipole moment, we have to know the hybridisation and shape.

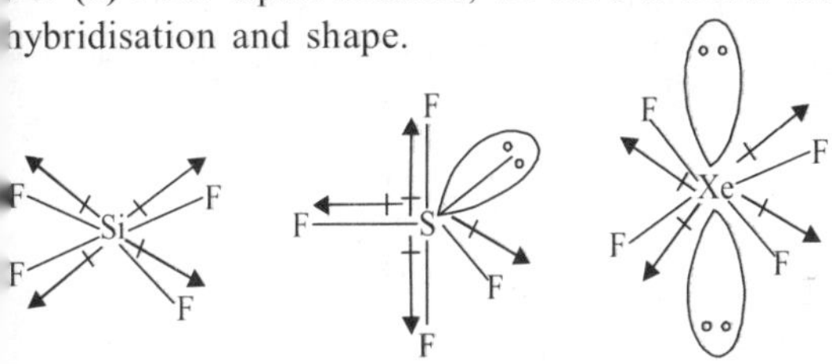

$\mu = 0$ $\mu \neq 0$ $\mu = 0$

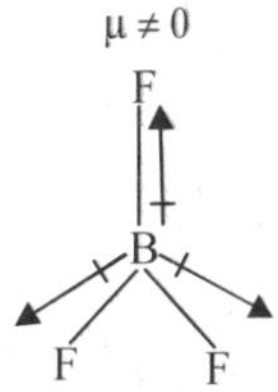

$\mu = 0$

35. (a) : A binary compound is one made of two different elements. These can be one of each element such as $CuCl_2$ or FeO. These can also be several of each element such as Fe_2O_3 or $SnBr_4$.

Metals which have variable oxidation number can form more than one type of binary compound like Fe shows the oxidation state +2 and +3. Hence it forms two types of binary compounds. *e.g.*, $FeCl_2$, $FeCl_3$.

36. (b) : Fluorine is more reactive than chlorine. So bond energy of chlorine is greater than fluorine.

Silicon exhibits 6 coordination number.

In aqueous state Mn(II) is more stable.

$$Mn \rightleftharpoons Mn^{2+} + 2e^-$$

37. (b) : Li, Be, B, C - these elements belong to the same period. Generally the value of 1st ionisation potential increases in moving from left to right in a period, since the nuclear charge of the elements also increase in the same direction. But the ionisation potential of boron ($B \rightarrow 2s^2 p^1$) is lower than that of beryllium ($Be \rightarrow 2s^2$), since in case of boron, $2p^1$ electron have to be removed to get B^+ [$B (2s^2 p^1) \rightarrow B^+ (2s^2) + e^-$], while in case of Be, $2s^2$ electron have to be removed to get Be^+ ($2s^1$). *p* electron can be removed more easily than *s* electron so the energy required to remove electron will be less in case of boron. The order will be

$$Li < B < Be < C.$$

38. (a) : The energy required to remove the most loosely bound electron from an isolated gaseous atom is called the ionisation energy.

The ionisation potential decreases as the size of the atom decreases. Atoms with fully or partly filled orbitals have high ionisation potential.

39. (a) : In XeF_4 the 'Xe' atom is sp^3d^2 hybridised, which contains two lone pair orbitals and four bond pair orbitals. Therefore the shape of XeF_4 molecule is square planar, with one lone pair orbital over and other below the plane.

40. (c) : As among N, P, As and Sb, the former has highest electronegativity (*EN*) so its oxide is most acidic.

As the electronegativity value of element increases, the acidic character of the oxide also increases.

41. (b) : White phosphorus has low ignition temperature so it is most reactive among all the allotropes.

42. (a) : $MnO_2 + 4HCl \rightarrow MnCl_2 + 2H_2O + Cl_2\uparrow$

$$2KMnO_4 + 16\,HCl \rightarrow 2KCl + 2MnCl_2 + 8H_2O + 5Cl_2\uparrow$$

43. (a) : Ammonium sulphate is a salt of strong acid (H_2SO_4) and weak base (NH_4OH). Therefore, repeated use of ammonium sulphate would increase the concentration of sulphuric acid, while ammonia from NH_4OH is used up by the plant. Hence the acidity of soil will increase.

44. (c) : Due to greater electronegativity of nitrogen, dipole moment for NH_3 is greater.

45. (c) : The formula of hypophosphorous acid is H_3PO_2 as shown in (c). It is monobasic acid.

46. (a):

B.E.	O – O	S – S	Se – Se	Te – Te
($kJmol^{-1}$) :	142	226	172	126

47. (a) : All the hydrides of group V elements have one lone pair of electrons on their central atom. Therefore, they can act as Lewis bases. The basic character of these hydrides decreases down the group.

48. (a) : The acidic character of the oxides decreases with the decrease in the oxidation state and also decreases down the group.

49. (d) : In general, the electron affinity decreases from top to bottom in a group. But in group 17, fluorine has lower electron affinity as compared to chlorine due to very small size of fluorine atom.

50. (b) : Since the valency of calcium is 2 and a chlorite ion is ClO_2^-, therefore calcium chlorite is $Ca(ClO_2)_2$.

51. (a) : $2Na_2S_2O_3 + I_2 \rightarrow Na_2S_4O_6 + 2\,NaI$.
(Sodium tetrathionate)

52. (a) : Ozone layer is very beneficial to us, because it stops harmful ultraviolet radiations to reach the earth.

53. (c) : Atomic number of the given element is 15 and it belongs to 5th group. Therefore atomic number of the element below the above element $= 15 + 18 = 33$.

54. (a) : NO_2 is paramagnetic due to the presence of unpaired electrons.

55. (c) : Since chlorine is more electronegative than bromine, therefore it will displace bromine from an aqueous solution containing bromide ions.

$$Cl_2 + 2Br^- \rightarrow 2Cl^- + Br_2$$

56. (a) : Except nitrogen and bismuth, all elements of fifth group form pentahalides especially pentafluorides. As mentioned earlier, nitrogen cannot form pentahalides because it cannot expand its octet due to non-availability of *d*-orbitals.

57. (b) : Outer electronic configuration of Cl $= 3s^2 3p_x^2 3p_y^2 3p_z^1$.

Outer electronic configuration of Cl^- $= 3s^2 3p_x^2 3p_y^2 3p_z^2$, *i.e.*, 4 lone pair of electrons.

58. (c) : N, O and F are highly electronegative non metals and will have the strongest tendency to form anions by gaining electrons from metal atoms.

59. (c) : A stronger oxidising agent (Cl_2) displaces a weaker oxidising agent (Br_2) from its salt solution.

$$2KBr + Cl_2 \rightarrow 2KCl + Br_2$$

60. (a) : Caustic soda is manufactured by the electrolysis of NaCl solution where Cl_2 is evolved at the anode and H_2 at the cathode.
At anode : $Cl^- \rightarrow Cl + e^-$, $Cl + Cl \rightarrow Cl_2 \uparrow$
At cathode : $Na^+ + e^- \rightarrow Na$.

61. (a) : Nitrogen molecule is diatomic containing a triple bond between two N atoms, $\ddot{N}{\equiv}\ddot{N}$. Therefore, nitrogen molecule is formed by sharing six electrons.

62. (b): $\underset{\text{Cane sugar}}{C_{12}H_{22}O_{11}} + \underset{\text{From } HNO_3}{18[O]} \longrightarrow \underset{\text{Oxalic acid}}{6(COOH)_2} + 5H_2O$

63. (d) : N_2 molecule contains triple bond between N atoms having very high dissociation energy ($946\ kJ\ mol^{-1}$) due to which it is relatively inactive.

64. (c) : H_3PO_2 is named as hypophosphorous acid. As it contains only one P–OH group, its basicity is one.

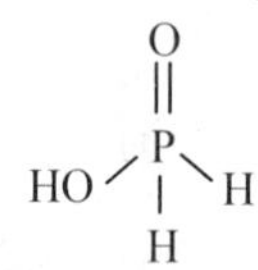

65. (c) : Polarity of the bond depends upon the electronegativity difference of the two atoms forming the bond. Greater the electronegativity difference more is the polarity of the bond.

N – Cl	O – F	N – F	N – N
3.04–3.16	3.5–4.0	3.04–4.0	3.04–3.04

66. (c) : As halogens have seven electrons (ns^2np^5) in the valence shell, they have a strong tendency to acquire the nearest inert gas configuration by gaining an electron from the metallic atom and form halide ions easily.

67. (c) : Fluorine because of its smaller size and highest electronegativity shows strongest hydrogen bonding.

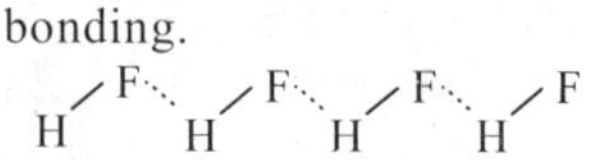

68. (c) : $Ca(OH)_2 + Cl_2 \rightarrow CaOCl_2 + H_2O$

69. (b) : Bromide in the mother liquor (containing $MgBr_2$) is oxidised to Br_2 by passing Cl_2 which is a stronger oxidising agent.

$$2Br^- + Cl_2 \rightarrow Br_2 + 2Cl^-$$

70. (a) : Alkaline solution of pyrogallol absorbs oxygen quickly.

1. (c) : Pyrosulphuric acid or oleum (+6) is $H_2S_2O_7$ vhich is obtained by dissolving SO_3 and is called uming sulphuric acid.

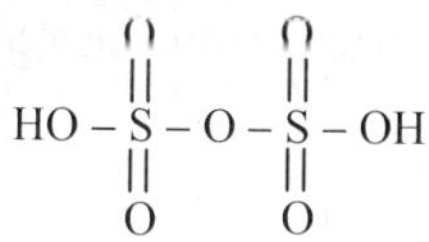

2. (d) : Aqueous solution of ammonia is obtained y passing NH_3 and OH^- ions.

$$NH_3 + H_2O \rightleftharpoons NH_4^+ + OH^-$$

3. (d) : $P_2O_5 + 3H_2O \xrightarrow{\Delta} 2H_3PO_4$

4. (b) : Orthophosphoric acid, H_3PO_4 contains ree P–OH groups and is therefore, tribasic.

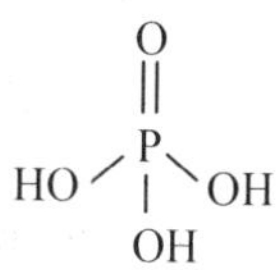

5. (b) : $PCl_3 + 3H_2O \rightarrow H_3PO_3 + 3HCl$

6. (a) : $PH_4I + NaOH \rightarrow NaI + PH_3 + H_2O$

7. (d) : $NH_4Cl + NaNO_2 \xrightarrow{Heat} NH_4NO_2 + NaCl$

$$NH_4NO_2 \xrightarrow{\Delta} N_2 + 2H_2O$$

8. (d) : Bleaching action of chlorine is due to idation in presence of moisture. It is permanent.

$$H_2O + Cl_2 \rightarrow 2HCl + [O]$$

olouring matter + [O] → colourless matter

). (b) : In case of nitrogen, *d*-orbitals are not ailable. Nitrogen belongs to *p*-block elements.

N : $1s^2\ 2s^2\ 2p^3$

. (a) : All the elements of group 15 form trihalides d pentahalides of the type MX_3 and MX_5 except trogen which forms only trihalides. Moreover, trogen does not form pentahalides due to the sence of *d*-orbitals in its valence shell.

. (a) : Red phosphorus is insoluble in CS_2 and ly white P is soluble in CS_2.

82. (d) : On heating, it gives pyrophosphoric acid at 525 K and metaphosphoric acid at 875 K.

$$2H_3PO_4 \xrightarrow[-H_2O]{525\ K} \underset{\text{Pyrophosphoric acid}}{H_4P_2O_7} \xrightarrow[-H_2O]{875\ K} \underset{\text{Metaphosphoric acid}}{2HPO_3}$$

83. (b) : Due to the absence of H-bonding, PH_3 has the lowest b.p. The boiling point of the V group hydrides is :

$$BiH_3 > SbH_3 > NH_3 > AsH_3 > PH_3$$

84. (b) : Chlorine does not react directly with oxygen.

85. (b) : Alkaline pyrogallol absorbs O_2 and oil of cinnamon absorbs O_3.

86. (c) : Air is liquefied by making use of the Joule - Thompson effect (cooling by expansion of the gas). Water vapour and CO_2 are removed by solidification. The remaining constituents of liquid air *i.e.*, liquid oxygen and liquid nitrogen are separated by means of fractional distillation (b.p. of O_2 = –183°C : b.p. of N_2 = –195.8°C).

87. (a) : $CaOCl_2 + 2HCl \rightarrow CaCl_2 + H_2O + Cl_2$. The liberated Cl_2 gives the disinfectant nature to bleaching powder.

$Cl_2 + H_2O \rightarrow HCl + HOCl$ (Kill germs)

88. (c) : When 2-molecules of nitric acid undergoes heating, loose a water molecule to form an anhydride.

$$\begin{matrix} HO \cdot NO_2 \\ HO \cdot NO_2 \end{matrix} \xrightarrow{\Delta} N_2O_5 + H_2O$$

Thus, N_2O_5 is nitric acid anhydride.

89. (d) : Cl_2 gas reacts with dry slaked lime, $Ca(OH_2)$ to give bleaching powder.

$Ca(OH)_2 + Cl_2 \xrightarrow{\Delta} CaOCl_2 + H_2O$

Chapter 22

d- and f-Block Elements

1. Which one of the following ions exhibits *d-d* transition and paramagnetism as well?

(a) CrO_4^{2-} (b) $Cr_2O_7^{2-}$

(c) MnO_4^- (d) MnO_4^{2-}

(NEET 2018)

2. Match the metal ions given in Column I with the spin magnetic moments of the ions given in Column II and assign the correct code :

Column-I	Column-II
A. Co^{3+}	(i) $\sqrt{8}$ B.M.
B. Cr^{3+}	(ii) $\sqrt{35}$ B.M.
C. Fe^{3+}	(iii) $\sqrt{3}$ B.M.
D. Ni^{2+}	(iv) $\sqrt{24}$ B.M.
	(v) $\sqrt{15}$ B.M.

	A	B	C	D
(a)	(iv)	(v)	(ii)	(i)
(b)	(i)	(ii)	(iii)	(iv)
(c)	(iv)	(i)	(ii)	(iii)
(d)	(iii)	(v)	(i)	(ii)

(NEET 2018)

3. Name the gas that can readily decolourise acidified $KMnO_4$ solution.

(a) SO_2 (b) NO_2

(c) P_2O_5 (d) CO_2

(NEET 2017)

4. $HgCl_2$ and I_2 both when dissolved in water containing I^- ions, the pair of species formed is

(a) HgI_2, I^- (b) HgI_4^{2-}, I_3^-

(c) Hg_2I_2, I^- (d) HgI_2, I_3^-

(NEET 2017)

5. The reason for greater range of oxidation states in actinoids is attributed to

(a) actinoid contraction

(b) 5*f*, 6*d* and 7*s* levels having comparable energies

(c) 4*f* and 5*d* levels being close in energies

(d) the radioactive nature of actinoids.

(NEET 2017)

6. Which one of the following statements related to lanthanons is incorrect?

(a) Europium shows +2 oxidation state.

(b) The basicity decreases as the ionic radius decreases from Pr to Lu.

(c) All the lanthanons are much more reactive than aluminium.

(d) Ce(+4) solutions are widely used as oxidizing agent in volumetric analysis.

(NEET-II 2016)

7. Which one of the following statements is correct when SO_2 is passed through acidified $K_2Cr_2O_7$ solution?

(a) SO_2 is reduced.

(b) Green $Cr_2(SO_4)_3$ is formed.

(c) The solution turns blue.

(d) The solution is decolourised.

(NEET-I 2016)

8. The electronic configurations of Eu (Atomic No. 63), Gd (Atomic No. 64) and Tb (Atomic No. 65) are

(a) $[Xe]4f^6 5d^1 6s^2$, $[Xe]4f^7 5d^1 6s^2$ and $[Xe]4f^8 5d^1 6s^2$

(b) $[Xe]4f^7 6s^2$, $[Xe]4f^7 5d^1 6s^2$ and $[Xe]4f^9 6s^2$

(c) $[Xe]4f^7 6s^2$, $[Xe]4f^8 6s^2$ and $[Xe]4f^8 5d^1 6s^2$

(d) $[Xe]4f^6 5d^1 6s^2$, $[Xe]4f^7 5d^1 6s^2$ and $[Xe]4f^9 6s^2$

(NEET-I 2016)

9. Gadolinium belongs to 4*f* series. Its atomic number is 64. Which of the following is the correct electronic configuration of gadolinium?

(a) $[Xe]\,4f^9 5s^1$ (b) $[Xe]\,4f^7 5d^1 6s^2$

(c) $[Xe]\,4f^6 5d^2 6s^2$ (d) $[Xe]\,4f^8 6d^2$

(2015)

10. Assuming complete ionisation, same moles of which of the following compounds will require the least amount of acidified $KMnO_4$ for complete oxidation?

(a) $FeSO_3$ (b) FeC_2O_4

(c) $Fe(NO_2)_2$ (d) $FeSO_4$ *(2015)*

11. Magnetic moment 2.84 B.M. is given by (At. nos. Ni = 28, Ti = 22, Cr = 24, Co = 27)

(a) Cr^{2+} (b) Co^{2+}

(c) Ni^{2+} (d) Ti^{3+}

(2015, Cancelled)

12. Which of the following processes does not involve oxidation of iron?
(a) Formation of $Fe(CO)_5$ from Fe.
(b) Liberation of H_2 from steam by iron at high temperature.
(c) Rusting of iron sheets.
(d) Decolourisation of blue $CuSO_4$ solution by iron. *(2015, Cancelled)*

13. Because of lanthanoid contraction, which of the following pairs of elements have nearly same atomic radii? (Numbers in the parenthesis are atomic numbers)
(a) Zr(40) and Hf(72) (b) Zr(40) and Ta(73)
(c) Ti(22) and Zr(40) (d) Zr(40) and Nb(41) *(2015, Cancelled)*

14. The reaction of aqueous $KMnO_4$ with H_2O_2 in acidic conditions gives
(a) Mn^{4+} and O_2 (b) Mn^{2+} and O_2
(c) Mn^{2+} and O_3 (d) Mn^{4+} and MnO_2. *(2014)*

15. Magnetic moment 2.83 BM is given by which of the following ions?
(At. nos. Ti = 22, Cr = 24, Mn = 25, Ni = 28)
(a) Ti^{3+} (b) Ni^{2+}
(c) Cr^{3+} (d) Mn^{2+} *(2014)*

16. Reason of lanthanoid contraction is
(a) negligible screening effect of '*f*'-orbitals
(b) increasing nuclear charge
(c) decreasing nuclear charge
(d) decreasing screening effect. *(2014)*

17. Which of the following statements about the interstitial compounds is incorrect?
(a) They are much harder than the pure metal.
(b) They have higher melting points than the pure metal.
(c) They retain metallic conductivity.
(d) They are chemically reactive. *(NEET 2013)*

18. Which of the following lanthanoid ions is diamagnetic?
(At. nos. Ce = 58, Sm = 62, Eu = 63, Yb = 70)
(a) Eu^{2+} (b) Yb^{2+}
(c) Ce^{2+} (d) Sm^{2+} *(NEET 2013)*

19. Identify the correct order of solubility in aqueous medium.
(a) $Na_2S > CuS > ZnS$
(b) $Na_2S > ZnS > CuS$
(c) $CuS > ZnS > Na_2S$
(d) $ZnS > Na_2S > CuS$ *(NEET 2013)*

20. Sc (Z = 21) is a transition element but Zn (Z = 30) is not because
(a) both Sc^{3+} and Zn^{2+} ions are colourless and form white compounds.
(b) in case of Sc, 3*d* orbitals are partially filled but in Zn these are filled.
(c) last electron is assumed to be added to 4*s* level in case of Zn.
(d) both Sc and Zn do not exhibit variable oxidation states. *(Karnataka NEET 2013)*

21. Identify the alloy containing a non-metal as a constituent in it.
(a) Invar (b) Steel
(c) Bell metal (d) Bronze *(2012)*

22. Which of the statements is not true?
(a) On passing H_2S through acidified $K_2Cr_2O_7$ solution, a milky colour is observed.
(b) $Na_2Cr_2O_7$ is preferred over $K_2Cr_2O_7$ in volumetric analysis.
(c) $K_2Cr_2O_7$ solution in acidic medium is orange.
(d) $K_2Cr_2O_7$ solution becomes yellow on increasing the pH beyond 7. *(2012)*

23. The catalytic activity of transition metals and their compounds is ascribed mainly to
(a) their magnetic behaviour
(b) their unfilled *d*-orbitals
(c) their ability to adopt variable oxidation states
(d) their chemical reactivity *(Mains 2012)*

24. Which of the following exhibits only + 3 oxidation state?
(a) U (b) Th
(c) Ac (d) Pa *(Mains 2012)*

25. Which one of the following does not correctly represent the correct order of the property indicated against it?
(a) Ti < V < Cr < Mn; increasing number of oxidation states
(b) $Ti^{3+} < V^{3+} < Cr^{3+} < Mn^{3+}$: increasing magnetic moment
(c) Ti < V < Cr < Mn : increasing melting points
(d) Ti < V < Mn < Cr : increasing 2nd ionization enthalpy *(Mains 2012)*

26. Four successive members of the first series of the transition metals are listed below. For which one of them the standard potential ($E^\circ_{M^{2+}/M}$) value has a positive sign?

(a) Co ($Z = 27$) (b) Ni ($Z = 28$)
(c) Cu ($Z = 29$) (d) Fe ($Z = 26$)
(Mains 2012)

27. For the four successive transition elements (Cr, Mn, Fe and Co), the stability of +2 oxidation state will be there in which of the following order?
(a) Mn > Fe > Cr > Co
(b) Fe > Mn > Co > Cr
(c) Co > Mn > Fe > Cr
(d) Cr > Mn > Co > Fe
(At. nos. Cr = 24, Mn = 25, Fe = 26, Co = 27)
(2011)

28. Acidified $K_2Cr_2O_7$ solution turns green when Na_2SO_3 is added to it. This is due to the formation of
(a) $Cr_2(SO_4)_3$ (b) CrO_4^{2-}
(c) $Cr_2(SO_3)_3$ (d) $CrSO_4$ *(2011)*

29. Which of the following ions will exhibit colour in aqueous solutions?
(a) La^{3+} ($Z = 57$) (b) Ti^{3+} ($Z = 22$)
(c) Lu^{3+} ($Z = 71$) (d) Sc^{3+} ($Z = 21$)
(2010)

30. Which of the following ions has electronic configuration $[Ar]3d^6$?
(a) Ni^{3+} (b) Mn^{3+}
(c) Fe^{3+} (d) Co^{3+}
(At. nos. Mn = 25, Fe = 26, Co = 27, Ni = 28)
(2010)

31. Which of the following pairs has the same size?
(a) Fe^{2+}, Ni^{2+} (b) Zr^{4+}, Ti^{4+}
(c) Zr^{4+}, Hf^{4+} (d) Zn^{2+}, Hf^{4+}
(2010)

32. Match List I (substances) with List II (processes) employed in the manufacture of the substances and select the correct option.

List I (Substances)	List II (Processes)
(A) Sulphuric acid	(i) Haber's process
(B) Steel	(ii) Bessemer's process
(C) Sodium hydroxide	(iii) Leblanc process
(D) Ammonia	(iv) Contact process

(a) A - (i), B - (iv), C - (ii), D - (iii)
(b) A - (i), B - (ii), C - (iii), D - (iv)
(c) A - (iv), B - (iii), C - (ii), D - (i)
(d) A - (iv), B - (ii), C - (iii), D - (i)
(Mains 2010)

33. Which of the following oxidation states is the most common among the lanthanoids?
(a) 4 (b) 2
(c) 5 (d) 3 *(Mains 2010)*

34. Which one of the elements with the following outer orbital configurations may exhibit the largest number of oxidation states?
(a) $3d^54s^1$ (b) $3d^54s^2$
(c) $3d^24s^2$ (d) $3d^34s^2$ *(2009)*

35. The correct order of decreasing second ionisation enthalpy of Ti(22), V(23), Cr(24) and Mn(25) is
(a) Mn > Cr > Ti > V (b) Ti > V > Cr > Mn
(c) Cr > Mn > V > Ti (d) V > Mn > Cr > Ti
(2008)

36. Which one of the following ions is the most stable in aqueous solution?
(At. No. Ti = 22, V = 23, Cr = 24, Mn = 25)
(a) V^{3+} (b) Ti^{3+}
(c) Mn^{3+} (d) Cr^{3+} *(2007)*

37. Identify the incorrect statement among the following:
(a) Lanthanoid contraction is the accumulation of successive shrinkages.
(b) As a result of lanthanoid contraction, the properties of 4*d* series of the transition elements have no similarities with the 5*d* series of elements.
(c) Shielding power of 4*f* electrons is quite weak.
(d) There is a decrease in the radii of the atoms or ions as one proceeds from La to Lu.
(2007)

38. In which of the following pairs are both the ions coloured in aqueous solution?
(At. no. : Sc = 21, Ti = 22, Ni = 28, Cu = 29, Co = 27)
(a) Ni^{2+}, Cu^{+} (b) Ni^{2+}, Ti^{3+}
(c) Sc^{3+}, Ti^{3+} (d) Sc^{3+}, Co^{2+}.
(2006)

39. Copper sulphate dissolves in excess of KCN to give
(a) $Cu(CN)_2$ (b) CuCN
(c) $[Cu(CN)_4]^{3-}$ (d) $[Cu(CN)_4]^{2-}$
(2006)

40. More number of oxidation states are exhibited by the actinoids than by the lanthanoids. The main reason for this is

(a) more active nature of the actinoids
(b) more energy difference between $5f$ and $6d$ orbitals than that between $4f$ and $5d$ orbitals
(c) lesser energy difference between $5f$ and $6d$ orbitals than that between $4f$ and $5d$ orbitals
(d) greater metallic character of the lanthanoids than that of the corresponding actinoids. *(2006, 2005)*

1. The number of moles of $KMnO_4$ reduced by one mole of KI in alkaline medium is
(a) one (b) two
(c) five (d) one fifth. *(2005)*

2. Four successive members of the first row transition elements are listed below with their atomic numbers. Which one of them is expected to have the highest third ionisation enthalpy?
(a) Vanadium ($Z = 23$)
(b) Chromium ($Z = 24$)
(c) Manganese ($Z = 25$)
(d) Iron ($Z = 26$) *(2005)*

3. The aqueous solution containing which one of the following ions will be colourless? (Atomic number : Sc = 21, Fe = 26, Ti = 22, Mn = 25)
(a) Sc^{3+} (b) Fe^{2+}
(c) Ti^{3+} (d) Mn^{2+} *(2005)*

4. Among the following series of transition metal ions, the one where all metal ions have $3d^2$ electronic configuration is [At. nos. Ti = 22, V = 23, Cr = 24, Mn = 25]
(a) Ti^{3+}, V^{2+}, Cr^{3+}, Mn^{4+}
(b) Ti^{+}, V^{4+}, Cr^{6+}, Mn^{7+}
(c) Ti^{4+}, V^{3+}, Cr^{2+}, Mn^{3+}
(d) Ti^{2+}, V^{3+}, Cr^{4+}, Mn^{5+} *(2004)*

5. Lanthanoids are
(a) 14 elements in the sixth period (atomic no. 90 to 103) that are filling $4f$ sublevel
(b) 14 elements in the seventh period (atomic number = 90 to 103) that are filling $5f$ sublevel
(c) 14 elements in the sixth period (atomic number = 58 to 71) that are filling the $4f$ sublevel
(d) 14 elements in the seventh period (atomic number = 50 to 71) that are filling $4f$ sublevel. *(2004)*

6. Which one of the following characteristics of the transition metals is associated with their catalytic activity?
(a) High enthalpy of atomization
(b) Paramagnetic behaviour
(c) Colour of hydrated ions
(d) Variable oxidation states *(2003)*

47. The basic character of the transition metal monoxides follows the order (Atomic no's. Ti = 22, V = 23, Cr = 24, Fe = 26)
(a) VO > CrO > TiO > FeO
(b) CrO > VO > FeO > TiO
(c) TiO > FeO > VO > CrO
(d) TiO > VO > CrO > FeO *(2003)*

48. The correct order of ionic radii of Y^{3+}, La^{3+}, Eu^{3+} and Lu^{3+} is (Atomic nos. Y = 39, La = 57, Eu = 63, Lu = 71)
(a) $Y^{3+} < La^{3+} < Eu^{3+} < Lu^{3+}$
(b) $Y^{3+} < Lu^{3+} < Eu^{3+} < La^{3+}$
(c) $Lu^{3+} < Eu^{3+} < La^{3+} < Y^{3+}$
(d) $La^{3+} < Eu^{3+} < Lu^{3+} < Y^{3+}$ *(2003)*

49. General electronic configuration of lanthanides is
(a) $(n-2)f^{1-14}(n-1)s^2p^6d^{0-1}ns^2$
(b) $(n-2)f^{10-14}(n-1)d^{0-1}ns^2$
(c) $(n-2)f^{0-14}(n-1)d^{10}ns^2$
(d) $(n-2)d^{0-1}(n-1)f^{1-14}ns^2$ *(2002)*

50. An atom has electronic configuration $1s^2\,2s^2\,2p^6\,3s^2\,3p^6\,3d^3\,4s^2$, you will place it in
(a) fifth (b) fifteenth
(c) second (d) third. *(2002)*

51. Which of the following shows maximum number of oxidation states?
(a) Cr (b) Fe
(c) Mn (d) V
(2002, 2000, 1994)

52. Zn gives H_2 gas with H_2SO_4 and HCl but not with HNO_3 because
(a) Zn act as oxidising agent when react with HNO_3
(b) HNO_3 is weaker acid than H_2SO_4 and HCl
(c) In electrochemical series Zn is above hydrogen
(d) $NO_3^{\ominus}$ is reduced in preference to hydronium ion. *(2002)*

53. Which of the following statement is not correct?
(a) $La(OH)_3$ is less basic than $Lu(OH)_3$.
(b) In lanthanide series ionic radius of Lu^{+3} ion decreases.
(c) La is actually an element of transition series rather lanthanides.
(d) Atomic radius of Zn and Hf are same because of lanthanide contraction.
(2001)

54. The most convenient method to protect the bottom of ship made of iron is

(a) coating it with red lead oxide
(b) white tin plating
(c) connecting it with Mg block
(d) connecting it with Pb block. *(2001)*

55. Which ion is colourless?
(a) Cr^{4+} (b) Sc^{3+}
(c) Ti^{3+} (d) V^{3+} *(2000)*

56. Which of the following configuration is correct for iron?
(a) $1s^2 2s^2 2p^6 3s^2 3p^6 4s^2 3d^7$
(b) $1s^2 2s^2 2p^6 3s^2 3p^6 4s^2 3d^5$
(c) $1s^2 2s^2 2p^6 3s^2 3p^6 3d^5$
(d) $1s^2 2s^2 2p^6 3s^2 3p^6 4s^2 3d^6$ *(1999)*

57. Which of the following has more unpaired *d*-electrons?
(a) N^{3+} (b) Fe^{2+}
(c) Zn^+ (d) Cu^+ *(1999)*

58. Bell metal is an alloy of
(a) Cu + Zn (b) Cu + Sn
(c) Cu + Pb (d) Cu + Ni *(1999)*

59. In which of the following compounds transition metal has zero oxidation state?
(a) $NOClO_4$ (b) $NH_2.NH_2$
(c) CrO_5 (d) $[Fe(CO)_5]$ *(1999)*

60. Which one of the following elements constitutes a major impurity in pig iron?
(a) Sulphur (b) Oxygen
(c) Silicon (d) Carbon *(1998)*

61. Which one of the following ionic species will impart colour to an aqueous solution?
(a) Zn^{2+} (b) Cu^+
(c) Ti^{4+} (d) Cr^{3+} *(1998)*

62. Which one of the following elements shows maximum number of different oxidation states in its compounds?
(a) Gd (b) La
(c) Eu (d) Am *(1998)*

63. Without losing its concentration, $ZnCl_2$ solution cannot be kept in contact with
(a) Pb (b) Al
(c) Au (d) Ag *(1998)*

64. Which of the following does not represent the correct order of the property indicated?
(a) $Mn^{2+} > Ni^{2+} < Co^{2+} < Fe^{2+}$
(b) $Fe^{2+} > Co^{2+} > Ni^{2+} > Cu^{2+}$
(c) $Ni^{2+} > Cr^{2+} > Fe^{2+} > Mn^{2+}$
(d) Se > Ti > Cr > Mn *(1997)*

65. The lanthanide contraction is responsible for the fact that
(a) Zr and Hf have about the same radius
(b) Zr and Zn have the same oxidation state
(c) Zr and Y have about the same radius
(d) Zr and Nb have similar oxidation state. *(1997)*

66. Which of the following element is responsible for oxidation of water to O_2 in biological processes?
(a) Cu (b) Mo
(c) Fe (d) Mn *(1997)*

67. The electronic configuration of gadolinium (Atomic No. = 64) is
(a) $[Xe]\ 4f^3\ 5d^5\ 6s^2$ (b) $[Xe]\ 4f^6\ 5d^2\ 6d^2$
(c) $[Xe\ 4f^8\ 5d^9\ 6s^2$ (d) $[Xe]\ 4f^7\ 5d^1\ 6s^2$ *(1997)*

68. $K_2Cr_2O_7$ on heating with aqueous NaOH gives
(a) $Cr_2O_7^{2-}$ (b) $Cr(OH)_2$
(c) CrO_4^{2-} (d) $Cr(OH)_3$ *(1997)*

69. A transition element *X* has a configuration $[Ar]3d^4$ in its +3 oxidation state. Its atomic number is
(a) 22 (b) 19
(c) 25 (d) 26 *(1996)*

70. When calomel reacts with NH_4OH, we get
(a) Hg_2O (b) HgO
(c) $HgNH_2Cl$ (d) $NH_2–Hg–Hg–Cl$ *(1996)*

71. The electronic configuration of transition elements is exhibited by
(a) ns^1 (b) ns^2np^5
(c) $ns^2\ (n-1)d^{1-10}$ (d) $ns^2\ (n-1)d^{10}$ *(1996)*

72. $KMnO_4$ reacts with oxalic acid according to the equation
$2MnO_4^- + 5C_2O_4^{2-} + 16H^+ \rightarrow 2Mn^{2+} + 10CO_2 + 8H_2O$
Here 20 mL of 0.1 M $KMnO_4$ is equivalent to
(a) 50 mL of 0.5 M $C_2H_2O_4$
(b) 20 mL of 0.1 M $C_2H_2O_4$
(c) 20 mL of 0.5 M $C_2H_2O_4$
(d) 50 mL of 0.1 M $C_2H_2O_4$ *(1996)*

73. Amongst TiF_6^{2-}, CoF_6^{3-}, Cu_2Cl_2 and $NiCl_4^{2-}$ which are the colourless species? (atomic number of Ti = 22, Co = 27, Cu = 29, Ni = 28)
(a) CoF_6^{3-} and $NiCl_4^{2-}$ (b) TiF_6^{2-} and Cu_2Cl_2
(c) Cu_2Cl_2 and $NiCl_4^{2-}$ (d) TiF_6^{2-} and CoF_6^{3-} *(1995)*

74. The mercury is the only metal which is liquid at 0°C. This is due to its

(a) high vapour pressure
(b) weak metallic bond
(c) high ionization energy
(d) both (b) and (c). *(1995)*

75. Which of the following statement concerning lanthanide elements is false?
(a) All lanthanides are highly dense metals.
(b) More characteristic oxidation state of lanthanide elements is +3.
(c) Lanthanides are separated from one another by ion exchange method.
(d) Ionic radii of trivalent lanthanides steadily increases with increase in the atomic number. *(1994)*

76. To protect iron against corrosion, the most durable metal plating on it, is
(a) copper plating (b) zinc plating
(c) nickel plating (d) tin plating. *(1994)*

77. When $CuSO_4$ is electrolysed using platinum electrodes,
(a) copper is liberated at cathode, sulphur at anode
(b) copper is liberated at cathode, oxygen at anode
(c) sulphur is liberated at cathode, oxygen at anode
(d) oxygen is liberated at cathode, copper at anode. *(1993)*

78. The transition elements have a general electronic configuration
(a) $ns^2np^6nd^{1-10}$
(b) $(n-1)d^{1-10}$, ns^{0-2}, np^{0-6}
(c) $(n-1)d^{1-10}$, ns^{1-2} (d) nd^{1-10} ns^{-2} *(1991)*

79. Photographic films and plates have an essential ingredient of
(a) silver nitrate (b) silver bromide
(c) sodium chloride (d) oleic acid. *(1989)*

80. Nitriding is the process of surface hardening of steel by treating it is an atmosphere of
(a) NH_3 (b) O_3
(c) N_2 (d) H_2S. *(1989)*

81. While extracting an element from its ore, the ore is ground and leached with dil. potassium cyanide solution to form the soluble product potassium argentocyanide. The element is
(a) lead (b) chromium
(c) manganese (d) silver. *(1989)*

82. A blue colouration is not obtained when
(a) ammonium hydroxide dissolves in copper sulphate
(b) copper sulphate solution reacts with $K_4[Fe(CN)_6]$
(c) ferric chloride reacts with sod. ferrocyanide
(d) anhydrous $CuSO_4$ is dissolved in water. *(1989)*

83. The electronic configurations of four elements are given below. Which element does not belong to the same family as others?
(a) $[Xe]4f^{14}5d^{10}6s^2$ (b) $[Kr]4d^{10}5s^2$
(c) $[Ne]3s^23p^5$ (d) $[Ar]3d^{10}4s^2$ *(1989)*

84. The oxidation state of Cr in $K_2Cr_2O_7$ is
(a) +5 (b) +3
(c) +6 (d) +7 *(1988)*

85. Hypo is used in photography to
(a) reduce AgBr grains to metallic silver
(b) convert metallic silver to silver salt
(c) remove undecomposed silver bromide as a soluble complex
(d) remove reduced silver. *(1988)*

Answer Key

1. (d)	**2.** (a)	**3.** (a)	**4.** (b)	**5.** (b)	**6.** (c)	**7.** (b)	**8.** (b)	**9.** (b)	**10.** (d)
11. (c)	**12.** (a)	**13.** (a)	**14.** (b)	**15.** (b)	**16.** (a)	**17.** (d)	**18.** (b)	**19.** (b)	**20.** (b)
21. (b)	**22.** (b)	**23.** (c)	**24.** (c)	**25.** (c)	**26.** (c)	**27.** (a)	**28.** (a)	**29.** (b)	**30.** (d)
31. (c)	**32.** (d)	**33.** (d)	**34.** (b)	**35.** (c)	**36.** (d)	**37.** (b)	**38.** (b)	**39.** (c)	**40.** (c)
41. (b)	**42.** (c)	**43.** (a)	**44.** (d)	**45.** (c)	**46.** (d)	**47.** (d)	**48.** (b)	**49.** (a)	**50.** (a)
51. (c)	**52.** (d)	**53.** (a)	**54.** (b)	**55.** (b)	**56.** (d)	**57.** (b)	**58.** (b)	**59.** (d)	**60.** (d)
61. (d)	**62.** (d)	**63.** (b)	**64.** (c)	**65.** (a)	**66.** (c)	**67.** (d)	**68.** (c)	**69.** (c)	**70.** (c)
71. (c)	**72.** (d)	**73.** (b)	**74.** (d)	**75.** (d)	**76.** (c)	**77.** (b)	**78.** (c)	**79.** (b)	**80.** (a)
81. (d)	**82.** (b)	**83.** (c)	**84.** (c)	**85.** (c)					

EXPLANATIONS

1. (d):

In CrO_4^{2-}	Cr^{+6} ($n = 0$)	diamagnetic
In $Cr_2O_7^{2-}$	Cr^{+6} ($n = 0$)	diamagnetic
In MnO_4^-	Mn^{+7} ($n = 0$)	diamagnetic
In MnO_4^{2-}	Mn^{+6} ($n = 1$)	paramagnetic

In MnO_4^{2-}, one unpaired electron(n) is present in d-orbital so, d-d transition is possible.

2. (a) : $Co^{3+} = [Ar]3d^6$, unpaired $e^-(n) = 4$

Spin magnetic moment $(\mu) = \sqrt{4(4+2)} = \sqrt{24}$ B.M.

$Cr^{3+} = [Ar]3d^3$, unpaired $e^-(n) = 3$

Spin magnetic moment $(\mu) = \sqrt{3(3+2)} = \sqrt{15}$ B.M.

$Fe^{3+} = [Ar]3d^5$, unpaired $e^-(n) = 5$

Spin magnetic moment $(\mu) = \sqrt{5(5+2)} = \sqrt{35}$ B.M.

$Ni^{2+} = [Ar]3d^8$, unpaired $e^-(n) = 2$

Spin magnetic moment $(\mu) = \sqrt{2(2+2)} = \sqrt{8}$ B.M.

3. (a) : SO_2 readily decolourises pink violet colour of acidified $KMnO_4$ solution.

$$\underset{\text{(Pink violet)}}{2KMnO_4} + 5SO_2 + 2H_2O \rightarrow K_2SO_4 + \underset{\text{(Colourless)}}{2MnSO_4} + 2H_2SO_4$$

4. (b) : $HgCl_2 + 4I^-_{(aq)} \rightarrow HgI^{2-}_{4(aq)} + 2Cl^-_{(aq)}$

$I_{2(s)} + I^-_{(aq)} \rightarrow I^-_{3(aq)}$

5. (b): Actinoids have a greater range of oxidation states due to comparable energies of $5f$, $6d$ and $7s$ orbitals. Hence, all their electrons can take part in bond formation.

6. (c) : The first few members of the lanthanoid series are quite reactive, almost like calcium. However, with increasing atomic number, their behaviour becomes similar to that of aluminium.

7. (b): $K_2Cr_2O_7 + H_2SO_4 + 3SO_2 \longrightarrow K_2SO_4 + \underset{\text{(Green)}}{Cr_2(SO_4)_3} + H_2O$

8. (b) **9. (b)**

10. (d) : $KMnO_4$ (Mn^{7+}) changes to Mn^{2+} *i.e.*, number of electrons involved per mole of $KMnO_4$ is 5.

(a) For $FeSO_3$,

$Fe^{2+} \longrightarrow Fe^{3+}$ (No. of e^-s involved = 1)

$SO_3^{2-} \longrightarrow SO_4^{2-}$ (No. of e^-s involved = 2)

Total number of e^-s involved = 1 + 2 = 3

(b) For FeC_2O_4,

$Fe^{2+} \longrightarrow Fe^{3+}$ (No. of e^-s involved = 1)

$C_2O_4^{2-} \longrightarrow 2CO_2$ (No. of e^-s involved = 2)

Total number of e^-s involved = 1 + 2 = 3

(c) For $Fe(NO_2)_2$,

$Fe^{2+} \longrightarrow Fe^{3+}$ (No. of e^-s involved = 1)

$2NO_2^- \longrightarrow 2NO_3^-$ (No. of e^-s involved = 4)

Total number of e^-s involved = 1 + 4 = 5

(d) For $FeSO_4$,

$Fe^{2+} \longrightarrow Fe^{3+}$ (No. of e^-s involved = 1)

Total number of e^-s involved = 1

As $FeSO_4$ requires least number of electrons thus, it will require least amount of $KMnO_4$.

11. (c) : Magnetic moment $(\mu) = \sqrt{n(n+2)}$

2.84 B.M. corresponds to 2 unpaired electrons.

Cr^{2+} – $3d^4$, 4 unpaired electrons

Co^{2+} – $3d^7$, 3 unpaired electrons

Ni^{2+} – $3d^8$, 2 unpaired electrons

Ti^{3+} – $3d^1$, 1 unpaired electron

12. (a) : Oxidation number of Fe in $Fe(CO)_5$ is zero.

13. (a) : Zr and Hf have nearly same radii due to lanthanoid contraction.

14. (b) : Hydrogen peroxide is oxidised to H_2O and O_2.

$$2KMnO_4 + 3H_2SO_4 + 5H_2O_2 \rightarrow K_2SO_4 + 2MnSO_4 + 8H_2O + 5O_2$$

or, $2MnO_4^- + 5H_2O_2 + 6H^+ \rightarrow 2Mn^{2+} + 8H_2O + 5O_2$

15. (b) : Magnetic moment is given by

$\mu = \sqrt{n(n+2)}$ B.M.

[where n = no. of unpaired electrons]

When $n = 2$, then $\mu = 2.83$ B.M.

For Ti^{3+} ($3d^1$), $n = 1$; Cr^{3+} ($3d^3$), $n = 3$

Ni^{2+} ($3d^8$), $n = 2$; Mn^{2+} ($3d^5$), $n = 5$

Hence, Ni^{2+} has two unpaired electrons, with magnetic moment 2.83 B.M.

16. (a) : Due to poor shielding effect of $4f$-orbitals, nucleus will exert a strong attraction and size of atom or ion goes on decreasing as move in the series with increase in atomic number.

17. (d) : Interstitial compounds are generally chemically inert.

18. (b) : Sm^{2+} $(Z = 62)$: $[Xe]4f^6$
Eu^{2+} $(Z = 63)$: $[Xe]4f^7$
Yb^{2+} $(Z = 70)$: $[Xe]4f^{14}$
Ce^{2+} $(Z = 58)$: $[Xe]4f^1 5d^1$

Only Yb^{2+} is diamagnetic.

19. (b) : Sodium sulphide is soluble in water. The solubility product (and hence solubility) of ZnS is larger than that of CuS.

20. (b) : Sc $(Z = 21)$ has incompletely filled 3d-orbitals in its ground state $(3d^1)$, it is considered as a transition element but Zn $(Z = 30)$ has completely filled d-orbitals $(3d^{10})$ in its ground state and its common oxidation state of (+2), it is not considered as a transition element.

21. (b) : Invar $\Rightarrow$ Ni(metal) + Fe(metal)
Steel $\Rightarrow$ C(non-metal) + Fe(metal)
Bell metal $\Rightarrow$ Cu(metal) + Sn(metal) + Fe(metal)
Bronze $\Rightarrow$ Cu(metal) + Sn(metal)

22. (b) **23. (c)**

24. (c) : U exhibits + 3, + 4, + 5, + 6
Th exhibits + 3, + 4 ; Ac exhibits + 3 only
Pa exhibits + 3, + 4, + 5

25. (c) :

Element	Ti < V < Cr < Mn
No. of oxidation states	3 4 5 6

Given order is correct.

Magnetic moment $(\mu) = \sqrt{n(n+2)}$ B.M.

For Ti^{3+} $n = 1$, $\mu = \sqrt{1(1+2)} = \sqrt{3}$ B.M.

For V^{3+} $n = 2$, $\mu = \sqrt{2(2+2)} = \sqrt{8}$ B.M.

For Cr^{3+} $n = 3$, $\mu = \sqrt{3(3+2)} = \sqrt{15}$ B.M.

For Mn^{3+} $n = 4$, $\mu = \sqrt{4(4+2)} = \sqrt{24}$ B.M.

Thus magnetic moment : $Ti^{3+} < V^{3+} < Cr^{3+} < Mn^{3+}$

Melting point order : Mn < Ti < Cr $\lessgtr$ V
1245°C 1668°C 1875°C 1900°C

2nd ionisation enthalpy order
Ti < V < Mn < Cr
(in kJ/mol) : 1320 1376 1513 1635

26. (c) :

Element	Co	Ni	Cu	Fe
$E^\circ_{M^{2+}/M}$ (V)	– 0.28	– 0.25	+ 0.34	– 0.44

27. (a) : The order can be explained using the idea of spin correlation. Spin correlation refers to lowering of energy for like (parallel) spins. Spin correlation leading to decrease in repulsion for electrons of like spins than for electrons of different spins is called exchange energy.

Spin correlation and its exchange energy gives an electronic configuration a special stability which is greatest for half-filled electronic configurations. Mn^{2+} (d^5) gets stabilisation due to half-filled configuration.

In Fe^{2+} (d^6) the placing of one extra electron in a subshell destabilises. Placing of 2 electrons in Co^{2+} (d^7) destabilises it more. Cr^{2+} (d^4) has one vacant subshell. Fe^{2+} gets more stabilisation compared to Cr^{2+} through exchange energy. So the order is as follows:

Mn > Fe > Cr > Co

28. (a) : $K_2Cr_2O_7 + 4H_2SO_4 \rightarrow K_2SO_4 + Cr_2(SO_4)_3 + 4H_2O + 3[O]$

$[Na_2SO_3 + [O] \rightarrow Na_2SO_4] \times 3$

$K_2Cr_2O_7 + 3Na_2SO_3 + 4H_2SO_4 \rightarrow 3Na_2SO_4 + K_2SO_4 + Cr_2(SO_4)_3 + 4H_2O$

or $Cr_2O_7^{2-} + 3SO_3^{2-} + 8H^+ \rightarrow 3SO_4^{2-} + 2Cr^{3+} + 4H_2O$

29. (b) : Ti^{3+} $(Z = 22)$

Ions which have unpaired electrons exhibit colour in solution. Ti^{3+} has an outer electronic configuration of $4s^0 3d^1$, *i.e.*, 1 unpaired electron.

Thus its solution will be coloured.

$Sc^{3+} \rightarrow d^0$

In case of La^{3+}, $4f^0$ configuration is present and in Lu^{3+}, $4f^{14}$ is present. So, there is no possibility of f-f transition, hence these ions do not appear coloured.

30. (d) : The electronic configuration of the given ions is :

Ni^{3+} : $[Ar]3d^7 4s^0$, Mn^{3+} : $[Ar]3d^4 4s^0$
Fe^{3+} : $[Ar]3d^5 4s^0$, Co^{3+} : $[Ar]3d^6 4s^0$

Thus, Co^{3+} is the ion with the desired configuration.

31. (c) : Hf^{4+} and Zr^{4+} belong to group IVB. But, Hf^{4+} has same size as Zr^{4+} due to the addition of 14 lanthanide elements before it in which electrons are added into the f-subshell which poorly shield the outer electrons and contraction in size occurs.

32. (d)

33. (d) : The common stable oxidation state of all the lanthanoids is +3. The oxidation state of +2 and +4 are also exhibited by some of the elements. These oxidation states are only stable in those cases where stable $4f^0$, $4f^7$ or $4f^{14}$ configurations are achieved.

34. (b) : Greater the number of valence electrons, more will be the number of oxidation states exhibited by the element.

Option (a) : $3d^5 4s^1$, can show a maximum of 6 oxidation states.
Option (b) : $3d^5 4s^2$, can show a maximum of 7 oxidation states.
Option (c) : $3d^2 4s^2$ can show a maximum of 4 oxidation states.
Option (d) : $3d^3 4s^2$ can show a maximum of 5 oxidation states.

35. (c) : Electronic configuration of the given elements are
$Mn \rightarrow 1s^2\, 2s^2\, 2p^6\, 3s^2\, 3p^6\, 3d^5\, 4s^2$
$Cr \rightarrow 1s^2\, 2s^2\, 2p^6\, 3s^2\, 3p^6\, 3d^5\, 4s^1$
$Ti \rightarrow 1s^2\, 2s^2\, 2p^6\, 3s^2\, 3p^6\, 3d^2\, 4s^2$
$V \rightarrow 1s^2\, 2s^2\, 2p^6\, 3s^2\, 3p^6\, 3d^3\, 4s^2$
In general, ionization potential (both 1st and 2nd) increases from left to right across the period due to increase in effective nuclear charge. On this basis, the second IP values should exhibit the trend:
$Mn > Cr > V > Ti$
But the actual observed order is:
$Cr > Mn > V > Ti$
Practically, only chromium is exceptional and rest others show the normal trend. This exceptional behaviour of chromium is due to the stable configuration ($3d^5$) that it achieves after the loss of first electron.

36. (d) : +4 is the most stable oxidation state of vanadium and titanium. Mn^{3+} is not stable. Mn^{2+}, rather than Mn^{3+} is much more stable in aqueous solution. For chromium, +3 oxidation state is most stable in aqueous solution.

37. (b) : In each vertical column of transition elements, the elements of second and third transition series resemble each other more closely than the elements of first and second transition series on account of lanthanide contraction. Hence the properties of elements of 4*d* series of the transition elements resemble with the properties of the elements of 5*d* series of the transition elements.

38. (b) : $Sc \rightarrow [Ar]\, 3d^1\, 4s^2$, $Sc^{3+} \rightarrow [Ar]$
$Ti \rightarrow [Ar]\, 3d^2\, 4s^2$, $Ti^{3+} \rightarrow [Ar]\, 3d^1$
$Ni \rightarrow [Ar]\, 3d^8\, 4s^2$, $Ni^{2+} \rightarrow [Ar]\, 3d^8$
$Cu \rightarrow [Ar]\, 3d^{10}\, 4s^1$, $Cu^+ \rightarrow [Ar]\, 3d^{10}$
$Co \rightarrow [Ar]\, 3d^7\, 4s^2$, $Co^{2+} \rightarrow [Ar]\, 3d^7$
Ti^{3+}, Ni^{2+} and Co^{2+} are coloured due to presence of unpaired electrons.

39. (c) : First cupric cyanide is formed which decomposes to give cuprous cyanide and cyanogen gas. Cuprous cyanide dissolves in excess of potassium cyanide to form a complex, potassium cyanide $[K_3Cu(CN)_4]$.
$[CuSO_4 + 2KCN \rightarrow Cu(CN)_2 + K_2SO_4] \times 2$
$2Cu(CN)_2 \rightarrow Cu_2(CN)_2 + (CN)_2$
$Cu_2(CN)_2 + 6KCN \rightarrow 2K_3Cu(CN)_4$
$2CuSO_4 + 10KCN \rightarrow 2K_3Cu(CN)_4 + 2K_2SO_4 + (CN)_2$

40. (c) : The 5*f*-orbitals extend into space beyond the 6*s* and 6*p*-orbitals and participate in bonding. This is in direct contrast to the lanthanides where the 4*f*-orbitals are buried deep inside in the atom, totally shielded by outer orbitals and thus unable to take part in bonding.

41. (b) : In alkaline medium :
$2KMnO_4 + H_2O \longrightarrow 2KOH + 2MnO_2$
$KI + 3[O] \longrightarrow KIO_3$
$2KMnO_4 + KI + H_2O \longrightarrow 2KOH + 2MnO_2 + KIO_3.$

42. (c) : V^{2+} (21) $[Ar]^{18}\, 3d^3\, 4s^0$
Cr^{2+} (22) $[Ar]^{18}\, 3d^4\, 4s^0$
Mn^{2+} (23) $[Ar]^{18}\, 3d^5\, 4s^0$
Fe^{2+} (24) $[Ar]^{18}\, 3d^5\, 4s^1$
To find ionization enthalpy we first see electronic configuration. Then we see shell. If shell are same then see charge. Then see extra stability (Half filled and fully filled)
$\Rightarrow\; I.E_3\,(Mn) > I.E_3\,(Fe) > I.E_3\,(Cr) > I.E_3\,(V)$

43. (a) : If the transition metal ion has unpaired electron then it shows colour.
$Sc^{3+}\, [Ar]^{18}\, 3d^0\, 4s^0$
$Fe^{2+}\, [Ar]^{18}\, 3d^5\, 4s^1$
$Ti^{3+}\, [Ar]^{18}\, 3d^1\, 4s^0$
$Mn^{2+}\, [Ar]^{18}\, 3d^5\, 4s^0$
Hence, Sc^{3+} do not contain unpaired electron and hence it will not undergo $d - d$ transition and do not show colour.

44. (d) : $_{22}Ti = 3d^2\, 4s^2$; $Ti^{2+} = 3d^2$
$_{23}V = 3d^3\, 4s^2$; $V^{3+} = 3d^2$
$_{24}Cr = 3d^4\, 4s^2$; $Cr^{4+} = 3d^2$
$_{25}Mn = 3d^5\, 4s^2$; $Mn^{5+} = 3d^2$

45. (c) : As sixth period can accommodate only 18 elements in the table, 14 members of 4*f* series (atomic number 58 to 71) are separately accommodated in a horizontal row below the periodic table. These are called as lanthanides.

46. (d) : The transition elements, on account of their variable valency, are able to form unstable intermediate compounds very readily.

47. (d) : Oxides of transition metals in low oxidation states +2 and +3 (MO, M_3O_4 and M_2O_3) are generally basic except Cr_2O_3 which is amphoteric in character. Basic character generally decreases with increase in atomic number.

48. (b) : On going from La^{3+} to Lu^{3+}, the ionic radius shrinks from 1.15 Å to 0.93 Å (lanthanide contraction). The radius of La^{3+} is also larger than that of Y^{3+} ion which lies immediately above it in periodic table.

9. (a) : The general electronic structure of lanthanides is

$(n-2)f^{1-14}(n-1)s^2p^6d^{0-1}ns^2$

0. (a) : The electronic configuration of an atom $s^2\ 2s^2\ 2p^6\ 3s^2\ 3p^6\ 3d^3\ 4s^2$.

In the configuration, the last electron of the atom is filled in d sub-shell as $3d^3$. Thus this element belongs to d-block of the periodic table with group no. V.

1. (c) : Each of the element in group III B to VII B can show the maximum oxidation state equal to its group number.

Mn is in group seven shows a maximum oxidation state of +7 in $KMnO_4$.

2. (d) : Zinc is on the top position of hydrogen in electrochemical series. So Zn displaces H_2 from dilute H_2SO_4 and HCl with liberation of H_2.

$Zn + H_2SO_4 \rightarrow ZnSO_4 + H_2$

On the other hand HNO_3 is an oxidising agent. Hydrogen obtained in this reaction is converted into H_2O.

$Zn + 2HNO_3 \rightarrow Zn(NO_3)_2 + 2H$

$HNO_3 \rightarrow H_2O + 2NO_2 + O$

$H + O \rightarrow H_2O$.

. (a) : $La(OH)_3$ is more basic than $Lu(OH)_3$. In lanthanides the basic character of hydroxides decreases as the ionic radius decreases.

. (b) : The most convenient method to protect the bottom of the ship made of iron is white tin coating preventing the build up of barnacles.

. (b) : $_{21}Sc \rightarrow 3d^1, 4s^2$ (valence shell)

Sc^{3+} there is no unpaired 'd' electrons, therefore is colourless ion in its solution.

. (d) : $_{26}Fe \rightarrow 1s^2, 2s^2, 2p^6, 3s^2, 3p^6, 4s^2, 3d^6$

According to '$n + l$' rule electron first enters to '$4s$' and then to $3d$ subshell.

. (b) : In Fe^{2+} there are 24 electrons and 2-electrons removed from $4s$-subshell.

There are 4-unpaired electrons in the $3d$-subshell.

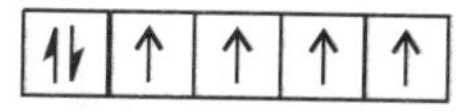

3d

58. (b) : Bell metal ⇒ Cu = 80%, Sn = 20%

It is used for making bells, utensils, etc.

59. (d) : In Iron carbonyl the oxidation number of 'Fe' is zero.

$[Fe(CO)_5] \rightarrow x + 5 \times 0 = 0 \Rightarrow x = 0$

60. (d) : Pig iron is the impure form of iron, which contains carbon as the major impurity, *i.e.* 2.5 to 5%.

61. (d) : $Cr^{3+}(21) \rightarrow 1s^2, 2s^2, 2p^6, 3s^2, 3p^6, 3d^3$.

As Cr^{3+} ion has three unpaired electrons in its valence shell, so it imparts green colour to an aqueous solution.

62. (d) : 'La' forms compounds in which its oxidation no. is +3.

'Eu' and 'Gd' exhibit +2 as well as +3 oxidation state and not higher than that, due to stable (f^7) configuration. whereas 'Am' exhibits the oxidation states +2, +3, +4, +5, +6, etc. due to extremely large size and low ionisation energy.

63. (b) : Only 'Al' lies above 'Zn' in electrochemical series, which can displace the latter from $ZnCl_2$ solution. Therefore conc. of $ZnCl_2$ will decrease when kept in 'Al' container.

$2Al + 3ZnCl_2 \rightarrow 2AlCl_3 + 3Zn$

64. (c) : The correct order is

$Cr^{2+} > Mn^{2+} > Fe^{2+} > Ni^{2+}$.

65. (a) : Due to lanthanide contraction, the elements of second and third *i.e.* Zr and Hf transition series resemble more with each other than the elements of first and second transition series.

66. (c)

67. (d) : Half-filled and fully filled orbitals are more stable.

68. (c) : $K_2Cr_2O_7 + 2NaOH \rightarrow K_2CrO_4 + Na_2CrO_4 + H_2O$

or $Cr_2O_7^{2-} + 2OH^- \rightarrow 2CrO_4^{2-} + H_2O$

69. (c) : It is the configuration of metal ion. The metal atom will have three more electrons. Therefore the atomic number of the metal = (18) + 4 + 3 = 25.

70. (c) : When calomel reacts with NH_4OH, it turns black due to the formation of a mixture of mercury and ammonium basic mercury (II) chloride.

$Hg_2Cl_2 + 2\ NH_4OH \rightarrow NH_4Cl + 2H_2O + Hg + HgNH_2Cl$

(calomel)

71. (c) : General electronic configuration of transition elements is $ns^2 (n - 1)d^{1-10}$.

72. (d) : $2MnO_4^- + 5C_2O_4^{2-} + 16H^+ \rightarrow 2Mn^{2+} + 10CO_2 + 8H_2O$

$\therefore$ 2 moles of $MnO_4^- \equiv$ 5 moles of $C_2O_4^{2-}$

20 mL of 0.1 M $KMnO_4$ = 2 mmol of $KMnO_4$

Also, 50 mL of 0.1 M $C_2H_2O_4 \equiv$ 5 mmol of $C_2O_4^{2-}$

Therefore, these are equivalent.

73. (b) : In TiF_6^{2-} titanium is in +4 state. In Cu_2Cl_2, the copper is in +1 state. Thus in both cases, transition from one *d*-orbital to other is not possible.

Ti - $3d^2, 4s^2 \rightarrow Ti^{4+}$ - $3d^0\ 4s^0$

Cu - $3d^{10}, 4s^1 \rightarrow Cu^+$ - $3d^{10}\ 4s^0$

74. (d) : Very high ionisation energy of Hg makes it difficult for electrons to participate in metallic bonding.

75. (d) : Ionic radii of trivalent lanthanides decreases with increase in atomic number.

76. (c) : A layer of oxide is formed on the surface of nickel, which protects nickel, below it and thus the iron underneath it.

77. (b) : $CuSO_4 \rightleftharpoons Cu^{2+} + SO_4^{2-}$

$H_2O \rightleftharpoons H^+ + OH^-$

At cathode : $Cu^{2+} + 2e^- \rightarrow Cu$

At anode : $4OH^- \rightarrow 2H_2O + O_2 + 4e^-$

78. (c) : The general electronic configuration o transition elements is $(n-1)d^{1-10}ns^{1-2}$

79. (b) : AgBr is highly photosensitive and i used as an ingredient for photographic films an plates.

80. (a) : When steel is heated in presence of NH_3 iron nitride on the surface of steel is formed whic imparts a hard coating. This process is called nitriding

81. (d) : Cyanide process is used in the metallurg of Ag.

$2Ag_2S + 8NaCN + O_2 + 2H_2O \rightarrow 4Na[Ag(CN)_2] + 4NaOH + 2$

$2Na[Ag(CN)_2] + Zn \rightarrow Na_2[Zn(CN)_4] + 2Ag\downarrow$

82. (b) : $2CuSO_4 + K_4[Fe(CN)_6] \rightarrow \underset{\text{chocolate pp}}{Cu_2[Fe(CN)_6]} + 2K_2SC$

83. (c) : $[Ne]3s^23p^5$ is the electronic configuratio of a *p*-block element whereas other configuratior are those of *d*-block elements.

84. (c) : Oxidation state of Cr in $K_2Cr_2O_7$ is

$2 + 2x - 14 = 0 \quad \therefore 2x = 14 - 2$

$2x = 12 \quad \therefore x = +6$

85. (c) : Undecomposed AgBr forms a solub complex with hypo and the reaction is given as:

$AgBr + 2Na_2S_2O_3 \rightarrow \underset{\text{soluble complex}}{Na_3[Ag(S_2O_3)_2]} + NaBr$

Chapter 23

Coordination Compounds

1. The type of isomerism shown by the complex $[CoCl_2(en)_2]$ is
(a) geometrical isomerism
(b) coordination isomerism
(c) ionization isomerism
(d) linkage isomerism. *(NEET 2018)*

2. The geometry and magnetic behaviour of the complex $[Ni(CO)_4]$ are
(a) square planar geometry and diamagnetic
(b) tetrahedral geometry and diamagnetic
(c) square planar geometry and paramagnetic
(d) tetrahedral geometry and paramagnetic. *(NEET 2018)*

3. Iron carbonyl, $Fe(CO)_5$ is
(a) tetranuclear (b) mononuclear
(c) trinuclear (d) dinuclear. *(NEET 2018)*

4. An example of a sigma bonded organometallic compound is
(a) Grignard's reagent (b) ferrocene
(c) cobaltocene (d) ruthenocene. *(NEET 2017)*

5. The correct order of the stoichiometries of AgCl formed when $AgNO_3$ in excess is treated with the complexes : $CoCl_3.6NH_3$, $CoCl_3.5NH_3$, $CoCl_3.4NH_3$ respectively is
(a) 3AgCl, 1AgCl, 2AgCl
(b) 3AgCl, 2AgCl, 1AgCl
(c) 2AgCl, 3AgCl, 2AgCl
(d) 1AgCl, 3AgCl, 2AgCl *(NEET 2017)*

6. Correct increasing order for the wavelengths of absorption in the visible region for the complexes of Co^{3+} is
(a) $[Co(H_2O)_6]^{3+}$, $[Co(en)_3]^{3+}$, $[Co(NH_3)_6]^{3+}$
(b) $[Co(H_2O)_6]^{3+}$, $[Co(NH_3)_6]^{3+}$, $[Co(en)_3]^{3+}$
(c) $[Co(NH_3)_6]^{3+}$, $[Co(en)_3]^{3+}$, $[Co(H_2O)_6]^{3+}$
(d) $[Co(en)_3]^{3+}$, $[Co(NH_3)_6]^{3+}$, $[Co(H_2O)_6]^{3+}$ *(NEET 2017)*

7. Pick out the correct statement with respect to $[Mn(CN)_6]^{3-}$.
(a) It is sp^3d^2 hybridised and tetrahedral.
(b) It is d^2sp^3 hybridised and octahedral.
(c) It is dsp^2 hybridised and square planar.
(d) It is sp^3d^2 hybridised and octahedral. *(NEET 2017)*

8. The correct increasing order of *trans*-effect of the following species is
(a) $NH_3 > CN^- > Br^- > C_6H_5^-$
(b) $CN^- > C_6H_5^- > Br^- > NH_3$
(c) $Br^- > CN^- > NH_3 > C_6H_5^-$
(d) $CN^- > Br^- > C_6H_5^- > NH_3$ *(NEET-II 2016)*

9. Jahn–Teller effect is not observed in high spin complexes of
(a) d^7 (b) d^8 (c) d^4 (d) d^9 *(NEET-II 2016)*

10. Which of the following has longest C—O bond length? (Free C—O bond length in CO is 1.128 Å.)
(a) $[Fe(CO)_4]^{2-}$ (b) $[Mn(CO)_6]^+$
(c) $Ni(CO)_4$ (d) $[Co(CO)_4]^-$ *(NEET-I 2016)*

11. The hybridization involved in complex $[Ni(CN)_4]^{2-}$ is (At. No. Ni = 28)
(a) sp^3 (b) d^2sp^2
(c) d^2sp^3 (d) dsp^2 *(2015)*

12. The name of complex ion, $[Fe(CN)_6]^{3-}$ is
(a) hexacyanitoferrate (III) ion
(b) tricyanoferrate (III) ion
(c) hexacyanidoferrate (III) ion
(d) hexacyanoiron (III) ion. *(2015)*

13. The sum of coordination number and oxidation number of the metal M in the complex $[M(en)_2(C_2O_4)]Cl$ (where *en* is ethylenediamine) is
(a) 6 (b) 7 (c) 8 (d) 9 *(2015)*

14. Number of possible isomers for the complex $[Co(en)_2Cl_2]Cl$ will be
(en = ethylenediamine)
(a) 1 (b) 3 (c) 4 (d) 2
(2015)

15. Cobalt (III) chloride forms several octahedral complexes with ammonia. Which of the following will not give test for chloride ions with silver nitrate at 25°C?
(a) $CoCl_3 \cdot 5NH_3$ (b) $CoCl_3 \cdot 6NH_3$
(c) $CoCl_3 \cdot 3NH_3$ (d) $CoCl_3 \cdot 4NH_3$
(2015, Cancelled)

16. Which of these statements about $[Co(CN)_6]^{3-}$ is true?
(a) $[Co(CN)_6]^{3-}$ has four unpaired electrons and will be in a high-spin configuration.
(b) $[Co(CN)_6]^{3-}$ has no unpaired electrons and will be in a high-spin configuration.
(c) $[Co(CN)_6]^{3-}$ has no unpaired electrons and will be in a low-spin configuration.
(d) $[Co(CN)_6]^{3-}$ has four unpaired electrons and will be in a low-spin configuration.
(2015, Cancelled)

17. Among the following complexes the one which shows zero crystal field stabilization energy (CFSE) is
(a) $[Mn(H_2O)_6]^{3+}$ (b) $[Fe(H_2O)_6]^{3+}$
(c) $[Co(H_2O)_6]^{2+}$ (d) $[Co(H_2O)_6]^{3+}$
(2014)

18. Which of the following complexes is used to be as an anticancer agent?
(a) *mer*-$[Co(NH_3)_3Cl_3]$ (b) *cis*-$PtCl_2(NH_3)_2]$
(c) *cis*-$K_2[PtCl_2Br_2]$ (d) Na_2CoCl_4
(2014)

19. A magnetic moment at 1.73 BM will be shown by one among of the following
(a) $TiCl_4$ (b) $[CoCl_6]^{4-}$
(c) $[Cu(NH_3)_4]^{2+}$ (d) $[Ni(CN)_4]^{2-}$
(NEET 2013)

20. An excess of $AgNO_3$ is added to 100 mL of a 0.01 M solution of dichlorotetraaqua-chromium (III) chloride. The number of moles of AgCl precipitated would be
(a) 0.003 (b) 0.01 (c) 0.001 (d) 0.002
(NEET 2013)

21. Crystal field splitting energy for high spin d^4 octahedral complex is
(a) $-1.2\ \Delta_o$ (b) $-0.6\ \Delta_o$
(c) $-0.8\ \Delta_o$ (d) $-1.6\ \Delta_o$
(Karnataka NEET 2013)

22. In a particular isomer of $[Co(NH_3)_4Cl_2]^0$, the Cl – Co – Cl angle is 90°, the isomer is known as
(a) optical isomer (b) *cis*-isomer
(c) position isomer (d) linkage isomer.
(Karnataka NEET 2013)

23. The anion of acetylacetone (acac) forms $Co(acac)_3$ chelate with Co^{3+}. The rings of the chelate are
(a) five membered (b) four membered
(c) six membered (d) three membered.
(Karnataka NEET 2013)

24. The correct IUPAC name for $[CrF_2(en)_2]Cl$ is
(a) chloro difluorido ethylene diaminechromium (III) chloride
(b) difluoridobis (ethylene diamine) chromium (III) chloride
(c) difluorobis-(ethylene diamine) chromium (III) chloride
(d) chloro difluoridobis (ethylene diamine) chromium (III) *(Karnataka NEET 2013)*

25. Which among the following is a paramagnetic complex?
(a) $[Co(NH_3)_6]^{3+}$ (b) $[Pt(en)Cl_2]$
(c) $[CoBr_4]^{2-}$ (d) $Mo(CO)_6$
(At. No. Mo = 42, Pt = 78)
(Karnataka NEET 2013)

26. Which is diamagnetic?
(a) $[Co(F)_6]^{3-}$ (b) $[Ni(CN)_4]^{2-}$
(c) $[NiCl_4]^{2-}$ (d) $[Fe(CN)_6]^{3-}$
(Karnataka NEET 2013)

27. Which one of the following is an outer orbital complex and exhibits paramagnetic behaviour?
(a) $[Ni(NH_3)_6]^{2+}$ (b) $[Zn(NH_3)_6]^{2+}$
(c) $[Cr(NH_3)_6]^{3+}$ (d) $[Co(NH_3)_6]^{3+}$
(2012)

28. Red precipitate is obtained when ethanol solution of dimethylglyoxime is added to ammoniacal Ni(II). Which of the following statements is not true?
(a) Red complex has a square planar geometry.
(b) Complex has symmetrical H-bonding.
(c) Red complex has a tetrahedral geometry.

(d) Dimethylglyoxime functions as bidentate ligand.

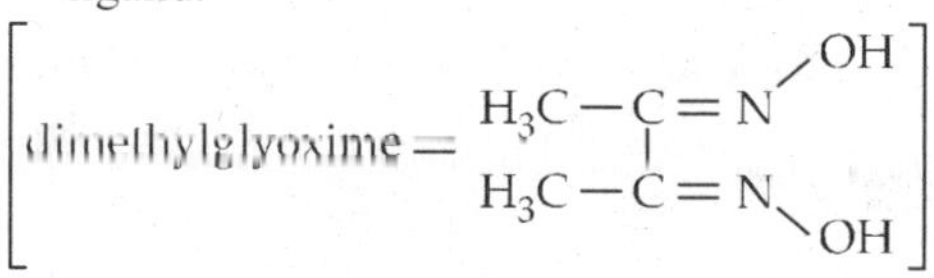

(Mains 2012)

29. Low spin complex of d^6-cation in an octahedral field will have the following energy

(a) $\frac{-12}{5}\Delta_o + P$ (b) $\frac{-12}{5}\Delta_o + 3P$

(c) $\frac{-2}{5}\Delta_o + 2P$ (d) $\frac{-2}{5}\Delta_o + P$

(Δ_o = crystal field splitting energy in an octahedral field, P = Electron pairing energy) *(2012)*

30. Of the following complex ions, which is diamagnetic in nature?

(a) $[NiCl_4]^{2-}$ (b) $[Ni(CN)_4]^{2-}$

(c) $[CuCl_4]^{2-}$ (d) $[CoF_6]^{3-}$

(2011)

31. The complexes $[Co(NH_3)_6][Cr(CN)_6]$ and $[Cr(NH_3)_6][Co(CN)_6]$ are the examples of which type of isomerism?

(a) Linkage isomerism

(b) Ionization isomerism

(c) Coordination isomerism

(d) Geometrical isomerism *(2011)*

32. The complex, $[Pt(Py)(NH_3)BrCl]$ will have how many geometrical isomers?

(a) 3 (b) 4 (c) 0 (d) 2

(2011)

33. The d-electron configurations of Cr^{2+}, Mn^{2+}, Fe^{2+} and Co^{2+} are d^4, d^5, d^6 and d^7 respectively. Which one of the following will exhibit minimum paramagnetic behaviour?

(a) $[Mn(H_2O)_6]^{2+}$ (b) $[Fe(H_2O)_6]^{2+}$

(c) $[Co(H_2O)_6]^{2+}$ (d) $[Cr(H_2O)_6]^{2+}$

(At. nos. Cr = 24, Mn = 25, Fe = 26, Co = 27) *(2011)*

34. Which of the following carbonyls will have the strongest C – O bond?

(a) $Mn(CO)_6^+$ (b) $Cr(CO)_6$

(c) $V(CO)_6^-$ (d) $Fe(CO)_5$ *(2011)*

35. Which of the following complex compounds will exhibit highest paramagnetic behaviour?

(a) $[Ti(NH_3)_6]^{3+}$ (b) $[Cr(NH_3)_6]^{3+}$

(c) $[Co(NH_3)_6]^{3+}$ (d) $[Zn(NH_3)_6]^{2+}$

(At. No. Ti = 22, Cr = 24, Co = 27, Zn = 30) *(2011)*

36. Which of the following complex ions is not expected to absorb visible light?

(a) $[Ni(CN)_4]^{2-}$ (b) $[Cr(NH_3)_6]^{3+}$

(c) $[Fe(H_2O)_6]^{2+}$ (d) $[Ni(H_2O)_6]^{2+}$

(2010)

37. Crystal field stabilization energy for high spin d^4 octahedral complex is

(a) $-1.8\ \Delta_o$ (b) $-1.6\ \Delta_o + P$

(c) $-1.2\ \Delta_o$ (d) $-0.6\ \Delta_o$ *(2010)*

38. The existance of two different coloured complexes with the composition of $[Co(NH_3)_4Cl_2]^+$ is due to

(a) linkage isomerism

(b) geometrical isomerism

(c) coordination isomerism

(d) ionization isomerism. *(2010)*

39. Which one of the following complexes is not expected to exhibit isomerism?

(a) $[Ni(NH_3)_4(H_2O)_2]^{2+}$ (b) $[Pt(NH_3)_2Cl_2]$

(c) $[Ni(NH_3)_2Cl_2]$ (d) $[Ni(en)_3]^{2+}$

(2010)

40. Out of TiF_6^{2-}, CoF_6^{3-}, Cu_2Cl_2 and $NiCl_4^{2-}$ (Z of Ti = 22, Co = 27, Cu = 29, Ni = 28) the colourless species are

(a) Cu_2Cl_2 and $NiCl_4^{2-}$

(b) TiF_6^{2-} and Cu_2Cl_2

(c) CoF_6^{3-} and $NiCl_4^{2-}$

(d) TiF_6^{2-} and CoF_6^{3-}. *(2009)*

41. Which of the following does not show optical isomerism?

(a) $[Co(NH_3)_3Cl_3]^0$

(b) $[Co(en)Cl_2(NH_3)_2]^+$

(c) $[Co(en)_3]^{3+}$

(d) $[Co(en)_2Cl_2]^+$

(en = ethylenediamine) *(2009)*

42. Which of the following complex ions is expected to absorb visible light?

(a) $[Ti(en)_2(NH_3)_2]^{4+}$ (b) $[Cr(NH_3)_6]^{3+}$

(c) $[Zn(NH_3)_6]^{2+}$

(d) $[Sc(H_2O)_3(NH_3)_3]^{3+}$

[At. nos. Zn = 30, Sc = 21, Ti = 22, Cr = 24]

(2009)

43. Which of the following complexes exhibits the highest paramagnetic behaviour?
(a) $[Co(ox)_2(OH)_2]^-$
(b) $[Ti(NH_3)_6]^{3+}$
(c) $[V(gly)_2(OH)_2(NH_3)_2]^+$
(d) $[Fe(en)(bpy)(NH_3)_2]^{2+}$
where *gly* = glycine, *en* = ethylenediamine and *bpy* = bipyridyl moities. (At. nos. Ti = 22, V = 23, Fe = 26, Co = 27) *(2008)*

44. In which of the following coordination entities the magnitude of Δ_o (CFSE in octahedral field) will be maximum?
(a) $[Co(CN)_6]^{3-}$ (b) $[Co(C_2O_4)_3]^{3-}$
(c) $[Co(H_2O)_6]^{3+}$ (d) $[Co(NH_3)_6]^{3+}$
(At. No. Co = 27) *(2008)*

45. Which of the following will give a pair of enantiomorphs?
(a) $[Cr(NH_3)_6][Co(CN)_6]$
(b) $[Co(en)_2Cl_2]Cl$
(c) $[Pt(NH_3)_4][PtCl_6]$
(d) $[Co(NH_3)_4Cl_2]NO_2$ *(2007)*
($en = NH_2CH_2CH_2NH_2$)

46. The *d* electron configurations of Cr^{2+}, Mn^{2+}, Fe^{2+} and Ni^{2+} are $3d^4$, $3d^5$, $3d^6$ and $3d^8$ respectively. Which one of the following aqua complexes will exhibit the minimum paramagnetic behaviour?
(a) $[Fe(H_2O)_6]^{2+}$ (b) $[Ni(H_2O)_6]^{2+}$
(c) $[Cr(H_2O)_6]^{2+}$ (d) $[Mn(H_2O)_6]^{2+}$.
(At. No. Cr = 24, Mn = 25, Fe = 26, Ni = 28) *(2007)*

47. $[Cr(H_2O)_6]Cl_3$ (At. no. of Cr = 24) has a magnetic moment of 3.83 B.M. The correct distribution of 3*d* electrons in the chromium of the complex is
(a) $3d^1_{xy}$, $3d^1_{yz}$, $3d^1_{z^2}$
(b) $3d^1_{(x^2-y^2)}$, $3d^1_{z^2}$, $3d^1_{xz}$
(c) $3d^1_{xy}$, $3d^1_{(x^2-y^2)}$, $3d^1_{yz}$
(d) $3d^1_{xy}$, $3d^1_{yz}$, $3d^1_{xz}$ *(2006)*

48. $[Co(NH_3)_4(NO_2)_2]Cl$ exhibits
(a) linkage isomerism, geometrical isomerism and optical isomerism
(b) linkage isomerism, ionization isomerism and optical isomerism
(c) linkage isomerism, ionization isomerism and geometrical isomerism
(d) ionization isomerism, geometrical isomerism and optical isomerism. *(2006)*

49. Which one of the following is an inner orbital complex as well as diamagnetic in behaviour?
(a) $[Zn(NH_3)_6]^{2+}$ (b) $[Cr(NH_3)_6]^{3+}$
(c) $[Co(NH_3)_6]^{3+}$ (d) $[Ni(NH_3)_6]^{2+}$
(Atomic number : Zn = 30, Cr = 24, Co = 27, Ni = 28) *(2005)*

50. Which one of the following is expected to exhibit optical isomerism?
(*en* = ethylenediamine)
(a) *cis*-$[Pt(NH_3)_2Cl_2]$
(b) *trans*-$[Pt(NH_3)_2Cl_2]$
(c) *cis*-$[Co(en)_2Cl_2]^+$
(d) *trans*-$[Co(en)_2Cl_2]^+$ *(2005)*

51. Which of the following is considered to be an anticancer species?

(a) 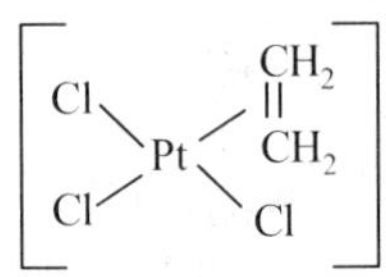

(b) 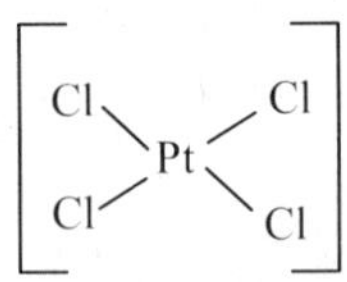

(c) 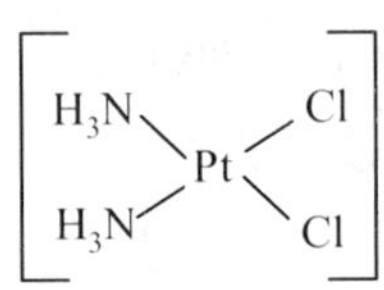

(d) 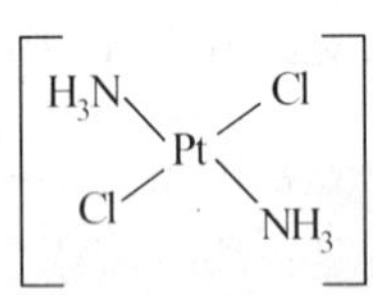 *(2004)*

52. Which of the following coordination compounds would exhibit optical isomerism?
(a) Pentaamminenitrocobalt(III) iodide
(b) Diamminedichloroplatinum(II)
(c) *trans*-Dicyanobis(ethylenediamine) chromium (III) chloride
(d) tris-(Ethylenediamine)cobalt(III) bromide *(2004)*

53. Among $[Ni(CO)_4]$, $[Ni(CN)_4]^{2-}$, $[NiCl_4]^{2-}$ species, the hybridisation states at the Ni atom are, respectively

(a) sp^3, dsp^2, dsp^2 (b) sp^3, dsp^2, sp^3

(c) sp^3, sp^3, dsp^2 (d) dsp^2, sp^3, sp^3.

[Atomic number of Ni = 28] *(2004)*

54. CN^- is a strong field ligand. This is due to the fact that

(a) it carries negative charge

(b) it is a pseudohalide

(c) it can accept electrons from metal species

(d) it forms high spin complexes with metal species. *(2004)*

55. Considering H_2O as a weak field ligand, the number of unpaired electrons in $[Mn(H_2O)_6]^{2+}$ will be (atomic number of Mn = 25)

(a) three (b) five

(c) two (d) four. *(2004)*

56. Which of the following does not have a metal - carbon bond?

(a) $Al(OC_2H_5)_3$ (b) C_2H_5MgBr

(c) $K[Pt(C_2H_4)Cl_3]$ (d) $Ni(CO)_4$ *(2004)*

57. In an octahedral structure, the pair of *d* orbitals involved in d^2sp^3 hybridisation is

(a) $d_{x^2-y^2}$, d_{z^2} (b) d_{xz}, $d_{x^2-y^2}$

(c) d_{z^2}, d_{xz} (d) d_{xy}, d_{yz}. *(2004)*

58. The number of unpaired electrons in the complex ion $[CoF_6]^{3-}$ is

(a) 2 (b) 3 (c) 4 (d) zero

(Atomic no. : Co = 27) *(2003)*

59. Among the following which is not the π-bonded organometallic compound?

(a) $K[PtCl_3(\eta^2-C_2H_4)]$

(b) $Fe(\eta^5-C_5H_5)_2$

(c) $Cr(\eta^6-C_6H_6)_2$

(d) $(CH_3)_4Sn$ *(2003)*

60. Atomic number of Cr and Fe are respectively 24 and 26, which of the following is paramagnetic with the spin of electron?

(a) $[Cr(CO)_6]$ (b) $[Fe(CO)_5]$

(c) $[Fe(CN)_6]^{4-}$ (d) $[Cr(NH_3)_6]^{3+}$

(2002)

61. The hypothetical complex chloro diaquatriammine cobalt(III) chloride can be represented as

(a) $[CoCl(NH_3)_3(H_2O)_2]Cl_2$

(b) $[Co(NH_3)_3(H_2O)Cl_3]$

(c) $[Co(NH_2)_3(H_2O)_2Cl]$

(d) $[Co(NH_3)_3(H_2O)_3]Cl_3$ *(2002)*

62. In the silver plating of copper, $K[Ag(CN)_2]$ is used instead of $AgNO_3$. The reason is

(a) a thin layer of Ag is formed on Cu

(b) more voltage is required

(c) Ag^+ ions are completely removed from solution

(d) less availability of Ag^+ ions, as Cu can not displace Ag from $[Ag(CN)_2]^-$ ion. *(2002)*

63. $CuSO_4$ when reacts with KCN forms CuCN, which is insoluble in water. It is soluble in excess of KCN, due to formation of the following complex

(a) $K_2[Cu(CN)_4]$ (b) $K_3[Cu(CN)_4]$

(c) $CuCN_2$ (d) $Cu[KCu(CN)_4]$.

(2002)

64. Which of the following will give maximum number of isomers?

(a) $[Co(NH_3)_4Cl_2]$

(b) $[Ni(en)(NH_3)_4]^{2+}$

(c) $[Ni(C_2O_4)(en)_2]^{2-}$

(d) $[Cr(SCN)_2(NH_3)_4]^+$ *(2001)*

65. Coordination number of Ni in $[Ni(C_2O_4)_3]^{4-}$ is

(a) 3 (b) 6 (c) 4 (d) 2

(2001)

66. Which of the following organometallic compounds is σ and π-bonded?

(a) $[Fe(\eta^5-C_5H_5)_2]$

(b) $K[PtCl_3(\eta^2-C_2H_4)]$

(c) $[Co(CO)_5NH_3]^{2+}$

(d) $Fe(CH_3)_3$ *(2001)*

67. Which statement is incorrect?

(a) $Ni(CO)_4$ - tetrahedral, paramagnetic

(b) $Ni(CN)_4^{2-}$ - square planar, diamagnetic

(c) $Ni(CO)_4$ - tetrahedral, diamagnetic

(d) $[Ni(Cl)_4]^{2-}$ - tetrahedral, paramagnetic.

(2001)

68. Which of the following will exhibit maximum ionic conductivity?

(a) $K_4[Fe(CN)_6]$ (b) $[Co(NH_3)_6]Cl_3$

(c) $[Cu(NH_3)_4]Cl_2$ (d) $[Ni(CO)_4]$

(2001)

69. Shape of $Fe(CO)_5$ is
(a) octahedral
(b) square planar
(c) trigonal bipyramidal
(d) square pyramidal. *(2000)*

70. Which complex compound will give four isomers?
(a) $[Fe(en)_3]Cl_3$ (b) $[Co(en)_2Cl_2]Cl$
(c) $[Fe(PPh_3)_3NH_3ClBr]Cl$
(d) $[Co(PPh_3)_3Cl]Cl_3$ *(2000)*

71. The total number of possible isomers for the complex compound $[Cu^{II}(NH_3)_4][Pt^{II}Cl_4]$ are
(a) 5 (b) 6 (c) 3 (d) 4 *(1998)*

72. A coordination complex compound of cobalt has the molecular formula containing five ammonia molecules, one nitro group and two chlorine atoms for one cobalt atom. One mole of this compound produces three mole ions in an aqueous solution. On reacting this solution with excess of $AgNO_3$ solution, we get two moles of AgCl precipitate. The ionic formula for this complex would be
(a) $[Co(NH_3)_5(NO_2)]Cl_2$
(b) $[Co(NH_3)_5Cl][Cl(NO_2)]$
(c) $[Co(NH_3)_4(NO_2)Cl](NH_3)Cl]$
(d) $(Co(NH_3)_5][(NO_2)_2Cl_2]$ *(1998)*

73. IUPAC name of $[Pt(NH_3)_3(Br)(NO_2)Cl]Cl$ is
(a) Triamminebromochloronitroplatinum(IV) chloride
(b) Triamminebromonitrochloroplatinum(IV) chloride
(c) Triamminechlorobromonitroplatinum(IV) chloride
(d) Triamminenitrochlorobromoplatinum(IV) chloride *(1998)*

74. The formula of dichlorobis(urea)copper(II) is
(a) $[Cu\{O=C(NH_2)_2\}Cl]Cl$
(b) $[CuCl_2]\{O=C(NH_2)_2\}$
(c) $[Cu\{O=C(NH_2)_2\}Cl_2$
(d) $[CuCl_2\{O=C(NH_2)_2\}_2]$. *(1997)*

75. The number of geometrical isomers of the complex $[Co(NO_2)_3(NH_3)_3]$ is
(a) 4 (b) 0 (c) 2 (d) 3 *(1997)*

76. The coordination number and oxidation state of Cr in $K_3Cr(C_2O_4)_3$ are respectively
(a) 3 and + 3 (b) 3 and 0
(c) 6 and + 3 (d) 4 and + 2 *(1995)*

77. The number of geometrical isomers for $[Pt(NH_3)_2Cl_2]$ is
(a) 3 (b) 4 (c) 1 (d) 2 *(1995)*

78. In metal carbonyl having general formula $M(CO)_x$ where M = metal, x = 4 and the metal is bonded to
(a) carbon and oxygen (b) $C\equiv O$
(c) oxygen (d) carbon. *(1995)*

79. Which of the following ligands is expected to be bidentate?
(a) CH_3NH_2 (b) $CH_3C\equiv N$
(c) Br (d) $C_2O_4^{2-}$ *(1994)*

Answer Key

1. (a)	2. (b)	3. (b)	4. (a)	5. (b)	6. (d)	7. (b)	8. (b)	9. (b)	10. (a)
11. (d)	12. (c)	13. (d)	14. (b)	15. (c)	16. (c)	17. (b)	18. (b)	19. (c)	20. (c)
21. (b)	22. (b)	23. (c)	24. (b)	25. (c)	26. (b)	27. (a)	28. (c)	29. (b)	30. (b)
31. (c)	32. (a)	33. (c)	34. (a)	35. (b)	36. (a)	37. (d)	38. (d)	39. (c)	40. (b)
41. (a)	42. (b)	43. (d)	44. (a)	45. (b)	46. (b)	47. (d)	48. (c)	49. (c)	50. (c)
51. (c)	52. (d)	53. (b)	54. (b)	55. (b)	56. (a)	57. (a)	58. (c)	59. (d)	60. (d)
61. (a)	62. (d)	63. (b)	64. (d)	65. (b)	66. (c)	67. (a)	68. (a)	69. (c)	70. (b)
71. (d)	72. (a)	73. (a)	74. (b)	75. (c)	76. (c)	77. (d)	78. (d)	79. (d)	

EXPLANATIONS

1. **(a)** : $[CoCl_2(en)_2]$, exhibit geometrical isomerism, as the coordination number of Co is 6 and this compound has octahedral geometry.

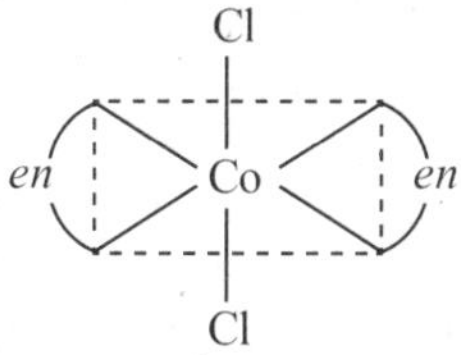

trans-form
(optically inactive)

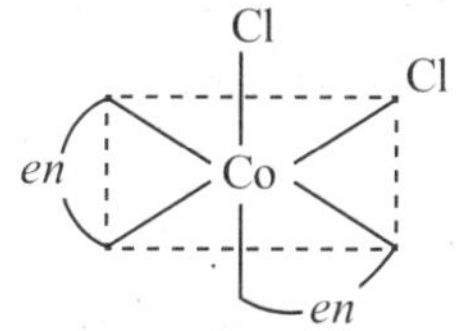

cis-form
(optically active)

2. **(b)** : Ni(28) : $[Ar]3d^8 4s^2$

∵ CO is a strong field ligand, so, unpaired electrons get paired.

In $[Ni(CO)_4]$:

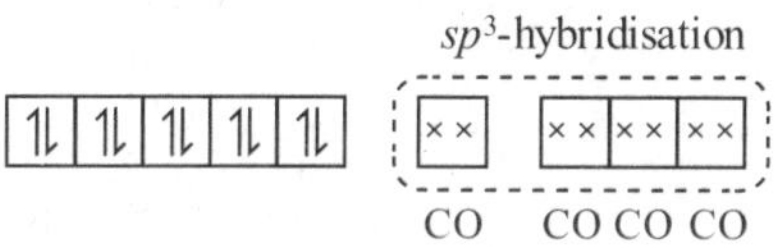

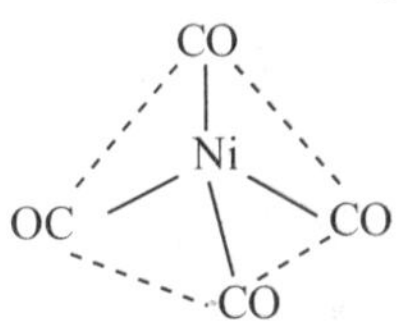

Thus, the complex is sp^3 hybridised with tetrahedral geometry and diamagnetic in nature.

3. **(b)** : Based on the number of metal atoms present in a complex, they are classified as :

e.g., : $Fe(CO)_5$: mononuclear

$Co_2(CO)_8$: dinuclear

$Fe_3(CO)_{12}$: trinuclear

4. **(a)**

5. **(b)** : $[Co(NH_3)_6]Cl_3 + 3AgNO_3 \rightarrow 3AgCl\downarrow + [Co(NH_3)_6](NO_3)_3$

$[Co(NH_3)_5Cl]Cl_2 + 2AgNO_3 \rightarrow 2AgCl\downarrow + [Co(NH_3)_5Cl](NO_3)_2$

$[Co(NH_3)_4Cl_2]Cl + AgNO_3 \rightarrow AgCl\downarrow + [Co(NH_3)_4Cl_2]NO_3$

6. **(d)**: Increasing order of crystal field splitting energy is : $H_2O < NH_3 < en$

Thus, increasing order of energy for the given complexes is :

$$[Co(H_2O)_6]^{3+} < [Co(NH_3)_6]^{3+} < [Co(en)_3]^{3+}$$

As, $E = \dfrac{hc}{\lambda}$

Thus, increasing order of wavelength of absorption is:

$$[Co(en)_3]^{3+} < [Co(NH_3)_6]^{3+} < [Co(H_2O)_6]^{3+}$$

7. **(b)**: $[Mn(CN)_6]^{3-}$: Let oxidation state of Mn be x.

$$x + 6 \times (-1) = -3 \Rightarrow x = +3$$

Electronic configuration of Mn : $[Ar]4s^2\ 3d^5$

Electronic configuration of Mn^{3+} : $[Ar]3d^4$

CN^- is a strong field ligand thus, it causes pairing of electrons in $3d$-orbital.

$[Mn(CN)_6]^{3-}$: [Ar]

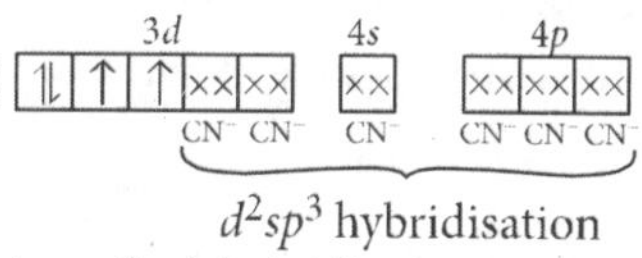

Then, $[Mn(CN)_6]^{3-}$ has d^2sp^3 hybridisation and has octahedral geometry.

8. **(b)**: The intensity of the *trans*-effect (as measured by the increase in rate of substitution of the *trans* ligand follows the sequence :

$CN^- > C_6H_5^- > Br^- > NH_3$

9. **(b)**: Jahn–Teller distortion is usually significant for asymmetrically occupied e_g orbitals since they are directed towards the ligands and the energy gain is considerably more.

In case of unevenly occupied t_{2g} orbitals, the Jahn–Teller distortion is very weak since the t_{2g} set does not point directly at the ligands and therefore, the energy gain is much less.

High spin complexes :

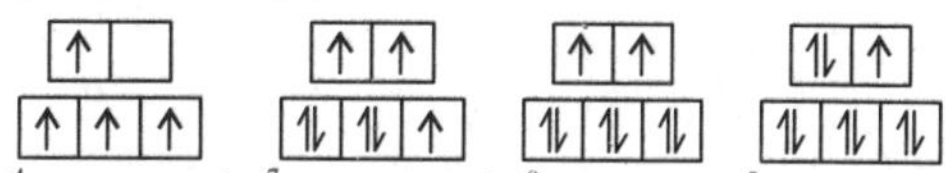

d^4, unsymmetrical d^7, unsymmetrical d^8, symmetrical d^9, unsymmetrical

10. **(a)** : The greater the negative charge on the carbonyl complex, the more easy it would be for the metal to permit its electrons to participate in the back bonding, the higher would be the *M*—C bond order and simultaneously there would be larger reduction in the C—O bond order. Thus, $[Fe(CO)_4]^{2-}$ has the lowest C—O bond order means the longest bond length.

11. **(d)** : $[Ni(CN)_4]^{2-}$: Oxidation number of Ni = +2

Electronic configuration of Ni^{2+} : $3d^8 4s^0$

$[Ni(CN)_4]^{2-}$ =

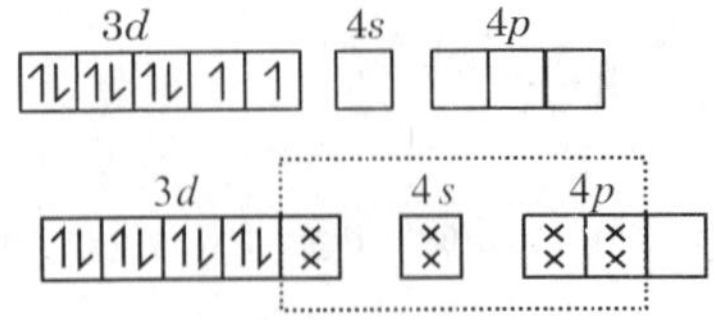

*dsp*² hybridization

[Pairing of electrons in *d*-orbital takes place due to the presence of strong field ligand (CN^-)]

12. (c)

13. (d) : $[M(en)_2(C_2O_4)]Cl$:

Oxidation number of metal = +3

Coordination number of metal = 6

∴ Sum of oxidation number and coordination number = 3 + 6 = 9

14. (b) : Possible isomers of $[Co(en)_2Cl_2]Cl$:

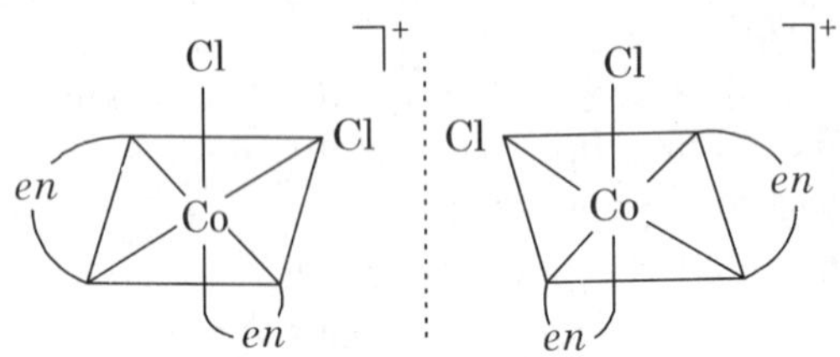

cis-isomer
(*d* and *l* forms)

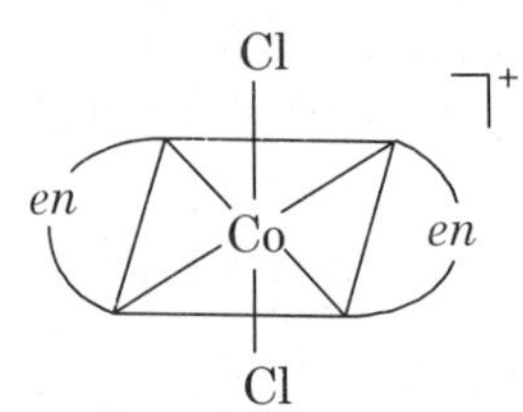

trans-isomer

15. (c) : For octahedral complexes, coordination number is 6.

Hence, $CoCl_3 \cdot 3NH_3$ *i.e.*, $[Co(NH_3)_3Cl_3]$ will not ionise and will not give test for Cl^- ion with silver nitrate.

16. (c) : $[Co(CN)_6]^{3-}$, oxidation no. of Co = +3

$Co^{3+} = 3d^6$

As CN^- is a strong field ligand, so all electrons will be paired up and complex will be low spin complex.

17. (b) : H_2O is a weak field ligand, hence

Δ_o < pairing energy.

CFSE = $(-0.4x + 0.6y)\Delta_o$

where, x and y are no. of electrons occupying t_{2g} and e_g orbitals respectively.

For $[Fe(H_2O)_6]^{3+}$ complex ion,

$Fe^{3+}(3d^5) = t_{2g}^3 e_g^2 = -0.4 \times 3 + 0.6 \times 2 = 0.0$ or 0 Dq

18. (b)

19. (c) : Oxidation state of Cu in $[Cu(NH_3)_4]^{2+}$ is +2

$Cu^{2+} = 3d^9$ 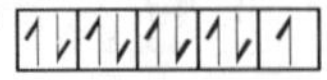

It has one unpaired electron (n = 1).

$\mu = \sqrt{n(n+2)} = \sqrt{1(1+2)} = \sqrt{3} = 1.73$ BM

20. (c) : $[Cr(H_2O)_4Cl_2]Cl + AgNO_3 \rightarrow [Cr(H_2O)_4Cl_2]NO_3 + \underset{\text{ppt.}}{AgCl}$

No. of mole = $\frac{100}{1000} = 10^{-3}$

So, mole of AgCl = 0.001

21. (b) : CFSE = $(-0.4x + 0.6y)\Delta_o$

where, x = No. of electrons occupying t_{2g} orbitals

y = No. of electrons occupying e_g orbitals

$= (-0.4 \times 3 + 0.6 \times 1)\Delta_o$ [∵ High spin $d^4 = t_{2g}^3 e_g^1$]

$= (-1.2 + 0.6)\Delta_o = -0.6\Delta_o$

22. (b) :

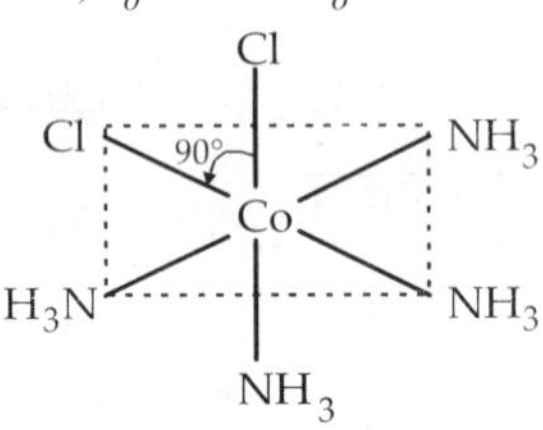

cis isomer

23. (c) : Chelating ligands having conjugated double bonds form more stable six membered rings.

24. (b)

25. (c) : $Co^{2+} = (3d^5)$

Bromine is a weak ligand but it is known that all tetrahedral complexes are high-spin regardless of the splitting power of the ligand. The low spin arrangement has five unpaired electrons in the *d*-orbital. So it is paramagnetic in nature.

26. (b) : In $[Ni(CN)_4]^{2-}$ all orbitals are doubly occupied, hence, it is diamagnetic.

$Ni^{2+} = 3d^8$

$[Ni(CN)_4]^{2-}$ = 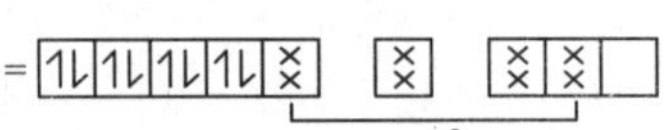

CN is a strong ligand and causes pairing of 3*d*-electrons of Ni^{2+}.

27. (a) : $[Ni(NH_3)_6]^{2+}$: sp^3d^2 (outer), octahedral, paramagnetic

$[Zn(NH_3)_6]^{2+}$: sp^3d^2 (outer), octahedral, diamagnetic

$[Cr(NH_3)_6]^{3+}$: d^2sp^3 (inner), octahedral, paramagnetic

$[Co(NH_3)_6]^{3+}$: d^2sp^3 (inner), octahedral, diamagnetic

28. (c) : $[Ni(dmg)_2]$ is square planar in structure not tetrahedral.

29. (b): C.F.S.E. = $(-0.4x + 0.6y)\Delta_o + zP$
where x = number of electrons occupying t_{2g} orbital
y = number of electrons occupying e_g orbital
z = number of pairs of electrons
For low spin d^6 complex electronic configuration
$= t_{2g}^6\, e_g^0$ or $t_{2g}^{2,2,2}\, e_g^0$
$\therefore\ x = 6, y = 0, z = 3$
C.F.S.E. $= (-0.4 \times 6 + 0 \times 0.6)\Delta_o + 3P$
$= \frac{-12}{5}\Delta_o + 3P$

30. (b): $[NiCl_4]^{2-}$:

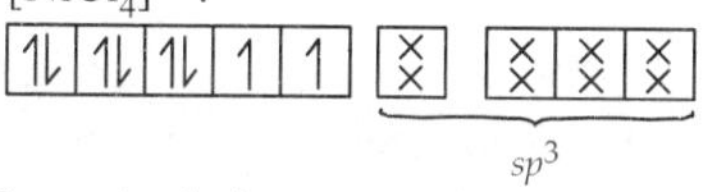

Number of unpaired electrons = 2
Hence $[NiCl_4]^{2-}$ is paramagnetic.

$[Ni(CN)_4]^{2-}$:

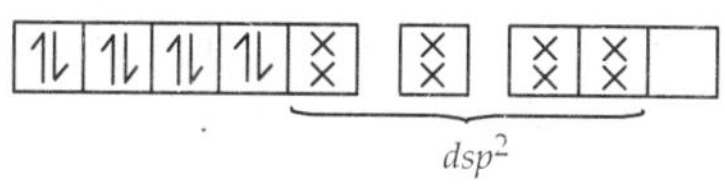

Number of unpaired electrons = 0, so it is diamagnetic in nature.

$[CuCl_4]^{2-}$:

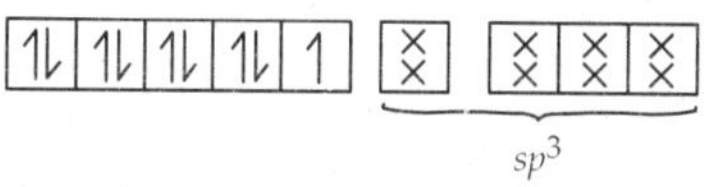

No. of unpaired electron = 1, so it is paramagnetic.

$[CoF_6]^{3-}$:

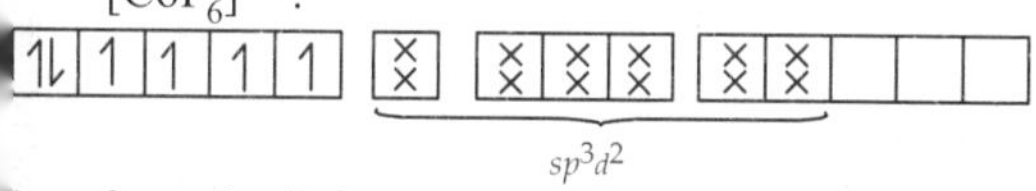

No. of unpaired electrons = 4, so it is paramagnetic.

31. (c): Coordination isomerism arises from the interchange of ligands between cationic and anionic entities of different metal ions present in the complex.
e.g., $[Co(NH_3)_6][Cr(CN)_6]$ and $[Cr(NH_3)_6][Co(CN)_6]$

32. (a): $[Pt(Py)(NH_3)BrCl]$ can have three isomers.

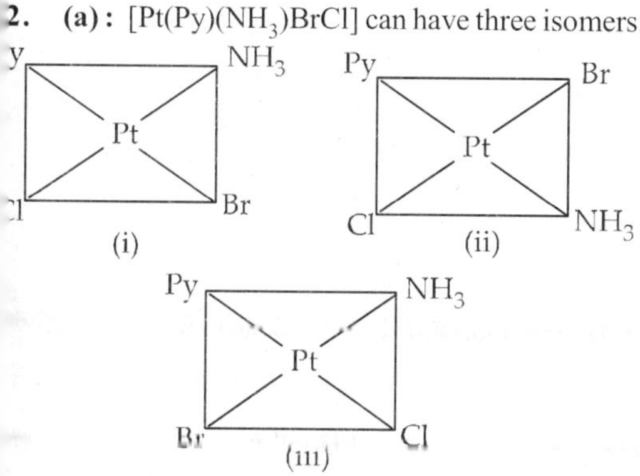

33. (c): $[Mn(H_2O)_6]^{2+}$: $Mn^{2+} = 3d^5$
Number of unpaired electron = 5
$[Fe(H_2O)_6]^{2+}$: $Fe^{2+} = 3d^6$
$\therefore$ Number of unpaired electrons = 4
$[Co(H_2O)_6]^{2+}$: $Co^{2+} = 3d^7$
$\therefore$ Number of unpaired electrons = 3
$[Cr(H_2O)_6]^{2+}$: $Cr^{2+} = 3d^4$
$\therefore$ Number of unpaired electrons = 4
Minimum paramagnetic behaviour is shown by $[Co(H_2O)_6]^{2+}$.

34. (a): The presence of positive charge on the metal carbonyl would resist the flow of the metal electron charge to π^* orbitals of CO. This would increase the CO bond order and hence CO in a metal carbonyl cation would absorb at a higher frequency compared to its absorption in a neutral metal carbonyl.

35. (b): $Ti \rightarrow [Ar]\,3d^2\,4s^2$, $Ti^{3+} \rightarrow [Ar]\,3d^1\,4s^0$
(1 unpaired electron)
$Cr \rightarrow [Ar]\,3d^4\,4s^2$, $Cr^{3+} \rightarrow [Ar]\,3d^3\,4s^0$
(3 unpaired electrons)
$Co \rightarrow [Ar]\,3d^7\,4s^2$, $Co^{3+} \rightarrow [Ar]\,3d^6\,4s^0$
(0 unpaired electrons because of pairing)
$Zn \rightarrow [Ar]\,3d^{10}\,4s^2$, $Zn^{2+} \rightarrow [Ar]\,3d^{10}$
(no unpaired electrons)
$[Cr(NH_3)_6]^{3+}$ exhibits highest paramagnetic behaviour as it contains 3 unpaired electrons.

36. (a): A transition metal complex absorbs visible light only if it has unpaired electrons.

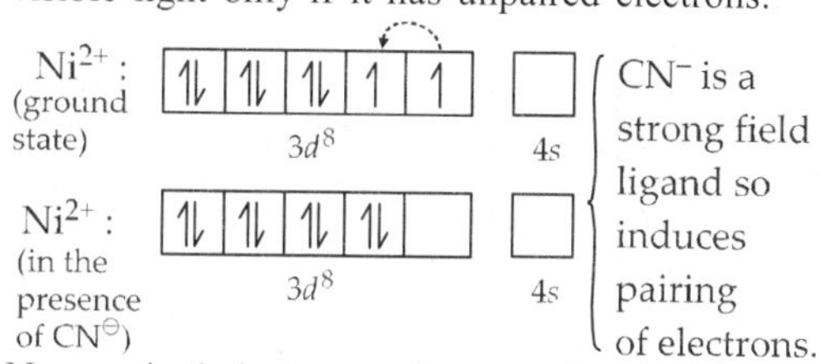

No unpaired electron so does not absorb visible light.

37. (d):

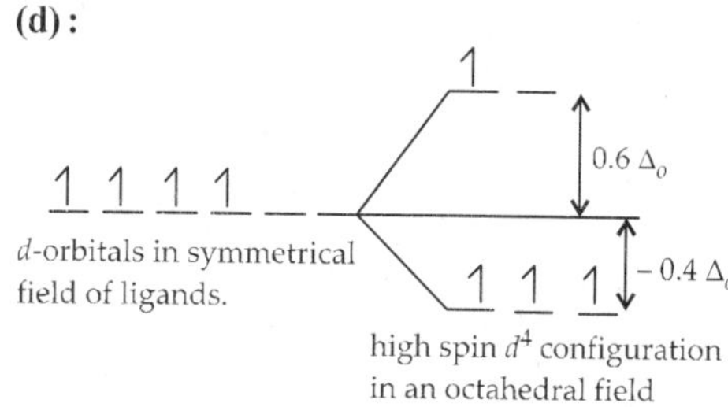

CFSE $= 3(-0.4)\Delta_o + 0.6\Delta_o = -1.2\Delta_o + 0.6\Delta_o = -0.6\Delta_o$

38. (d)

39. (c)

40. (b): A species is coloured when it contains unpaired d-electrons which are capable of undergoing d-d transition on adsorption of light of a particular wavelength.
In TiF_6^{2-}, Ti^{4+} : $3d^0$, colourless
In CoF_6^{3-}, Co^{3+} : $3d^6$, coloured

In Cu_2Cl_2, $Cu^+ : 3d^{10}$, colourless
In $NiCl_4^{2-}$, $Ni^{2+} : 3d^8$, coloured.
Thus TiF_6^{2-} $(3d^0)$ and Cu_2Cl_2 $(3d^{10})$ with empty and fully filled *d*-orbitals appear colourless as they are not capable of undergoing *d-d* transition.

41. **(a) :** Optical isomerism is shown by :
(i) complexes of the type $[M(AA)X_2Y_2]$, *i.e.*, $[Co(en)Cl_2(NH_3)_2]^+$ containing one symmetrical bidentate ligand.
(ii) complexes of the type $[M(AA)_3]$, *i.e.*, $[Co(en)_3]^{3+}$ containing a symmetrical bidentate ligand.
(iii) complexes of the type $[M(AA)_2X_2]$, *i.e.*, $[Co(en)_2Cl_2]^+$. However compexes of the type $[MA_3B_3]$ show geometrical isomerism, known as *fac-mer* isomerism.
∴ $[Co(NH_3)_3Cl_3]$ exhibits *fac-mer* isomerism.

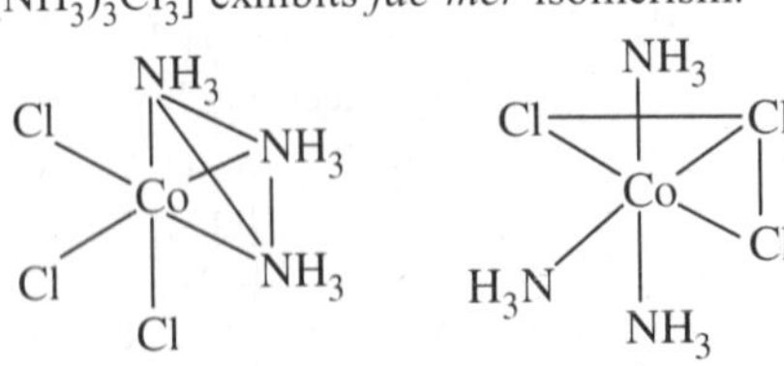

42. **(b):** $Ti^{4+} \rightarrow 3d^0$, $Cr^{3+} \rightarrow 3d^3$
$Zn^{2+} \rightarrow 3d^{10}$, $Sc^{3+} \rightarrow 3d^0$
Transition metal ions containing completely filled *d*-orbitals or empty *d*-orbitals are colourless species.

43. **(d) :** O.S of Ti in the complex $[Ti(NH_3)_6]^{3+}$
$Ti^{3+} = 1s^2\,2s^2\,2p^6\,3s^2\,3p^6\,3d^1$
no. of unpaired electron in *d* orbital is one.
O.S of V in complex $[V(gly)_2(OH)_2(NH_3)_2]^+$
$= x + 2 \times 0 + 2 \times (-1) + 2 \times 0 = +1$
$\therefore x = +3$
$V^{3+} = 1s^2\,2s^2\,2p^6\,3s^2\,3p^6\,3d^2$
no. of unpaired electron in *d* orbital is two.
O.S of Fe in the given complex is +2
∴ $Fe^{2+} = 1s^2\,2s^2\,2p^6\,3s^2\,3p^6\,3d^6$
no. of unpaired electron in *d* orbital is four.
O.S of Co in the given complex $[Co(ox)_2(OH)_2]^-$
$= x + 2 \times (-2) + 2 \times (-1) = -1 = x - 4 - 2 = -1$
$\therefore x = +5$
(not possible, common ox. no. of Co = +2, +3, +4)
$Co^{5+} = 1s^2\,2s^2\,2p^6\,3s^2\,3p^6\,3d^4$
It should be an inner orbital complex (d^2sp^3 hybridisation) containing only one unpaired electron. So the complex having highest paramagnetism would be the complex of iron containing four unpaired electrons.

44. **(a) :** When the ligands are arranged in order of the magnitude of crystal field splitting, the arrangement, thus, obtained is called spectrochemical series.
Arranged in increasing field strength as
$I^- < Br^- < Cl^- < NO_3^- < F^- < OH^- < C_2O_4^{2-} < H_2O < NH_3 < en < NO_2^- < CN^- < CO$
It has been observed that ligands before H_2O are weak field ligands while ligands after H_2O are strong field ligands.

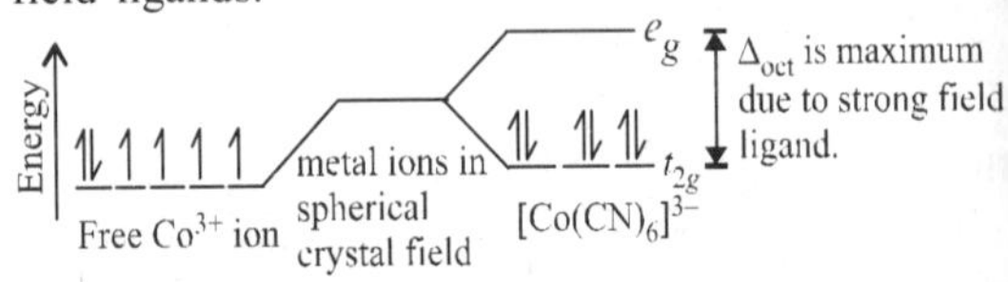

CFSE in octahedral field depends upon the nature of ligands. Stronger the ligands larger will be the value of Δ_{oct}.

45. **(b) :** Either a pair of crystals, molecules or compounds that are mirror images of each other but are not identical, and that rotate the plane of polarised light equally, but in opposite directions are called as enantiomorphs.

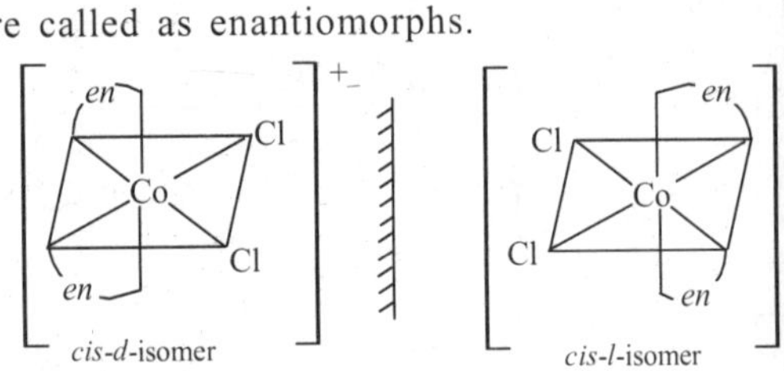

46. **(b) :** 3*d*

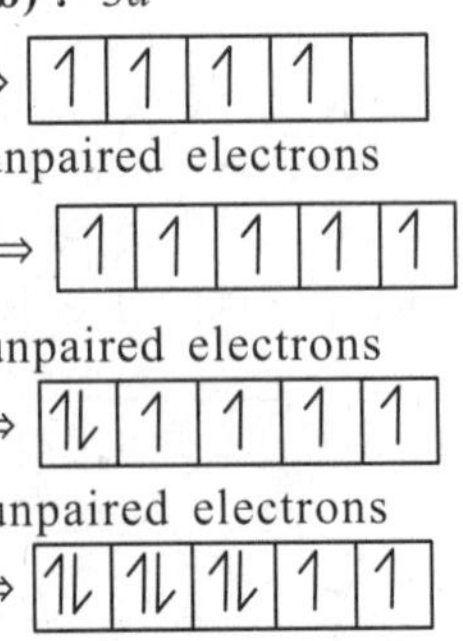

$Cr^{2+} \Rightarrow$ ↿ ↿ ↿ ↿ _
⇒ 4 unpaired electrons
$Mn^{2+} \Rightarrow$ ↿ ↿ ↿ ↿ ↿
⇒ 5 unpaired electrons
$Fe^{2+} \Rightarrow$ ⥮ ↿ ↿ ↿ ↿
⇒ 4 unpaired electrons
$Ni^{2+} \Rightarrow$ ⥮ ⥮ ⥮ ↿ ↿
⇒ 2 unpaired electrons
Greater the number of unpaired electrons, higher is the paramagnetism. Hence Ni^{2+} will exhibit the minimum paramagnetic behaviour.

47. **(d) :** Magnetic moment = $\sqrt{n(n+2)}$
$3.83 = \sqrt{n(n+2)} \Rightarrow (3.83)^2 = n(n+2)$
$\Rightarrow 14.6689 = n^2 + 2n$
On solving the equation, $n = 3$

$Cr^{3+} \rightarrow [Ar]\ 3d^3$

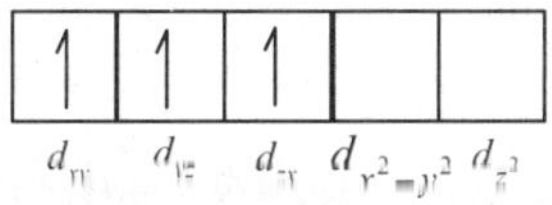

48. **(c)** : Ionization isomerism arises when the coordination compounds give different ions in solution.

$[Co(NH_3)_4(NO_2)]Cl \rightleftharpoons [Co(NH_3)_4(NO_2)_2]^+ + Cl^-$

Linkage isomerism occurs in complex compounds which contain ambidentate ligands like NO_2^-, SCN^-, CN^-, $S_2O_3^{2-}$ and CO.

$[Co(NH_3)_4(NO_2)_2]Cl$ and $[Co(NH_3)_4(ONO)_2]Cl$ are linkage isomers as NO_2^- is linked through N or through O.

Octahedral complexes of the type Ma_4b_2 exhibit geometrical isomerism.

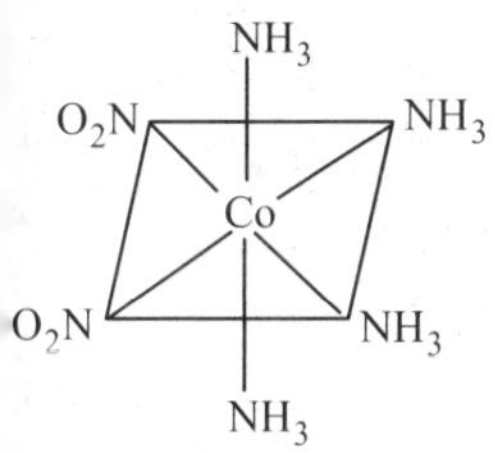

cis-

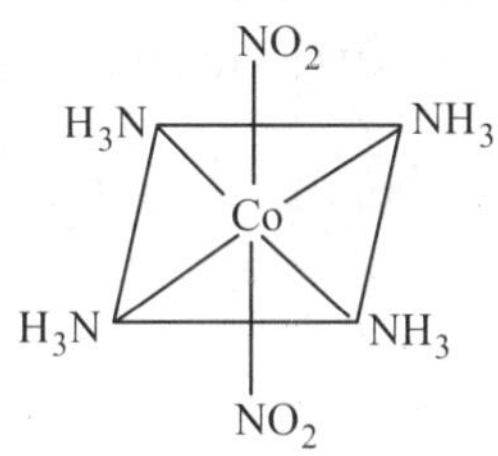

trans-

49. **(c)** : $[Co(NH_3)_6]^{3+}$: Co(27) $[Ar]^{18}$

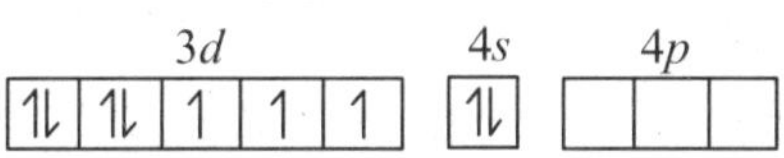

Co^{3+} : (24) $[Ar]^{18}$

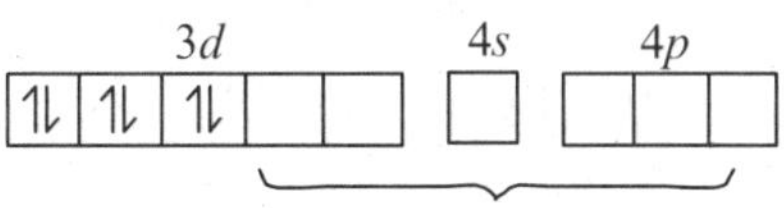

d^2sp^3

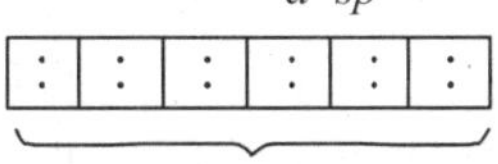

electron pair from six ligands (NH_3)

$d^2sp^3 \rightarrow$ inner octahedral complex and diamagnetic.

$[Zn(NH_3)_6]^{2+} \longrightarrow sp^3d^2$ (outer)and diamagnetic.

$[Cr(NH_3)_6]^{3+} \longrightarrow d^2sp^3$ (inner)and paramagnetic.

$[Ni(NH_3)_6]^{2+} \longrightarrow sp^3d^2$ (outer)and paramagnetic.

50. **(c)** : Optical isomerism is not shown by square planar complexes.

Octahedral complexes of general formulae, $[Ma_2b_2c_2]^{n\pm}$, $[Mabcdef]$, $[M(AA)_3]^{n\pm}$, $[M(AA)_2a_2]^{n\pm}$ (where AA = symmetrical bidentate ligand), $[M(AA)_2ab]^{n\pm}$ and $[M(AB)_3]^{n\pm}$ (where AB = unsymmetrical ligands) show optical isomerism.

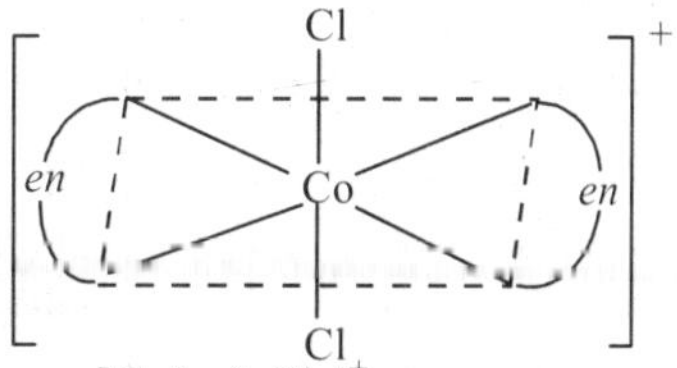

trans - $[Co(en)_2Cl_2]^+$

does not show optical isomerism (superimposable mirror image). But *cis*-form shows optical isomerism.

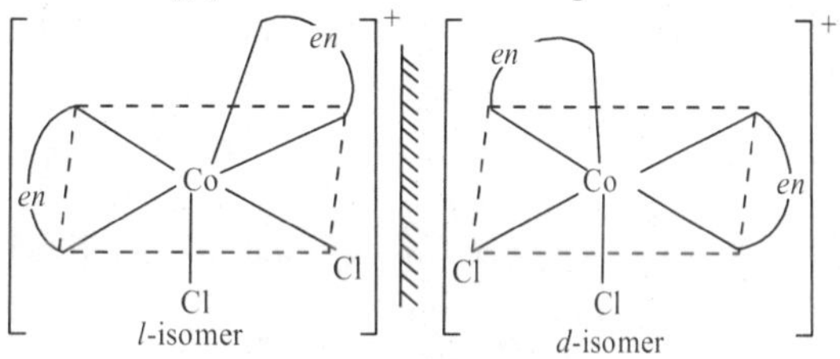

l-isomer *d*-isomer

cis - $[Co(en)_2Cl_2]^+$

51. **(c)** : *Cis* isomer of $[Pt(NH_3)_2Cl_2]$ is used as an anticancer drug for treating several types of malignant tumours. When it is injected into the blood stream, the more reactive Cl groups are lost. So the Pt atom bonds to a N atom in guanosine (a part of DNA). This molecule can bond to two different guanosine units and by bridging between them it upsets the normal reproduction of DNA.

52. **(d)** : $[Co(en)_3]^{3+}$:

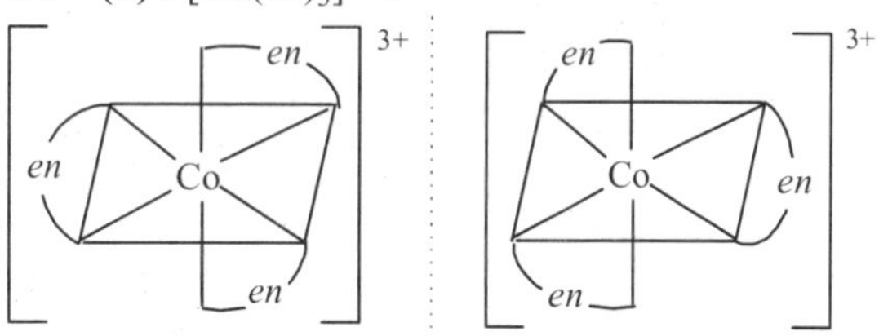

d-form mirror *l*-form

53. **(b)** :

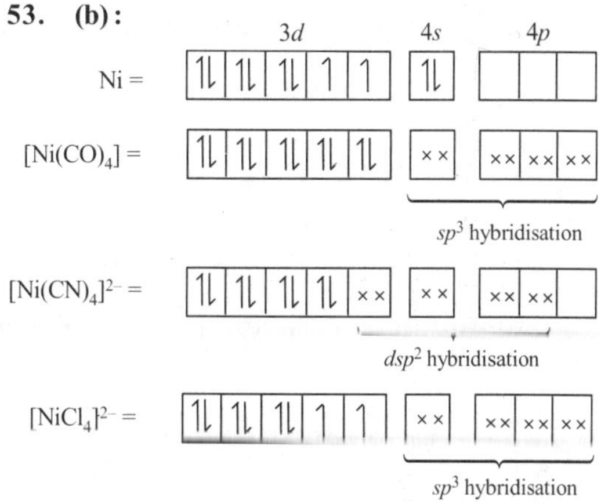

54. **(b)** : Cyanide ion is strong field ligand because it is a pseudohalide ion. Pseudohalide ions are stronger coordinating ligands and they have the ability to form σ-bond (from the pseudohalide to the metal) and π bond (from the metal to pseudohalide).

55. (b) : Mn 25 → $3d^5 4s^2$

Mn^{2+} → $3d^5$ 

In presence of weak field ligand, there will be no pairing of electrons. So it will form a high spin complex, *i.e.* the number of unpaired electrons = 5.

56. (a) : $Al(OC_2H_5)_3$ contains bonding through O and thus it does not have metal - carbon bond.

57. (a) : In the formation of d^2sp^3 hybrid orbitals, two $(n-1)d$ orbitals of e_g set [*i.e.* $(n-1)d_{z^2}$ and $(n-1)d_{x^2-y^2}$ orbitals)], one *ns* and three *np* (np_x, np_y and np_z) orbitals combine together and form six d^2sp^3 hybrid orbitals.

58. (c) : $[CoF_6]^{3-}$:

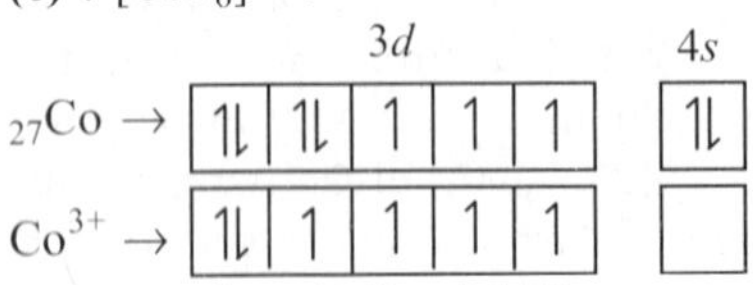

(in weak ligand field)

Thus, the number of unpaired electrons = 4.

59. (d) : π-bonded organometallic compound includes organometallic compounds of alkenes, alkynes and some other carbon containing compounds having electrons in their *p* orbitals.

60. (d) : Odd electrons, ions and molecules are paramagnetic.
In $Cr(CO)_6$ molecule 12 electrons are contributed by CO group and it contains no odd electron.
Cr → $3d^5\ 4s^1$
$Fe(CO)_5$ molecule also does not contain odd electron.
Fe → $3d^6\ 4s^2$
In $[Fe(CN)_6]^{4-}$ ion Fe(+II) → $3d^6\ 4s^0$
∴ No odd electrons.
In $[Cr(NH_3)_6]^{3+}$ ion Cr(+III) → $3d^3\ 4s^0$
This ion contains odd electron so it is paramagnetic.

61. (a) : Chlorodiaquatriamminecobalt(III)chloride can be represented as $[CoCl(NH_3)_3(H_2O)_2]Cl_2$.

62. (d) : Copper being more electropositive readily precipitate silver from their salt (Ag^+) solution.
$Cu + 2AgNO_3 \rightarrow Cu(NO_3)_2 + Ag$
In $K[Ag(CN)_2]$ solution a complex anion $[Ag(CN)_2]^-$ is formed so Ag^+ ions are less available in the solution and Cu cannot displace Ag from this complex ion.

63. (b) : Copper sulphate reacts with potassium cyanide giving a white precipitate of cuprous cyanide and cyanogen gas. The cuprous cyanide dissolves in excess of KCN forming potassium cuprocyanide $K_3[Cu(CN)_4]$.
$2CuSO_4 + 4KCN \rightarrow 2CuCN + (CN)_2 + 2K_2SO_4$
$CuCN + 3KCN \rightarrow K_3[Cu(CN)_4]$

64. (d): $[Cr(SCN)_2(NH_3)_4]^+$ shows linkage, geometrical and optical isomerisms.

65. (b) : C_2O_4 → bidentate ligand.
3 molecules attached from two sides with Ni makes co-ordination number 6.

66. (c) : $[Co(CO)_5NH_3]^{2+}$: In this complex, Co-atom is attached with NH_3 through σ bonding and with CO with dative π-bond.

67. (a) : In $Ni(CO)_4$ complex, $Ni(CO)_4$ will have $3d^{10}$ configuration.

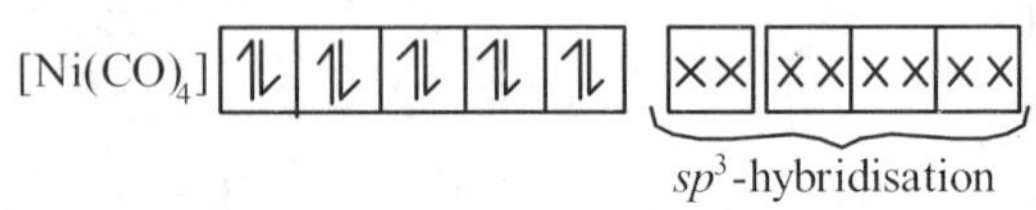

Hence $[Ni(CO)_4]$ will have tetrahedral geometry but diamagnetic as there are no unpaired electrons.

68. (a) : Ionic conductance increases with increasing the number of ions, produced after decomposition.

Compound	No. of ions produced
$K_4[Fe(CN)_6]$	5
$[Co(NH_3)_6]Cl_3$	4
$[Cu(NH_3)_4]Cl_2$	3
$[Ni(CO)_4]$	0

69. (c) : In $Fe(CO)_5$, the 'Fe' atom is dsp^3 hybridised, therefore shape of the molecule is trigonal bipyramidal.

Fe atom in $Fe(CO)_5$

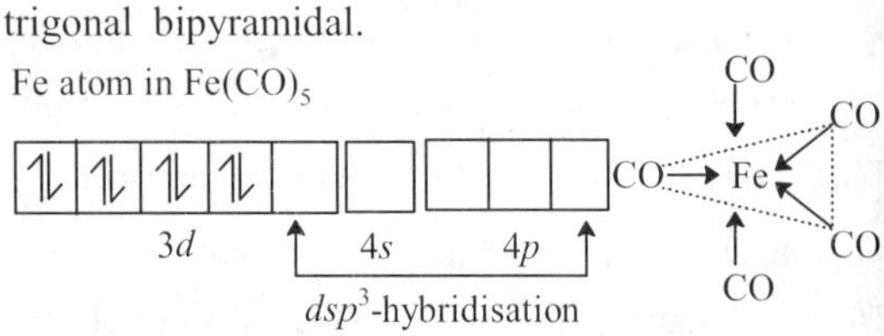

70. (c) : $[Fe(PPh_3)NH_3ClBr]Cl$ can give two optical and two geometrical isomers. While other complexes do not form geometrical isomers.

71. (d) : The isomers of the complex compound $[Cu^{II}(NH_3)_4][Pt^{II}Cl_4]$ are :

(i) $[Cu(NH_3)_3Cl][Pt(NH_3)Cl_3]$
(ii) $[Pt(NH_3)_3Cl][Cu(NH_3)Cl_3]$
(iii) $[Pt(NH_3)_4][CuCl_4]$
So, the total no. of isomers are – 4.

72. (a) : As the complex gives two moles of AgCl ppt. with $AgNO_3$ solution, so the complex must have two ionisable Cl atoms. Hence the probable complex, which gives three mole ions may be $[Co(NH_3)_5NO_2]Cl_2$.
$[Co(NH_3)_5NO_2]Cl_2 \rightarrow [Co(NH_3)_5NO_2]^{2+} + 2Cl^-$
one mole $\rightarrow$ 3 mole ions.

73. (a) : The ligands are named in the alphabatic order according to latest IUPAC system. So the name of $[Pt(NH_3)_3Br(NO_2)Cl]Cl$ is Triamminebromochloronitroplatinum(IV) chloride. (The oxidation no. of 'Pt' is +4).

74. (b)

75. (c) : Possible geometrical isomers are :

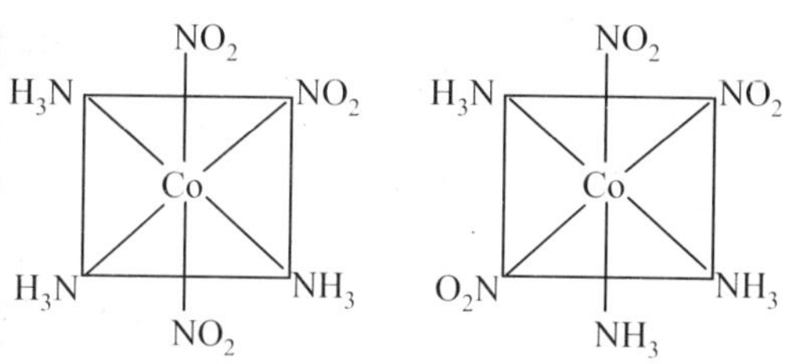

76. (c) :

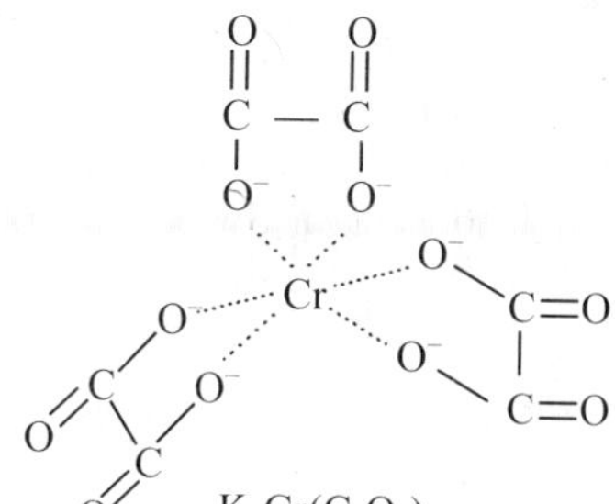

$K_3Cr(C_2O_4)_3$

As the number of atoms of the ligands that are directly bound to the central metal is known as coordination number. It is six here (see in figure).
Oxidation state :
Let oxidation state of Cr be x.
$\Rightarrow \quad 3(+1) + x + 3(-2) = 0 \Rightarrow 3 + x - 6 = 0 \Rightarrow x = 3$

77. (d) :

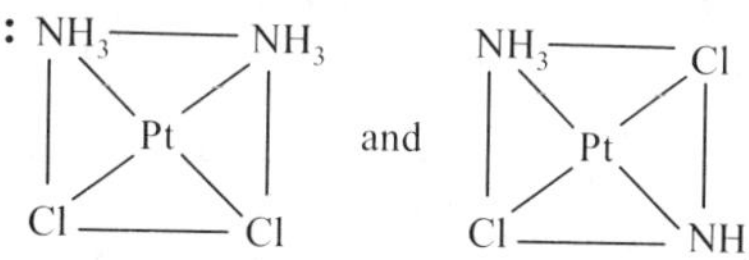

The two geometrical isomers are given above.

78. (d) : In $M(CO)_4$ metal is bonded to the ligands via carbon atoms with both σ and π-bond character. Both metal to ligand and ligand to metal bonding are possible.

79. (d) : When a ligand has two groups that are capable of bonding to the central atom, it is said to be bidentate. Thus the only ligand,which is expected to be bidentate is $C_2O_4^{2-}$ as

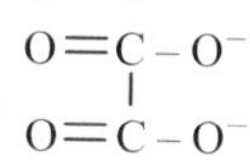

.

Chapter 24

Haloalkanes and Haloarenes

1. The compound *A* on treatment with Na gives *B*, and with PCl_5 gives *C*. *B* and *C* react together to give diethyl ether. *A*, *B* and *C* are in the order
   (a) C_2H_5OH, C_2H_6, C_2H_5Cl
   (b) C_2H_5OH, C_2H_5Cl, C_2H_5ONa
   (c) C_2H_5Cl, C_2H_6, C_2H_5OH
   (d) C_2H_5OH, C_2H_5ONa, C_2H_5Cl
   (NEET 2018)

2. The compound C_7H_8 undergoes the following reactions :

   $$C_7H_8 \xrightarrow{3Cl_2/\Delta} A \xrightarrow{Br_2/Fe} B \xrightarrow{Zn/HCl} C$$

   The product *C* is
   (a) *m*-bromotoluene
   (b) *o*-bromotoluene
   (c) 3-bromo-2,4,6-trichlorotoluene
   (d) *p*-bromotoluene. *(NEET 2018)*

3. Identify *A* and predict the type of reaction.

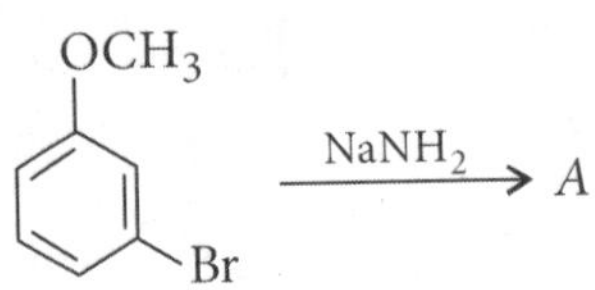

(a) 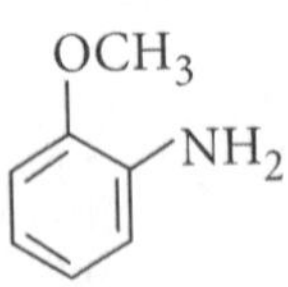

and elimination addition reaction

(b) 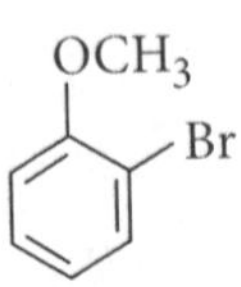

and cine substitution reaction

(c) 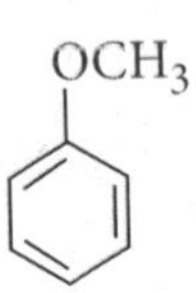

and cine substitution

(d) 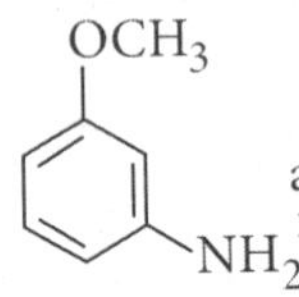

and substitution reaction

(NEET 2017,

4. Consider the reaction,
   $CH_3CH_2CH_2Br + NaCN \rightarrow CH_3CH_2CH_2CN + NaB$
   This reaction will be the fastest in
   (a) ethanol
   (b) methanol
   (c) *N*, *N*′-dimethylformamide (DMF)
   (d) water. *(NEET-II 2016*

5. Which of the following biphenyls is opticall active?

(a) 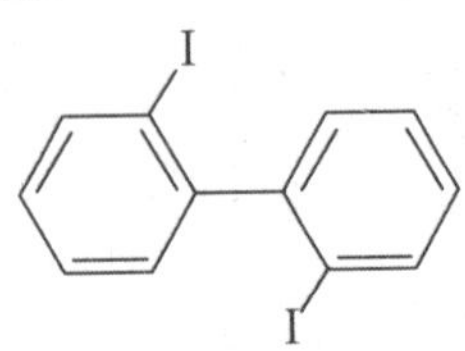

(b) 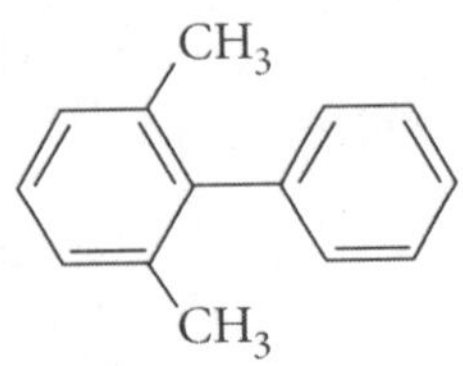

(c) 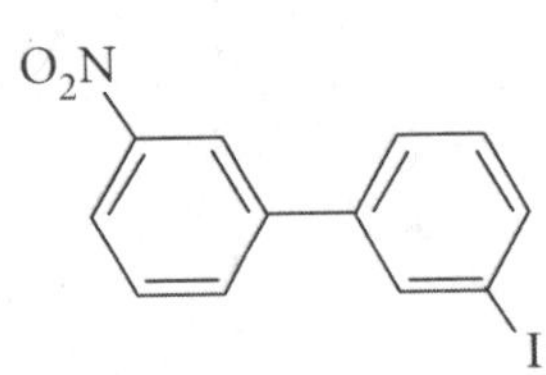

(d) 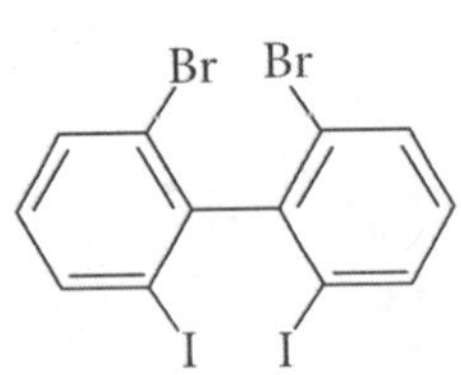

(NEET-I 201

6. For the following reactions :

(A) $CH_3CH_2CH_2Br + KOH \longrightarrow CH_3CH = CH_2 + KBr + H_2O$

(B)

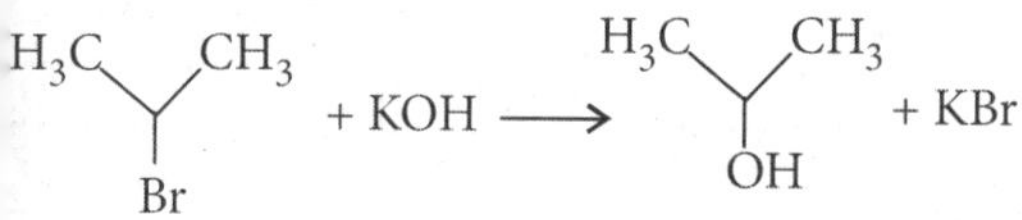

(C)

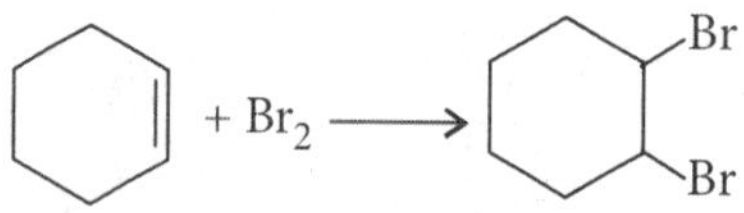

Which of the following statements is correct?

(a) (A) is elimination, (B) and (C) are substitution reactions.

(b) (A) is substitution, (B) and (C) are addition reactions.

(c) (A) and (B) are elimination reactions and (C) is addition reaction.

(d) (A) is elimination, (B) is substitution and (C) is addition reaction. *(NEET-I 2016)*

7. Two possible stereo-structures of $CH_3CHOHCOOH$, which are optically active, are called

(a) atropisomers (b) enantiomers

(c) mesomers (d) diastereomers. *(2015)*

8. In an S_N1 reaction on chiral centres, there is

(a) inversion more than retention leading to partial racemisation

(b) 100% retention (c) 100% inversion

(d) 100% racemisation. *(2015)*

9. The reaction of $C_6H_5CH{=}CHCH_3$ with HBr produces

(a) $C_6H_5CH_2CH_2CH_2Br$

(b)

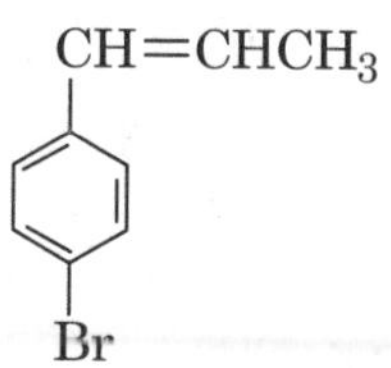

(c) $C_6H_5CH(Br)CH_2CH_3$

(d) $C_6H_5CH_2CH(Br)CH_3$ *(2015, Cancelled)*

10. Which of the following compounds will undergo racemisation when solution of KOH hydrolyses?

(i)

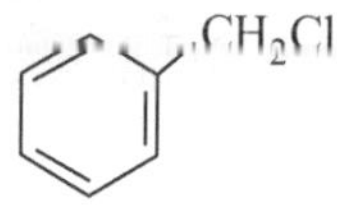

(ii) $CH_3CH_2CH_2Cl$

(iii) $H_3C-CH(CH_3)-CH_2Cl$

(iv)

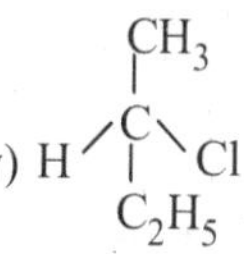

(a) (i) and (ii) (b) (ii) and (iv)

(c) (iii) and (iv) (d) (i) and (iv) *(2014)*

11. Given:

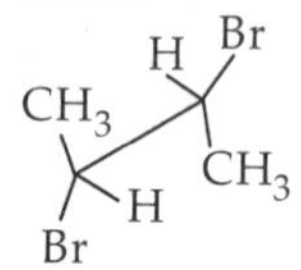

I

and

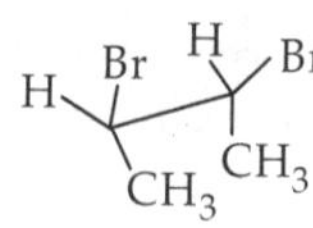

II

I and II are

(a) identical

(b) a pair of conformers

(c) a pair of geometrical isomers

(d) a pair of optical isomers *(Karnataka NEET 2013)*

12. Which of the following acids does not exhibit optical isomerism?

(a) Maleic acid (b) α-amino acids

(c) Lactic acid (d) Tartaric acid *(2012)*

13. In the replacement reaction

$$>C-I + MF \longrightarrow >C-F + MI$$

The reaction will be most favourable if *M* happens to be

(a) Na (b) K

(c) Rb (d) Li *(Mains 2012)*

14. Consider the reactions.

(i) $(CH_3)_2CH-CH_2Br \xrightarrow{C_2H_5OH} (CH_3)_2CH-CH_2OC_2H_5 + HBr$

(ii) $(CH_3)_2CH-CH_2Br \xrightarrow{C_2H_5O^-} (CH_3)_2CH-CH_2OC_2H_5 + Br^-$

The mechanisms of reactions (i) and (ii) are respectively

(a) S_N1 and S_N2 (b) S_N1 and S_N1

(c) S_N2 and S_N2 (d) S_N2 and S_N1 *(Mains 2011)*

15. Which one is most reactive towards S_N1 reaction?
(a) $C_6H_5CH(C_6H_5)Br$
(b) $C_6H_5CH(CH_3)Br$
(c) $C_6H_5C(CH_3)(C_6H_5)Br$
(d) $C_6H_5CH_2Br$ *(2010)*

16. The correct order of increasing reactivity of

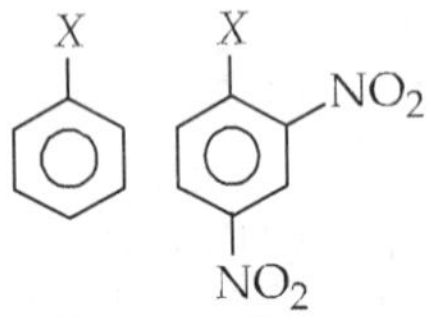

$(CH_3)_3C-X$ $(CH_3)_2CH-X$

I II III IV

C—*X* bond towards nucleophile in the following compounds is
(a) I < II < IV < III (b) II < III < I < IV
(c) IV < III < I < II (d) III < II < I < IV
(2010)

17. In the following reaction
$C_6H_5CH_2Br \xrightarrow[2.\ H_3O^+]{1.\ Mg,\ Ether} X$, the product '*X*' is
(a) $C_6H_5CH_2OCH_2C_6H_5$
(b) $C_6H_5CH_2OH$
(c) $C_6H_5CH_3$
(d) $C_6H_5CH_2CH_2C_6H_5$ *(Mains 2010)*

18. Which of the following reactions is an example of nucleophilic substitution reaction?
(a) $2RX + 2Na \rightarrow R - R + 2NaX$
(b) $RX + H_2 \rightarrow RH + HX$
(c) $RX + Mg \rightarrow RMgX$
(d) $RX + KOH \rightarrow ROH + KX$ *(2009)*

19. How many stereoisomers does this molecule have?
$CH_3CH{=}CHCH_2CHBrCH_3$
(a) 8 (b) 2
(c) 4 (d) 6 *(2008)*

20. In a S_N2 substitution reaction of the type
$R\text{—}Br + Cl^- \xrightarrow{DMF} R\text{—}Cl + Br^-$
which one of the following has the highest relative rate?
(a) $CH_3-C(CH_3)_2-CH_2Br$ (b) CH_3CH_2Br
(c) $CH_3CH_2CH_2Br$
(d) $CH_3-CH(CH_3)-CH_2Br$ *(2008)*

21. If there is no rotation of plane polarised light by a compound in a specific solvent, though to be chiral, it may mean that
(a) the compound is certainly meso
(b) there is no compound in the solvent
(c) the compound may be a racemic mixture
(d) the compound is certainly a chiral. *(2007)*

22. $CH_3 - CHCl - CH_2 - CH_3$ has a chiral centre. Which one of the following represents its *R*-configuration?
(a) C_2H_5 on top, H – C – CH_3, Cl below
(b) C_2H_5 on top, Cl – C – CH_3, H below
(c) CH_3 on top, H – C – Cl, C_2H_5 below
(d) C_2H_5 on top, H_3C – C – Cl, H below
(2007)

23. Which of the following is not chiral?
(a) 2-Hydroxypropanoic acid
(b) 2-Butanol
(c) 2,3-Dibromopentane
(d) 3-Bromopentane *(2006)*

24. Which of the following undergoes nucleophilic substitution exclusively by S_N1 mechanism?
(a) Ethyl chloride (b) Isopropyl chloride
(c) Chlorobenzene (d) Benzyl chloride
(2005)

25. The chirality of the compound

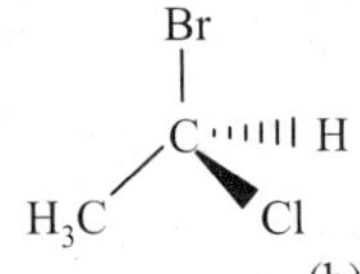

is
(a) *R* (b) *S*
(c) *E* (d) *Z* *(2005)*

26. Which of the following is least reactive in a nucleophilic substitution reaction?
(a) $(CH_3)_3C - Cl$ (b) $CH_2{=}CHCl$
(c) CH_3CH_2Cl
(d) $CH_2{=}CHCH_2Cl$ *(2004)*

27. Which of the following pairs of compounds are enantiomers?

(a) 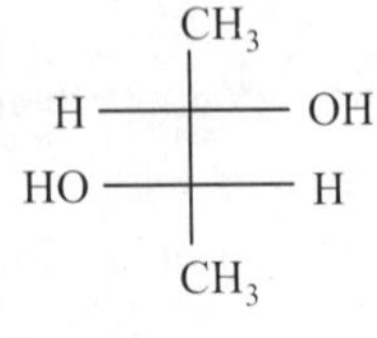

and
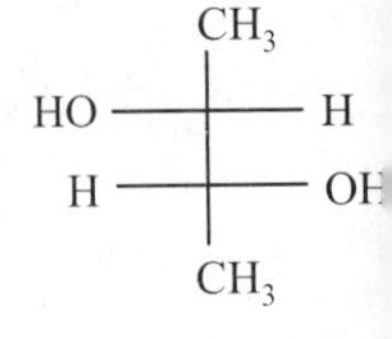

(b) 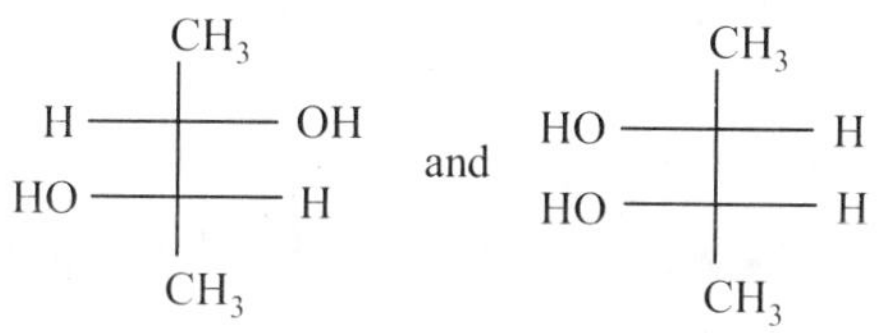

(c) 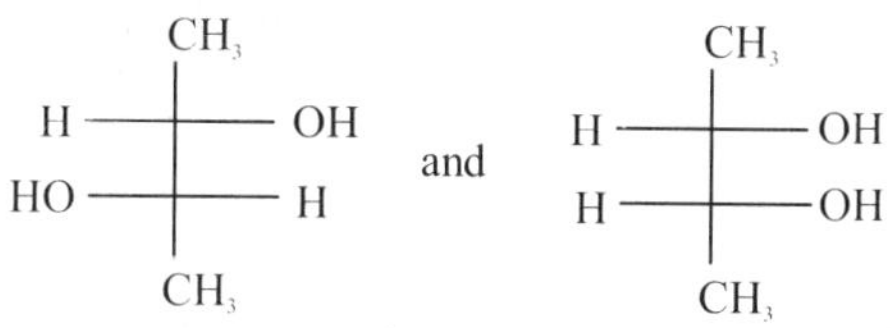

(d) 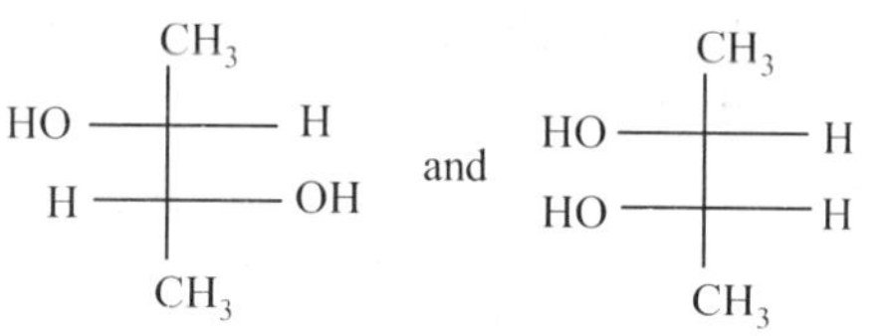

(2003)

28. Reactivity order of halides for dehydrohalogenation is

(a) $R - F > R - Cl > R - Br > R - I$
(b) $R - I > R - Br > R - Cl > R - F$
(c) $R - I > R - Cl > R - Br > R - F$
(d) $R - F > R - I > R - Br > R - Cl$ *(2002)*

29. $CH_3CH_2Cl \xrightarrow{NaCN} X \xrightarrow{Ni/H_2} Y \xrightarrow{\text{acetic anhydride}} Z$

Z in the above reaction sequence is

(a) $CH_3CH_2CH_2NHCOCH_3$
(b) $CH_3CH_2CH_2NH_2$
(c) $CH_3CH_2CH_2CONHCH_3$
(d) $CH_3CH_2CH_2CONHCOCH_3$ *(2002)*

30. $CH_3 - CH_2 - \underset{\displaystyle Cl}{\underset{|}{CH}} - CH_3$ obtained by chlorination of *n*-butane will be

(a) meso form (b) racemic mixture
(c) *d*-form (d) *l*-form. *(2001)*

31. An organic compound A (C_4H_9Cl) on reaction with Na/diethyl ether gives a hydrocarbon which on monochlorination gives only one chloro derivative then, A is

(a) *t*-butyl chloride (b) *s*-butyl chloride
(c) *iso*-butyl chloride (d) *n*-butyl chloride
(2001)

32. A compound of molecular formula C_7H_{16} shows optical isomerism, compound will be

(a) 2,3-dimethylpentane
(b) 2,2-dimethylbutane
(c) 2-methylhexane
(d) none of these. *(2001)*

33. Ethyl chloride is converted into diethyl ether by

(a) Perkins reaction
(b) Grignard reaction
(c) Wurtz synthesis
(d) Williamson's synthesis *(1999)*

34. Which of the following compounds is not chiral?

(a) CH_3CHDCH_2Cl (b) CH_3CH_2CHDCl
(c) $DCH_2CH_2CH_2Cl$ (d) $CH_3CHClCH_2D$
(1998)

35. Replacement of Cl of chlorobenzene to give phenol requires drastic conditions. But chlorine of 2,4-dinitrochlorobenzene is readily replaced because

(a) NO_2 donates e^- at *meta* position
(b) NO_2 withdraws e^- from *ortho/para* positions
(c) NO_2 make ring electron rich at *ortho* and *para*
(d) NO_2 withdraws e^- from *meta* position.
(1997)

36. The alkyl halide is converted into an alcohol by

(a) elimination
(b) dehydrohalogenation
(c) addition
(d) substitution. *(1997)*

37. In the reaction

$CH_3CHO + HCN \rightarrow CH_3CH(OH)CN$,

a chiral centre is produced. This product is

(a) dextrorotatory (b) racemic mixture
(c) meso compound (d) laevorotatory.
(1995)

38. Reaction of *t*-butyl bromide with sodium methoxide produces

(a) sodium *t*-butoxide
(b) *t*-butyl methyl ether
(c) isobutane (d) isobutylene.
(1994)

39. Grignard reagent is prepared by the reaction between

(a) magnesium and alkane
(b) magnesium and aromatic hydrocarbon
(c) zinc and alkyl halide
(d) magnesium and alkyl halide. *(1994)*

40. Benzene reacts with *n*-propyl chloride in the presence of anhydrous $AlCl_3$ to give
(a) 3-propyl-1-chlorobenzene
(b) *n*-propylbenzene
(c) no reaction
(d) isopropylbenzene. *(1993)*

41. Industrial preparation of chloroform employs acetone and
(a) phosgene
(b) calcium hypochlorite
(c) chlorine gas
(d) sodium chloride. *(1993)*

42. Chlorobenzene reacts with Mg in dry ether to give a compound (*A*) which further reacts with ethanol to yield
(a) phenol (b) benzene
(c) ethyl benzene (d) phenyl ether. *(1993)*

43. When chlorine is passed through propene at 400°C, which of the following is formed?
(a) PVC
(b) Allyl chloride
(c) Propyl chloride
(d) 1, 2-Dichloroethane *(1993)*

44. Which chloro derivative of benzene among the following would undergo hydrolysis most readily with aqueous sodium hydroxide to furnish the corresponding hydroxy derivative?

(a) 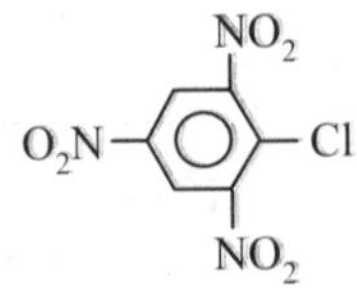

(b) 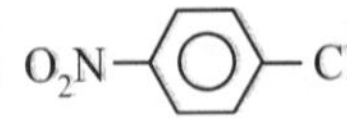

(c) 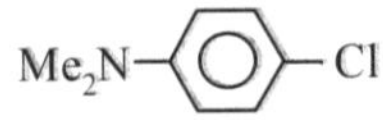

(d) C_6H_5Cl *(1989)*

45. Which of the following is an optically active compound?
(a) 1-Butanol
(b) 1-Propanol
(c) 2-Chlorobutane
(d) 4-Hydroxyheptane *(1989)*

46. Phosgene is a common name for
(a) phosphoryl chloride
(b) thionyl chloride
(c) carbon dioxide and phosphine
(d) carbonyl chloride. *(1988)*

47. Which one is formed when sodium phenoxide is heated with ethyl iodide?
(a) Phenetole
(b) Ethyl phenyl alcohol
(c) Phenol
(d) None of these *(1988)*

Answer Key

1. (d)	2. (a)	3. (d)	4. (c)	5. (d)	6. (d)	7. (b)	8. (a)	9. (c)	10. (None
11. (b)	12. (a)	13. (c)	14. (c)	15. (c)	16. (a)	17. (c)	18. (d)	19. (c)	20. (b)
21. (a)	22. (b)	23. (d)	24. (d)	25. (a)	26. (b)	27. (a)	28. (b)	29. (a)	30. (b)
31. (a)	32. (a)	33. (d)	34. (c)	35. (b)	36. (d)	37. (b)	38. (d)	39. (d)	40. (d)
41. (b)	42. (b)	43. (b)	44. (a)	45. (c)	46. (d)	47. (a)			

EXPLANATIONS

1. **(d) :** $C_2H_5OH \xrightarrow{Na} C_2H_5O^-Na^+$ — C_2H_5OH (A), $C_2H_5O^-Na^+$ (B)

C_2H_5OH (A) $\xrightarrow{PCl_5}$ C_2H_5Cl (C)

$$\underset{(B)}{C_2H_5O^-Na^+} + \underset{(C)}{C_2H_5Cl} \xrightarrow[\text{Williamson's synthesis}]{S_N2} \underset{\text{Diethyl ether}}{C_2H_5OC_2H_5}$$

2. **(a) :**

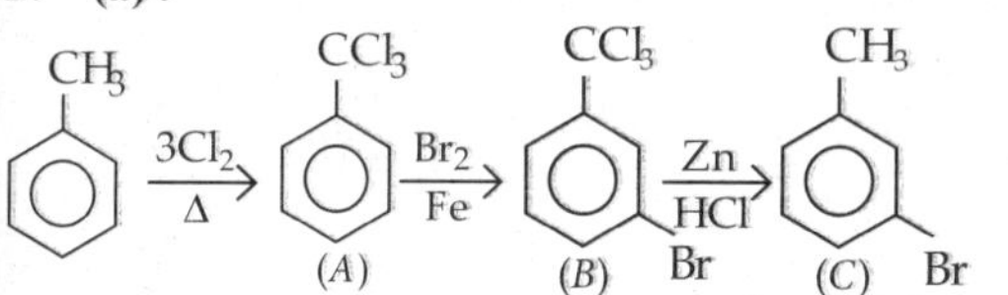

m-bromotoluene

3. **(d) :** *m*-Bromoanisole gives only the respective *meta* substituted aniline. This is a substitution reaction which goes by an elimination-addition pathway.

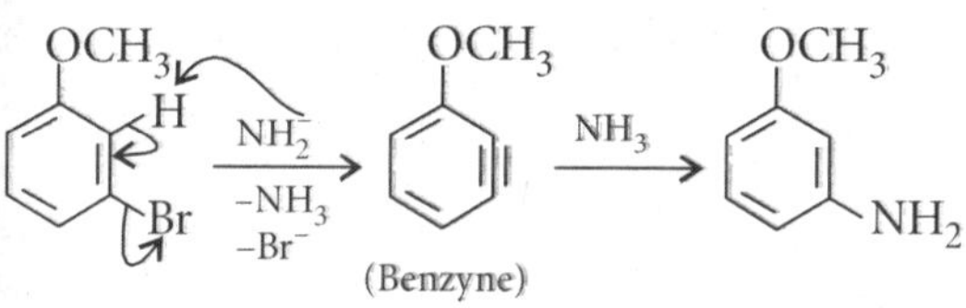

4. **(c) :** The reaction,

$$CH_3CH_2CH_2Br + NaCN \longrightarrow CH_3CH_2CH_2CN + NaBr$$

follows S_N2 mechanism which is favoured by polar aprotic solvent *i.e.*, *N*, *N'*–dimethylformamide (DMF),

$$H-\overset{\overset{\large O}{\|}}{C}-N(CH_3)_2.$$

5. **(d) :** *o*-Substituted biphenyls are optically active as both the rings are not in one plane and their mirror images are non-superimposable.

6. **(d) :** $CH_3CH_2CH_2Br + KOH \longrightarrow CH_3CH=CH_2 + KBr + H_2O$

Saturated compound is converted into unsaturated compound by removal of group of atoms hence, it is an elimination reaction.

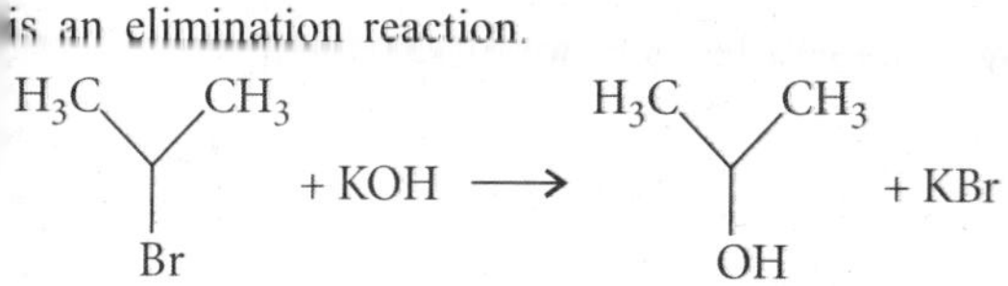

—Br group is replaced by — OH group hence, it is a substitution reaction.

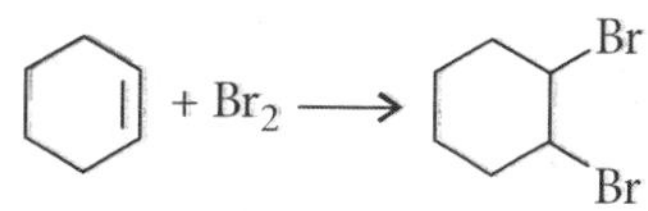

Addition of Br_2 converts an unsaturated compound into a saturated compound hence, it is an addition reaction.

7. **(b) :**

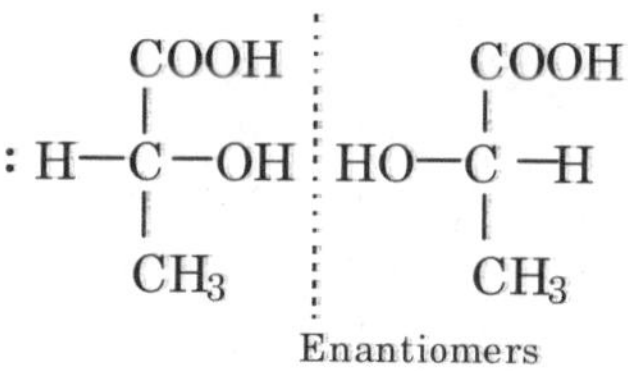

8. **(a) :** In case of optically active alkyl halides, S_N1 reaction is accompanied by racemisation. The carbocation formed in the slow step being sp^2 hybridised is planar and attack of nucleophile may take place from either side resulting in a mixture of products, one having the same configuration and other having inverted configuration.
The isomer corresponding to inversion is present in slight excess because S_N1 also depends upon the degree of shielding of the front side of the reacting carbon.

9. **(c) :**

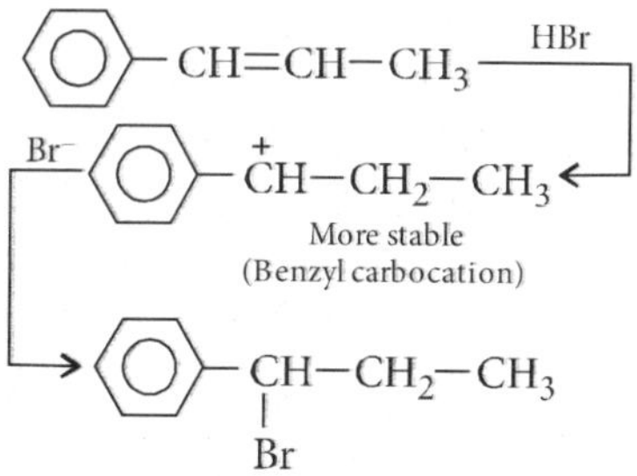

10. **(None) :** Due to chirality 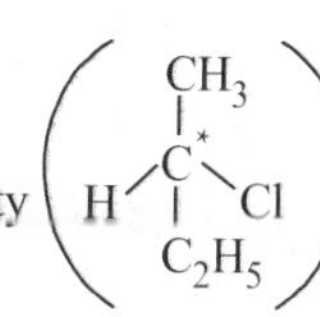, only compound (iv) will undergo racemisation. Hence, all the given options are incorrect.

11. **(b) :** I and II are staggered and eclipsed conformers.

12. (a) : Maleic acid shows geometrical isomerism and not optical isomerism.

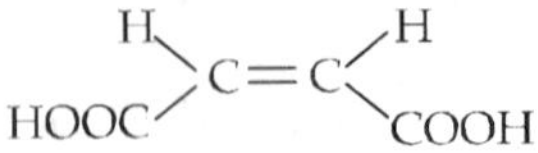

Maleic acid

13. (c) : Tertiary halide shows S_N1 mechanism *i.e.*, ionic mechanism. In the given reaction negative ion will attack on carbocation. Thus greater the tendency of ionisation (greater ionic character in $M - F$ bond) more favourable will be reaction. The most ionic bond is Rb – F in the given examples thus most favourable reaction will be with Rb–F.

14. (c) : If reaction is S_N1, there will be the formation of carbocation and the rearrangement takes place. In these reactions there is no rearrangement hence both are S_N2 mechanism.

15. (c) : S_N1 reactions proceed *via* the formation of a carbocation intermediate.
More stable is the carbocation more reactive is the alkyl/aryl halide towards S_N1.
In $C_6H_5C^+(CH_3)(C_6H_5)$ carbocation, the two phenyl rings by their $-R$ effect and —CH_3 by its $+I$ effect diminish the positive charge and make it stable.

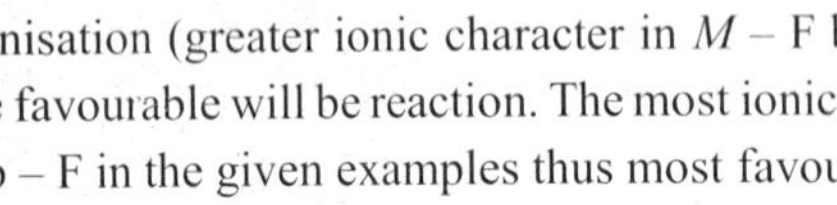

16. (a) : I < II < IV < III
The order of reactivity is dependent on the stability of the intermediate carbocation formed by cleavage of C—*X* bond. The 3° carbocation (formed from III) will be more stable than its 2° counter part (formed from IV) which in turn will be more stable than the arenium ion (formed from I). Also, the aryl halide has a double bond character in the C—*X* bond which makes the cleavage more difficult. However, inspite of all the stated factors, II will be more reactive than I due to the presence of the electron withdrawing $-NO_2$ group. C—*X* bond becomes weak and undergoes nucleophilic substitution reaction.

17. (c) : $C_6H_5CH_2Br \xrightarrow{\text{Mg, ether}} C_6H_5CH_2MgBr$

$$\downarrow H_3O^+$$

$$C_6H_5CH_3 + Mg\begin{matrix} Br \\ OH \end{matrix}$$

18. (d)

19. (c) : The given compound may be written as

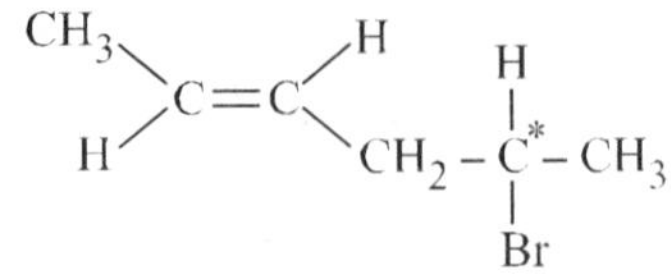

Both geometrical isomerism (*cis-trans* form) and optical isomerism is possible in the given compound.
No. of optical isomer = $2^n = 2^1 = 2$
(where n = no. of asymmetric carbon)
Hence total no. of stereoisomers = 2 + 2 = 4

20. (b) : S_N2 mechanism is followed in case of primary and secondary alkyl halides *i.e.* S_N2 reaction is favoured by small groups on the carbon atoms attached to halogen so,

$$CH_3 - X > R - CH_2 - X > R_2CH - X > R_3C - X.$$

Primary is more reactive than secondary and tertiary alkyl halides.
S_N2 order : Methyl > Ethyl > Isopropyl > Tertiary butyl > Allyl > Benzyl

21. (a) : Meso compound does not rotate plane polarised light. Compound which contains tetrahedral atoms with four different groups but the whole molecule is achiral, is known as meso compound. It possesses a plane of symmetry and is optically inactive. One of the asymmetric carbon atoms turns the plane of polarised light to the right and other to the left and to the same extent so that the rotation due to upper half is compensated by the lower half, *i.e.*, internally compensated, and finally there is no rotation of plane polarised light.

22. (b) :

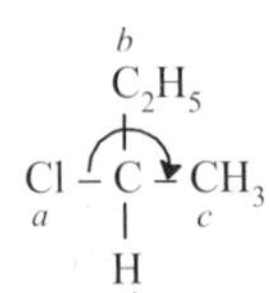

R-configuration

23. (d) : $H_3C - CH_2 - \underset{\displaystyle}{\overset{\displaystyle Br}{\overset{|}{C}H}} - CH_2 - CH_3$
Due to absence of asymmetric carbon atom.

24. (d) : S_N1 reaction is favoured by heavy (bulky) groups on the carbon atom attached to halogens and nature of carbonium ion in substrate is
Benzyl > Allyl > Tertiary > Secondary > Primary > Methyl halides.

25. (a) :

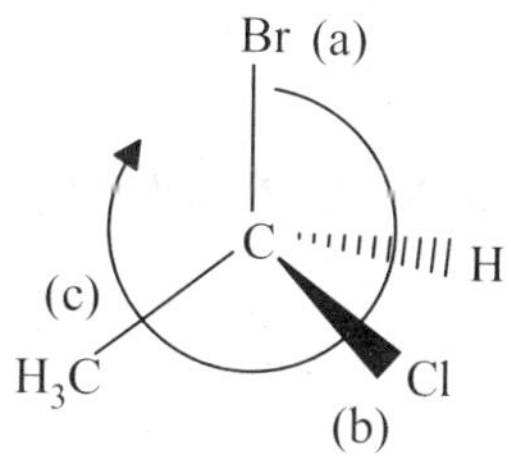

Lowest priority atom is always away from the viewer. Priority is seen on the basis of atomic no. and if atomic no. are same then on the basis of atomic mass. See in the order of higher to lower priority.
If clockwise then it is *R*.
If anticlockwise then it is *S*.
Full name of the molecule is
(*R*) 1-bromo-1-chloroethane.

26. (b) : The non-reactivity of the chlorine atom in vinyl chloride may be explained from the molecular orbital point of view as follows. If the chlorine atom has sp^2 hybridisation, the C – Cl bond will be a σ-bond and the two lone pairs of electrons would occupy the other two sp^2 orbitals. This would leave a *p* orbital containing a lone pair, and this orbital could now conjugate with the π-bond of the ethylenic link. Thus two M.O's will be required to accommodate these four π-electrons. Furthermore, since chlorine is more electronegative than carbon, the electrons will tend to be found in the vicinity of the chlorine atom. Nevertheless, the chlorine atom has now lost full control of the lone pair and so, is less negative than it would have been had there been no conjugation. Since two carbon atoms have acquired a share in the lone pair, each carbon atom acquires a small negative charge. Hence, owing to delocalisation of bonds (through conjugation), the vinyl chloride molecule has an increased stability. Before the chlorine atom can be displaced by some other group, the lone pair must be localised again on the chlorine atom. This requires energy, and so the chlorine is more firmly bound.

$$H_2C{=}CH{-}\ddot{C}l: \longleftrightarrow \bar{C}H_2{-}CH{=}\overset{+}{C}l$$

7. **(a) :** These two are non-superimposable mirror images of each other, so they are enantiomers.

8. **(b) :** I > Br > Cl > F → atomic radii

, Cl, Br, I belongs to the same group orderly. Atomic radii go on increasing as the nuclear charge increases in preceeding downwards in a group. The decreasing order of bond length C – I > C – Br > C – Cl > C – F. The order of bond dissociation energy *R* – F > *R* – Cl > *R* – Br > *R* – I. During dehydrohalogenation C – I bond breaks more easily than C – F bond. So reactivity order of halides

$R - I > R - Br > R - Cl > R - F$.

29. (a): $CH_3CH_2Cl \xrightarrow{NaCN} \underset{(X)}{CH_3CH_2CN} \xrightarrow{Ni/H_2}$

$\underset{(Y)}{CH_3CH_2CH_2NH_2} \xrightarrow[\text{anhydride}]{\text{acetic}} \underset{(Z)}{CH_3CH_2CH_2NHCOCH_3}$

30. (b) : Chlorination of *n*-butane takes place via free radical formation. *i.e.* $Cl_2 \rightarrow {}^{\bullet}Cl + {}^{\bullet}Cl$

$CH_3CH_2CH_2CH_3 \xrightarrow{{}^{\bullet}Cl} CH_3\dot{C}HCH_2CH_3 + HCl$

sp^2- hybrid planar shape intermediate and ${}^{\bullet}Cl$ may attack from either side to give

$$CH_3\dot{C}HCH_2CH_3 + \dot{C}l \longrightarrow$$

$$CH_3-\underset{Cl}{\overset{H}{C}}-CH_2CH_3 + CH_3-\underset{H}{\overset{Cl}{C}}-CH_2CH_3$$

Racemic mixture
(Mixture of 50% *d*-form and 50% *l*-form)

31. (a) : Wurtz reaction → It involves the reaction of alkyl halides with Na in ethanol solution to form higher alkanes.

$2R - X + 2Na \rightarrow R - R + 2NaX$

In the given problem,

$2C_4H_9Cl + 2Na \xrightarrow{\text{ethanol}} C_4H_9{\cdot}C_4H_9 + 2NaCl$

Compound *A* is *t*-butyl chloride in this all – CH_3 groups have primary hydrogen only and able to give only one chloro derivative.

$(CH_3)_3CC(CH_3)_3 \xrightarrow{Cl_2} CH_2Cl(CH_3)_2C{-}C(CH_3)_3$

32. (a) : Organic compounds exhibit the property of enantiomerism (optical isomerism) only when their molecules are chiral. Most chiral compounds have a chiral centre, which is an atom bonded to four different atoms or groups.

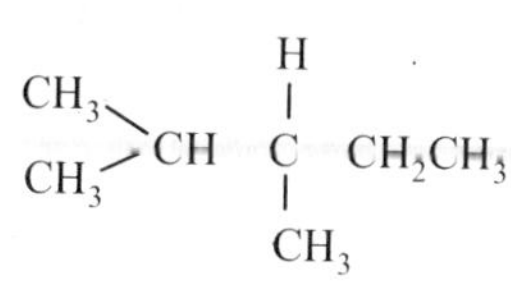

2,3 Dimethylpentane has one chiral C atom and do not have any symmetric element.

33. (d) : $C_2H_5 - Cl + Na - O - C_2H_5 \rightarrow$

$C_2H_5 - O - C_2H_5 + NaCl$

The above reaction is called as Williamson's synthesis.

34. (c) : 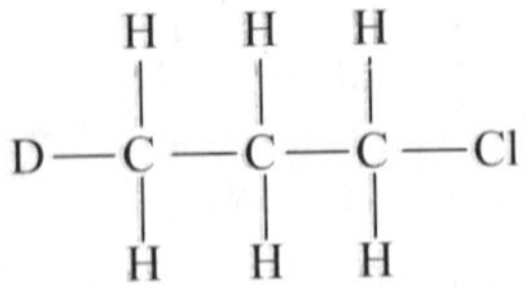

The above compound has no chiral 'C'-atom. All the 'C' atoms are attached to two identical 'H' atoms, so they are not asymmetrical.

35. (b) : 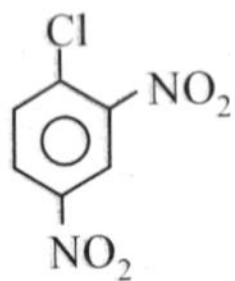

Withdrawal of electrons by $-NO_2$ groups from *ortho/para* positions cause easier removal of $-Cl$ atom due to the development of positive charge on *o*- and *p*- positions.

36. (d) : $C_2H_5Br + KOH \rightarrow C_2H_5OH + KBr$
Ethyl bromide (aqueous) Ethyl alcohol

37. (b) :

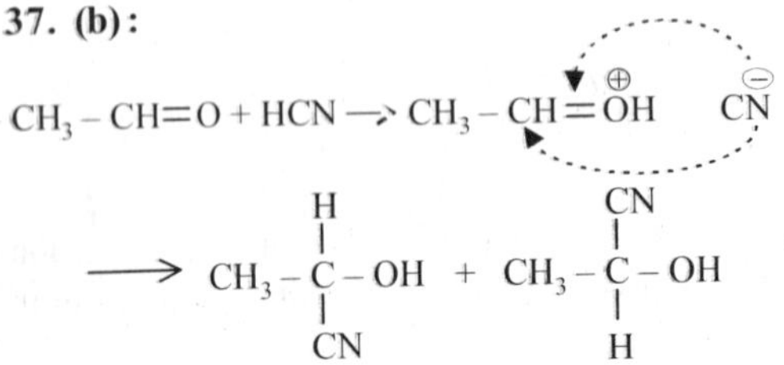

(Racemic mixture)

38. (d) : Isobutylene is obtained.

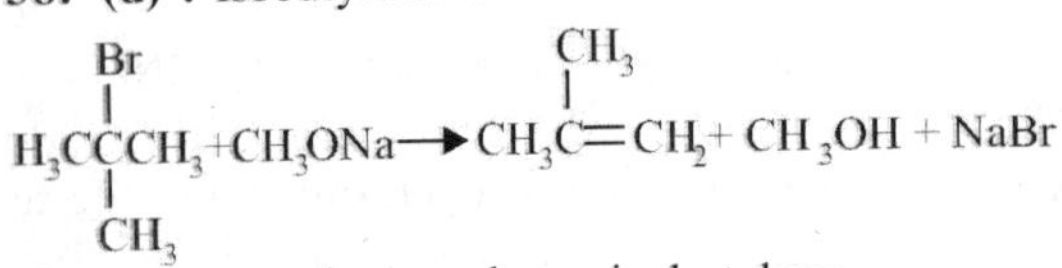

Thus, the reaction produces isobutylene.

39. (d) : Grignard reagent is prepared by heating an alkyl halide with dry magnesium powder in dry ether.

$$R-X+Mg \xrightarrow{\text{Dry ether}} \underset{\text{Grignard reagent}}{R-Mg-X}$$

40. (d) : $C_6H_6 + CH_3CH_2CH_2Cl \xrightarrow[\text{AlCl}_3]{\text{Anhy.}} \underset{\text{Isopropylbenzene}}{C_6H_5-CH(CH_3)-CH_3}$

41. (b) : $CaOCl_2 + H_2O \rightarrow Ca(OH)_2 + Cl_2$
Cl_2, so obtained acts as a mild oxidising as well as chlorinating agent.

$$CH_3-\underset{\underset{O}{\|}}{C}-CH_3 + CaOCl_2 \longrightarrow CHCl_3$$

42. (b) : $C_6H_5Cl \xrightarrow{Mg} \underset{(A)}{C_6H_5MgCl} \xrightarrow{CH_3CH_2OH} C_6H_6 + CH_3CH_2OMgCl$

43. (b) :

$$CH_3CH{=}CH_2 \xrightarrow[-HCl]{Cl_2,\ 400°C} ClCH_2CH{=}CH_2$$

At 400°C temperature, substitution occurs instead of addition.

44. (a) : Cl in 2, 4, 6-trinitrochlorobenzene is activated by three $-NO_2$ groups at *o* and *p*-positions and hence undergoes hydrolysis most readily.

45. (c) : $CH_3-CH_2-\overset{*}{C}H(Cl)-CH_3$

2-Chlorobutane contains a chiral carbon atom and hence is optically active compound.

46. (d) : Carbonyl chloride ($COCl_2$)

47. (a) : Phenetole is formed when sodium phenoxide is heated with ethyl iodide.

$$C_6H_5ONa + C_2H_5I \xrightarrow{\Delta} \underset{\text{Phenetole}}{C_6H_5OC_2H_5}$$

Chapter 25

Alcohols, Phenols and Ethers

1. In the reaction,

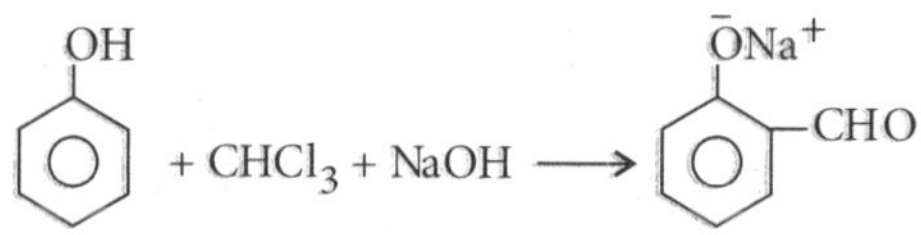

the electrophile involved is

(a) dichloromethyl cation ($\overset{+}{C}HCl_2$)

(b) formyl cation ($\overset{+}{C}HO$)

(c) dichloromethyl anion ($\overset{-}{C}HCl_2$)

(d) dichlorocarbene ($:CCl_2$) *(NEET 2018)*

2. Compound A, $C_8H_{10}O$, is found to react with NaOI (produced by reacting Y with NaOH) and yields a yellow precipitate with characteristic smell. A and Y are respectively

(a) 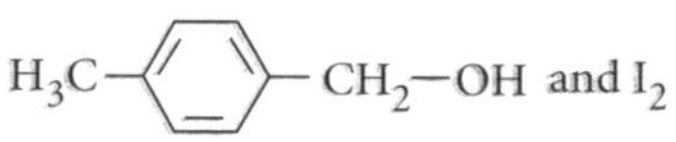

(b) 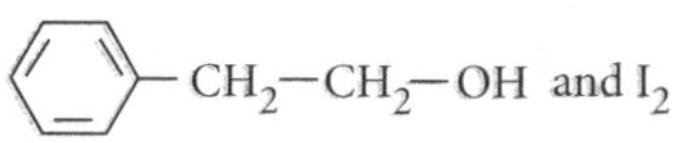

(c) 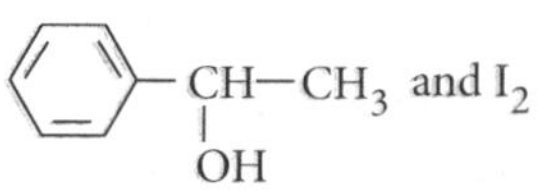

(d) 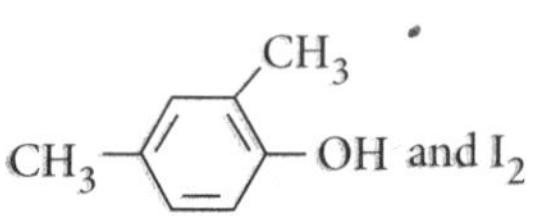 *(NEET 2018)*

3. Identify the major products P, Q and R in the following sequence of reactions :

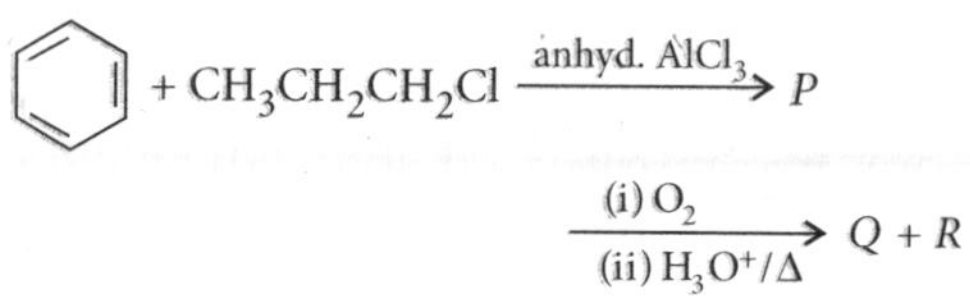

(a) $P =$ 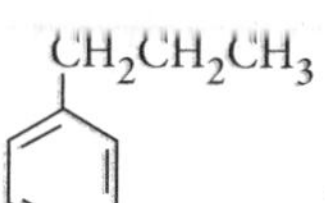, $Q =$ 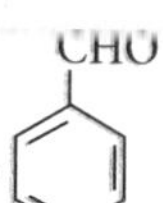,

$R = CH_3CH_2—OH$

(b) $P =$ 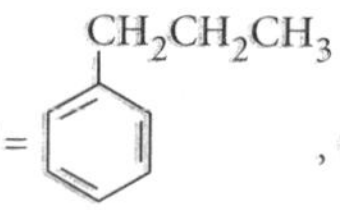, $Q =$ 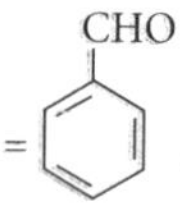, $R =$ 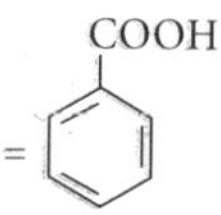

(c) $P =$ 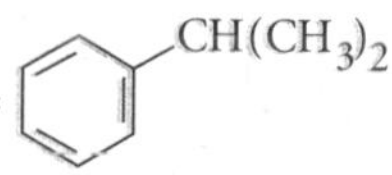 $Q =$ 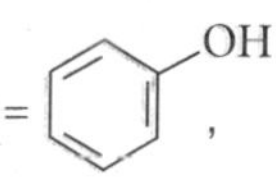,

$R = CH_3CH(OH)CH_3$

(d) $P =$ 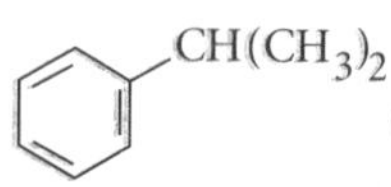 $Q =$ 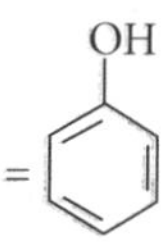,

$R = CH_3 — CO — CH_3$

(NEET 2018)

4. The heating of phenyl methyl ether with HI produces

(a) iodobenzene (b) phenol

(c) benzene (d) ethyl chloride.

(NEET 2017)

5. Which one is the most acidic compound?

(a) 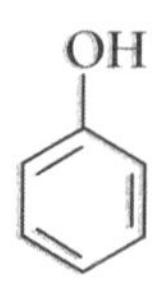

(b) 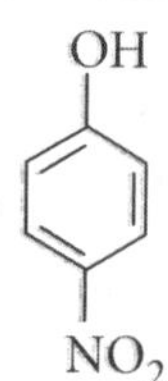

(c) 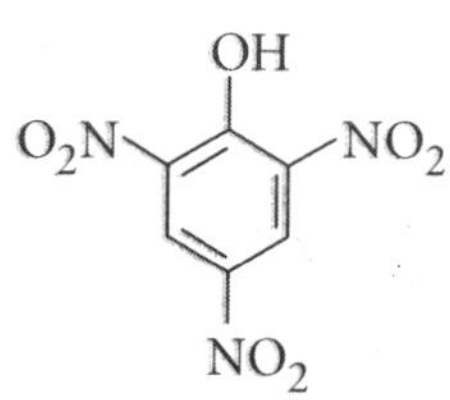

(d) 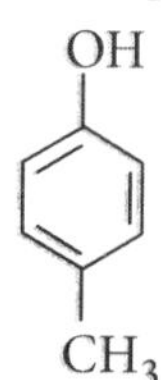

(NEET 2017)

6. The reaction

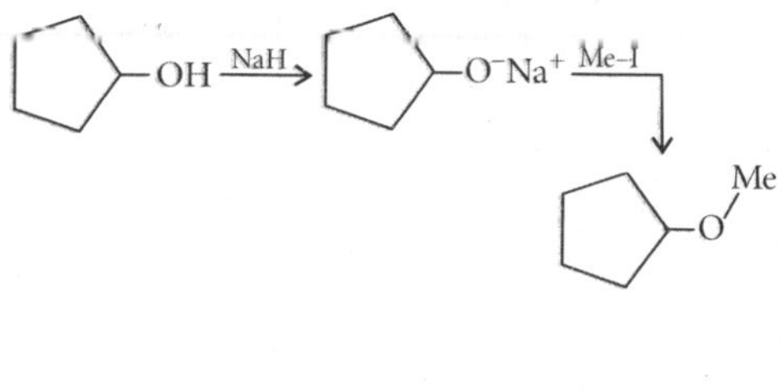

can be classified as
(a) dehydration reaction
(b) Williamson alcohol synthesis reaction
(c) Williamson ether synthesis reaction
(d) alcohol formation reaction.
(NEET-I 2016)

7. Reaction of phenol with chloroform in presence of dilute sodium hydroxide finally introduces which one of the following functional group?
(a) $-COOH$ (b) $-CHCl_2$
(c) $-CHO$ (d) $-CH_2Cl$ *(2015)*

8. Which of the following reaction(s) can be used for the preparation of alkyl halides?
(I) $CH_3CH_2OH + HCl \xrightarrow{\text{Anh. } ZnCl_2}$
(II) $CH_3CH_2OH + HCl \longrightarrow$
(III) $(CH_3)_3COH + HCl \longrightarrow$
(IV) $(CH_3)_2CHOH + HCl \xrightarrow{\text{Anh. } ZnCl_2}$
(a) (I) and (II) only
(b) (IV) only
(c) (III) and (IV) only
(d) (I), (III) and (IV) only *(2015)*

9. The reaction,

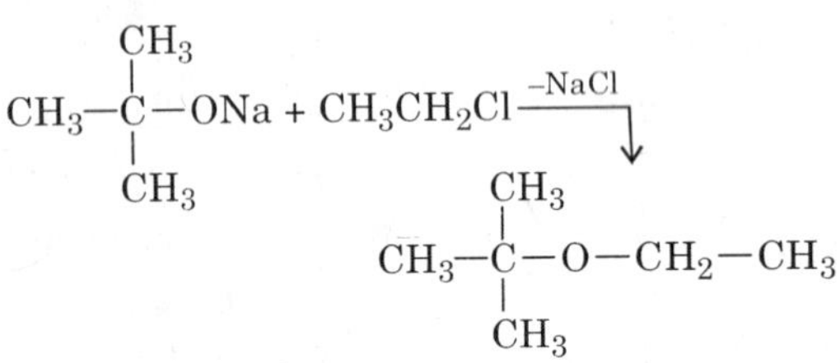

is called
(a) Etard reaction
(b) Gattermann-Koch reaction
(c) Williamson synthesis
(d) Williamson continuous etherification process. *(2015, Cancelled)*

10. Among the following sets of reactants which one produces anisole?
(a) CH_3CHO ; $RMgX$
(b) C_6H_5OH ; $NaOH$; CH_3I
(c) C_6H_5OH ; neutral $FeCl_3$
(d) $C_6H_5CH_3$; CH_3COCl ; $AlCl_3$ *(2014)*

11. Which of the following will not be soluble in sodium hydrogen carbonate?
(a) 2,4,6-Trinitrophenol
(b) Benzoic acid
(c) *o*-Nitrophenol
(d) Benzenesulphonic acid *(2014)*

12. Among the following ethers, which one will produce methyl alcohol on treatment with hot concentrated HI?

(a) 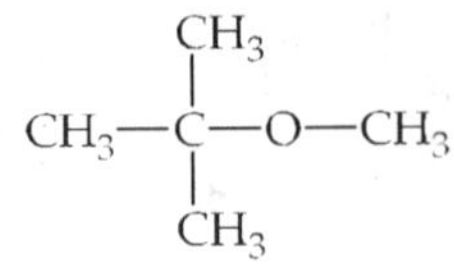

(b) 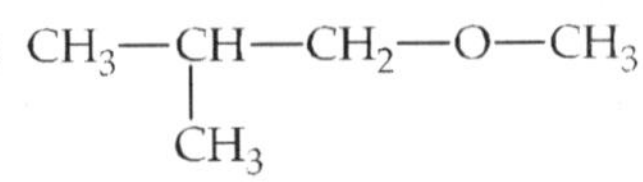

(c) $CH_3-CH_2-CH_2-O-CH_3$

(d) 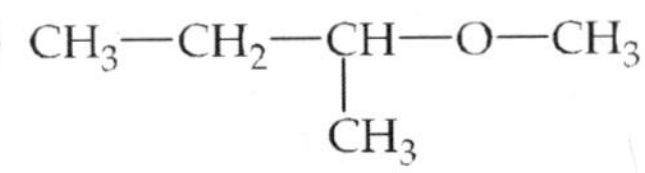

(NEET 2013)

13. Number of isomeric alcohols of molecular formula $C_6H_{14}O$ which give positive iodoform test is
(a) three (b) four
(c) five (d) two
(Karnataka NEET 2013)

14. In the following sequence of reactions
$CH_3-Br \xrightarrow{KCN} A \xrightarrow{H_3O^+} B \xrightarrow[\text{ether}]{LiAlH_4} C$
the end product (C) is
(a) acetone (b) methane
(c) acetaldehyde (d) ethyl alcohol.
(2012)

15. Which of the following compounds can be used as antifreeze in automobile radiators?
(a) Methyl alcohol
(b) Glycol
(c) Nitrophenol
(d) Ethyl alcohol
(Mains 2012)

16. In the following reactions,

(i) 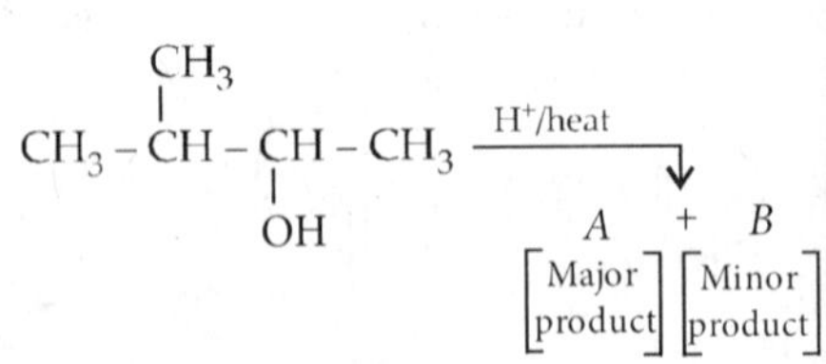

(ii) 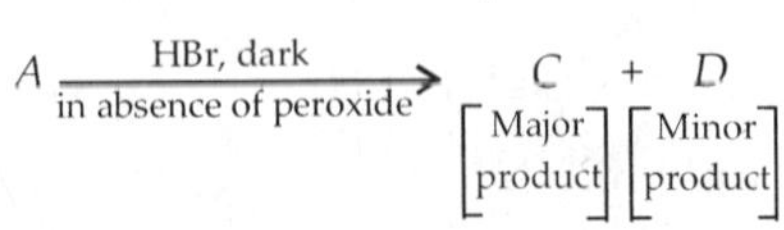

the major products (A) and (C) are respectively

(a) $CH_2=C(CH_3)-CH_2-CH_3$ and $CH_2(Br)-CH(CH_3)-CH_2-CH_3$

(b) $CH_3-C(CH_3)=CH-CH_3$ and $CH_3-C(CH_3)(Br)-CH_2-CH_3$

(c) $CH_2=C(CH_3)-CH_2-CH_3$ and $CH_3-C(CH_3)(Br)-CH_2-CH_3$

(d) $CH_3-C(CH_3)=CH-CH_3$ and $CH_3-CH(CH_3)-CH(Br)-CH_3$ *(2011)*

17. Given are cyclohexanol (I), acetic acid (II), 2,4,6-trinitrophenol (III) and phenol (IV). In these the order of decreasing acidic character will be

(a) III > II > IV > I (b) II > III > I > IV
(c) II > III > IV > I (d) III > IV > II > I *(2010)*

18. Which of the following compounds has the most acidic nature?

(a) 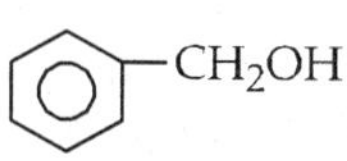 (b) 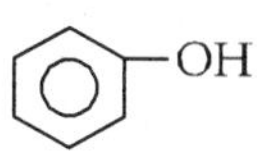

(c) 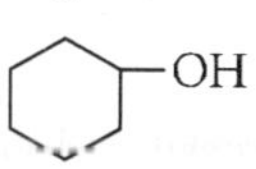

(d) 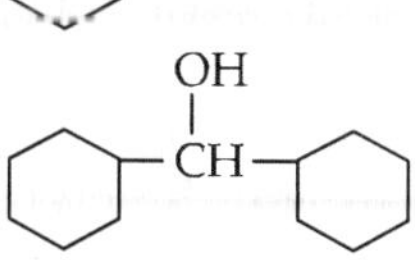 *(2010)*

19. Among the following four compounds
(i) Phenol
(ii) Methyl phenol
(iii) *Meta*-nitrophenol
(iv) *Para*-nitrophenol
The acidity order is
(a) (iv) > (iii) > (i) > (ii)
(b) (iii) > (iv) > (i) > (ii)
(c) (i) > (iv) > (iii) > (ii)
(d) (ii) > (i) > (iii) > (iv) *(2010)*

20. When glycerol is treated with excess of HI, it produces
(a) 2-iodopropane (b) allyl iodide
(c) propene (d) glycerol triiodide *(Mains 2010)*

21. Following compounds are given
(i) CH_3CH_2OH (ii) CH_3COCH_3
(iii) $CH_3-CHOH(CH_3)$ (iv) CH_3OH

Which of the above compound(s), on being warmed with iodine solution and NaOH, will give iodoform?
(a) (i), (iii) and (iv) (b) Only (ii)
(c) (i), (ii) and (iii) (d) (i) and (ii) *(Mains 2010)*

22. Match the compounds given in List I with their characteristic reactions given in List II. Select the correct option.

List I (Compounds)		List II (Reactions)
A. $CH_3(CH_2)_3NH_2$	(i)	Alkaline hydrolysis
B. $CH_3C\equiv CH$	(ii)	With KOH (alcohol) and $CHCl_3$ produces bad smell
C. $CH_3CH_2COOCH_3$	(iii)	Gives white ppt. with ammoniacal $AgNO_3$
D. $CH_3CH(OH)CH_3$	(iv)	With Lucas reagent cloudiness appears after 5 minutes

(a) A-(ii), B-(i), C-(iv), D-(iii)
(b) A-(iii), B-(ii), C-(i), D-(iv)
(c) A-(ii), B-(iii), C-(i), D-(iv)
(d) A-(iv), B-(ii), C-(iii), D-(i) *(Mains 2010)*

23. Consider the following reaction:

$$\text{Ethanol} \xrightarrow{PBr_3} X \xrightarrow{\text{alc. KOH}} Y \xrightarrow[\text{(ii) } H_2O\text{, heat}]{\text{(i) } H_2SO_4\text{, room temperature}} Z$$

the product Z is
(a) $CH_3CH_2-O-CH_2-CH_3$
(b) $CH_3-CH_2-O-SO_3H$
(c) CH_3CH_2OH
(d) $CH_2{=}CH_2$ *(2009)*

24. $HOCH_2CH_2OH$ on heating with periodic acid gives
(a) 2HCOOH (b) $\underset{CHO}{\overset{CHO}{|}}$
(c) 2 $H_2C{=}O$ (d) $2CO_2$ *(2009)*

25. Consider the following reaction:

$$\text{Phenol} \xrightarrow{\text{Zn dust}} X \xrightarrow[\text{Anhyd. AlCl}_3]{CH_3Cl} Y \xrightarrow{\text{Alkaline KMnO}_4} Z$$

the product Z is
(a) benzaldehyde (b) benzoic acid
(c) benzene (d) toluene *(2009)*

26. In the reaction:

$$CH_3-\overset{CH_3}{\overset{|}{CH}}-CH_2-O-CH_2-CH_3 + HI \xrightarrow{\text{heated}}$$

Which of the following compounds will be formed?
(a) $CH_3-\underset{CH_3}{\underset{|}{CH}}-CH_3 + CH_3CH_2OH$
(b) $CH_3-\underset{CH_3}{\underset{|}{CH}}-CH_2OH + CH_3CH_3$
(c) $CH_3-\overset{CH_3}{\overset{|}{CH}}-CH_2OH + CH_3CH_2I$
(d) $CH_3-\overset{CH_3}{\overset{|}{CH}}-CH_2-I + CH_3CH_2OH$
(2007)

27. The general molecular formula, which represents the homologous series of alkanols is
(a) $C_nH_{2n+2}O$ (b) $C_nH_{2n}O_2$
(c) $C_nH_{2n}O$ (d) $C_nH_{2n+1}O$
(2006)

28. Ethylene oxide when treated with Grignard reagent yields
(a) primary alcohol
(b) secondary alcohol
(c) tertiary alcohol
(d) cyclopropyl alcohol. *(2006)*

29. The major organic product in the reaction is
$CH_3-O-CH(CH_3)_2 + HI \rightarrow$ products
(a) $CH_3I + (CH_3)_2CHOH$
(b) $CH_3OH + (CH_3)_2CHI$
(c) $ICH_2OCH(CH_3)_2$ (d) $CH_3O\underset{I}{\underset{|}{C}}(CH_3)_2$
(2006)

30. Which one of the following compounds is most acidic?
(a) $Cl-CH_2-CH_2-OH$
(b) 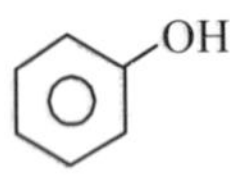
(c) 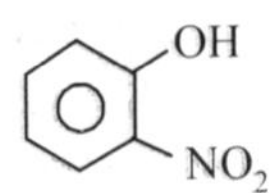
(d) 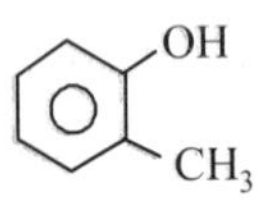 *(2005)*

31. Which one of the following will not form a yellow precipitate on heating with an alkaline solution of iodine?
(a) $CH_3CH(OH)CH_3$
(b) $CH_3CH_2CH(OH)CH_3$
(c) CH_3OH
(d) CH_3CH_2OH *(2004)*

32. *n*-propyl alcohol and isopropyl alcohol can be chemically distinguished by which reagent
(a) PCl_5 (b) reduction
(c) oxidation with potassium dichromate
(d) ozonolysis. *(2002)*

33. When phenol is treated with $CHCl_3$ and NaOH the product formed is
(a) benzaldehyde (b) salicylaldehyde
(c) salicylic acid (d) benzoic acid.
(2002)

34. Which of the following is correct?
(a) On reduction, any aldehyde gives secondary alcohol.
(b) Reaction of vegetable oil with H_2SO_4 gives glycerine.
(c) Alcoholic iodine with NaOH gives iodoform.
(d) Sucrose on reaction with NaCl gives invert sugar. *(2001)*

35. Reaction of 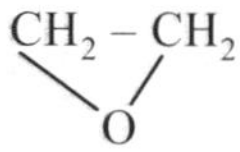 with $RMgX$ leads to the formation of
(a) RCH_2CH_2OH (b) $RCHOHCH_3$
(c) $RCHOHR$ (d) 
(1998)

36. Which one of the following compounds is resistant to nucleophilic attack by hydroxyl ions?
(a) Diethyl ether (b) Acetonitrile
(c) Acetamide (d) Methyl acetate
(1998)

37. When 3,3-dimethyl-2-butanol is heated with H_2SO_4, the major product obtained is
(a) 2,3-dimethyl-2-butene
(b) *cis* and *trans* isomers of 2,3-dimethyl-2-butene
(c) 2,3-dimethyl-1-butene
(d) 3,3-dimethyl-1-butene. *(1995)*

38. On heating glycerol with conc. H_2SO_4, a compound is obtained which has bad odour. The compound is
(a) acrolein (b) formic acid
(c) allyl alcohol
(d) glycerol sulphate. *(1994)*

39. The compound which does not react with sodium is
(a) CH_3COOH (b) $CH_3CHOHCH_3$
(c) C_2H_5OH (d) CH_3OCH_3
(1994)

40. Ethanol and dimethyl ether form a pair of functional isomers. The boiling point of ethanol is higher than that of dimethyl ether, due to the presence of
(a) H-bonding in ethanol
(b) H-bonding in dimethyl ether
(c) CH_3 group in ethanol
(d) CH_3 group in dimethyl ether. *(1993)*

41. Increasing order of acid strength among *p*-methoxyphenol, *p*-methylphenol and *p*-nitrophenol is
(a) *p*-nitrophenol, *p*-methoxyphenol, *p*-methylphenol
(b) *p*-methylphenol, *p*-methoxyphenol, *p*-nitrophenol
(c) *p*-nitrophenol, *p*-methylphenol, *p*-methoxyphenol
(d) *p*-methoxyphenol, *p*-methylphenol, *p*-nitrophenol. *(1993)*

42. Which one of the following on oxidation gives a ketone?
(a) Primary alcohol
(b) Secondary alcohol
(c) Tertiary alcohol
(d) All of these. *(1993)*

43. What is formed when a primary alcohol undergoes catalytic dehydrogenation?
(a) Aldehyde (b) Ketone
(c) Alkene (d) Acid *(1993)*

44. How many isomers of $C_5H_{11}OH$ will be primary alcohols?
(a) 5 (b) 4
(c) 2 (d) 3 *(1992)*

45. Methanol is industrially prepared by
(a) oxidation of CH_4 by steam at 900°C
(b) reduction of HCHO using $LiAlH_4$
(c) reaction HCHO with a solution of NaOH
(d) reduction of CO using H_2 and $ZnO–Cr_2O_3$.
(1992)

46. HBr reacts fastest with
(a) 2-methylpropan-1-ol
(b) methylpropan-2-ol
(c) propan-2-ol
(d) propan-1-ol. *(1992)*

47. When phenol is treated with excess bromine water. It gives
(a) *m*-bromophenol
(b) *o*- and *p*-bromophenols
(c) 2,4-dibromophenol
(d) 2,4,6-tribromophenol. *(1992)*

48. The compound which reacts fastest with Lucas reagent at room temperature is
(a) butan-1-ol
(b) butan-2-ol
(c) 2-methylpropan-1-ol
(d) 2-methylpropan-2-ol. *(1989)*

49. Which one of the following compounds will be most readily attacked by an electrophile?
(a) Chlorobenzene (b) Benzene
(c) Phenol (d) Toluene
(1989)

50. Propene, $CH_3CH{=}CH_2$ can be converted into 1-propanol by oxidation. Indicate which set of reagents amongst the following is ideal for the above conversion?
(a) $KMnO_4$ (alkaline)
(b) Osmium tetroxide (OsO_4/CH_2Cl_2)
(c) B_2H_6 and alk. H_2O_2
(d) O_3/Zn. *(1989)*

51. Phenol is heated with $CHCl_3$ and aqueous KOH when salicylaldehyde is produced. This reaction is known as
(a) Rosenmund's reaction
(b) Reimer-Tiemann reaction
(c) Friedel-Crafts reaction
(d) Sommelet reaction. *(1989,1988)*

52. Lucas reagent is
(a) conc. HCl and anhydrous $ZnCl_2$
(b) conc. HNO_3 and hydrous $ZnCl_2$
(c) conc. HCl and hydrous $ZnCl_2$
(d) conc. HNO_3 and anhydrous $ZnCl_2$. *(1988)*

Answer Key

1. (d)	**2.** (c)	**3.** (d)	**4.** (b)	**5.** (c)	**6.** (c)	**7.** (c)	**8.** (d)	**9.** (c)	**10.** (b)
11. (c)	**12.** (a)	**13.** (b)	**14.** (d)	**15.** (b)	**16.** (b)	**17.** (a)	**18.** (b)	**19.** (a)	**20.** (a)
21. (c)	**22.** (c)	**23.** (c)	**24.** (c)	**25.** (b)	**26.** (c)	**27.** (a)	**28.** (a)	**29.** (a)	**30.** (c)
31. (c)	**32.** (c)	**33.** (b)	**34.** (c)	**35.** (a)	**36.** (a)	**37.** (a)	**38.** (a)	**39.** (d)	**40.** (a)
41. (d)	**42.** (b)	**43.** (a)	**44.** (b)	**45.** (d)	**46.** (b)	**47.** (d)	**48.** (d)	**49.** (c)	**50.** (c)
51. (b)	**52.** (a)								

EXPLANATIONS

1. **(d)** : It is Reimer–Tiemann reaction. The electrophile formed is dichlorocarbene ($:CCl_2$) which is formed according to the following mechanism :

$$CHCl_3 + OH^- \rightleftharpoons \bar{\ddot{C}}Cl_3 + H_2O \xrightarrow{-Cl^-\ (\alpha\text{-Elimination})} :CCl_2$$

$:CCl_2$ Dichlorocarbene (electrophile)

2. **(c)** : As the compound is giving yellow precipitate with NaOI that shows it is undergoing haloform reaction. Haloform reaction is shown by the compounds having

$CH_3-\underset{\underset{O}{\|}}{C}-$ or $CH_3-\underset{\underset{OH}{|}}{CH}-$ group.

Hence, the compound A is 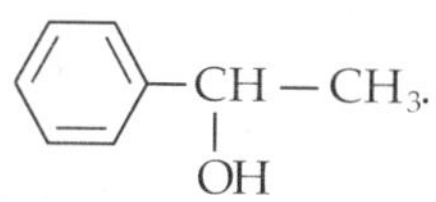

$$2NaOH + \underset{'Y'}{I_2} \longrightarrow NaOI + NaI + H_2$$

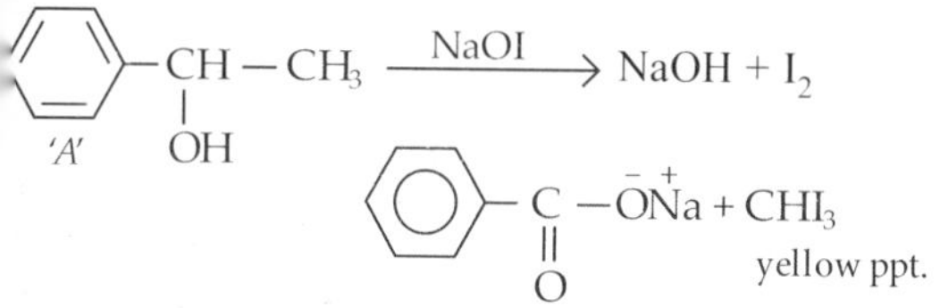

3. **(d)** :

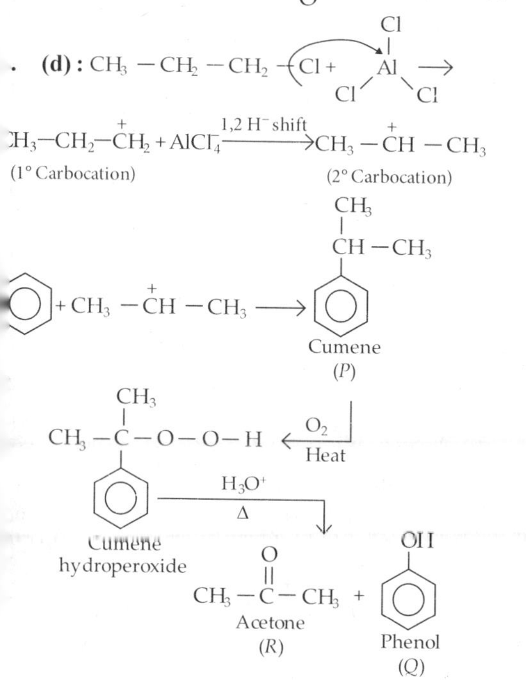

4. **(b)** : In case of phenyl methyl ether, methyl phenyl oxonium ion $\left(C_6H_5-\overset{+}{\underset{\underset{H}{|}}{O}}-CH_3\right)$ is formed by protonation of ether. The $O-CH_3$ bond is weaker than $O-C_6H_5$ bond as $O-C_6H_5$ has partial double bond character. Therefore, the attack by I^- ion breaks $O-CH_3$ bond to form CH_3I.

Step I :

$$C_6H_5-\ddot{\underset{..}{O}}-CH_3 + HI \rightleftharpoons C_6H_5-\overset{\overset{H}{|}}{\underset{..}{\overset{+}{O}}}-CH_3 + I^-$$

Oxonium ion

Step II :

$$I^- + CH_3-\overset{\overset{H}{|}}{\underset{..}{\overset{+}{O}}}-C_6H_5 \longrightarrow CH_3I + C_6H_5OH$$

5. **(c)** : Electron withdrawing groups increase the acidity while electron donating groups decrease the acidity of phenol.

6. **(c)** : Williamson's ether synthesis reaction involves the treatment of sodium alkoxide with a suitable alkyl halide to form an ether.

7. **(c)** : This is Reimer–Tiemann reaction.

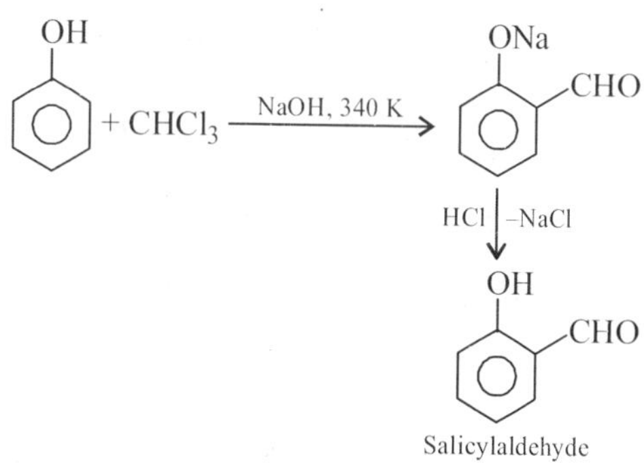

8. **(d)** : 1° and 2° alcohols react with HCl in presence of anhydrous $ZnCl_2$ as catalyst while in case of 3° alcohols $ZnCl_2$ is not required.

9. **(c)** : Williamson synthesis is the best method for the preparation of ethers.

10. **(b)** : (a) $CH_3CHO + RMgX$

$$\xrightarrow{\text{ether}} CH_3-\overset{\overset{R}{|}}{CH}-OH$$

2° alcohol

(b) $C_6H_5OH + NaOH \xrightarrow[-H_2O]{} C_6H_5ONa$ (Sodium phenoxide)

$C_6H_5ONa \xrightarrow[\Delta]{CH_3I} C_6H_5OCH_3 + NaI$

Methyl phenyl ether (Anisole) — (Williamson's synthesis)

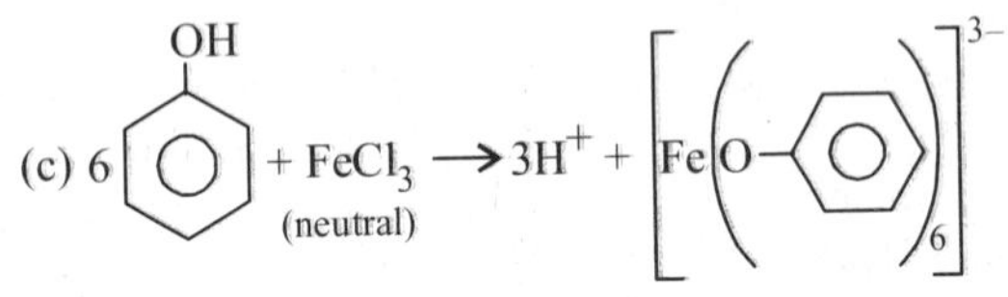

Violet colour complex

+ 3HCl

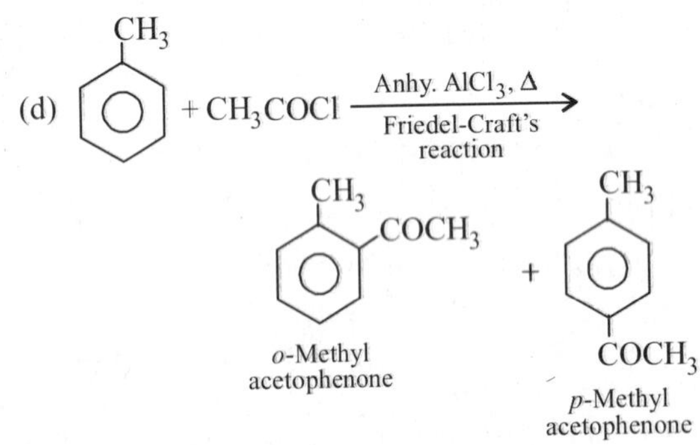

11. (c) : The reaction is as follows:

Acid + $NaHCO_3 \longrightarrow$ Sodium salt of acid (soluble) + H_2CO_3

Among all the given compounds, *o*-nitrophenol is weaker acid than HCO_3^-. Hence, it does not react with $NaHCO_3$.

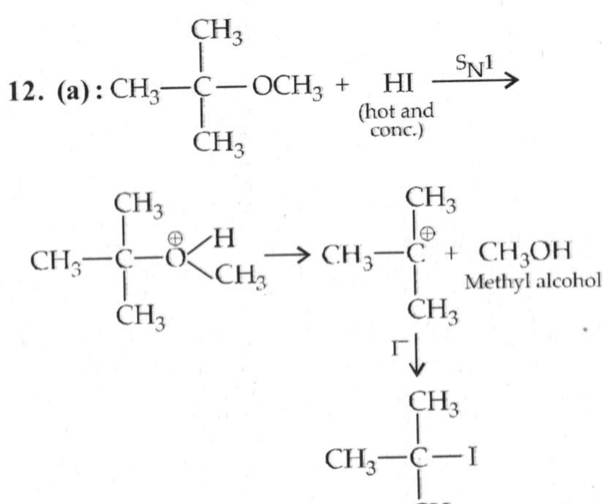

13. (b) : The iodoform test is positive for alcohols with formula R — CHOH — CH_3. Among $C_6H_{14}O$ isomers, the ones with positive iodoform test are:

I. $CH_3—CH_2—CH_2—CH_2—CHOH—CH_3$
2- Hexanol

II. $CH_3—CH_2—CH(CH_3)—CHOH—CH_3$
3- Methyl-2-pentanol

III. $(CH_3)_2CH—CH_2—CHOH—CH_3$
4- Methyl-2-pentanol

IV. $(CH_3)_3C—CHOH—CH_3$
3, 3- Dimethyl-2-butanol

14. (d) : $CH_3Br \xrightarrow{KCN} \underset{(A)}{CH_3CN} \xrightarrow{H_3O^+} \underset{(B)}{CH_3COOH} \xrightarrow[\text{ether}]{LiAlH_4} \underset{(C)}{CH_3CH_2OH}$

15. (b)

16. (b) :

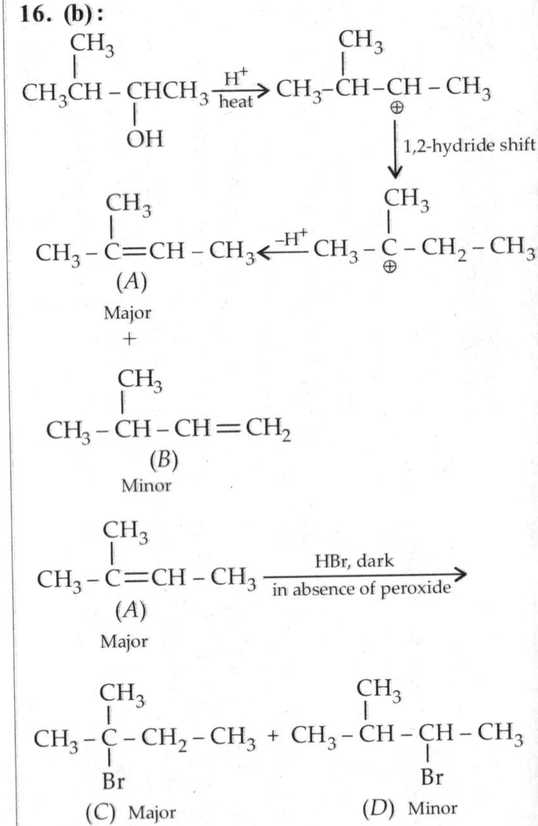

17. (a) : III > II > IV > I

Since, phenols and carboxylic acids are more acid than aliphatic alcohols, we find that cyclohexan (I) is least acidic. Out of the two given phenols, III more acidic than IV. This is because of the presen of three highly electron withdrawing NO_2 grou on the benzene ring which makes the O—H bor extremely polarized. This facilitates the release of as H^+. Thus, III > IV.

In acetic acid the electron withdrawing $-\overset{\overset{\displaystyle O}{\|}}{C}-$ in the —COOH group polarises the O—H bond and increases the acidic strength. Acetic acid is therefore more acidic than phenol or cyclohexanol.

$\therefore$ The order is III > II > IV > I.

18. (b): Phenol is most acidic of all the given compounds.

In phenol, the electron withdrawing phenyl ring polarizes the O—H bond thereby facilitating the release of H as H^+ and hence phenol is most acidic.

In 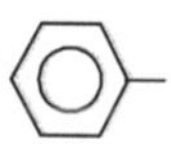 $-CH_2OH$ the electron withdrawing effect of phenyl ring is somewhat diminished by the $-CH_2$ group and it is therefore less acidic than phenol. In (c) and (d), —OH group is attached to alkyl groups which, due to their $+I$ effect reduce the polarity of —OH bond and so the acidic strength is low.

19. (a): In phenols, the presence of electron releasing groups decrease the acidity, whereas presence of electron withdrawing groups increase the acidity, compared to phenol. Among the *meta* and *para*-nitrophenols, the latter is more acidic as the presence of $-NO_2$ group at *para* position stabilises the phenoxide ion to a greater extent than when it is present at *meta* position. Thus, correct order of acidity is :

para-nitrophenol (iv) > *meta*-nitrophenol (iii) > phenol (i) > methyl phenol (ii)

20. (a):

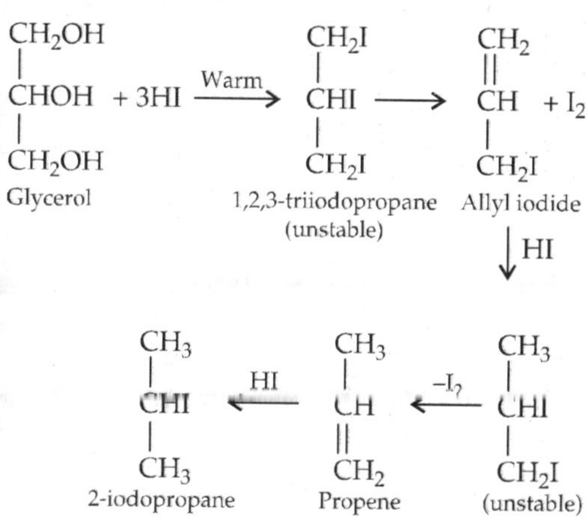

21. (c) : Methyl alcohol does not respond to the iodoform test. The iodoform test is exhibited by ethyl alcohol, acetaldehyde, acetone, methyl ketones, those alcohols which possess $CH_3CH(OH)-$ group, acetophenone, α-hydroxypropionic acid, keto acid, 2-aminoalkanes, etc.

22. (c) : $\underset{1^\circ \text{ Amine}}{CH_3CH_2CH_2CH_2NH_2} \xrightarrow[CHCl_3]{KOH \text{ (alc.)}} \underset{\text{Bad smell}}{CH_3CH_2CH_2CH_2NC} + 3KCl + 3H_2O$

$$CH_3C\equiv CH + \text{Amm. } AgNO_3 \longrightarrow \underset{\text{White ppt.}}{CH_3C\equiv \bar{C}Ag^+} + HNO_3$$

$$CH_3CH_2COOCH_3 + NaOH \xrightarrow{\text{Heat}} CH_3CH_2COONa + CH_3OH$$

$$\underset{2^\circ \text{ Alcohol}}{CH_3CH(OH)CH_3} + \text{Conc. HCl} \xrightarrow{\text{anhy. } ZnCl_2} CH_3-\underset{\underset{\displaystyle Cl}{|}}{CH}-CH_3 + H_2O$$

cloudiness appears in 5 minutes

23. (c) :

$$\underset{\text{Ethanol}}{C_2H_5OH} \xrightarrow{PBr_3} \underset{(X)}{C_2H_5Br} \xrightarrow[\text{dehydro-halogenation}]{\text{alc. KOH}}$$

$$\underset{\underset{(Y)}{\text{Ethene}}}{CH_2=CH_2} \xrightarrow{H_2SO_4} CH_3CH_2-HSO_4 \xrightarrow{H_2O} \underset{(Z)}{C_2H_5-OH}$$

24. (c) : When 1,2-diol like ethylene glycol is treated with HIO_4, each alcoholic group is oxidised to a carbonyl group by HIO_4. Since in glycol, both the –OH groups are terminal, so oxidation would yield two formaldehyde molecules.

i.e., $\begin{matrix} CH_2-OH \\ | \\ CH_2-OH \end{matrix} \xrightarrow{HIO_4} 2HCHO$

25. (b) :

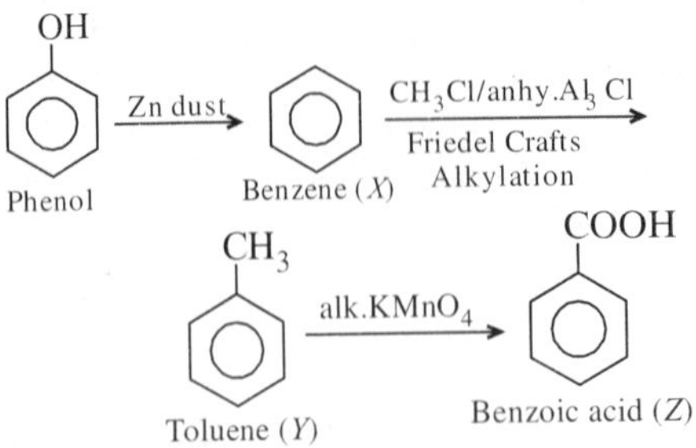

26. (c) : The alkyl iodide produced depends on the nature of the alkyl groups. If one group is Me and the other a primary or secondary alkyl group, it is methyl iodide which is produced. This can be explained on the assumption that the mechanism is S_N2, and because of the steric effect of the larger group, I^- attacks the smaller methyl group.

When the substrate is a methyl *t*-alkyl ether, the products are *t*-*R*I and MeOH. This can be explained by an S_N1 mechanism, the carbonium ion produced being the *t*-alkyl since tertiary carbonium ion is more stable than a primary or secondary carbonium ion.

27. (a) : All alcohols follow the general formula $C_nH_{2n+2}O$.

$CH_3OH\ [CH_{2+2}O]$; $C_2H_5OH\ [C_2H_{(2\times2)+2}O]$
$n = 1$, $n = 2$

28. (a) : $H_2C\overset{O}{—}CH_2 + CH_3MgBr \longrightarrow$

$CH_3CH_2CH_2OMgBr \xrightarrow{H^+} \underset{\text{primary alcohol}}{CH_3CH_2CH_2OH}$

29. (a) : With cold HI, a mixture of alkyl iodide and alcohol is formed. In the case of mixed ethers, the halogen atom attaches to a smaller and less complex alkyl group.

$CH_3OCH(CH_3)_2 + HI \rightarrow CH_3I + (CH_3)_2CHOH$

30. (c) : Phenols are much more acidic than alcohols, due to the stabilisation of phenoxide ion by resonance.

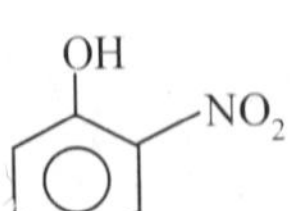

—NO_2 is the electron withdrawing group and helps in stabilizing the negative charge on the oxygen hence equilibrium shifts in forward direction and more H^+ remove easily. Hence, it is most acidic.

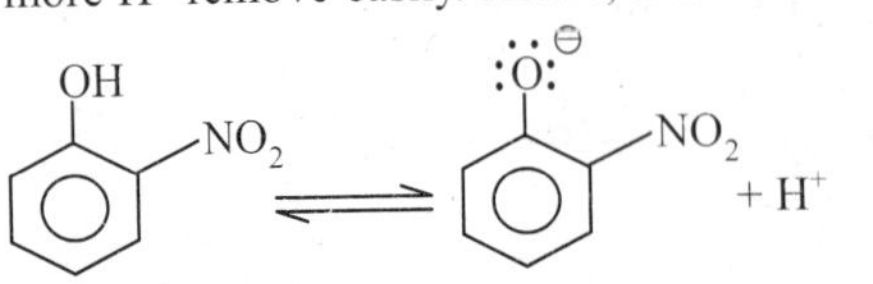

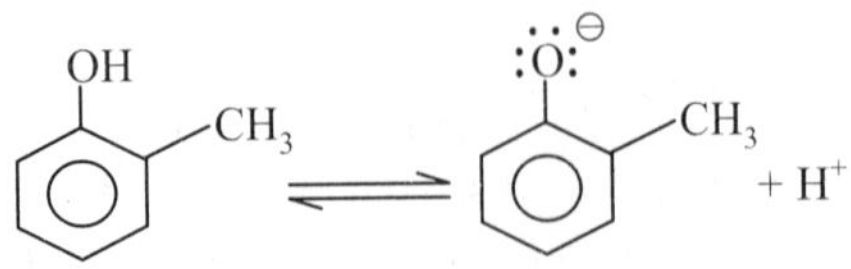

—CH_3 is the electron donating group.
Hence electron density increases on the oxygen and destabilizes the product. Thus, equilibrium shifts in backward direction.

31. (c) : Formation of a yellow precipitate on heating a compound with an alkaline solution of iodine is known as iodoform reaction. Methyl alcohol does not respond to this test. Iodoform test is exhibited by ethyl alcohol, acetaldehyde, acetone, methyl ketones and those alcohols which possess $CH_3CH(OH)$ – group.

32. (c) : *n*-Propyl alcohol on oxidation with potassium dichromate gives an aldehyde which on further oxidation gives an acid. Both aldehyde and acid contain the same number of C atoms as the original alcohol.

$$CH_3CH_2CH_2OH \xrightarrow[K_2Cr_2O_7/H_2SO_4]{25°C}$$

$$CH_3CH_2CHO \xrightarrow{K_2Cr_2O_7/H_2SO_4} CH_3CH_2COOH$$

Isopropyl alcohol on oxidation gives a ketone with the same number of C atoms as the original alcohol.

$$CH_3-\overset{OH}{\underset{CH_3}{CH}} \xrightarrow{K_2Cr_2O_7/H_2SO_4} CH_3-\underset{O}{\overset{}{\underset{\|}{C}}}-CH_3$$

33. (b) : This reaction is called Reimer-Tiemann reaction.

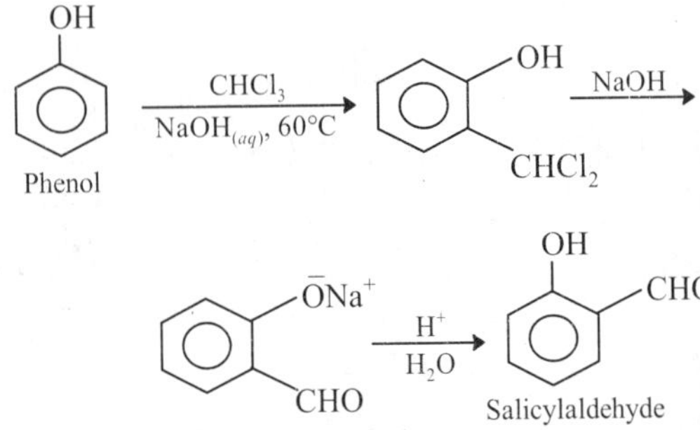

34. (c) : $C_2H_5OH + 4I_2 + NaOH \longrightarrow$
$CHI_3 + NaI + HCOONa + H_2O$

Iodoform is a pale yellow solid which crystallises in hexagonal plates.

5. **(a) :**

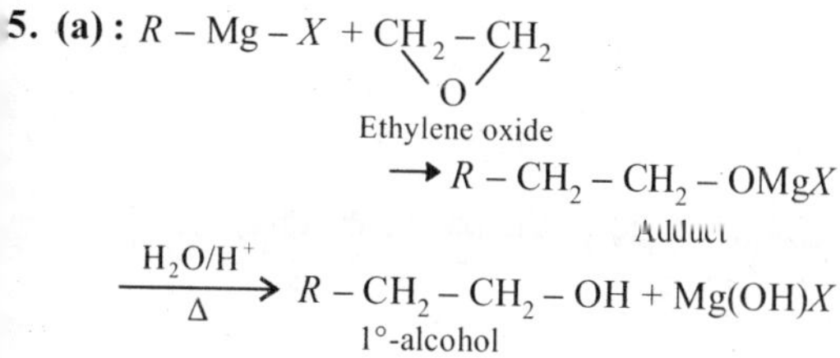

6. **(a) :** Diethyl ether is a saturated compound, so is resistant to nucleophilic attack by a hydroxyl n (OH^-).

ther compounds have unsaturation and the ısaturated 'C' atom bears partial +ve charge, erefore they undergo easy nucleophilic attack by H^- ion.

'. **(a):**

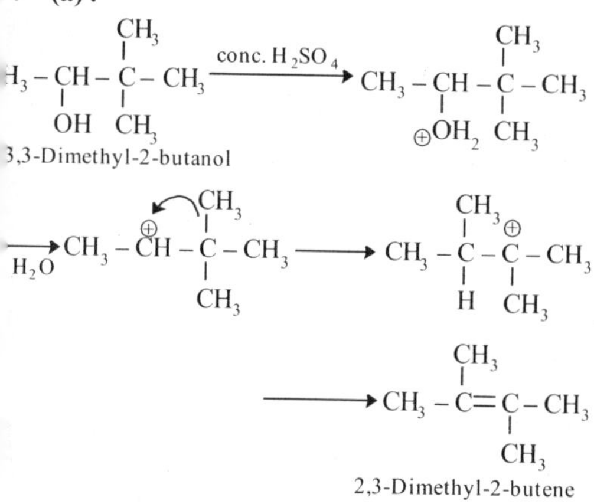

. **(a):**

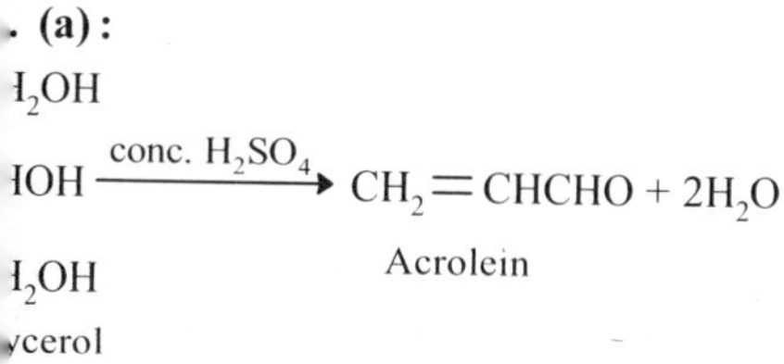

(d) : Ethers are very inert. The chemical inertness ethers is due to absence of active group in their lecules. Since $CH_3 - O - CH_3$ is an inert and it s not contain active group, therefore it does not ct with sodium.

(a) : Hydrogen bonding in ethanol.

(d) : $- OCH_3$, $-CH_3$ are electron donating groups reases the acidic character of phenols. $-NO_2$, N are electron withdrawing groups, tend to rease the acidic character. Thus, the order is ethoxyphenol < *p*-methylphenol < *p*-nitrophenol.

(b) : 2° alcohols on oxidation give ketones, lcohols form aldehydes.

43. **(a) :** Primary alcohol undergoes catalytic dehydrogenation to give aldehyde.

44. **(b) :** 4-isomers are possible for $C_5H_{11}OH$.

(i) $CH_3CH_2CH_2CH_2CH_2OH$

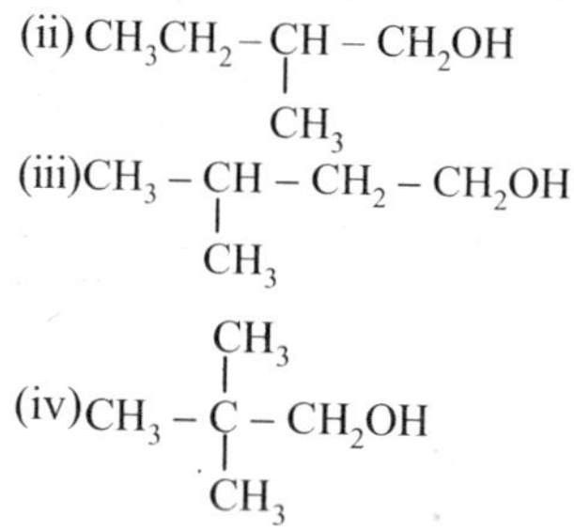

45. **(d) :** $CO + 2H_2 \xrightarrow{ZnO - Cr_2O_3} CH_3OH$

46. **(b) :** 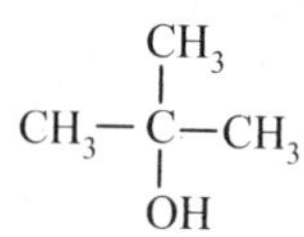 generates 3° carbocation which is very stable intermediate, thus it will react more rapidly with HBr.

47. **(d) :** Phenol on reaction with excess bromine water gives 2,4,6-tribromophenol.

48. **(d) :** 2-Methylpropan-2-ol reacts rapidly with Lucas reagent at room temperature.

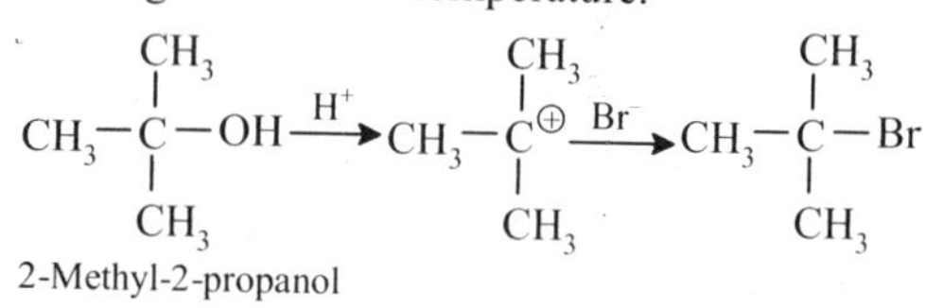

49. **(c) :** –OH group being electron donor increases the electron density in phenol. Thus, the electron density in phenol is higher than that of toluene, benzene and chlorobenzene.

50. **(c) :**

$$CH_3-CH=CH_2 \xrightarrow[\text{Hydroboration}]{BH_3,\ THF} \underset{\text{Tripropyl borane}}{(CH_3CH_2CH_2)_3B} \xrightarrow[OH^-]{H_2O_2} \underset{\text{Propan-1-ol}}{3CH_3CH_2CH_2OH}$$

51. **(b) :** Treatment of phenol with $CHCl_3$ and aqueous hydroxide introduces – CHO group, onto the aromatic ring generally *ortho* to the – OH group. This reaction is known as Reimer Tiemann reaction.

52. **(a) :** Conc. HCl and anhydrous $ZnCl_2$–Lucas reagent.

Chapter 26

Aldehydes, Ketones and Carboxylic Acids

1. Carboxylic acids have higher boiling points than aldehydes, ketones and even alcohols of comparable molecular mass. It is due to their
   (a) formation of intramolecular H-bonding
   (b) formation of carboxylate ion
   (c) more extensive association of carboxylic acid *via* van der Waals' forces of attraction
   (d) formation of intermolecular H-bonding. *(NEET 2018)*

2. Consider the reactions,

$$\underset{(C_2H_6O)}{X} \xrightarrow[573\ K]{Cu} A \xrightarrow[^-OH,\ \Delta]{[Ag(NH_3)_2]^+} \text{Silver mirror observed}$$
$$A \xrightarrow{^-OH,\ \Delta} Y$$
$$A \xrightarrow{NH_2NHCONH_2} Z$$

   Identify *A, X, Y* and *Z*.
   (a) *A*-Methoxymethane, *X*-Ethanol, *Y*-Ethanoic acid, Z-Semicarbazide.
   (b) *A*-Ethanal, *X*-Ethanol, *Y*-But-2-enal, Z-Semicarbazone.
   (c) *A*-Ethanol, *X*-Acetaldehyde, *Y*-Butanone, Z-Hydrazone.
   (d) *A*-Methoxymethane, *X*-Ethanoic acid, *Y*-Acetate ion, *Z*-Hydrazine. *(NEET 2017)*

3. Of the following, which is the product formed when cyclohexanone undergoes aldol condensation followed by heating?

(a) 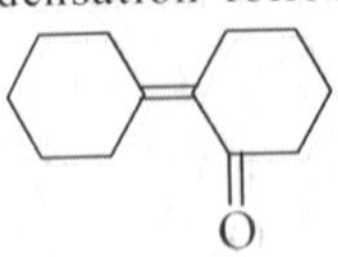
(b) 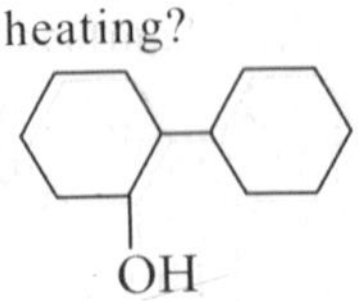
(c) 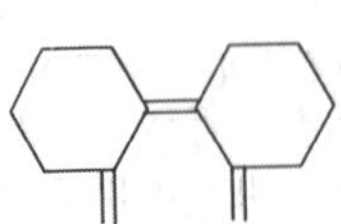
(d) 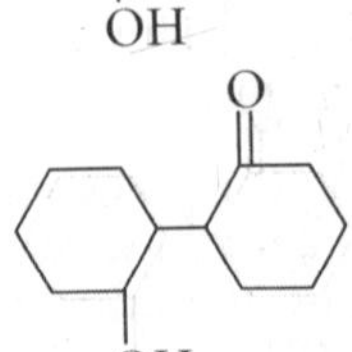

(NEET 2017)

4. The correct structure of the product '*A*' formed in the reaction

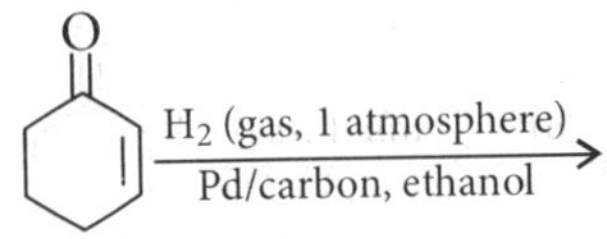 *A* is

(a) 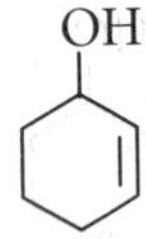
(b) 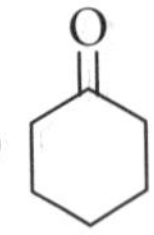
(c) 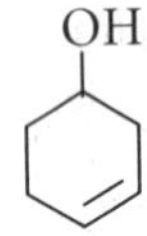
(d) 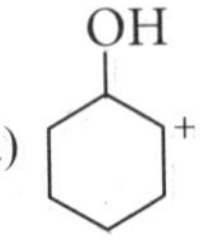

(NEET-II 201

5. The correct order of strengths of the carboxyl acids

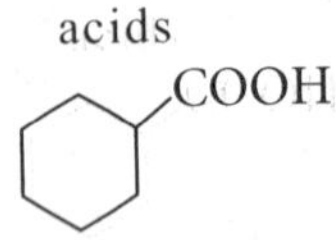
I
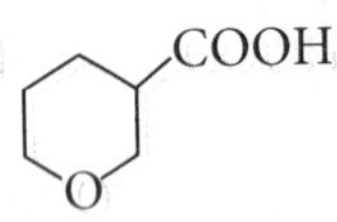
II
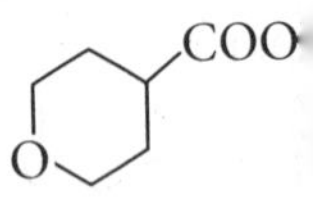
III

is
   (a) I > II > III (b) II > III > I
   (c) III > II > I (d) II > I > III *(NEET-II 201*

6. Which of the following reagents wou distinguish *cis*-cyclopenta-1-2-diol from t *trans*-isomer?
   (a) MnO_2
   (b) Aluminium isopropoxide
   (c) Acetone
   (d) Ozone *(NEET-I 20*

7. The correct statement regarding a carbo compound with a hydrogen atom on its alp carbon, is
   (a) a carbonyl compound with a hydrogen at on its alpha-carbon rapidly equilibra with its corresponding enol and t process is known as carbonylation
   (b) a carbonyl compound with a hydrogen at on its alpha-carbon rapidly equilibra with its corresponding enol and t process is known as keto-enol tautomer

(c) a carbonyl compound with a hydrogen atom on its alpha-carbon never equilibrates with its corresponding enol

(d) a carbonyl compound with a hydrogen atom on its alpha-carbon rapidly equilibrates with its corresponding enol and this process is known as aldehyde-ketone equilibration. *(NEET-I 2016)*

8. The oxidation of benzene by V_2O_5 in the presence of air produces

(a) maleic anhydride (b) benzoic acid

(c) benzaldehyde

(d) benzoic anhydride. *(2015)*

9. Reaction of a carbonyl compound with one of the following reagents involves nucleophilic addition followed by elimination of water. The reagent is

(a) hydrazine in presence of feebly acidic solution

(b) hydrocyanic acid

(c) sodium hydrogen sulphite

(d) a Grignard reagent. *(2015)*

10. Which one of the following esters gets hydrolysed most easily under alkaline conditions?

(a) 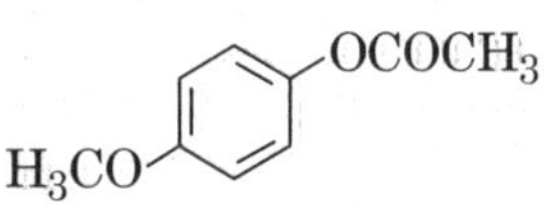

(b) 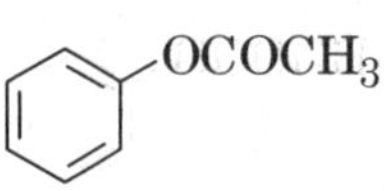

(c) 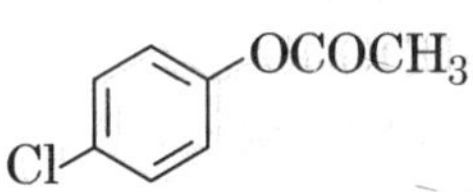

(d) 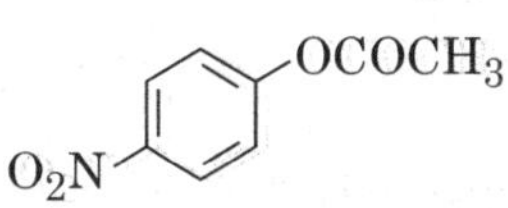 *(2015)*

11. An organic compound '*X*' having molecular formula $C_5H_{10}O$ yields phenylhydrazone and gives negative response to the iodoform test and Tollens' test. It produces *n*-pentane on reduction. '*X*' could be

(a) 3-pentanone (b) *n*-amyl alcohol

(c) pentanal (d) 2-pentanone. *(2015, Cancelled)*

12. Which one is most reactive towards nucleophilic addition reaction?

(a) 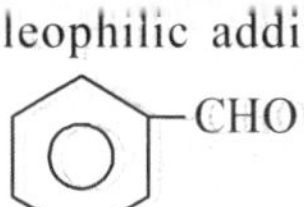 (b) 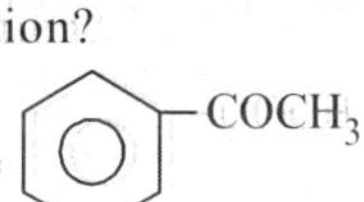

(c)  (d)  *(2014)*

13. The order of stability of the following tautomeric compounds is

$$\underset{(I)}{CH_2=C(OH)-CH_2-C(=O)-CH_3} \rightleftharpoons \underset{(II)}{CH_3-C(=O)-CH_2-C(=O)-CH_3} \rightleftharpoons \underset{(III)}{CH_3-C(OH)=CH-C(=O)-CH_3}$$

(a) II > I > III (b) II > III > I

(c) I > II > III (d) III > II > I *(NEET 2013)*

14. Reaction by which benzaldehyde cannot be prepared

(a)  + CO + HCl in presence of anhydrous $AlCl_3$

(b) 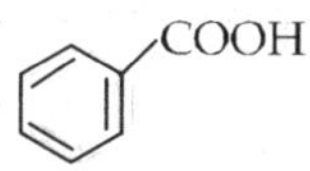 + Zn/Hg and conc. HCl

(c) 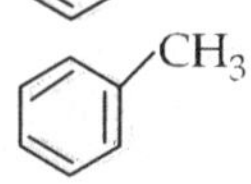 + CrO_2Cl_2 in CS_2 followed by H_3O^+

(d) 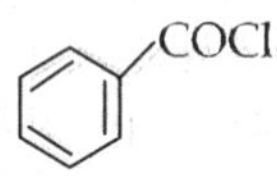 + H_2 in presence of Pd-$BaSO_4$ *(NEET 2013)*

15. Predict the products in the given reaction.

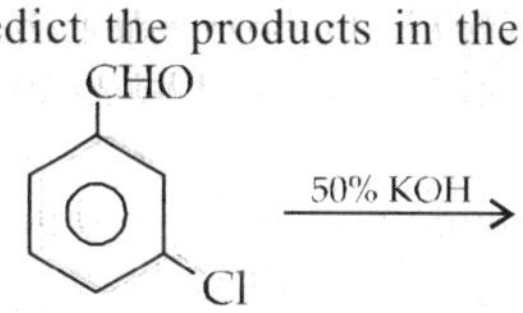

(a) 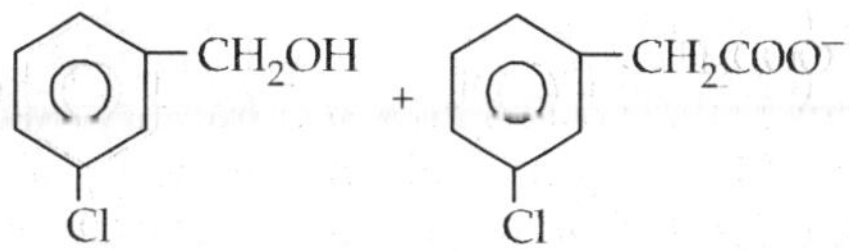

(b) 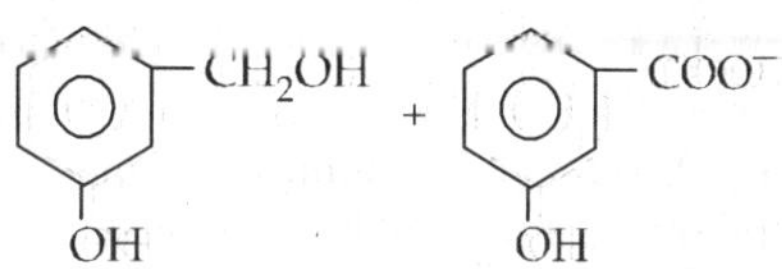

(c) 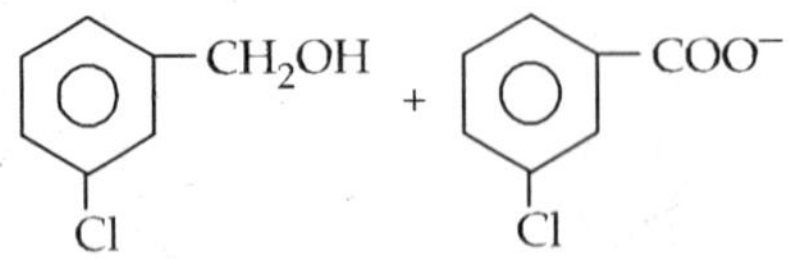

(d) 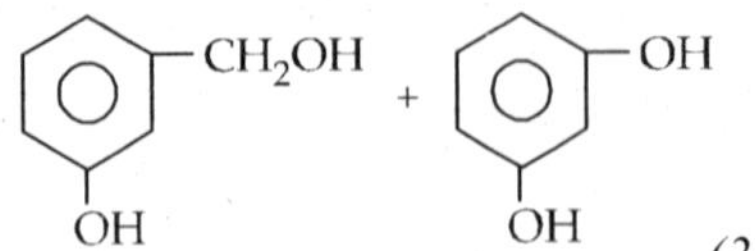

(2012)

16. Acetone is treated with excess of ethanol in the presence of hydrochloric acid. The product obtained is

(a) $CH_3CH_2CH_2-\overset{O}{\overset{||}{C}}-CH_3$

(b) $CH_3CH_2CH_2-\overset{O}{\overset{||}{C}}-CH_2CH_2CH_3$

(c) $(CH_3)_2C<^{OH}_{OC_2H_5}$

(d) $(CH_3)_2C<^{OC_2H_5}_{OC_2H_5}$ (2012)

17. CH_3CHO and $C_6H_5CH_2CHO$ can be distinguished chemically by
(a) Benedict's test
(b) Iodoform test
(c) Tollens' reagent test
(d) Fehling's solution test (2012)

18. The correct order of decreasing acid strength of trichloroacetic acid (A), trifluoroacetic acid (B), acetic acid (C) and formic acid (D) is
(a) $B > A > D > C$ (b) $B > D > C > A$
(c) $A > B > C > D$ (d) $A > C > B > D$
(2012)

19. Consider the following reaction

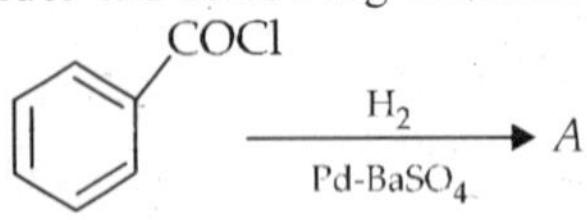

The product A is
(a) C_6H_5CHO (b) C_6H_5OH
(c) $C_6H_5COCH_3$ (d) C_6H_5Cl
(Mains 2012)

20. Consider the reaction :
$RCHO + NH_2NH_2 \rightarrow RCH{=}N-NH_2$
What sort of reaction is it?
(a) Electrophilic addition-elimination reaction
(b) Free radical addition-elimination reaction
(c) Electrophilic substitution-elimination reaction
(d) Nucleophilic addition-elimination reaction
(Mains 2012)

21. Which of the following compounds will give a yellow precipitate with iodine and alkali?
(a) Acetophenone (b) Methyl acetate
(c) Acetamide
(d) 2-Hydroxypropane (Mains 2012)

22. Clemmensen reduction of a ketone is carried out in the presence of which of the following?
(a) Glycol with KOH (b) Zn-Hg with HCl
(c) $LiAlH_4$
(d) H_2 and Pt as catalyst (2011)

23. In a set of reactions m-bromobenzoic acid gave a product D. Identify the product D.

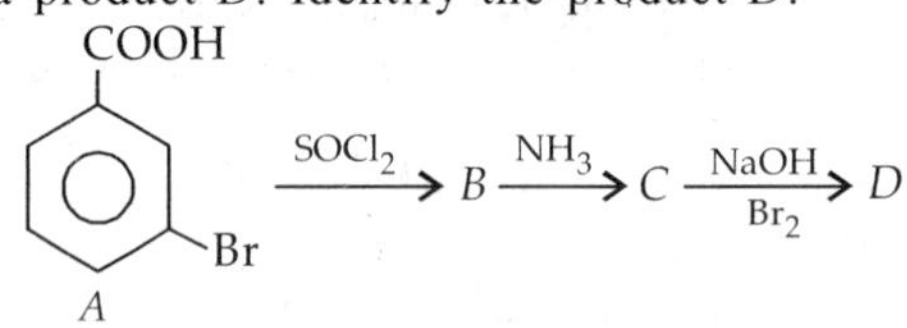

(a) 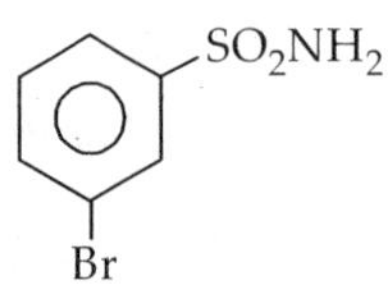

(b) 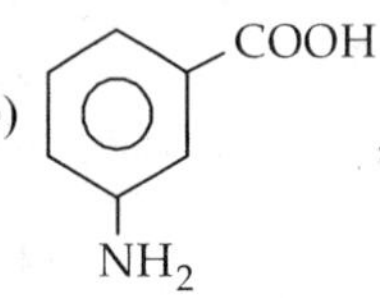

(c) 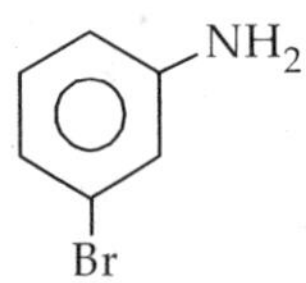

(d) 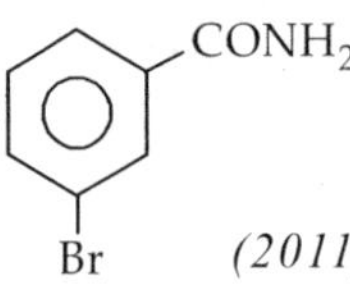

(2011)

24. The order of reactivity of phenyl magnesium bromide (PhMgBr) with the following compounds:

$\begin{matrix}CH_3\\H\end{matrix}>C=O$, $\begin{matrix}CH_3\\CH_3\end{matrix}>C=O$ and $\begin{matrix}Ph\\Ph\end{matrix}>C=O$

I II III

(a) III > II > I (b) II > I > III
(c) I > III > II (d) I > II > III
(Mains 2011)

25. Match the compounds given in List-I with List-II and select the suitable option using the code given below.

List-I	List-II
(A) Benzaldehyde	(i) Phenolphthalein
(B) Phthalic anhydride	(ii) Benzoin condensation
(C) Phenyl benzoate	(iii) Oil of wintergreen
(D) Methyl salicylate	(iv) Fries rearrangement

(a) (A)-(iv), (B)-(i), (C)-(iii), (D)-(ii)
(b) (A)-(iv), (B)-(ii), (C)-(iii), (D)-(i)
(c) (A)-(ii), (B)-(iii), (C)-(iv), (D)-(i)
(d) (A)-(ii), (B)-(i), (C)-(iv), (D)-(iii)

(Mains 2011)

26. An organic compound *A* on treatment with NH_3 gives *B*, which on heating gives *C*. *C* when treated with Br_2 in the presence of KOH produces ethyl amine. Compound *A* is
(a) CH_3COOH
(b) $CH_3CH_2CH_2COOH$
(c) $CH_3-\underset{\displaystyle CH_3}{\underset{|}{C}}HCOOH$
(d) CH_3CH_2COOH *(Mains 2011)*

27. Which of the following reactions will not result in the formation of carbon-carbon bonds?
(a) Reimer–Tiemann reaction
(b) Cannizzaro reaction
(c) Wurtz reaction
(d) Friedel–Crafts acylation *(2010)*

28. Acetamide is treated with the following reagents separately. Which one of these would yield methyl amine?
(a) NaOH-Br_2 (b) Sodalime
(c) Hot conc.H_2SO_4 (d) PCl_5 *(2010)*

29. Among the given compounds, the most susceptible to nucleophilic attack at the carbonyl group is
(a) CH_3COOCH_3 (b) CH_3CONH_2
(c) $CH_3COOCOCH_3$ (d) CH_3COCl *(2010)*

30. Which one of the following compounds will be most readily dehydrated?

(a) 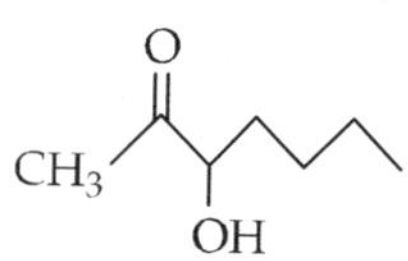

(b) 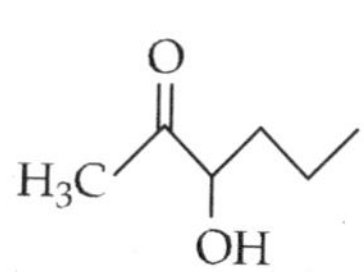

(c) 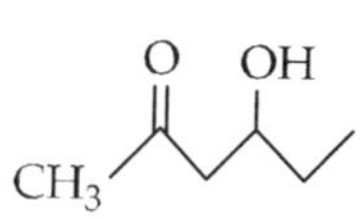

(d) 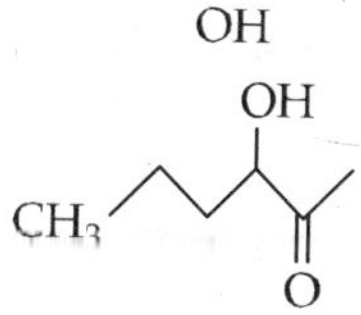

(Mains 2010)

31. Trichloroacetaldehyde, CCl_3CHO reacts with chlorobenzene in presence of sulphuric acid and produces

(a) 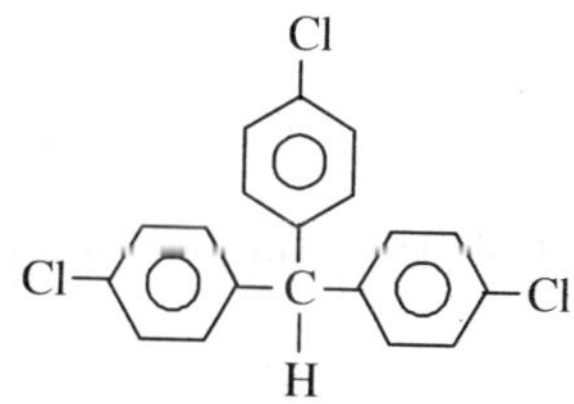

(b) 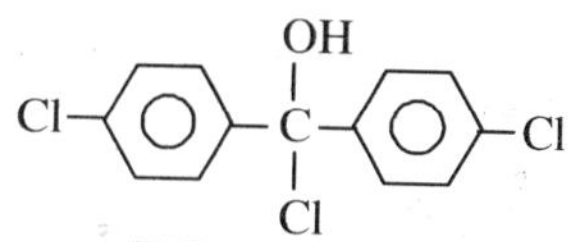

(c) 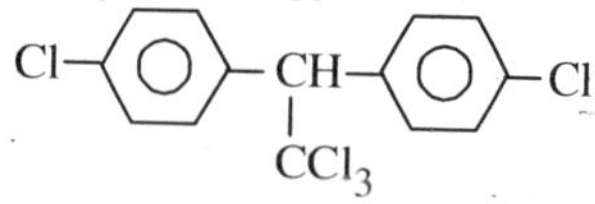

(d) 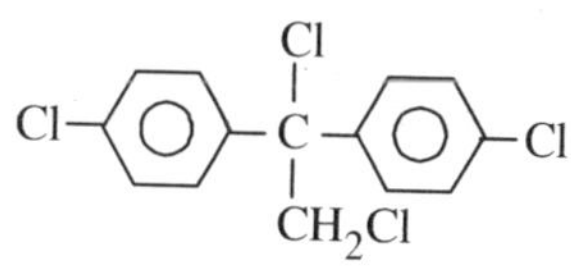

(2009)

32. Propionic acid with Br_2/P yields a dibromo product. Its structure would be
(a) $H-\underset{Br}{\overset{Br}{\underset{|}{\overset{|}{C}}}}-CH_2COOH$
(b) $CH_2(Br)-CH_2-COBr$
(c) $CH_3-\underset{Br}{\overset{Br}{\underset{|}{\overset{|}{C}}}}-COOH$
(d) $CH_2(Br)-CH(Br)-COOH$ *(2009)*

33. Acetophenone when reacted with a base, C_2H_5ONa, yields a stable compound which has the structure

(a) 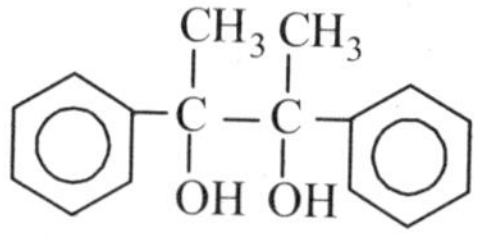

(b) 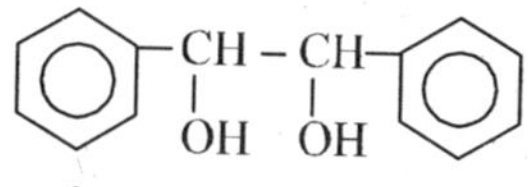

(c) 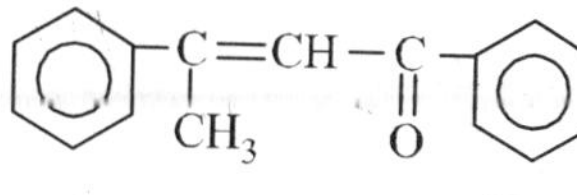

(d) 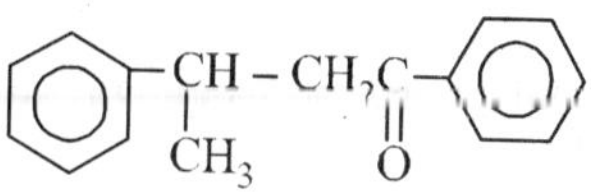

(2008)

34. A strong base can abstract an α-hydrogen from
(a) ketone (b) alkane
(c) alkene (d) amine. *(2008)*

35. The relative reactivities of acyl compounds towards nucleophilic substitution are in the order of
(a) Acid anhydride > Amide > Ester > Acyl chloride
(b) Acyl chloride > Ester > Acid anhydride > Amide
(c) Acyl chloride > Acid anhydride > Ester > Amide
(d) Ester > Acyl chloride > Amide > Acid anhydride. *(2008)*

36. Reduction of aldehydes and ketones into hydrocarbons using zinc amalgam and conc. HCl is called
(a) Cope reduction (b) Dow reduction
(c) Wolff–Kishner reduction
(d) Clemmensen reduction. *(2007)*

37. Which one of the following on treatment with 50% aqueous sodium hydroxide yields the corresponding alcohol and acid?
(a) C_6H_5CHO
(b) $CH_3CH_2CH_2CHO$
(c) $CH_3-\overset{O}{\overset{\|}{C}}-CH_3$
(d) $C_6H_5CH_2CHO$ *(2007)*

38. The product formed in Aldol condensation is
(a) a beta-hydroxy aldehyde or a beta-hydroxy ketone
(b) an alpha-hydroxy aldehyde or ketone
(c) an alpha, beta unsaturated ester
(d) a beta-hydroxy acid. *(2007)*

39. Consider the following compounds
(i) C_6H_5COCl
(ii) 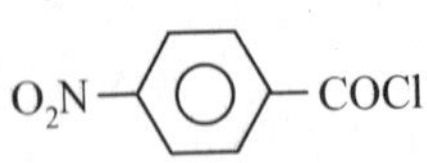
(iii) 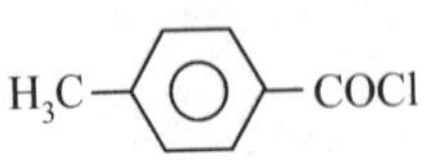
(iv) 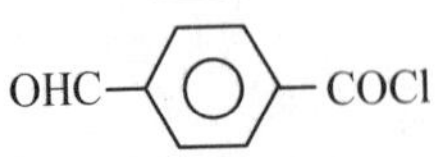

The correct decreasing order of their reactivity towards hydrolysis is
(a) (i) > (ii) > (iii) > (iv)
(b) (iv) > (ii) > (i) > (iii)
(c) (ii) > (iv) > (i) > (iii)
(d) (ii) > (iv) > (iii) > (i) *(2007)*

40. Which of the following represents the correct order of the acidity in the given compounds?
(a) $FCH_2COOH > CH_3COOH > BrCH_2COOH > ClCH_2COOH$
(b) $BrCH_2COOH > ClCH_2COOH > FCH_2COOH > CH_3COOH$
(c) $FCH_2COOH > ClCH_2COOH > BrCH_2COOH > CH_3COOH$
(d) $CH_3COOH > BrCH_2COOH > ClCH_2COOH > FCH_2COOH$ *(2007)*

41. Nucleophilic addition reaction will be most favoured in
(a) CH_3CHO
(b) $CH_3-CH_2-CH_2\overset{O}{\overset{\|}{C}}-CH_3$
(c) $(CH_3)_2C=O$
(d) CH_3CH_2CHO *(2006)*

42. A carbonyl compound reacts with hydrogen cyanide to form cyanohydrin which on hydrolysis forms a racemic mixture of α-hydroxy acid. The carbonyl compound is
(a) formaldehyde (b) acetaldehyde
(c) acetone (d) diethyl ketone. *(2006)*

43. In a set of reactions propionic acid yielded a compound *D*.

$$CH_3CH_2COOH \xrightarrow{SOCl_2} B \xrightarrow{NH_3} C \xrightarrow[Br_2]{KOH} D$$

The structure of *D* would be
(a) $CH_3CH_2NH_2$ (b) $CH_3CH_2CH_2NH_2$
(c) $CH_3CH_2CONH_2$ (d) $CH_3CH_2NHCH_3$ *(2006)*

44. Self condensation of two moles of ethyl acetate in presence of sodium ethoxide yields
(a) ethyl propionate
(b) ethyl butyrate
(c) acetoacetic ester
(d) methyl acetoacetate. *(2006)*

45. The major organic product formed from the following reaction :

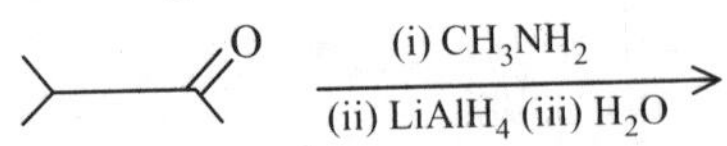

.... is

(a) 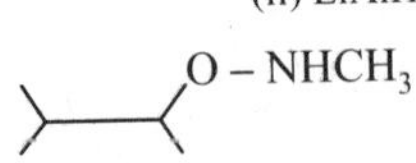
(b) 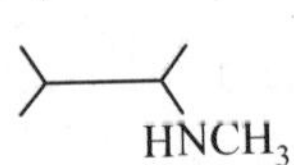
(c) 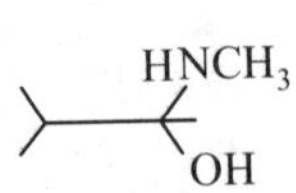
(d) 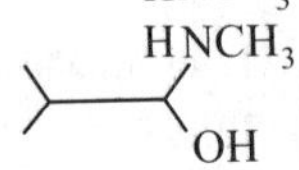
(2005)

46. In a set of reactions acetic acid yielded a product D.

$$CH_3COOH \xrightarrow{SOCl_2} A \xrightarrow[\text{anhy. } AlCl_3]{\text{benzene}} B \xrightarrow{HCN} C \xrightarrow{HOH} D$$

The structure of D would be

(a) 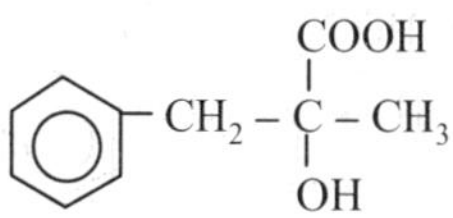

(b) 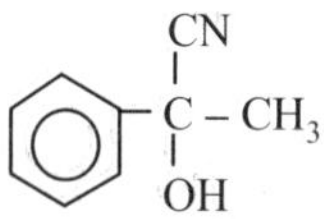

(c) 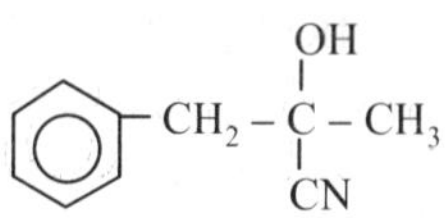

(d) 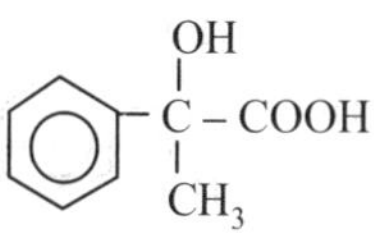 *(2005)*

47. Which one of the following can be oxidised to the corresponding carbonyl compound?
(a) 2-Hydroxypropane
(b) *ortho*-Nitrophenol
(c) Phenol
(d) 2-Methyl-2-hydroxypropane *(2004)*

48. In this reaction :
$CH_3CHO + HCN \rightarrow CH_3CH(OH)CN \xrightarrow{HOH} CH_3CH(OH)COOH$
an asymmetric centre is generated. The acid obtained would be
(a) D-isomer
(b) L-isomer
(c) 50% D + 50% L-isomer
(d) 20% D + 80% L-isomer *(2003)*

49. When m-chlorobenzaldehyde is treated with 50% KOH solution, the product(s) obtained is (are)

(a) 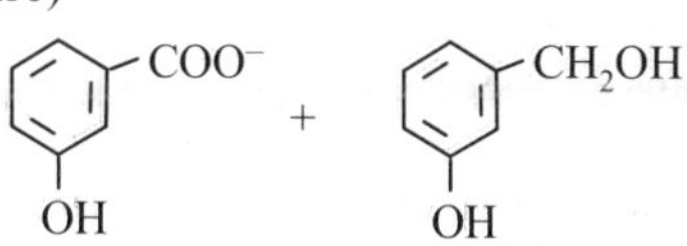

(b) 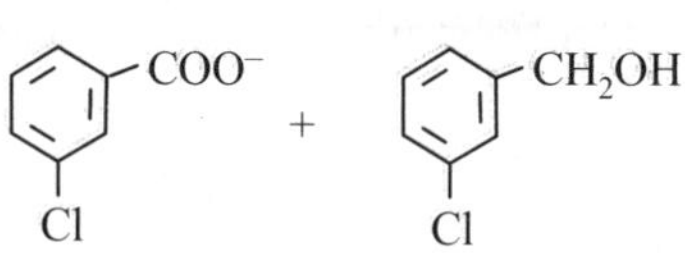

(c) 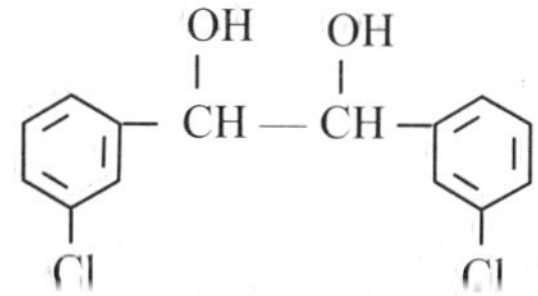

(d) 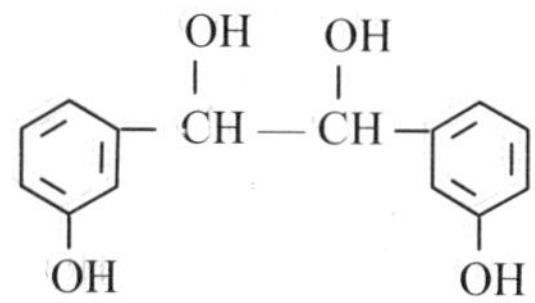 *(2003)*

50. A and B in the following reactions are :

$$R-\underset{\underset{O}{||}}{C}-R' \xrightarrow[KCN]{HCN} A \xrightarrow{B} RR'C{<}^{OH}_{CH_2NH_2}$$

(a) $A = RR'C{<}^{OH}_{COOH}$, $B = NH_3$
(b) $A = RR'C{<}^{CN}_{OH}$, $B = H_3O^{\oplus}$
(c) $A = RRCH_2CN$, $B = NaOH$
(d) $A = RR'C{<}^{CN}_{OH}$, $B = LiAlH_4$ *(2003)*

51. In a set of the given reactions, acetic acid yielded a product C.

$$CH_3COOH + PCl_5 \rightarrow A \xrightarrow[\text{Anh. } AlCl_3]{C_6H_6} B \xrightarrow[\text{ether}]{C_2H_5MgBr} C$$

Product C would be
(a) $CH_3CH(OH)C_2H_5$
(b) $CH_3COC_6H_5$
(c) $CH_3CH(OH)C_6H_5$
(d) $CH_3-\overset{\overset{C_2H_5}{|}}{C}(OH)C_6H_5$ *(2003)*

52. $\overset{\ominus}{\ddot{C}}H_2-\underset{\underset{O}{||}}{C}-CH_3$ and $CH_2{=}\underset{\underset{O^{\ominus}}{|}}{C}-CH_3$ are
(a) resonating structures
(b) tautomers
(c) geometrical isomers
(d) optical isomers. *(2002)*

53. In the following reaction product P is

$$R-\underset{\underset{O}{||}}{C}-Cl \xrightarrow[Pd\text{-}BaSO_4]{H_2} P$$

(a) RCH_2OH (b) $RCOOH$
(c) $RCHO$ (d) RCH_3 *(2002)*

54. 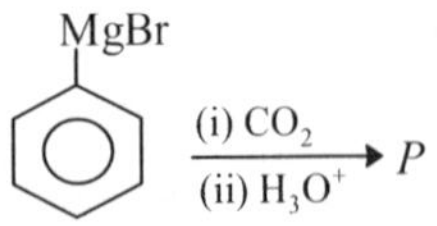

In the above reaction product P is

(a) 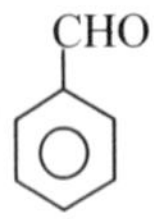

(b) 

(c) 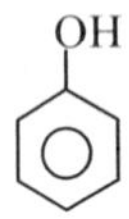

(d) $C_6H_5-\overset{O}{\overset{||}{C}}-C_6H_5$

(2002)

55. Which alkene on ozonolysis gives CH_3CH_2CHO and CH_3COCH_3?

(a) $CH_3CH_2CH=C(CH_3)_2$
(b) $CH_3CH_2CH=CHCH_2CH_3$
(c) $CH_3CH_2CH=CHCH_3$
(d) $CH_3-C(CH_3)=CHCH_3$ *(2001)*

56. Which of the following give positive Fehling solution test?
(a) Sucrose (b) Glucose
(c) Fats (d) Protein *(2001)*

57. Which of the following is incorrect?
(a) $FeCl_3$ is used in detection of phenol.
(b) Fehling solution is used in detection of glucose.
(c) Tollens' reagent is used in detection of unsaturation.
(d) $NaHSO_3$ is used in detection of carbonyl compound. *(2001)*

58. Polarisation in acrolein can be described as
(a) $\overset{+\delta}{C}H_2=CH-\overset{+\delta}{C}HO$
(b) $\overset{-\delta}{C}H_2=CH-\overset{+\delta}{C}HO$
(c) $\overset{-\delta}{C}H_2=CH-CH\overset{+\delta}{O}$
(d) $\overset{+\delta}{C}H_2=CH-CH\overset{-\delta}{O}$ *(2000)*

59. First product of the reaction between RCHO and NH_2NH_2 is
(a) $RCH=NNH_2$ (b) $RCH=NH$
(c) RCH_2NH_2 (d) $RCON_3$ *(2000)*

60. Ethyl benzoate can be prepared from benzoic acid by using
(a) ethyl alcohol
(b) ethyl alcohol and dry HCl
(c) ethyl chloride
(d) sodium ethoxide. *(2000)*

61. Reduction by $LiAlH_4$ of hydrolysed produc of an ester gives
(a) two alcohols (b) two aldehydes
(c) one acid and one alcohol
(d) two acids. *(2000*

62. In the reaction, $CH_3CN + 2H \xrightarrow[\text{Ethers}]{\text{HCl}}$ X $\xrightarrow{\text{Boiling } H_2O} Y$; the term Y is
(a) acetaldehyde (b) ethanamine
(c) acetone (d) dimethylamine
(1999

63. Aldol condensation will not take place in
(a) CH_3COCH_3 (b) CH_3CHO
(c) HCHO (d) CH_3CH_2CHO
(1999, 1996

64. Which one of the following compounds wil react with $NaHCO_3$ solution to give sodiun salt and carbon dioxide?
(a) Acetic acid (b) n-Hexanol
(c) Phenol (d) Both (b) and (c
(1999

65. Which one of the following esters canno undergo Claisen self-condensation?
(a) $C_6H_5CH_2COOC_2H_5$
(b) $C_6H_5COOC_2H_5$
(c) $CH_3CH_2CH_2CH_2COOC_2H_5$
(d) $C_6H_{11}CH_2COOC_2H_5$ *(1998*

66. An ester (A) with molecular formula, $C_9H_{10}O$ was treated with excess of CH_3MgBr and th complex so formed, was treated with H_2SO to give an olefin (B). Ozonolysis of (C) gav a ketone with molecular formula C_8H_8O whic shows +ve iodoform test. The structure o (A) is
(a) $H_3CCH_2COC_6H_5$ (b) $C_2H_5COOC_6H_5$
(c) $C_6H_5COOC_2H_5$
(d) p-$H_3CO-C_6H_4-COCH_3$ *(1998*

67. Iodoform test is not given by
(a) ethanal (b) ethanol
(c) 2-pentanone (d) 3-pentanone.
(1998

68. Ketones [$RCOR_1$] where $R = R_1$ = alkyl grou It can be obtained in one step by
(a) oxidation of tertiary alcohol
(b) reaction of acid halide with alcohols
(c) hydrolysis of esters
(d) oxidation of primary alcohol. *(1997*

69. Phenylmethanol can be prepared by reducin the benzaldehyde with

(a) CH_3Br and Na (b) CH_3I and Mg
(c) CH_3Br (d) Zn and HCl. *(1997)*

70. The oxidation of toluene to benzaldehyde by chromyl chloride is called
(a) Etard reaction
(b) Riemer–Tiemann reaction
(c) Wurtz reaction
(d) Cannizzaro's reaction. *(1996)*

71. Which of the following compound gives benzoic acid on hydrolysis?
(a) Chlorobenzene (b) Benzoyl chloride
(c) Chlorophenol (d) Chlorotoluene *(1996)*

72. The order of reactivity of carbonyl compounds for nucleophilic addition is
(a) $Ar_2C=O > R_2C=O > ArCHO > RCHO > H_2C=O$
(b) $H_2C=O > R_2C=O > Ar_2C=O > RCHO > ArCHO$
(c) $H_2C=O > RCHO > ArCHO > R_2C=O > Ar_2C=O$
(d) $ArCHO > Ar_2C=O > RCHO > R_2C=O > H_2C=O$ *(1995)*

73. Which one of the following product is formed when adipic acid is heated?

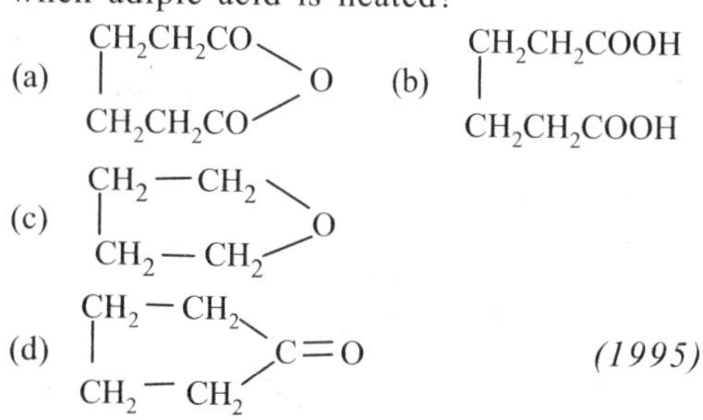

(1995)

74. The oxidation of toluene with CrO_3 in the presence of $(CH_3CO)_2O$ gives a product *A*, which on treatment with aqueous NaOH produces
(a) C_6H_5COONa
(b) 2, 4-diacetyl toluene
(c) C_6H_5CHO
(d) $(C_6H_5CO)_2O$. *(1995)*

75. Compound *A* has a molecular formula C_2Cl_3OH. It reduces Fehling's solution and on oxidation, it gives a monocarboxylic acid *B*. If *A* is obtained by the action of chlorine on ethyl alcohol, then compound *A* is
(a) methyl chloride
(b) monochloro acetic acid
(c) chloral
(d) chloroform. *(1994)*

76. Which of the following compound will undergo self aldol condensation in the presence of cold dilute alkali?
(a) $CH\equiv C-CHO$ (b) $CH_2=CHCHO$
(c) C_6H_5CHO (d) CH_3CH_2CHO *(1994)*

77. Which of the following compounds will give positive test with Tollens' reagent?
(a) Acetic acid (b) Acetone
(c) Acetamide (d) Acetaldehyde *(1994)*

78. An acyl halide is formed when PCl_5 reacts with an
(a) amide (b) ester
(c) acid (d) alcohol. *(1994)*

79. Sodium formate on heating yields
(a) oxalic acid and H_2
(b) sodium oxalate and H_2
(c) CO_2 and NaOH
(d) sodium oxalate. *(1993)*

80. $(CH_3)_2C=CHCOCH_3$ can be oxidised to $(CH_3)_2C=CHCOOH$ by
(a) chromic acid (b) NaOI
(c) Cu at 300°C (d) $KMnO_4$ *(1993)*

81. In which of the following, the number of carbon atoms does not remain same when carboxylic acid is obtained by oxidation?
(a) CH_3COCH_3 (b) CCl_3CH_2CHO
(c) $CH_3CH_2CH_2OH$ (d) CH_3CH_2CHO *(1992)*

82. Benzoic acid gives benzene on being heated with *X* and phenol gives benzene on being heated with *Y*. Therefore *X* and *Y* are respectively
(a) soda-lime and copper
(b) Zn dust and NaOH
(c) Zn dust and soda-lime
(d) soda-lime and zinc dust. *(1992)*

83. *A* is a lighter phenol and *B* is an aromatic carboxylic acid. Separation of a mixture of *A* and *B* can be carried out easily by using a solution of
(a) sodium hydroxide
(b) sodium sulphate
(c) calcium chloride
(d) sodium bicarbonate. *(1992)*

84. Acetaldehyde reacts with
(a) electrophiles only
(b) nucleophiles only
(c) free radicals only
(d) both electrophiles and nucleophiles. *(1991)*

85. The reagent (s) which can be used to distinguish acetophenone from benzophenone is (are)
(a) 2,4-dinitrophenylhydrazine
(b) aqueous solution of $NaHSO_3$
(c) Benedict reagent
(d) I_2 and NaOH. *(1990)*

86. 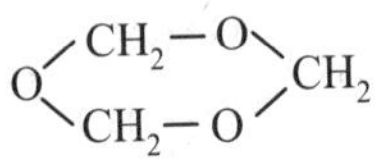

The above shown polymer is obtained when a carbonyl compound is allowed to stand. It is a white solid. The polymer is
(a) trioxane (b) formose
(c) paraformaldehyde (d) metaldehyde. *(1989)*

87. 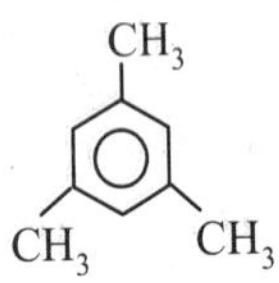 The given compound describes a condensation polymer which can be obtained in two ways : either treating 3 molecules of acetone (CH_3COCH_3) with conc. H_2SO_4 or passing propyne ($CH_3C \equiv CH$) through a red hot tube. The polymer is
(a) phorone
(b) mesityl oxide
(c) deacetonyl alcohol
(d) mesitylene. *(1989)*

88. $\underset{(A)}{3CH_3COCH_3} \xrightarrow[-3H_2O]{HCl}$

$$\underset{(B)}{(CH_3)_2C = CH - CO - CH = C(CH_3)_2}$$

This polymer (*B*) is obtained when acetone is saturated with hydrogen chloride gas, *B* can be
(a) phorone (b) formose
(c) diacetone alcohol (d) mesityl oxide. *(1989)*

89. The compound formed when malonic acid is heated with urea is
(a) cinnamic acid (b) butyric acid
(c) barbituric acid (d) crotonic acid. *(1989)*

90. If formaldehyde and KOH are heated, then we get
(a) methane (b) methyl alcohol
(c) ethyl formate (d) acetylene. *(1988)*

91. Formalin is an aqueous solution of
(a) fluorescein (b) formic acid
(c) formaldehyde (d) furfuraldehyde. *(1988)*

92. Among the following the strongest acid is
(a) CH_3COOH (b) CH_2ClCH_2COOH
(c) $CH_2ClCOOH$ (d) CH_3CH_2COOH. *(1988)*

93. Which of the following is the correct decreasing order of acidic strength of
(i) methanoic acid (ii) ethanoic acid
(iii) propanoic acid (iv) butanoic acid
(a) (i) > (ii) > (iii) > (iv)
(b) (ii) > (iii) > (iv) > (i)
(c) (i) > (iv) > (iii) > (ii)
(d) (iv) > (i) > (iii) > (ii). *(1988)*

Answer Key

1.	(d)	2.	(b)	3.	(a)	4.	(b)	5.	(b)	6.	(c)	7.	(b)	8.	(a)	9.	(a)	10.	(d)
11.	(a)	12.	(d)	13.	(d)	14.	(b)	15.	(c)	16.	(d)	17.	(b)	18.	(a)	19.	(a)	20.	(d)
21.	(a,d)	22.	(b)	23.	(c)	24.	(d)	25.	(d)	26.	(d)	27.	(b)	28.	(a)	29.	(d)	30.	(c)
31.	(c)	32.	(c)	33.	(c)	34.	(a)	35.	(c)	36.	(d)	37.	(a)	38.	(a)	39.	(c)	40.	(c)
41.	(a)	42.	(b)	43.	(a)	44.	(c)	45.	(b)	46.	(d)	47.	(a)	48.	(c)	49.	(b)	50.	(d)
51.	(d)	52.	(a)	53.	(c)	54.	(b)	55.	(a)	56.	(b)	57.	(c)	58.	(d)	59.	(a)	60.	(b)
61.	(a)	62.	(a)	63.	(c)	64.	(a)	65.	(b)	66.	(c)	67.	(d)	68.	(a)	69.	(d)	70.	(a)
71.	(b)	72.	(c)	73.	(a)	74.	(c)	75.	(c)	76.	(d)	77.	(d)	78.	(c)	79.	(b)	80.	(b)
81.	(a)	82.	(d)	83.	(d)	84.	(b)	85.	(d)	86.	(a)	87.	(d)	88.	(a)	89.	(c)	90.	(b)
91.	(c)	92.	(c)	93.	(a)														

EXPLANATIONS

1. **(d) :** Due to the formation of intermolecular H-bonding, association occurs in carboxylic acids.

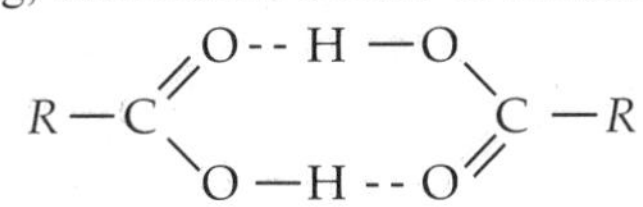

So, they have higher boiling points than aldehydes, ketones and even alcohols of comparable molecular mass.

2. **(b) :** Since, A gives silver mirror test, it must be an aldehyde and aldehydes are formed by oxidation of 1° alcohols. Thus, 'X' is a 1° alcohol, *i.e.*, CH_3CH_2OH.

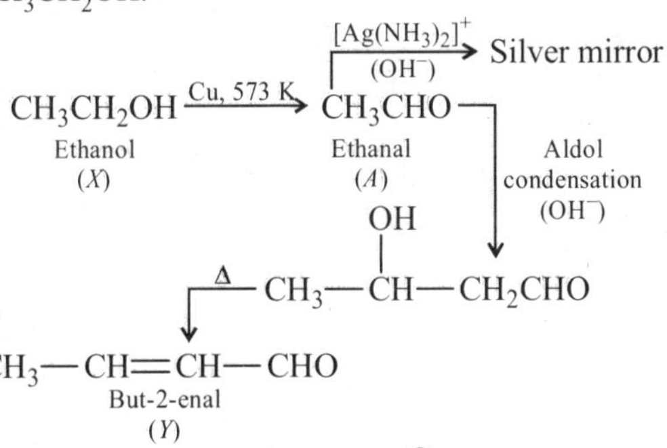

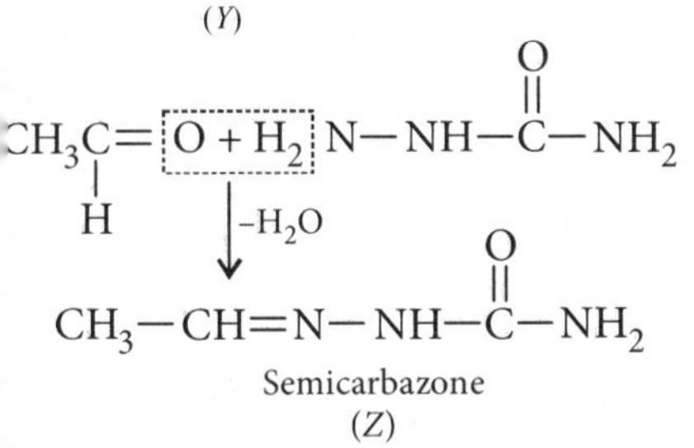

3. **(a) :**

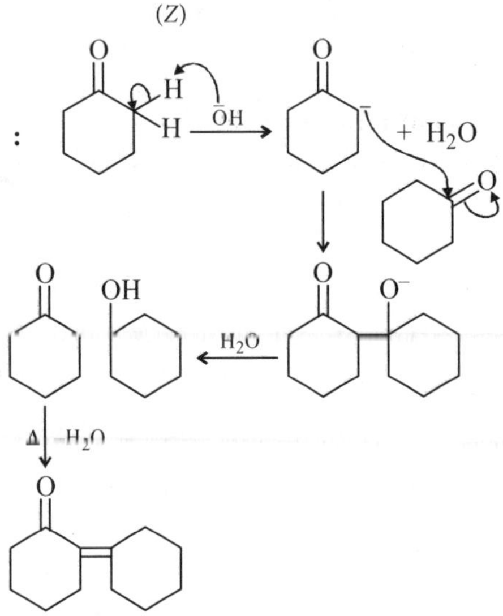

4. **(b) :**

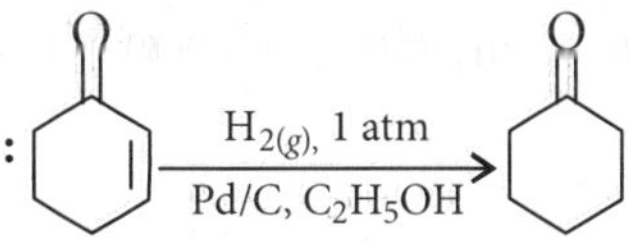

C=C bond is reduced faster than C=O bond with H_2(Pd—C).

5. **(b) :** Acidic strength ∝ – I effect
As oxygen is more electron withdrawing (II) and (III) show greater – I effect than (I). Thus, (I) is least acidic. Out of (II) and (III), (II) is more acidic than (III) as distance of O increases from —COOH group and acidic strength decreases.

6. **(c) :**

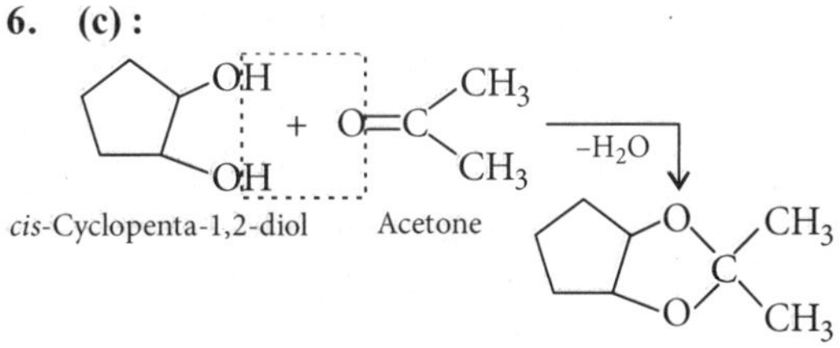

Trans-isomer does not react with acetone.

7. **(b) :** Keto-enol tautomerism :

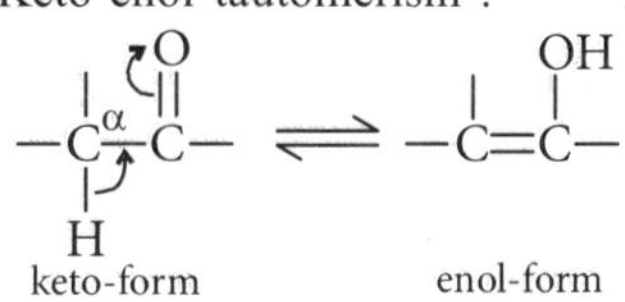

8. **(a) :**

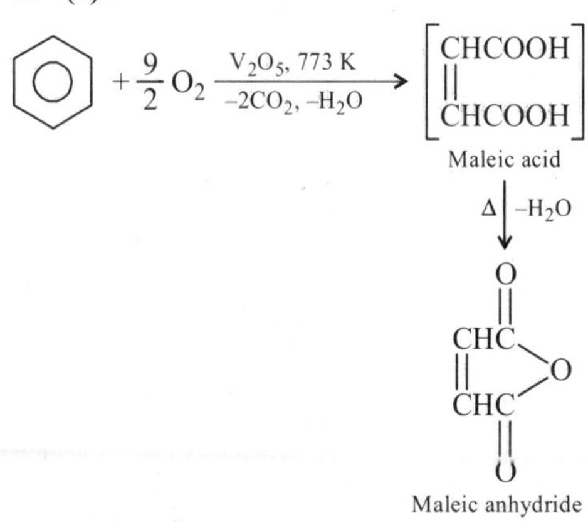

9. **(a) :** Carbonyl compounds react with ammonia derivatives in weakly acidic medium as follows :

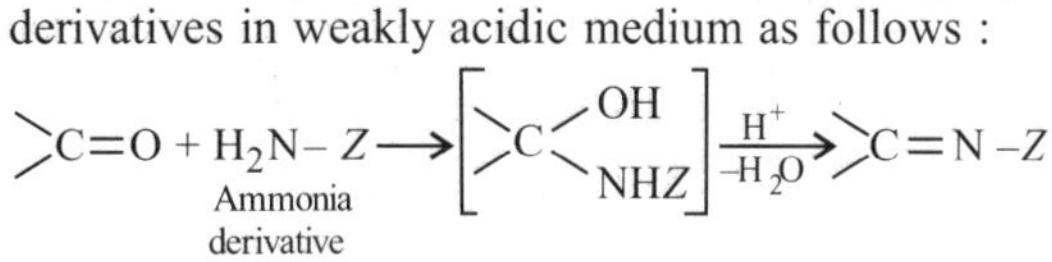

10. (d) : Electron withdrawing groups increase the reactivity towards nucleophilic substitution reaction and $-NO_2$ is a strong electron withdrawing group.

11. (a) : Compound 'X' yields phenylhydrazone

$\Rightarrow -\overset{O}{\overset{||}{C}}-$ group.

Negative iodoform test $\Rightarrow CH_3-\overset{O}{\overset{||}{C}}-$group is absent.

Negative Tollens' test $\Rightarrow$ ketone

Hence, the compound is 3-pentanone.

$$\underset{\substack{\text{3-Pentanone}\\ (C_5H_{10}O)\\ (X)}}{CH_3CH_2-\overset{O}{\overset{||}{C}}-CH_2CH_3} \xrightarrow{\text{Reduction}} \underset{n\text{-Pentane}}{CH_3CH_2CH_2CH_2CH_3}$$

12. (d): Aromatic aldehydes are more reactive than alkyl aryl ketones. Electron withdrawing group ($-NO_2$) increases the reactivity towards nucleophilic addition reactions whereas, electron donating group ($-CH_3$) decreases the reactivity towards nucleophilic addition reactions. Therefore, the order is :

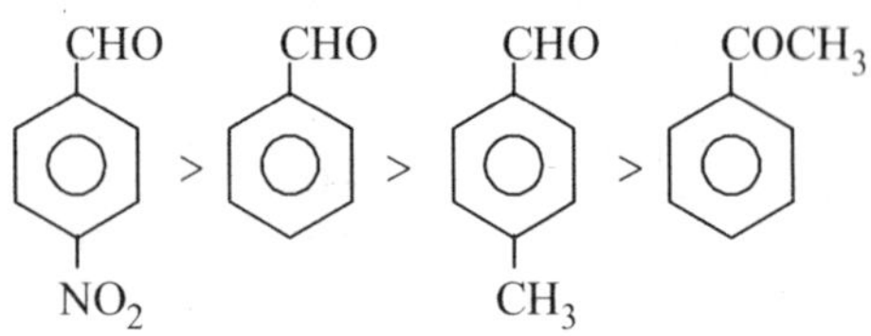

13. (d): $\underset{\substack{\text{(II)}\\ \text{Acetylacetone}\\ \text{[Keto form (24\%)]}}}{CH_3-\overset{O}{\overset{||}{C}}-CH_2-\overset{O}{\overset{||}{C}}-CH_3} \rightleftharpoons$

$$\underset{\text{(III)}}{CH_3-\overset{O-H\cdots\cdots}{\overset{|}{C}}=CH-\overset{O}{\overset{||}{C}}-CH_3}$$

[Enol form (76%) more stable due to intramolecular hydrogen bonding]

14. (b): Reduction in presence of Zn-Hg and conc. HCl is useful for aldehyde and ketone but carboxylic acid group remains unaffected.

15. (c): Aldehyde having no α-hydrogen atoms on heating with concentrated alkali solution (50%) undergo Cannizzaro's reaction.

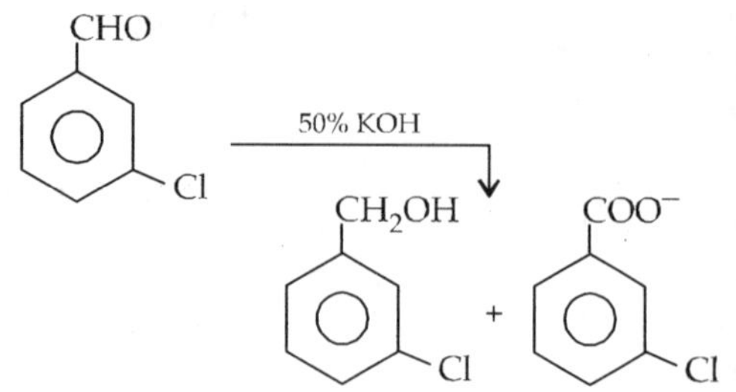

16. (d): $\underset{\text{Acetone}}{(CH_3)_2C=O} + \begin{matrix} H\,OC_2H_5 \\ H\,OC_2H_5 \end{matrix} \xrightarrow[\Delta]{HCl_{(g)}} \underset{\text{Acetal}}{(CH_3)_2C\begin{matrix} \diagup OC_2H_5 \\ \diagdown OC_2H_5 \end{matrix}}$

17. (b): Acetaldehyde, acetone and methyl ketone having CH_3CO- group undergo haloform reaction. Thus CH_3CHO will give yellow precipitate with I_2 and NaOH but $C_6H_5CH_2CHO$ will not.

18. (a): As $-I$ effect increases, COOH group becomes more electron deficient and tendency to loose H^+ ions increases *i.e.*, acid strength increases. As $+I$ effect increases, acid strength decreases. Thus, correct order of acid strength is

$$\underset{(B)}{CF_3COOH} > \underset{(A)}{CCl_3COOH} > \underset{(D)}{HCOOH} > \underset{(C)}{CH_3COOH}$$

19. (a): 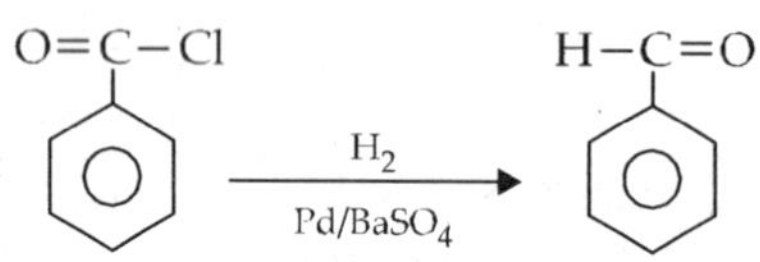

It is Rosenmund's reaction.

20. (d)

21. (a,d) : This example shows iodoform reaction. The compound with $CH_3-\underset{O}{\underset{||}{C}}-$ group or $CH_3-\underset{OH}{\underset{|}{CH}}-$ group give yellow precipitate of iodoform (CHI_3) when react with iodine and alkali.

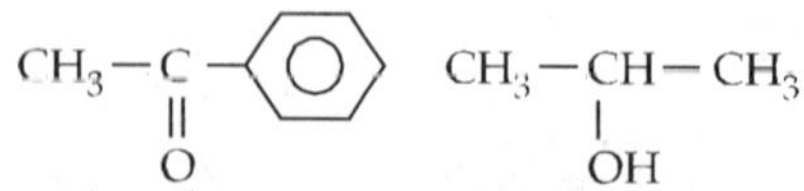

Acetophenone (+ve iodoform) 2-Hydroxypropane (+ve iodoform)

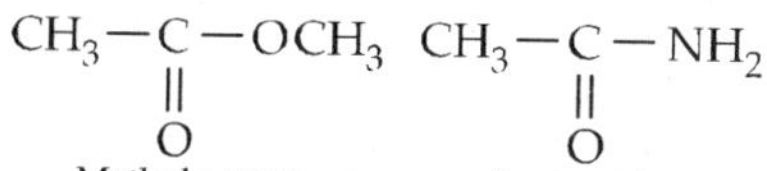

Methyl acetate   Acetamide

– ve iodoform

(Acid derivatives do not give iodoform test)

2. (b): Carbonyl group is reduced to – CH_2 group, hen treated with amalgamated zinc and conc. HCl. his process is called Clemmensen's reduction.

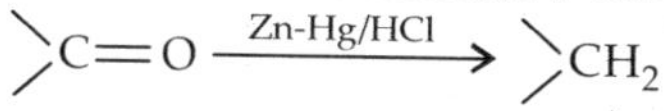

3. (c):

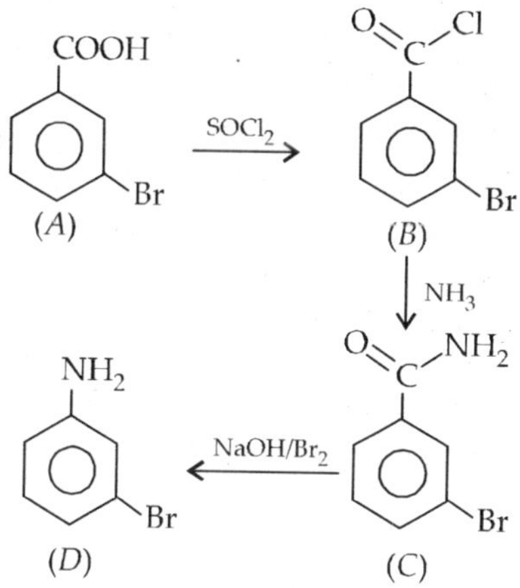

. (d): Greater the number of alkyl groups attached the carbonyl groups and hence, lower will be its ctivity.

I > II > III

. (d):

(A) Benzaldehyde	(ii) Benzoin condensation
(B) Phthalic anhydride	(i) Phenolphthalein
(C) Phenyl benzoate	(iv) Fries rearrangement
(D) methyl salicylate	(iii) Oil of wintergreen

(d): The compound will be CH_3CH_2COOH.

$$\underset{A}{CH_3CH_2COOH} \xrightarrow{NH_3} \underset{B}{CH_3CH_2COONH_4}$$

$$\downarrow \Delta$$

$$\underset{\text{ethyl amine}}{CH_3-CH_2-NH_2} \xleftarrow{Br_2/KOH} \underset{C}{CH_3CH_2CONH_2}$$

(b): (a) Reimer–Tiemann reaction :

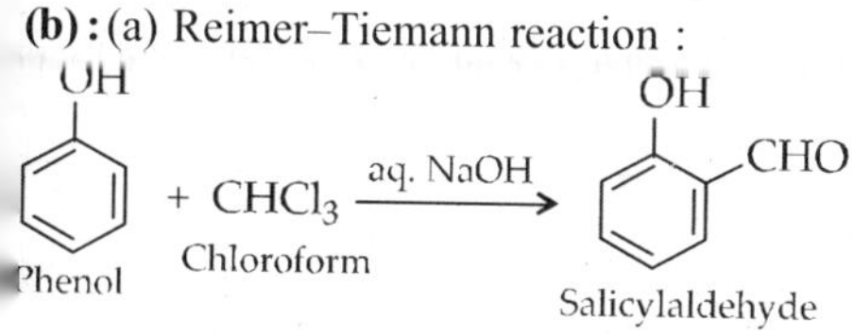

(b) Cannizzaro reaction :

$$\underset{\text{Formaldehyde}}{HCHO} \xrightarrow{50\%\ NaOH} \underset{\text{Sodium formate}}{HCOO^{\ominus}Na^{\oplus}} + \underset{\text{Methanol}}{CH_3OH}$$

(c) Wurtz reaction :

$$\underset{\text{Methyl iodide}}{H_3C—I} + 2Na + I—CH_3 \rightarrow \underset{\text{Ethane}}{CH_3—CH_3} + 2NaI$$

(d) Friedel–Crafts acylation :

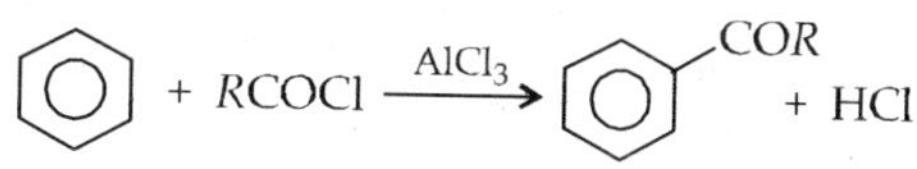

From the above examples it is evident that C—C bond formation does not takes place in Cannizzaro reaction.

28. (a): $\underset{\text{Acetamide}}{CH_3CONH_2} + 4NaOH + Br_2 \rightarrow$

$$\underset{1^\circ \text{ Amine}}{CH_3NH_2} + 2KBr + K_2CO_3 + 2H_2O$$

This reaction is called Hofmann Bromamide reaction.

29. (d): CH_3COCl is most susceptible to nucleophilic attack. The susceptibility of a substrate towards nucleophilic attack depends on how good a leaving group is attached to it. Cl^- is a weak base and therefore a good leaving group.

30. (c): The ease of dehydration of the given compounds can be explained on the basis of the stability of the carbocation formed. In case of options (a), (b) and (d), a secondary carbocation is formed but the presence of an electron withdrawing >C=O group adjacent to the positively charged carbon, intensifies the charge and hence destabilises the species.

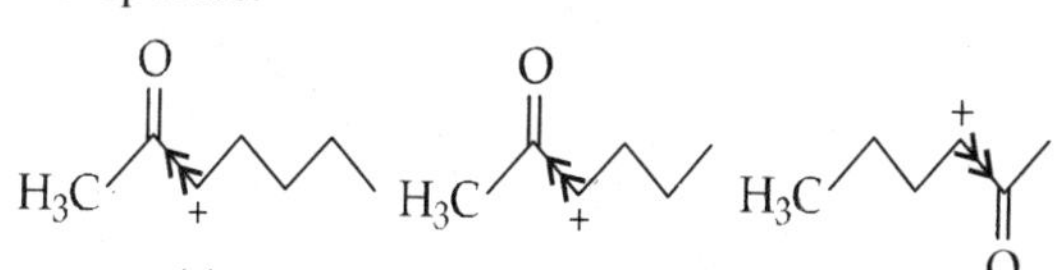

(a)   (b)   (d)

However, in case of option (c), a secondary carbocation is formed, but the electron withdrawing >C=O group is present farther away, as a result, the effect of this group is diminished and hence the carbocation is relatively more stable.

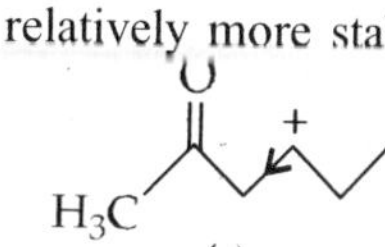

(c)
(more stable)

31. (c) : It gives D.D.T (*p,p*- dichlorodipheny-ltrichloroethane)

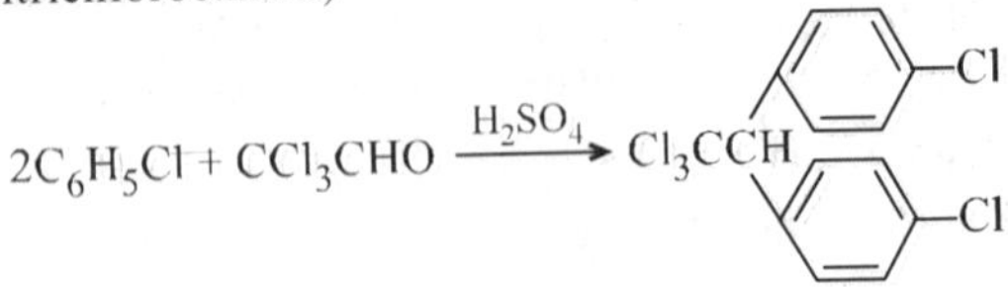

32. (c) : This is Hell–Volhard–Zelinsky reaction. In this reaction, acids containing α-H react with X_2/red P giving product in which the α-hydrogens are substituted by *X*.

$$\therefore\ CH_3CH_2COOH \xrightarrow{Br_2/P} CH_3-\underset{Br}{\overset{Br}{\underset{|}{\overset{|}{C}}}}-COOH$$

33. (c) : The first step is a simple condensation reaction. The last step is an example of E1cB mechanism and the leaving group is hydroxide, which is unusual. Still this step manages to take place owing to the stability incorporated therein the product, which is a conjugated carbonyl compound.

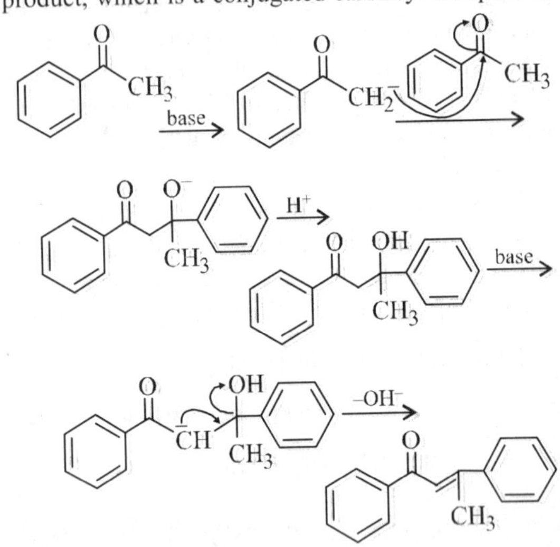

34. (a) : The base (OH^-) ion removes one of the α-hydrogen atom (which is some what acidic) from aldehyde and ketones to form a carbanion or the enolate ion. The acidity of α-hydrogen is due to reasonance stabilization of enolate anion.

35. (c) :

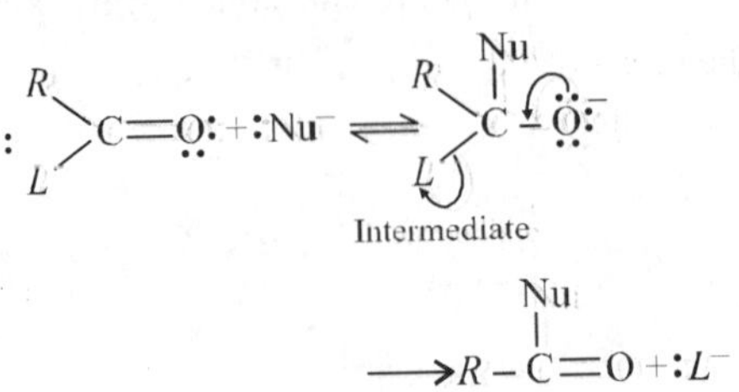

$$(L = X,\ NH_2,\ O-\overset{O}{\overset{||}{C}}-R \text{ or } OR)$$

The relative reactivities of various compounds hav been found to be in the following order :

$$\underset{X}{\overset{R}{>}}C{=}O > R-\overset{O}{\overset{||}{C}}-O-\overset{O}{\overset{||}{C}}-R > R-C\overset{\nearrow O}{\searrow OR} > R-C\overset{\nearrow O}{\searrow NH}$$

36. (d) : Aldehydes and ketones are converted t alkane when treated with zinc amalgam and con HCl. This is known as Clemmensen reduction. He $>C{=}O$ group is reduced to $>CH_2$ group.

$$R-\overset{O}{\overset{||}{C}}-H + 4\,[H] \xrightarrow[\text{conc. HCl}]{\text{Zn-Hg}} R-CH_3 + H_2O$$

37. (a) : Aldehydes which do not have α-H atom, presence of 50% NaOH or 50% KOH undergo disproportionation reaction to produce alcohol a sodium salt of acid. This reaction is known Cannizzaro reaction. C_6H_5CHO containing no α- atom undergoes Cannizzaro reaction to produ benzyl alcohol and sodium benzoate.

$$C_6H_5CHO \xrightarrow{50\%\ NaOH} C_6H_5CH_2OH + C_6H_5COONa$$

38. (a) : The aldehydes or ketones containing α atom in presence of dilute alkali undergo s condensation reaction to form β-hydroxyaldehy or β-hydroxyketone. This reaction is known as Al condensation.

39. (c) : The ease of hydrolysis depends upon magnitude of the +ve charge on the carbonyl gro Electron-withdrawing groups increase magnitude of positive charge and electron donat groups decrease the magnitude of positive char Hence, the decreasing order of reactivity towa hydrolysis is

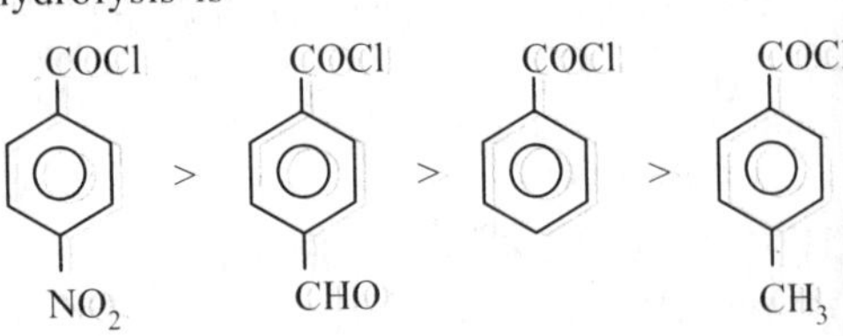

40. (c) : $FCH_2COOH > ClCH_2COOH > BrCH_2CO$ $> CH_3CO$

Acidity decreases as the –*I* effect of the gr decreases, F is the most electronegative atom hence it has highest –*I* effect among the halog

41. (a) : The reactivity of the carbonyl group towards the addition reactions depends upon the magnitude of the positive charge on the carbonyl carbon atom. Hence aryl substituent that increases the positive charge on the carbonyl carbon must increase its reactivity towards addition reactions. The introduction of negative group ($-I$ effect) increases the reactivity while introduction of alkyl group ($+I$ effect) decreases the reactivity.

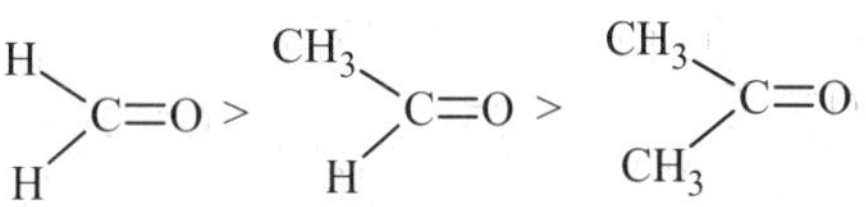

$+I$ effect and steric hindrance increases

42. (b) : $CH_3CHO + HCN \longrightarrow CH_3-CH(OH)-CN \xrightarrow{H_2O} CH_3-CH(OH)-COOH$

Lactic acid

43. (a) : $CH_3CH_2COOH \xrightarrow{SOCl_2} \underset{(B)}{CH_3CH_2COCl} \xrightarrow{NH_3} \underset{(C)}{CH_3CH_2CONH_2} \xrightarrow[Br_2]{KOH} \underset{(D)}{CH_3CH_2NH_2}$

44. (c) : Ethyl acetate undergoes Claisen condensation in presence of sodium ethoxide involving α-hydrogen atom in which two molecules of ethyl acetate combine together to form acetoacetic ester.

$$CH_3COOC_2H_5 + CH_3COOC_2H_5 \xrightarrow{C_2H_5ONa} \underset{\text{Acetoacetic ester}}{CH_3COCH_2COOC_2H_5} + C_2H_5OH$$

45. (b) :

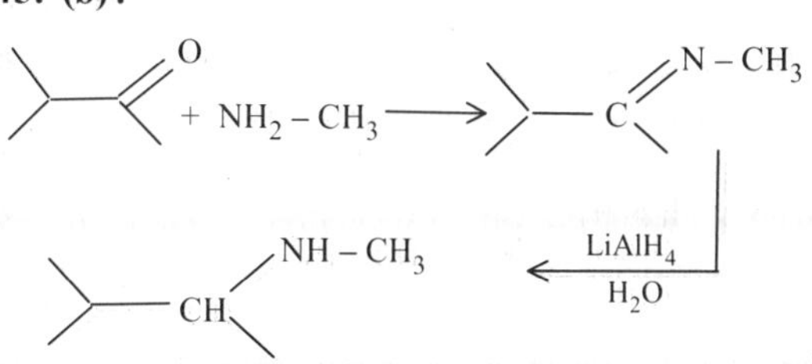

46. (d) :

$$CH_3-COOH \xrightarrow{SOCl_2} \underset{(A)}{CH_3-\overset{O}{\overset{||}{C}}-Cl} + SO_2\uparrow$$

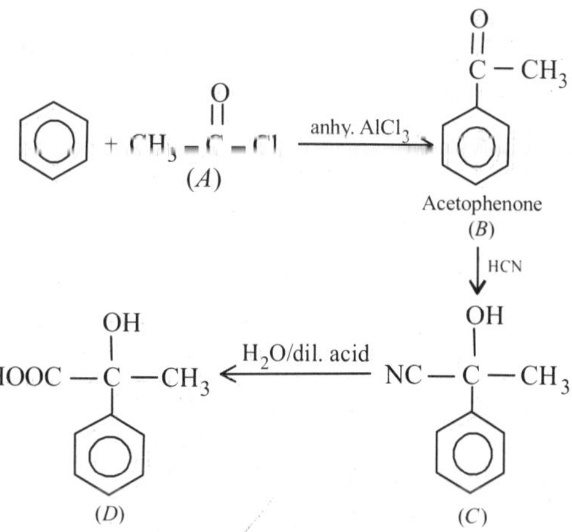

47. (a) : Secondary alcohol on oxidation gives a ketone containing the same number of carbon atoms.

$$CH_3-\overset{CH_3}{CHOH} \xrightarrow{[O]} CH_3-\overset{CH_3}{C}=O$$

48. (c) : Lactic acid ($CH_3CH(OH)COOH$) is an optically active compound due to the presence of asymmetric carbon atom. It exists in D-and L-form, the ratio of which is found to be (1 : 1), *i.e.*, a racemic mixture is obtained.

49. (b) :

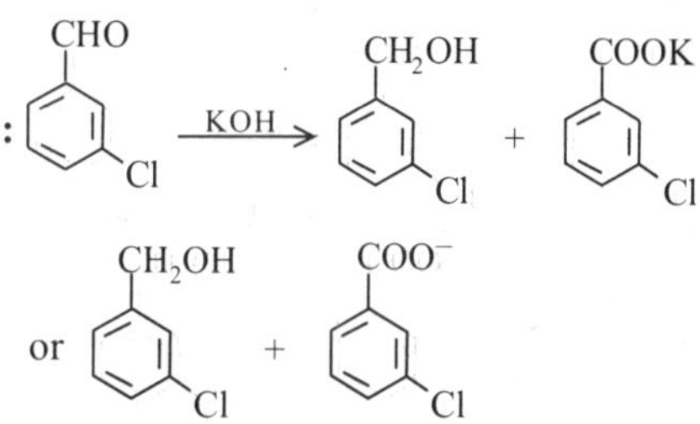

The above reaction is known as Cannizzaro's reaction.

50. (d) : $R-\underset{O}{\underset{||}{C}}-R' \xrightarrow{HCN/KCN} \underset{(A)}{R-C(CN)(OH)-R'} \xrightarrow[(B)]{LiAlH_4} R-C(CH_2NH_2)(OH)-R'$

51. (d) : $CH_3COOH + PCl_5 \rightarrow \underset{(A)}{CH_3COCl} \xrightarrow[\text{anhy. } AlCl_3]{C_6H_6} \underset{(B)}{C_6H_5COCH_3} \xrightarrow[\text{ether}]{C_2H_5MgBr} \underset{(C)}{C_6H_5C(C_2H_5)(OH)-CH_3}$

52. (a) : They are resonating forms because the position of the atomic nuclei remain the same and only electron redistribution has occurred.

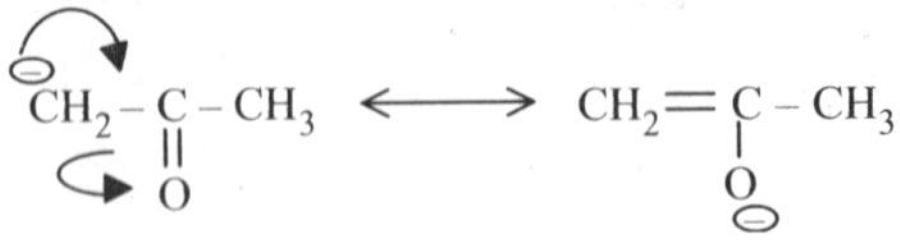

53. (c) : This is Rosenmund reaction.

$$R-\underset{\underset{O}{||}}{C}-Cl \xrightarrow[Pd/BaSO_4]{H_2} \underset{P}{RCHO}$$

$BaSO_4$ prevents the aldehyde from being reduced and acts as a poison to the palladium catalyst in this reaction.

54. (b) :

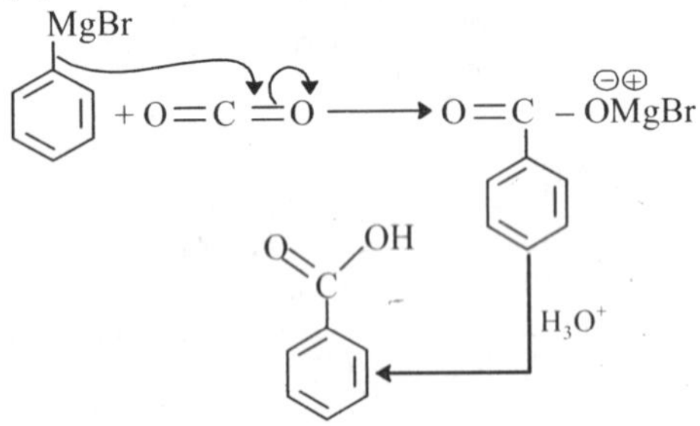

P

The product is benzoic acid.

55. (a) : On passing a steam of ozone through a solution of olefin in an organic solvent, an ozonide is obtained.

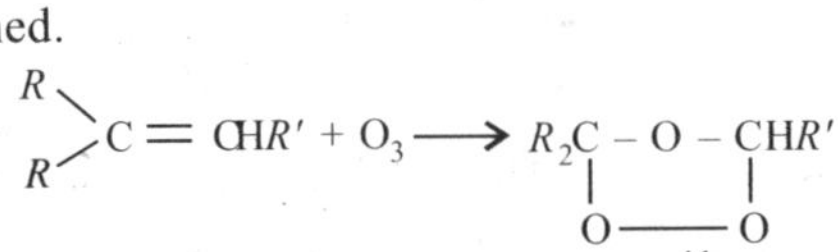

ozonide

The ozonide on reduction with Zn and acid or H_2/Ni gives aldehydes and/or ketones.

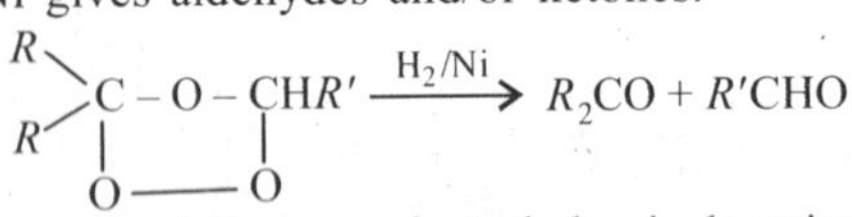

The nature of these products helps in locating the position of the double bond in olefin.

56. (b) : Glucose reduces Fehling solution because glucose has free –CHO group which is readily oxidised.

57. (c) : Tollens' reagent is a solution of ammoniacal silver nitrate and used for the detection of –CHO group. Aldehydes reduce Tollens' reagent and itself get oxidised to give Ag^+ ions to Ag powder which forms the silver coloured mirror in the test tube. So this test is also known as silver mirror test.

$$R-CHO + [Ag(NH_3)_2]^+ \rightarrow R\text{–}COO^- + \underset{\text{(Powder)}}{Ag}$$

58. (d) : O-atom is more electronegative than C-atom, therefore O-atom bears partial –ve charge and C-atom to which it is attached bear partial +ve charge.

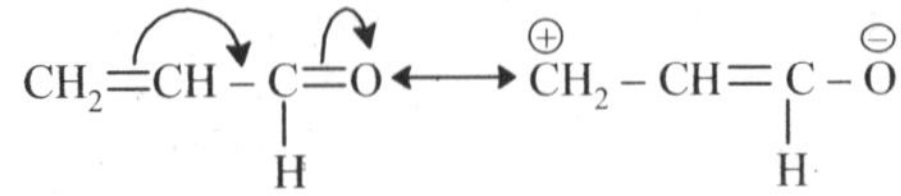

59. (a) : It is a simple condensation reaction which proceeds with elimination of water.

$$R-CH=O + H_2N-NH_2 \xrightarrow{-H_2O} RCH=N-NH_2$$

60. (b) : Ethyl benzoate can be prepared by heating benzoic acid with ethyl alcohol in presence of dry HCl or conc. H_2SO_4. The reaction is called as esterification reaction.

$$C_6H_5-COOH + C_2H_5-OH \xrightarrow[-H_2O]{\text{dry HCl}} \underset{\text{Ethyl benzoate}}{C_6H_5COOC_2H_5}$$

61. (a) : Reduction of hydrolysed product of ester by $LiAlH_4$ produces two alcohols.

$$R-COOR' \xrightarrow{H_2O} R-COOH + R'OH \xrightarrow[\text{ether}]{LiAlH_4} R-CH_2OH + R'OH$$

62. (a) : $CH_3-C\equiv N + 2H \xrightarrow[\text{ether}]{HCl} \underset{(X)}{CH_3-CH=NH}$

$$CH_3-CH=NH \xrightarrow[\Delta]{H_2O} \underset{(Y)}{CH_3-CHO} + NH_3$$

Y = Acetaldehyde

63. (c) : The carbonyl compounds having atleast one α-hydrogen atom undergo condensation reaction in presence of dilute NaOH solution. This reaction is called as aldol condensation reaction. As formaldehyde (HCHO) has no α-hydrogen atom attached to carbonyl group, it does not respond to this test.

64. (a) : $NaHCO_3$ is weakly basic, so it can only react with the acid CH_3COOH. While phenol is weakly acidic and *n*-hexanol is neutral, they do not react with $NaHCO_3$.

$$CH_3COOH + NaHCO_3 \rightarrow CH_3COONa + CO_2 + H_2O$$

65. (b) : The esters having active methylene group (– CH_2 –), show Claisen Condensation reaction. As $C_6H_5-COOC_2H_5$ has no α-hydrogen atom or active methylene group, so it cannot undergo Claisen-Condensation reaction.

66. (c) : $\underset{(A)}{C_6H_5-COOC_2H_5} \xrightarrow{CH_3MgBr}$

$C_6H_5-\overset{OMgBr}{\underset{CH_3}{C}}-OC_2H_5 \xrightarrow{-Mg(OC_2H_5)Br}$

$C_6H_5-\overset{O}{\overset{||}{C}}-CH_3 \xrightarrow{CH_3MgBr} C_6H_5-\overset{OMgBr}{\underset{CH_3}{C}}-CH_3 \xrightarrow{H_2O}$

$C_6H_5-\overset{OH}{\underset{CH_3}{C}}-CH_3 \xrightarrow[-H_2O]{conc.\ H_2SO_4} C_6H_5-\underset{\underset{(B)}{CH_3}}{C}=CH_2 \xrightarrow[Zn]{O_3/H_2O}$

$\underset{(C_8H_8O)}{C_6H_5-CO-CH_3} \xrightarrow{I_2/NaOH} \underset{Iodoform}{CHI_3} + C_6H_5-COONa$

67. (d) : Ethyl alcohol, 2-alkanols, and carbonyl compounds containing $CH_3-\underset{\underset{O}{||}}{C}-$ group show iodoform test, *i.e.*, acetaldehyde and 2-ketones etc. So iodoform test is not given by 3-pentanone.

68. (a) : A tertiary alcohol is difficult to oxidise. But when it is treated with an acidic oxidising agent under some conditions, it is oxidised to ketone and then to acids. Both the ketone and acid contain the lesser number of carbon atoms than the starting alcohol.

69. (d) : $\underset{Benzaldehyde}{C_6H_5CHO} + 2[H] \xrightarrow{Zn/HCl} \underset{\substack{Phenylmethanol\\(Benzyl\ alcohol)}}{C_6H_5CH_2OH}$

70. (a) : The oxidation of toluene ($C_6H_5CH_3$) with chromyl chloride (CrO_2Cl_2) in CCl_4 or CS_2 to give benzaldehyde is called Etard reaction. In this reaction, the chromyl chloride first forms a brown complex, which is separated and then decomposed with H_2O to give benzaldehyde (C_6H_5CHO).

71. (b) : $\underset{Benzoyl\ chloride}{C_6H_5COCl} + H_2O \rightarrow \underset{Benzoic\ acid}{C_6H_5COOH} + HCl$

72. (c) : With each substitution of hydrogen atom, reactivity of carbonyl compound decreases. This is due to inductive effect in case of alkyl groups and resonance in case of aromatic groups.

73. (a) : 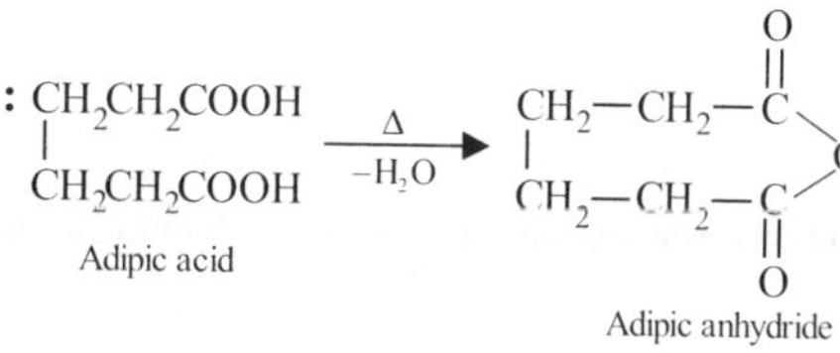

Adipic acid → Adipic anhydride

74. (c) : 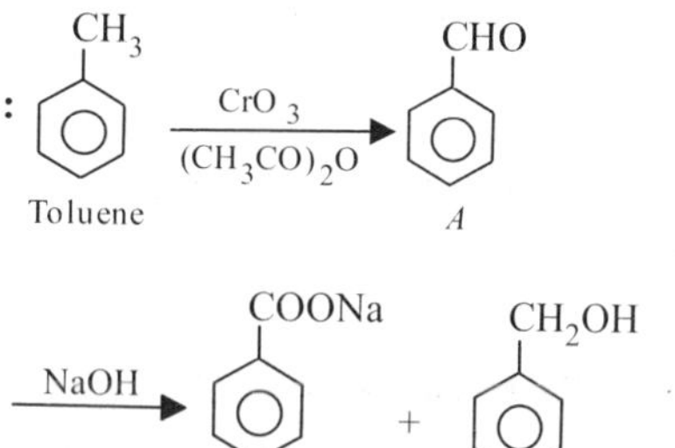

Toluene, *A*, (Cannizzaro product)

75. (c) : $\underset{(Ethylalcohol)}{CH_3CH_2OH} \xrightarrow[-2\ HCl]{Cl_2} \underset{(Acetaldehyde)}{CH_3CHO} \xrightarrow[-3\ HCl]{3Cl_2} \underset{(Chloral)}{CCl_3CHO}$

Thus, the compound *A* is chloral.

76. (d) : Since CH_3CH_2CHO has α-hydrogen atom, therefore it will undergo aldol condensation in the presence of cold dilute alkali.

77. (d) : Acetaldehyde reduces Tollens' reagent to silver mirror.

$$\underset{(Acetaldehyde)}{CH_3CHO} + \underset{(Tollens'\ reagent)}{2[Ag(NH_3)_2]^+} + 3OH^- \rightarrow CH_3COO^- + 2H_2O + \underset{(Silver\ mirror)}{2Ag} + 4NH_3$$

78. (c) : $\underset{Acetic\ acid}{3CH_3COOH} + PCl_5 \rightarrow \underset{Acetyl\ chloride}{3CH_3COCl} + POCl_3 + HCl$

79. (b) : Sodium oxalate and H_2

$$2HCOONa \xrightarrow{\Delta} \underset{Sodium\ oxalate}{\begin{matrix}COONa\\|\\COONa\end{matrix}} + H_2$$

80. (b) : $(CH_3)_2C=CHCOCH_3 \xrightarrow{NaOI} (CH_3)_2C=CHCOOH + CHI_3$

($NaOH + I_2$)/NaOI is the best suitable reagent for the above reaction.

81. (a) : Ketones on oxidation give carboxylic acids with lesser number of carbon atoms *i.e,*

$CH_3COCH_3 \xrightarrow{[O]} CH_3COOH + CO_2 + H_2O$

82. (d) : $C_6H_5COOH \xrightarrow[(X)]{Soda\ lime} C_6H_6 + ZnO$

$C_6H_5OH \xrightarrow[(Y)]{Zn\ dust} C_6H_6 + ZnO$

X = soda-lime and *Y* = Zn dust

83. (d) : Carboxylic acids dissolve in $NaHCO_3$ but phenols do not.

84. (b) : Acetaldehyde reacts only with nucleophiles. Since the mobile π-electrons of carbon oxygen double bond are strongly pulled towards oxygen, carbonyl carbon is electron-deficient and carbonyl oxygen is electron-rich. Thus, the electron deficient carbonyl carbon is most susceptible to attack by electron rich nucleophilic reagent, *i.e.* by base.

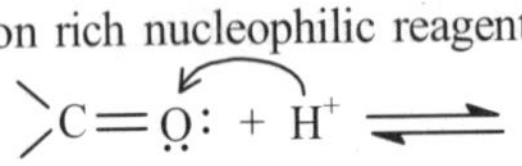

from acidic medium

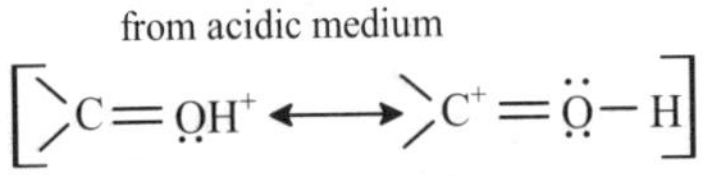

The nucleophile, then attacks the protonated carbonyl group to form addition product.

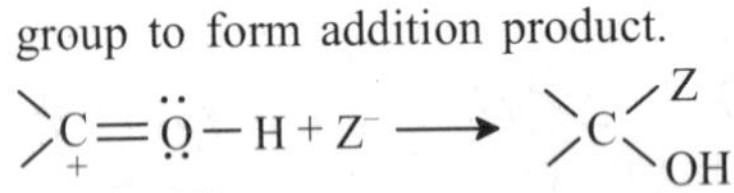

Nucleophile → Addition product

85. (d) : Acetophenone reacts with NaOH and I_2 to give yellow ppt. of CHI_3 but benzophenone ($C_6H_5COC_6H_5$) does not. Hence, it can be used to distinguish between them.

$$C_6H_5COCH_3 \xrightarrow{I_2,\ NaOH} \underset{\text{yellow ppt.}}{CHI_3} + C_6H_5COONa$$

86. (a) :

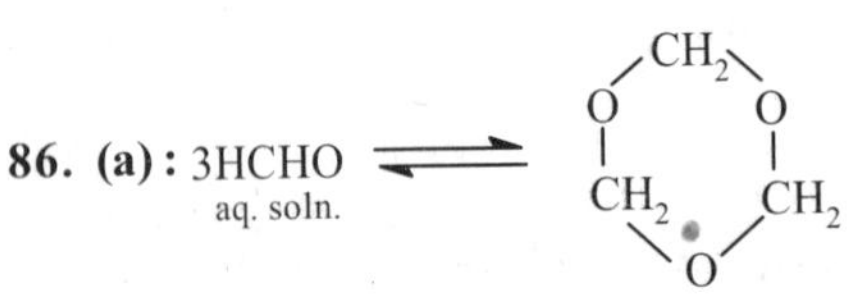

Trioxane (metaformaldehyde)

87. (d) : Acetone forms mesitylene (1, 3, 5-trimethyl benzene) on distillation with conc. H_2SO_4.

88. (a) :

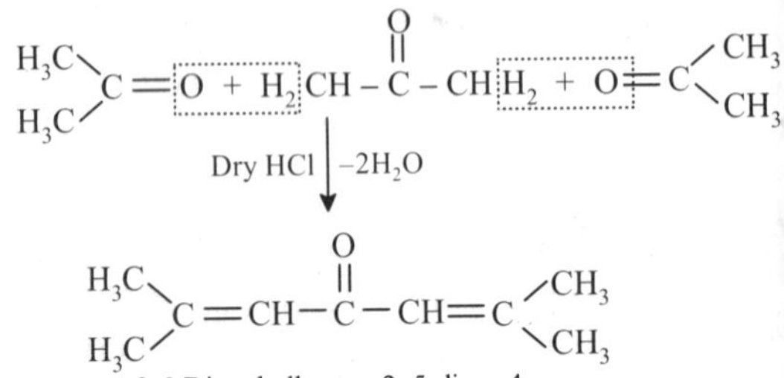

2,6-Dimethylhepta - 2, 5-diene-4-one
(phorone)

89. (c) :

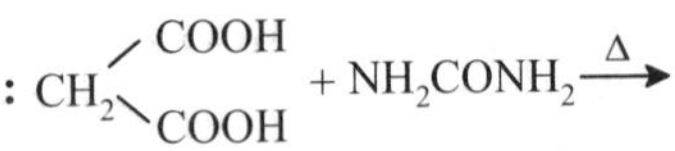

Malonic acid

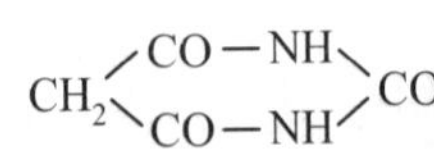

Barbituric acid

90. (b) : $HCHO + KOH \xrightarrow{50\%\ KOH} HCOOK + CH_3OH$
The above reaction is called as Cannizzaro's reaction.

91. (c) : 40% HCHO

92. (c) : Strongest acid is $CH_2ClCOOH$. $-I$ effect of Cl atom decreases with the increase in distance therefore, $CH_2ClCOOH$ is strongest acid.

93. (a) : $+I$ effect of the alkyl group increases from CH_3 to CH_3CH_2 to $CH_3CH_2CH_2$, resulting the acid character decreases. Therefore, the order is (i) > (ii) > (iii) > (iv).

Chapter 27 Organic Compounds Containing Nitrogen

1. Nitration of aniline in strong acidic medium also gives m-nitroaniline because
   (a) inspite of substituents nitro group always goes to only m-position
   (b) in electrophilic substitution reactions amino group is *meta* directive
   (c) in absence of substituents nitro group always goes to m-position
   (d) in acidic (strong) medium aniline is present as anilinium ion. *(NEET 2018)*

2. The correct increasing order of basic strength for the following compounds is

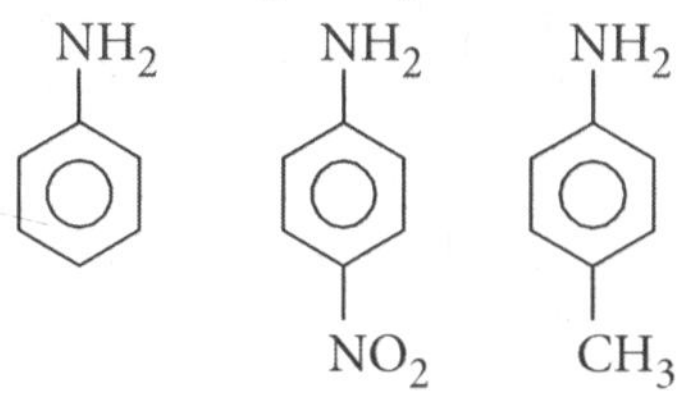

(I) (II) (III)

   (a) III < I < II (b) III < II < I
   (c) II < I < III (d) II < III < I *(NEET 2017)*

3. Which of the following reactions is appropriate for converting acetamide to methanamine?
   (a) Hoffmann hypobromamide reaction
   (b) Stephen's reaction
   (c) Gabriel phthalimide synthesis
   (d) Carbylamine reaction *(NEET 2017)*

4. Which one of the following nitro-compounds does not react with nitrous acid?

(a) 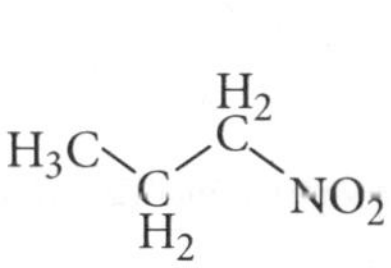 (b) 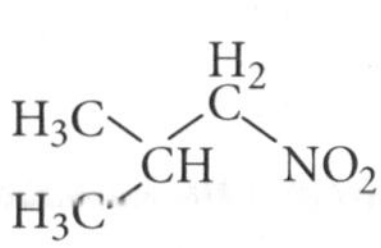

(c) 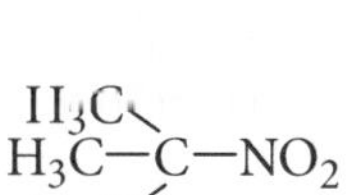 (d) 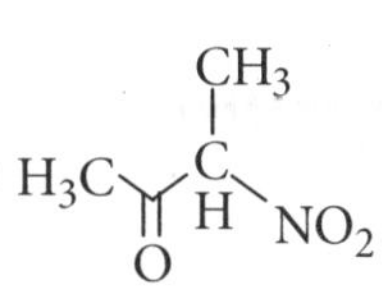

(NEET-II 2016)

5. A given nitrogen-containing aromatic compound '*A*' reacts with Sn/HCl, followed by HNO_2 to give an unstable compound '*B*'. '*B*', on treatment with phenol, forms a beautiful coloured compound '*C*' with the molecular formula $C_{12}H_{10}N_2O$. The structure of compound '*A*' is

(a) 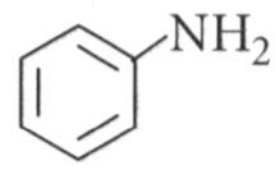 (b) 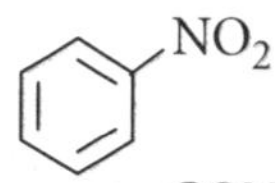

(c) 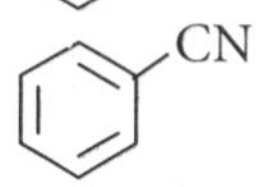 (d) 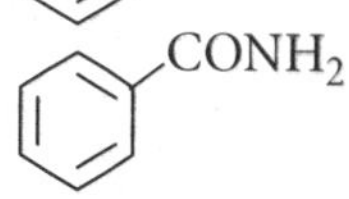

(NEET-II 2016)

6. The correct statement regarding the basicity of arylamines is
   (a) arylamines are generally more basic than alkylamines because of aryl group
   (b) arylamines are generally more basic than alkylamines, because the nitrogen atom in arylamines is sp-hybridised
   (c) arylamines are generally less basic than alkylamines because the nitrogen lone-pair electrons are delocalised by interaction with the aromatic ring π-electron system
   (d) arylamines are generally more basic than alkylamines because the nitrogen lone-pair electrons are not delocalised by interaction with the aromatic ring π-electron system. *(NEET-I 2016)*

7. The product formed by the reaction of an aldehyde with a primary amine is
   (a) carboxylic acid (b) aromatic acid
   (c) Schiff's base (d) ketone. *(NEET I 2016)*

8. The following reaction

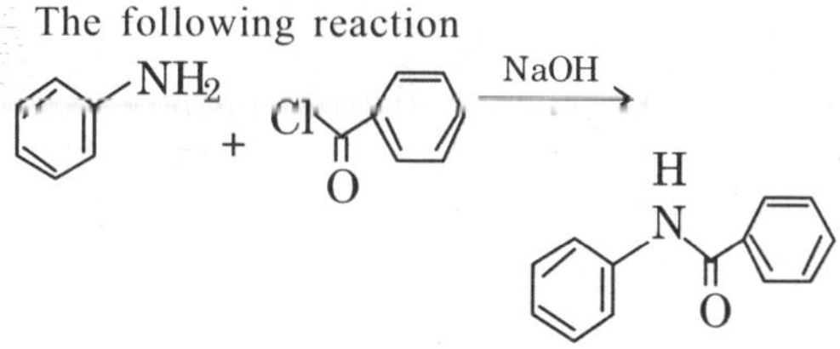

is known by the name
(a) Perkin's reaction
(b) Acetylation reaction
(c) Schotten-Baumann reaction
(d) Friedel-Crafts reaction. *(2015)*

9. Method by which aniline cannot be prepared is
(a) degradation of benzamide with bromine in alkaline solution
(b) reduction of nitrobenzene with H_2/Pd in ethanol
(c) potassium salt of phthalimide treated with chlorobenzene followed by hydrolysis with aqueous NaOH solution
(d) hydrolysis of phenylisocyanide with acidic solution. *(2015)*

10. The number of structural isomers possible from the molecular formula C_3H_9N is
(a) 5 (b) 2
(c) 3 (d) 4 *(2015)*

11. The electrolytic reduction of nitrobenzene in strongly acidic medium produces
(a) azobenzene (b) aniline
(c) *p*-aminophenol (d) azoxybenzene. *(2015, Cancelled)*

12. In the following reaction, the product (A) is

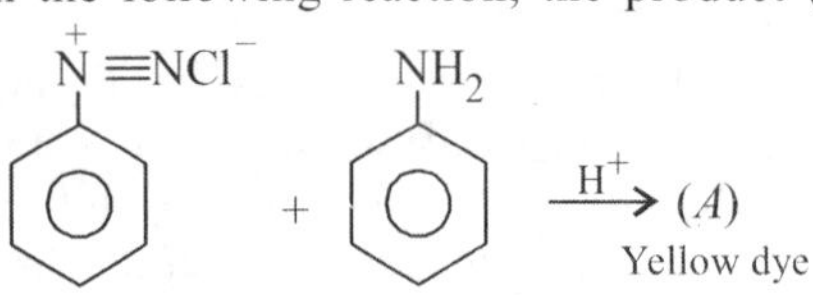

(a) 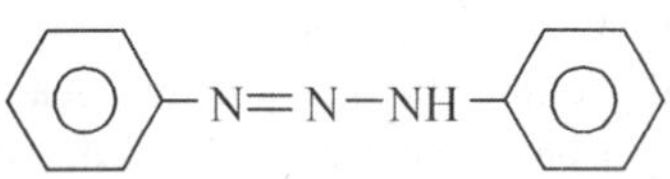

(b) 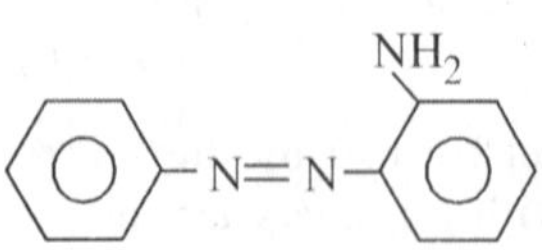

(c) 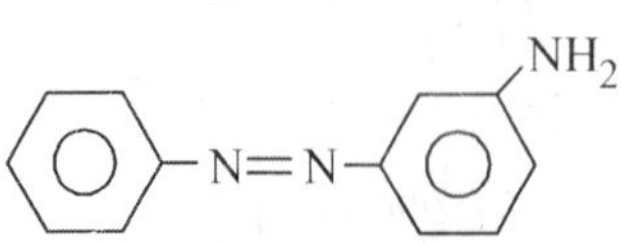

(d) 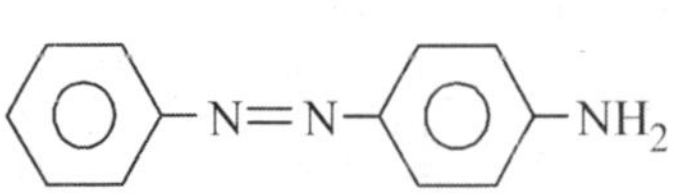

(2014)

13. Which of the following will be most stable diazonium salt $RN_2^+X^-$?
(a) $CH_3N_2^+X^-$ (b) $C_6H_5N_2^+X^-$
(c) $CH_3CH_2N_2^+X^-$ (d) $C_6H_5CH_2N_2^+X^-$ *(2014)*

14. Nitrobenzene on reaction with conc. HNO_3/H_2SO_4 at 80–100°C forms which one of the following products?
(a) 1, 4-Dinitrobenzene
(b) 1, 2, 4-Trinitrobenzene
(c) 1, 2-Dinitrobenzene
(d) 1, 3-Dinitrobenzene *(NEET 2013)*

15. In the reaction 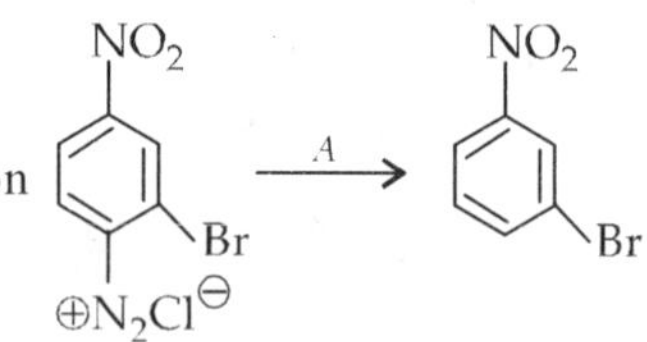

A is
(a) H_3PO_2 and H_2O (b) H^+/H_2O
(c) $HgSO_4/H_2SO_4$ (d) Cu_2Cl_2 *(NEET 2013)*

16. On hydrolysis of a "compound", two compounds are obtained. One of which on treatment with sodium nitrite and hydrochloric acid gives a product which does not respond to iodoform test. The second one reduces Tollens reagent and Fehling's solution. The "compound" is
(a) $CH_3CH_2CH_2NC$
(b) $CH_3CH_2CH_2CN$
(c) $CH_3CH_2CH_2ON{=}O$
(d) $CH_3CH_2CH_2CON(CH_3)_2$ *(Karnataka NEET 2013)*

17. Some reactions of amines are given. Which one is not correct?

(a) 

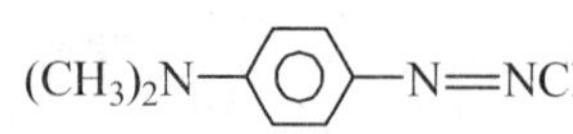

(b) $CH_3CH_2NH_2 + HNO_2 \rightarrow CH_3CH_2OH + N_2$
(c) $CH_3NH_2 + C_6H_5SO_2Cl \rightarrow CH_3NHSO_2C_6H_5$
(d) $(CH_3)_2NH + NaNO_2 + HCl \rightarrow (CH_3)_2N{-}N{=}O$ *(Karnataka NEET 2013)*

18. An organic compound (C_3H_9N) (A), when treated with nitrous acid, gave an alcohol and N_2 gas was evolved. (A) on warming with $CHCl_3$ and caustic potash gave (C) which on reduction gave isopropylmethylamine. Predict the structure of (A).

(a) 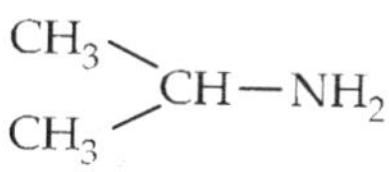

(b) $CH_3CH_2-NH-CH_3$

(c) 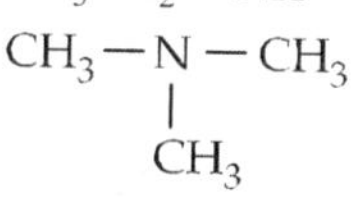

(d) $CH_3CH_2CH_2-NH_2$ *(2012)*

19. What is the product obtained in the following reaction?

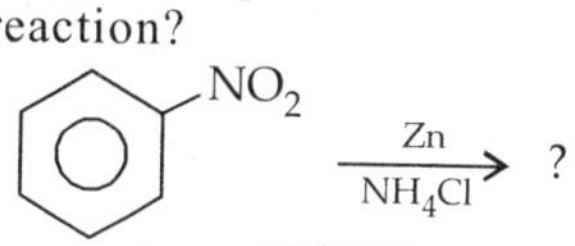

(a) 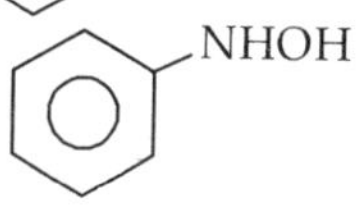

(b) 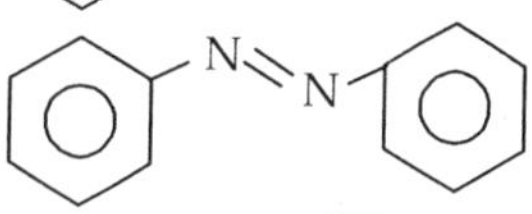

(c) 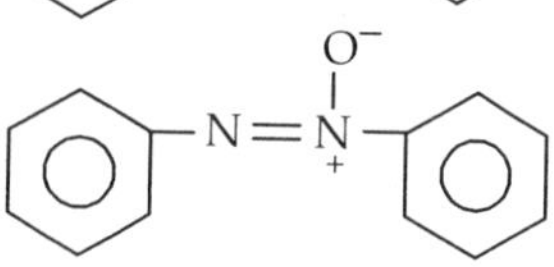

(d) 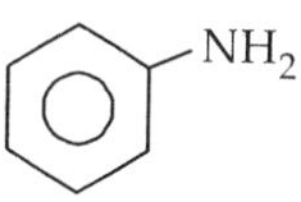 *(2011)*

20. Which of the following compounds is most basic?

(a) 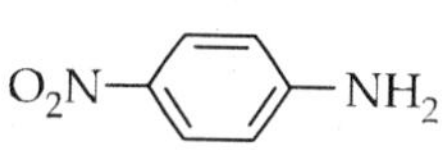

(b) 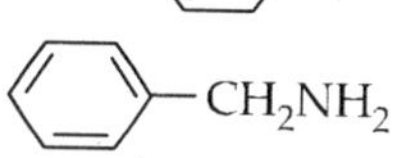

(c) 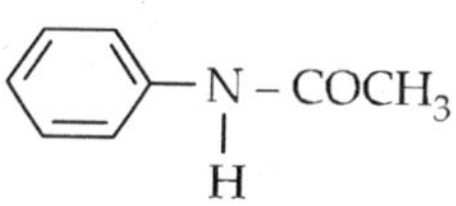

(d) 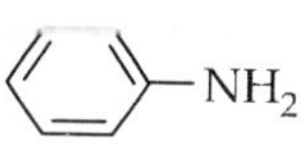 *(Mains 2011)*

21. Aniline in a set of the following reactions yielded a coloured product Y.

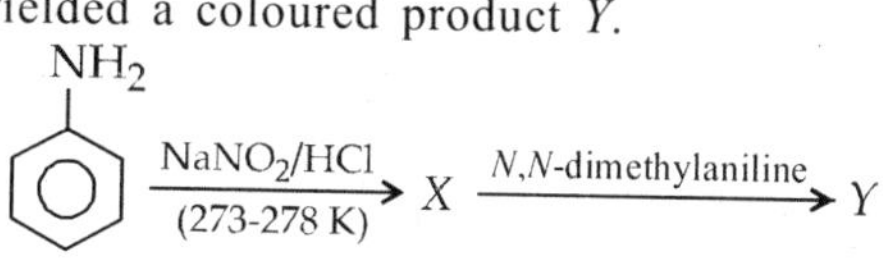

The structure of 'Y' would be

(a) 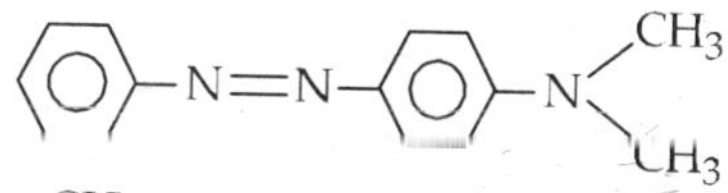

(b) 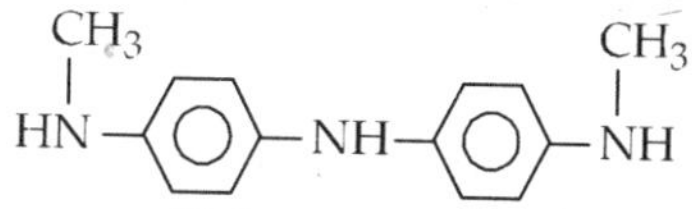

(c) 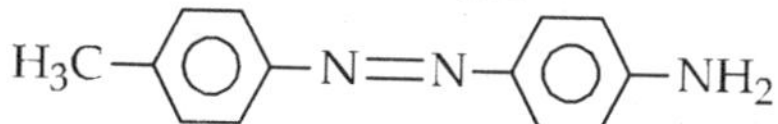

(d) 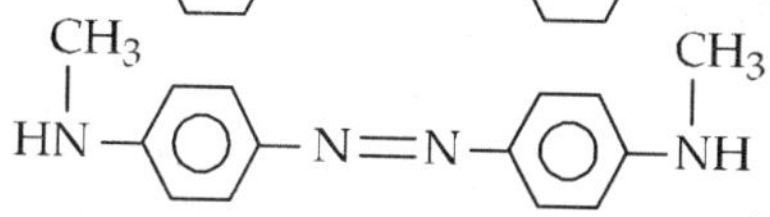

(2010)

22. Which of the following statements about primary amines is false?

(a) Alkyl amines are stronger bases than aryl amines.

(b) Alkyl amines react with nitrous acid to produce alcohols.

(c) Aryl amines react with nitrous acid to produce phenols.

(d) Alkyl amines are stronger bases than ammonia. *(2010)*

23. Predict the product.

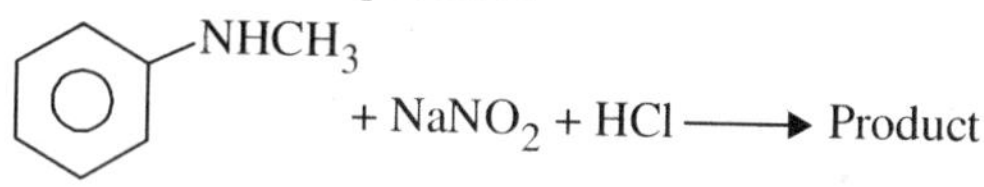

(a) 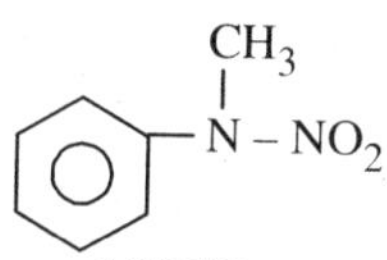

(b) 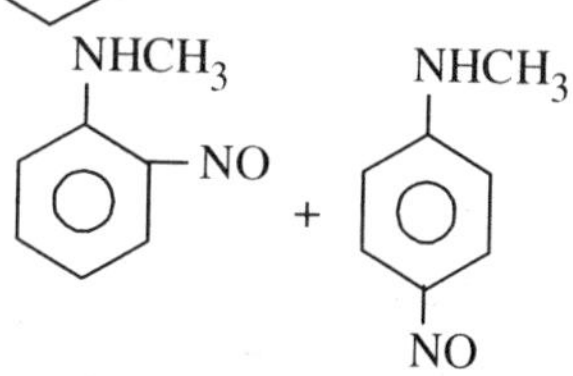

(c) 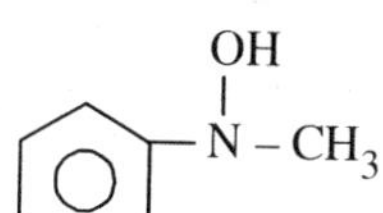

(d) 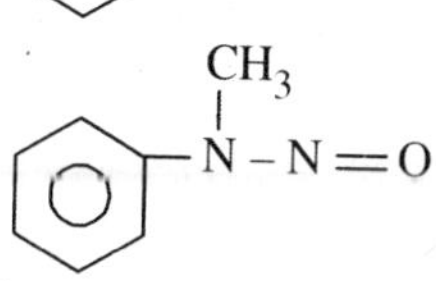 *(2009)*

24. Nitrobenzene can be prepared from benzene by using a mixture of conc. HNO_3 and conc. H_2SO_4. In the mixture, nitric acid acts as a/an

(a) acid (b) base

(c) catalyst (d) reducing agent.

(2009)

25. In a reaction of aniline a coloured product C was obtained.

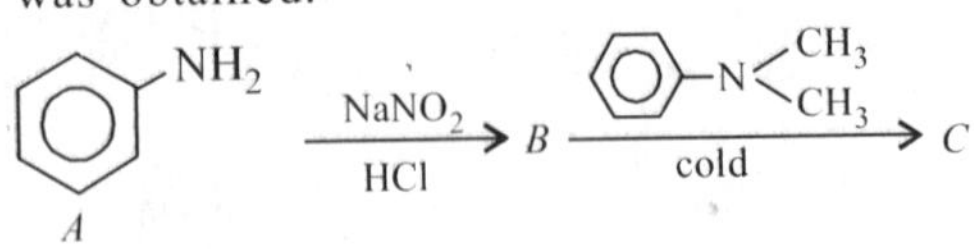

The structure of C would be

(a) 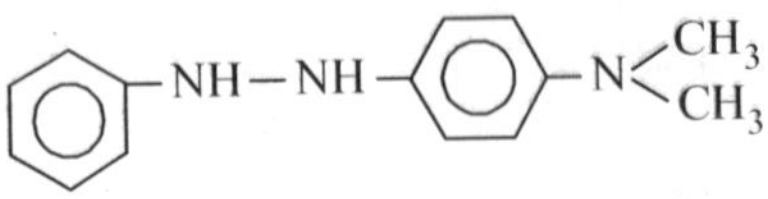

(b) 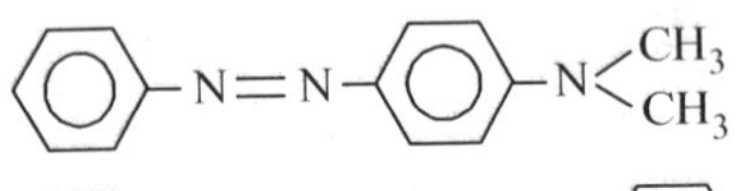

(c) 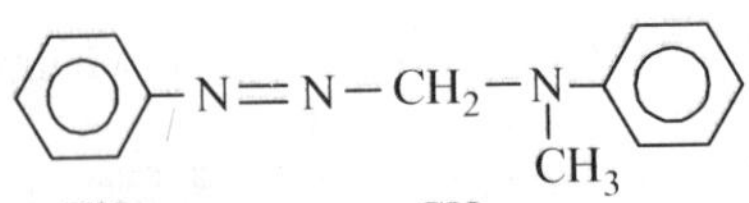

(d) 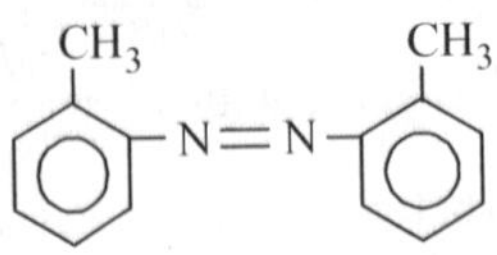 *(2008, 2004)*

26. Which one of the following on reduction with lithium aluminium hydride yields a secondary amine?
(a) Methyl isocyanide (b) Acetamide
(c) Methyl cyanide (d) Nitroethane *(2007)*

27. Which of the following is more basic than aniline?
(a) Benzylamine (b) Diphenylamine
(c) Triphenylamine (d) *p*-Nitroaniline *(2006)*

28. Electrolytic reduction of nitrobenzene in weakly acidic medium gives
(a) *N*-phenylhydroxylamine
(b) nitrosobenzene
(c) aniline
(d) *p*-hydroxyaniline. *(2005)*

29. Aniline in a set of reactions yielded a product D.

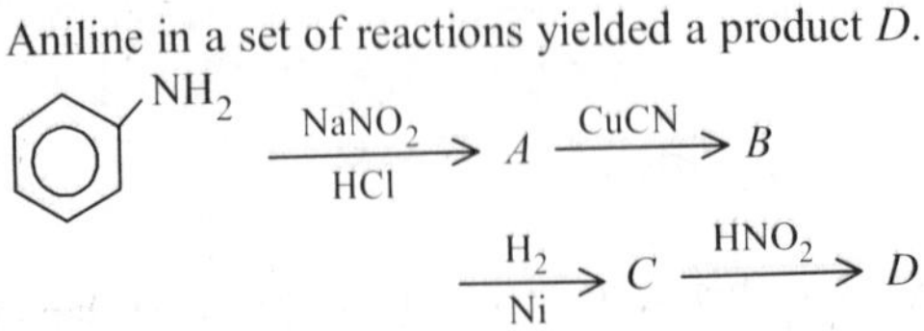

The structure of the product D would be
(a) C_6H_5NHOH (b) $C_6H_5NHCH_2CH_3$
(c) $C_6H_5CH_2NH_2$ (d) $C_6H_5CH_2OH$ *(2005)*

30. The final product C, obtained in this reaction

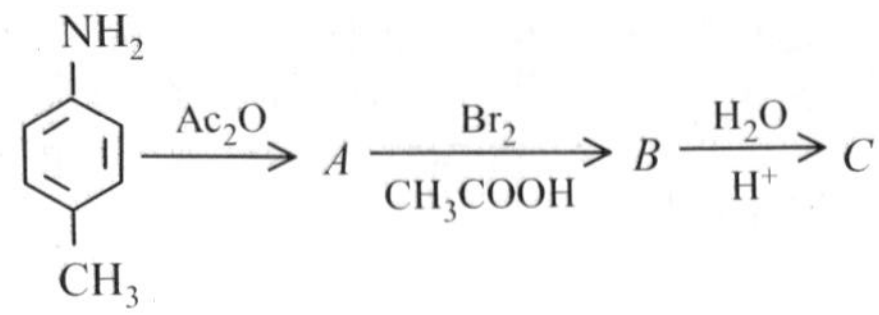

would be

(a) 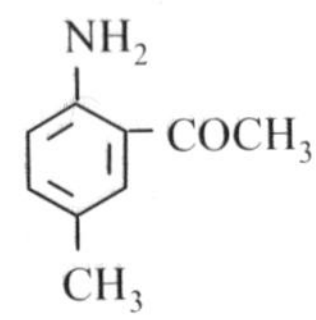 (b) 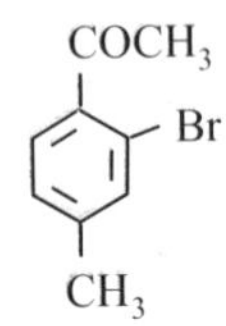

(c) 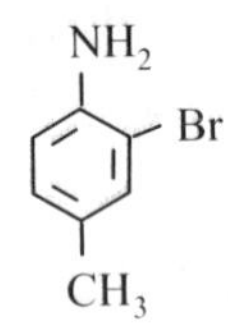 (d) 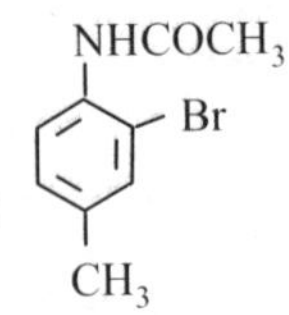

(2003

31. 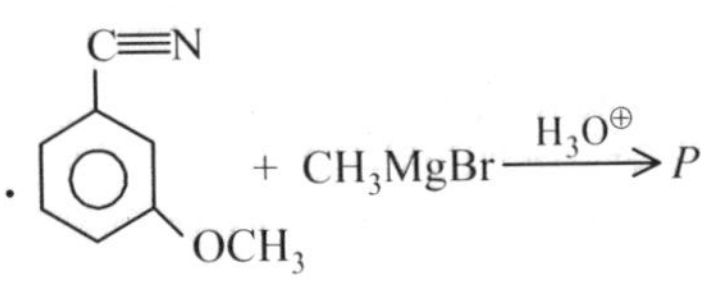

Product 'P' in the above reaction is

(a) 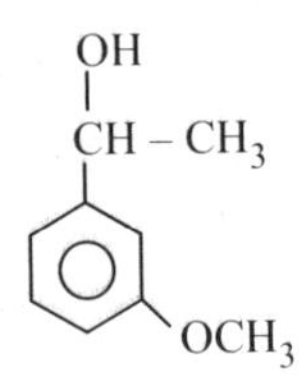 (b) 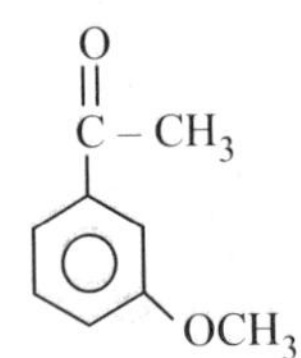

(c) 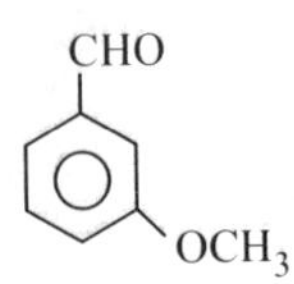 (d) 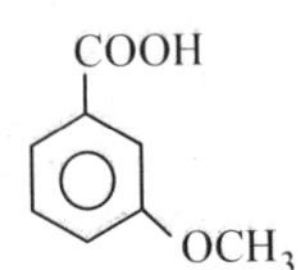

(2002

32. Intermediates formed during reaction c $RCONH_2$ with Br_2 and KOH are
(a) $RCONHBr$ and $RNCO$
(b) $RNHCOBr$ and $RNCO$
(c) $RNH - Br$ and $RCONHBr$
(d) $RCONBr_2$ *(200*

33. $A \xrightarrow{\text{reduction}} B \xrightarrow{CHCl_3/KOH} C \xrightarrow{\text{reduction}}$ *N*-methylanilin

then A is

(a) 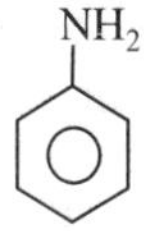

(b) 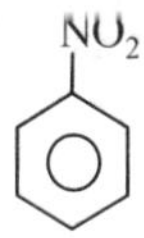

(c) CH_3NH_2

(d)  *(2000)*

34. Amides may be converted into amines by a reaction named after

(a) Hoffmann (b) Claisen
(c) Perkin (d) Kekule

(1999)

35. Phenyl isocyanides are prepared by which of the following reaction?

(a) Reimer-Tiemann reaction
(b) Carbylamine reaction
(c) Rosenmund's reaction
(d) Wurtz reaction

(1999)

36. Aniline is reacted with bromine water and the resulting product is treated with an aqueous solution of sodium nitrite in presence of dilute hydrochloric acid. The compound so formed is converted into a tetrafluoroborate which is subsequently heated dry. The final product is

(a) *p*-bromoaniline
(b) *p*-bromofluorobenzene
(c) 1, 3, 5-tribromobenzene
(d) 2, 4, 6-tribromofluorobenzene.

(1998)

37. The compound obtained by heating a mixture of ethyl amine and chloroform with ethanolic potassium hydroxide (KOH) is

(a) an amide
(b) an amide and nitro compound
(c) an ethyl isocyanide
(d) an alkyl halide. *(1997)*

38. An aniline on nitration gives

(a) 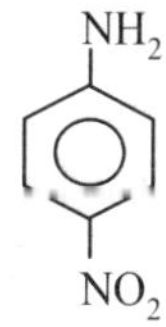

(b) 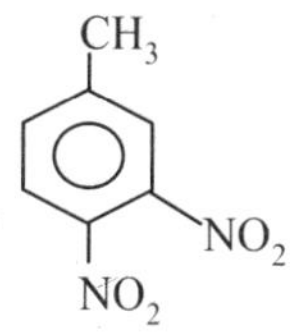

(c) 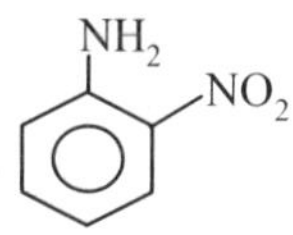

(d) both (a) and (c). *(1996)*

39. Which product is formed, when acetonitrile is hydrolysed partially with cold concentrated HCl?

(a) Methyl cyanide
(b) Acetic anhydride
(c) Acetic acid
(d) Acetamide *(1995)*

40. When aniline reacts with oil of bitter almonds (C_6H_5CHO) condensation takes place and benzal derivative is formed. This is known as

(a) Schiff's base
(b) Benedict's reagent
(c) Millon's base
(d) Schiff's reagent. *(1995)*

41. The action of nitrous acid on an aliphatic primary amine gives

(a) secondary amine (b) nitro alkane
(c) alcohol (d) alkyl nitrite.

(1994)

42. Which one of the following order is wrong, with respect to the property indicated?

(a) Benzoic acid > phenol > cyclohexanol (acid strength)
(b) Aniline > cyclohexylamine > benzamide (basic strength)
(c) Formic acid > acetic acid > propanoic acid (acid strength)
(d) Fluoroacetic acid > chloroacetic acid > bromoacetic acid (acid strength)

(1994)

43. For carbylamine reaction, we need hot alcoholic KOH and

(a) any primary amine and chloroform
(b) chloroform and silver powder
(c) a primary amine and an alkyl halide
(d) a monoalkylamine and trichloromethane. *(1992)*

44. Indicate which nitrogen compound amongst the following would undergo Hofmann reaction (*i.e.*, reaction with Br_2 and strong KOH) to furnish the primary amine (R–NH_2)?

(a) $RCONHCH_3$ (b) $RCOONH_4$
(c) $RCONH_2$ (d) $R - CO - NHOH$ *(1989)*

Answer Key

1. (d)	**2.** (c)	**3.** (a)	**4.** (c)	**5.** (b)	**6.** (c)	**7.** (c)	**8.** (c)	**9.** (c)	**10.** (d)
11. (c)	**12.** (d)	**13.** (b)	**14.** (d)	**15.** (a)	**16.** (a)	**17.** (a)	**18.** (a)	**19.** (a)	**20.** (b)
21. (a)	**22.** (c)	**23.** (d)	**24.** (b)	**25.** (b)	**26.** (a)	**27.** (a)	**28.** (c)	**29.** (d)	**30.** (c)
31. (b)	**32.** (a)	**33.** (b)	**34.** (a)	**35.** (b)	**36.** (d)	**37.** (c)	**38.** (d)	**39.** (d)	**40.** (a)
41. (c)	**42.** (b)	**43.** (a)	**44.** (c)						

EXPLANATIONS

1. **(d)** :

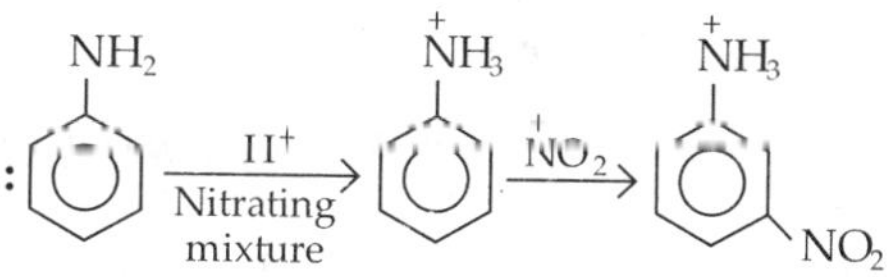

The reason for formation of an unexpected amount of *m*-nitroaniline is that under strongly acidic condition of nitration, most of the aniline is converted into anilinium ion and since, $-\overset{+}{N}H_3$ is a *m*-directing group, therefore, a large amount of *m*-nitroaniline is also obtained.

2. **(c)**

3. **(a)** :

$$\underset{\text{Acetamide}}{CH_3-\overset{O}{\overset{\|}{C}}-NH_2} + Br_2 + 4KOH \xrightarrow{\text{Hoffmann bromamide reaction}} \underset{\text{Methanamine}}{CH_3NH_2} + 2KBr + K_2CO_3 + 2H_2O$$

4. **(c)** : Tertiary nitroalkanes do not react with nitrous acid as they do not contain α-hydrogen atom.

5. **(b)** :

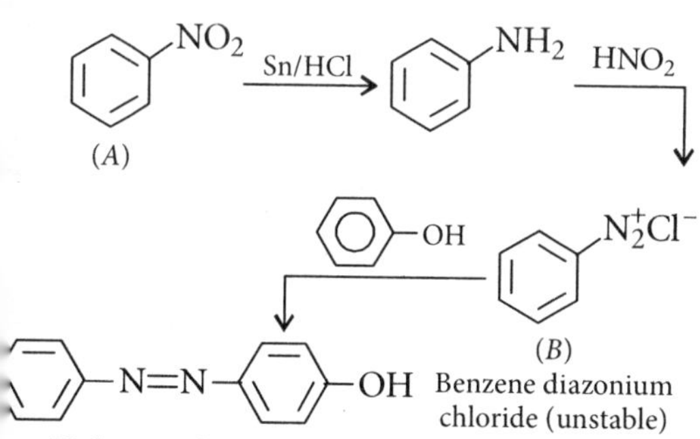

p-Hydroxyazobenzene (red colour dye)

6. **(c)** : In arylamines, lone pair of electrons on nitrogen atom is delocalised over the benzene ring, thus, not available for donation. So, arylamines are less basic than alkylamines .

7. **(c)** : $>C{=}O + H_2NR \longrightarrow \underset{\text{Schiff's base}}{>C{=}N{-}R}$

8. **(c)** : Benzoylation of compounds containing active hydrogen atom such as alcohols, phenols and amines with benzoyl chloride in the presence of dilute aq. NaOH solution is called Schotten-Baumann reaction.

9. **(c)** : Aniline cannot be prepared by this method because aryl halides do not undergo nucleophilic substitution reaction with potassium phthalimide under mild conditions.

10. **(d)** : The possible structural isomers are :

1. $CH_3CH_2CH_2NH_2$ — Propanamine
2. $CH_3-\underset{NH_2}{\underset{|}{CH}}-CH_3$ — Isopropylamine
3. $CH_3CH_2NHCH_3$ — *N*-Methylethanamine
4. $CH_3-\overset{CH_3}{\overset{|}{N}}-CH_3$ — *N,N*-Dimethylmethanamine

11. **(c)** :

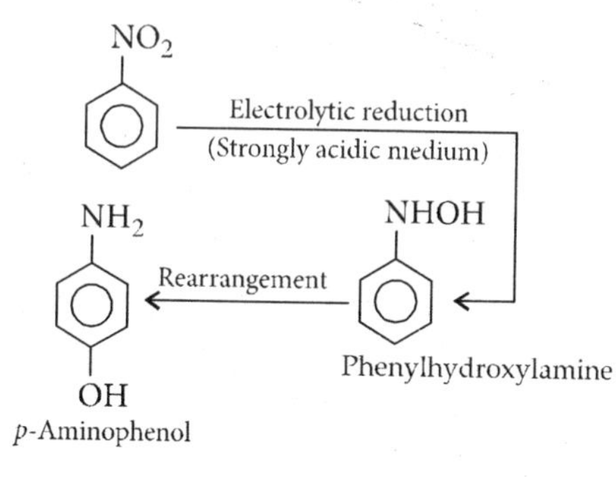

12. **(d)** :

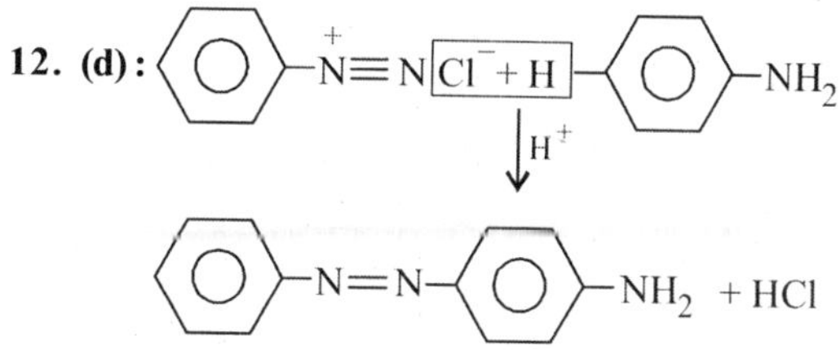

p-Aminoazobenzene (yellow dye)
(*A*)

13. **(b)** : Aromatic diazonium salts are more stable due to dispersal of the positive charge in benzene ring.

14. (d): 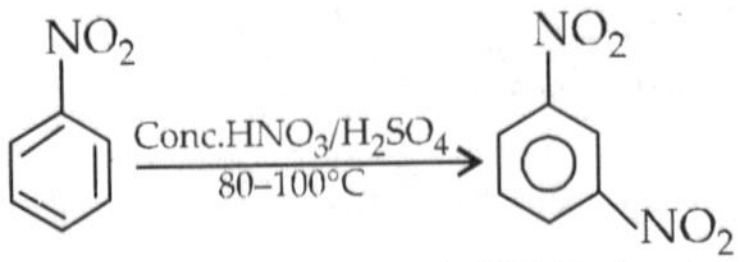

1, 3-Dinitrobenzene

15. (a): H_3PO_2 and H_2O reduces the $-\overset{+}{N}_2\overset{-}{Cl}$ to –H.

16. (a): $CH_3CH_2CH_2NC + 2H_2O \xrightarrow{H^+} \underset{I}{CH_3CH_2CH_2NH_2} + \underset{II}{HCOOH}$

II (HCOOH) reduces Tollens' reagent and Fehling's solution.

17. (a): Aromatic tertiary amines undergo electrophilic substitution with nitrosonium ion at *p*-position of the phenyl ring to form green-coloured *p*-nitrosoamines.

$NaNO_2 + HCl \rightarrow HNO_2 + NaCl$

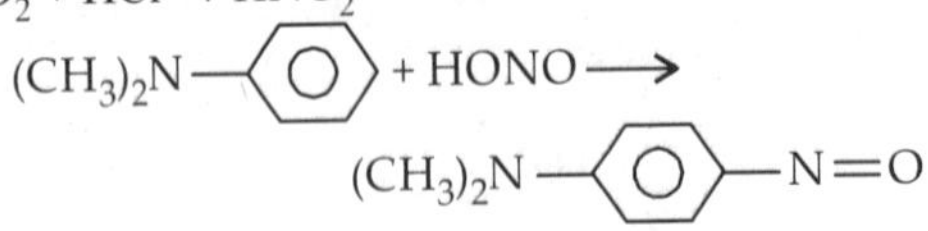

p-Nitro-*N*, *N*-dimethyl aniline (green)

18. (a): As *A* gives alcohol on treatment with nitrous acid thus it should be primary amine. C_3H_9N has two possible structure with $-NH_2$ group.

$CH_3-CH_2-CH_2-NH_2$ or $CH_3-CH(CH_3)-NH_2$

As it gives isopropylmethylamine thus it should be isopropyl amine not *n*-propyl amine.

$\underset{(A)}{CH_3-CH(CH_3)-NH_2} \xrightarrow{HNO_2} CH_3-CH(OH)-CH_3 + N_2\uparrow$

$(A) \xrightarrow{CHCl_3/KOH} \underset{(C)}{CH_3-CH(CH_3)-NC} \xrightarrow{\text{Reduction}} CH_3-CH(CH_3)-NH-CH_3$

Isopropylmethylamine

19. (a):

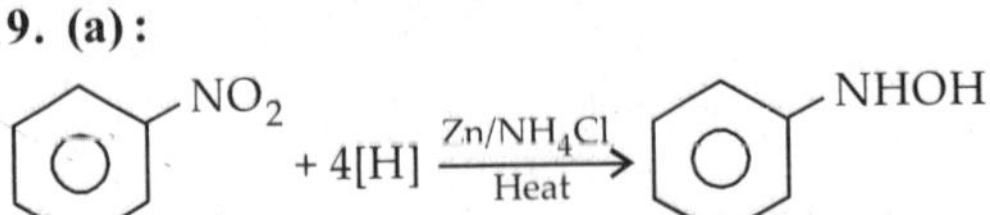

20. (b): In benzylamine the electron pair present on the nitrogen is not delocalised with the benzene ring.

21. (a): 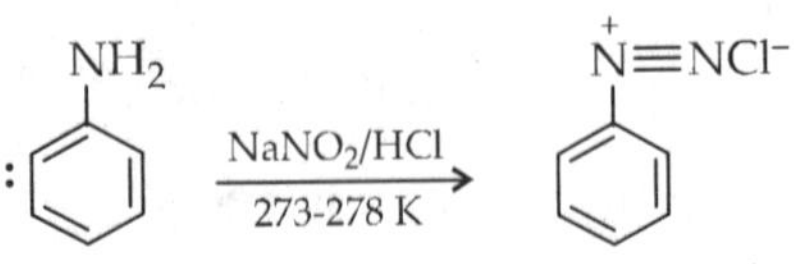

(diazonium salt) (*X*)

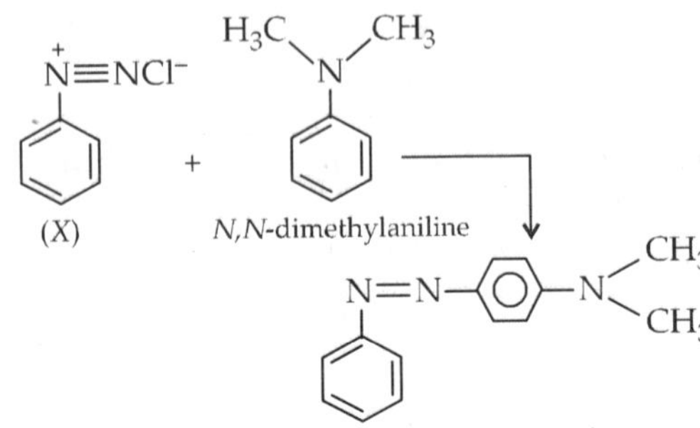

(*X*) *N*,*N*-dimethylaniline

(*Y*) (azo compound)

22. (c): Aryl amines react with nitrous acid to produce diazonium salts.

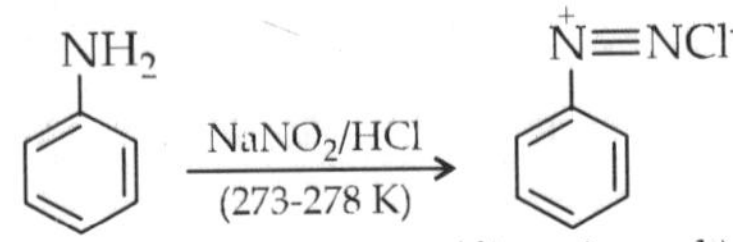

(diazonium salt)

23. (d): 2° aliphatic and aromatic amines react with nitrous acid to form *N*-nitrosoamine.

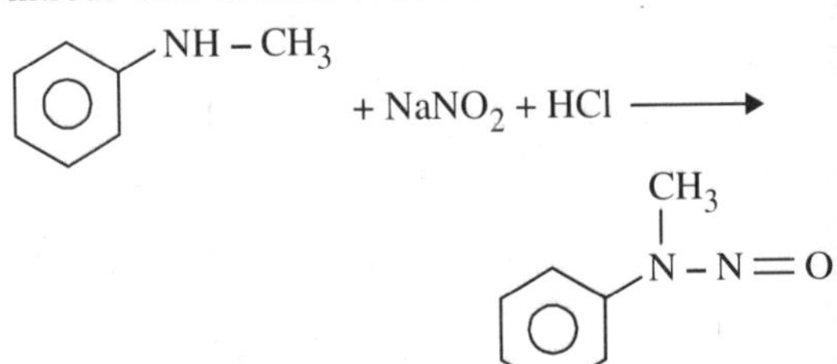

N-nitroso-*N*-methylaniline

24. (b): $\underset{(\text{from } H_2SO_4)}{H^+} + \underset{(\text{Base})}{H\ddot{O}-NO_2} \longrightarrow [H_2O^+-NO_2] \longrightarrow H_2O + \overset{+}{NO_2}$

25. (b):

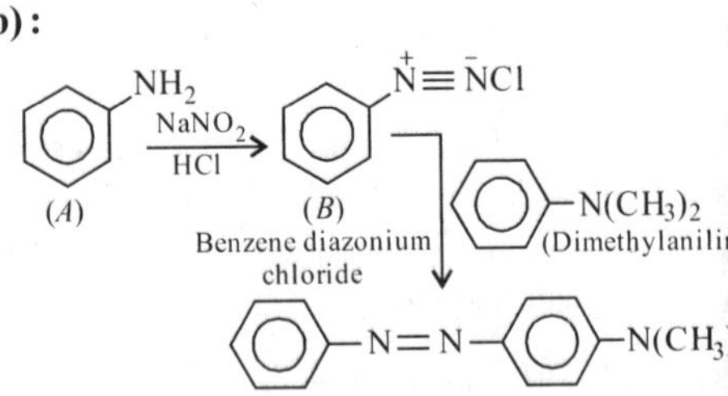

(*A*) (*B*) Benzene diazonium chloride (Dimethylaniline)

p-Dimethylaminoazobenzene (Butter yellow) (*C*)

26. (a): Alkyl isocyanides on reduction with lithium aluminium hydride forms secondary amine containing methyl as one of the the alkyl groups.

$$R-N \overset{\rightarrow}{\underset{\leftarrow}{=}} C + [H] \xrightarrow{LiAlH_4} RNHCH_3$$

Alkyl isocyanide Secondary amine

$$H_3C-N \overset{\rightarrow}{\underset{\leftarrow}{=}} C + 4[H] \xrightarrow{LiAlH_4} H_3C-NH-CH_3$$

Methyl isocyanide Dimethylamine

27. (a) : Any group which when present on benzene ring has electron withdrawing ($-NO_2$, $-CN$, $-SO_3H$, $-COOH$, $-Cl$, $-C_6H_5$, etc.) group decreases basicity of aniline. *e.g.* Aniline is more basic than nitroaniline and diphenyl amine. While a group which has electron repelling effect ($-NH_2$, $-OR$, $-R$, etc.) increases basicity of aniline.

Thus, benzylamine is more basic than aniline.

28. (c) : Electrolytic reduction of nitrobenzene in weakly acidic medium gives aniline but in strongly acidic medium it gives *p*-aminophenol through the acid-catalysed rearrangement of the initially formed phenylhydroxylamine.

$$\underset{\text{Nitrobenzene}}{C_6H_5NO_2} \xrightarrow[\text{Weakly acidic medium}]{\text{Electrolytic reduction}} \underset{\text{Aniline}}{C_6H_5NH_2}$$

29. (d) :

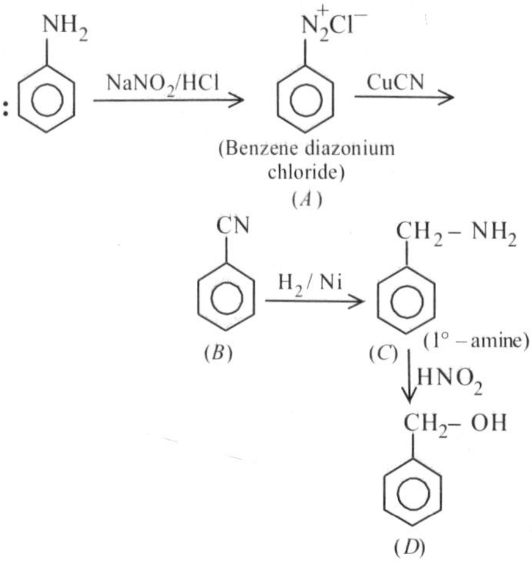

30. (c) :

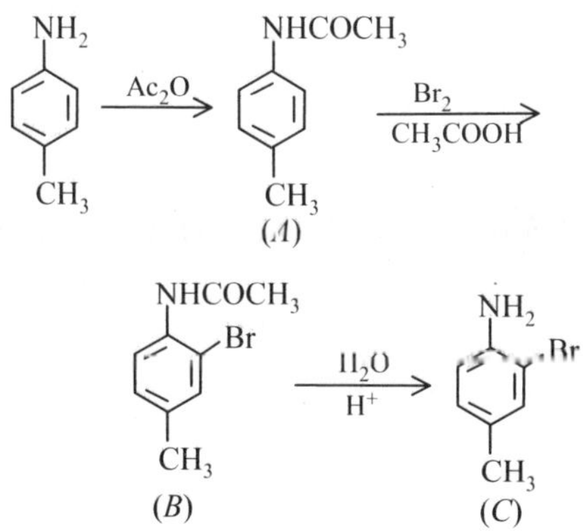

31. (b) :

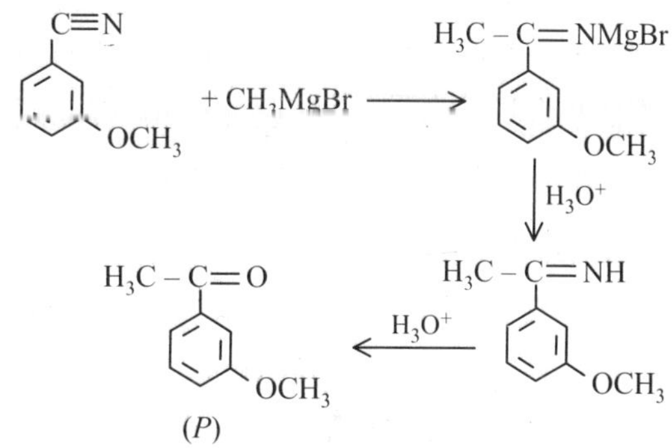

32. (a) : The reaction $RCONH_2 + Br_2 + KOH \rightarrow RNH_2$ is known as Hoffmann-bromamide reaction. The mechanism of the reaction is

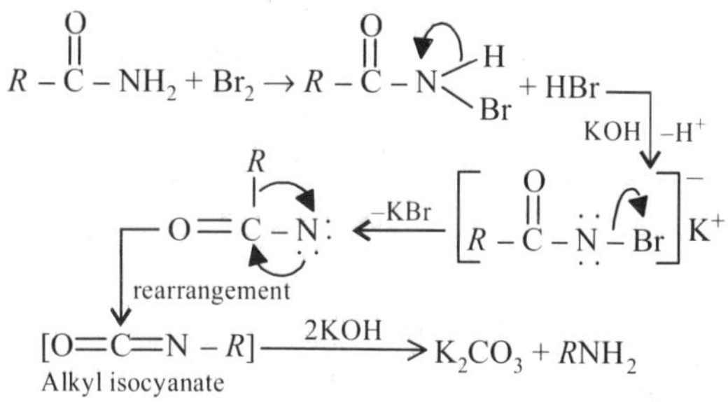

This reaction is used in the descent of series, *i.e.* for preparing a lower homologue from a higher one.

33. (b) : '*C*' must be an isocyanide and obtained from a 1° amine by Carbylamine reaction ($CHCl_3$ + KOH). Further 1° amine must be obtained by reduction of nitrohydrocarbon. So '*A*' is nitrobenzene.

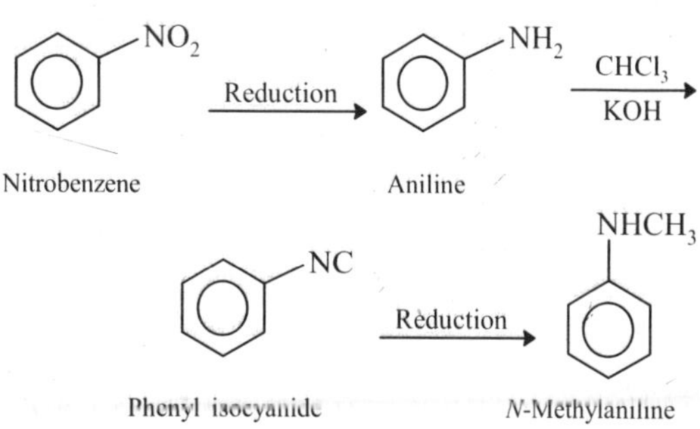

34. (a) :

$$\underset{\text{Acid amide}}{R-\overset{\overset{O}{\|}}{C}-NH_2} + Br_2 + 4KOH \longrightarrow \underset{1^\circ \text{ amine}}{R-NH_2} + K_2CO_3 + 2KBr + 2H_2O$$

This reaction is called Hoffmann bromamide reaction.

35. (b) : $C_6H_5-NH_2 + CHCl_3 + 3KOH \rightarrow C_6H_5-NC + 3KCl + 3H_2O$

The above reaction is called as carbylamine reaction, which is a specific reaction of 1°-amine. In this reaction aniline is treated with an alkaline solution of chloroform to give phenyl isocyanide.

36. (d) :

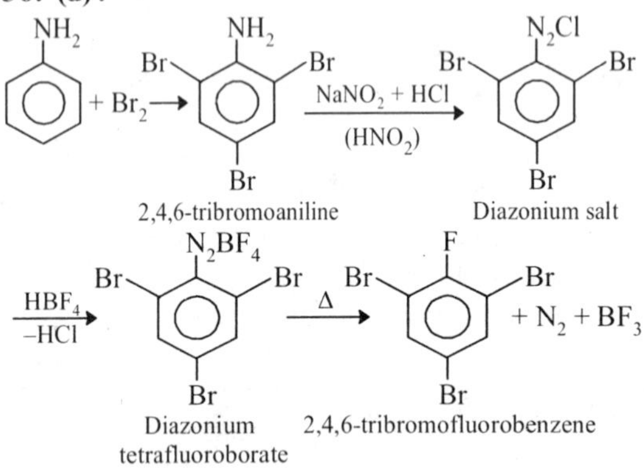

37. (c) : $\underset{\text{Ethyl amine}}{CH_3CH_2NH_2} + \underset{\text{Chloroform}}{CHCl_3} + 3KOH \rightarrow \underset{\text{Ethyl isocyanide}}{CH_3CH_2NC} + 3KCl + 3H_2O$

Isocyanide can be easily characterised by their offensive odour. The reaction is called carbylamine test.

38. (d) :

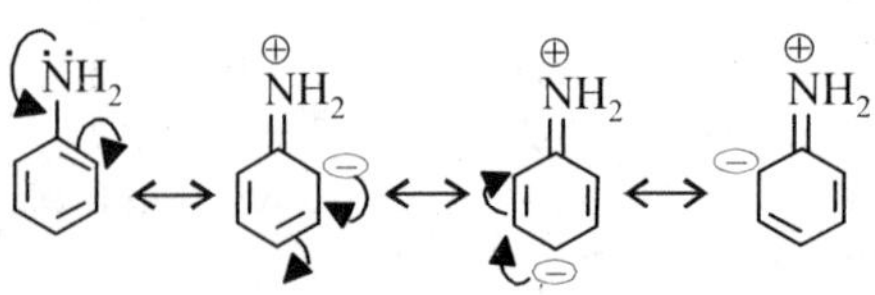

As, NO_2^+ electrophile can attack both *ortho* and *para* positions, therefore both (a) and (c) product will be obtained.

39. (d): $\underset{\text{Acetonitrile}}{CH_3-C\equiv N} \xrightarrow[H_2O]{\text{conc. HCl}} \underset{\text{Acetamide}}{CH_3-CO-NH_2}$

40. (a) : Benzaldehyde reacts with primary aromatic amines to form Schiff's base (Benzylidene aniline).

$\underset{\text{Benzaldehyde}}{C_6H_5HC{=}O} + \underset{\text{Aniline}}{C_6H_5NH_2} \rightarrow \underset{\text{Benzylidene aniline}}{C_6H_5HC{=}NC_6H_5} + H_2O$

41. (c) :

$\underset{\text{Primary amine}}{R-NH_2} + \underset{\text{Nitrous acid}}{HNO_2} \longrightarrow \underset{\text{Alcohol}}{ROH} + N_2 + H_2O$

42. (b) : Basic strength decreases as,

cyclohexylamine > aniline > benzamide.

Lesser basicity in aniline and benzamide is due to participation of lone pair of electron of $-NH_2$ group.

43. (a) : In carbylamine reaction, primary amines on heating with chloroform in presence of alcoholic KOH form isocyanides (or carbylamines). It is used to distinguish 1° amines from 2° and 3° amines.

$R\text{–}NH_2 + CHCl_3 + \underset{\text{(alc.)}}{3KOH} \rightarrow RNC + 3KCl + 3H_2O$

44. (c) : The amide (–$CONH_2$) group is converted into primary amino group (–NH_2) by Hofmann's bromamide reaction.

$RCONH_2 + Br_2 + 4KOH \xrightarrow{\Delta} \underset{1^\circ\text{ amine}}{R-NH_2} + KBr + K_2CO_3 + 2H_2O$

Chapter 28

Biomolecules

1. The difference between amylose and amylopectin is
   (a) amylopectin have $1 \rightarrow 4$ α-linkage and $1 \rightarrow 6$ α-linkage
   (b) amylose have $1 \rightarrow 4$ α-linkage and $1 \rightarrow 6$ β-linkage
   (c) amylopectin have $1 \rightarrow 4$ α-linkage and $1 \rightarrow 6$ β-linkage
   (d) amylose is made up of glucose and galactose. *(NEET 2018)*

2. Which of the following compounds can form a zwitter ion?
   (a) Aniline (b) Acetanilide
   (c) Benzoic acid (d) Glycine
   (NEET 2018)

Which of the following statements is not correct?
(a) Ovalbumin is a simple food reserve in egg-white.
(b) Blood proteins thrombin and fibrinogen are involved in blood clotting.
(c) Denaturation makes the proteins more active.
(d) Insulin maintains sugar level in the blood of a human body. *(NEET 2017)*

The central dogma of molecular genetics states that the genetic information flows from
(a) Amino acids $\rightarrow$ Proteins $\rightarrow$ DNA
(b) DNA $\rightarrow$ Carbohydrates $\rightarrow$ Proteins
(c) DNA $\rightarrow$ RNA $\rightarrow$ Proteins
(d) DNA $\rightarrow$ RNA $\rightarrow$ Carbohydrates
(NEET-II 2016)

The correct corresponding order of names of four aldoses with configuration given below

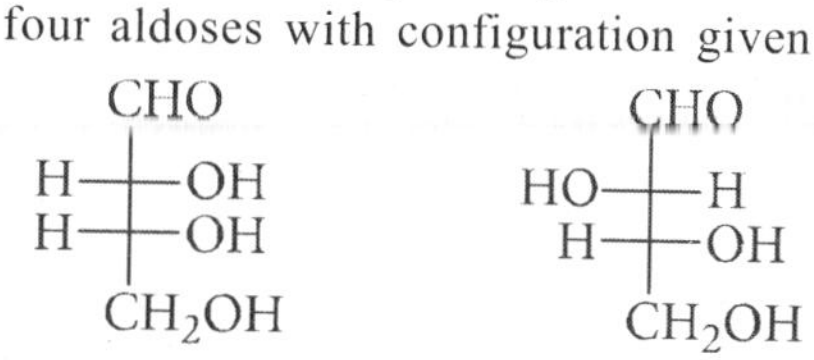

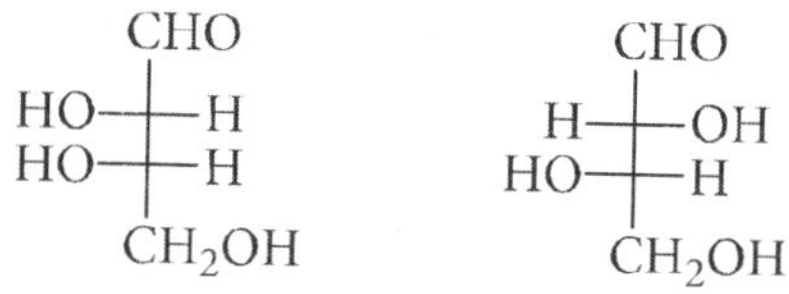

respectively, is
(a) *L*-erythrose, *L*-threose, *L*-erythrose, *D*-threose
(b) *D*-threose, *D*-erythrose, *L*-threose, *L*-erythrose
(c) *L*-erythrose, *L*-threose, *D*-erythrose, *D*-threose
(d) *D*-erythrose, *D*-threose, *L*-erythrose, *L*-threose.
(NEET-II 2016)

6. The correct statement regarding RNA and DNA, respectively is
   (a) the sugar component in RNA is a arabinose and the sugar component in DNA is ribose
   (b) the sugar component in RNA is 2′-deoxyribose and the sugar component in DNA is arabinose
   (c) the sugar component in RNA is arabinose and the sugar component in DNA is 2′-deoxyribose
   (d) the sugar component in RNA is ribose and the sugar component in DNA is 2′-deoxyribose. *(NEET-I 2016)*

7. In a protein molecule various amino acids are linked together by
   (a) peptide bond (b) dative bond
   (c) α-glycosidic bond
   (d) β-glycosidic bond. *(NEET-I 2016)*

8. Which one given below is a non-reducing sugar?
   (a) Glucose (b) Sucrose
   (c) Maltose (d) Lactose
   (NEET-I 2016)

9. *D*(+)-glucose reacts with hydroxyl amine and yields an oxime. The structure of the oxime would be

(a) 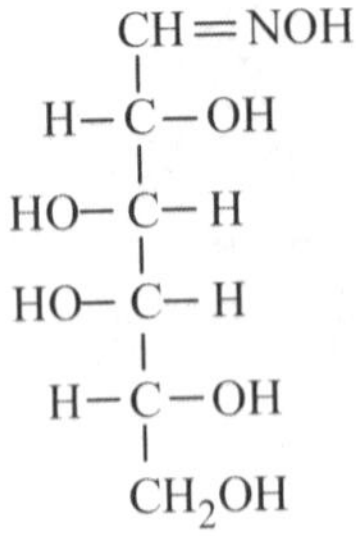 (b) 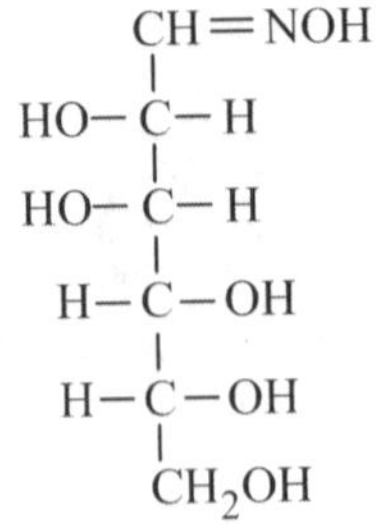

(c) 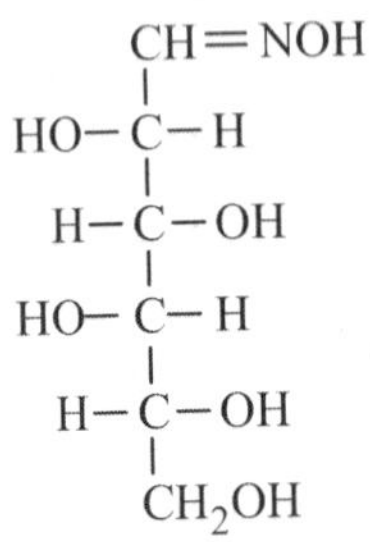 (d) 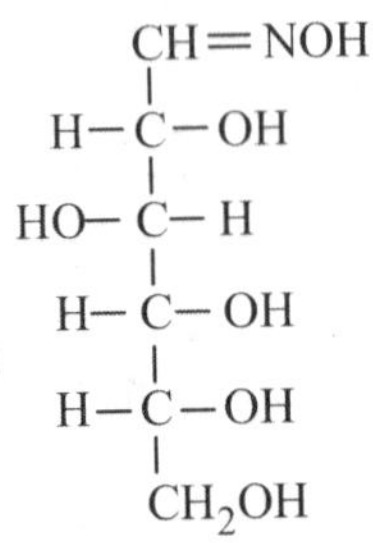

(2014)

10. Which of the following hormones is produced under the conditions of stress which stimulate glycogenolysis in the liver of human beings?
(a) Thyroxin (b) Insulin
(c) Adrenaline (d) Estradiol *(2014)*

11. In DNA, the linkages between different nitrogenous bases are
(a) phosphate linkage (b) H-bonding
(c) glycosidic linkage (d) peptide linkage *(Karnataka NEET 2013)*

12. Deficiency of vitamin B_1 causes the disease
(a) convulsions (b) beri-beri
(c) cheilosis (d) sterility *(2012)*

13. Which one of the following sets of monosaccharides forms sucrose?
(a) α-*D*-galactopyranose and α-*D* glucopyranose
(b) α-*D*-glucopyranose and β-*D*-fructofuranose
(c) β-*D*-glucopyranose and α-*D*-fructofuranose
(d) α-*D*-glucopyranose and β-*D*-fructopyranose. *(2012)*

14. Which one of the following statements is not true regarding (+) lactose?
(a) On hydrolysis (+) lactose gives equal amount of D(+) glucose and D(+) galactose.
(b) (+) Lactose is a β-glucoside formed by the union of a molecule of D(+) glucose and a molecule of D(+) galactose.
(c) (+) Lactose is a reducing sugar and does not exihibit mutarotation.
(d) (+) Lactose, $C_{12}H_{22}O_{11}$ contains 8-OH groups *(2011)*

15. Which of the following is not a fat soluble vitamin?
(a) Vitamin B complex
(b) Vitamin D
(c) Vitamin E
(d) Vitamin A *(Mains 2011)*

16. Which of the statements about "Denaturation" given below are correct?
(1) Denaturation of proteins causes loss of secondary and tertiary structures of the protein.
(2) Denaturation leads to the conversion of double strand of DNA into single strand
(3) Denaturation affects primary structure which gets distorted.
(a) (2) and (3) (b) (1) and (3)
(c) (1) and (2) (d) (1), (2) and (3) *(Mains 2011)*

17. Which one of the following does not exhibit the phenomenon of mutarotation?
(a) (+) Sucrose (b) (+) Lactose
(c) (+) Maltose (d) (–) Fructose *(2010)*

18. Fructose reduces Tollens' reagent due to
(a) asymmetric carbons
(b) primary alcoholic group
(c) secondary alcoholic group
(d) enolisation of fructose followed by conversion to aldehyde by base *(Mains 2010)*

19. The segment of DNA which acts as the instrumental manual for the synthesis of the protein is
(a) ribose (b) gene
(c) nucleoside (d) nucleotide. *(200*

20. Which of the following hormones contains iodine?
(a) Testosterone (b) Adrenaline
(c) Thyroxine (d) Insulin *(200*

21. In DNA, the complimentary bases are
(a) adenine and guanine; thymine and cytosine
(b) uracil and adenine; cytosine and guanine
(c) adenine and thymine; guanine and cytosine
(d) adenine and thymine; guanine and uracil.
(2008, 1998)

22. Which of the following is an amine hormone?
(a) Insulin (b) Progesterone
(c) Thyroxine (d) Oxypurin
(2008)

23. RNA and DNA are chiral molecules, their chirality is due to
(a) chiral bases
(b) chiral phosphate ester units
(c) *D*-sugar component
(d) *L*-sugar component. *(2007)*

24. Which of the following vitamins is water-soluble?
(a) Vitamin E (b) Vitamin K
(c) Vitamin A (d) Vitamin B
(2007)

25. The human body does not produce
(a) enzymes (b) DNA
(c) vitamins (d) hormones.
(2006)

26. During the process of digestion, the proteins present in food materials are hydrolysed to amino acids. The two enzymes involved in the process

$$\text{proteins} \xrightarrow{\text{enzyme } (A)} \text{polypeptides} \xrightarrow{\text{enzyme } (B)} \text{amino acids,}$$

are respectively
(a) invertase and zymase
(b) amylase and maltase
(c) diastase and lipase
(d) pepsin and trypsin. *(2006)*

27. Which one of the following is a peptide hormone?
(a) Adrenaline (b) Glucagon
(c) Testosterone (d) Thyroxine
(2006)

28. Which functional group participates in disulphide bond formation in proteins?
(a) Thioester (b) Thioether
(c) Thiol (d) Thiolactone
(2005)

29. The cell membranes are mainly composed of
(a) fats (b) proteins
(c) phospholipids (d) carbohydrates.
(2005)

30. Which of the following structures represents the peptide chain?

(a) 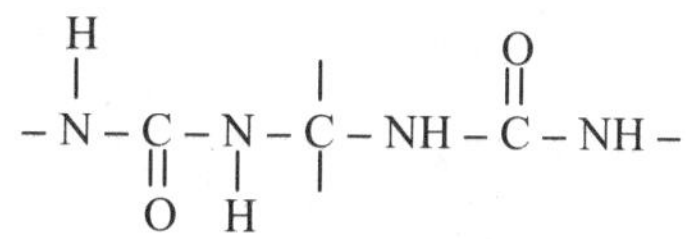

(b) 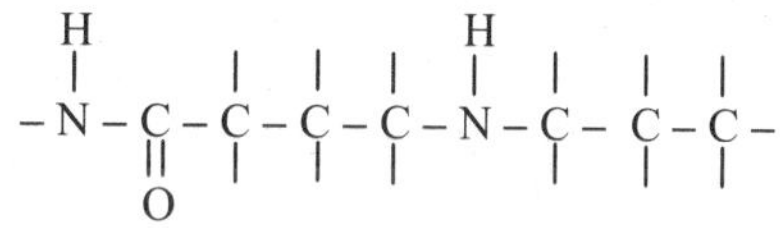

(c) 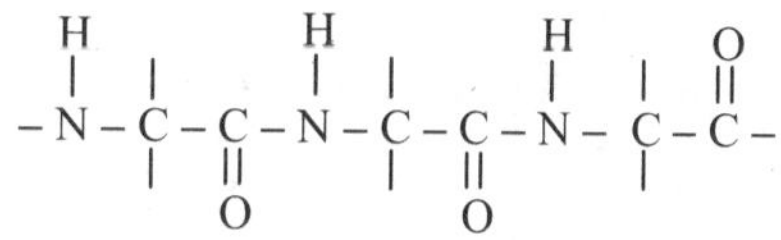

(d) 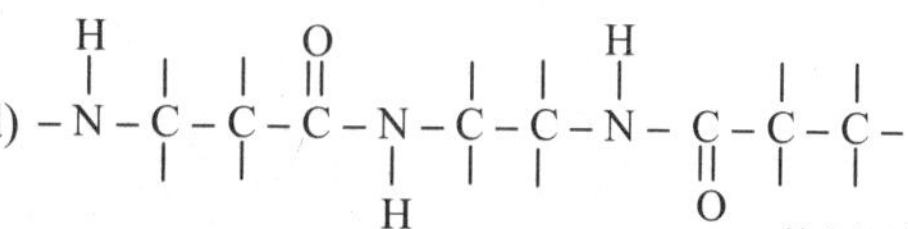

(2004)

31. A sequence of how many nucleotides in messenger RNA makes a codon for an amino acid?
(a) Three (b) Four
(c) One (d) Two *(2004)*

32. The hormone that helps in the conversion of glucose to glycogen is
(a) cortisone (b) bile acids
(c) adrenaline (d) insulin. *(2004)*

33. The correct statement in respect of protein haemoglobin is that it
(a) functions as a catalyst for biological reactions
(b) maintains blood sugar level
(c) acts as an oxygen carrier in the blood
(d) forms antibodies and offers resistance to diseases. *(2004)*

34. Number of chiral carbons in β-*D*-(+) glucose is
(a) five (b) six
(c) three (d) four *(2004)*

35. The helical structure of protein is stabilised by
(a) dipeptide bonds (b) hydrogen bonds
(c) ether bonds (d) peptide bonds.
(2004)

36. Vitamin B_{12} contains
(a) Fe (II) (b) Co (III)
(c) Zn (II) (d) Ca (II) *(2003)*

37. Glycolysis is
(a) oxidation of glucose to glutamate
(b) conversion of pyruvate to citrate
(c) oxidation of glucose to pyruvate
(d) conversion of glucose to haem. *(2003)*

38. Phospholipids are esters of glycerol with
(a) three carboxylic acid residues
(b) two carboxylic acid residues and one phosphate group
(c) one carboxylic acid residue and two phosphate groups
(d) three phosphate groups. *(2003)*

39. Chargaff's rule states that in an organism
(a) amount of adenine (A) is equal to that of thymine (T) and the amount of guanine (G) is equal to that of cytosine (C)
(b) amount of adenine (A) is equal to that of guanine (G) and the amount of thymine (T) is equal to that of cytosine (C)
(c) amount of adenine (A) is equal to that of cytosine (C) and the amount of thymine (T) is equal to that of guanine (G)
(d) amounts of all bases are equal. *(2003)*

40. Enzymes are made up of
(a) edible proteins
(b) proteins with specific structure
(c) nitrogen containing carbohydrates
(d) carbohydrates. *(2002)*

41. Cellulose is polymer of
(a) glucose (b) fructose
(c) ribose (d) sucrose. *(2002)*

42. Which is not true statement?
(a) α-carbon of α-amino acid is asymmetric.
(b) All proteins are found in *L*-form.
(c) Human body can synthesise all proteins they need.
(d) At pH = 7 both amino and carboxylic groups exist in ionised form. *(2002)*

43. Which of the following is correct about H-bonding in nucleotide?
(a) A – T, G – C (b) A – G, T – C
(c) G – T, A – C (d) A – A, T – T
(2001)

44. Which is the correct statement?
(a) Starch is a polymer of α-glucose.
(b) Amylose is a component of cellulose.
(c) Proteins are composed of only one type of amino acid.
(d) In cyclic structure of fructose, there are four carbons and one oxygen atom.
(2001)

45. $-\overset{\overset{O}{||}}{C}-\ddot{N}H-$ (peptide bond).
Which statement is incorrect about peptide bond?
(a) C – N bond length in proteins is longer than usual bond length of N – C bond.
(b) Spectroscopic analysis shows planar structure of $-\underset{\underset{O}{||}}{C}-NH-$ group.
(c) C – N bond length in proteins is smaller than usual bond length of C – N bond.
(d) None of the above. *(2001)*

46. Which of the following is correct?
(a) Cycloheptane is an aromatic compound.
(b) Diastase is an enzyme.
(c) Acetophenone is an ether.
(d) All of these. *(2001)*

47. α-*D*-glucose and β-*D*-glucose are
(a) epimers (b) anomers
(c) enantiomers (d) diastereomers.
(2000)

48. Which one is responsible for production of energy in bio-reaction?
(a) Thyroxine (b) Adrenaline
(c) Oestrogen (d) Progesterone
(2000)

49. Which of the following is the sweetest sugar?
(a) Fructose (b) Glucose
(c) Sucrose (d) Maltose *(1999)*

50. The number of molecules of ATP produced in the lipid metabolism of a molecule of palmitic acid is
(a) 56 (b) 36
(c) 130 (d) 86 *(1998)*

51. Glucose molecule reacts with *X* number of molecules of phenyl hydrazine to yield osazone. The value of *X* is
(a) two (b) one
(c) four (d) three *(1998)*

52. Haemoglobin is
(a) a vitamin (b) a carbohydrate
(c) an enzyme (d) a globular protein. *(1997)*

53. The function of enzymes in the living system is to
(a) catalyse biochemical reactions
(b) provide energy
(c) transport oxygen
(d) provide immunity. *(1997)*

54. The secondary structure of a protein refers to
(a) regular folding patterns of continuous portions of the polypeptide chain
(b) three-dimensional structure, specially the bond between amino acid residues that are distant from each other in the polypeptide chain
(c) mainly denatured proteins and structures of prosthetic groups
(d) linear sequence of amino acid residues in the polypeptide chain. *(1995)*

55. The oxidation of glucose is one of the most important reactions in a living cell. What is the number of ATP molecules generated in cells from one molecule of glucose?
(a) 28 (b) 38
(c) 12 (d) 18 *(1995)*

56. The α-*D*-glucose and β-*D*-glucose differ from each other due to difference in carbon atom with respect to its
(a) number of OH groups
(b) size of hemiacetal ring
(c) conformation
(d) configuration. *(1995)*

57. Which of the following statements about enzymes are true?
(a) Enzymes catalyse chemical reactions by increasing the activation energy.
(b) Enzymes are highly specific both in binding chiral substrates and in catalysing their reactions.
(c) Enzymes lack in nucleophilic groups.
(d) Pepsin is proteolytic enzyme. *(1995)*

58. Chemically considering digestion is basically
(a) anabolism
(b) hydrogenation
(c) hydrolysis
(d) dehydrogenation. *(1994)*

59. An example of biopolymer is
(a) teflon (b) neoprene
(c) nylon-66 (d) DNA. *(1994)*

60. Enzymes take part in a reaction and
(a) decrease the rate of a chemical reaction
(b) increase the rate of a chemical reaction
(c) both (a) and (b)
(d) none of these. *(1993)*

61. The couplings between base units of DNA is through
(a) hydrogen bonding
(b) electrostatic bonding
(c) covalent bonding
(d) van der Waals forces. *(1992)*

62. On hydrolysis of starch, we finally get
(a) glucose (b) fructose
(c) both (a) and (b) (d) sucrose. *(1991)*

Answer Key

1. (a) **2.** (d) **3.** (c) **4.** (c) **5.** (d) **6.** (d) **7.** (a) **8.** (b) **9.** (d) **10.** (c)
11. (b) **12.** (b) **13.** (b) **14.** (c) **15.** (a) **16.** (c) **17.** (a) **18.** (d) **19.** (b) **20.** (c)
21. (c) **22.** (c) **23.** (c) **24.** (d) **25.** (c) **26.** (d) **27.** (b) **28.** (c) **29.** (c) **30.** (c)
31. (a) **32.** (d) **33.** (c) **34.** (d) **35.** (b) **36.** (b) **37.** (c) **38.** (b) **39.** (a) **40.** (b)
41. (a) **42.** (b) **43.** (a) **44.** (a) **45.** (a) **46.** (b) **47.** (b) **48.** (a) **49.** (a) **50.** (c)
51. (d) **52.** (d) **53.** (a) **54.** (a) **55.** (b) **56.** (d) **57.** (b) **58.** (c) **59.** (d) **60.** (b)
61. (a) **62.** (a)

EXPLANATIONS

1. (a) : Amylose is a linear polymer of α-*D*-glucose held by C_1-C_4 glycosidic linkage whereas amylopectin is branched chain polymer of α-*D* glucose units in which chain is held by C_1-C_4 glycosidic linkage while branching occurs by C_1-C_6 glycosidic linkage.

2. (d) : $\underset{\text{Glycine}}{HOOC-CH_2-NH_2} \rightleftharpoons \underset{\text{Zwitter ion}}{{}^{-}OOC-CH_2-\overset{+}{N}H_3}$

3. (c) : Denaturation changes the structure of a protein and protein loses its activity.

4. (c) : Genetic information flows from

$$\text{DNA} \xrightarrow{\text{Transcription}} \text{RNA} \xrightarrow{\text{Translation}} \text{Proteins}$$

5. (d) :

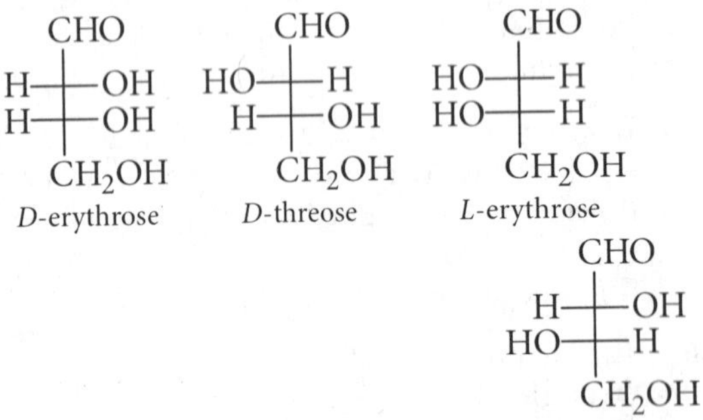

D-erythrose *D*-threose *L*-erythrose *L*-threose

6. (d) **7. (a)**

8. (b) : All monosaccharides whether aldoses or ketoses are reducing sugars. Disaccharides such as sucrose in which the two monosaccharide units are linked through their reducing centres *i.e.*, aldehydic or ketonic groups are non-reducing.

9. (d) :

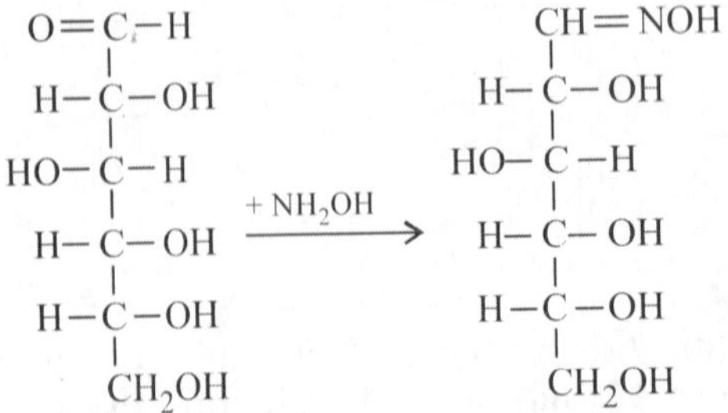

D(+)-Glucose Glucoxime

10. (c) : Adrenaline hormone helps to release fatty acids from fat and glucose from liver glycogen under the condition of stress. Hence, it is also called 'flight or fight hormone'.

11. (b) : Nitrogeneous bases are linked together by hydrogen bonds.

12. (b) :

Deficiency disease	Vitamin
Convulsions	B_6
Beri-beri	B_1
Cheilosis	B_2
Sterility	E

13. (b) : Sucrose is formed by the condensation o α-*D*-glucopyranose and β-*D*-fructofuranose.

14. (c) : (+) Lactose is a reducing sugar and al reducing sugar shows mutarotation.

15. (a) : Vitamin B complex is not a fat solubl vitamin. It is a water soluble vitamin.

16. (c) : Denaturation does not change the primar structure of protein.

17. (a) : Sucrose does not show mutarotation. Mutarotation is the phenomenon of change i optical rotation shown by freshly prepared solution of sugars. However, this property is not exhibite by all sugars. Only those sugars which have a fre aldehyde (—CHO) or ketone (>C=O) group ar capable of showing mutarotation. Sucrose lack free aldehyde or ketone group and is therefor incapable of showing mutarotation.

18. (d) : Under alkaline conditions of the reagen fructose gets converted into a mixture of glucos and mannose (Lobry de Bruyn van Ekenstei rearrangement) both of which contain the –CH group and hence reduce Tollens' reagent to giv silver mirror test.

19. (b) : Genes are responsible for protein synthesi

20. (c) :

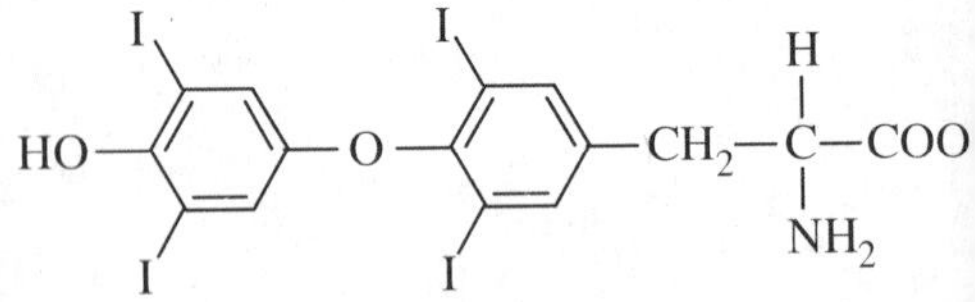

Thyroxine

21. (c) : DNA contains two types of nitrogeneo bases

Purine $\rightarrow$ Adenine (A) and guanine (G)

Pyrimidine $\rightarrow$ Cytosine (C) and thymine (T)

The purine and pyrimidine bases pair only in certa combination. Adenine pairs with thymine (A : T) two hydrogen bonds and guanine with cytosine

(G : C) by three hydrogen bonds.

22. (c) : Thyroxine is an amine hormone and water soluble hormone containing amino group.

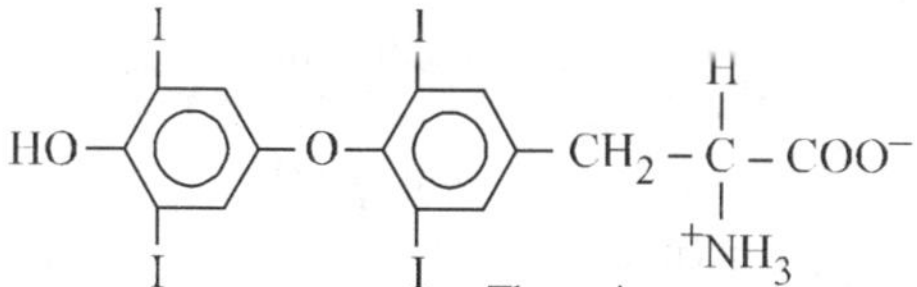

Thyroxine

23. (c) : The constituents of nucleic acids are nitrogenous bases, sugar and phosphoric acid. The sugar present in DNA is *D*(–)-2-deoxyribose and the sugar present in RNA is *D*(–)-ribose. Due to these *D*(–)-sugar components, DNA and RNA molecules are chiral molecules.

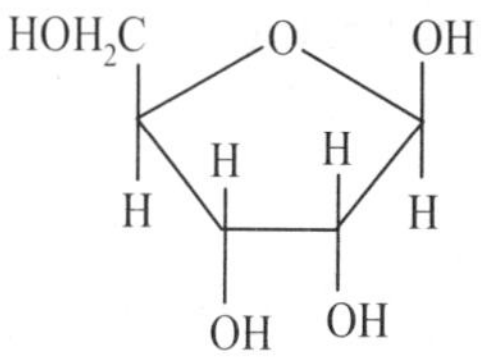

D(–)-ribose

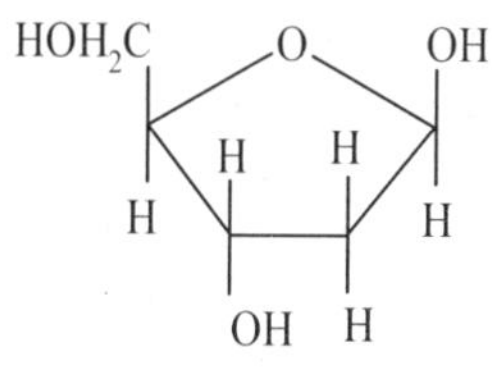

D(–)-2-deoxyribose

24. (d) : Vitamin B and C are water-soluble whereas vitamin A, D, E and K are fat soluble.

25. (c) : Certain organic substances required for regulating some of the body processes and preventing certain diseases are called vitamins, which cannot be synthesised by the organism.

26. (d) : $\text{Proteins} \xrightarrow[\text{proteases}]{\text{pepsin}} \text{Polypeptides} \xrightarrow[\text{chemotrypsin}]{\text{trypsin}} \text{Amino acids}$

27. (b) : Glucagon is a single chain peptide of 29 amino acids, synthesised by the α-cells in the islets of Langerhans of the pancreas.

28. (c) : Disulphide bond may be reduced to thiol by means of reagents *i.e.*, $NaBH_4$, which shows the presence of thiol group in disulphide bond formation.

29. (c) : Cell membranes are mainly composed of phospholipids.

30. (c) : In peptide linkage *i.e.*, – CONH – group, the carboxyl group of one amino acid molecule forms an amide by combination with the amino group of the next amino acid molecule with the liberation of water molecule.

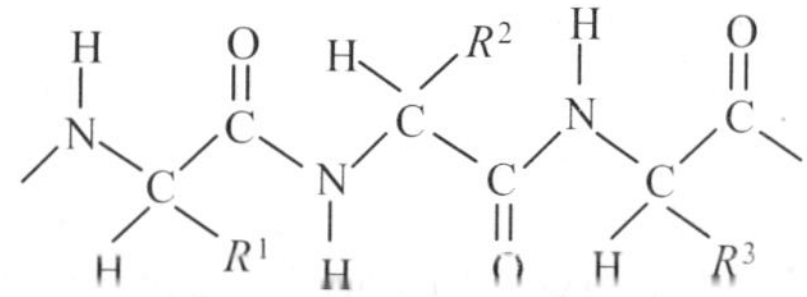

31. (a) : The four bases in *m*RNA : adenine, cytosine, guanine and uracil have been shown to act in the form of triplets; each triplet behaving as a code for the synthesis of a particular amino acid.

32. (d) : Insulin is a hormone secreted by the pancreas that lowers blood glucose level by promoting the uptake of glucose by cells and the conversion of glucose to glycogen by the liver and skeletal muscle.

33. (c) : Four Fe^{2+} ions of each haemoglobin can bind with 4 molecules of O_2 and it is carried as oxyhaemoglobin.

$$Hb_4 + 4O_2 \rightarrow Hb_4O_8.$$

34. (d) :

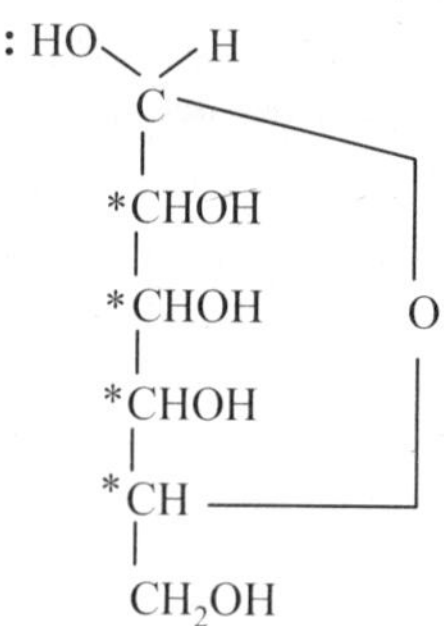

This structure of β-*D*-glucose has four asymmetric carbon atoms.

35. (b) : α-helix structure is formed when the chain of α-amino acids coil as a right handed screw because of the formation of hydrogen bonds between amide groups of the same peptide chain, *i.e.* NH group in one unit is linked to carbonyl oxygen of the third unit by hydrogen bonding. This H-bonding is responsible for holding helix in a position.

36. (b) : Vitamin B_{12} is chemically named as cyanocobalamine having molecular formula $C_{63}H_{88}O_{14}N_{14}PCo$.

37. (c) : Glycolysis is the first stage in the oxidation of glucose. It is an anaerobic process and involves the degradation of glucose into two molecules of pyruvate with the generation of two molecules of ATP.

38. (b) : Phospholipids may be regarded as derivatives of glycerol in which two of the hydroxyl groups are esterified with fatty acids while the third is esterified with some derivatives of phosphoric acid.

39. (a) : Amount of A = T and that of G = C.

40. (b) : Enzymes are proteins that act as catalyst for bio-chemical processes of life. They speed up these reactions enormously and with a high degree of selectivity.

41. (a) : Cellulose is a straight chain polysaccharide composed of *D*-glucose units joined by β-glycosidic linkage between C_1 of one glucose unit and C_4 of the next glucose unit. The number of *D*-glucose units in cellulose ranges from 3000 to 50000.

42. (b) : Some proteins are also found in the *D*-form.

43. (a)

44. (a) : Starch is also known as amylum which occurs in all green plants. A molecule of starch $(C_6H_{10}O_5)_n$ is built of a large number of α-glucose rings joined through oxygen atoms.

45. (a) : Peptide bond is formed by the reaction of one – COOH group of one amino acid with the – NH_2 group of another amino acid and represented as

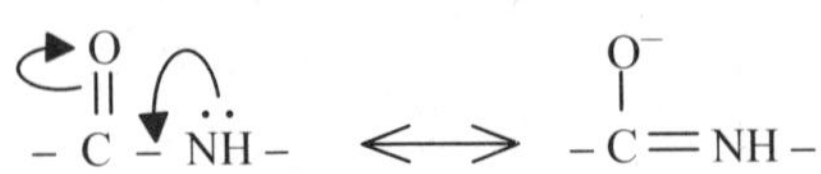

As some double bond character is found between C – N bond the bond length of C–N in protein should be smaller than the usual C–N bond.

46. (b) : Diastase is an enzyme. (The protein produced by living systems which acts as a biological catalyst). Enzymes are characterised by the name ending with *-ase*.

47. (b) : Glucose forms a stable hemiacetal between the -CHO group and the -OH group on the 5th carbon. In this process the 1st 'C' atom becomes asymmetric giving two isomers which differ in the configuration of the asymmetric carbon. These two isomers are called as anomers.

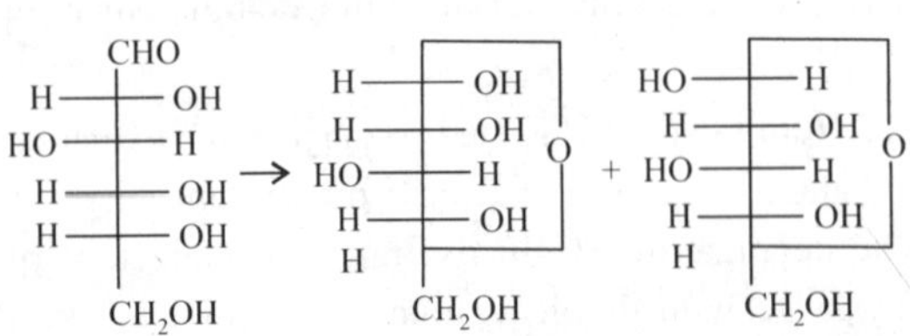

D-glucose α-*D*-glucose β-*D*-glucose

Anomers

48. (a) : It is a hormone secreted from thyroid gland. It controls various biochemical reactions involving burning of proteins, carbohydrates, fats to release energy.

49. (a) : Fructose is the sweetest among all the sugars and is highly soluble in water.

50. (c) : In the lipid metabolism a molecule of palmitic acid ($C_{15}H_{31}$ – COOH) produces 130 adenosine triphosphate molecule (ATP).

51. (d) : Glucose first reacts with phenyl hydrazine giving phenylhydrazone. Then the adjacent –CHOH group is oxidized by a 2nd phenyl hydrazine molecule and itself is reduced to aniline. The resulting carbonyl group reacts with 3rd phenyl hydrazine molecule giving osazone.

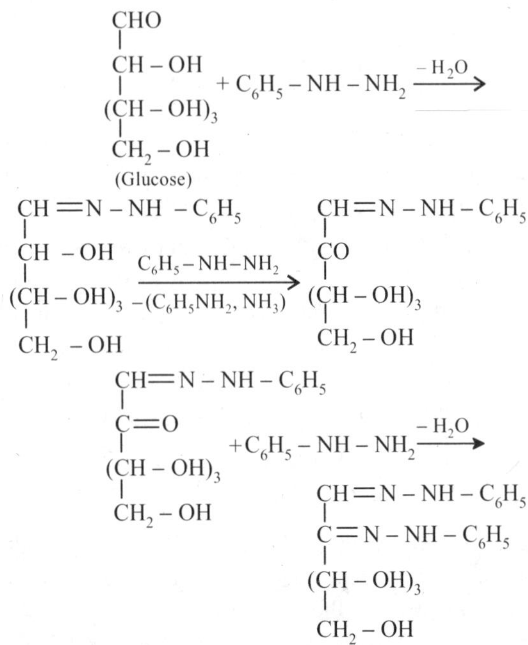

(Glucosazone)

52. (d) : Haemoglobin is a globular protein of four subunits, each subunit having a heme moiety and a polypeptide chain (Two α and two β chains).

53. (a) : The enzymes are globular proteins which catalyse chemical reactions in the living systems.

54. (a)

55. (b) : $C_6H_{12}O_6 + 6O_2 \rightarrow 6CO_2 + 6H_2O + 38ATP$

56. (d):

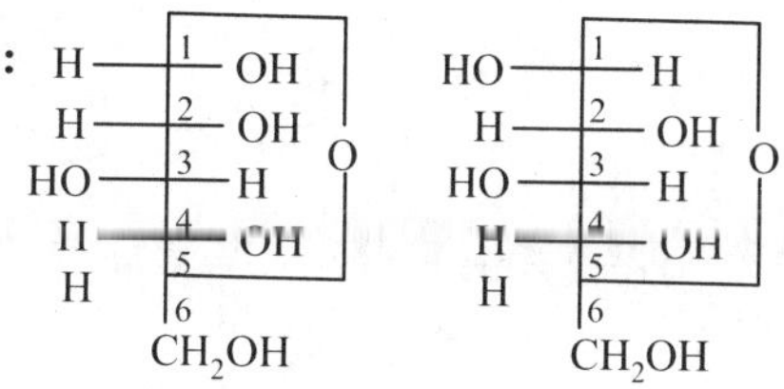

α-*D*-glucose β-*D*-glucose

These isomers differ only in the orientation (or configuration) at C_1 atom.

57. (b)

58. (c)

59. (d) : DNA is an example of biopolymer.

60. (b) : Enzymes being biocatalyst increases the rate of a chemical reaction by providing alternative lower activation energy pathways.

61. (a) : Hydrogen bonding

Double helical structure of DNA : Double helix is composed of two right handed helical polynucleotide chains coiled around the same central axis. The two strands are antiparallel. The bases are stacked inside the helix in planes perpendicular to the helical axis. The two strands are held together by hydrogen bonds. Two hydrogen bonds between A and T(A=T) and three are formed between C and G (C≡G).

62. (a) : Glucose is produced commercially by the hydrolysis of starch by boiling it with dil. H_2SO_4 at 393 K under presssure of 2-3 bar.

$$\underset{\text{Starch}}{(C_6H_{10}O_5)_n} + nH_2O \xrightarrow[393,\ 2\text{-}3\text{bar}]{H^+} \underset{\text{Glucose}}{nC_6H_{12}O_6}$$

Chapter 29

Polymers

1. Regarding cross-linked or network polymers, which of the following statements is incorrect?
(a) They contain covalent bonds between various linear polymer chains.
(b) They are formed from bi- and tri-functional monomers.
(c) Examples are bakelite and melamine.
(d) They contain strong covalent bonds in their polymer chains. *(NEET 2018)*

2. Which one of the following structures represents nylon 6, 6 polymer?

(a) 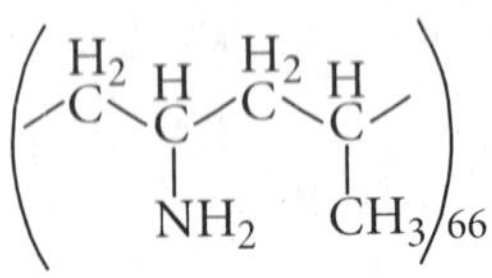

(b) 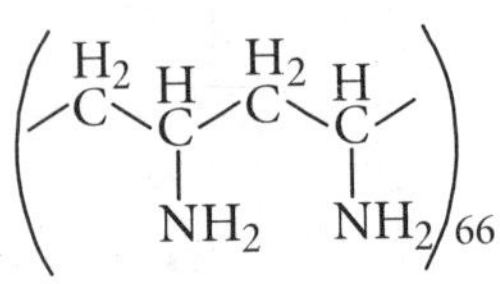

(c) 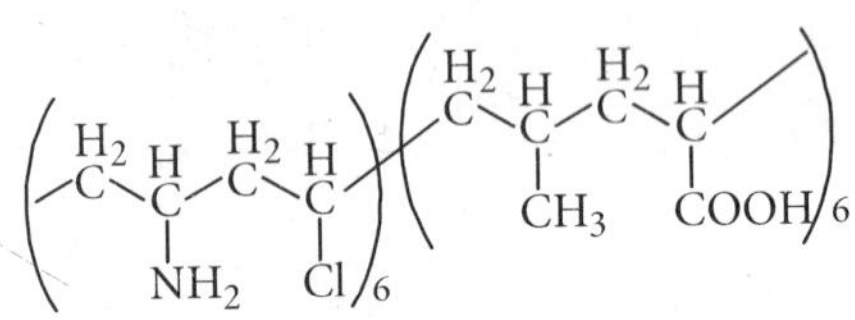

(d) 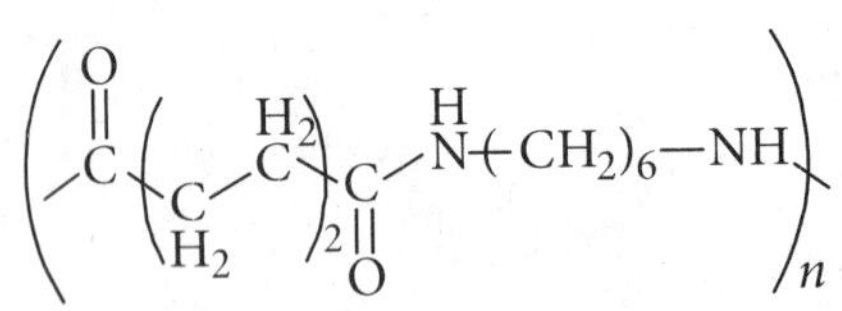

(NEET-II 2016)

3. Natural rubber has
(a) alternate *cis*- and *trans*-configuration
(b) random *cis*- and *trans*-configuration
(c) all *cis*-configuration
(d) all *trans*-configuration. *(NEET-I 2016)*

4. Caprolactam is used for the manufacture of
(a) teflon (b) terylene
(c) nylon 6, 6 (d) nylon 6. *(2015)*

5. Biodegradable polymer which can be produced from glycine and aminocaproic acid is
(a) buna-N (b) nylon 6,6
(c) nylon 2-nylon 6 (d) PHBV.
(2015, Cancelled)

6. Which one of the following is an example of thermosetting polymer?
(a) $+CH_2-\underset{Cl}{\underset{|}{C}}=CH-CH_2+_n$
(b) $+CH_2-\underset{Cl}{\underset{|}{CH}}+_n$
(c) $+\overset{H}{\overset{|}{N}}-(CH_2)_6-\overset{H}{\overset{|}{N}}-\overset{O}{\overset{||}{C}}-(CH_2)_4-\overset{O}{\overset{||}{C}}+_n$
(d) 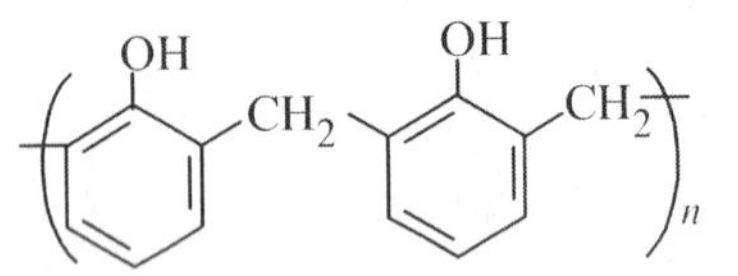

(2014)

7. Which of the following organic compounds polymerizes to form the polyester dacron?
(a) Propylene and *para* HO—(C_6H_4)—OH
(b) Benzoic acid and ethanol
(c) Terephthalic acid and ethylene glycol
(d) Benzoic acid and *para* HO—(C_6H_4)—OH
(2014)

8. Nylon is an example of
(a) polyamide (b) polythene
(c) polyester (d) polysaccharide.
(NEET 2013)

9. Which is the monomer of neoprene in the following?
(a) $CH_2=\underset{Cl}{\underset{|}{C}}-CH=CH_2$
(b) $CH_2=CH-C\equiv CH$
(c) $CH_2=CH-CH=CH_2$

(d) $CH_2{=}C(CH_3){-}CH{=}CH_2$ *(NEET 2013)*

10. Which one of the following is not a condensation polymer?
(a) Melamine (b) Glyptal
(c) Dacron (d) Neoprene
(2012)

11. Which of the following statements is false?
(a) Artificial silk is derived from cellulose.
(b) Nylon-6,6 is an example of elastomer.
(c) The repeat unit in natural rubber is isoprene.
(d) Both starch and cellulose are polymers of glucose. *(2012)*

12. Which one of the following sets forms the biodegradable polymer?
(a) $CH_2{=}CH-CN$ and $CH_2{=}CH-CH{=}CH_2$
(b) H_2N-CH_2-COOH and $H_2N-(CH_2)_5-COOH$
(c) $HO-CH_2-CH_2-OH$ and

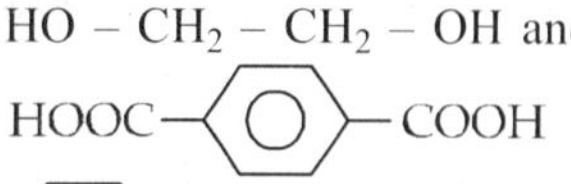

(d) 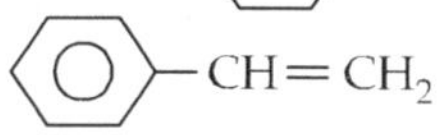 and
$CH_2{=}CH-CH{=}CH_2$ *(Mains 2012)*

13. Of the following which one is classified as polyester polymer?
(a) Terylene (b) Bakelite
(c) Melamine (d) Nylon-6,6
(2011)

14. Which of the following structures represents neoprene polymer?
(a) $-[CH_2-C(Cl){=}CH-CH_2]_n-$
(b) $-[CH_2-CH(Cl)]_n-$ (c) $-[CH_2-CH(CN)]_n-$
(d) $-[CH(C_6H_5)-CH_2]_n-$ *(2010)*

15. Structures of some common polymers are given. Which one is not correctly presented?
(a) Neoprene-
$\left[CH_2-C(Cl){=}CH-CH_2-CH_2\right]_n$
(b) Terylene -

(c) Nylon 6,6 -
$-[NH(CH_2)_6NHCO(CH_2)_4-CO]_n-$
(d) Teflon - $-[CF_2-CF_2]_n-$
(2009)

16. Which one of the following statements is not true?
(a) Buna-S is a copolymer of butadiene and styrene.
(b) Natural rubber is a 1,4-polymer of isoprene.
(c) In vulcanization, the formation of sulphur bridges between different chains make rubber harder and stronger.
(d) Natural rubber has the *trans*-configuration at every double bond.
(2008)

17. Which one of the following polymers is prepared by condensation polymerisation?
(a) Teflon (b) Natural rubber
(c) Styrene (d) Nylon-6,6
(2007)

18. $\sim\!\!\sim[NH(CH_2)_6NHCO(CH_2)_4CO]_n\sim\!\!\sim$ is a
(a) homopolymer
(b) copolymer
(c) addition polymer
(d) thermosetting polymer.
(2006)

19. The monomer of the polymer
$\sim\!\sim CH_2-C(CH_3)_2-CH_2-\overset{\oplus}{C}(CH_3)_2$ is
(a) $H_2C{=}C(CH_3)_2$
(b) $CH_3CH{=}CHCH_3$
(c) $CH_3CH{=}CH_2$
(d) $(CH_3)_2C{=}C(CH_3)_2$ *(2005)*

20. Which one of the following is a chain growth polymer?
(a) Starch (b) Nucleic acid
(c) Polystyrene (d) Protein *(2004)*

21. Acrilan is a hard, horny and a high melting material. Which one of the following represents its structure?

(a) $\left[-CH_2-\underset{CN}{\underset{|}{CH}}-\right]_n$

(b) $\left[-CH_2-\overset{CH_3}{\overset{|}{\underset{COOCH_3}{\underset{|}{C}}}}-\right]_n$

(c) $\left[-CH_2-\underset{COOC_2H_5}{\underset{|}{CH}}-\right]_n$

(d) $\left[-CH_2-\underset{Cl}{\underset{|}{CH}}-\right]_n$ *(2003)*

22. Which one of the following monomers gives the polymer neoprene on polymerization?
(a) $CH_2{=}CHCl$ (b) $CCl_2{=}CCl_2$
(c) $CH_2{=}\overset{Cl}{\overset{|}{C}}-CH{=}CH_2$ (d) $CF_2{=}CF_2$ *(2003)*

23. Monomer of $\left[-\overset{CH_3}{\overset{|}{\underset{CH_3}{\underset{|}{C}}}}-CH_2-\right]$ is
(a) 2-methylpropene (b) styrene
(c) propylene (d) ethene. *(2002)*

24. Which of the following is not correctly matched?

(a) Neoprene : $\left[-CH_2-\underset{Cl}{\underset{|}{C}}{=}CH-CH_2-\right]_n$

(b) Nylon-6,6 : $\left[-NH-(CH_2)_6-NH-CO-(CH_2)_4-\overset{O}{\overset{||}{C}}-O-\right]_n$

(c) Terylene : $\left[-OCH_2-CH_2-\overset{O}{\overset{||}{C}}-C_6H_4-\overset{O}{\overset{||}{C}}-\right]_n$

(d) PMMA : $\left[-CH_2-\overset{CH_3}{\overset{|}{\underset{COOCH_3}{\underset{|}{C}}}}-\right]_n$. *(2001)*

25. $CF_2 = CF_2$ is monomer of
(a) teflon (b) orlon
(c) polythene (d) nylon-6. *(2000)*

26. Which compound forms linear polymer due to H-bond?
(a) H_2O (b) NH_3
(c) HF (d) HCl *(2000)*

27. Natural rubber is a polymer of
(a) styrene (b) ethyne
(c) butadiene (d) isoprene. *(1999)*

28. Terylene is a condensation polymer of ethylene glycol and
(a) salicylic acid (b) phthalic acid
(c) benzoic acid (d) terephthalic acid. *(1999)*

29. Which one of the following is used to make 'non-stick' cookware?
(a) Poly-ethylene terephthalate
(b) Polytetrafluoroethylene
(c) PVC
(d) Polystyrene *(1997)*

30. The bakelite is prepared by the reaction between
(a) phenol and formaldehyde
(b) tetramethylene glycol
(c) urea and formaldehyde
(d) ethylene glycol. *(1995)*

Answer Key

1. (d)	**2.** (d)	**3.** (c)	**4.** (d)	**5.** (c)	**6.** (d)	**7.** (c)	**8.** (a)	**9.** (a)	**10.** (d)
11. (b)	**12.** (b)	**13.** (a)	**14.** (a)	**15.** (a)	**16.** (d)	**17.** (d)	**18.** (b)	**19.** (a)	**20.** (c)
21. (a)	**22.** (c)	**23.** (a)	**24.** (c)	**25.** (a)	**26.** (c)	**27.** (d)	**28.** (d)	**29.** (b)	**30.** (a)

EXPLANATIONS

1. **(d)** : Cross-linked or network polymers are usually formed from bi-functional and tri-functional monomers and contains strong covalent bonds between various linear polymer chains like melamine, bakelite, etc.

2. **(d)** : Nylon 6,6 is obtained by condensing adipic acid ($HOOC(CH_2)_4COOH$) with hexamethylenediamine ($H_2N(CH_2)_6NH_2$).

3. **(c)** : Natural rubber is *cis*-polyisoprene.

4. **(d)** :

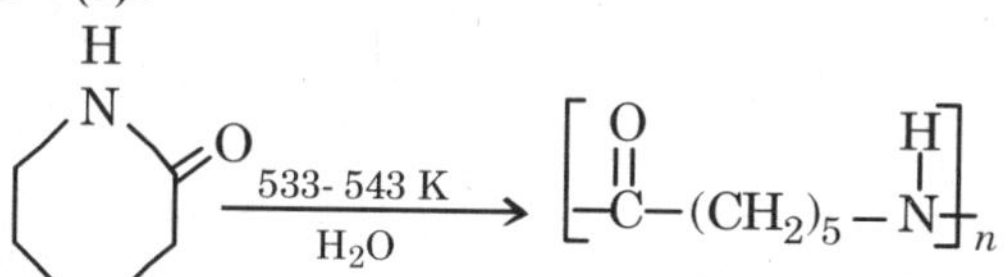

Nylon 6

5. **(c)** : $nH_2N—CH_2—COOH + nH_2N—(CH_2)_5—COOH$
Glycine Aminocaproic acid
$\longrightarrow (—HN—CH_2—CO—NH—(CH_2)_5—CO—)_n$
Nylon 2-nylon 6

6. **(d)** : (a) - Neoprene rubber (elastomer)
(b) - PVC (thermoplastic polymer)
(c) - Nylon-6,6 (fibre)
(d) - Novolac which further undergoes cross linking to produce bakelite (thermosetting polymer).

7. **(c)** :

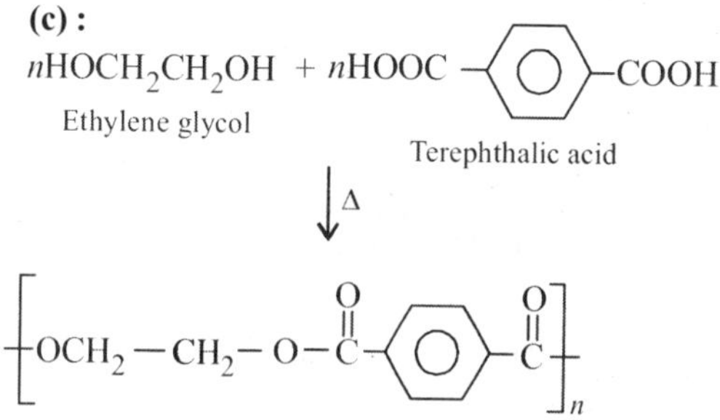

Terylene (Dacron)

8. **(a)**

9. **(a)** : $CH_2{=}C(Cl){-}CH{=}CH_2$ is the monomer of neoprene.

$$nCH_2{=}\underset{\text{Chloroprene}}{C(Cl)}{-}CH{=}CH_2 \xrightarrow{\text{Polymerisation}} \underset{\text{Neoprene}}{{-}\!\!\left[CH_2{-}C(Cl){=}CH{-}CH_2\right]\!\!{-}_n}$$

10. **(d)** : Neoprene is an addition polymer.

11. **(b)** : Nylon 6,6 is an example of fibre.

12. **(b)**

13. **(a)** : Terylene (Dacron) is a polyester polymer because it is made by monomer units ethylene glycol and dimethyl terephthalate.

14. **(a)** : Neoprene is :

$$-\!\!\left[CH_2{-}\underset{Cl}{\underset{|}{C}}{=}CH{-}CH_2\right]\!\!-_n$$

It is a polymer of chloroprene.

$$CH_2{=}\overset{Cl}{\overset{|}{C}}{-}CH{=}CH_2$$

15. **(a)** : Neoprene is a polymer of chloroprene.

$$\underset{\text{Chloroprene}}{nCH_2{=}CH{-}\overset{Cl}{\overset{|}{C}}{=}CH_2} \xrightarrow{\text{Polymerisation}} \underset{\text{Neoprene}}{-\!\!\left[CH_2{-}CH{=}\overset{Cl}{\overset{|}{C}}{-}CH_2\right]\!\!-_n}$$

Rest of the polymers are correctly represented.

16. **(d)** : Natural rubber is *cis*-1,3 polyisoprene and has only *cis* configuration about the double bond as shown below.

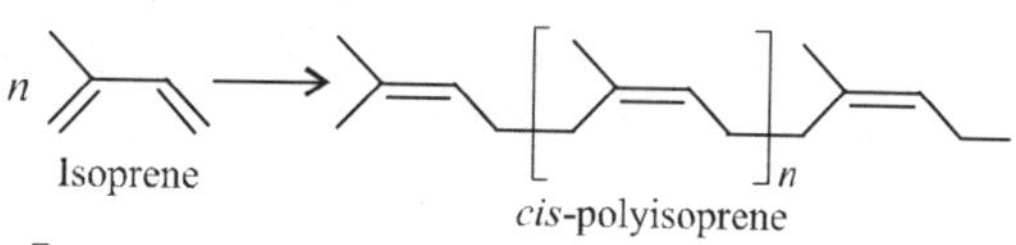

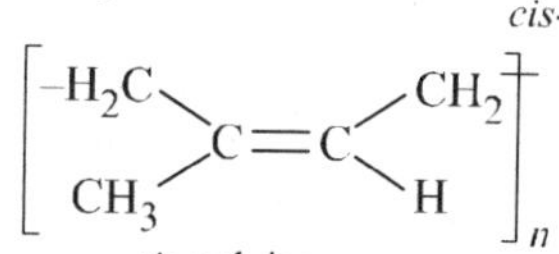

cis-polyisoprene
(Natural rubber)

whereas in Gutta-percha, only *trans*-configuration exists about the double bond.

17. **(d)** : Nylon-6,6 is a condensation polymer of adipic acid and hexamethylene diamine.

$$\underset{\text{Adipic acid}}{n\,HOOC-(CH_2)_4-COOH} + \underset{\text{Hexamethylene diamine}}{n\,H_2N-(CH_2)_6-NH_2}$$

$$\xrightarrow[-H_2O]{\Delta} \underset{\text{Nylon-6,6}}{\left(\overset{H}{\overset{|}{N}}-(CH_2)_6-\overset{H}{\overset{|}{N}}-\underset{O}{\underset{||}{C}}-(CH_2)_4-\underset{O}{\underset{||}{C}}\right)_n}$$

18. (b) : $\sim\!\!\sim[NH(CH_2)_6NHCO(CH_2)_4CO]_n\!\sim\!\!\sim$ is formed by the condensation of adipic acid and hexamethylene diamine. It is a copolymer (a polymer made from more than one type of monomer molecules is referred to as copolymer).

19. (a) :

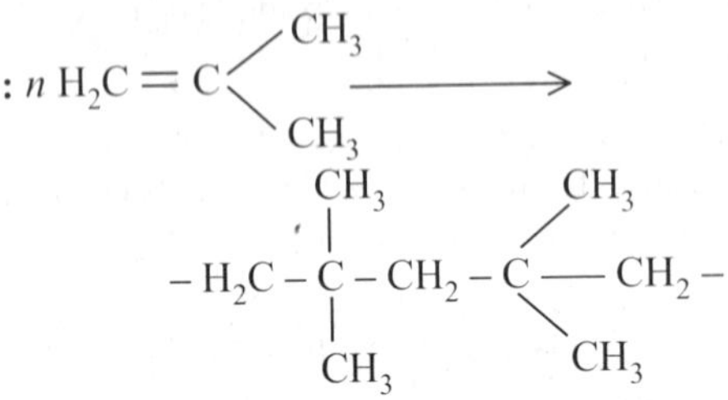

20. (c) : Chain-growth polymers involve a series of reactions each of which consume a reactive particle and produces another similar one. The reactive particles may be free radicals or ions (cation or anion) to which monomers get added by a chain reaction. It is an important reaction of alkenes and conjugated dienes or indeed of all kinds of compounds that contains C – C double bonds.

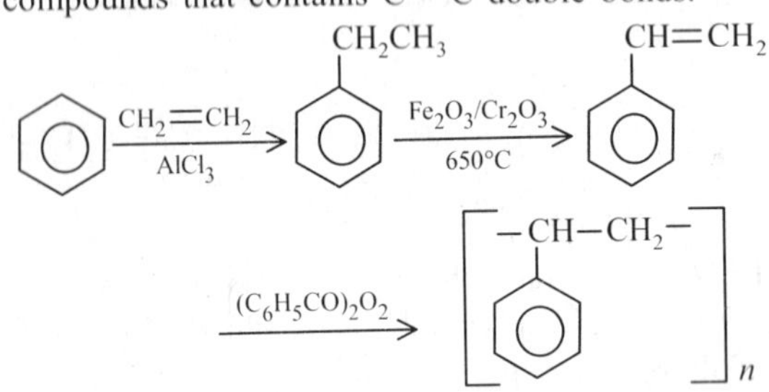

polystyrene

21. (a) : Acrilan is an addition polymer of acrylonitrile.

$$nCH_2{=}CH-CN \longrightarrow \left[CH_2-\underset{\displaystyle CN}{\underset{|}{CH}}\right]_n$$

22. (c) : Chloroprene or 2-chloro-1,3-butadiene on addition polymerisation gives neoprene.

23. (a) : The monomer of

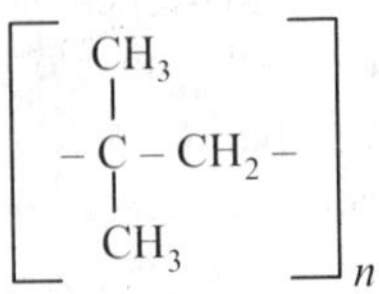

is

$$H_3C-\underset{\displaystyle CH_3}{\underset{|}{C}}{=}CH_2$$

(2-methylpropene)

24. (c) : Terylene is an example of condensation polymer and formed by the condensation of methyl terephthalate and glycol.

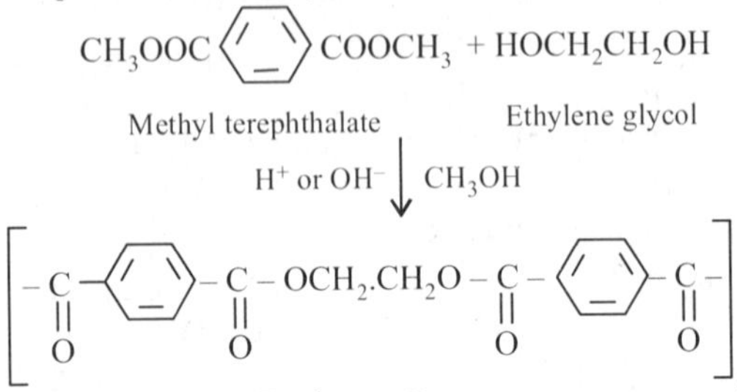

Terylene or Dacron

25. (a) : $n(CF_2{=}CF_2) \rightarrow [CF_2-CF_2]_n$

polytetrafluoroethylene (teflon)

26. (c) : H-F – – – H-F– – – H-F– – – H-F
Dotted lines represent hydrogen bond between HF molecule and hence it is a linear polymer. Due to high electronegativity value of 'F' atom it forms effective hydrogen bonds.

27. (d) :

$$n\left(CH_2{=}CH-\underset{\displaystyle CH_3}{\underset{|}{C}}{=}CH_2\right) \rightarrow \left[CH_2-CH{=}\underset{\displaystyle CH_3}{\underset{|}{C}}-CH_2\right]_n$$

Isoprene   Polyisoprene

Polyisoprene is the natural rubber, which is the polymer of isoprene.

28. (d) : $n(HO—CH_2—CH_2—OH)$ +

Ethylene glycol

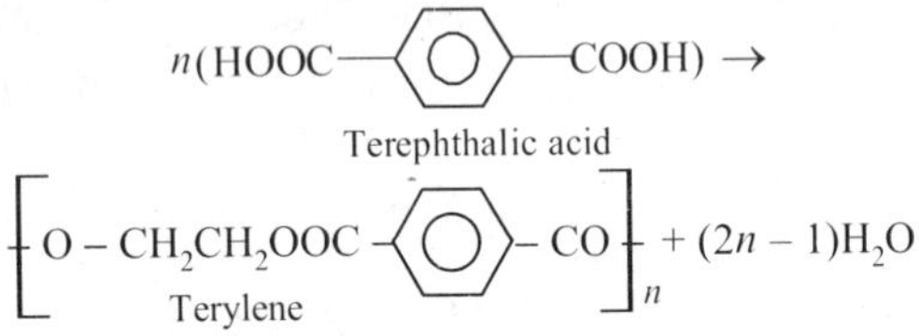

Terylene is the condensation polymer of ethylene glycol and terephthalic acid.

29. (b) : Polytetrafluoroethylene or teflon is a tough material, resistance to heat and bad conductor of electricity. It is used for coating the cookware to make them non-sticky.

30. (a) : Phenol and formaldehyde undergo condensation polymerisation under two different conditions to give a cross linked polymer called bakelite

Chapter 30

Chemistry in Everyday Life

Mixture of chloroxylenol and terpineol acts as
(a) antiseptic (b) antipyretic
(c) antibiotic (d) analgesic
(NEET 2017)

Which of the following is an analgesic?
(a) Streptomycin (b) Chloromycetin
(c) Novalgin (d) Penicillin
(NEET-I 2016)

Bithional is generally added to the soaps as an additive to function as a/an
(a) buffering agent (b) antiseptic
(c) softener (d) dryer.
(2015, Cancelled)

Artificial sweetner which is stable under cold conditions only is
(a) saccharine (b) sucralose
(c) aspartame (d) alitame.
(2014)

Antiseptics and disinfectants either kill or prevent growth of microrganisms. Identify which of the following statements is not true.
(a) Dilute solutions of boric acid and hydrogen peroxide are strong antiseptics.
(b) Disinfectants harm the living tissues.
(c) A 0.2% solution of phenol is an antiseptic while 1% solution acts as a disinfectant.
(d) Chlorine and iodine are used as strong disinfectants.
(NEET 2013)

Dettol is the mixture of
(a) chloroxylenol and bithionol
(b) chloroxylenol and terpineol
(c) phenol and iodine
(d) terpineol and bithionol
(Karnataka 2013)

7. Chloroamphenicol is an
(a) antifertility drug
(b) antihistaminic
(c) antiseptic and disinfectant
(d) antibiotic-broad spectrum *(Mains 2012)*

8. Which one of the following is employed as Antihistamine?
(a) Chloramphenicol
(b) Diphenylhydramine
(c) Norothindrone
(d) Omeprazole *(2011)*

9. Which one of the following is employed as a tranquilizer drug?
(a) Promethazine (b) Valium
(c) Naproxen (d) Mifepriston
(2010)

10. Which one of the following is employed as a tranquilizer?
(a) Naproxen (b) Tetracycline
(c) Chlorpheninamine (d) Equanil
(2009)

11. Chloropicrin is obtained by the reaction of
(a) steam on carbon tetrachloride
(b) nitric acid on chlorobenzene
(c) chlorine on picric acid
(d) nitric acid on chloroform. *(2004)*

12. Which of the following forms cationic micelles above certain concentration?
(a) Sodium dodecyl sulphate
(b) Sodium acetate
(c) Urea
(d) Cetyltrimethylammonium bromide.
(2004)

13. Gammexane is
(a) bromobenzene
(b) benzyl chloride

(c) chlorobenzene
(d) benzene hexachloride *(1999)*

14. The decomposition of organic compounds, in the presence of oxygen and without the development of odoriferous substances, is called
(a) nitrification (b) N_2-fixation
(c) decay (d) denitrification *(1999)*

15. Aspirin is an acetylation product of
(a) *m*-Hydroxybenzoic acid
(b) *o*-Dihydroxybenzene
(c) *o*-Hydroxybenzoic acid
(d) *p*-Dihydroxybenzene *(1998)*

16. Which of the following can possibly be used as analgesic without causing addiction and moon modification?
(a) Diazepam
(b) Tetrahydrocatinol
(c) Morphine
(d) N-Acetyl-para-aminophenol. *(1997*

17. Diazo coupling is useful to prepare some
(a) pesticides
(b) dyes
(c) proteins
(d) vitamins. *(1994*

18. Which one of the following statements is no true?
(a) Ampicillin is a natural antibiotic
(b) Aspirin is both analgesic and antipyreti
(c) Sulphadiazine is a synthetic antibacteria drug
(d) Some disinfectants can be used a antiseptics. *(1994*

Answer Key

1. (a) **2.** (c) **3.** (b) **4.** (c) **5.** (a) **6.** (b) **7.** (d) **8.** (b) **9.** (b) **10.** (d)
11. (d) **12.** (b) **13.** (d) **14.** (c) **15.** (c) **16.** (d) **17.** (b) **18.** (a)

EXPLANATIONS

. **(a)** : Dettol which is a well known antiseptic is mixture of chloroxylenol and α-terpineol in a uitable solvent.

. **(c)** : Streptomycin, chloromycetin and penicillin re antibiotics while novalgin is an analgesic.

. **(b)**

. **(c)** : Aspartame is stable under cold conditions nd unstable at cooking temperature.

(a) : Dilute solutions of boric acid and hydrogen eroxide are weak antiseptics.

(b) : Dettol is the mixture of chloroxylenol and -terpineol.

(d)

(b) : Diphenylhydramine is employed as ntihistamine drug.

(b) : Valium is a tranquilizer.

. **(d)** : Equanil is used for the treatment of stress, ild and severe mental diseases *i.e.*, as a tranquilizer.

. **(d)** : When chloroform is treated with ncentrated nitric acid, its hydrogen is replaced nitro group.

$$HCl_3 + HONO_2 \rightarrow \underset{\text{chloropicrin}}{CNO_2Cl_3} + H_2O$$

. **(b)** : Sodium acetate forms cationic micelles. In molecule of soaps and detergents the negative s aggregate to form a micelle of colloidal size. e negative ion has a long hydrocarbon chain and olar group (COO^-) at one end.

. **(d)** : Gammexane is an isomeric form of nzenehexachloride (BHC).

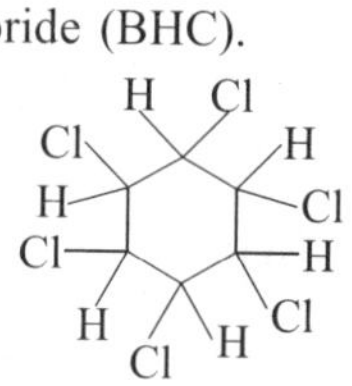

14. (c) : The other three type of reactions takes place only in the presence of bacteria, in which the nitrogen compound is decomposed either to nitrogen or nitrates or nitrites. While in decay reaction an organic compound is decomposed in presence of oxygen.

15. (c) : Aspirin is acetyl salicylic acid, which is formed by acetylation of *o*-hydroxybenzoic acid.

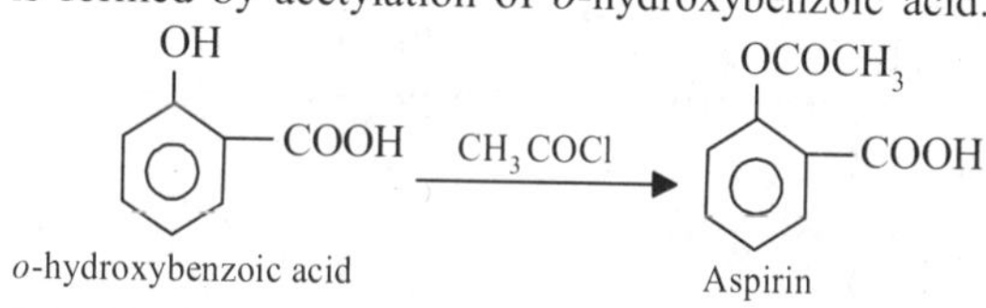

16. (d) : N-Acetyl-para-aminophenol (or paracetamol) is an antipyretic which can also be used as an analgesic to relieve pains.

17. (b) : Azo dyes are derived by coupling of a phenol adsorbed on the surface of a fabric with a diazonium salt. Dyes can be prepared by diazo coupling for example

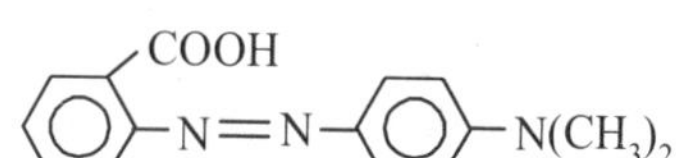

Methyl red

18. (a) : Ampicillin is a modification of penicillin and thus is not a natural antibiotic. These semisynthetic penicillin (SSP) like ampicillin, cloxacillin, etc. are produced by chemically combining specific side chains (in place of benzyl side chain of penicillin group) or by incorporating specific precursors in the mould cultures. The aim of producing SSP's is to overcome penicillin's shortcomings such as poor oral efficacy, hyper sensitivity, susceptibility to penicillinase, narrow spectrum of activity, etc.

Chapter 31

Nuclear Chemistry*

1. A nuclide of an alkaline earth metal undergoes radioactive decay by emission of the α-particles in succession. The group of the periodic table to which the resulting daughter element would belong is
(a) Gr. 13 (b) Gr. 17
(c) Gr. 14 (d) Gr. 16 *(2005)*

2. The radioactive isotope $^{60}_{27}Co$ which is used in the treatment of cancer can be made by (n, p) reaction. For this reaction the target nucleus is
(a) $^{59}_{28}Ni$ (b) $^{59}_{27}Co$
(c) $^{60}_{28}Ni$ (d) $^{60}_{27}Co$ *(2004)*

3. The radioisotope, tritium $\left(^{3}_{1}H\right)$ has a half-life of 12.3 years. If the initial amount of tritium is 32 mg, how many milligrams of it would remain after 49.2 years?
(a) 1 mg (b) 2 mg
(c) 4 mg (d) 8 mg *(2003)*

4. $^{235}_{92}U$, nucleus absorbs a neutron and disintegrate in $^{139}_{54}Xe$, $^{94}_{38}Sr$ and x so, what will be product x?
(a) 3-neutrons (b) 2-neutrons
(c) α-particle (d) β-particle
(2002)

5. A human body required 0.01 m activity of radioactive substance after 24 hours. Half life of radioactive substance is 6 hours. Then injection of maximum activity of radioactive substance that can be injected is
(a) 0.08 (b) 0.04
(c) 0.16 (d) 0.32 *(2001)*

6. If a $^{a}_{b}X$ species emits first a positron, then two α and two β particles and in the last, one α, is also emitted and gets converts to $^{c}_{d}Y$ species. So correct relation is
(a) $c = a - 12, d = b - 5$
(b) $c = a - 5, d = b - 1$
(c) $c = a - 6, d = b - 0$
(d) $c = a - 4, d = b - 2$ *(200*

7. A 300 gram radioactive sample at initial ha life is 3 hours. After 18 hours remaining quanti
(a) 4.68 gram (b) 2.34 gram
(c) 3.34 gram (d) 9.37 gram
(200

8. Sulphur-35 (34.96903 a.m.u.) emits a β-partic but no γ-ray. The product is chlorin 35 (34.96885 a.m.u.). The maximum ener emitted by the β-particle is
(a) 0.16758 MeV
(b) 1.6758 MeV
(c) 16.758 MeV
(d) 0.016758 MeV
(199

9. In the following radioactive dec $^{232}_{92}X \rightarrow ^{220}_{89}Y$, how many α and β particles ejected from X to form Y?
(a) 3α and 5β
(b) 5α and 3β
(c) 3α and 3β
(d) 5α and 5β *(19*

10. The half-life of $^{14}_{6}C$, if its λ is 2.31×10^{-4}
(a) 3.5×10^4 years
(b) 3×10^3 years
(c) 2×10^2 years
(d) 4×10^3 years *(19*

11. Number of neutrons in a parent nucleus which gives $^{14}_{7}N$ nucleus after two success β emissions, would be
(a) 7 (b) 6
(c) 9 (d) 8 *(19*

* *Not included in the syllabus of AIPMT since 2*

12. Carbon-14 dating method is based on the fact that
(a) ratio of carbon-14 and carbon-12 is constant
(b) carbon-14 is the same in all objects
(c) carbon-14 is highly insoluble
(d) all of these. *(1997)*

13. $^{235}_{92}U + n \rightarrow$ fission product + neutron $+ 3.20 \times 10^{-11}$ J.
The energy undergoes fission is
(a) 8.21×10^{7} kJ (b) 6.55×10^{6} kJ
(c) 12.75×10^{8} kJ (d) 18.60×10^{9} kJ *(1997)*

14. After the emission of one α-particle followed by one β-particle from the atom of $^{238}_{92}X$, the number of neutrons in the atom will be
(a) 144 (b) 143
(c) 148 (d) 146 *(1996)*

15. Half-life for radioactive ^{14}C is 5760 years. In how many years 200 mg of ^{14}C will be reduced to 25 mg?
(a) 17280 years (b) 23040 years
(c) 5760 years (d) 11520 years *(1995)*

16. In a radioactive decay, an emitted electron comes from
(a) outermost orbit of the atom
(b) orbit having principal quantum number one
(c) nucleus of the atom
(d) inner orbital of the atom. *(1994)*

17. If an isotope of hydrogen has two neutrons in its atom, its atomic number and atomic mass number will respectively be
(a) 2 and 1 (b) 3 and 1
(c) 1 and 1 (d) 1 and 3 *(1992)*

18. The age of most ancient geological formations is estimated by
(a) potassium - argon method
(b) carbon - 14 dating method
(c) radium - silicon method
(d) uranium - lead method. *(1989)*

19. Emission of an alpha particle leads to a
(a) decrease of 2 units in the charge of the atom
(b) increase of 2 units in the mass of the atom
(c) decrease of 2 units in the mass of the atom
(d) increase of 4 units in the mass of the atom. *(1989)*

Answer Key

1. (c) **2.** (c) **3.** (b) **4.** (a) **5.** (c) **6.** (a) **7.** (a) **8.** (a) **9.** (c) **10.** (b)
11. (c) **12.** (a) **13.** (a) **14.** (b) **15.** (a) **16.** (c) **17.** (d) **18.** (d) **19.** (a)

EXPLANATIONS

1. (c) : Most stable product of radioactive disintegration is lead which belongs to group 14.

2. (c) : ${}^{60}_{28}\text{Ni} + {}^{1}_{0}n \rightarrow {}^{60}_{27}\text{Co} + {}^{1}_{1}p$

3. (b) : $T = t_{1/2} \times n$; $n = \frac{49.2}{12.3} = 4$

$N = N_0(1/2)^n = 32(1/2)^4 = 32 \times \frac{1}{2} \times \frac{1}{2} \times \frac{1}{2} \times \frac{1}{2} = 2$ mg

4. (a) : ${}^{235}_{92}\text{U} + {}^{1}_{0}n \rightarrow {}^{139}_{54}\text{Xe} + {}^{94}_{38}\text{Sr} + 3{}^{1}_{0}n$

Product x is 3 neutron.

5. (c) : At the end of 24 hrs. activity = 0.01 M

Half life = 6 hrs.

In 24 hrs. there are 24/6 = 4 half life.

Activity of substance after n half-life = $\frac{(A)}{2^n}$

$\Rightarrow \frac{(A)}{2^4} = 0.01$. $\therefore (A) = 0.16$

6. (a) :

$${}^{a}_{b}X \xrightarrow{-{}^{0}_{+1}\beta} {}^{a}_{b-1}X \xrightarrow{-2{}^{4}_{2}\text{He}} {}^{a-8}_{b-5}X \xrightarrow{-2{}^{0}_{-1}\beta}$$

$${}^{a-8}_{b-3}X \xrightarrow{-{}^{4}_{2}\text{He}} {}^{a-12}_{b-5}X \equiv {}^{c}_{d}X$$

$\therefore$ $c = a - 12$ and $d = b - 5$

7. (a) : no. of half life's gone $= \frac{18}{3} = 6$, $N_0 = 300$ g.

$$N_t = N_0 \times \left(\frac{1}{2}\right)^n$$

$$= 300 \times \left(\frac{1}{2}\right)^6 = 300 \times \frac{1}{64} = 4\cdot 68 \text{ g}$$

8. (a) : Mass defect = 34.96903 – 34.96885
= 0.00018 amu

Energy emitted = 0.00018 × 931 MeV
= 0.16758 MeV

9. (c) : ${}^{232}_{92}X \rightarrow {}^{220}_{89}Y \rightarrow m{}^{4}_{2}\alpha + n{}^{0}_{-1}\beta$

$\Rightarrow 232 = 220 + 4m \Rightarrow m = 3; 92 = 89 + 2m - n$

$\Rightarrow n = 89 + 6 - 92 = 3$

Hence 3α and 3β particles are ejected.

10. (b) : $t_{1/2} = \frac{0.693}{\lambda} = \frac{0.693}{2.31 \times 10^{-4}} = \frac{6.93}{2.31} \times 10^3$
$= 3 \times 10^3$ yr.

11. (c) : ${}^{b}_{a}X \rightarrow {}_{7}\text{N}^{14} + 2{}_{-1}\beta^0 \Rightarrow b = 14$ and

$a = 7 + 2(-1) = 5 \Rightarrow {}^{14}_{5}X$

Number of neutrons = 14 – 5 = 9

12. (a) : With the passage of time, calculated amount of carbon-14 degrades. This fact is the basis of C-14 dating method.

13. (a) : 1 atom of ${}^{235}_{92}\text{U}$ on fission gives energy
$= 3.2 \times 10^{-11}$ J

6.023×10^{23} atom (1 mole) on fission gives energy
$= 3.2 \times 10^{-11} \times 6.023 \times 10^{23}$ J $= 3.2 \times 6.023 \times 10^{12}$ J

235 g of ${}^{235}_{92}\text{U}$ on fission gives energy

$$= \frac{6.023}{235} \times 3.2 \times 10^{12} \text{ J} = 8.2 \times 10^7 \text{ kJ}$$

14. (b) : ${}^{238}_{92}X \xrightarrow{-\alpha} {}^{234}_{90}Y \xrightarrow{-\beta} {}^{234}_{91}Z$

Therefore, number of neutrons in ${}^{234}_{91}Z$
$= 234 - 91 = 143$

15. (a) : Quantity left after 5760 years $\frac{200}{2} = 100$ mg

Similarly quantity left after another 5760 years (*i.e.* 11520 years) $= \frac{100}{2} = 50$ mg and the quantity left after another 5760 years (*i.e.* 17280 years) $= \frac{50}{2} = 25$ mg

Thus time taken by 200 mg of ^{14}C to reduce to 25 mg

= (5760 + 5760 + 5760)years = 17280 years

16. (c): Since radioactivity is a nuclear phenomenon, therefore electron comes from nucleus of the atom. During this process a neutron breaks down into a proton and an electron.

$$n \rightarrow p + {}^{0}_{-1}e$$

17. (d) : Hydrogen has 3 isotopes ${}^{1}_{1}\text{H}, {}^{2}_{1}\text{H}, {}^{3}_{1}\text{H}$

Here $Z = 1, A = 3$ viz. Tritium $({}^{3}_{1}\text{H})$

So, it has $1p$ and $2n$.

18. (d) : The age of minerals and rocks is estimated by U-Pb method which is also known as helium dating.

Remember : C-14 dating method is used to predict the age of fossils or dead animals or a fallen tree.

19. (a) : Emission of α-particle $({}^{4}_{2}\text{He})$ leads to decrease of 2 units of charge

Example : ${}^{238}_{92}\text{U} \rightarrow {}^{234}_{90}\text{Th} + {}^{4}_{2}\text{He}$